Food& Beverage
COST
CONTROL

6TH EDITION

Food& Beverage COST CONTROL

6TH EDITION

LEA R. DOPSON • DAVID K. HAYES

WILEY

Library of Congress Cataloging-in-Publication Data

Dopson, Lea R., author.
  Food and beverage cost control / Lea R. Dopson, David K. Hayes.—Sixth edition.
    pages cm
  Includes bibliographical references and index.
  ISBN 978-1-118-98849-7 (hardback) 1. Food service—Cost control. I. Hayes, David K., author. II. Title.
  TX911.3.C65D66 2016
  647.95068—dc23
                                        2014039225

ISBN: 978-1-118-98849-7

Printed in the United States of America

10   9   8   7   6   5   4   3   2   1

DEDICATION

This edition is dedicated to the memory of Jack E. and Anita Miller.

CONTENTS

PREFACE

Many years have passed rapidly since the first edition of *Food and Beverage Cost Control* was released. Publication of the first edition fulfilled original lead author Professor Jack Miller's vision for a college-level text that would provide students and practicing managers the essential tools needed to effectively manage costs in food and beverage operations. His steadfast insistence that the original text be easy-to-read, easy-to-understand, and easy-to-remember is no doubt the primary reason for its continued tremendous success.

The authors hope that the study of cost management creates in readers the same interest and excitement for the topic that the authors experience. If so, we will have been successful in our attempt to be true to this text's original vision of creating an outstanding learning tool that prepares students to be successful managers in the exciting hospitality industry.

It has been said that there are three kinds of managers: those who know what has happened in the past, those who know what is happening now, and those who know what will happen in the future. Clearly, the manager who possesses all three traits is best prepared to manage effectively and efficiently. This text will give the reader the tools required to maintain sales and cost histories (the past), develop systems for monitoring current activities (the present), and learn the techniques required to anticipate what is to come (the future).

Previous revisions of the text focused primarily on ensuring that any new cost control–related information included was relevant, up-to-date, and accurate. All of those things remain true in the sixth edition. And indeed, much new and important information has been added to this edition. But recalling Professor Miller's original vision for the book meant we needed to do even more for this revision. The result was a renewed commitment on our part to carefully reexamine every chapter and word while revising this edition.

Today's professional foodservice managers face increasingly complex challenges in their jobs. As in the past, the tools and information they need to properly address these challenges must be easily understood if they are to be readily applied. Students will find this edition significantly easier to read. Instructors will find the information in it easier to present. Practicing managers will find the information in it easier to apply. We are convinced that is exactly what Professor Miller would have wanted for the *Sixth Edition* of *Food and Beverage Cost Control,* and we are delighted to play our part in sustaining his original vision.

TO THE STUDENT •────────────────

This book will provide you all the cost control–related information and tools you will need to achieve success levels that match your own highest career goals. If you work hard and do your best, you will find you have the ability to master all of the information in this text. When you do, you will have gained an invaluable set of management skills and tools that will enhance your knowledge of the hospitality management industry. These skills and tools will ensure that your hospitality career will consistently be rewarding for you both personally and professionally.

TO THE INSTRUCTOR •────────────────

Today's hospitality students are the most diverse, multicultural generation yet produced. How are today's students different from their counterparts of 20 years ago? Studies indicate that instead of focusing on material wealth and professional status, people in their 20s and early 30s are more likely to seek a rewarding and spiritually fulfilling life. Their genders are also different. From 1975 to 1985, the typical hospitality cost control class would have been overwhelmingly male. Today, females will often make up the majority of students in the same type class. Their ethnic backgrounds are different. National demographic projections suggest that about 65 percent of the growth in the US population through the year 2020 will be in ethnic minority groups, particularly Hispanic and Asian populations. Meeting the needs of today's students required us to carefully reexamine two extremely important characteristics of the text:

- Readability
- Presentation of mathematical concepts

READABILITY

Another difference of today's students from those of previous generations relates to the way students read.

If you were to survey a wide range of hospitality instructors today, you would find a nearly universal answer to the question of whether they believe their current students read as much, or as well, as did students from earlier generations. That uniform answer would be, "No; they do not." It would be a big mistake, however, to conclude from this that modern students are ill-informed or do not learn as readily as those in prior generations. For today's students, the use of smart devices and other highly advanced technology tools is a snap, but tweeting and texting are far more popular than textbooks. To ensure that our text continues to reach students who are used to reading concise messages, it was especially important to carefully review it for its readability. There were several main goals of this reading-related review:

- Eliminate redundancy.
- Identify and remove pedantic wording.
- Reexamine the presentation order of information to ensure maximum comprehension.
- Simplify the presentation and explanation of mathematical procedures.

PRESENTATION OF MATHEMATICAL CONCEPTS

Experienced managers know that effective cost control in a foodservice operation is built on a variety of systems that depend on the skillful use of mathematics.

In many cases, however, hospitality students may be unsure of their mathematical abilities. Because that is so, any textbook addressing cost control must possess two essential traits:

1. *It must be accurate.* The authors are grateful to the number of editors and reviewers who helped us ensure the mathematical formulas and examples presented in this edition are as error-free as humanly possible. We are grateful, as well, to the number of students and instructors who, in editions 1 through 5, provided feedback that helped ensure all mathematical examples and end-of-chapter questions and answers retained in this edition are clearly presented and accurate.

2. *The mathematical concepts included in the text must be presented clearly.* In a heightened effort to address this key concern, a new feature titled "Here's How It's Done" has been added to this edition. This new feature was created in direct response to instructors' desire that their students have step-by-step explanations and illustrations within every chapter of some of the text's more challenging math concepts. In this unique feature, students are shown, using real work-setting examples, how the math concepts presented in the chapter are applied and their results evaluated. We are convinced this new feature will be extremely popular with students and their instructors due to its ability to enhance the understanding and comprehension of the mathematical procedures upon which many of a manager's cost control efforts are based.

TO MANAGERS

While *Food and Beverage Cost Control* has always been produced in a textbook format, it has also consistently been an invaluable tool for the practicing manager. The easy, step-by-step approach used to estimate future customer counts (Chapter 2) and apply measures of labor productivity (Chapter 7) are just two examples of its very practical application. The formulas used to calculate edible portion (EP) product yields (Chapter 5) and the information utilized to properly establish prices for menu items (Chapter 6) are two more such examples.

From information needed to convert standardized recipes from the US system of weights and measures to the metric system (Chapter 3), to tips for calculating and analyzing variances on profit and loss statements (Chapter 9), managers responsible for the operation of high-volume foodservice units will find the information that is vitally important and easily applicable to their operations.

Effective foodservice managers are skilled problem solvers. The information found in the exciting new *Sixth Edition* of *Food and Beverage Cost Control* is designed especially to provide professional problem solvers with the tools they need to manage efficient and highly profitable foodservice operations.

NEW IN THE SIXTH EDITION

Sixth Edition readers will be pleased to find major enhancements both in the text's content and in its structure.

NEW CONTENT

One of the continuing strengths of *Food and Beverage Cost Control* has been the authors' commitment to continually and carefully monitoring the field of food and beverage cost control to identify changes that must be made to ensure the book presents the most up-to-date and accurate information available. Significant changes made in this edition include:

- Incorporating new and vital information from the US Food and Drug Administration (FDA) modification of the model "Food Code."
- Revising all financial statements presented in the text to conform to the recommendations contained in the new eighth edition of the *Uniform System of Accounts for Restaurants (USAR)*.
- Expanding information related to the increasingly popular farm-to-table, green technology, and sustainability movements.
- Addressing the potential impact on labor costs of the Patient Protection and Affordable Care Act (Affordable Care Act).
- Identifying advancements in handheld point-of-sale (POS) and payment systems technology.
- Expanding, by approximately 20 percent, the number of chapter-ending **Test Your Skills** exercises.
- Addition of the new chapter feature: **Here's How It's Done.** This unique feature was added to help readers understand key mathematical concepts.
- Addition of the new feature: **Cost Control Around the World.** This feature, present in each chapter, directly addresses the international aspects of cost control management. In our global environment, students will be increasingly called on to demonstrate their understanding of how ethics, culture, and business practices around the world directly affect cost control efforts in foodservice units located outside the United States.

NEW STRUCTURE

In a book such as this one, the presentation order of information is extremely important. Development of the *Sixth Edition* allowed the authors to carefully reexamine content presentation in the text and undertake a major improvement related to three key text chapters. In the most previously released *Fifth Edition*, these chapters were:

    Chapter 3: Managing the Cost of Food

    Chapter 4: Managing the Cost of Beverages

    Chapter 5: Managing the Food and Beverage Production Process

While this structure presented key information in a logical manner, chapter length was not consistent, and this caused difficulty for some instructors. In the new *Sixth Edition*, the structure of these three key chapters has been reorganized as follows:

    Chapter 3: Purchasing and Receiving

    Chapter 4: Managing Inventory and Production

    Chapter 5: Monitoring Food and Beverage Product Costs

This structural change allowed the authors to eliminate duplication and to combine key information. Thus, for example, information regarding the use of purchase orders (Chapter 3) and the taking of inventories (Chapter 4) are presented in such a way as to address their use in the management of both food and alcoholic beverage costs.

Similarly, because the procedures and tools that managers can use to monitor and control product costs are analogous for both food and beverages, this information was combined (Chapter 5). The result of this significant structural change in content presentation is greater consistency in chapter length and elimination of content redundancy with no loss of important information presented.

RETAINED IN THE SIXTH EDITION

Much of the popularity of this text is no doubt due to the quality of the elements and features developed for it in prior editions. In this *Sixth Edition,* the authors were pleased to update and retain from the previous edition the following key text elements:

OVERVIEW: Each chapter begins with a brief overview of what the chapter contains. The overview focuses on why students will benefit from learning the information presented in the chapter. Thus, this element directly informs readers about what is to be presented in the chapter and why it is important to know it.

CHAPTER OUTLINE: One-tier outlines are presented at the beginning of each chapter to inform readers about the specific topics to be addressed. This helpful feature also makes it easier to find specific material contained in the chapter.

LEARNING OUTCOMES: Students want to know how the information they learn will be useful to them in their careers. This feature specifically identifies what readers will know and what they will know how to do when they have mastered the material in the chapter.

GREEN AND GROWING: More than ever, students and customers alike recognize that environmental consciousness is as important at work as it is at home. As a result, hospitality professionals are increasingly adopting "green" practices and policies that aid the planet as well as their own bottom lines. In this feature, students become familiar with the whys and hows of responsibly growing their businesses by implementing Earth-friendly business practices specific to the hospitality industry.

CONSIDER THE COST: One of the most exciting things about learning any new skill is the ability to directly apply what has been learned to situations the learners will actually encounter. To give students an opportunity to do just that, "Consider the Cost" micro-case studies have been developed to present students with common cost control–related challenges they will likely encounter at work. Each case study poses questions that allow readers to apply information learned in the chapter to these "real world" work situations and problems. Instructors will also find these micro-case studies are fun for their students to read and discuss in class.

FUN ON THE WEB!: This important feature of the text adds to student learning by integrating the use of the Internet into the study of cost control. This feature provides Web-based resources that can help managers more effectively do their jobs.

TECHNOLOGY TOOLS: These updated listings of real-life application examples demonstrate to students that they can utilize advanced smart device applications, sophisticated wired and wireless communication tools, and much more to help manage costs and improve operating efficiencies. While not all managers will use all of the tools suggested, it is important for students to understand the rapidly expanding technology-based resources available to them today.

APPLY WHAT YOU HAVE LEARNED: This exciting pedagogical feature allows students to draw on their own problem-solving skills, ideas, and opinions using the concepts explored within each chapter. Challenging and realistic, yet purposely brief, these industry-specific scenarios provide excellent starting points for class discussions or, if the instructor prefers, outstanding written homework assignments.

KEY TERMS AND CONCEPTS: Students often need help in identifying key terms and concepts that should be mastered after reading a section of a book. These are listed at the conclusion of each chapter and in the order in which they appeared in the chapter to make finding them easier.

TEST YOUR SKILLS: This popular feature has been retained and expanded. As was true in previous editions, predesigned Microsoft Excel spreadsheets are employed in most of the questions to allow students to practice problem-solving. Doing so enhances the instructor's ability to evaluate student mastery of cost control concepts and student skill in understanding and using spreadsheets. The Excel spreadsheets are downloadable from the student companion website at www.wiley.com/college/dopson.

MANAGERIAL TOOLS

It is the authors' hope that all readers find the book as helpful to use as we found it exciting to develop. To that end, appendices are provided that we believe will be of great value.

Appendix A: Frequently Used Formulas for Managing Costs is included on the student companion website (www.wiley.com/college/dopson) as an easy reference guide. This feature allows readers to look up mathematical formulas for any of the computations presented in the text.

Appendix B: Management Control Forms provides simplified cost control–related forms. This popular appendix has been retained from previous editions of this text. Included on the student companion website at www.wiley.com/college/dopson, these forms can be used as guideposts in the development of property-specific forms. They may be implemented as-is or modified as the manager sees fit.

A *Glossary* of key terms used in the chapters and in the industry is included in the back of the text to help the reader with the operational vocabulary necessary to understand the language of hospitality cost control management. The glossary is also included on the book companion site at www.wiley.com/college/dopson.

COMPANION WEBSITES

To help instructors effectively manage their time and to enhance student learning opportunities, several significant educational tools have been developed specifically for this text:

> Instructor's Materials
> Student Materials

INSTRUCTOR'S MATERIALS

A password-protected online *Instructor's Manual* (www.wiley.com/college/dopson) has been meticulously developed and classroom tested for this text. The manual includes the following, each of which is presented in a stand-alone format:

- *Lecture Outlines* for each chapter.
- *Lecture PowerPoints* for each chapter: These easy-to-read teaching aids are excellent tools for instructors presenting their lectures in class or online. These are available to students as well, as a chapter review aid.

- Suggested answers to each chapter's *Consider the Cost* micro-case studies.
- Suggested answers for *Apply What You Have Learned* questions for each chapter.
- Suggested answers to chapter-ending *Test Your Skills* problems. Instructors will be able to access answers and formulas to the "Test Your Skills" spreadsheet exercises at the end of each chapter.
- A *Test Bank* including 20 multiple choice (four-alternative) and 10 True and False (two-alternative) exam questions developed for each chapter. The authors recognize the importance that instructors place on well-designed exam questions. For this edition, a major revision of the test bank was undertaken. The result was a significant improvement in the quality, validity, and reliability of the exam questions and each question's correct answer.

The Test Bank for this text has been specifically formatted for *Respondus*, an easy-to-use software for creating and managing exams that can be printed or published directly to Blackboard, WebCT, Desire2Learn, eCollege, ANGEL, and other eLearning systems. Instructors who adopt *Food and Beverage Cost Control, Sixth Edition,* can download the Test Bank for free.

Additional Wiley resources can be uploaded, at no charge, into the learning management system (LMS) used by course instructors. To view and access these resources and the *Test Bank*, visit www.wiley.com/college/dopson, select the correct title, and click on the "Instructor Companion Website" link, then click on "Respondus Test Bank." Instructions on how to use Respondus and upload additional materials into the LMS appear in this section of the companion site.

STUDENT MATERIALS

A newly revised *Study Guide* (978-1-119-06157-1) provides several additional resources to help students review the material and exercises to test their knowledge of key concepts and topics. Study guides are popular with students and instructors alike because they provide yet another tool for those professionals seeking to maximize their learning of this text's important material.

A robust companion website contains additional support materials for students and is available at www.wiley.com/college/dopson.

Lecture PowerPoints

Test Your Skills

Frequently Used Formulas for Managing Costs

Management Control Forms

WILEYPLUS LEARNING SPACE

A place where students can define their strengths and nurture their skills, *WileyPLUS Learning Space* transforms course content into an online learning community. *WileyPLUS Learning Space* invites students to experience learning activities, work through self-assessment, ask questions and share insights. As students interact with the course content, each other, and their instructor, *WileyPLUS Learning Space* creates a personalized study guide for each student. Through collaboration, students make deeper connections to the subject matter and feel part of a community.

Through a flexible course design, instructors can quickly organize learning activities, manage student collaboration, and customize your course—having full control over content as well as the amount of interactivity between students.

WileyPLUS Learning Space lets the instructor:

- Assign activities and add your own materials
- Guide your students through what's important in the interactive e-textbook by easily assigning specific content
- Set up and monitor group learning
- Assess student engagement
- Gain immediate insights to help inform teaching

Defining a clear path to action, the visual reports in *WileyPLUS Learning Space* help both you and your students gauge problem areas and act on what's most important.

ACKNOWLEDGMENTS

The first five editions of this text have been very popular. As a result, this book has now become one of the market leaders among hospitality cost control texts. This success has stemmed in large part from the testing of its concepts and materials in classes at the University of North Texas, Purdue University, Texas Tech University, the University of Houston, California State Polytechnic University at Pomona, and Lansing Community College, as well as from those original St. Louis Community College students who received their instruction under Jack Miller.

We are also extremely grateful to the various professionals in institutional, commercial, and hotel foodservice operations who contributed to the original concept and idea for the book and who so freely gave of their time and advice in this endeavor. For comment, collaboration, and constructive criticism on the manuscript, we thank the reviewers who have generously given their feedback through six editions of the book. In addition, we also want to acknowledge the hundreds of instructors who provided key information in a survey of the Cost Control course. This greatly impacted how we revised this *Sixth Edition*.

This edition could not have been produced without the assistance of a great many colleagues, friends, and family who supported our efforts. As always, a special thank you goes to those who have been so supportive of us throughout our careers: Loralei, Terry, and Laurie, as well as Peggy, Scott, Trishauna, Joshua, Pauline, M.D., and J.J.C. We appreciate all of you!

A special thanks also goes to Allisha A. Miller, consulting author and project manager at Panda Professionals Hospitality Education and Training, for her meticulous attention to detail in carefully reviewing each of the mathematical formulas and problem solutions presented in this edition and for her assistance in developing this text's instructor materials.

We know the value of a quality publisher in the development of an outstanding text revision. We are continually impressed with the high standards exhibited by JoAnna Turtletaub, Wiley vice president and publisher, and the patient support provided by her staff, including Melissa Edwards, our outstanding editor. Their efforts helped ensure that this text met the high standards Wiley sets for its own publications and, by doing so, helped us contribute our very best efforts as well. As always, we are deeply grateful to all of the staff at Wiley for their intellect, patience, and faithfulness in producing this sixth, and best ever, edition of *Food and Beverage Cost Control*.

Lea Dopson, Ed.D. David K. Hayes, Ph.D.
Pomona, CA *Okemos, MI*

WileyPLUS Learning Space

An easy way to help your students **learn, collaborate,** and **grow.**

Personalized Experience

Students create their own study guide while they interact with course content and work on learning activities.

Flexible Course Design

Educators can quickly organize learning activities, manage student collaboration, and customize their course—giving them full control over content as well as the amount of interactivity among students.

Clear Path to Action

With visual reports, it's easy for both students and educators to gauge problem areas and act on what's most important.

Instructor Benefits

- Assign activities and add your own materials
- Guide students through what's important in the interactive e-textbook by easily assigning specific content
- Set up and monitor collaborative learning groups
- Assess learner engagement
- Gain immediate insights to help inform teaching

Student Benefits

- Instantly know what you need to work on
- Create a personal study plan
- Assess progress along the way
- Participate in class discussions
- Remember what you have learned because you have made deeper connections to the content

We are dedicated to supporting you from idea to outcome.

WILEY

Food & Beverage COST CONTROL

6TH EDITION

CHAPTER 1

Managing Revenue and Expense

OVERVIEW

This chapter presents the relationship among a foodservice business's revenue, expense, and profit. As a professional foodservice manager, you must understand the relationship that exists between controlling these three areas and the resulting success of your operation. In addition, the chapter presents the mathematical foundation you must know to report your operating results and express them as a percentage of your revenue or budget. This method is standard within the hospitality industry.

Chapter Outline

- Professional Foodservice Manager
- Profit: The Reward for Service
- Getting Started
- Understanding the Income (Profit and Loss) Statement
- Understanding the Budget
- Technology Tools
- Apply What You Have Learned
- Key Terms and Concepts
- Test Your Skills

LEARNING OUTCOMES

At the conclusion of this chapter, you will be able to:

- Apply the formula used to determine business profits.
- Express business expenses and profits as a percentage of revenue.
- Compare actual operating results with budgeted operating results.

PROFESSIONAL FOODSERVICE MANAGER

To be a successful foodservice manager, you must be a talented individual. Consider, for a moment, your role in the operation of a profitable foodservice facility. As a foodservice manager, you are both a manufacturer and a retailer. A professional foodservice manager is unique because all of the functions of a product's sale, from menu development to guest service, are in the hands of the same individual. As a manager, you are in charge of securing raw materials, producing a product, and selling it—all under the same roof. Few other managers are required to have the breadth of skills that effective foodservice operators must have. Because foodservice operators are in the service sector of business, many aspects of management are more challenging for them than for their manufacturing or retailing management counterparts.

A foodservice manager is one of the few types of managers who actually have contact with the ultimate consumer. This is not true for the managers of a cell phone factory or automobile production line. These individuals produce a product, but they do not sell it to the person who will actually use it. In a like manner, furniture and clothing store managers will sell products to those who use them, but they have had no role in actually producing the products they sell. The face-to-face guest contact in the hospitality industry requires that you assume the responsibility of standing behind your own work and the work of your staff, in a one-on-one situation with the ultimate consumer, or end user, of your products and services.

The management task checklist in Figure 1.1 shows some of the areas in which foodservice, manufacturing, and retailing managers differ in their responsibilities.

In addition to your role as a food factory supervisor, you must serve as a cost control manager, because if you fail to perform this vital role, your business will perform poorly or may even cease to exist. Foodservice management provides the opportunity for creativity in a variety of settings. The control of revenue and expenses is just one more area in which an effective foodservice operator can excel. In fact, in most areas of foodservice, excellence in operation is measured in terms of a manager's ability to produce and deliver quality products in a way that ensures an appropriate operating profit for the owners of the business.

FIGURE 1.1 Management Task Checklist

Task	Foodservice Manager	Manufacturing Manager	Retail Manager
1. Secure raw materials	Yes	Yes	No
2. Manufacture product	Yes	Yes	No
3. Distribute to end user	Yes	No	Yes
4. Market to end user	Yes	No	Yes
5. Reconcile problems with end user	Yes	No	Yes

PROFIT: THE REWARD FOR SERVICE

In the foodservice industry a manager's primary responsibility is to deliver quality products and services to guests at a price mutually agreeable to both parties. In addition, the quality must be such that buyers of the product or service feel that excellent value was received for the money they spent. When they do, a business will prosper. If, however, management focuses more on reducing costs than providing value to guests, problems will inevitably occur.

It is important to remember that serving guests causes businesses to incur costs. It is wrong to think that "low" costs are good and "high" costs are bad. A restaurant with $5 million in sales per year will have higher costs than the same-size restaurant achieving only $500,000 in sales per year. The reason is quite clear. The amount of products, labor, and equipment needed to sell $5 million worth of food and beverages is greater than that required to sell only $500,000.

Remember, if there are fewer guests, there are likely to be lower costs, but less sales and profit as well! Because that is true, a business will suffer if management attempts to reduce costs with no regard for the impact on the balance between managing costs and maintaining high levels of guest satisfaction. In addition, efforts to reduce costs that result in unsafe physical conditions for guests or employees are never wise. Although some short-term savings may result, the expense of a lawsuit resulting from a guest or employee injury can be very high. Managers who, for example, neglect to spend the money to shovel and salt a snowy restaurant entrance area may find that they spend thousands of dollars more defending themselves in a lawsuit brought by an individual who slipped and fell on the ice than they would have spent clearing the snowy walkway.

For an effective manager, the question to be considered is not whether costs are high or low. The question is whether costs are *too high* or *too low*, given the value a business seeks to create for its guests. Managers can eliminate nearly all costs by closing the operation's doors. Obviously, however, when you close the doors to nearly all expenses, you also close the doors to sales and, more importantly, to profits. Expenses, then, must be incurred, but managed in a way that allows the operation to achieve its desired profit levels.

It is especially important for you to understand profits. Some people assume that if a business purchases an item for $1.00 and sells it for $3.00, the profit generated is $2.00. In fact, this is not true. As a business operator, you must realize that the difference between what you have paid for the goods you sell and the price at which you sell them does not represent your profit. Instead, all expenses, including advertising, the building that houses your operation, management salaries, and the labor required to generate the sale, just to name but a few, are among the many expenses that must be subtracted from your income before you can determine your profits accurately.

Every foodservice operator is faced with, and must understand well, the profit formula:

$$\text{Revenue} - \text{Expenses} = \text{Profit}$$

Thus, when you manage your facility, you will receive **revenue**—the money you take in—and you will incur **expenses**—the cost of everything required to operate the business and generate your revenue. **Profit** is represented by the amount that remains after all expenses have been paid. Because doing so is common in the industry, in this book the authors will use the following terms interchangeably: revenues and sales; expenses and costs.

The profit formula holds true even for managers in the nonprofit sectors of foodservice such as schools, hospitals, military bases, and businesses providing meals to their workers. For example, consider the situation of Hector Bentevina. Hector is the foodservice manager at the headquarters of a large corporation that employs many office workers. Hector supplies the foodservice to a large group of these workers, each of whom is employed by the corporation that owns the facility Hector manages. In this situation, Hector's employer may not have profits as its primary motive. That is so because, in most **business dining** situations, food is provided as a service to the company's employees either as a no-cost (to the employee) benefit or at a greatly reduced price. In all cases, however, some provision for profit must be made by nonprofit operations such as the one operated by Hector, although it is not likely their primary motive.

Figure 1.2 shows the flow of business for the typical foodservice operation. Note that profit dollars must be taken out at some point in the process, or management will be in a position of simply trading equal amounts of cash for cash.

FIGURE 1.2 Foodservice Business Flowchart

In your own operation, if you find that revenue is consistently less than your expenses, with no reserve for the future, you will also find that there is no money for new equipment; needed facility maintenance may not be performed and employee raises (including your own) may be few and far between. In addition, your facility will eventually become outdated due to a lack of funds for remodeling and upgrading. The fact is, all foodservice operations must generate revenue in excess of expenses if they are to thrive.

An appropriate level of business profits is always the result of solid planning, sound management, and careful decision making. The purpose of this text is to give you the information and tools you need to make good decisions about managing your operation's revenue and expenses.

It is important to understand that profit should not be viewed as what is left over after all bills are paid. In fact, careful planning is necessary to earn a profit. In most cases, investors will not invest in businesses that do not generate enough profit to make their investment worthwhile. The restaurant business can be very profitable; however, there is no guarantee that an individual restaurant will make a profit. Some restaurants do, and others do not. Because that is true, a more appropriate formula that recognizes and rewards the business owner for the risk associated with ownership is:

> Revenue − Desired profit = Ideal expense

In this case, **ideal expense** is defined as management's view of the correct or appropriate amount of expense necessary to generate a given level of sales. **Desired profit** is defined as the profit that the owner wants to achieve at that level of revenue. This formula clearly places profit as a reward for providing service, not as a leftover. When foodservice managers deliver quality and value to their guests, anticipated revenue levels and desired profits can be achieved. Desired profit and ideal expense levels are not, however, easily achieved. It takes a talented foodservice operator to consistently make good decisions that will maximize revenue while holding expenses to the ideal or appropriate amount. This book will teach you how to make those good decisions.

REVENUE

Revenue dollars are the result of units sold to customers. Units may consist of individual menu items, lunches, dinners, drinks, or any other item produced by your operation. Revenue varies with both the number of guests coming to your business and the amount of money spent by each guest. You can increase revenue by increasing the number of guests you serve, by increasing the amount each guest you serve spends, or by a combination of both approaches. Adding seating or drive-through windows, extending operating hours, and building additional foodservice units are all examples of management's efforts to increase the number of guests served. Suggestive selling by service staff, creative menu pricing techniques, and discounts for very large purchases are examples of efforts to increase the amount of money each guest spends.

Management's primary task is to take the steps necessary to attract guests to the foodservice operation. This is true because the profit formula begins with sales made to guests. Experienced foodservice operators know that adding guests and selling more to each guest are extremely effective ways of increasing overall profitability, but *only* if effective cost management systems are also in place.

The focus of this text is on managing and controlling costs, not on generating additional revenue. While the two topics are related, they are very different. Marketing efforts, restaurant design, site selection, employee training, and proper food preparation methods are good examples of factors that directly impact an operation's ability to increase sales levels. Effective expense control cannot solve the problems caused by inadequate revenue resulting from inferior marketing, food quality or service levels. Effective cost control when coupled with management's aggressive attitude toward meeting and exceeding guests' expectations, however, can result in outstanding revenue and profit performance.

Green and Growing!

Good food and service will attract foodservice customers. So will other important factors customers care about, including location, unusual décor, and, increasingly, how "green" an operation is perceived to be. *Green* is the term used to describe those foodservice operations that incorporate environmentally conscious activities into the design, construction, and operation of their businesses. These activities can be related to packaging and shipping materials reduction, energy conservation, or **sustainable development,** a term used to describe a variety of Earth-friendly practices and policies as "development that meets the needs of the present population without compromising the ability of future generations to meet their own needs."

The positive benefits that accrue when businesses incorporate green activities are significant, and are increasing. Managers of green operations help protect the environment. For example, did you know that every ton of 100 percent post-consumer waste recycled paper saves 12 trees, 1,976 pounds of greenhouse gases, and 390 gallons of oil? Green operating is also gaining in popularity because more and more guests seek out and frequent green restaurants simply because they are committed to preserving the environment.

The Green Restaurant Association[SM] (GRA) is a nonprofit, national environmental organization founded to help restaurants and their customers become more "green" (environmentally sustainable) in ways that are convenient and cost-effective. The GRA's agenda includes issues related to:

Research

Environmental consulting

Education

Public relations and marketing

Community organizing and consumer activism

To learn more about this increasingly high-profile group, visit the GRA's website, dinegreen.com. To learn more about how your foodservice operation can increase profits by implementing sustainable activities, watch for the "Green and Growing" feature in each upcoming chapter of this book.

UN Brundtland Commission, "Report of the World Commission on Environment and Development: Our Common Future," 42nd session, *Development and International Cooperation: Environment,* August 4, 1987, chapter 2 opener.

EXPENSES

Expenses are used to generate revenue. But managers must carefully control their expenses. There are four major foodservice expense categories that you must learn to control:

1. Food costs
2. Beverage costs
3. Labor costs
4. Other expenses

FOOD COSTS

Food costs are the costs associated with actually producing the menu items sold to guests. They include the expense of meats, dairy, fruits, vegetables, and other categories of food items produced by the foodservice operation. When calculating their food costs, some managers include the cost of minor paper and plastic items, such as the paper wrappers used to wrap sandwiches. In most cases, food costs will make up the largest or second-largest expense category you must learn to manage.

BEVERAGE COSTS

Beverage costs are those expenses related to the sale of alcoholic beverages. It is common practice in the hospitality industry to consider beverage costs of a nonalcoholic nature as an expense in the food cost category, not the beverage category. Thus, milk, tea, coffee, waters, carbonated beverages, and other nonalcoholic beverage items are *not* generally considered a beverage cost.

Alcoholic beverages accounted for in the beverage cost category include beer, wine, and liquor. This cost category may also include the expenses of other ingredients such as cherries, lemons, olives, limes, mixers like carbonated beverages, and the juices needed to produce alcoholic drinks. It may also include miscellaneous items such as stir sticks, napkins, and coasters.

LABOR COSTS

Labor costs include the cost of all nonmanagement as well as management employees needed to run a business. This expense category also includes the amount of any taxes you are required to pay when you have employees on your payroll, as well as the cost of benefits they may receive. In many foodservice operations, labor costs are an operator's highest cost or they are second only to food and beverage costs in the total number of dollars spent.

Consider the Cost

"I'm feeling pretty good about our cost management efforts," said Rachel. "Our labor cost is higher than our food cost."

"I'm pleased with our efforts, too," said Julie. "Our food cost is higher than our labor cost."

"That's great, Julie," said Joseph. "I just calculated our monthly costs, and our food and labor expenses are just about equal. Sounds like we are all doing well!"

Rachel, Julie, and Joseph had all attended hospitality school together. Each had taken a job in the same large city, so they often got together over coffee to talk about their businesses and their jobs. One manages Chez Paul's, a fine-dining French-style restaurant known for impeccable service. Another manages Fuby's, a family-style cafeteria known for its tasty, home-style cooking. The third manages Gardinos, a national restaurant chain that offers mid-priced Italian cuisine in a beautiful Tuscan-style decor.

1. Which foodservice operation do you think Rachel manages? Why? *Chez Paul – Service*
2. Which foodservice operation do you think Julie manages? Why? *Fubys – Quantity*
3. Which foodservice operation do you think Joseph manages? Why? *Gardinos – Avg*

FUN ON THE WEB!

The foodservice industry is large and continues to grow. The trade association representing many foodservice businesses is the National Restaurant Association (NRA). Enter "National Restaurant Association" in your favorite browser to visit the website.

When you arrive at the site, click on "News & Research" to see the association's current revenue projections for the restaurant industry, which now has annual sales of over $650 billion.

OTHER EXPENSES

Other expenses comprise all of the expenses that are not included as a food, beverage, or labor costs. Examples include business insurance, utilities, rent, and such items as linens, china, glassware, kitchen knives, and pots and pans.

Although this expense category is sometimes incorrectly referred to by some as "minor expenses," your ability to successfully control this expense area is critical to the overall profitability of your foodservice operation.

GETTING STARTED •——————————————————————

Good managers must learn to understand, control, and manage their expenses. Consider the case of Tabreshia Larson, the food and beverage director of the 200-room Renaud Hotel, located in a college town and built near an interstate highway. Tabreshia has just received her end-of-the-year operating reports for the current year. She is interested in comparing these results to those of the prior year. The numbers she received are shown in Figure 1.3.

Tabreshia is concerned about her operation, but she is not sure if she should be. Revenue is higher than last year, so she feels her guests must like the products and services they receive. In fact, repeat business from corporate meetings and special-events meals is increasing. Profits are greater than last year also, but Tabreshia has the uneasy feeling that things are not going as well as they could. The kitchen appears to run smoothly. The staff, however, often runs out of needed items, and there sometimes seems to be a large amount of leftover food that must be thrown away. Also, at times, there seems to be too many employees on the property and not enough work for them to do; at other times, there seems to be too few employees and her guests have to wait too long to get served. Tabreshia also feels that employee theft may be occurring, but she certainly doesn't have the time to watch every storage area within her operation. She would really like to get a handle on the problems (if there are any)—but how and where should she start?

The answer for Tabreshia, and for you, if you want to develop a serious expense control system, is very simple. You start with basic mathematics skills that you must have to properly analyze your revenue and expenses. The mathematics required, and used in this text, are not very hard. They consist of addition, subtraction, multiplication, and division. These tools will be sufficient to build a cost control system that will help you professionally manage the expenses you incur.

To see why managers must be able to analyze their businesses, consider what it would mean to you if a fellow foodservice manager told you that yesterday he spent $500 on food. Obviously, it means very little unless you know more about his operation. Should he have spent $500 yesterday? Was that too much? Too little? Was it a "good" day or a "bad" day? These questions raise a challenging problem. How can you properly compare your expenses today with those of yesterday, or your own foodservice unit with another, so that you can see how well you are doing?

The answer to that question becomes even more complex because we know that the value of dollars changes over time. For example, a restaurant that generated revenue of $1,000 per day in 1954 would be very different from that same restaurant with daily revenue of $1,000 today because the value of the dollar today

FIGURE 1.3 Renaud Hotel Operating Results

	This Year	Last Year
Revenue	$1,106,040	$850,100
Expenses	1,017,557	773,591
Profit	$ 88,483	$ 76,509

is quite different from what it was in 1954. Generally, inflation causes the purchasing power of a dollar today to be less than that of a dollar from a previous time period. Inflation can make it challenging to answer the simple question, "Am I doing as well today as I was doing five years ago?"

Alternatively, consider the problem of an individual responsible for the management of several foodservice units. She owns two food carts that sell tacos on either side of a large city. One food cart uses $500 worth of food products each day; the other uses $600 worth of food products each day. Are both units being efficiently operated? Does the second food cart use an additional $100 worth of food each day because it serves more customers or because it is less efficient in utilizing its food?

The answer to all of the preceding questions, and many more, can be determined if we use percentages to relate the expenses of an operation to the revenue it generates. Percentage calculations are important for at least two major reasons. First and foremost, percentages are the most common tools used to evaluate costs in the foodservice industry. Therefore, knowledge of what a percent is and how it is calculated is vital. Second, as a manager in the foodservice industry, you will be evaluated primarily on your ability to compute, analyze, and control these percentages.

Although it is true that many basic management tools such as Microsoft Excel, OpenOffice's Calc, Lotus 1-2-3, and other software programs can compute percentages for you, it is important that you understand what the percentages mean and how they should be interpreted. Percent calculations are used extensively in this text and are a cornerstone of any effective cost control system.

REVIEWING PERCENTAGES

Understanding percentages and how they are mathematically computed is essential for all managers. The following review may be helpful for some readers. If you already thoroughly understand the percent concept, you may skip this section and the "Computing Percentages" section and proceed directly to the "Using Percentages" section.

Percent (%) means "out of each hundred." Thus, 10 percent would mean 10 out of each 100. If we asked how many guests would buy blueberry pie on a given day, and the answer is 10 percent, then 10 people out of each 100 we serve will select blueberry pie. If 52 percent of your employees are female, then 52 out of each 100 employees are female. If 15 percent of your employees will receive a raise this month, then 15 out of each 100 employees will get their raise. There are three basic ways to express percent:

1. Common form
2. Fractional form
3. Decimal form

Figure 1.4 shows these three forms, or ways, of writing a percentage.

FIGURE 1.4 Forms of Expressing Percent

Form	Percent		
	1%	10%	100%
Common	1%	10%	100%
Fraction	1/100	10/100	100/100
Decimal	0.01	0.10	1.00

COMMON FORM

In its common form, the % sign is used to express the percentage. If we say 10 percent (or 10%), then we mean "10 out of each 100," and no further explanation is necessary. If we say 50 percent (or 50%), then we mean "50 out of each 100," and no further explanation is necessary. In the common form, the percent is equivalent to the same amount expressed in either the fraction or the decimal form.

FRACTION FORM

In fraction form, the percentage is expressed as the part, or a portion of 100. Thus, 10 percent is written as 10 "over" 100 (10/100). Similarly, 50 percent is written as 50 "over" 100 (50/100). When using the fraction form, the "part" is the numerator and is always placed "on top," while the "whole" is the denominator and it is always placed "on the bottom."

Despite the fact that it looks different, when writing 10 percent, or any other percent, use of the fraction form is simply another way of expressing the relationship between, in this example, the part (10) and the whole (100).

DECIMAL FORM

A decimal is a number developed directly from the counting system we use. It is based on the fact that we count to 10, then start over again. In other words, each of our major units—10s, 100s, 1,000s, and so on—is based on the use of 10s, and each number can easily be divided by 10.

Unlike the common or fraction form, the decimal form of expressing a percentage uses the decimal point (.) to present the percent relationship. Thus, 10 percent is expressed as 0.10 in decimal form; 50 percent is expressed as 0.50. When utilizing the decimal form, the numbers to the right of the decimal point express the percentage.

Professionals throughout the foodservice industry use each of these three methods of expressing percentages. To be successful, you must develop a clear understanding of how a percentage is computed and when it is properly used. Once you know that, you can express the percentage in any form that is required or that is useful to you.

COMPUTING PERCENTAGES

To determine what percent one number is of another number, you divide the number that is the part by the number that is the whole. Usually, but not always, this means dividing the smaller number by the larger number. For example, assume that 840 guests were served during a banquet at your hotel and that 420 of them asked for coffee with their meal. To find what percent of your guests ordered coffee, divide the part of the group who ordered coffee (420) by the size of the whole group (840).

The process looks like this:

$$\frac{\text{Part}}{\text{Whole}} = \text{Percent, or} \quad \frac{420}{840} = 0.50, \text{ or } 50\%$$

Recall that a percentage can be expressed in three ways. Thus, 50% (common form), 50/100 (fraction form), and 0.50 (decimal form) all represent the proportion of people at the banquet who ordered coffee.

Some new foodservice managers have difficulty computing percent figures. That's because sometimes it is easy to forget which number goes "on the top" and which number goes "on the bottom." In general, if you attempt to compute a percentage and get a whole number (a number larger than 1), either a mistake has been made or revenue is extremely low and/or costs are extremely high!

FIGURE 1.5 Percent Computation

Possibilities	Examples	Results
Part is smaller than the whole	$\frac{61}{100} = 61\%$	Always less than 100%
Part is equal to the whole	$\frac{35}{35} = 100\%$	Always equals 100%
Part is larger than the whole	$\frac{125}{50} = 250\%$	Always greater than 100%

Some people also become confused when converting from one form of percent to another. If that is a problem for you, remember the following conversion rules:

1. To convert from common form to decimal form, move the decimal two places to the left; that is, 50.00% = 0.50.
2. To convert from decimal form to common form, move the decimal two places to the right; that is, 0.40 = 40.00%.

In a restaurant, the "whole" is most often a revenue (sales) figure. Expenses and profits are the "parts," which are usually expressed in terms of a percent. It is interesting to note that, in the United States, the same system in use for our numbers is in use for our money. Each dime contains 10 pennies; each dollar contains 10 dimes, and so on. Thus, in discussions of money, it is true that a percent refers to "cents out of each dollar" as well as "out of each 100 dollars." When we say 10 percent of a dollar, we mean 10 cents, or "10 cents out of each dollar." Likewise, 25 percent of a dollar represents 25 cents, 50 percent of a dollar represents 50 cents, and 100 percent of a dollar represents $1.00.

Sometimes, when using percentages to express the relationship between portions of a dollar and the whole dollar, we can find that the part is indeed larger than the whole. Figure 1.5 demonstrates the three possibilities associated with computing a percentage. Great care must always be taken when computing percentages, so that the percentage arrived at does not represent an error in mathematics. In turn, the mathematical errors could cause you to make poor foodservice decisions.

HERE'S HOW IT'S DONE *1.1*

When a manager calculates a food expense percentage, labor expense percentage, or any other expense percentage, the mathematical result is usually a number less than 1. In most cases, the mathematical formula used to calculate a percentage will result in the percentage being expressed in decimal form.

For example, if the cost of food for a menu item is $3.60 and the menu item sells for $12.00, the percentage that represents the cost of food is calculated as:

$$\frac{\$3.60 \text{ Cost of food}}{\$12.00 \text{ Selling price}} = 0.30$$

In this example, the menu item's food cost is expressed in decimal form (0.30).

When a percentage is expressed in decimal form, the numbers to the right of the decimal represent the size of the percentage. To convert the percentage from decimal form to common form, simply multiply the decimal form amount times 100.

In this example, the conversion from decimal form to common form would be:

$$0.30 \times 100 = 30\%$$

Therefore, the menu item's food cost percentage, when expressed in common form, is 30%.

If the percentage in this example is to be expressed in fractional form, the part (30) is the numerator and would be placed on top of the whole (100). 100 is the whole and thus is the denominator. The denominator is always placed on the bottom. In this example, the result would be expressed as 30/100.

USING PERCENTAGES

The ability to calculate a percentage is important because percentages are useful tools. To illustrate, consider a restaurant that you are operating. Imagine that your revenue for a week is $1,600. Expenses for that same week are $1,200. Given these facts and the information presented earlier in this chapter, your profit formula for the week would be as follows:

$$\text{Revenue} - \text{Expenses} = \text{Profit}$$
$$\text{or}$$
$$\$1,600 - \$1,200 = \$400$$

If you had planned for a $500 profit for the week, you would have been "short" by $100. Using the alternative profit formula that identifies desired profit and presented earlier, you would find:

$$\text{Revenue} - \text{Desired profit} = \text{Ideal expense}$$
$$\text{or}$$
$$\$1,600 - \$500 = \$1,100$$

Note that your expense in this example ($1,200) exceeded your ideal expense ($1,100), and as a result, too little profit was achieved.

These numbers can also be expressed in terms of percentages. If we want to know what percentage of our revenue went to pay for our expenses, we would compute it as follows:

$$\frac{\text{Expense}}{\text{Revenue}} = \text{Expense \%}$$
$$\text{or}$$
$$\frac{\$1,200}{\$1,600} = 0.75, \text{ or } 75\%$$

In this example, expenses are 75 percent of revenue. Another way to state this relationship is to say that each dollar of revenue costs 75 cents to produce. As a result, each revenue dollar taken in results in 25 cents profit:

$$\$1.00 \text{ Revenue} - \$0.75 \text{ Expense} = \$0.25 \text{ Profit}$$

As long as your business's expenses are smaller than its revenues, some profit will be generated, even if it is not as much as you had planned.

Managers can calculate their expense percentages, and they can also calculate their profit percentages. You can compute profit percentages using the following formula:

$$\frac{\text{Profit}}{\text{Revenue}} = \text{Profit \%}$$

In our example:

$$\frac{\$400 \text{ Profit}}{\$1,600 \text{ Revenue}} = 25\% \text{ Profit}$$

We can compute what we had planned our profit percentage to be by dividing desired profit ($500) by revenue ($1,600):

$$\frac{\$500 \text{ Desired profit}}{\$1,600 \text{ Revenue}} = 31.25\% \text{ Desired profit}$$

In simple terms, we had planned to make 31.25 percent profit, but instead made only a 25 percent profit. Excess costs account for the difference. If these costs could be identified and corrected, we could perhaps achieve the desired profit percentage in the future. Expenses expressed as cost percentages are important, and most foodservice operators compute many cost percentages, not just one. The major cost divisions used in foodservice are:

1. Food and beverage costs
2. Labor costs
3. Other expenses

Because these are the major cost categories, in foodservice operations a modified profit formula can be developed as follows:

Revenue − (Food and beverage costs + Labor costs + Other expenses) = Profit

Put in another format, the equation would look like this:

	Revenue (100%)
Minus (−)	Food and beverage cost %
Minus (−)	Labor cost %
Minus (−)	Other expenses %
Equals (=)	Profit %

This expression of the profit formula makes sense because it clearly shows that managers start with 100 percent of their revenue, subtract their expense percentages, and the amount that remains represents the operation's profit percentage. Regardless of the form in which percentages are reported, professional foodservice managers carefully evaluate their revenue and expenses, and they use percentages to do so.

UNDERSTANDING THE INCOME (PROFIT AND LOSS) STATEMENT

Foodservice operations generate revenue and incur expenses whenever they are open for business. Periodically, these operations will want to report their income and expense activity. To see how this is typically done, consider Figure 1.6, a summary of revenue, expense, and profits generated by Dan's Steakhouse.

All of Dan's expenses and profits can be computed as percentages by using the revenue figure of $400,000 as the whole and the food and beverage costs, labor costs, other expenses, and profit representing the parts as follows:

$$\frac{\text{Food and beverage costs}}{\text{Revenue}} = \text{Food and beverage cost \%}$$

or

$$\frac{\$150,000}{\$400,000} = 37.50\%$$

$$\frac{\text{Labor costs}}{\text{Revenue}} = \text{Labor cost } \%$$

or

$$\frac{\$175,000}{\$400,000} = 43.75\%$$

$$\frac{\text{Other expenses}}{\text{Revenue}} = \text{Other expenses } \%$$

or

$$\frac{\$25,000}{\$400,000} = 6.25\%$$

$$\frac{\text{Total expenses}}{\text{Revenue}} = \text{Total expenses } \%$$

or

$$\frac{\$350,000}{\$400,000} = 87.50\%$$

$$\frac{\text{Profit}}{\text{Revenue}} = \text{Profit } \%$$

or

$$\frac{\$50,000}{\$400,000} = 12.50\%$$

The accounting tool that managers use to report their operations' revenue, expenses, and profit for a specific time period is called the **statement of income and expense**. The statement of income and expense is also commonly known as the **income statement** or the **profit-and-loss statement**, which is very often shortened by foodservice managers to simply the **P&L**.

The P&L lists all of an operation's revenue, food and beverage costs, labor costs, and other expenses. The P&L also identifies profits by using the profit formula. Recall that the profit formula is:

$$\text{Revenue} - \text{Expenses} = \text{Profit}$$

Figure 1.7 is a simplified P&L statement for Dan's Steakhouse (*Note:* detailed information on properly preparing and analyzing an income statement will be addressed in Chapter 9, "Analyzing the Income Statement"). Notice the similarity of Figure 1.7 to Figure 1.6. In Figure 1.7, expenses and profits are expressed in terms of both dollar amounts and percentages of revenue.

Another way of looking at Dan's simplified P&L is shown in Figure 1.8. The pieces of the pie represent Dan's cost and profit categories. Costs and profit total 100 percent, which is equal to Dan's total revenues. Put another way, out of every sales dollar Dan generates, 100 percent is designated as either costs or profit.

FIGURE 1.6 Dan's Steakhouse

Revenue		$400,000
Expenses		
Food and Beverage Cost	$150,000	
Labor Cost	175,000	
Other Expenses	25,000	
Total Expenses		$350,000
Profit		$ 50,000

FIGURE 1.7 Dan's Steakhouse P&L

Revenue		$400,000	100%
Food and Beverage Cost	$150,000		37.5%
Labor Cost	175,000		43.75%
Other Expenses	25,000		6.25%
Total Expenses		$350,000	87.5%
Profit		$ 50,000	12.5%

FIGURE 1.8 Dan's Steakhouse Costs and Profit as a Percentage of Revenues

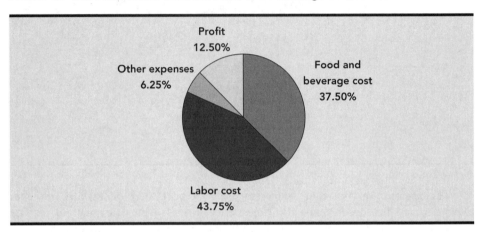

Dan knows from the P&L that revenues represent 100 percent of the total dollars available to cover expenses and provide for a profit. Food and beverage costs are 37.50 percent, and labor costs are 43.75 percent. Other expenses percentage equals 6.25 percent, and the total expenses percentage is 87.50 percent (37.50 + 43.75 + 6.25 = 87.50%). The steakhouse profit equals 12.50 percent. Thus, for each dollar in revenue, Dan earns a profit of 12.50 cents.

In restaurants that serve alcohol, food revenues and beverage revenues are most often reported separately. Likewise, food costs and beverage costs are most often separated into two categories in the P&L. This is done so that food costs can easily be compared to food revenues, and beverage costs can be easily compared to beverage revenues. This is helpful when, for example, one manager is responsible for controlling food costs in the restaurant and another manager is responsible for controlling beverage costs in the bar.

The P&L is an important management tool because it indicates the efficiency and profitability of a business. It is important that they are accurate and easily understood. Because so many individuals and groups are interested in a facility's performance, it is important that the P&L and other financial statements are prepared in a manner that is consistent with other facilities. If, for example, you own two Italian restaurants, it would be very confusing if the units' two managers used different methods for preparing and reporting their P&Ls. You, your investors, accountants, governmental taxing entities, and your creditors will all be interested in your operational results, and unless you report and account for these in a manner that is consistent and that can be easily understood, confusion is likely to result.

To avoid such a set of circumstances, **The Uniform System of Accounts for Restaurants (USAR)** is used to report financial results in many foodservice units. This system was created to ensure uniform reporting of financial results. A *Uniform System of Accounts* exists for restaurants, another for hotels, and another for clubs.

These uniform accounting systems are continually reviewed and periodically revised. This text was prepared using reporting principles contained in the 8th edition of the *USAR*, which was released in 2010. Important specific recommendations of the *USAR* will be addressed in detail in the appropriate portions of this text.

The use of the *USAR* when producing a P&L is not mandatory, but its use is highly recommended. This is so because the primary purpose of preparing a P&L is to clearly identify revenue, expenses, and profits for a specific time period. As a manager, your individual efforts will greatly influence your operation's profitability. Good managers want to provide excellent value to their guests, which will cause guests to return. When they do, sales will increase. In addition, good managers know how to analyze, manage, and control their costs. When costs are controlled well an operation's expenses are held to the amounts that were preplanned by its manager. The final result is the desired profit level.

Good managers influence the success of their units and their own employees. The results for them personally are promotions, added responsibilities, and salary increases. If you wish to succeed in the hospitality industry, it is important to remember that your performance will be evaluated primarily on your ability to achieve the profit levels your operation has planned for.

In addition to your own efforts, many factors influence profit dollars and profit percent, and you must be aware, and in control, of all of them. All of the factors that make up professional food and beverage cost control and that will impact your profits are directly addressed in later chapters of this text.

FUN ON THE WEB!

For restaurant managers, learning is an ongoing process. Fortunately, a large number of sources of important information are readily available to managers who seek to continue their education. To examine some of these resources, enter "restaurant industry financial results" in your favorite search engine and review current data about how the restaurant industry is performing.

UNDERSTANDING THE BUDGET

Some foodservice managers do not generate revenue on a daily basis. Consider, for a moment, the foodservice manager who operates Camp Eureka, a children's summer camp. In this case, parents pay a fixed fee to cover housing, activities, and meals for a set period of time. The foodservice manager, in this situation, is just one of several camp managers who must share this revenue. If too many dollars are spent on providing housing or play activities, too few dollars may be available to provide an adequate quantity or quality of meals. On the other hand, if too many dollars are spent on providing foodservice, there may not be enough left to cover other needed expense areas. In a case like this, as in many other cases, foodservice operators must prepare a budget.

A **budget** is simply an estimate of projected revenue, expenses, and profit. In some hospitality companies, the budget is known as the forecast, or the **plan,** referring to the fact that the budget details the operation's estimated, or "planned for," revenue and expenses for a given accounting period. An **accounting period** is any specific hour, day, week, or month in which an operator wishes to report and analyze an operation's revenue and expenses.

All effective managers, whether in the commercial (for-profit) or nonprofit sector, should use budgets. Budgeting is simply planning for an operation's revenue, expenses, and profit. If these items are planned for, you can determine how close your actual performance is to your plan or budget.

To illustrate the importance of a budget using the summer camp example, assume the following information is known:

1. Number of campers to be served each day is 180.
2. Number of meals served to each camper per day is 3.
3. Length of campers' stay is 7 days.

With 180 campers eating 3 meals each day for 7 days, 3,780 meals will be served (180 campers × 3 meals per day × 7 days = 3,780 meals).

Generally, in a case such as the summer camp, the foodservice manager is given a dollar amount that represents the allowed expense for each meal to be served. For example, if $1.85 per meal is the amount budgeted for this food-service manager, the total revenue budget would equal $6,993 ($1.85 per meal × 3,780 meals = $6,993).

From this figure, an expense budget can begin to be developed. In this case, we would be interested in the amount of expenses budgeted and the amount actually spent on those expenses. Equally important, we are interested in the percent of the budget we actually used, a concept known as comparing **performance to budget.**

A simple example may help to explain the idea of budget and performance to budget. Assume that a child has $1.00 per day to spend on candy. On Monday morning, the child's parents give the child $1.00 for each day of the week, or $7.00 total ($1.00 × 7 days = $7.00).

If the child spends exactly $1.00 per day, he or she will be able to buy candy all week. If, however, too much is spent on any one day, there might not be any money left at the end of the week. To ensure a full week of candy eating, a good "candy purchasing" budget could be created, such as the one shown in Figure 1.9.

To prepare this budget, the "% of Total" column is computed by dividing $1.00 (the part) by $7.00 (the whole). Notice that we can determine the percent of total that should have been spent by any given day; that is, each day equals 14.28 percent, or 1/7 of the total.

This same logic applies to a foodservice operation. Managers determine how much of their total budgets can be spent in any specific time period. Figure 1.10 represents commonly used budget periods and their accompanying proportional amounts.

In the foodservice industry, the use of monthly budgets is very popular. Some foodservice operations, however, recognize that different months include different numbers of days. As a result, some operators are changing from one-month budget periods to budget periods of 28 days. The **28-day-period approach** divides a year into 13 equal periods of 28 days each. Therefore, each period has four Mondays, four Tuesdays, four Wednesdays, and so on. This helps the manager compare performance from one period to the next without having to compensate for extra days in any one month.

FIGURE 1.9 Budgeting Candy Purchases

Weekday	Budgeted Amount	% of Total
Monday	$1.00	14.28%
Tuesday	1.00	14.28%
Wednesday	1.00	14.28%
Thursday	1.00	14.28%
Friday	1.00	14.28%
Saturday	1.00	14.28%
Sunday	1.00	14.28%
Total	$7.00	100.00%

FIGURE 1.10 Common Foodservice Budget Periods

Budget Period	Portion	% of Total
One week	One day	1/7 or 14.28%
Two-week period	One day	1/14 or 7.14%
	One week	1/2 or 50.0%
One month	One week	1/4 or 25.0%
28 days	One day	1/28 or 3.6%
30 days	One day	1/30 or 3.3%
31 days	One day	1/31 or 3.2%
Six months	One month	1/6 or 16.7%
One year (365 days)	One day	1/365 or 0.3%
	One week	1/52 or 1.9%
	One month	1/12 or 8.3%

The disadvantage of the 28-day period approach is that managers can no longer talk about the month of April, because, if a budget began at the first of the year, "Period 4" would occur during part of March and part of April. Although using the 28-day-period approach takes a while to get used to, it is often an effective way to measure performance and plan from period to period.

Managers are interested in comparing actual performance to budgeted performance. At Camp Eureka, after one week's camping was completed, we calculated the results shown in Figure 1.11.

We used the expense records from the previous summer as well as our solid industry knowledge and experience to develop initial budget amounts. Detailed information about this budgeting process is addressed in Chapter 10, "Planning for Profits." When, as in this case, an accurate budget has been developed we can directly compare our budgeted (planned) performance to our actual performance.

Figure 1.12 shows a performance-to-budget summary with revenue and expenses presented in terms of both the budget amount and the actual amount. In all cases, percentages are used to compare actual expenses with the budgeted amount, using the formula:

$$\frac{\text{Actual}}{\text{Budget}} = \%\ \text{of Budget}$$

Note that, in this example, fewer meals were actually served than were originally budgeted. Revenue remained the same, but some campers skipped (or slept through!) some of their meals. This is often the case when one fee or price buys

FIGURE 1.11 Camp Eureka One-Week Budget

Item	Budget	Actual
Meals Served	3,780	3,700
Revenue		$6,993
Food Expense	$2,600	$2,400
Labor Expense	$2,800	$2,900
Other Expenses	$ 700	$ 965
Total Expenses	$6,100	$6,265
Profit	$ 893	$ 728

FIGURE 1.12 Camp Eureka Performance to Budget Summary

Item	Budget	Actual	% of Budget
Meals Served	3,780	3,700	97.9%
Revenue	$6,993	$6,993	100.0%
Food Expense	$2,600	$2,400	92.3%
Labor Expense	$2,800	$2,900	103.6%
Other Expenses	$ 700	$ 965	137.9%
Total Expenses	$6,100	$6,265	102.7%
Profit	$ 893	$ 728	81.5%

a number of meals, whether they are eaten or not. In some other cases, managers will receive revenue only for meals actually served. This, of course, is true in a traditional restaurant setting. In either case, budgeted amount, actual expenses, and the concept of percent of budget, or performance to budget, are important management tools.

In looking at the Camp Eureka performance-to-budget summary, we can see that the manager served fewer meals than planned and, thus, spent less on food than estimated, but spent more on labor than was originally thought necessary. In addition, much more was spent than estimated for other expenses—that is, 137.9 percent of the budgeted amount. As a result, profit dollars were lower than planned. This manager has some problems, but note that there are not problems everywhere in the operation.

How do we know that? If our budget is accurate and we are within reasonable limits of our budget, we are said to be "in line," or in compliance, with our budget. It is difficult to budget exact revenue and expenses, so if we determine that plus (more than) or minus (less than) 10 percent of budget in each category is considered in line, or acceptable, then a close examination of Figure 1.12 shows we are in line with regard to meals served, food expense, labor expense, and total expenses. We are not in line with other expenses, however, because they were 137.9 percent of the amount originally planned. Thus, they far exceed the 10 percent variation that was reasonably allowed. Profit was also outside the acceptable boundary we established because it was only 81.5 percent of the amount budgeted. Note that, in this illustration, figures over 100 percent mean too much (other expenses), and figures below 100 percent mean too little (profit).

Many operators use the concept of "significant" variation to determine whether a cost control problem exists. In this case, a significant variation is any variation in expected costs that management feels is an area of concern. This variation can be caused by costs that were either higher or lower than the amount originally budgeted or planned for.

In the foodservice industry, the essence of cost control is identifying actual costs, comparing them to planned costs, and taking corrective action when necessary. When you manage a foodservice operation and you find that significant variations from your planned results occur, you must:

1. Identify the problem.
2. Determine the cause.
3. Take corrective action.

It is crucial to know the kind of problem you have if you are to be an effective problem solver. Management's attention must be focused on the proper area of concern. In the summer camp example, the proper areas for management's concern are **other expenses** and **profit**. If, in the future, food expense became *too* low, it too would be an area of concern. Why? Remember that expenses create revenue; thus, it is not your goal to eliminate expense. In fact, managers who focus too much on eliminating expense, instead of building revenue, often find that their expenses are completely eliminated when they are forced to close their operation's doors permanently because guests did not feel they received good value for the money spent at that restaurant! Control and management of revenue and expenses are important. Elimination of either is not desired.

As you have seen, revenue and expenses directly impact profit. Your important role as a hospitality manager is to analyze, manage, and control your costs so that you achieve planned results. It can be done, and it can be fun.

The remainder of this text discusses how you can best manage and account for foodservice revenue and expenses. With a good understanding of the relationship among revenue, expenses, and profit, and your ability to analyze these areas using percentages, you are ready to begin the cost control and cost management process.

Technology Tools

Most hospitality managers would agree that an accurate and timely income statement (P&L) is an invaluable aid to their management efforts. There are a variety of software programs on the market that can be used to develop this statement for you. You simply fill in the revenue and expense portions of the program, and a P&L is produced. Variations include programs that compare your actual results to budgeted figures or forecasts, to prior-month performance, or to prior-year performance. In addition, P&Ls can be produced for any time period, including days, weeks, months, quarters, or years. Most income statement programs will have a budgeting feature and the ability to maintain historical sales and cost records. Some of these have been developed specifically for restaurants, but cost-effective generic products are also available.

A second issue, and one that must be kept foremost in mind, is that of information accessibility. For example, an executive chef would certainly need to have information readily available on food costs, however, it may not be wise to allow servers or cooks access to payroll information. While labor expenses certainly affects costs, individual worker pay should be shared only with those who need to know. Thus, as you examine (in this chapter and others) the cost control technology tools available to you, keep in mind that not all information should be accessible to all parties, and that security of your cost and customer information can be just as critical as its accuracy.

FUN ON THE WEB!

Intuit is the company that produces the popular *QuickBooks* line of accounting software. QuickBooks can help you create a monthly income statement (P&L) and do much more. To view QuickBooks product offerings, go to the Intuit company website and review the features available in its newest version of QuickBooks.

Cost Control Around the World

Food and beverage cost control is truly a topic of international importance. Consider that there are now over 33,500 McDonald's restaurants operating in 119 countries. The operations serve over 69 million customers per day. Although there are over 13,500 McDonald's located in the United States, nearly twice that number of McDonald's restaurants are located outside the United States.

Although McDonald's is among the best known, many other hospitality companies operate in the international market and the number of those doing so increases each year. Burger King, KFC, Wendy's, Hilton Hotels & Resorts, Hyatt, Marriott, Aramark, Subway, Dunkin' Donuts, Baskin-Robbins, Pizza Hut, Taco Bell, and Rainforest Cafe are just a few examples of the increasingly large number of US-based companies expanding their international presence. As a result, more and more foodservice professionals working in restaurants, hotels, and contract foodservice businesses are being given cost control–related assignments in their companies' rapidly expanding international divisions.

Apply What You Have Learned

*J*ennifer Caratini has recently accepted the job as the foodservice director for Techmar Industries, a corporation with 1,000 employees. As their foodservice director, Jennifer's role is to operate a company cafeteria, serving 800 to 900 meals per day, as well as an executive dining room, serving 100 to 200 meals per day. All of the meals are provided "free of charge" to the employees of Techmar. One of Jennifer's first jobs is to prepare a budget for next year's operations.

1. In addition to the cost of food products and foodservice employees, what other expenses will Techmar incur by providing free meals to its employees?

2. Since employees do not pay for their food directly, what will Jennifer likely use as the "revenue" portion of her budget? How do you think this number should be determined?

3. In addition to her know-how as a foodservice director, what skills will Jennifer likely need as she interacts with the executives at Techmar who must approve her operating budget?

Key Terms and Concepts

*T*he following are terms and concepts discussed in the chapter that are important for you as a manager. To help you review, please define the terms below.

revenue	beverage costs	P&L
expenses	labor costs	The Uniform System
profit	other expenses	of Accounts for
business dining	percent	Restaurants (USAR)
ideal expense	statement of income and	budget/plan
desired profit	expense	accounting period
sustainable development	income statement	performance to budget
food costs	profit and loss statement	28-day-period approach

Test Your Skills

You may download the Excel spreadsheets for the Test Your Skills exercises from the student companion website at www.wiley.com/college/dopson. Complete the exercises by placing your answers in the shaded boxes and answering the questions as indicated.

1. Last month, Lani's Pizza Parlor generated $75,000 in revenues. Her total expenses last month were $63,000. Create the formula Lani needs to calculate the amount of profit she made last month. How much profit did she make?

Lani's Pizza Parlor	
Revenue	
Expenses	
Profit	

2. At the conclusion of her first month of operating Val's Donut Shop, Val computed the following revenue and expense figures:

Week	Revenue	Expenses	Profit/Loss
1	$ 894.50	$ 761.80	
2	1,147.60	522.46	
3	1,261.80	879.14	
4	1,345.11	1,486.20	
Month			
To Receive $1,200.00 Profit for the Month			
Month			

Prepare both weekly and monthly profit formulas so that Val has a good idea about her current profit situation. Also, given her sales for the month, tell her how much her ideal expense should have been to realize her desired profit of $1,200.

3. Su Chan manages a popular restaurant called the Bungalow. Her P&L for the month of March is as follows:

The Bungalow's March P&L		
Revenue	$100,000.00	100.0%
F&B Expense	$ 34,000.00	34.0%
Labor Expense	40,000.00	40.0%
Other Expenses	21,000.00	21.0%
Total Expenses	$ 95,000.00	95.0%
Profit	$ 5,000.00	5.0%

Su has a meeting with the owner of the Bungalow next week, so she decided to create a pie chart showing the percentage of her costs in relation to her total sales (see the following diagram).

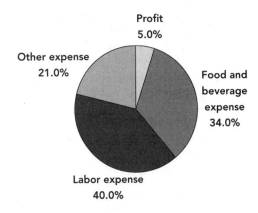

At the meeting with the owner, Su is asked to change the information on the pie chart to reflect the next month's projections. The owner suggests that April revenue and costs should be as follows:

April revenue = $120,000
Food and beverage expense = $44,000
Labor and other expenses remain constant.

Using these numbers, is the owner's profit percentage going to be higher or lower than that in March? By how much?

After looking at the owner's projections, she thinks it might be too difficult (and not so good for her guests) if she cannot increase labor costs along with sales. She proposes a compromise and tells the owner that if he will agree to increase labor costs, she will try to decrease other expenses. So Su proposes the following:

April revenue = $120,000
Food and beverage expense = $44,000
Labor expense = $50,000
Other expenses = $19,000

Using these numbers, is the owner's profit percentage going to be higher or lower than that in March? By how much?

Which set of projections has more reasonable goals?

Note: If you use the Excel spreadsheets from this book's student resources site, the changes you make to the numbers should be reflected on the pie charts as well.

4. The dining room at the Roadrock Inn is extremely popular. Terry Ray, the food and beverage director, is pleased to see that his revenue is higher than last year's. Of course, expenses are higher also. Express Terry's expenses and profit as a percentage of total revenue, for both this year and last year (fill in all empty blanks).

	This Year	%	Last Year	%
Total Revenue	$965,971.00		$875,421.00	
F&B Expense	$367,069.00		$350,168.00	
Labor Expense	338,090.00		315,151.00	
Other Expenses	144,896.00		140,068.00	
Total Expenses				
Profit				

How is Terry doing in managing his expenses this year compared to last year? How do changes in revenue affect his performance?

5. Pamela Cantu operates a school foodservice department in a small, rural community. She feeds approximately 1,000 students per day in three different locations. She receives an average of $1.20 in revenues per meal. Her budget, set at the beginning of the school year by the superintendent, is developed in such a way that a small amount is to be reserved for future equipment purchases and dining-room renovation. These funds are available, however, only if Pamela meets her budget. She hopes to use this year's reserve (profit) to buy a $5,000 refrigerated salad bar for the high school. Because it is the midpoint of her school year, help her determine her "performance to budget" thus far (fill in all blanks).

Item	Budget	Actual	% of Budget
Meals Served	300,000	149,800	
Revenue			
Food Expense	$170,000	$84,961	
Labor Expense	125,000	63,752	
Other Expenses	60,000	31,460	
Total Expenses	$355,000		
Reserve	$ 5,000		

Assuming that the year is 50 percent completed and Pamela continues doing what she is doing, is she likely to meet the reserve requirement and thus be able to purchase the salad bar by the end of the year? If not, what changes should she make over the next six months to ensure that she will have the $5,000 in reserve?

6. Sam Guild operates a dining room reserved for doctors in a large hospital in the Northeast. Sam's boss has given Sam a target of 33 percent food cost but has indicated that the target might be adjusted. Currently, the doctors' meals sell for $15.00. Sam knows he currently can spend $4.95 for the food required to produce each meal. Fill out the chart below to help Sam find out how much he will be able to spend on each meal at various food cost percentage levels if his boss adjusts his target.

Meal Selling Price	Food Cost %	Amount That Can Be Spent for Food
$15.00	20%	
$15.00	25%	
$15.00	30%	
$15.00	33%	$4.95
$15.00	35%	
$15.00	40%	

How will the doctors' meals likely be affected if the target cost percentage is reduced? What if it is increased?

7. Dawne Juan is the food and beverage director for a mid-size hotel in a beach destination area. The general manager of the hotel has given Dawne a target of 10 percent profit for this year. Dawne's staff is predominantly composed of her beach buddies. Although she is good at controlling most of her costs, she has a hard time telling her friends to go home when business slows down, and she needs to reduce her staff. If she doesn't make her profit goal, her general manager will likely reprimand her, and she could possibly lose her job. Express Dawne's expenses and profit as a percentage of total revenue, both this year and last year, to determine if she met her profit goal (fill in all blanks).

	This Year	%	Last Year	%
Total Revenue	$1,448,956		$1,094,276	
F&B Expense	463,666			35%
Labor Expense	652,030			40%
Other Expenses		15%	186,027	
Total Expenses				
Profit				8%

Was Dawne effective at controlling her expenses? Did she meet the profit goal set by the general manager? If not, what could Dawne do in the future to help her make her target profit?

8. Lee Ray operates the Champs Steak and Seafood restaurant. Last month, Lee budgeted $3,500 for food, in the specific categories listed on the following page. It was a busy month, but Lee thought he did a good job managing his costs. Imagine his surprise when, at the end of the month, Lee calculated

his actual expenses and entered them in the chart below. He found he was way over budget! Calculate Lee's % of Budget in each category listed on the chart, as well as the total.

	Budget	Actual	% of Budget
Meats and Poultry	$1,500	$1,600	
Seafood	1,200	1,500	
Fruits and Vegetables	350	370	
Dairy Products	200	210	
Groceries	250	270	
Total			

By how much money was Lee over his total budget? In which categories did Lee's costs vary more than 10 percent from the amount he had originally budgeted? Lee said it was a busy month. Would the number of customers he served affect his actual costs? What would you recommend he do next to further analyze the reasons for his restaurant's budget performance last month?

9. Daudi owns and manages a restaurant featuring Middle Eastern cuisine. His operating results for this year are listed below. For next year, Daudi expects that his revenue will increase 5 percent. He also expects that the percentage of revenue he spends on food will remain unchanged, but that employee raises and rising health care costs will mean he will spend 10 percent more for the cost of labor next year than he spent this year. Because of new cost control measures he plans to implement, Daudi expects the total amount that he will spend for other expenses next year will be unchanged from this year.

Help Daudi prepare a budget for next year that will show the amount of revenue, expenses, and profit his operation will likely experience. Show each amount in dollars and as a percentage of revenue. Should Daudi's profits next year be greater or lesser than this year? By how much?

	This Year Actual	Percent	Next Year Budget	Next Year Percent
Revenue	$1,500,000	100%		
Cost of Food		35%		
Cost of Labor		30%		
Other Expenses		20%		
Total Expenses		85%		
Profit	$ 225,000	15%		

10. Some foodservice professionals feel the best way to improve profits is to reduce costs. Others feel that increasing revenue is the best way to increase profits. Name three specific steps a manager can take to reduce current costs. Name three specific steps a manager can take to increase revenues. Which approach do you feel would be best for the type of foodservice operation you want to manage in the future?

CHAPTER 2

Creating Sales Forecasts

OVERVIEW

This chapter presents the methods and procedures you must learn to create accurate records of what you have sold in the past as well as forecasts of how much business you will do in the future. This includes predicting the total amount of revenue you will generate, the number of guests you will serve, and the amount of money each guest will spend. Knowledge of these management techniques will provide the information you must have to analyze your historical sales and to serve your future guests professionally.

Chapter Outline

- Importance of Forecasting Sales
- Sales Histories
- Maintaining Sales Histories
- Sales Variances
- Predicting Future Sales
- Technology Tools
- Apply What You Have Learned
- Key Terms and Concepts
- Test Your Skills

LEARNING OUTCOMES

At the conclusion of this chapter, you will be able to:

- Develop a procedure to record current sales.
- Compute percentage increases or decreases in sales over time.
- Develop a procedure to predict future sales.

IMPORTANCE OF FORECASTING SALES •————

When they open their facility's doors at the beginning of the day, the first questions most foodservice managers must ask themselves are very simple: "How many guests will I serve today?—This week?—This year?" The answers to questions such as these are critical because the guests you serve will provide the revenue from which you will need to pay basic operating expenses and create a profit. Simply put, if too few guests are served, total revenue may not be enough to cover your costs, even if these costs are well managed. In addition, decisions regarding the type and quantity of food or beverages to purchase depend on knowing the number of guests who will be coming to buy those products. The labor required to serve guests is also determined based on the manager's "best guess" of the projected number of customers to arrive, as well as what these guests will buy. In an ongoing operation, it is often true that future sales estimates, or **projected sales**, will be heavily based on sales history. This is true because what has happened in the past in your operation is often the best predictor of what will happen in the future. Those managers who can best predict the future are those who are most prepared to control how it will affect them.

In the hospitality industry, we have many ways of counting or defining sales. In the simplest case, sales are defined as the dollar (or other currency) amount of revenue collected during a predetermined time period. The time period might be defined as an hour, a shift, a day, a week, a month, or a year. When used this way, sales and revenue are considered interchangeable terms.

When you predict the future number of guests you will serve and the revenue they will generate in a given time period, you have created a **sales forecast.** You can calculate your actual sales for a current time period in several ways. Most foodservice managers utilize a computerized system called a **point-of-sale (POS) system**, which, among other tasks, is programmed to record sales and payment information. Alternatively, manually produced guest checks or head counts are another method foodservice managers can use to help identify how many sales were completed. Today, however, even the smallest of foodservice operations should take advantage of the speed and accuracy provided by computerized programs used for recording sales.

FUN ON THE WEB!

A number of companies sell hospitality industry–specific POS systems used to record historical sales information and more. Some of the most popular companies include:

Oracle (previously Micros)

Squirrel Systems

NCR

To review their product offerings, enter the company name followed by "POS" into your favorite search engine.

It is important to remember that a distinction is made in the hospitality industry between sales (revenue) and **sales volume.** Sales volume is the number of units sold. Consider Manuel, a bagel shop manager, whose Monday business consists of $2,000 in sales (revenue) because he actually sold 1,000 bagels (sales volume). It is important for Manuel to know how much revenue was taken in, so he can evaluate the expenses required to generate his revenue and the number of units that have been sold. With this information, he can also be prepared to serve additional guests the next day.

In many areas of the hospitality industry such as in retirement centers and college and university residence halls, it is customary that no cash actually changes

FIGURE 2.1 Advantages of Accurate Sales Forecasts

- **Accurate revenue estimates**
- **Improved ability to predict expenses**
- **Greater efficiency in scheduling needed workers**
- **Greater efficiency in scheduling menu item production schedules**
- **Better accuracy in purchasing the correct amount of food for immediate use**
- **Improved ability to maintain proper levels of perishable and nonperishable food inventories**
- **Improved budgeting ability**
- **Lower selling prices for guests because of increased operational efficiencies**
- **Increased dollars available for current facility maintenance and future growth**
- **Increased profit levels and stockholder value**

hands during a particular meal period. However, the manager of such a facility still created sales during that meal period and would be interested in sales volume or how much food was actually consumed by the residents or students on any particular day. This is critical information because all foodservice managers must be prepared to answer the questions, "How many individuals did I serve today, and how many should I expect tomorrow?" In some cases, a food and beverage operation is a blend of cash and noncash sales.

Consider Tonya Brown, a hospital foodservice director. It is very likely that Tonya will be involved in serving both cash-paying guests (in an open-to-the-public cafeteria) and noncash patients (with tray-line-assembled meals that are then delivered to patients' rooms). In addition, meals for hospital employees might be cash sales but at a reduced or subsidized rate. Clearly, Tonya's operation will create sales each day, and it will be important for her and her staff to know, as accurately as possible, how many of each type of guest she will serve and which menu items these guests will be served.

An understanding of anticipated sales, in terms of revenue dollars, guest counts, or both, will help you have the right number of staff members working, with the right amounts of products available to them, at the right time. In this way, you can begin to effectively manage your costs. In addition to the importance of accurate sales records for purchasing and staffing, sales records are valuable to the operator when developing labor standards that improve efficiency.

Consider, for example, managing a large restaurant with 400 seats. If an individual server can serve 25 guests at lunch, you would need 400/25, or 8, servers per lunch shift if all your seats were filled. If management keeps no accurate sales histories and makes no sales forecasts, too few or too many servers might be scheduled to work. With accurate sales records, a sales history can be developed for each foodservice outlet you operate, and better decisions can be made with regard to planning for each unit's operation. Figure 2.1 lists some of the advantages that you gain when you can accurately predict the number of people you will serve in any future time period.

SALES HISTORIES

A **sales history** is the systematic recording of all sales achieved during a predetermined time period. It is an accurate record of what and how much your operation has sold. Before you can develop a sales history, however, you must think about the definition of sales that is most helpful to you and your understanding of how your operation functions.

The simplest type of sales history records revenue only. The sales history format used by Rae's Restaurant and shown in Figure 2.2 is a typical one for an operation recording its sales revenue on a daily and weekly basis.

FIGURE 2.2 Sales History

Rae's Restaurant			
Sales Period	Date	Daily Sales	Sales to Date
Monday	1/1	$ 851.90	$ 851.90
Tuesday	1/2	974.37	1,826.27
Wednesday	1/3	1,004.22	2,830.49
Thursday	1/4	976.01	3,806.50
Friday	1/5	856.54	4,663.04
Saturday	1/6	1,428.22	6,091.26
Sunday	1/7	1,241.70	7,332.96
Week's Total			$7,332.96

Notice that, if you managed Rae's Restaurant you would determine daily sales either from your POS system or from manually adding the information recorded on your guest checks. You then transfer that number on a daily basis to your sales history by entering the amount of your daily sales in the column titled Daily Sales.

Sales to date is the cumulative total of sales reported in the unit. **Sales to date** is the number you will get when you add today's Daily Sales to the sales of all prior days in the **reporting period**—the time period for which sales records are being maintained.

To illustrate, Sales to Date on Tuesday, January 2, is computed by adding Tuesday's sales to those of Monday (the prior day) to arrive at a Sales to Date total of $1,826.27 ($851.90 + $974.37 = $1,826.27). As a result, the Sales to Date column is a running total of the sales achieved by Rae's Restaurant for the week.

Should Rae's manager prefer it, the reporting period could be defined in time blocks other than one week. Common alternatives are meal periods (breakfast, lunch, dinner, and so forth), days, weeks, two-week periods, four-week (28-day) periods, months, quarters (three-month periods), or any other unit of time that helps managers better understand their business. Most modern POS systems allow you to choose the specific reporting period of most interest to you.

In some situations, you will not have the ability to consider your sales in terms of revenue generated. Figure 2.3 is the type of sales history you can use when no cash sales are typically reported. Consider this example: The manager of Camp Eureka, our summer camp introduced in Chapter 1, is interested in recording sales

FIGURE 2.3 Sales History

Camp Eureka								
	Guests Served							
Serving Period	Mon	Tues	Wed	Thurs	Fri	Sat	Sun	Total
7:00–9:00 A.M.	121							
9:00–11:00 A.M.	40							
11:00–1:00 P.M.	131							
1:00–3:00 P.M.	11							
3:00–5:00 P.M.	42							
5:00–7:00 P.M.	161							
Total Served	506							

based on serving periods rather than an alternative time frame, such as a 24-hour (one-day) period. This approach is often used in such settings as all-inclusive hotels and resorts, extended-care facilities for senior citizens, nursing homes, college dormitories, correctional facilities, military bases, hospitals, summer camps, or any other situation where knowledge of the number of actual guests served during a given period is critical for planning purposes.

Given the data in Figure 2.3, the implications for staffing food servers at the camp are very clear. Fewer servers are needed from 9:00 to 11:00 A.M. than from 7:00 to 9:00 A.M. The reason is obvious. Fewer campers eat between 9:00 and 11:00 A.M. (40) than between 7:00 and 9:00 A.M. (121). As a knowledgeable manager, if you were operating this camp, you could either reduce serving staff during the slower service period or move those workers to some other necessary task.

You might also decide not to produce as many menu items for consumption during the 9:00 to 11:00 A.M. period. In that way, you could make more efficient use of both your labor and food products. It is simply easier to manage well when you know the answer to the question, "How many guests will I serve?"

Sales histories can be created to record revenue, guests served, or both. It is important, however, that you keep good records of how much you have sold in the past, because doing so is one key to accurately predicting the amount of sales you will achieve in the future.

COMPUTING AVERAGES FOR SALES HISTORIES

In some cases, knowing the average number of revenue dollars generated in a past time period, or the average number of guests served in that period, may be a real benefit to you. This is because in many operations, future guest activity can often be very similar to past guest activity. As a result, using historical sales averages from your operation can be useful as you project future guest sales and counts.

HERE'S HOW IT'S DONE *2.1*

An **average**, which is also called a **mean**, is simply a value computed by identifying the number of items in a series, adding the quantities of each item in the series, and then dividing the total of the quantities by the number of items in the series. It's easy.

The first and most important thing to do when you calculate an average is to identify exactly how many items will be included in the series. The number of quantities in the series you are examining is important because it will be the denominator in the calculation of the average. The sum of the assigned values of these quantities will be the numerator.

For example, if a manager wants to calculate her operation's average electric bill last year, she must first determine that the number of items in the series will be 12—the number of months in last year and the number of electric bills to be added.

Similarly, if a manager wants to calculate the average sales per day last week, the number of items in the series will be the number of days the restaurant operated last week. After the number of items in the series is identified, the quantity of each item in the series must be totaled.

To illustrate how managers calculate an average, assume a manager buys three different knives. One knife costs $6.00, another costs $9.00, and the third costs $18.00. To calculate the average cost of a single knife, the manager first recognizes that there are three quantities (knives purchased) in the series of items. Then the sum of the quantities (the cost of the 3 knives) is calculated.

In this example the sum of the quantities equals $33.00 ($6.00 + $9.00 + $18.00 = $33.00).

Next, the manager divides the arrived-at sum by 3; which is the number of items in this series:

$$\frac{\$33.00 \text{ sum of the knives' cost}}{3 \text{ knives purchased}} = \$11.00 \text{ average price per knife}$$

Thus, $11.00 is the average of $6.00 + $9.00 + $18.00—that is, the average price paid by the manager for the knives. The number of items in the series is 3 (i.e., they are 6, 9, and 18).

The sum of the quantities in this case equals 33 (6 + 9 + 18 = 33). Thus, in this example $33.00 ÷ 3 = $11.00; the average price paid by the manager for knives.

The two major types of averages you are likely to encounter as a foodservice manager are:

- Fixed average
- Rolling average

FIXED AVERAGE

A **fixed average** is an average for a specific (fixed) time period—for example, the first 14 days of a given month. In this case, you would compute the average amount of sales or guest activity for this 14-day period. Note that this average is called fixed because the first 14 days of the month will always consist of the same days (the 1st through the 14th), as shown in Figure 2.4.

Figure 2.4 details the sales activity of Lauraina's Take-Out Coffee. The calculation of this average (total revenue/number of days) is fixed, or constant, because Lauraina's management has identified the 14 specific days used to make up the average. The number $427.14 might be very useful because it might, if management wishes, be used as a good predictor of the revenue volume that should be expected for the first 14 days of next month.

FIGURE 2.4 14-Day Fixed Average

Lauraina's Take-Out Coffee	
Day	Daily Sales
1	$ 350.00
2	322.00
3	388.00
4	441.00
5	419.00
6	458.00
7	452.00
8	458.00
9	410.00
10	434.00
11	476.00
12	460.00
13	418.00
14	494.00
14-Day Total	$5,980.00

$$\frac{\$5,980}{14 \text{ days}} = \$427.14$$

ROLLING AVERAGE

A **rolling average** is the average amount of sales or volume over a changing time period. A fixed average is computed using a specific or constant set of data, but a rolling average is computed using data that will change. To illustrate, consider the case of Ubalda Salas, who operates a sports bar. Ubalda is interested in knowing what the average revenue dollars were in her operation for each prior seven-day period.

In this case, the prior seven-day period changes, or rolls forward by one day, as each day passes. It is important to note that Ubalda could have been interested in her average daily revenue last week (fixed average), but she prefers to know her average sales for the last seven days. This means that she will, at times, be using data from both last week and this week to compute the last seven-day average.

Using the sales data recorded in Figure 2.5, the seven-day rolling average for Ubalda's Sports Bar is computed as shown in Figure 2.6.

FIGURE 2.5 14-Day Sales Levels

Ubalda's Sports Bar	
Day	Sales
1	$3,500.00
2	$3,200.00
3	$3,900.00
4	$4,400.00
5	$4,200.00
6	$4,580.00
7	$4,500.00
8	$4,600.00
9	$4,100.00
10	$4,400.00
11	$4,700.00
12	$4,600.00
13	$4,180.00
14	$4,940.00

FIGURE 2.6 Seven-Day Rolling Average

Ubalda's Sports Bar								
Day	1–7	2–8	3–9	4–10	5–11	6–12	7–13	8–14
1	$ 3,500	—						
2	3,200	$ 3,200	—					
3	3,900	3,900	$ 3,900	—				
4	4,400	4,400	4,400	$ 4,400	—			
5	4,200	4,200	4,200	4,200	$ 4,200	—		
6	4,580	4,580	4,580	4,580	4,580	$ 4,580	—	
7	4,500	4,500	4,500	4,500	4,500	4,500	$ 4,500	—
8		4,600	4,600	4,600	4,600	4,600	4,600	$ 4,600
9			4,100	4,100	4,100	4,100	4,100	4,100
10				4,400	4,400	4,400	4,400	4,400
11					4,700	4,700	4,700	4,700
12						4,600	4,600	4,600
13							4,180	4,180
14								4,940
Total	$ 28,280	$ 29,380	$ 30,280	$ 30,780	$ 31,080	$ 31,480	$ 31,080	$ 31,520
7-Day	$4,040.00	$4,197.14	$4,325.71	$4,397.14	$4,440.00	$4,497.14	$4,440.00	$4,502.86

Note that each seven-day period is made up of a group of daily revenue numbers that changes over time. The first seven-day rolling average is computed by summing the first seven days' revenue (revenue on days 1–7 = $28,280) and dividing that number by seven to arrive at a seven-day rolling average of $4,040 ($28,280 revenue ÷ 7 days = $4,040 average).

Each day, Ubalda adds her daily revenue to that of the prior seven-day total and drops the day that is now eight days past. This gives her the effect of continually "rolling" the most current seven days' data forward. The rolling average, although more complex and time-consuming to calculate than a fixed average, can be extremely useful in recording data to help you make effective predictions about the sales levels you can expect in the future. This is true because, in many cases, rolling data are more current and, thus, more relevant than some fixed historical averages.

To best predict future sales in operations you manage you may choose to compute fixed averages for some time periods and rolling averages for others. For example, it may be helpful to know your average daily sales for the first 14 days of last month as well as your average sales for the most recently past 14 days. If, for example, these two numbers are very different, you will know whether the number of sales you can expect in the future is increasing or declining. Regardless of the type of average you feel is best for your operation, you should always document your sales history because it is from your sales history that you will be better able to predict future sales levels.

RECORDING REVENUE, GUEST COUNTS, OR BOTH

Some foodservice operations do not record revenue as the primary measure of their sales activity. For them, developing sales histories by recording the number of individuals they serve each day makes the most sense. Thus, **guest count,** the term used in the hospitality industry to indicate the number of people served, is recorded on a regular basis.

You may decide that your operation is best managed by tracking both generated revenue and guest counts. In fact, if you do decide to record both revenue and guest counts, you have the information you need to compute **average sales per guest,** a term sometimes referred to as **check average.**

Average sales per guest is determined by the following formula:

$$\frac{\text{Total sales}}{\text{Number of guests served}} = \text{Average sales per guest}$$

HERE'S HOW IT'S DONE *2.2*

The average sales per guest, or check average, is one of a foodservice manager's most commonly utilized formulas. And it's not hard to calculate it. To compute an operation's check average, managers uses these steps:

Step 1. Identify the amount of sales achieved in a specific time period.

Step 2. Identify the number of guests served in the same time period.

Step 3. Apply the Average Sales per Guest formula.

For example, assume a manager recorded that the amount of sales achieved last week was $18,750 (Step 1).

Further, assume that 1,500 guests were served last week (Step 2). Applying the Average Sales per Guest formula (Step 3), the manager would find that last week's check average was $12.50.

$$\frac{\$18,750 \text{ total sales last week}}{\$12.50 \text{ average sales per guest}} = 1,500 \text{ guests served last week}$$

One reason why the ability to accurately calculate an average sales per guest, or check average, is so important is that managers are often evaluated on the success of their efforts to maintain, or to increase, the average amount spent by each guest visiting their operations.

FIGURE 2.7 Sales History for Brothers' Family Restaurant

Sales Period	Date	Day	Sales	Guests Served	Average Sales per Guest
Monday	Jan 1	Monday	$1,365.00	190	$7.18
Tuesday	Jan 2	Tuesday	$2,750.00	314	$8.76
Two-Day Average			$2,057.50	252	$8.16

Consider the information in Figure 2.7 in which the manager of Brothers' Family Restaurant has decided to monitor and record the following:

1. Sales
2. Guests served
3. Average sales per guest

Most POS systems are programmed to report the amount of revenue generated in a selected time period, the number of guests served, and the average sales per guest. In the case of Brothers' Family Restaurant, Monday's revenue was $1,365; the restaurant served 190 guests, and thus the average sales per guest that day was $7.18 ($1,365/190 = $7.18). On Tuesday, the average sales per guest was $8.76 ($2,750/314 = $8.76).

To compute the two-day revenue average, the Brothers' manager would add Monday's revenue and Tuesday's revenue and then divide by 2, yielding a two-day revenue average of $2,057.50 [($1,365 + $2,750)/2 = $2,057.50].

In a like manner, the two-day average for the number of guests served is computed by adding the number of guests served on Monday to the number served on Tuesday and then dividing by 2, yielding a two-day average of guests served of 252 [(190 + 314)/2 = 252].

It might be logical to think that the manager of Brothers' could compute the Monday and Tuesday combined average sales per guest by adding the averages from each day and then dividing by 2. It is important to understand that this would *not* be correct.

A formula consisting of Monday's average sales per guest plus Tuesday's average sales per guest divided by 2 [($7.18 + $8.76)/2] yields $7.97. In fact, the actual two-day average sales per guest is $8.16 [($1,365 + $2,750)/(190 + 314) = ($4,115/504) = $8.16].

Although the difference of $0.19 might, at first glance, appear to be an inconsequential amount, assume that you are the president of a restaurant chain with 4,000 units worldwide. If each unit served 1,000 guests per day and you miscalculated average sales per guest by $0.19, your daily revenue assumption would be "off" by $760,000 per day [(4,000 units × 1,000 guests × $0.19) = $760,000]!

Returning to the Brothers' Family Restaurant example, the correct procedure for computing the two-day average sales per guest is as follows:

$$\frac{(\text{Monday sales} + \text{Tuesday sales})}{(\text{Monday guests} + \text{Tuesday guests})} = \text{Two-day average sales per guest}$$

or

$$(\$1,365 + \$2,750)/(190 + 314) = \$8.16$$

The correct computation in this example is a **weighted average**—that is, an average that weighs the number of guests served in different time periods with how much they spend in those same time periods.

To demonstrate further the importance of weighted averages, consider the data in Figure 2.8 and assume that you want to answer the question, "What is the combined average sales per guest?"

FIGURE 2.8 Weighted Average

	Sales	Guests Served	Average Sales per Guest
Day 1	$ 100.00	20	$ 5.00
Day 2	$4,000.00	400	$10.00
Two-Day Average	$2,050.00	210	???

From the data in Figure 2.8, it is easy to see that the two-day average would not be $7.50 [($5.00 + $10.00)/2 = $7.50] because many more guests were served on the day the average sales per guest was $10.00 than on the day the average sales per guest was $5.00. With so many guests spending an average of $10.00, and so few spending an average of $5.00, the overall average should be much closer to $10.00 than to $5.00.

In fact, utilizing the average sales per guest formula, the correct weighted average sales per guest would be $9.76, as follows:

$$\frac{(\text{Day 1 sales} + \text{Day 2 sales})}{(\text{Day 1 guests} + \text{Day 2 guests})} = \text{Two-day average sales per guest}$$

or

$$\frac{\$100 + \$4,000}{20 + 400 \text{ guests}} \quad \$9.76 \text{ per guest}$$

MAINTAINING SALES HISTORIES

Although a sales history might consist of revenue, number of guests served, and average sales per guest, depending on the type of operation you manage, you might want to know even more detailed information about your sales. This could include information such as the number of guests served in a specific meal or time period (e.g., breakfast, lunch, or dinner), or the method of meal delivery (e.g., drive-through sales versus carry-out or dine-in sales).

The important concept to remember is that you have the power to develop the sales history information that best suits your operation. That information should be updated at least daily, and a cumulative total for the appropriate time periods should also be maintained. In most cases, your sales histories should be kept for a period of at least two years. This allows you to have a good sense of what has happened to your business in the recent past.

Of course, if you are the manager of a new operation, or one that has recently undergone a major concept change, you may not have the advantage of reviewing meaningful sales histories because they simply do not exist. If you find yourself in such a situation, it is imperative that you begin to build and maintain your sales histories as soon as possible so you will, as quickly as possible, have good sales information on which to base your future managerial decisions.

SALES VARIANCES

After an accurate sales history system has been established, you may begin to see that your operation experiences some **sales variance** or differences from previous sales levels. These sales variances are normal and will give you an indication of whether your sales are increasing, declining, or staying the same. Because that information is so important to predicting future sales levels, many foodservice managers

FIGURE 2.9 Sales History and Variance

Quick Wok			
Month	Sales This Year	Sales Last Year	Variance
January	$ 54,000	$ 51,200	$ 2,800
February	57,500	50,750	6,750
March	61,200	57,500	3,700
First-Quarter Total	$172,700	$159,450	$13,250

improve their sales history information by including sales variance as an additional component of the history.

Figure 2.9 details a portion of a sales history that has been modified to include a sales Variance column, which allows the manager to see how sales are different from a prior period. In this case, the manager of Quick Wok wants to compare sales for the first three months of this year to sales for the first three months of last year, as recorded in that period's sales history report.

The variance in Figure 2.9 is determined by subtracting sales last year from sales this year. In January, the variance figure is obtained as follows:

Sales this year − Sales last year = Variance

or

$54,000 − $51,200 = $2,800

Thus, the manager of Quick Wok can see that the sales for the first quarter are greater than last year's first quarter. In fact, all three months in the first quarter of the year showed revenue increases over the prior year.

The total sales improvement for the first quarter was $13,250 ($172,700 − $159,450 = $13,250). The sales history and variance format used in Figure 2.9 lets a manager know the dollar value of revenue variance. But many good managers want to know even more because simply knowing the dollar value of a variance has limitations.

To illustrate, consider two restaurant managers. One manager's restaurant had revenue of $1,000,000 last year. The second manager's restaurant generated one-half as much revenue, or $500,000. This year both managers had sales increases of $50,000. But it is clear that while both experienced a $50,000 sales increase, that increase represents a much greater proportional change in the second restaurant than in the first. Because that is true, effective managers are often interested in the **percentage variance,** or percentage change, in their sales from one time period to the next.

Figure 2.10 shows how the sales history data at the Quick Wok can be expanded to include percentage variance as part of that operation's complete sales history.

FIGURE 2.10 Sales History, Variance, and Percentage Variance

Quick Wok				
Month	Sales This Year	Sales Last Year	Variance	Percentage Variance (%)
January	$ 54,000	$ 51,200	$ 2,800	5.5%
February	57,500	50,750	6,750	13.3%
March	61,200	57,500	3,700	6.4%
First-Quarter Total	$172,700	$159,450	$13,250	8.3%

Percentage variance is obtained by subtracting sales last year from sales this year and dividing the resulting number by sales last year. Thus, in the month of January, the percentage variance is calculated as:

$$\frac{\text{Sales this year} - \text{Sales last year}}{\text{Sales last year}} = \text{Percentage variance}$$

or

$$\frac{\$54,000 - \$51,200}{\$51,200} = 0.055, \text{ or } 5.5\%$$

Note that the resulting decimal form percentage can be converted to the more frequently used common form discussed in Chapter 1 by moving the decimal point two places to the right, or through multiplying it by 100.

Note that when a sales history includes a variance column, an alternative, and shorter, formula for computing the percentage variance for January is:

$$\frac{\text{January variance}}{\text{January sales last year}} = \text{January percentage variance}$$

or

$$\frac{\$2,800}{\$51,200} = 0.055, \text{ or } 5.5\%$$

Yet another way to compute the sales percentage variance for January is to use a math shortcut, as follows:

$$\frac{\text{January sales this year}}{\text{January sales last year}} - 1 = \text{January percentage variance}$$

or

$$\frac{\$54,000}{\$51,200} - 1 = 0.055, \text{ or } 5.5\%$$

Regardless of the mathematical method you use, calculating percentage variance is invaluable when you want to compare the operating results of two foodservice operations of different sizes.

Returning to our previous example of the two restaurant managers, each of whom achieved $50,000 revenue increases by using the first percentage variance formula presented, you will see that the restaurant with higher sales increased its revenue by 5.0 percent [($1,050,000 − $1,000,000)/$1,000,000 = 0.05] or 5 percent in common form. The restaurant with less original revenue and the same $50,000 increase in sales, however, achieved a 10 percent increase [($550,000 − 500,000)/$500,000 = 0.10] or 10% in common form.

As your level of expertise increases, you will find additional areas in which knowing the percentage variance in revenue and in your expenses (addressed later in this text) will greatly assist you in your management decision making.

PREDICTING FUTURE SALES

It has been pointed out that truly outstanding managers have an ability to see the future in regard to the revenue figures they will achieve and the number of guests they expect to serve. You, too, can learn to do this when you apply your knowledge of percentage variances to estimating your operation's future sales. Depending on the type of facility you manage, you may be interested in predicting future revenues, guest counts, or average sales per guest levels. We will examine the procedures for all three of these in detail.

FORECASTING FUTURE REVENUES

Erica Tullstein is the manager of Rock's Pizza Pub on the campus of State College. Her guests consist of college students, most of whom come to the Rock to talk, surf the web, text, eat, and study. Erica has done a good job maintaining sales histories in the two years she has managed the Rock. She records the revenue dollars she achieves on a daily basis, as well as the number of students frequenting the Rock. Revenue data for the last three months of the year are recorded in Figure 2.11.

As can be seen in Figure 2.11, fourth-quarter revenues for Erica's operation have increased from the previous year. Of course, there could be a variety of reasons for this. Erica may have extended her hours of operation to attract more students. She may have increased the size of pizzas and held her prices constant, thus creating more value for her guests and thus more customers. She may have raised the selling price of pizzas. Or perhaps a competing pizza parlor was closed during this time period. Using all of her knowledge of her own operation and her market, Erica would like to predict the sales level she will likely experience in the first three months of next year. This sales forecast will be most helpful as she plans for next year's anticipated expenses, staffing levels, and profits.

The first question Erica must address is the amount her sales have actually increased. Revenue increases range from a low in October of 3.4 percent, to a high in December of 13.9 percent. The overall quarter average of 7.5 percent is the figure that Erica elects to use as she predicts her sales revenue for the first quarter of the coming year. She feels it is neither too conservative, as would be the case if she used the October percentage increase, nor too aggressive, as would be the case if she used the December figure.

If Erica were to use the 7.5 percent average increase from the fourth quarter of last year to predict her revenues for the first quarter of this year, a revenue forecast could be developed for the first quarter of next year as shown in Figure 2.12.

FIGURE 2.11 Revenue History

Rock's Pizza Pub				
Month	Sales This Year	Sales Last Year	Variance	Percentage Variance (%)
October	$ 75,000	$ 72,500	$ 2,500	3.4%
November	64,250	60,000	4,250	7.1%
December	57,500	50,500	7,000	13.9%
Fourth-Quarter Total	$196,750	$183,000	$13,750	7.5%

FIGURE 2.12 First-Quarter Revenue Forecast

Rock's Pizza Pub				
Month	Sales Last Year	% Increase Estimate	Increase Amount	Revenue Forecast
January	$ 68,500	7.5%	$ 5,137.50	$ 73,637.50
February	72,000	7.5%	5,400.00	77,400.00
March	77,000	7.5%	5,775.00	82,775.00
First-Quarter Total	$217,500	7.5%	$16,312.50	$233,812.50

The revenue forecast for this time period is determined by multiplying sales last year by the percentage increase estimate, and then adding the percentage increase amount to sales last year.

For the month of January, the revenue forecast is calculated using the following formula:

> Sales last year + (Sales last year × % increase estimate) = Revenue forecast
>
> or
>
> $68,500 + ($68,500 × 0.075) = $73,637.50

An alternative way to compute the revenue forecast is to use a math shortcut as follows:

> Sales last year × (1 + % Increase estimate) = Revenue forecast
>
> or
>
> $68,500 × (1 + 0.075) = $73,637.50

Erica is using the increases she has experienced in the past to predict increases she may experience in the future. Monthly revenue figures from last year's sales history plus percentage increase estimates based on those histories can give Erica a very good idea of the revenue levels she may achieve in January, February, and March of the coming year.

Cost Control Around the World

Experienced foodservice managers working in the United States know that Mother's Day is the busiest day of the year for restaurants. An American foodservice manager's revenue forecast for that day would reflect this fact. But not every country celebrates Mother's Day, and there are some who do celebrate it but choose to do so on a day other than the second Sunday in May. As a result, predicting future revenues when operating a restaurant in a foreign country requires managers to have a good understanding of that country's holidays, festivals, and special events. In many cases, these will be very different from those holidays celebrated or events held in the United States.

To cite just one example, consider that on April 12, 1952, the Organization of American States (OAS) and the United Nations Children's Fund (UNICEF) asked each country to declare a Children's Day (*Dia del Nino* in Spanish).

Bolivia selected April 12, the same day on which the Declaration was drafted, and Dia del Nino has been celebrated in Bolivia since 1955. Argentina celebrates Dia del Nino the second Sunday in August. In both Ecuador and Nicaragua, this holiday is celebrated on June 1.

Although it is not celebrated in the United States, Dia del Nino is one of South America's biggest holidays. On that day, it is common for parents to visit their children at school, give the children small presents, and then take their families out to eat to celebrate the day. Certainly, foodservice managers working in South America need to be aware of when this special day is celebrated and plan accordingly if they are to accurately estimate their revenue and be ready for the big Dia del Nino crowds!

FORECASTING FUTURE GUEST COUNTS

Using the same techniques employed in estimating increases in sales, you can estimate increases or decreases in the number of guests you will serve. Figure 2.13 shows how Erica, the manager of Rock's Pizza Pub, used last year's fourth quarter guest counts to determine the variance and percentage variance for the guest counts she achieved in her facility in the fourth quarter of this year.

FIGURE 2.13 Guest Count History

Rock's Pizza Pub				
Month	Guests This Year	Guests Last Year	Variance	Percentage Variance (%)
October	14,200	13,700	+500	3.6%
November	15,250	14,500	+750	5.2%
December	16,900	15,500	+1,400	9.0%
Fourth-Quarter Total	46,350	43,700	+2,650	6.1%

FIGURE 2.14 First-Quarter Guest Count Forecast

Rock's Pizza Pub				
Month	Guests Last Year	% Increase Estimate	Guest Increase Estimate	Guest Count Forecast
January	12,620	6.1%	770	13,390
February	13,120	6.1%	800	13,920
March	13,241	6.1%	808	14,049
First-Quarter Total	38,981	6.1%	2,378	41,359

If Erica were to use the 6.1 percent average increase from the fourth quarter of last year to predict her guest counts for the first quarter of the coming year, a planning sheet could be developed as presented in Figure 2.14. It is important to note that Erica is not required to use the same percentage increase estimate for each coming month. Any forecasted increase management feels is appropriate can be used to predict future sales.

The guest count forecast is determined by multiplying guest count last year by the percentage increase estimate this year, and then adding the result to the guest count last year. In the month of January, the guest count forecast is calculated using the following formula:

Guest count last year + (Guest count last year × % Increase estimate) = Guest count forecast

or

12,620 + (12,620 × 0.061) = 13,390

This process can be simplified by using a math shortcut, as follows:

Guests last year × (1.00 + % Increase estimate) = Guest count forecast

or

12,620 × (1.00 + 0.061) = 13,390

You may notice that in January, the guest increase estimate is rounded from 769.82 to 770. This is because you cannot serve "0.82" people! Utilizing normal rounding procedures, you should choose and use the guest count forecast formula you feel most comfortable with.

Consider the Cost

"A 60-minute wait! You've got to be kidding!" said the guest.

"I'm sorry sir," replied Romy. "We'll seat your party as quickly as possible."

Romy was the dining room host at the Al-Amir restaurant. The Al-Amir featured Middle Eastern and North African Cuisine. Guests loved the Al-Amir's chicken shawarma, baba gannouj, tabouleh, and kibbeh. As a result, the restaurant often was very busy. When that happened, the line of guests waiting to be seated got long and, sometimes, waiting customers got upset.

"Listen" replied the guest, "I understand when places are busy. It can take a while to serve everyone. But look, nearly half your dining room is empty. The tables just need to be cleared and reset."

"Yes sir," replied Romy. "But the workers we do have are clearing tables as fast as they can."

"Then you need more dining room help. We'll just come back another time," said the guest, as he left the restaurant, along with his female dining companion, and two small children in hand.

"I'm really very sorry, sir," said Romy to the guest's back as he watched him leave. Romy thought to himself, "This happens way too often!"

Assume the Al-Amir does not have an effective sales forecast system in place.

1. What will be the long-term impact on the revenue-generating ability of the restaurant if it consistently understaffs its dining room?

2. What would be the long-term impact on Al-Amir's staff?

3. Sometimes even the best sales forecasts are inaccurate. What steps can managers take to ease the difficulties encountered when their sales forecasts prove to be incorrect?

FORECASTING FUTURE AVERAGE SALES PER GUEST

Recall that average sales per guest (check average) is simply the average amount of money each guest spends during a visit. The same formula is used to forecast an operation's average sales per guest, as was used in forecasting total revenue and guest counts. Using data taken from the sales history, the following formula is used:

Last year's average sales per guest
+ Estimated increase in sales per guest
= Sales per guest forecast

Alternatively, the manager of Rocks Pizza Pub could compute average sales per guest using the data collected from revenue forecasts (Figure 2.12) and combine that data with the guest count forecasts you created (Figure 2.14). If that is done, the revenue forecast data presented in Figure 2.15 would result.

FIGURE 2.15 First-Quarter Average Sales per Guest Forecast

Rock's Pizza Pub			
Month	Revenue Forecast	Guest Count Forecast	Average Sales per Guest Forecast
January	$ 73,637.50	13,390	$5.50
February	77,400.00	13,920	$5.56
March	82,775.00	14,049	$5.89
First-Quarter Total	$233,812.50	41,359	$5.65

An average sales per guest forecast is obtained by dividing the revenue forecast by the guest count forecast. Thus, in the month of January, the average sales per guest forecast is determined by the following formula:

$$\frac{\text{Revenue forecast}}{\text{Guest count forecast}} = \text{Average sales per guest forecast}$$

or

$$\frac{\$73,637.50}{13,390 \text{ guests}} = \$5.50 \text{ per guest}$$

Increasingly, sophisticated POS systems not only analyze how many guests were served on a given day but also provide data that help managers better understand why that number was served. For example, historical weather patterns can be analyzed to discover if rainy days affect total sales volume (and, thus, perhaps indicate that a forecast adjustment should be made on a day on which rain is predicted). Weather, day of the month, and day of the week are just some of the many factors that may affect sales volume and should be carefully considered by sophisticated foodservice managers as they prepare their sales forecasts.

It is important to note that sales histories, regardless of how well they have been developed and maintained, may not provide all of the information needed to accurately predict future sales. Your knowledge of potential price changes, new or lost competitors, facility renovations, and improved selling programs are additional factors that you might need to consider when predicting future sales. There is no question, however, that a sales history report is easily developed and will serve as the cornerstone of other management systems you will design. Without accurate sales data, the control systems you implement, regardless of their sophistication, will perform poorly.

FUN ON THE WEB!

Maintaining a membership in a professional trade organization is a good way to stay up-to-date on new techniques for reporting and forecasting sales. One excellent way to do this is by attending the organization's annual meetings and trade shows. Visit the websites of these popular trade associations to find out when and where they will be holding their next trade show or convention.

Association

National Restaurant Association

American Hotel and Lodging Association

Asian American Hotel Owner's Association

The Academy of Nutrition and Dietetics

Dietary Managers Association

American Culinary Federation

Club Managers Association of America

American School Foodservice Association

National Association of Catering Executives

National Association of College and University Food Services

Hospitality Financial and Technology Professionals

International Hotel and Restaurant Association

Green and Growing!

If your operation is "going green" and your customer counts are going up, don't be surprised. Customers are increasingly concerned about the quality of their environment. These customers also prefer to frequent foodservice operations that share their concerns and act on them. As a result, guest counts can be increased by undertaking green initiatives and then proudly letting customers know about what your operation is doing.

It is important to market your products and services directly to the rapidly growing market segment of educated, savvy customers who care about the food they eat and their impact on the world around them. Implementing sustainable practices that focus on conservation as well as utilizing organic, seasonal, and locally grown products can help build customer and employee loyalty, as well as boost profits.

FUN ON THE WEB!

POS systems continually undergo development to meet the evolving needs of hospitality managers. To explore product offerings for progressive POS companies, enter "Restaurant POS" and any one of the following terms into your favorite search engine:

Cloud computing

Tableside payment

Mobile payment

Online payment services

When you arrive and review the POS product offerings, pay especially close attention to the features related to the maintenance of sales histories.

Technology Tools

The importance of accurate sales histories when forecasting future sales is unquestionable and invaluable. Your POS system can be very instrumental in this effort. Many POS systems today can be programmed to:

1. Track sales by guest count
2. Track sales by date
3. Monitor cash vs. credit sales
4. Maintain products-sold histories
5. Maintain check average data
6. Compare actual sales to prior-period sales
7. Maintain rolling sales averages
8. Forecast future sales in predetermined increments:
   a. Monthly
   b. Weekly
   c. Daily
   d. By meal period
   e. Hourly
   f. Portions of an hour (e.g., 15 min., 30 min., etc.)

9. Maintain actual sales to forecasted sales variance reports

10. Maintain reservations systems:

   a. Automate advanced bookings up to two years in advance

   b. Track no-shows and cancellations

   c. Build a guest database for mailings and e-mailings

   d. Track guest birthdays, favorite tables, food preferences, etc.

For those operations that rely on reservations to control guest seating, software is available to instantly identify repeat guests, giving the operator a display screen that can include such information as frequency of visit, purchase preferences, and total dollars spent in the operation. In addition, reservations software makes it possible for operators to reward repeat guests by developing their own "frequent dining" programs, similar to a hotel or airline's frequent-traveler program. In addition, restaurants can track customer complaints and, if desired, provide coupons to compensate guests for difficulties. Also, reservations-related programs such as these can store information on reservation demand, predict optimal reservation patterns, identify frequent no-show guests, and even allow guests to make their own reservations online through the operation's website or through the company's mobile applications.

When added to your knowledge of the unique factors that impact your unit, properly maintained sales histories can help you answer two important control questions, namely, "How many people are coming tomorrow?" and "How much is each person likely to spend?" The judgment of management is critical in forecasting answers to these questions. Since you can now answer those questions, you are ready to develop systems that will allow you to prepare an efficient and cost-effective way of serving your guests. You want to be ready to provide your arriving guests with quality food and beverage products and enough staff to serve them properly. You have done your homework with regard to the number of individuals who may be coming to your operation. You also know how much they are likely to spend while they are there. Now you must prepare for their arrival. That is the topic addressed in the next chapter!

Apply What You Have Learned

*P*auline Cooper is a registered dietitian and the foodservice director at Memorial Hospital. Increasingly, the hospital's marketing efforts have emphasized its skill in treating diabetic patients. As a result, the number of diabetic meals served by Pauline's staff has been increasing. As a professional member of the hospital's management team, Pauline has been asked to report on how the hospital's diabetic treatment marketing efforts have affected her area.

1. How important is it that Pauline have historical records of the type (i.e., vegetarian, low-sodium, gluten-free, and the like) of meals served by her staff and not merely the number of meals served? Why?

2. Assume that Pauline's per-meal cost has been increasing because diabetic meals are more expensive to produce than regular meals. Could Pauline use sales histories to estimate the financial impact of serving additional diabetic meals in the future? How?

3. What are other reasons that managers in a foodservice operation might keep detailed records of meal types served, as well as the total number of meals served?

Key Terms and Concepts

The following are terms and concepts discussed in the chapter that are important for you as a manager. To help you review, please define the terms below.

sales forecast/projected
  sales
point-of-sale (POS)
  system
sales volume
sales history

sales to date
reporting period
average (mean)
fixed average
rolling average
guest count

average sales per guest
  (check average)
weighted average
sales variance
percentage variance

Test Your Skills

You may download the Excel spreadsheets for the Test Your Skills exercises from the student companion website at www.wiley.com/college/dopson. Complete the exercises by placing your answers in the shaded boxes and answering the questions as indicated.

1. Vanessa is the snack bar manager at the Silver Glen Country Club. Each day, Vanessa records the revenue generated and the number of guests served in the snack bar. Using the information below, calculate her total revenue, the total number of guests served, her average revenue per day, and the average number of guests served per day.

	Revenue	Guests Served
Monday	$480.00	45
Tuesday	535.00	50
Wednesday	595.00	60
Thursday	395.00	40
Friday	940.00	85
Saturday	1,450.00	120
Sunday	1,120.00	90
Week's Total		
Daily Average		

2. Laurie Fitsin owns a small sandwich shop called Laurie's Lunch Box. She has developed a sales history for the first week of March using total sales and guests served. Help Laurie calculate her average sales per guest for each day of the week and calculate her totals. Laurie has decided that she could take a shortcut and calculate the average sales per guest for the week by adding Monday through Sunday's average sales per guest and dividing by seven. Would this shortcut make a difference in her total average sales per guest for the week? If so, how much of a difference? Should she take this short-cut? Why or why not?

Laurie's Lunch Box				
Sales Period	Date	Sales	Guests Served	Average Sales per Guest
Monday	3/1	$1,248.44	200	
Tuesday	3/2	1,686.25	360	
Wednesday	3/3	1,700.00	350	
Thursday	3/4	1,555.65	300	
Friday	3/5	1,966.31	380	
Saturday	3/6	2,134.65	400	
Sunday	3/7	2,215.77	420	
Total				

3. Peggy Richey operates Peggy's Pizza Place in southern California. She has maintained a sales history from January through June, and wants to compare this year's sales with last year's sales. Calculate her sales variances and percentage variances for the first six months of the year.

Peggy's Pizza Place				
Month	Sales This Year	Sales Last Year	Variance	Percentage Variance
January	$37,702.73	$34,861.51		
February	33,472.03	31,485.60		
March	36,492.98	33,707.79		
April	35,550.12	32,557.85		
May	36,890.12	37,852.42		
June	37,482.52	37,256.36		
6-Month Total				

4. Peggy (from the preceding exercise) reviews the sales and variance information from her first six months of the year to forecast her revenues for the last six months of the year. She decides to forecast a sales increase of 4.75 percent to predict her upcoming changes in sales. Help her calculate the projected sales and revenue forecasts for the last six months of the year.

Peggy's Pizza Place				
Month	Sales Last Year	Predicted Change	Projected Sales Increase	Revenue Forecast
July	$36,587.91	4.75%		
August	36,989.73	4.75%		
September	40,896.32	4.75%		
October	37,858.63	4.75%		
November	37,122.45	4.75%		
December	37,188.71	4.75%		
6-Month Total				

5. The Lopez brothers, Angelo, Antonio, and Isaiah, own the Lopez Cantina. Angelo is in charge of marketing, and he is developing his sales forecast for next year. Because of his marketing efforts, he predicts a 5 percent increase in his monthly guest counts. Angelo is not aware of any anticipated menu price increases and assumes, therefore, that his weighted check average will remain stable.

   A. Using last year's sales and guest counts, estimate Angelo's weighted check average (average sales per guest) for the year. (*Spreadsheet hint:* Use the ROUND function to two decimal places on the cell containing the weighted check average, cell D18, because it will be used in another formula in part B.)

Month	Sales Last Year	Guest Count Last Year	Check Average
January	$45,216.00	4,800	
February	48,538.00	5,120	
March	50,009.00	5,006	
April	45,979.00	4,960	
May	49,703.00	5,140	
June	48,813.00	5,300	
July	55,142.00	5,621	
August	59,119.00	6,002	
September	55,257.00	5,780	
October	50,900.00	5,341	
November	54,054.00	5,460	
December	50,998.00	5,400	
Total			

   B. Using the weighted check average calculated in part A, determine Angelo's projected sales, assuming a 5 percent increase in guest counts. (*Spreadsheet hint:* Use the ROUND function to zero decimal places in the Guest Count Forecast column, cells C23:C34. Use the SUM function for the total, cell C35. Otherwise, your answers will not be correct.)

Month	Guest Count Last Year	Guest Count Forecast	Weighted Check Average	Projected Sales
January	4,800			
February	5,120			
March	5,006			
April	4,960			
May	5,140			
June	5,300			
July	5,621			
August	6,002			
September	5,780			
October	5,341			
November	5,460			
December	5,400			
Total				

6. Donna Berger is a hotel food and beverage director at a 500-room hotel. Donna knows that as the number of rooms sold in the hotel increases, the number of guests she serves for breakfast increases also. Based on historical records, Donna will serve breakfast to 55 percent of the hotel's registered guests. Help Donna plan for the number of breakfasts she will serve by completing the following chart:

Number of Guests in Hotel	Historical % of Guests Eating Breakfast	Estimated Number of Guests to Be Served
100	55%	
175	55%	
225	55%	
275	55%	
325	55%	
375	55%	
425	55%	
475	55%	
500	55%	

What information will Donna need to determine the historical percentage of guests who eat breakfast?

7. Lakota Vela operates Hall's House, a mid-priced restaurant with a $30.00 check average. Her clientele consists of business people and tourists visiting her city. Based on the historical sales records she keeps, Lakota believes her business will achieve a food sales increase next year of 4 percent per month for each of the first six months of the year. She feels this increase will be the result of increases in guest counts (not check averages).

At mid-year (July 1), Lakota intends to increase her menu prices (and thus, her check average) by 2 percent. She feels that although these price increases could result in a slight, short-term reduction in her guest counts, the restaurant's guest counts will still increase 3 percent for the last six months of the year.

Taking into account her guest count growth estimates and mid-year price increases, Lakota would like to estimate her predicted year-end food revenues. Prepare the revenue estimates for Hall's House. (*Spreadsheet hint:* Use the ROUND function to zero decimal places in the Guest Count Forecast columns, cells D5 through D10 (D5:D10) and D15 through D20 (D15:D20). Use the SUM function for the totals, cells D11 and D21. Otherwise, your answers will not be correct.)

Months January through June					
Month	Guest Count Last Year	Guest Count % Increase Estimate	Guest Count Forecast	Original Check Average	Revenue Forecast
January	6,270				
February	6,798				
March	6,336				
April	6,400				
May	6,930				
June	6,864				
6-Month Total					

Months July through December					
Month	Guest Count Last Year	Guest Count % Increase Estimate	Guest Count Forecast	New Check Average	Revenue Forecast
July	6,845				
August	6,430				
September	6,283				
October	6,402				
November	6,938				
December	7,128				
6-Month Total					

8. Raktida is the manager a popular Italian Restaurant on Mott Street. She wants to predict her guest counts for the first week of November so that she can estimate an accurate number of servers to schedule. Business is very good, but her sales history from last month indicates that fewer guests are served during the first few days of the week compared to last year, whereas more guests per day are served in the later part of the week. Raktida has entered the guest counts from last year and the estimated percentage change in guest counts for this year in the chart below. Because good service is so important to her, she wants to ensure that enough servers are scheduled to work each day. One server can provide excellent service to 50 guests. Help Raktida calculate how many servers to schedule each day by completing the following chart. Note: Raktida always rounds the number of servers required up to the next whole number to ensure the best service possible for her guests! (*Spreadsheet hint:* Use ROUNDUP to 0 decimal places in the Estimated Guest Count This Year column and in the Number of Servers Needed This Year columns.)

    How would Raktida's server scheduling efforts this year be affected if last year she had recorded only her weekly (not daily) guest counts?

Raktida's Guest Forecast and Server Scheduling Worksheet for the First Week of November				
	Guest Count Last Year	Estimated Change This Year	Estimate Guest Count This Year	Number of Servers Needed This Year
Sunday	625	–5%		
Monday	750	–5%		
Tuesday	825	0%		
Wednesday	850	5%		
Thursday	775	5%		
Friday	1250	10%		
Saturday	1400	10%		

9. Marcia Curtis is the vice president of development for "Tamales to Go," a rapidly expanding chain of restaurants featuring takeout tamales and other Mexican food specialties. Currently, the chain has 150 units and average unit volume is $800,000 per year. Annual per-unit revenue growth for opened units is 5 percent per year.

Tonya Gamez, the chain's president, has promised company stockholders the chain will experience 12 percent overall revenue growth in the next year. Assuming that per-unit growth on existing units continues to average 5 percent, calculate how many total operating units Marcia will need to have open next year to meet Tonya's goal of a 12 percent overall increase in the chain's revenue.

	This Year	Next Year
Total Revenue	$120,000,000	
Per Unit Revenue	$ 800,000	
Total Number of Units	150	

10. Sales forecasts are important because knowing how many people you will serve is important. What are three specific problems that will occur when managers consistently *underestimate* the number of guests they will serve on a given day? What are three specific difficulties that will likely result if managers consistently *overestimate* the number of guests they will serve?

CHAPTER 3

Purchasing and Receiving

OVERVIEW

In this chapter, you will learn the professional techniques and methods that managers use to accurately estimate the future sales of an operation's individual food and beverage menu items. Doing so is important because those estimates, when used in conjunction with standardized recipes, give managers the information they must have to purchase the quality and amount of ingredients needed to properly service their guests.

When ordered items are delivered to an operation, great care must be taken to ensure that the delivered items exactly match those that management intended to buy. In this chapter, you will also learn the procedures managers must implement to verify all items delivered to their operations are identical in quantity, quality, and price to those originally ordered.

Chapter Outline

- Forecasting Food Sales
- Forecasting Beverage Sales
- Importance of Standardized Recipes
- Purchasing Food
- Purchasing Beverages
- Purchase Orders
- Receiving Food and Beverage Products
- Technology Tools
- Apply What You Have Learned
- Key Terms and Concepts
- Test Your Skills

At the conclusion of this chapter, you will be able to:

- Use sales histories and standardized recipes to determine the amount of food products to buy in anticipation of forecasted sales.
- Purchase food and beverage products in a cost-effective manner.
- Implement proper procedures for receiving food and beverage products.

FORECASTING FOOD SALES

The US Department of Agriculture Food Expenditure Series reports that in 2012, sales of food consumed away from home exceeded 49 percent of total food purchases and has steadily increased over time.[1] According to the National Restaurant Association's current forecasts,[2] continued economic growth, gains in consumers' real disposable income, and changes in the lifestyles of today's busy American families are all spurring the sustained rise in the number of meals served away from home. This is good news for your career as a hospitality manager.

All this growth, activity, and consumer demand, however, will also create challenges for you. Consider the situation you would encounter if you used sales histories (see Chapter 2) to project that 300 guests will visit today for lunch at the restaurant you manage. Your restaurant serves only three entrée items: roast chicken, roast pork, and roast beef. The question you face is this: "How many servings of each item should we produce so that we do not run out of any one item nor have too many of each item left after the lunch period is over?"

If you were to run out of one of your three menu items, guests who wanted that item would undoubtedly become upset. They might even leave your restaurant (and perhaps take with them dining companions who would have ordered the other items you had plenty of!). Producing too much of any one item would, on the other hand, result in unsold items that could cause your costs to rise to unacceptable levels unless these remaining items could be sold for their full price at a later time.

Clearly, in this situation, it would be unwise to produce 300 portions of each item. Although you would never run out of any one item (each of your 300 estimated guests could order the same item and you would still have produced enough), you would also have 600 total portions left over at the end of your lunch period.

What you would really like to do, of course, is instruct your staff to make the "right" amount of each menu item. The right amount would be the number of servings that minimizes your chances of running out of an item before lunch is over as well as minimizing your chances of having excessive amounts unsold when the meal period is completed.

Just as estimating the number of guests who will arrive at your restaurant depends on an accurate forecast of guest counts, the answer to the question of how many servings of roast chicken, pork, and beef you should prepare lies in accurate menu item sales forecasting.

Let us return to the three-item menu example cited previously. This time, however, assume that you were wise enough to have recorded last week's menu item sales on a form similar to the one presented in Figure 3.1.

A review of the data in Figure 3.1 indicates that an estimate of 300 guests for next Monday makes good sense because the weekly sales total last week of 1,500 guests served averages 300 guests per day (1,500 guests served/5 days = 300/guests served per day). You also know that on an average day, you sold 73 roast chicken (365 sold/5 days = 73 per day), 115 roast pork (573 sold/5 days = 115 per day), and 112 roast beef (562 sold/5 days = 112 per day).

---

[1] US Department of Agriculture Economic Research Service, "Table 1, Food and Alcoholic Beverages: Total Expenditures," *Food Expenditures, Overview*, last updated Nov. 13, 2013.

[2] National Restaurant Association, "Restaurant Industry Forecast," *News and Research*, accessed Sept. 25, 2014.

FIGURE 3.1 Menu Item Sales History

Date: 1/2–1/6				Menu Items Sold			
Menu Item	Mon	Tues	Wed	Thurs	Fri	Week's Total	Average Sold
Roast Chicken	70	72	61	85	77	365	73
Roast Pork	110	108	144	109	102	573	115
Roast Beef	100	140	95	121	106	562	112
Total	280	320	300	315	285	1,500	300

Once you know the average number of people selecting a given menu item, and you know the total number of guests who made the selections, you can compute each menu item's **popularity index**, or the percentage of total guests choosing a given menu item from a list of alternative or competing menu items.

In this example, you can improve your estimate about the quantity of each item to prepare if you use the sales history to help guide your production decision. If you assume that future guests will select menu items in a manner similar to that of past guests, the sales history information can be used to improve your predictions:

$$\text{Popularity index} = \frac{\text{Total number of a specific menu item sold}}{\text{Total number of all menu items sold}}$$

In this example, the popularity index calculated for roast chicken last week would be 24.3 percent (365 roast chicken sold/1,500 total guests = 0.243, or 24.3%). Similarly, 38.2 percent (573 roast pork sold/1,500 total guests = 38.2%) preferred roast pork, and 37.5 percent (562 roast beef sold/1,500 total guests = 37.5%) selected roast beef.

In most cases, if you know what menu items your future guests will select, then you are better prepared to make good decisions about the quantity of each item that should be made available to serve them. In this example, Figure 3.2 illustrates your best estimate of what your 300 guests are likely to order when they arrive.

The basic formula for individual menu item forecasting is based on an item's individual sales history:

$$\text{Number of guests expected} \times \text{Item popularity index} = \text{Predicted number to be sold}$$

The **predicted number to be sold** is simply the quantity of a specific food or beverage item likely to be sold given an estimate of the total number of guests expected to be served.

Once you know what items your guests are likely to select, you can then determine how much of each menu item your production staff should be instructed to prepare or have ready to serve.

FIGURE 3.2 Forecasting Item Sales

Menu Item	Guest Forecast	Popularity Index	Predicted Number to Be Sold
Roast Chicken	300	0.243	73
Roast Pork	300	0.382	115
Roast Beef	300	0.375	112
Total			300

It is important to recognize that, as a foodservice manager, you may face a great deal of uncertainty when attempting to estimate the number of guests who will arrive at your operation on any given day because a variety of factors can influence that number, such as these:

- Competition
- Weather
- Special events in your area
- Holidays
- Facility occupancy (in hospitals, dormitories, hotels, and the like) and/or the availability of parking (in selected situations such as shopping malls and strip shopping centers)
- Your own advertising and promotional offers
- Your competitor's advertising and promotional offerings
- Quality of service
- Changes in operating hours
- Operational consistency

These factors, as well as others that can affect sales volume, can make accurate guest count prediction very challenging.

In addition, remember that sales histories track only the general trends of an operation. They are not able to estimate precisely the number of guests who may arrive on any given day. That is the job of the manager. Because they document what has happened in the past, however, sales histories can be a helpful guide to what can be expected to happen in the future.

In Chapter 2, we examined the concept of sales forecasting. You learned that forecasting can involve estimating the number of guests you expect and the dollar amount of sales you expect. Menu item forecasting helps predict what menu items guests will purchase when they arrive at your operation. Menu item forecasting is crucial if you are to effectively purchase needed food and beverage items.

FORECASTING BEVERAGE SALES

Alcoholic beverages are those products that are meant for consumption as a beverage and that contain a significant amount of alcohol. These products are generally classified as beer, wine, or spirits:

1. **Beer**: Fermented beverages made from grain and flavored with hops.
2. **Wine**: Fermented beverages made from grapes, other berries and fruits.
3. **Spirits**: Fermented beverages that are distilled to increase the alcohol content of the product; these are also referred to as **liquors.**

In most cases, estimating the predicted number to be sold for menu items is easier than for beverage items. This is so because the number of possible "menu items" available in the average bar or lounge is staggering. Human imagination has few limits; thus, the number of different alcoholic beverage mixtures a skilled bartender can produce makes forecasting popularity indexes for individual beverages a difficult process, indeed. Doing so effectively means utilizing the formulas for popularity index and predicted number to be sold, but these formulas must be used somewhat differently when they are applied to alcoholic beverage sales.

FORECASTING BEER SALES

Given a choice of beverage products, some of your guests will likely choose beer. The questions you must answer to effectively manage your beverage costs are, "What percentage of my guests will choose beer?" and "Which kind of beer?" and, "In what packaging format will they choose that beer?"

To illustrate, assume that you are the owner of LeRae, a small bar in a trendy section of a large West Coast city. Your clientele generally consists of upscale office and managerial professionals. For the time period January 2 through January 9, you served an alcoholic beverage to a total of 1,600 guests: 400, or 25 percent, selected a beer product; 160, or 10 percent, selected a wine product; and 1,040, or 65 percent, selected some type of spirit-based drink.

You have monitored your historical sales data and found that, in the past, one out of four guests (25 percent) coming to LeRae's will order beer. But, given the several brands of beer that you offer, you need to determine the specific brand of beer your guests will buy. In addition, it is very likely that at least some of the beer you serve will come packaged in more than one form. That is, a specific beer brand might be sold in individual cans, bottles, or in kegs. **Keg beer** is also known as **draft beer**, or beer in a form of packaging in which the beer is shipped to you in multigallon units for bulk sale.

By recording individual beer sales, you will know what your guests' beer preferences are. Figure 3.3 shows that, for the period January 2 to January 9, LeRae's served 400 beers to guests. The figure details which specific beer those guests ordered as well as each product's percentage of the total number of sales.

By reviewing data from your point of sales (POS) system, you will know exactly which beers, by brand and by packaging form, you have sold in the bar on a daily basis. This information can be used to estimate the number of specific beer products that will be ordered by your guests in the future. For example, from the data shown in Figure 3.3, if you estimated that 800 guests will purchase beer in a future time period, 90 of those guests would likely order Budweiser in a bottle (800 estimated guests × 11.25% popularity index = 90 orders predicted to be sold).

FIGURE 3.3 LeRae's Bar Detailed Beer Sales

Beverage Sales		Date: 1/2–1/9
Product: Beer	Number Sold	Popularity Index (%)
Budweiser bottles	45	11.25
Coors bottles	18	4.50
Miller cans	61	15.25
Coors cans	68	17.00
Budweiser draft	115	28.75
Harp's draft	93	23.25
Total	400	100.00

FORECASTING WINE SALES

The ability to accurately forecast wine sales is important. In many operations the forecasting of wine sales must be divided into two parts:

1. Forecasting bottled-wine sales
2. Forecasting wine-by-the-glass sales

FIGURE 3.4 LeRae's Bar Wine-by-the-Glass Sales

Beverage Sales		Date: 1/2–1/9
Product: Wine by the Glass	Number Sold	Popularity Index (%)
Chardonnay	30	18.75
Merlot	16	10.00
Zinfandel	62	38.75
House Zinfandel	52	32.50
Total	160	100.00

FORECASTING BOTTLED-WINE SALES

When forecasting wine sales by the bottle, you treat an individual type of bottled wine exactly as you would treat a menu item. A wine listing or wine menu detailing the selection of wines available is presented to the guest, who then makes a choice. Popularity indexes for bottled wines are computed exactly as they would be when analyzing food item sales. You might find, however, that it is possible and quite desirable to offer wines with rather low sales levels because unopened wines in a bottle are not highly perishable. Thus, many operators develop extensive wine lists consisting of a large number of wines, many of which sell only infrequently.

FORECASTING WINE-BY-THE-GLASS SALES

Generally, forecasting the sale of **house wines** refers to estimating the sales of modestly priced wines offered by the glass. Once you have estimated the number of guests who will select wine served by the glass, the type of wine they will select can then be forecasted.

The popularity of different wine types changes frequently, as newer styles and varieties gain in popularity and newer wine-producing regions (such as Argentina, Australia, and South Africa) improve the quality and marketing of their locally produced wines.

Figure 3.4 details the by-the-glass sales of wine at LeRae's for the period January 2 to January 9. LeRae's manager can use that information to forecast future sales. For example, if LeRae's manager forecasts that 200 guests who purchase wine by the glass will be served in the future, 20 of those guests will likely select the house Merlot (200 estimated guests × 10.0% popularity index = 20 orders predicted to be sold).

If guests remain fairly consistent in their buying habits, managers can have a good idea of the total demand for their wine-by-the-glass products and will be better able to determine the amount of each wine type that must be on hand for any given day.

FORECASTING SPIRIT SALES

Like beer and wine, the number of guests who order a **mixed drink** (a drink made with a spirit) can be recorded and analyzed. Unlike beer and wine, however, using that information to estimate the exact drink guests will request can be difficult to determine. To illustrate, assume that two guests order bourbon and soda; one guest specifies Jack Daniel's brand of bourbon, whereas the other one prefers the lower-cost Heaven Hill brand. From the guests' point of view, they both ordered a bourbon-and-soda mixed drink. From the operator's point of view, two distinct items were selected.

To make matters even more complicated, assume a third guest arrives and orders bourbon and soda without preference as to the type of bourbon used. This can result in a third type of bourbon and soda drink being served. Obviously, a different method of sales forecasting is necessary in a situation such as this, and, in fact, several are available.

FIGURE 3.5 LeRae's Bar Spirit Sales

Beverage Sales		Date: 1/2–1/8
Product: Spirits	Number Sold	Popularity Index (%)
Scotch	210	13.1
Bourbon	175	10.9
Vodka	580	36.3
Gin	375	23.4
Coffee liqueur	175	10.9
Tequila	85	5.3
Total	1,600	100.0

One method requires that the bar operator view guest selection not in terms of the drink requested, such as bourbon and soda, gin and tonic, Sea Breeze, and so on, but rather, in terms of the particular spirit product that forms the base of the drink. To illustrate, consider a table of four guests who order the following:

1. Kahlúa on the rocks
2. Kahlúa and coffee
3. Kahlúa and cream
4. Kahlúa and Coke

Each guest could be considered as having ordered the same item: a drink in which Kahlúa, a coffee-flavored liqueur from Mexico, forms the base of the drink. The purpose of this method is, of course, to simplify the process of recording guests' preferences and to aid in reordering needed spirit products.

An alternative method of tracking drink sales is to consider spirit types such as:

- Bourbon
- Scotch
- Vodka
- Gin
- Rum
- Tequila
- Coffee liqueur

Managers who use this approach are recognizing that literally hundreds of different spirit drinks can be made. These managers are more interested, for example, in knowing the total number of coffee liqueur drinks served than in knowing the number of coffee liqueur drinks served using Kahlúa. Figure 3.5 illustrates spirit sales and popularity index results at LeRae's utilizing such a system.

As the amount of time and effort required to track specific drink sales increases, so does accuracy. Each operator must determine the level of control appropriate for his or her own operation. This is because there is a relationship between the time, money, and effort required to maintain a control system and its cost-effectiveness.

IMPORTANCE OF STANDARDIZED RECIPES

Although it is the menu that determines what is to be sold and at what price, the **standardized recipe** controls both the quantity and the quality of what a kitchen or bar will produce. A standardized recipe details the procedures to be used in

FIGURE 3.6 Standardized Recipe

Roast Chicken		

Special Instructions: Serve with Crabapple Garnish _____ Recipe Yield: 48 _____

(see Crabapple Garnish Standardized Recipe). _____ Portion Size: ¼ chicken

_____ Portion Cost: See cost sheet

Serve on 10-in. plate. _____

Ingredients	Amount	Method
Chicken quarters (twelve 3–3½-lb. chickens)	48 ea.	Step 1. Wash chicken; check for pinfeathers; tray on 24 in. × 20 in. baking pans.
Butter (melted)	1 lb. 4 oz.	Step 2. Clarify butter; brush liberally on chicken quarters; combine all seasonings; mix well; sprinkle all over chicken quarters.
Salt	¼ C	
Pepper	2 T	
Paprika	3 T	
Poultry seasoning	2 t	
Ginger	1½ t	
Garlic powder	1 T	Step 3. Roast at 325°F in oven for 2½ hours, to an internal temperature of at least 165°F.

preparing and serving each of your food or beverage items. The standardized recipe ensures that each time guests order an item they receive exactly what you intended them to receive.

A quality standardized recipe contains the following information:

1. Menu item name
2. Total yield (number of portions produced)
3. Portion size
4. Ingredient list
5. Preparation/method section
6. Cooking time and temperature
7. Special instructions, if necessary
8. Recipe cost (optional)*

Figure 3.6 shows a sample standardized recipe for roast chicken. If this standardized recipe represents the quality and quantity that management wishes its guests to have and if it is followed carefully each time, then guests will always receive the value management intended.

Despite their tremendous advantages, some managers resist taking the time to develop and implement standardized recipes. The excuses they use are many, but the following list contains arguments often used against standardized recipes:

1. They take too long to use.
2. My employees don't need recipes; they know how we do things here.
3. My chef refuses to reveal his or her secrets.
4. They take too long to write up.

---

*This information is optional. If the recipe cost is not included in the standardized recipe, a standardized cost sheet must be developed for each recipe item (see Chapter 5).

5. We tried them but lost some, so we stopped using them.

6. They are too hard to read, or many of my employees cannot read English.

Of the preceding arguments, only the last one, an inability to read English, has any validity. Even in that case, the effective operator should have recipes printed in the language of his or her production employees. Standardized recipes have far more advantages than disadvantages.

The best managers enforce the use of standardized recipes for these reasons:

1. Accurate purchasing is impossible without the existence and use of standardized recipes.

2. Dietary concerns require some foodservice operators to know the exact ingredients and the correct amount of nutrients in each serving of a menu item.

3. Accuracy in menu laws requires that foodservice operators be able to tell guests about the type and amount of ingredients in their recipes.

4. The responsible service of alcohol is impossible without adhering to appropriate portion sizes in standardized drink recipes.

5. Accurate recipe costing and menu pricing is impossible without standardized recipes.

6. Matching food used to cash sales is impossible to do without standardized recipes.

7. New employees can be trained faster and better with standardized recipes.

8. The computerization of a foodservice operation is impossible unless the elements of standardized recipes are in place; thus, the advantages of advanced technological tools available to the operation are restricted or even eliminated if standardized recipes are not used.

Standardized recipes are essential to any serious effort to produce consistent, high-quality food and beverage products at a known cost.

Any recipe can be standardized. The process can sometimes be complicated, however, especially in the areas of baking and sauce production. To create a standardized recipe, it is always best to begin with a recipe of proven quality. Frequently, you may have a recipe designed for 10 servings, but you want to expand it to serve 100 people. In cases like this, it may not be possible to simply multiply the amount of each ingredient by 10. A great deal has been written regarding various techniques used to expand recipes. Computer software designed for that purpose is also now on the market. As a general rule, however, any item that can be produced in quantity can be standardized in recipe form and can be adjusted, up or down, in quantity.

FUN ON THE WEB!

A variety of good companies offer software programs that ease the process of standardized recipe development and conversion. To review such products, type "standardized recipe development software" in your favorite search engine and explore the results.

ADJUSTING STANDARDIZED RECIPES

When adjusting standardized recipes to produce greater, or fewer, numbers of portions, it is important that recipe modifications be made properly. For example, weighing ingredients on a pound or an ounce scale is the most accurate method of measuring many ingredients. It is also important to note that the food item to be measured must be **recipe-ready**. That is, the item must be cleaned, trimmed, cooked, and generally made completely ready to be added to the recipe.

For liquid items, measurement of volume (e.g., ounce, cup, quart, or gallon) is usually preferred. Some operators like to weigh all ingredients, even liquids, for improved accuracy.

When adjusting recipes for proper quantity (number of servings to be produced), two general methods are typically used:

1. Factor method
2. Percentage method

FACTOR METHOD

When using the factor method to adjust a recipe's yield, you first utilize the following formula to arrive at the proper recipe **conversion factor (CF)**:

$$\frac{\text{Yield desired}}{\text{Current desired}} = \text{Conversion factor}$$

If, for example, our current recipe makes 50 portions, and the number of portions we wish to make is 125, the formula would be as follows:

$$\frac{125 \text{ desired portions}}{50 \text{ current portions}} = 2.5 \text{ Conversion factor (CF)}$$

Thus, 2.5 would be the conversion factor. To produce 125 portions, you would multiply each ingredient in the recipe by 2.5 to arrive at the required amount of that ingredient.

Figure 3.7 illustrates the use of this method for a three-ingredient recipe.

PERCENTAGE METHOD

The percentage method addresses ingredient weights, rather than a conversion factor, when adjusting standardized recipes. It is sometimes more accurate than using the conversion factor method. For that reason, the percentage method is a favorite among bakers and others to whom accuracy in recipe ingredient amounts is especially critical.

Essentially, the percentage method involves weighing all ingredients and then computing the percentage weight of each recipe ingredient in relation to the total weight of all ingredients.

To make their calculations easier, many operators convert pounds to ounces prior to making their percentage calculations. These amounts are converted back from ounces to pounds when the conversion is completed.

To illustrate the use of the percentage method, assume that you have a recipe with a total weight of 10.5 pounds, or 168 ounces (10.5 lb. × 16 oz. per lb. = 168 oz.).

FIGURE 3.7 Factor Method Usage

Ingredient	Original Amount	Conversion factor	New Amount
A	4 lb.	2.5	10 lb.
B	1 qt.	2.5	2½ qt.
C	1½ T	2.5	3¾ T

HERE'S HOW IT'S DONE *3.1*

In some cases, a professionally produced standardized recipe will already include the ingredient amounts needed to make a number of different quantities. For example, a standardized recipe may indicate the ingredients needed to produce 25, 50, 75, and 100 portions of the recipe. In other cases, however, a standardized recipe must be adjusted from its current yield to produce the number of portions you need. Because that is true, you must know how to properly increase and decrease the amount produced by a standardized recipe. It's easy to do.

Increasing Yields in Standardized Recipes

To illustrate the process used to *increase* the yield of standardized recipes, assume a recipe yields 80 portions and you need to make 120 portions. Increasing the recipe yield from 80 portions to 120 portions is a two-step process.

Step 1: Calculate the conversion factor using the following formula:

$$\frac{\text{Yield desired}}{\text{Current yield}} = \text{Conversion factor}$$

In this example, that is:

$$\frac{120 \text{ desired portions}}{80 \text{ current portions}} = 1.5 \text{ Conversion factor}$$

Step 2: Multiply each ingredient amount by the conversion factor. For example, if the original recipe required 12 eggs and the recipe conversion factor is 1.5, the number of eggs needed would be 18 eggs.

In this example, the calculation is:

$$12 \text{ eggs} \times 1.5 \text{ Conversion factor} = 18 \text{ eggs}$$

Decreasing Yields in Standardized Recipes

Decreasing the yield in a standardized recipe is also easy. To illustrate, assume a recipe yields 80 portions and you need to make 40 portions. To decrease the recipe yield from 80 portions to 40 portions, you use the same two-step process.

Step 1: Calculate the conversion factor using the formula:

$$\frac{\text{Yield desired}}{\text{Current yield}} = \text{Conversion factor}$$

In this example, that is:

$$\frac{40 \text{ desired portions}}{80 \text{ current portions}} = 0.5 \text{ Conversion factor}$$

Step 2: Multiply each ingredient amount by the conversion factor. For example, if the original recipe required 12 eggs and the recipe conversion factor is 0.5, the number of eggs needed would be 6:

$$12 \text{ eggs} \times 0.5 \text{ Conversion factor} = 6 \text{ eggs}$$

Here's a tip to help you remember how it is done:
If a recipe is being *increased,* the recipe conversion factor (CF) will always be *greater than 1.0.* If a recipe is being *decreased,* the recipe conversion factor (CF) will always be *less than 1.0.*

If the portion size for this recipe is 4 ounces, the total recipe yield would be 168/4 = 42 servings. If you want your kitchen to prepare 75 portions, you would need to supply it with a standardized recipe consisting of the following total recipe weight:

$$75 \text{ servings} \times 4 \text{ oz. per serving} = 300 \text{ oz.}$$

You now have all the information necessary to use the percentage method of recipe conversion. Figure 3.8 details how the process would be accomplished. Note that amounts in the percentage of total column are computed by dividing the ingredient weight by the total recipe weight. The percentage result is then rounded to one decimal place, as shown in the following equations.

FIGURE 3.8 Percentage Method

Ingredient	Original Amount	Ounces	% of Total	Total Amount Required	% of Total	New Recipe Amount
A	6 lb. 8 oz.	104 oz.	61.9	300 oz.	61.9	185.7 oz.
B	12 oz.	12 oz.	7.1	300 oz.	7.1	21.3 oz.
C	1 lb.	16 oz.	9.5	300 oz.	9.5	28.5 oz.
D	2 lb. 4 oz.	36 oz.	21.5	300 oz.	21.5	64.5 oz.
Total	10 lb. 8 oz.	168 oz.	100.0	300 oz.	100.0	300.0 oz.

Thus, for example, ingredient A's percent of total is computed as:

$$\frac{\text{Item A ingredient weight}}{\text{Total recipe weight}} = \% \text{ of total}$$

or

$$\frac{104 \text{ oz.}}{168 \text{ oz.}} = 0.619, \text{ or } 61.9\%$$

Cost Control Around the World

Some managers find it difficult to adjust recipes when they include measurements such as teaspoons, tablespoons, pints, and the like. Although the general US population has been slow to adopt the international metric system for everyday use, foodservice managers working internationally, and increasingly foodservice managers working in the United States, often encounter standardized recipes developed using metric measurements. When metric measurements are used, standardized recipe adjustment is easier. Because that is true, it is a good idea for all managers to memorize (or keep on file) a table, such as the following, that helps them convert *metric* volume and weight measurements to *standard*, or *English*, measurements commonly used to develop standardized recipes in the United States.

Volume Measures	
Standard Units	**Metric Units**
1.05 quarts	1 liter
Gallon	3.79 liters
Quart	0.95 liters
Pint	473 milliliters
Cup	237 milliliters
Tablespoon (T)	14.8 milliliters
Teaspoon (t)	4.9 milliliters

Weight Measures	
Standard Units	**Metric Units**
2.2 pounds	1 kilogram
1 pound	453.6 grams
¾ pound	340.2 grams
½ pound	226.8 grams
¼ pound	113.4 grams
1 ounce	28.4 grams

Note: 1 liter (L) = 1,000 milliliters (ml)
1 kilogram (K) = 1,000 grams (g)
1 pound (lb.) = 16 ounces (oz.)

Temperature Conversions

To convert Celsius to Fahrenheit temperatures:

(Celsius temperature × 1.8) + 32 = Fahrenheit temperature

Example: Convert 100 degrees Celsius to Fahrenheit.

(100 degrees Celsius × 1.8) + 32 = 212°F

To compute the ingredient amounts needed in the adjusted recipe, we multiply the percentage total amount for each ingredient by the total amount required. For example, with ingredient A, the process is:

Item A % of total × Total amount required = New recipe amount
or
61.9% × 300 oz. = 185.7 oz.

The proper conversion of weights and measurements is important in recipe expansion or reduction. The judgment of the recipe writer is also critical because such factors as cooking time, cooking temperature, and utensil selection may vary as recipe sizes are increased or decreased. In addition, some recipe ingredients, such as spices or flavorings, may not respond well to mathematical conversions. In the final analysis, it is your assessment of product taste that should ultimately determine ingredient ratios in standardized recipes. But in all cases, every recipe in use in an operation should be standardized.

FUN ON THE WEB!

A number of websites provide metric-to-US measurement conversion tools. To visit such sites, enter "metric standardized recipe conversion tools" in your favorite search engine and view the results.

PURCHASING FOOD

Menu item forecasts and the use of standardized recipes allow managers to know exactly what must be purchased to ensure their operations have the available menu items their guests will want to buy. Entire books have been written about foodservice purchasing; however, proper purchasing is essentially a matter of determining the following:

1. What should be purchased?
2. What is the best price to pay?
3. How can a steady supply be ensured?

WHAT SHOULD BE PURCHASED?

The question of what should be purchased is answered by the use of a product specification or *spec* for each item purchased. A **product specification** (spec) is simply a detailed description of a recipe ingredient or menu item. A spec is a way for you to communicate with a vendor, in a very precise way, so that your operation receives the exact item you have requested, every time you request it.

It is very important to note that a product specification determines neither the best product to buy nor the product that costs the least. Rather, it is the product that you have determined to be the *most appropriate* product for its intended use in terms of both quality and cost.

A product specification that is not detailed enough can be a problem because the needed level of item quality may not be delivered. However, if your product specifications are too tight (i.e., overly and unnecessarily specific), too few vendors may be able to supply the product you need, resulting in excessively high costs that you will have to pay to receive that item.

FIGURE 3.9 Sample Product Specification

Product Name:	Bacon, sliced	Spec #: 117
Pricing Unit:	lb.	
Standard/Grade:	Select No. 1	
	Moderately thick slice	
	Oscar Mayer item 2040 or equal	
Weight Range:	14–16 slices per lb.	
Packaging:	2/10 lb. Cryovac packed	
Container Size:	Not to exceed 20 lb.	
Intended Use:	Bacon, lettuce, and tomato sandwiches	
Other Information:	Flat packed on oven-proofed paper, never frozen	
Product Yield:	60% yield	

Figure 3.9 is an example of a professionally prepared product specification for bacon used in a foodservice operation that produces bacon, lettuce, and tomato (BLT) sandwiches.

A properly prepared product specification will include the following information:

1. Product name or specification number
2. Pricing unit
3. Standard or grade
4. Weight range/size
5. Processing and/or packaging
6. Container size
7. Intended use
8. Other information such as product yield

PRODUCT NAME

This may seem self-explanatory, but, in reality, it is not. For example, a *mango* is a tropical fruit to those in the Southwestern United States, but may mean a bell pepper to those in the Midwest. Further, bell peppers do not just come in green, their most common color, but can also be purchased in yellow, orange, and red forms. Thus, the product name used on a specification must be specific enough to clearly and precisely identify the item you wish to buy.

When developing product specifications, you might find it helpful to assign a number, as well as a name, to the item you wish to buy. This can be useful when, for example, many forms of the same ingredient or menu item may be purchased.

To illustrate, a deli-restaurant might use 10 to 20 different types of bread, depending on the intended use of the bread. In this example, each type of bread may be given a specific name and number. The same is true with a number of other items, such as cheese, which come in a variety of forms (e.g., block, sliced, shredded) and types (Colby, cheddar, Swiss, and others). Note that, in Figure 3.9, bacon is given a name and a specification number, indicating that more than one form of bacon is purchased by this operation.

PRICING UNIT

A product's pricing unit may be pounds, quarts, gallons, cases, or any other commonly used measurement unit in which the item is sold. Many pricing units are

FIGURE 3.10 Selected Produce Container Net Weights

Items Purchased	Container	Approximate Net Weight (lb.)
Apples	Cartons, tray pack	40–45
Asparagus	Pyramid crates, loose pack	32
Beets, bunched	½ crate, 2 dozen bunches	36–40
Cabbage, green	Flat crates (1¾ bushels)	50–60
Cantaloupe	½ wirebound crate	38–41
Corn, sweet	Cartons, packed 5 dozen ears	50
Cucumbers, field grown	Bushel cartons	47–55
Grapefruit, FL	⅘-bushel cartons and wirebound crates	42½
Grapes, table	Lugs and cartons, plain pack	23–24
Lettuce, loose leaf	⅘-bushel crates	8–10
Limes	Pony cartons	10
Onions, green	⅘-bushel crates (36 bunches)	11
Oranges, FL	⅘-bushel cartons	45
Parsley	Cartons, wax treated, 5 dozen bunches	21
Peaches	2-layer cartons and lugs, tray pack	22
Shallots	Bags	5
Squash	1-layer flats, place pack	16
Strawberries, CA	12 one-pint trays	11–14
Tangerines	⅘-bushel cartons	47½
Tomatoes, pink and ripe	3-layer lugs and cartons, place pack	24–33

easily understood. Parsley, however, is typically sold in the United States by the bunch. Grapes are sold by the lug.

Unless managers are very familiar with the variety of pricing unit terms used in their geographic areas, they may not be able to buy products in an effective way. Figure 3.10 lists some of the more common pricing units for produce in the United States. You should insist that all your vendors supply you with definitions of each pricing unit upon which they base their selling prices.

STANDARD OR GRADE

Many food items are sold with varying degrees of quality. Because that is true, the US Department of Agriculture (USDA), the Bureau of Fisheries, and the Food and Drug Administration have developed standards, or grades, for many food items. In addition, grading programs are in place for many commonly used foodservice items. Trade groups such as the National Association of Meat Purveyors publish item descriptions for many of these products. Consumers also are aware of many of these distinctions. One example is the USDA's grades for beef used in most foodservice operations. In descending order of quality, these are:

- Prime
- Choice
- Select
- Standard

In some cases, managers may prefer to develop a specification identifying a particular product's brand name (e.g., Minor's beef base, or A-1 Steak Sauce) or a specific point of origin (e.g., Maine lobster or Idaho potatoes) as an alternative or supplement to a product standard or grade.

WEIGHT RANGE/SIZE

Weight range or size is important when purchasing some meats, fish, poultry, fruits, and vegetables. In our standardized recipe example of roast chicken, the chicken quarters were to have come from chickens in the 3- to 3½-pound range. This will make them very different in cost and cooking time than if they came from chickens in the 4- to 4½-pound range. In the case of products requiring specific trim or maximum fat covering, that should be designated also, such as 10-ounce strip steak, maximum tail 1 inch, fat covering ½ inch. Four-ounce hamburger patties, 16-ounce T-bones, and ¼-pound hot dogs are examples of the type of item that require an exact size, not a weight range.

Count, in the hospitality industry, is a term that is often used to designate product size. For example, 16- to 20-count shrimp refers to the fact that, for this size shrimp, 16 to 20 of the individual shrimp would be required to make 1 pound. In a like manner, 30- to 40-count shrimp means that it takes 30 to 40 of this size shrimp to make a pound. In addition to seafoods such as shrimp and scallops, many fruits and vegetables are also sold by count. In general, the larger the count, the smaller the size of the individual food items.

PROCESSING AND/OR PACKAGING

Processing and packaging refers to a product's state when you buy it. Apples, for example, may be purchased fresh, dried, canned, or frozen. Each form will carry a price appropriate for its processed or packaged state.

Food can come packed in a large number of forms and styles, including slab packed, layered cell packed, fiberboard divided, shrink packed, individually wrapped, and bulk packed. Although it is beyond the scope of this text to detail all of the many varieties of food processing and packing styles available to foodservice managers, it is important for you to know about them. Your vendors will be pleased to explain to you all the types of item processing and packaging alternatives for the products they sell.

Green and Growing!

Farm to Fork is a term increasingly important to those in foodservice. It refers to the path that food follows from those who grow or raise it to those who will prepare and serve it. Ideally, this path is short, to maximize freshness, minimize health risks, and be environmentally friendly. For that reason, many foodservice operators prefer to seek out and buy locally grown foods whenever possible.

In addition to their freshness, locally grown foods are most often good for the environment because less storing, shipping, and packaging results in less energy to transport and less solid waste from excessive packing materials. Reduced transportation and packaging costs often translate into lower prices charged to foodservice operators.

Locally grown and organic products also help support the same local economies from which many foodservice operations draw their customers. Buying locally is an option that all foodservice managers should thoroughly examine for its benefits to their communities and the environment, as well as the health of their customers and their own bottom lines!

CONTAINER SIZE

Container size refers to the can size, number of cans per case, or weight of the container in which the product is delivered. Most operators know that a

50-pound bag of flour should contain 50 pounds of flour. Some might not be sure, however, what the appropriate weight for a "lug" of tomatoes would be (see Figure 3.10).

INTENDED USE

Different types of the same item are often used in the same foodservice operation but in a variety of ways. Consider, for example, the operator who uses strawberries in a variety of ways. Perfectly colored and shaped large berries are best for chocolate-dipped strawberries served on a buffet table. Less-than-perfect berries, however, may cost less and be a perfectly acceptable form for sliced strawberries used to top strawberry shortcake. Frozen berries might make a good choice for a baked strawberry pie and might be of even lower cost.

Breads, dairy, apples, and other fruits are additional examples of foods that come in a variety of forms. It is important to recognize that the best form of a food product is not necessarily the most expensive form. Rather, it is the form that is best for a product's intended use.

OTHER INFORMATION SUCH AS PRODUCT YIELD

Additional information may be included in a specification if it helps the vendor understand exactly what you have in mind when your order is placed. An example is product yield. **Product yield** is the amount of product that you will have remaining after subtracting losses resulting from cleaning, trimming, cooking, and portioning. Knowing an item's product yield will help you and your vendor determine how much product you must purchase initially to have the desired product quantity you need after accounting for any product lost in an item's preparation. You will learn how to accurately calculate product yields in Chapter 5.

WHAT IS THE BEST PRICE TO PAY?

Once purchase specifications have been developed and quantities to be purchased are known, your next step is to determine how to buy these items at the best price. Some would say that determining the best price should be a simple matter of finding the vendor with the lowest-cost product and placing an order with that vendor. In fact, that is almost always a sure sign of a manager who lacks understanding of the way business, and vendors, operate.

The best price, in fact, is more accurately stated as the lowest price that meets the product specifications of the operation and achieves the long-term goals of both the foodservice operation and its vendors.

When you have a choice of vendors, each supplying the same product (your operation's specification), it is possible to engage in comparison shopping. The management tool used to do this is called the **bid sheet** (see Figure 3.11).

The bid sheet includes vendor information, buyer information, item description, purchase unit, bid price, salesperson's signature, and date. It also includes the dates that the bid prices will be *fixed,* which means the dates during which the supplier agrees to keep the bid price in effect.

Using the example shown in Figure 3.11, the bid sheet could be sent to all approved meat vendors each week on Friday to be returned to you by Monday. Then you could compare the item prices offered to identify the vendor(s) with whom you will place your orders.

After you have received bids from your suppliers, you can compare those bids on a **price comparison sheet,** such as the one shown in Figure 3.12. A price comparison sheet typically has a place to list the category being bid—namely, produce, dairy, and meats products. It also identifies the name of the vendors authorized to bid; the bid date; item descriptions; units of purchase; best bid price; best company

FIGURE 3.11 Bid Sheet

Vendor: _____	Buyer: _____		
Vendor's Address: _____	Buyer's Address: _____		
Vendor's Telephone #: _____	Buyer's Telephone #: _____		
Vendor's Fax #: _____	Buyer's Fax #: _____		
Vendor's E-mail: _____	Buyer's E-mail: _____		

Item Description	Unit	Bid Price
109 Rib, 19–22 lb., Choice	Pound	
110 Rib, 16–19 lb., Choice	Pound	
112A Rib Eye lip on 9–11 lb., Choice	Pound	
120 Brisket, 10–12 lb. deckle off, Choice	Pound	
164 Steamship Round, 60 lb., square bottom, Choice	Pound	
168 Inside Round, 17–20 lb., Choice	Pound	
184 Top Butt, 9–11 lb., Choice	Pound	
189A Tender, 5 lb. avg.	Pound	
193 Flank Steak, 2 lb. avg., Choice	Pound	
1184b Top Butt Steak, 8 oz., Choice	Pound	
1190a Tenderloin Steak, 8 oz., Choice	Pound	
109 Rib, 19–22 lb., Certified Angus Beef, Choice	Pound	
123 Short Ribs, 10 lb.	Pound	
180 Strip, 10–12 lb., Choice	Pound	

Bid Prices Fixed From: _____ **To:** _____

Salesperson Signature: _____ **Date:** _____

quote; and last price paid. This information may then be used to select a vendor based on the prices charged for needed items. When this process is completed, a *purchase order* or PO (addressed later in this chapter) can be developed for each vendor selected.

Bid sheets and price comparison sheets may be used to determine the specific vendor who can supply the lowest price, but they do not give enough information to determine the best price. This makes sense when you realize that your own guests do not necessarily go to the lowest-priced restaurants for all of their meals. If they did, there would be no hope of success for the operator who tried to provide a better food product, in a better environment, with better service.

In most cases, any product can be sold a little cheaper if quality is allowed to vary. Even with the use of product specifications, vendor dependability, ease of order placement, ability to access important account information via the Internet, the quality of a vendor's service, accuracy in delivery, and payment terms can all be determining factors when attempting to determine the "best" price available from the best supplier.

In some cases, specific item vendors to be used by a foodservice operator have been determined in advance. This is often true in a large corporate organization or in a franchise situation. Contracts to provide goods may be established by the central purchasing department of these organizations. When that happens, the designated vendor may have a national or a long-term contract to supply, at a predetermined price, items that meet the operation's specifications.

FIGURE 3.12 Price Comparison Sheet

Vendors   Category: Produce

A. Bill's Produce   Date Bid: 1/2

B. Davis Foods

C. Ready Boy

Item Description	Unit	A	B	C	Best Bid ($)	Best Company	Last Price Paid
Lettuce, Iceberg, 24 ct.	Case	$9.70	$10.20	$9.95	$9.70	A	$9.50
Lettuce, Red Leaf, 24 ct.	Case	$10.50	$10.25	$10.75	$10.25	B	$10.10
Mushroom, Button, 10 lb.	Bag	$15.50	$15.75	$16.10	$15.50	A	$15.75
Mushroom, Portobello, 5 lb.	Bag	$19.00	$19.80	$18.90	$18.90	C	$19.00
Onion, White, Medium, 50 lb.	Bag	$20.25	$20.00	$20.50	$20.00	B	$19.80
Pepper, Green Bell, 85 ct.	Case	$28.90	$29.50	$30.10	$28.90	A	$27.00
Potato, Russet Idaho, 60 ct.	Case	$12.75	$12.50	$12.20	$12.20	C	$12.85

Reviewed By: D. Miller

FUN ON THE WEB!

Houston, Texas, is home to one of the nation's largest foodservice suppliers. Sysco Foods, or one of its regional operational partners, delivers a wide array of foodservice products to virtually every part of the United States and, as a result, is often chosen to service nationwide accounts. An innovative company, Sysco was one of the first to utilize the Internet to simplify an operator's ordering processes. To learn more about Sysco and its product lines, visit the company website by entering "Sysco Corporation" in your favorite search engine.

HOW CAN A STEADY SUPPLY BE ENSURED?

Unfortunately, very little has been written in the field of foodservice about managing costs through cooperation with vendors. Your food and beverages sales persons can be some of your most important allies in controlling costs. Operators who determine their supplier only on the basis of lowest cost will find that they receive only the product they have purchased, whereas their competitors may be buying more than just food! Or, as one food salesperson said when asked why he should be selected as the primary food vendor for business, "*With my products, you also get my knowledge!*"

Just as good foodservice operators know that their guests appreciate high-quality personal service levels, the best vendors also know that operators appreciate high-quality customer service. In many foodservice operations suppliers can be of immense value in ensuring a steady supply of quality products at a fair price if managers remember the following points.

SUPPLIERS HAVE MANY PRICES, NOT JUST ONE

Unlike the restaurant business, which generally charges the same price to all who come in the door, suppliers have a variety of prices based on the customer to whom they are quoting them. The price you pay will most often be based on a variety of factors, including the total amount of food and other products you buy from the vendor and the promptness with which you pay your bills.

SUPPLIERS REWARD VOLUME GUESTS

It is simply in the best interest of a supplier to give a better price to a high-volume customer. The cost to deliver a $1,000 food order to a restaurant is not that much different from the cost to deliver a $100 order. Each order would require one truck and one driver. Those operators who decide to concentrate their business in the hands of fewer suppliers will, as a general rule, pay lower prices.

CHERRY PICKERS ARE SERVICED LAST

Cherry pickers is the term used by suppliers to describe the customers who get bids from multiple vendors and then buy only the items that each vendor has "on sale" or for the lowest price. If an operator buys only a vendor's "on sale" items, the vendor will usually respond by providing limited service. It is a natural reaction to the foodservice operator's failure to take into account varying service levels, long-term relationships, dependability, or any other vendor characteristic except cheapest price.

SLOW PAY MEANS HIGH PAY

In most cases, operators who are slow to pay their bills will find that vendors will charge them more than they charge other operators who pay their bills in a more timely manner.

ONE VENDOR VERSUS MANY VENDORS

Many operators are faced with the decision of whether to buy from one vendor or many vendors. In general, the more vendors used, the more time managers must spend in ordering, receiving, and paying vendor invoices. Many operators, however, fear that if they give all their business to only one supplier, their costs may rise because of a lack of competition. In reality, the likelihood of this occurring is extremely small. Just as foodservice operators are unlikely to take advantage of their best guests (and, in fact, would tend to offer additional services not available to the occasional guest) so, too, does the vendor make extra effort on behalf of the operator who does most of his or her buying from that vendor. In fact, it makes good business sense for the vendor to do so.

Using one or perhaps two primary vendors tends to bring the average delivery size up and should result in lower per-item prices. On the other hand, giving one vendor all of the operation's business can be dangerous and costly if the items to be purchased from that vendor vary widely in quality and price. Staples such as flour, sugar, spices, and other nonperishables are most often best purchased in bulk from one vendor. Orders for meats, produce, and some bakery products are best split among several vendors, perhaps with a primary and a secondary vendor in each category so that you have a second alternative should the need arise. If you are using bid buying as a purchasing method, having at least three vendors is advisable so that you have an adequate choice of prices and services.

PURCHASING ETHICS

Ethics is defined as the choices of proper conduct made by individuals in their relationships with others. Ethics come into play in purchasing foodservice products because of the tendency for some suppliers to seek an unfair advantage over their competition by providing "personal" favors to buyers. These favors can range from small holiday gifts given in appreciation for another year's business to outright offers of cash bribes or kickbacks to the buyer in exchange for volume purchases.

Foodservice buyers often face ethical dilemmas related to gifts or favors from vendors. A quick way to review the ethics of a situation is to consider whom you would tell about it. If you are comfortable telling your boss and your other suppliers about a favor or gift you received from a vendor, it is likely ethical to accept it. If you would prefer that your actions go undetected, accepting the item might require you to compromise your ethics.

It is the job of foodservice managers to establish and communicate to their employees and to their suppliers the ethical standards of purchasing for their own operations. Some large foodservice organizations have formal standards, or codes, of ethical conduct for their buyers. When these are in place, they should, of course, be carefully reviewed and followed by all managers. If your organization does not have a formal set of ethical guidelines for buying, the following self-test can be helpful in determining whether a considered course of action with your suppliers is indeed ethical.

Ethical Guidelines

1. *Is it legal?* Any course of action that violates written law or company policy and procedure is wrong.

2. *Does it hurt anyone?* Are benefits that rightfully belong to the owner of the business accruing to the buyer? Discounts, rebates, and free products are the property of the business, not the buyer.

3. *Am I being honest?* Is the activity one that you can comfortably say reflects well on your integrity as a professional, or will the activity actually diminish your reputation with other suppliers?

4. *Would I care if it happened to me?* If you owned the business, would you be in favor of your buyer behaving in the manner you are considering? If you owned multiple units, would it be good for the business if all of your buyers followed the considered course of action?

5. *Does it compromise my freedom as a buyer?* If your action negatively influences the way you perform as a buyer, then you shouldn't do it. For example, you accept a gift from a supplier and then the supplier provides you poor service. Will you feel comfortable reprimanding the supplier even though he has given you a gift? If you do feel uncomfortable, then maybe you shouldn't accept the gift.

6. *Would I publicize my action?* A quick way to review the ethical merit of a situation is to consider whom you would tell about it. If you are comfortable telling your boss and your other suppliers about the considered course of action, it is likely ethical. If you would prefer that your actions go undetected, you are probably on shaky ethical ground. If you wouldn't want your action to be read aloud in a court of law (even if your action is legal), you probably shouldn't do it.

PURCHASING BEVERAGES

Most foodservice operators select only one quality level for food products. Once a determination on the proper quality level has been made and a product specification written, then only that quality of meat, lettuce, milk, bread, and so on is purchased. In the area of alcoholic beverage products, however, several levels of quality and packaging format are generally chosen. This ensures that a beverage product is available for those guests who wish to purchase the very best, and a product is also offered for those guests who prefer to spend less. Thus, the beverage buyer is faced with deciding not only whether, for example, to carry wine on the menu but also how many different kinds of wine and their quality levels. The same process is necessary for spirits and, to a lesser degree, for beers.

WINE PURCHASING

Determining which wines to buy is a matter of selecting both the right product and packaging form for your operation's needs. To do so, you must first determine if you will sell wine by the:

- Glass
- Split or half-bottle
- Carafe
- Bottle

Wines sold by the glass or carafe can be served from bottles opened specifically for that purpose or they can be drawn from specially boxed wine containers. Wines in a box typically are house wines sold to the beverage manager in multiliter-sized boxes to ease handling, speed, and service and to reduce packaging costs. Bottled wines of many sizes and varieties can also be purchased. The most commonly purchased wine bottle sizes for use in food service are shown in Figure 3.13.

In addition, you may find that you must purchase specific wines for cooking. In general, these products will be secured from your beverage wholesaler rather than your grocery wholesaler.

WINE LISTS

As a good manager, you will build a **wine list**, the term used to describe your menu of wine offerings selected for your own particular operation and guest expectations. Figure 3.14 is an example of a wine list used at Toliver's Terrace, a mid-priced fast casual restaurant.

At Toliver's Terrace, the wine list is first divided by types of wines/grape varietals: Sparkling Wine and Champagne, Chardonnay, Other White Wines, Cabernet Sauvignon, Merlot, and Pinot Noir.

Each category of wines is then numbered as follows: 100s for sparkling wine and champagne, 200s for white wines (Chardonnay and Other white wines), and 300s for red wines (Cabernet Sauvignon, Merlot, and Pinot Noir). The numbering system is used to assist the guest in ordering and to help the server identify the

FIGURE 3.13 Wine Bottle Sizes

Bottle Size (Capacity)	Common Name	Description
0.100 liters	Miniature (mini)	A single-serving bottle
0.187 liters	Split	¼ a standard bottle
0.375 liters	Half-bottle	½ a standard bottle
0.750 liters	Bottle	A standard wine bottle
1.5 liters	Magnum	Two bottles in one
3.0 liters	Double Magnum	Four bottles in one

Note: 1 US quart = 0.946 liters
　　　1 US gallon = 3.785 liters

FIGURE 3.14 Sample Wine List from Toliver's Terrace

	Sparkling Wine and Champagne	Price per Glass/ Price per Bottle
101	Gloria Ferrer, Brut, Sonoma County	$7.00/$26.00
102	Pommery, Reims, France	$43.00
103	Jordan "J," Sonoma	$48.00
104	Moët & Chandon, Epernay, France	$55.00
105	Dom Perignon, Epernay, France	$125.00
	Chardonnay	
201	Kendall-Jackson, California	$5.00/$20.00
202	Camelot, California	$6.00/$22.00
203	St. Francis, Sonoma	$7.00/$26.00
204	Cartlidge & Browne, California	$30.00
205	Stag's Leap, Napa Valley	$52.00
	Other White Wines	
206	Fall Creek, Chenin Blanc, Texas	$5.00/$18.00
207	Max Richter, Riesling, Germany	$6.00/$22.00
208	Honig, Sauvignon Blanc, Napa Valley	$7.00/$25.00
209	Tommasi, Pinot Grigio, Italy	$7.00/$25.00
210	Santa Margherita, Pinot Grigio, Italy	$34.00
	Cabernet Sauvignon	
301	Tessera, California	$5.00/$20.00
302	Guenoc, California	$7.00/$27.00
303	Sebastiani Cask, Sonoma	$35.00
304	Franciscan, Napa Valley	$38.00
305	Chateau Ste. Michelle, Cold Creek, Washington	$45.00
	Merlot	
306	Talus, California	$5.00/$20.00
307	Tapiz, Argentina	$6.00/$22.00
308	Ironstone, Sierra Foothills	$7.00/$26.00
309	Solis, Santa Clara County	$35.00
	Pinot Noir	
310	Firesteed, Oregon	$6.00/$23.00
311	Carneros Creek, Carneros	$31.00
312	Iron Horse, Sonoma	$39.00
313	Domain Drouhin, Willamette Valley, Oregon	$55.00

correct wine in storage. Guests sometimes feel intimidated by the French, Italian, or German names of wines and, thus, might not order them for fear of pronouncing the words incorrectly. A numbering system allows guests to choose a number rather than a name and so reduces the amount of anxiety they might have in ordering wine.

The second column in Figure 3.14 lists the name and place of the **vintner**, or wine producer. The third column lists the price by the glass and/or the price per bottle. Usually, it is an operation's less expensive wines that are available by the glass.

This is so because it is much more cost-effective to offer wine by the glass from a $20.00 bottle of wine than from an $80.00 bottle of wine since, once the bottle is opened, it has a relatively short storage life and if any product remains unsold, it may have to be discarded in a short period of time.

In wine list development, several points must be kept in mind. First, you must seek to provide alternatives for the guest who wants the best, as well as the guest who prefers to spend less. Second, wines that either complement the food or, in the case of a bar, are popular with the guests must be available. Tastes in wines change, and you must keep up with these changes. Subscribing to at least one wine journal in the hospitality field is a good way to do so. You must also avoid the temptation to offer too many wines on a wine list. Excess inventory and use of valuable storage space make this a poor idea. In addition, when selling wine by the glass, those items that sell poorly can lose quality and flavor rapidly. Third, wine sales can be diminished due to the complexity of the product itself.

You should strive to make the purchase of wine by the bottle a pleasant, non-threatening experience. Wait staff, who help in selling wine, should be knowledgeable but not pretentious. You can enlist the aid of your own wine supplier to help you train your staff in the effective marketing of wine, whether it is sold by the bottle or by the glass.

FUN ON THE WEB!

There are many websites that operators can visit to gain information about wines and wine production. To identify such sites, enter "wines" in your favorite search engine; after browsing in that category, follow up with a search of "wine lists." Pay special attention to any online publications your search identifies.

SPIRITS PURCHASING

Spirits have an extremely long **shelf life;** the period of time they can be stored with no significant reduction in quality. Thus, you can make a "mistake" and purchase the wrong spirit product without disastrous results, but only if that product can be sold over a reasonable period of time. Guest preference will dictate the types of liquors that are appropriate for any given operation, but it is your responsibility to determine product quality levels in the beverage area.

Consumer preferences concerning alcoholic beverages can change rapidly. The wise beverage buyer stays abreast of changing consumption trends by reading professional journals and staying active in his or her professional associations. These associations can be major providers of information related to changes in consumer buying behavior. Nowhere is this more important than in the area of spirits.

Spirits used in foodservice are purchased by the bottle. In the United States, as in most parts of the world, bottle sizes for spirits are standardized. The bottle sizes shown in Figure 3.15 represent those most commonly offered for sale to the hospitality market.

In the hospitality industry, 750-milliliter and 1-liter bottles are the two most commonly purchased spirit bottle sizes. In general, restaurant operators will buy spirits in two major categories. These are well liquors and call liquors.

WELL LIQUORS

Well liquors are those spirits that are served when the guest does not specify a particular brand name when ordering. The name stems from the concept of the *well,* or the bottle-holding area in the bar. Buyers must choose their well liquors very carefully. Guests who order well liquors may be price conscious, but that does not mean they are not quality conscious, also. Managers who shop for well liquors

FIGURE 3.15 Spirit Bottle Sizes and Capacities

Common Bottle Name	Metric Capacity	Fluid Ounce Capacity
Miniature	50 ml	1.7
Half-pint	200 ml	6.8
Pint	500 ml	16.9
Fifth	750 ml	25.4
Quart	1.0 L	33.8
Half-gallon	1.75 L	59.2

Note: 1 liter (L) equals 1000 milliliters (ml)

considering only the lowest possible price as the main criterion for selection will find that guest reaction can be extremely negative. Alternatively, if exceptionally high-quality products are chosen as well items, liquor costs may be excessive unless an adequate selling price structure is maintained.

CALL LIQUORS

Call liquors are those spirits that guests request by name, such as Jack Daniel's, Kahlúa, and Chivas Regal. Extremely expensive call liquors are sometimes referred to as **premium liquors**.

You will generally charge a higher price for those drinks prepared with call or premium liquors. Guests understand this and, in fact, by specifying call liquors indicate their preference to pay the higher prices these special products command.

FUN ON THE WEB!

The Internet is a great source of information about cocktails and bartending. If you are 21 or over, you can also explore numerous informational sites developed by liquor companies. To learn more about spirits and spirit production, go to your favorite search engine and enter the words "liquor and spirits." From there, you will readily be launched into a world of "spirited" information!

BEER PURCHASING

Beer is the most highly perishable of alcoholic beverage products. The **pull date**, or expiration date, on these products can be as short as a few months or even a few weeks. Because of this, it is important that the beverage operator only stock those items that will sell relatively quickly. This generally means selecting both appropriate brands and popular packaging forms.

Beverage operators typically carry between 3 and 10 types of beer. Some operations, however, stock as many as 50 or more! Generally speaking, geographic location, clientele, ambience, and menu help determine the beer product that will be selected. Obviously, we would not expect to see the same beer products at Hunan Gardens Chinese Restaurant that we would at Three Pesos Mexican Restaurant. Most foodservice operators find that one or two brands of light beer, two or three national domestic brands, and one or two quality import beers meet the great majority of their guests' demand. One must be very careful in this area not to stock excessive amounts of products that sell poorly.

Beer typically is sold to foodservice operators in cans, bottles, or kegs. Although each of these containers has its advantages and disadvantages, many foodservice operators with active beverage operations will select a variety of these packaging

FIGURE 3.16 Draft Beer Containers

Size (US Gal)	Size (Liters)	No. of 12-oz. Drinks	No. of 16-oz. Drinks	No. of 20-oz. Drinks	Weight	Common Name
1.32	5	14	10	8	–	Mini-Keg/(single use/recyclable)
5	18.9	53	40	32		Home Keg
5.23	19.8	55	41	33		Sixth Barrel
6.6	25	70	52	42		"Half Barrel" (Europe)
7.75	29.3	82	62	49	90 lb.	Quarter Barrel/Pony Keg
13.2	50	140	105	84		Import Keg (standard European "Barrel")
15.5	58.7	165	124	99	140–170 lb.	Half Barrel/Full Keg

methods. It makes little sense to carry the same beer product in both bottles and cans; however, many operators choose to serve some brands of their bottled or canned beer in draft form as well.

Many beer drinkers prefer draft beer (beer from kegs) over bottled and canned beer, and the per-glass cost to you is lower with beer sold from a keg. Special equipment and serving techniques are, however, required if quality draft beer is to be sold to guests. Also, the shelf life of keg beer is the shortest of all packaging types, ranging from 30 to 45 days for an untapped keg—that is, one that has not yet been opened by the bartender—and even fewer days for a tapped (opened) keg. Also, full kegs can be difficult to handle because of their weight, and it can be hard to keep an exact count of the product served without special metering equipment. Despite these drawbacks, many operators serve draft beer. Draft beer is sold in a variety of keg and barrel sizes, as listed in Figure 3.16.

FUN ON THE WEB!

Beers, and especially locally crafted beers, are increasingly popular with foodservice guests. To learn more about the beers brewed in your own area, enter the words "craft beers" and your state name into your favorite search engine. Also, search the web to find regularly produced online publications that are devoted to beers and information about how they are produced.

Green and Growing!

Eco-oriented drink programs present challenges and opportunities for restaurant and bar owners. Increasingly, customers ask for (or even demand!) organic beverages. Available organic spirits products include vodka, gin, tequila, scotch, and rum. Although more expensive than nonorganic versions of the same product, these items are increasingly available for purchase from mainline beverage distributors. Organic wines and beers are also becoming increasingly common.

Concerns about costs can plague green beverage initiatives because organic product costs are historically higher, and in the past, the number of interested customers has been smaller. Today, however, using seasonal and local produce and juices for drink production can help moderate every operation's costs while increasing quality. In addition, consumers are increasingly willing to pay the extra costs incurred by operations that choose to go green. The result? Delighted guests and increased profit margins.

PURCHASE ORDERS •————————————————————

Regardless of the food or beverage items to be purchased, managers should use a purchase order to request delivery of needed items. A **purchase order (PO)** is a detailed listing of products requested by a buyer. A PO may include a variety of product information but must always include the quantity ordered and the price quoted by the supplier. Figure 3.17 is an example of a simple yet effective PO form.

When ordering products, you may be able to choose from a variety of ways to tell suppliers what you want to buy. These may include ordering via the Internet, by telephone, or by placing orders in person. Regardless of your communication method, however, it is critical that you prepare a written purchase order because it serves as a record of what you have decided to buy.

In most cases, the PO should be made out in triplicate (three copies). One copy goes to the receiving area for use by the receiving clerk. Management retains one

FIGURE 3.17 Purchase Order (PO)

Item Purchased	Spec #	Quantity Ordered	Quoted Price	Extended Price
1.				
2.				
3.				
4.				
5.				
6.				
7.				
8.				
9.				
10.				
11.				
12.				
13.				
14.				
15.				
16.				
Total				

Vendor: _____   Purchase Order #: _____

Vendor's Address: _____   Delivery Date: _____

Vendor's Telephone #: _____

Vendor's Fax #: _____

Vendor's E-mail: _____

Order Date: _____   Comments: _____

Ordered By: _____   _____

Received By: _____

Delivery Instructions: _____   _____

copy for the bookkeeping area. The original is, of course, sent to the vendor. If the PO is communicated by telephone, management retains the original copy, with a notation (in the Comments section in the example in Figure 3.17), stating that the vendor has not seen the PO. In all cases, however, it is important to place all orders using a formal PO. If this is not done, the receiving clerk will have no record of what should be coming in on the delivery.

PO preparation can be simple or complex, but should always contain space for the following information:

Purchase Order Information

1. Vendor information
2. Purchase order number
3. Date ordered
4. Delivery date
5. Name of person who placed order
6. Name of person who received order
7. Name of ordered item
8. Item specification #, if appropriate
9. Quantity ordered
10. Quoted price per unit
11. Extension price
12. Total price of order
13. Delivery instructions
14. Comments

The advantages of a written purchase order are many and include:

- Written verification of quoted price
- Written verification of quantity ordered
- Written verification of the receipt of all goods ordered
- Written and special instructions to the receiving clerk, as needed
- Written verification of conformance to product specifications
- Written authorization to prepare vendor invoice for payment

Figure 3.18 shows a PO developed after a thorough inspection of a produce walk-in at a mid-sized hotel. The chef has used a sales forecast to determine the quantity of products needed for next Thursday's delivery. A check of the produce walk-in lets the chef know what is on hand and the quantity, if any, of each product that must be purchased. This information allows for the accurate preparation of the PO. In this case, the order is then placed using the vendor's website. The receiving clerk at the hotel is now prepared with the information necessary to effectively receive the products that have been ordered.

FUN ON THE WEB!

The best foodservice operators are also skilled buyers. The Internet provides a variety of product information sources. You can learn a lot about fruits, vegetables, dairy products, meats, and seafoods. Simply enter the item you are interested in buying in your favorite search. Two particularly good sites for you to visit are those of the United Fresh Fruit and Vegetable Association and the North American Meat Processors Association. Check them out.

FIGURE 3.18 Purchase Order

Vendor: Scooter's Produce			Purchase Order #: 56	
Vendor's Address: 123 Anywhere			Delivery Date: 1/18	
Vendor's Telephone #: 1-800-999-0000				
Vendor's Fax #: 1-800-999-0001				
Vendor's E-mail: scootersproduce@isp.org				

Item Purchased	Spec #	Quantity Ordered	Quoted Price	Extended Price
1. Bananas	81	30 lb.	$0.44 lb.	$ 13.20
2. Parsley	107	4 bunches	$0.80/bunch	$ 3.20
3. Oranges	101	3 cases	$31.50/case	$ 94.50
4. Lemons	35	6 cases	$29.20/case	$175.20
5. Cabbages	85	2 bags	$13.80/bag	$ 27.60
6.				
7.				
8.				
9.				
10.				
11.				
12.				
13.				
14.				
15.				
16.				
Total				$313.70

Order Date: 1/15   Comments:

Ordered By: Joshua Jenn   Faxed on 1/15

Received By: Transmitted by Joshua Jenn

Delivery Instructions: After 1:00 p.m.

RECEIVING FOOD AND BEVERAGE PRODUCTS

After the PO has been submitted to the vendor, it is time to prepare for the acceptance or receiving of the order. The receiving clerk in a large operation performs this function; in a smaller operation, you, as manager, may perform it, or you can designate a staff member to receive the order. In all cases, however, it is wise for you to establish the purchasing and receiving functions so that one individual places the order and another individual is responsible for verifying delivery and acceptance of the order. If this is not done, the potential for purchasing fraud or theft is substantial.

Auditors, those individuals responsible for reviewing and evaluating proper operational procedures, frequently find that the purchasing agent in an operation ordered a product, signed for its acceptance, and authorized payment for it when, in fact, no product was ever delivered! In this case, the purchasing agent could be getting cash payment from the supplier without the manager's knowledge. When purchasing duties are split among two or more individuals in the purchasing chain, this is much less likely to happen. If it is not possible to have more than one person involved in the buying process, management must carefully monitor the work of the purchasing agent/receiving clerk to prevent fraud.

Proper receiving is important, but there is probably no area of the foodservice establishment more ignored than the physical area in which receiving takes place. This is unfortunate, because this is the area where you ensure the quality and quantity of the products you have ordered. There are four requirements for effective receiving:

1. Proper location
2. Proper tools and equipment
3. Proper delivery schedules
4. Proper staff training

PROPER LOCATION

The "back door," which is most often used for receiving, is frequently no more than that, just an entrance to the kitchen. In fact, the receiving area must be adequate to handle the job of receiving, or product loss and inconsistency will result.

First, the receiving area must be large enough to allow for checking products delivered against both the **delivery invoice,** which is the seller's record of what is being delivered, and the PO, the buyer's record of what was ordered. In addition to space required to count and weigh incoming items, accessibility to equipment required to move products to their proper storage area and to dispose of excess packaging is important. A location near refrigerated storage areas is desirable for maintaining deliveries of refrigerated and frozen products at their optimal temperatures.

You should make sure the receiving area stays free of trash and clutter, which can make it too easy to hide delivered food items that may be taken home at the end of a dishonest employee's shift. It is important to remember that the delivery person is also a potential thief. Although most suppliers are extremely careful to screen their delivery personnel for honesty, it is a fact that a delivery person has access to products and has a truck available to remove as well as deliver goods. For this reason, it is important that the receiving clerk work in an area that has a clear view of delivery personnel and their vehicles.

The receiving area should be kept extremely clean; you do not want to contaminate incoming food or provide a carrying vehicle for pests. Sometimes suppliers deliver goods that can harbor roach eggs or other insects. A clean receiving area makes it easier to both prevent and detect this type of problem. The area should be well lit and properly ventilated. Too little light may cause product defects to go unnoticed, and excessive heat in the receiving area can quickly damage delivered goods, especially if they are refrigerated or frozen products.

Flooring in receiving areas should be light in color and of a type that is easily cleaned. In colder climates, it is important that the receiving area be warm enough to allow the receiving clerk to carefully inspect products. For example, if the outside temperature is below freezing, the outside loading dock is no place for an employee to conduct a thorough inspection of incoming products!

PROPER TOOLS AND EQUIPMENT

Although the tools and equipment needed for effective receiving vary by type and size of operation, some items are standard in any receiving operation. These include the following.

- *Scales:* Scales should be of two types: those accurate to the fraction of a pound (for large items) and those accurate to the fraction of an ounce (for smaller items and pre-portioned meats). Scales should be calibrated (adjusted) regularly to ensure their accuracy.

- *Wheeled equipment:* These items, whether hand trucks or carts, should be available so that goods can be moved quickly and efficiently to their proper storage areas.

- *Box cutters:* These tools, properly maintained and used, allow the receiving clerk to quickly remove excess packaging and thus accurately verify the quality of delivered products. Of course, care must be taken when using this tool, so proper training is essential to minimize any safety hazards.

- *Thermometers:* Foods must be delivered at their proper storage temperatures. You must establish the range of temperatures you deem acceptable for product delivery. For most operators, those temperatures are:

Acceptable Temperature Range for Delivered Products		
Item	°F	°C
Frozen Foods	10°F or less	−12°C or less
Refrigerated Foods	30°F to 45°F	−1°C to 7°C

- *Calculator:* Vendor calculations should always be checked, especially if the invoice has been prepared by hand. It is most helpful if the calculator used has a physical tape (as on an adding machine) that can be used by the receiving clerk when needed. The calculator should also be available in case the original invoice is either increased or decreased in amount because of incorrect vendor pricing or because items listed on the invoice were not delivered. In addition, invoice totals will change when all or a portion of the delivery was rejected because the items were of substandard quality.

PROPER DELIVERY SCHEDULES

In an ideal world, you would accept delivery of products only during the hours you choose. These times would likely be during your slow periods, when there would be plenty of time for a thorough checking of the products delivered. In fact, some operators are able to demand that deliveries be made only at certain times, say between 9:00 A.M. and 10:30 A.M. These are called **acceptance hours**. The operation may refuse to accept delivery of products at any other time. Some large operations prefer to establish times in which they will *not* accept deliveries, say between 11:00 A.M. and 1:00 P.M. These are called **refusal hours**. A busy lunchtime may make it inconvenient to accept deliveries at this time, and some operators will simply not take deliveries then. In both cases, however, the assumption is that the operator is either a large enough or a good enough customer to make demands such as these. If your operation does establish either acceptance hours or refusal hours, these should be enforced equally with all vendors.

In many operations it is the supplier will determine when goods are delivered. Although this may seem inconvenient (and often is), remember that all foodservice units would like to have their deliveries made during the slow periods; between their peak meal times. In many cases, it is simply not possible for the supplier to stop his or her trucks for several hours to wait for a good delivery time. In fact, in remote locations, some foodservice operators will be told only the day a delivery will be made, not a specific time!

The key to establishing a successful delivery schedule with suppliers is, quite simply, to work with them. Although every relationship between operator and supplier is somewhat different, both sides, working together, can generally come to an acceptable solution about the timing of deliveries.

PROPER STAFF TRAINING

Receiving personnel should be properly trained. When they are well trained, they can verify the four key characteristics of delivered items:

1. Weight
2. Quantity
3. Quality
4. Price

WEIGHT

One of the most important items to verify when receiving food products is their weight. Doing so is not always easy. For example, a 14-pound package of ground beef will look exactly like 15 pounds. There is no way to tell the difference without putting the product on the scale. Because that is true, receiving clerks should be required to weigh all meat, fish, and poultry delivered. The only exception to this rule would be unopened Cryovac (sealed) packages containing items such as hot dogs, bacon, and the like. In this situation, the entire case should be weighed to detect shortages in content.

Often, meat deliveries consist of several items, all of which are packaged together. When the receiving clerk or supplier is very busy, the temptation exists to weigh all of the products together. The following example shows why it is important to weigh each item rather than the entire group of items as a whole.

Assume that you ordered 40 pounds of product from Bruno's Meats. The portion of the PO detailing the items you ordered is displayed in Figure 3.19.

When the Bruno's delivery person arrived, all three items were in one box and the deliverer was in a hurry. He, therefore, suggested that your receiving clerk simply weigh the entire box. Your receiving clerk did just that and found that the contents weighed 40.5 pounds. Since the box itself weighed about ½ pound, she signed for the delivery. When she began to put the meat away, however, she weighed each item individually and found the information in Figure 3.20.

If you called the supplier to complain about the overcharge ($248.50 total price per the PO—$232.75 actual value of delivered items = $15.75 overcharge), you would likely be told that the misdelivery was simply a mistake caused by human error. It may well have been, but the lesson here is to always instruct your receiving personnel to weigh delivered items individually, even if your staff member is in a hurry.

FIGURE 3.19 Ordered Items

Item Ordered	Unit Price	Total Ordered	Total Price
Hamburger	$2.25/lb.	10 lb.	$ 22.50
New York Strip Steak	$7.00/lb.	20 lb.	$ 140.00
Corned Beef	$8.60/lb.	10 lb.	$ 86.00
Total		40 lb.	$ 248.50

FIGURE 3.20 Delivered Items

Item Ordered	Unit Price	Total Delivered	Actual Value
Hamburger	$2.25/lb.	15 lb.	$ 33.75
New York Strip Steak	$7.00/lb.	10 lb.	$ 70.00
Corned Beef	$8.60/lb.	15 lb.	$129.00
Total		40 lb.	$232.75

When an item is ordered by weight, its delivery should be verified by weight. It is up to the operator to train receiving clerks to always verify that the operation is charged only for the product weight delivered. Excess packaging, ice, or water in the case of produce can all serve to increase the delivered weight. The effective receiving clerk must be aware of and be on guard against deceptive delivery practices.

QUANTITY

The proper counting of products is as important as proper weighing. Suppliers typically make more mistakes in not delivering products than they do in excessive delivery. Products delivered but not charged for cost the supplier money. Products not delivered but charged for cost you money.

If you order five cases of Scotch, then, of course, you want to receive and pay for five cases. This is important for two reasons. First, you only want to pay for products that have been delivered. Second, and just as important, if you have prepared your PO correctly, you truly need five cases of Scotch. If only three are delivered, you may not be able to prepare enough of the Scotch-based drinks ordered by your guests. If this means you will run out of an item or have to make a substitute, you may be forced to deal with unhappy guests.

Shorting is the term used in the industry to indicate that an ordered item has not been delivered as requested. When a vendor shorts the delivery of an item you ordered, that item may or may not appear on the delivery invoice. If it does not appear, it must be noted so that management knows that the item is missing and appropriate reorder action can be taken.

If the item is listed on the delivery invoice, the delivery driver should sign a **credit memo**. A credit memo indicates an adjustment to a delivery invoice must be made. Credit memos should be filled out in triplicate (three copies). One copy is retained in the receiving area to be filed. Management retains one copy for proper bill payment. The original is sent to the vendor.

Figure 3.21 is an example of a credit memo. Note that the credit memo has a place for the signature of not only a representative from your operation but also that of the vendor—both must sign it.

The credit memo is a formal way of notifying a vendor that an item listed on the original delivery invoice is missing, and, thus, the value of that item should be reduced from the invoice's total. If a supplier consistently shorts your operation, that supplier is suspect in terms of both honesty and lack of concern for your operation's long-term success.

The counting of boxes, cases, bags, and the like must be routine behavior for the receiving clerk. Counting items such as the number of lemons or oranges in a box should be done on a periodic basis, but the value of counting items such as these on a regular basis is questionable. Although an unscrupulous supplier might be able to remove one or two lemons from each box delivered, the time it would take for an employee to detect such behavior is often not worth the effort required to spot it. It is preferable to do a thorough item count only periodically and to work with reputable vendors.

The direct delivery of products to a foodservice operator's storeroom or holding area is another area for concern. The delivery person may deliver some items, such as bread, milk, and carbonated beverage mixes, directly to the storage areas, thus bypassing the receiving clerk. This should not be allowed because, after such an activity, it may be impossible to verify the accurate quantity of items delivered. If this process must be used, product dates on each item can help ensure that all products listed on the delivery invoice were received.

QUALITY

No area of your operation should be of greater concern to you than that of the appropriate quality of product delivered. If you go to the trouble of developing product specifications but then accept delivery of products that do not match these

FIGURE 3.21 Credit Memo

CREDIT MEMO

Unit Name: _____

Vendor: _____ Delivery Date: _____

Invoice #: _____ Credit Memo #: _____

Correction					
Item	Quantity	Short	Refused	Price	Amount
Total					

Original Invoice Total: _____

Less: Credit Memo Total: _____

Adjusted Invoice Total: _____

Additional Information: _____

_____

_____

Vendor Representative: _____

Vendor Representative Telephone #: _____

Operation Representative: _____

Operation Representative Telephone #: _____

specifications, you are simply wasting time and effort. Without product specifications, verification of quality is difficult because the receiving staff, and management itself, is unsure of the quality level that is desired. Suppliers know their products. They also know their customers. Some customers will accept only those items they have specified. Others will accept virtually anything because they do not inspect or verify deliveries. If you were a supplier and you had a sack of onions that was getting a bit old, which customer would you deliver it to?

Unscrupulous suppliers can cost your operation guests because of both overcharging and shortchanging. Consider, for example, the restaurant manager who specifies that no more than a ¼-inch fat cover on all New York strip steaks ordered is acceptable. Instead, the meat company delivers steaks with a ½-inch fat cover. The operation will, of course, pay too much for the product because steaks with a ¼-inch fat covering sell at a higher price per pound than those with a ½-inch covering.

Checking for quality means checking the entire shipment for conformance to established product specifications. If only the top row of tomatoes in the box conforms to the operation's specification, it is up to the receiving clerk or manager to point that out to the vendor. If the remaining tomatoes in the box do not meet the specification, the product should be refused. The credit memo can then be used to reduce the total on the invoice to the proper amount.

Sometimes, quality deficiencies are not discovered until after a delivery driver has left your establishment. When that is the case, you should notify the vendor that a thorough inspection has uncovered substandard product. The vendor is then instructed to pick up the nonconforming items. Many managers use the Additional Information section of the credit memo form shown in Figure 3.21 to record this requested pickup. When the product is picked up, the pickup information is recorded. Alternatively, a separate memo to the vendor requesting a product pickup could be produced. It is best, however, to keep the number of cost control forms to a minimum whenever possible, especially when minor modifications of one form will allow that form to serve two purposes.

Experienced managers know that the skill required to receive beverage products is somewhat less than what is needed for receiving food. The reason is that alcoholic beverage products do not typically vary in quality in the same manner food products do. As with food, the receiving clerk needs a proper location, tools, and equipment. In addition, proper delivery schedules must be maintained. The training required in beverage receiving, however, is reduced due to the consistent nature of the product received. A case of freshly produced Coors beer, for example, will be consistent in quality regardless of the vendor. And if the product clearly displays a pull date very little inspection is required to ensure that the product is exactly what was ordered. In fact, when matching a beverage PO to the vendor's delivery invoice, only container size, quantity ordered and price must be verified, unlike food deliveries that require the verification of weight, quantity, quality, and price.

When receiving beverage products, the following items are of special concern and should be verified:

Key Beverage Receiving Checkpoints
- Correct brand
- Correct bottle size
- No broken bottles or bottle seals
- Pull dates (beer)
- Correct vintage or year produced (wine)
- Correct unit price
- Correct price extension
- Correct invoice total

Whether the item purchased is a food item or an alcoholic beverage, vendors are sometimes out of a product, just as you may sometimes run out of a menu item. In cases such as these, the receiving clerk must know whether it is management's preference to accept a product of higher quality, lower quality, or no product at all as a substitute. If this information is not known, one can expect that suppliers will be able to downgrade quality simply by saying that they were "out" of the requested product and did not want the operator to be "shorted" on the delivery.

Training to assess and evaluate quality products is a continuous process. The effective receiving clerk should develop a keen eye for quality. This is done to ensure that both the operation and the guests it serves receive the quality products intended by management.

PRICE

In the area of training staff to verify proper pricing, two major concerns should be addressed:

1. Matching PO unit price to delivery invoice unit price
2. Verifying price extensions and total

Matching PO Unit Price to Delivery Invoice Unit Price

When the person responsible for purchasing food for the operation places a purchase order, the confirmed quoted price should be carefully recorded on it because it is never safe to assume that the delivered price will match the price on the PO. As an ethical manager, you should not be happy with either an overcharge or an undercharge for a purchased product. Just as you would hope that a guest would inform you if a waiter forgot to add the correct price of a bottle of wine to the dinner check, a good receiving clerk works with the supplier to ensure that the operation is fairly charged for all items delivered. The proper acceptance of products puts the integrity of both supplier and operator on the line. Honesty and fair play must govern the actions of both parties.

If the receiving clerk has access to the PO, it is a simple matter to verify the quoted price and the delivered price. If these numbers do not match, management should be notified immediately. If management notification is not possible, both the driver and the receiving clerk should initial the Comments section of the PO, showing the difference in the two prices, and a credit memo should be prepared.

Obviously, if the receiving clerk has no record of the quoted price, from either a PO or an equivalent document, price verification of this type is not possible. An inability to verify the quoted price and the delivered price at the time of delivery is a sure indication of a poorly designed food cost control system.

Some operators deal with suppliers in such a way that a contract price is established. A **contract price** is simply an agreement between buyer and seller to hold the price of a product constant over a defined period of time. For example, Bernardo uses Dairy O Milk. Dairy O agrees to supply Bernardo with milk at the price of $2.55 per gallon for three months from January 1 through March 31. Bernardo is free to buy as much or as little as he needs. The milk will always be billed at their contract price of $2.55 per gallon. The advantage to Bernardo of such an arrangement is that he knows exactly what his per-gallon milk cost will be for the three-month period. The advantage to Dairy O is that it can offer a lower price in the hope of securing all of Bernardo's milk business. Even in the case of a contract price, however, the receiving clerk should verify the invoice delivery price against the established contract price.

Verifying Price Extensions and Total

Price extension is just as important for you to monitor as is the ordered/delivered price. Price extension is the process by which you compute extended price. **Extended price** is simply the unit price multiplied by the number of units delivered. For example, if the price for a case of lettuce is $18.00 and the number of cases delivered is six, the extended price is calculated as:

Unit price × Number of units delivered = Extended price

$18.00 × 6 cases = $108.00

Extended price verification is extremely important. It is critical that the receiving clerk verify:

- Unit prices
- Number of units delivered
- Extended price computations (Unit price × Number of units delivered)
- Invoice totals

There seems to be two major reasons why operators do not always insist that the receiving clerk verify the extended prices and invoice totals. The most common reason is the belief that there is not enough time to do so. The driver may be in a hurry and the operation may be very busy. If that is the case, the process of verifying the extended price can be moved to a slower time. Why? Because there is a written record provided by the vendor of both the unit price and the number of units delivered. Thus, extension errors are vendor errors, recognized by the vendor in the vendor's own handwriting! Or, more accurately, today they are in the vendor's own computer.

The second reason operators sometimes ignore price extensions is related to these same computers. Some operators believe that if an invoice is computer generated, the mathematics of price extension must be correct. Nothing could be further from the truth. Anyone familiar with the process of using computers knows that there are many possible entry errors that can result in extension errors (even formulas entered into Excel-type spreadsheets can be entered in error). Once all extension prices have been verified as correct, receiving clerks should check the invoice total against the sum of the individual price extensions. Managers must ensure that delivery clerks verify both extension prices and invoice totals. If this cannot be done at the time of delivery, it must be done as soon thereafter as possible.

RECEIVING RECORD OR DAILY RECEIVING SHEET

Some large operations use a receiving record when receiving food and beverage products. This method, although taking extra administrative time to both prepare and monitor, has some advantages.

A receiving record generally contains the following information:

1. Name of supplier
2. Invoice number
3. Item description
4. Unit price

5. Number of units delivered

6. Total cost

7. Storage area (unit distribution)

8. Date of activity

Figure 3.22 is an example of a receiving record, specifically designed for the receiving area of a large hotel. Note that some items are placed directly into production areas (direct use), whereas others may be used in specific units or sent to the storeroom. Sundry items, such as paper products, ashtrays, matches, and cleaning supplies, may be stored in specific nonfood areas. Note, also, that subtotals for storage areas can be determined in terms of either units or dollars, as the operator prefers. In all cases, the sums for each distribution area should equal the total for all items received during the day.

Receiving reports can be useful to management if it is important to record where items are to be delivered or where they have been delivered. Although some foodservice operators will find the receiving report useful, some will not because most of the information it contains is also included in the receiving clerk's copy of the PO.

FIGURE 3.22 Receiving Record for Hotel Pennycuff

									Distribution	
Supplier	Invoice #	Item	Unit Price	No. of Units	Total Cost	A	B	C	D	E
Dairy O	T-16841	½ pt. milk	$ 0.24	800	$192.00	75	600	125	—	
Tom's Rice	12785	Rice (bags)	$12.00	3	$ 36.00	—	1	—	2	—
Barry's Bread	J-165	Rye	$ 0.62	25	$ 15.50	—	25	—	—	—
		Wheat	$ 0.51	40	$ 20.40	20	—	20	—	—
		White	$ 0.48	90	$ 43.20	40	10	—	40	—
Total units				958		135	636	145	42	0
Total cost					$307.10					

Receiving Report   Date: 1/2

Distribution Key:

A = Coffee Shop   D = Storeroom

B = Banquet Kitchen   E = Sundry (nonfood items)

C = Direct Use

Comments: _____

Technology Tools

This chapter focused on managing food-related costs by controlling the areas of forecasting future sales, using standardized recipes, effective purchasing, and proper receiving.

Recipe Software

1. Maintain standardized recipes.
2. Cost standardized recipes.
3. Allow for computer-assisted recipe quantity conversion.
4. Maintain and supply dietary information by portion.
5. Create ingredient lists for purchase or issue from storeroom.
6. Suggest alternative cooking methods.
7. Supply color pictures of the finished product.
8. Create purchase orders based on production forecasts.
9. Determine suggested selling prices based on product costs.

Purchasing Software

1. Create vendor bid sheets based on forecasted ingredient needs.
2. Compare bids and make purchase recommendations based on best cost/best value.
3. Maintain vendor price histories.
4. Establish minimum and maximum par values by ingredient.
5. Create purchase orders and auto-order based on established par levels with automatic electronic order confirmation.
6. Interface (if desirable) with other systems to create aggregate purchase orders (in multiunit settings).
7. Create purchase recap by item and/or vendor.
8. Maintain a "red-flag" system for product purchasing variances that exceed forecasted usage.
9. Utilize purchase orders to predict actual profitability.
10. Purchase directly from vendor using vendor-supplied software.

Receiving Software

1. Prepare a daily receiving report.
2. Compare product received (receiving records) with purchase orders (PO) in areas of:
   a. Weight
   b. Quantity
   c. Quality
   d. Price
3. Maintain outage and shortage records by vendor.
4. Verify vendor price extensions.
5. Maintain receiving histories.

Managing the purchasing of needed food and beverage products is a process in which a great number of advanced technology tools are available. Remember, however, that the amount of information that can be generated in this area is vast, and you should elect to gather and maintain only information that is of real value to you.

Apply What You Have Learned

*T*onya Johnson is the regional manager for Old Town Buffets. Each of the five units she supervises is in a different town. Produce for each unit is purchased locally by each buffet manager. One day, Tonya gets a call from Danny Trevino, one of the buffet managers reporting to her. Danny states that one of the local produce suppliers he uses has offered Danny the use of two season tickets to the local university's home football games. Danny likes football and wants to accept the tickets.

1. Would you allow Danny to accept the tickets? Why or why not?
2. Would you allow your managers to accept a gift of any kind (including holiday gifts) from a vendor?
3. Draft a "gifts" policy that you would implement in your region. Would you be subject to the same policy?

Key Terms and Concepts

*T*he following are terms and concepts discussed in the chapter that are important for you as a manager. To help you review, please define the terms below.

popularity index	conversion factor (recipe)	call liquor
predicted number to be sold	product specification (spec)	premium liquor
alcoholic beverages	count (product size)	pull date (beer)
beer	product yield	purchase order (PO)
wine	bid sheet	auditor
spirits	price comparison sheet	delivery invoice
liquors	cherry pickers	acceptance hours
keg beer	ethics	refusal hours
draft beer	wine list	shorting
house wines	vintner	credit memo
mixed drink	shelf life	contract price
standardized recipe	well liquor	extended price
recipe-ready		

Test Your Skills

You may download the Excel spreadsheets for the Test Your Skills exercises from the student companion website at www.wiley.com/college/dopson. Complete the exercises by placing your answers in the shaded boxes and answering the questions as indicated.

1. Nikki Rauguth is the food and beverage manager at Harrison Residence Hall, the largest student housing facility on State University campus. Once each month, Nikki features an "Italian night," a themed dinner, for her students. She serves the following four menu items listed. Nikki has maintained sales histories showing the number of individual menu items selected for each of her last three "Italian nights." Calculate the total number of each menu items served over the past three months then use that information to calculate each menu item's popularity index.

	Month 1	Month 2	Month 3	3-Month Total	Popularity Index
Menu Item					
Lasagna	215	130	164		
Pasta Carbonara	65	52	74		
Seafood Shells	35	62	64		
Pork Milanese	98	145	116		
Total Served					

Over the entire three-month period, which Italian-themed menu item was the most popular with Nikki's students? Which menu item was the least popular?

2. Jean Alexander is the F&B director at the City Plaza Hotel. This year, Jean's hotel was selected as the host site for the Delmar Electronics company's annual holiday party. Jean asked her bartenders to keep careful records of the alcoholic and nonalcoholic beverages they served the guests during the event. This year, 1,350 drinks were served. Calculate the popularity indexes for each of the individual drink options offered to the party attendees, as well as total popularity indexes for the beer, wine, cocktails and nonalcoholic drink categories.

Delmar Electronics Holiday Party Drink Consumption		
Drink Type	**Number Served**	**Popularity Index**
Beer		
Bottled	145	
Draft	210	
Beer Total		
Wine		
Red		
White	150	
Wine Total	360	
Cocktails		
Whiskey	85	
Vodka	248	
Gin	45	
Rum	65	
Cocktail Total		
Nonalcoholic		
Coffee	62	
Soda	130	
Nonalcoholic Total		
Total Drinks	1,350	100%

Why would this information be important to Jean if the City Plaza Hotel is chosen to host the same event next year?

3. Rob Stewart is the director of foodservice at the 600-bed Memorial Hospital. Rob carefully maintains cumulative records of individual entrées served in the past when these menu items were offered, and these are listed in the "Number Served" column below. Today, Rob is preparing kitchen production orders for tomorrow's dinner meal where he will offer the same four menu items listed. He estimates that 500 dinners will be served. Help Rob forecast the number of each entrée his patients will likely request when they make their menu selections for tomorrow's dinner.

Entrée	Number Served	Popularity Index	Number to Produce
Roast Turkey	3,848		
Pasta Primavera	1,332		
Broiled Tilapia	3,700		
Sliced Beef with Mushroom Sauce	5,920		
Total Served		100%	

4. Joshua is the chef at the Metzger House restaurant. At a private dinner tomorrow, Joshua will be serving Medallion of Veal Sauté to 24 guests. The standardized recipe Joshua has for Medallion of Veal Sauté only makes 12 portions. Calculate the recipe conversion factor (CF) Joshua will utilize to convert the recipe to 24 servings, then calculate the amounts of ingredients he will need to have on hand to prepare this entrée for tomorrow's guests.

Standardized Recipe Worksheet: Medallion of Veal Sauté					
Medallion of Veal Sauté	**For 12 Servings**			**For 24 Servings**	
Ingredients	Amount	Unit	CF	Amount	Unit
Veal loin, boneless, 6 oz. each	12	each			each
Flour	2	cups			cups
Butter, clarified	2/3	cups			cups
Mushrooms, fresh, sliced	6	cups			cups
Shallots, finely chopped	3	T			T
White wine, dry	1	cups			cups
Heavy cream	1½	cups			cups
Veal veloute	2	cups			cups
Salt/pepper	To taste			To taste	

Method

1. Season veal medallions with salt and pepper. Dip in flour and sauté in clarified butter over medium heat until golden brown. Remove to tray.
2. Sauté sliced mushrooms and shallots until just wilted.
3. Add white wine, cream, and veloute sauce, then simmer to reduce sauce by half.
4. Season sauce with salt and pepper and spoon onto individual plated veal portions.
5. Garnish with fluted mushroom cap and sprig of fresh rosemary.

5. Cynthia is the F&B director at the Shady Grove assisted living facility. This Saturday, Cynthia is serving Chutney Raisin Chicken Salad to the residents of the facility. Her standardized recipe makes 8 pounds of salad but she only needs to make 6 pounds. Calculate the recipe conversion factor (CF) Cynthia will utilize to convert the recipe from 8 pounds to 6 pounds, then calculate the amounts of ingredients she will need to have on hand to prepare this item for her residents.

Standardized Recipe Worksheet: Chutney Raisin Chicken Salad					
Chutney Raisin Chicken Salad	For 8 Pounds			For 6 Pounds	
Ingredients	Amount	Unit	CF	Amount	Unit
Cooked chicken	5	lb.			lb.
Celery, diced	8	oz.			oz.
Green onions, chopped	4	oz.			oz.
Mango chutney	12	oz.			oz.
Raisins	1	cup			cup
Mayonnaise	1	lb.			lb.
Seedless grapes	12	oz.			oz.

Method

1. Remove bones, fat, and skin from cooked chicken and dice into quarter-inch pieces.
2. Combine the chicken, celery, green onions, mango chutney, raisins and mayonnaise in a bowl. Mix well.
3. Slice grapes in half. Add grapes to the chicken mixture and combine gently.
4. Refrigerate for two hours before serving.

6. Eli owns his own upscale bakeshop. He sells high-quality breads, cakes, and pastries to a select group of clientele that includes restaurants and hotels. One of Eli's best-selling items is his locally famous "Tasty Dinner Rolls." The standardized recipe for Tasty Dinner Rolls produces approximately 64 rolls. One of Eli's clients has requested 128 rolls for tomorrow. Eli's standardized recipes are developed based on ingredient weights. Use the percentage method to adjust Eli's Tasty Dinner Rolls recipe to calculate the amounts of ingredients he will need to have on hand to prepare the rolls his client has requested for tomorrow.

Recipe Ingredient Worksheet: Eli's Tasty Dinner Rolls					
Ounces Based on 64 Rolls			Ounces Based on 128 Rolls		
Number of Rolls	Total Ounces	Ounces per Roll	Number of Rolls	Ounces per Roll	Total Ounces
64	80		128		

Recipe Ingredient Worksheet: Eli's Tasty Dinner Rolls						
Tasty Dinner Rolls	For 64 Rolls				For 128 Rolls	
Ingredient	Original Amount	Unit	Original Ingredient Amount (Ounces)	% of Total	Total Ounces	New Ingredient Amount (Ounces)
Water, warm	20	fl. oz.	20			
Active dry yeast	2	oz.	2			
Bread flour	2½	lb.	40			
Salt	1	oz.	1			
Granulated sugar	¼	lb.	4			
Nonfat dry milk	3	oz.	3			
Shortening	2	oz.	2			
Unsalted butter	4	oz.	4			
Eggs	4	oz.	4			
Total			80			

7. Renée Radloff is the owner of an intimate Italian bistro located in Northern California. While traveling in Tuscany on vacation, Renée Radloff was served a garden salad with garlic croutons. Renée was so impressed with the croutons she asked the restaurant's manager for the recipe, and he was delighted to give it to her. Renée wants to use the recipe to prepare the croutons in her own restaurant but must first convert the recipe ingredient amounts from metric to US measurements. Help Renée to convert the recipe into a measurement form that can be easily used by her own production staff. (Spreadsheet hints: Use the ROUND function to 0 decimals for ounces, tablespoons, and teaspoons. Use the ROUND function to 1 decimal for pounds.)

Standardized Recipe: Tuscan Garlic Croutons				
Tuscan Garlic Croutons	Yield: 900 g		US Conversion	
Ingredients	Metric Amount	Metric Unit	US Amount	US Unit
Butter, unsalted	170	g		oz.
Garlic, chopped	15	ml		T
Sourdough bread cubes	680	g		lb.
Parmesan Reggiano, grated	30	g		oz.
Fresh basil	30	ml		T
Fresh oregano	5	ml		t

Method

1. Melt the butter in a small sauté pan and add the garlic. Sauté the garlic in butter over low heat for 5 minutes.
2. Place the bread cubes in a mixing bowl. Add the Parmesan Reggiano and fresh herbs.
3. Pour the garlic butter over the bread cubes and toss gently to combine.
4. Spread bread cubes in a single layer on a sheet pan and bake, stirring occasionally, at 175°C until dry and lightly brown (approximately 15 minutes).

At approximately what temperature (in Fahrenheit) should Renée's staff bake the croutons?

8. Billie Mendoza is the purchasing manager for a medium-sized all-suite hotel with a restaurant and a banquet hall. She needs to create the food purchase orders for tomorrow, and she wants to make sure that she is getting the best price for the best quality and service. At the beginning of this week, Billie received bids on produce items from Village Produce, City Produce, and Country Produce. She has listed these prices in the following price comparison sheet.

Identify the best bid price and best company for each of Billie's produce items. (Spreadsheet hint: Use the MIN function in the Best Bid $ column.)

If Billie was going to create a purchase order just for Village Produce, what items would she likely put on the purchase order based solely on bid prices?

Price Comparison Sheet								
Item	Description	Unit	Village Produce	City Produce	Country Produce	Best Bid $	Best Company Quote	Last Price Paid
Avocados	48 ct.	Case	$61.80	$60.30	$59.46			$57.94
Cauliflower	12 ct.	Case	$12.80	$12.90	$13.27			$13.26
Cucumbers	Medium	Case	$11.10	$11.52	$10.91			$11.34
Grapes	Red Seedless	Lug	$19.32	$19.50	$19.14			$18.72
Lettuce	Green Leaf, 24 ct.	Case	$ 9.53	$ 9.84	$10.27			$10.02
Lettuce	Romaine, 24 ct.	Case	$17.75	$17.82	$18.22			$18.10
Pears	D'Anjou	Case	$20.82	$20.58	$20.64			$20.62
Peppers	Green Bell, med.	Case	$ 8.30	$ 8.38	$ 9.28			$ 9.02
Pineapples	7 ct.	Case	$10.50	$10.38	$10.68			$10.08
Potatoes	B Reds	50-lb. Bag	$15.06	$14.82	$14.88			$14.98
Potatoes	Peeled, large	25-lb. Bag	$17.52	$17.22	$17.28			$17.18
Squash	Yellow #2	30-lb. Case	$ 8.55	$ 8.71	$ 8.98			$ 9.10
Strawberries	Driscoll	Flat	$18.29	$18.06	$17.10			$18.30

9. Loralei operates the foodservice for a large elementary school. She buys produce from Shady Tree Produce Company. Wayne, Shady Tree's owner, makes many errors when he prepares invoices for his customers, but he is the only vendor who has the ability to deliver daily. Loralei needs daily delivery. Because she knows Wayne is careless with the invoices, Loralei checks each one carefully. For Monday, Loralei needs the items listed as follows.

Monday Order		
Item	Unit Price	Number of Cases Needed
Tomatoes	$18.50	3
Potatoes	$12.90	6
Carrots	$18.29	4

Using this information, complete her purchase order for Monday.

Purchase Order							
Supplier				**Purchase Order**			
Company Name:	Shady Tree			PO Number	123		
Street Address:	123 Somewhere			Order Date:	1/15		
City, State, Zip:	Village, TX 12345			Delivery Date:	1/16		
Phone Number:	555-5555			Phone Number:	555-5557		
Fax Number:	555-5556			Fax Number:	555-5558		
E-Mail:	Shady@isp.org			E-mail:	Lora@isp.org		
Contact:	Wayne			Buyer:	Loralei		
Item	**Description**	**Unit**	**Quantity**	**Unit Price $**	**Extension**		
Tomatoes	4 × 5, layered	Case					
Potatoes	Peeled, large	Case					
Carrots	Julienne, 5-lb. bag	Case					
Total							

Upon delivery, Loralei checks her invoice from Wayne to see if he has, once again, made any errors.

Review the following invoice extended prices and total.

Shady Tree Produce Company Invoice for Monday Order			
Item	**Unit price**	**Number Delivered**	**Extended Price**
Tomatoes	$18.50	3	$ 55.55
Potatoes	$19.20	6	$115.20
Carrots	$18.92	4	$ 75.68
Total Amount Due			$256.43

Does the invoice contain errors? If so, what are they? What is the total amount of "error" on the invoice, if any? How can Loralei detect such errors in the future?

10. Restaurant managers use standardized recipes to help enhance product quality and to assist in controlling costs. If standardized recipes are not used, all aspects of a foodservice operation can be affected. What is a likely impact on guests if standardized recipes are not used? What is a likely impact on servers? On profits? On future revenues?

CHAPTER 4

Managing Inventory and Production

OVERVIEW

This chapter begins with an overview of the procedures used to properly store food and beverage products until they are ready for use. The careful control of products while in storage is important to help minimize product loss due to waste, spoilage, and theft. The chapter then addresses the steps that managers must take to ensure product inventories are kept secure. When stored products are needed by production staff, these products must be properly issued and their issue amounts carefully recorded to assist in future cost calculation and purchasing efforts. Finally, managers must ensure that the procedures used for producing food and beverage items for their guests result in the desired product quality and proper cost control. This chapter directly addresses these important procedures.

Chapter Outline

- Product Storage
- Inventory Control
- Product Issuing and Restocking
- Managing Food Production
- Managing Beverage Production
- Technology Tools
- Apply What You Have Learned
- Key Terms and Concepts
- Test Your Skills

LEARNING OUTCOMES

At the conclusion of this chapter, you will be able to:
- Implement an effective product storage and inventory system.
- Control the issuing of products from storage.
- Manage the food and beverage production process.

PRODUCT STORAGE •

In Chapter 3, you learned the procedures you will use to properly purchase and receive foodservice products. In most cases, after purchased items have been received, they must be immediately placed into storage. Food and beverage product quality rarely improves with increased storage time. In fact, the quality of most products you buy will be at its peak when the product you ordered is delivered to you. From then on, these products will often decline in freshness, quality, and nutritional value.

It is important to understand that all of the stored food and beverage products that make up your **inventory** are the same as money to you. In fact, you should think of items placed in storage in exactly that same way. The apple in a produce walk-in is not just an apple. It represents, at a selling price of $2.00, that amount in revenue to the airport foodservice director, who hopes to sell a crisp, fresh apple to a weary traveler. If the apple disappears, revenue of $2.00 will disappear also. When you think of inventory items in terms of their sales value, it becomes clear why food and beverage products must be stored and maintained carefully.

STORING FOOD PRODUCTS

The ideal situation for you and your operation would be for you to store only the food you will use between the time of a vendor's delivery and the time of that vendor's next delivery. This is true because storage costs money, in terms of providing both the storage space for inventory items and the money that is tied up in inventory items and thus unavailable for use elsewhere. It is always best, whenever possible, to order only the products that are absolutely needed by the operation. In that way, the vendor's storeroom actually becomes your storeroom. The vendor then absorbs the costs of storing your needed products. In all cases, however, you must have an adequate supply of products on hand to service your guests. They are your main concern. If you are doing your job well, you will have many guests and will need many items in storage!

After receiving staff has properly accepted the food products you have purchased, the next step in the control of food costs is that of storing those items. The storage process, in most foodservice establishments, consists of three main tasks:

1. Placing products in storage
2. Maintaining food and beverage storage areas
3. Maintaining product security

PLACING PRODUCTS IN STORAGE

Food products are highly perishable items. As such, they must be moved quickly from your receiving area to the area selected for storage. This is especially true for refrigerated and frozen items. An item such as ice cream, for example, can deteriorate substantially in quality if it remains at room temperature for only a few minutes. Most often, in foodservice, this high perishability means that the same individual responsible for receiving the items is the one responsible for their storage.

Consider the situation of Kathryn, the receiving clerk at Fairview Estates, an extended care facility with 400 residents. She has just taken delivery of seven loaves of bread. They were delivered in accordance with the purchase order her manager prepared. The bread must now be put in storage. When Kathryn stores these items, she must know whether management requires her to use the LIFO (last in, first out) or FIFO (first in, first out) method of product rotation.

LIFO System

When using the **LIFO** storage system, the storeroom manager intends to use the most recently delivered product (last in) before he or she uses any part of that same product previously on hand. If Kathryn decides, for example, to use the just delivered bread prior to using other bread already in storage, she would be utilizing the LIFO system. In all cases, you must strive to maintain a consistent product standard. In the case of some bread, pastry, fruit, and vegetable items, the storeroom clerk could be instructed to utilize the LIFO system. With LIFO, you will need to take great care to order only the quantity of product needed between deliveries. If too much product is ordered, loss rates will be very high. For most of the items you will buy, however, the best storage system to use is the FIFO system.

FIFO System

Using a **FIFO** (first in, first out) storage system means that you intend to rotate your stock in such a way that product already on hand is sold prior to the sale of more recently delivered product. With FIFO, oldest products (first in) are used before newer products. When the FIFO system is used, the storeroom clerk must take great care to place new stock behind, underneath, or at the bottom of old stock. It is often the tendency of employees not to do this. Consider, for example, the storeroom clerk who must put away six cases of tomato sauce. The cases weigh about 40 pounds each. The FIFO method dictates that these six cases be placed *under* the five cases already stacked in the storeroom. Will the clerk place the six newly delivered cases underneath the five older cases? In many instances, the answer is no. Unless management strictly enforces the FIFO rule, employees may be tempted to use the faster and easier, but improper, way of storing newly delivered products on top of those already in storage. Figure 4.1 demonstrates the difference between LIFO and FIFO when dealing with storing cases of food products.

FIFO is the preferred storage technique for most perishable and nonperishable items. Failure to implement a FIFO system of storage management can result in excessive product loss due to spoilage, shrinkage, and deterioration of product quality.

Decisions about storing food items according to the LIFO or FIFO method are management decisions. Once these decisions have been made, they should be communicated to storeroom staff and monitored on a regular basis to ensure compliance. To assist them in their efforts, some foodservice managers require the storeroom clerk to mark or tag each delivered item with the date of delivery. These markings provide a visual aid in determining which products should be used first. This is especially critical in the area of highly perishable and greater-cost items such as fresh meats and seafood. Special meat and seafood date tags should be available from your vendor. These tags contain a space for writing in the item's name, quantity, and delivery date. The use of these tags or an alternative date tracking system is strongly recommended. If the supplier has computerized his or her delivery, the box or case may already bear a bar code strip identifying both the product and the delivery date. When this is not the case, however, the storeroom clerk should perform this function.

FIGURE 4.1 FIFO and LIFO Storage Systems

Oldest	Newest
Oldest	Newest
Oldest	Newest
Newest	Oldest
Newest	Oldest
Newest	Oldest
FIFO	**LIFO**

FIGURE 4.2 FIFO Stocking System

Tomato sauce	2/10	Beets	2/10	Egg noodles	2/18
Tomato sauce	2/18	Beets	2/10	Egg noodles	2/18
Tomato sauce	2/18	Beets	2/18	Egg noodles	2/22
Tomato sauce	2/22	Beets	2/22	Egg noodles	2/22

FIGURE 4.3 Product Storage Label

Figure 4.2 shows products in a dry-storage area when management requires that the storeroom clerk mark each stored item with its date of delivery.

Some operators prefer to go even further when labeling products in storage. These operators date the item and then also indicate the day (or hour) in which the product should be pulled from storage, thawed, or even discarded (disc.).

Figure 4.3 is an example of a typical storage label utilized for this process.

FUN ON THE WEB!

Daydots is a line of labeling products developed especially for the restaurant industry. To learn more about how these storage labels can help your operation ensure product quality and save money, type "daydot foodservice labels" in your favorite search engine.

MAINTAINING FOOD STORAGE AREAS

To maintain the quality and security of delivered food items, they should be immediately placed into one of three storage areas:

1. Dry storage
2. Refrigerated storage
3. Frozen storage

Dry Storage

Dry storage areas should be maintained at a temperature ranging between 65°F and 75°F (18°C and 24°C). Temperatures below that range can be harmful to food products. More often, however, dry-storage temperatures get very high, exceeding by far the upper limit of temperature acceptability. This is because storage areas are frequently in poorly ventilated and closed-in areas of an operation. Excessively high or low temperatures will damage dry-storage products.

Shelving in dry-storage areas must be easily cleaned and sturdy enough to hold the weight of dry products. Slotted shelving is preferred over solid shelving when storing food because slotted shelving allows for better air circulation around stored products. All shelving should be placed at least six inches above the ground to allow for proper cleaning beneath the shelving and to ensure proper ventilation. Dry-goods products should never be stored directly on the floor. Dry goods may not be stored:

- In locker rooms
- In toilet rooms
- In dressing rooms
- In garbage rooms
- In mechanical rooms
- Under sewer lines that are not shielded to intercept potential drips
- Under leaking water lines, including leaking automatic fire sprinkler heads, or under lines on which water has condensed
- Under open stairwells

When placed into storage, all can and case labels should face out for easy identification. Bulk items such as flour or sugar should be stored in wheeled bins whenever possible so that heavy lifting and the potential for employee injuries related to lifting can be avoided. Most importantly, dry-storage space must be sufficient in size to handle your operation's needs. Cramped and cluttered dry-storage areas tend to increase costs because inventory cannot be easily rotated, maintained, located, or counted. Hallways leading to storage areas should always be kept cleared and free of excess storage materials and empty boxes. This helps both in accessing the storage area and in reducing the number of potential hiding places for insects and rodents.

Refrigerated Storage

Potentially hazardous foods are those that must be carefully handled for time and temperature control to keep them safe. Refrigerator temperatures used to store potentially hazardous foods should be maintained at 41°F (5°C) or less. In most cases, the lower areas tend to be coldest in refrigerators because warm air rises and cold air falls. In fact, the refrigerator itself may vary as much as four degrees (°F) between its coldest spot (near the bottom) and its warmest spot (near the top).

Walk-in refrigerators should have easily cleaned shelving units that are at least six inches off the floor and are slotted to allow for good air circulation. They should be properly cleaned on a regular basis. Refrigerators should be opened and closed quickly when used, both to lower operational costs and to ensure that the items in the refrigerator stay at their peak of quality. Condensation drainage systems in refrigerators should be checked at least weekly to ensure that they are kept clean and are functioning properly.

Freezer Storage

Freezer temperatures should be maintained at 0°F (−18°C) or less. Newly delivered products should be carefully checked with a thermometer when received to ensure that they are frozen and have been delivered at the proper temperature. In addition, these items should be carefully inspected to ensure that they have not been thawed and refrozen. This is because refrigerators and frozen-food holding units remove significant amounts of stored product moisture, causing shrinkage and **freezer burn** in meats and produce. Freezer burn refers to deterioration in product quality resulting from poorly wrapped or stored items kept at freezing temperatures.

Unless they are built in, frozen-food holding units as well as refrigerators should be high enough off the ground to allow for easy cleaning around and under them to prevent cockroaches and other insects from living beneath them. Stand-alone units should be placed 6 to 10 inches away from walls to allow for the free circulation of air around, and efficient operation of, the units.

Frozen-food holding units must be regularly maintained, a process that includes cleaning inside and out, as well as constant temperature monitoring to detect possible improper operation. A thermometer permanently placed in the unit or one easily read from outside the unit is best. It is also a good idea to periodically check that gaskets on freezers, as well as on refrigerators, tightly seal the food cabinet. This will not only reduce operating costs but will also maintain food quality for a longer period of time.

FUN ON THE WEB!

The US Food and Drug Administration (FDA) produces and regularly updates a food code containing information about the proper handling of foods stored and prepared for sale in foodservice operations. The 2009 *Food Code* is the first full edition to publish since the 2005 edition. To review the most recent food code recommendations produced by the FDA, go to: http://www.fda.gov/Food/FoodSafety/RetailFoodProtection/FoodCode.

MAINTAINING BEVERAGE STORAGE AREAS

Although the storage life for most beverage products is relatively long, alcoholic beverages, especially wine, must be stored carefully. Beverage storage rooms should be easily secured from unauthorized entrance because beverages are often expensive items and are a favorite target for both employee and guest theft.

Many beverage managers use a **two-key system** to control access to beverage storage areas. In this system, one key (or, in the case of electronic locks, one preprogrammed key or key code) is in the possession of the individual responsible for the beverage area. The other key, used when the beverage manager is not readily available, is kept in a sealed envelope in the safe or other secured area of the operation. Should this key be needed, management will be aware of its use because the envelope will have been opened.

Recodable electronic locks include features that allow management to issue multiple keys or codes and to identify precisely the time an issued key was used to access the lock and to whom that key or code was issued. For beverage storage areas, the use of recodable electronic locks is highly recommended.

FUN ON THE WEB!

The recodable electronic lock was introduced by VingCard in 1979. Today, its locks are popular in hotels, where guest room security is extremely important, as well as in many other situations (such as liquor and wine storage areas), where traceable access and high levels of security are critical. To view its current product offerings, visit the Ving Card Elsafe company website.

BEER STORAGE

Beer in kegs should be stored at refrigeration temperatures of 36°F to 38°F (2°C to 3°C). Keg beer is unpasteurized and, thus, must be handled carefully to avoid spoilage. Pasteurized beer in either cans or bottles should be stored in a cool, dark room at 50°F to 70°F (10°C to 21°C) and does not require refrigeration.

Storage areas should be kept clean and dust free. Canned beer, especially, should be covered when stored to eliminate the chance of dust or dirt settling on the rims of the cans. Product rotation is critical if beer is to be served at its maximum freshness, and it is important that you and your storage areas team devise a system to ensure that this happens. The best method is to date each case or six-pack as it is delivered. In this manner, you can, at a glance, determine whether proper FIFO product rotation is occurring.

WINE STORAGE

Wine storage is the most complex and time-consuming activity required of beverage storage personnel. Depending on the type and sales volume of the restaurant, extremely large quantities of wine may be stored. Regardless of the amount of wine to be stored, however, the principles of proper wine storage must be followed if the quality of the wine is to be maintained and product losses are to be kept at a minimum. Despite the mystery too often associated with wine storage, in most cases you will find that proper wine storage can be achieved if you monitor the following areas:

1. Temperature
2. Light
3. Cork condition

Temperature

A great deal of debate has centered on the proper temperature at which to store wine. But, generally speaking, most experts would agree that wines should be stored at a **cellar temperature** or approximately 50°F to 57°F (10°C to 14°C). White wines, however, are often stored at refrigerator temperatures. If you find that your wines must be stored at higher temperatures than these, the wine storage area should be as cool as can reasonably be achieved, and it is important to remember that, although many wines may improve with age, it improves only if it is properly stored. Excessive heat is always an enemy of effective wine storage.

Light

Just as wine must be protected from excess heat, it must be protected from direct sunlight. In olden times, this was achieved by storing wines in underground cellars or caves. In your own foodservice establishment, this means using a storage area where sunlight cannot penetrate and where the wine will not be subject to excessive fluorescent or incandescent lighting. The general rule for wine storage is that wine bottles should be exposed only to the minimum amount of light needed.

Cork Condition

It is the wine's cork that protects it from oxygen, its greatest enemy, and from the effects of oxidation. **Oxidation** occurs when oxygen comes in direct contact with bottled wine. You and your guests can detect a wine that has been overly oxidized because it smells somewhat like vinegar. Oxidation deteriorates the quality of bottled wines. Keeping oxygen out of the wine is a prime consideration of the vintner, and it should be important to you as well.

While some wine makers now seal their bottles with screw-type caps, cork continues to be the bottle sealer of choice for most wine producers. Quality wines demand quality corks. Traditionally, the best wines are fitted with corks that will last many years if they are not allowed to dry out. This is the reason wine should be stored so that the cork remains in contact with the wine and, thus, it stays moist. In an effort to accomplish this, most foodservice managers store wines on their sides.

Corks should be inspected at the time wine is received and periodically thereafter to ensure that there are no leaks resulting in oxidation and, thus, damaged products. If a leak is discovered at delivery, the wine should be refused. If the leak occurs during storage, the wine should be examined for quality and then either consumed or discarded, as appropriate.

In general, you can effectively manage the storage of wines if you think about how you should treat the cork that is protecting the wine. Always keep the cork (and thus the wine):

1. Cool
2. Moist
3. In the dark

LIQUOR STORAGE

Spirits should be stored between 70°F and 80°F (21°C to 27°C) in a locked or highly secure and dry storage area. Since these products do not generally require refrigeration, they may be stored along with food products, if necessary. An organized, well-maintained area for storing spirits will also ensure that purchasing decisions will be simplified because no product is likely to be overlooked or lost in inventory.

MAINTAINING PRODUCT SECURITY

Inventoried items are the same as money to you. In fact, you should think of inventory items in exactly that way. As already noted, the apple in a produce walk-in is not just an apple. It represents, at a selling price of $2.00, that amount in revenue to the airport foodservice director, who hopes to sell a crisp, fresh apple to a weary traveler. If the apple disappears, revenue of $2.00 will disappear also. When you think of inventory items in terms of their sales value, it becomes clear why product security is of the utmost importance.

All foodservice establishments will experience some amount of theft, in its strictest sense. The reason is very simple. Some employee theft is impossible to detect. Even the most sophisticated, computerized control system is not able to determine if an employee or vendor's employee walked into the produce walk-in and ate one green grape. Similarly, an employee who takes home two small sugar packets per night will likely go undetected for a great length of time. In neither of these cases, however, is the amount of loss significant, and certainly not enough to install security cameras in the walk-in or to search employees as they leave for home at the end of their shifts. What you do want to do, however, is to make it difficult to remove significant amounts of food or beverage items from storage without authorization, so that you can know when those items have been removed. Good cost control systems must be in place if you are to achieve this goal.

It is amazing how large the impact of theft can be on profitability. Consider the following example. Jesse is the receiving clerk at the Irish Voice sports bar. On a daily basis, Jesse takes home $2.00 worth of food products. How much, then, does Jesse cost the bar in one year? The answer is a surprising $14,600 in sales revenue! If Jesse or others pilfer $2.00 per day for 365 days, the total theft amount is $730 (365 days × $2.00 per day = $730). If the bar makes an after-tax profit of 5 percent on each dollar of food products sold, to recover the lost $730, the operation must sell $1.00/0.05 × $730 = $14,600!

To recover the dollar amount of Jesse's theft, the sports bar must sell $14,600 of food per year and make five cents per dollar sold on these sales. In the case of a smaller bar, $14,600 may well represent several days' sales revenue. Clearly, small thefts can add up to large dollar losses!

INVENTORY CONTROL

You should attempt to carefully control access to the location of your stored products. In some areas, this may be done by a process as simple as keeping the dry-storage area locked and requiring employees to "get the keys" from a manager or supervisor when products are needed. In other situations, cameras may be mounted in both storage areas and employee exit areas. Sometimes the physical layout of the foodservice operation may prevent management from being able to effectively lock and secure all storage areas, but too-easy access is sure to cause theft problems. This is not because employees are basically dishonest. Most are not. Theft problems develop because of the few employees who feel either that management will not miss a few of whatever is being stolen or that they "deserve" to take a few things because they work so hard.

It is your responsibility to see to it that your product inventories remain secure. As a general rule, if storerooms are to be locked, only one individual should have access to them during any shift. In reality, however, it is difficult to keep all inventory items under lock and key. Some items must be received and immediately sent to the kitchen for processing or use. As a result, most managers find that it is impossible to operate under a system where all food products are locked away from all employees. Storage areas should, however, not be accessible to guests or vendor employees. If proper control procedures are in place, employees will know that you can determine if theft has occurred. Without such control, employees might think that theft will go undetected. This must, and can, be avoided.

Proper inventory management seeks to provide appropriate **working stock,** which is the amount of an ingredient you anticipate using before purchasing that item again, and a minimal **safety stock,** the extra amount of that ingredient you decide to keep on hand to meet higher-than-anticipated demand. Demand for a given menu item can fluctuate greatly between supplier deliveries, even when the delivery occurs daily. With too little inventory on hand, you might run out of products and, therefore, reduce guest satisfaction and increase employee frustration. When too much inventory is on hand, waste, theft, and spoilage can become excessive. The ability to effectively manage the inventory process is one of the best skills a foodservice manager can acquire.

DETERMINING PROPER INVENTORY LEVELS

The actual amount of products you should keep in your inventory will vary based on a number of factors. These include:

1. Storage capacity
2. Item perishability
3. Vendor delivery schedule
4. Potential savings from increased purchase size
5. Operating calendar
6. Relative importance of stock outages
7. Value of inventory dollars

STORAGE CAPACITY

Inventory items must be purchased in quantities that can be adequately stored and secured. Many times, kitchens may lack adequate storage facilities. This may mean more frequent deliveries and holding less of each product on hand than would otherwise be desired. When storage space is too great, however, the tendency by some managers is to fill the space. It is important that this not be done, because increased inventory of items generally leads to greater spoilage and loss due to theft. Moreover, large quantities of goods on the shelf tend to send a message to employees that there is "plenty" of everything. This may result in the careless use of valuable and expensive products. It is also unwise to overload refrigerators or freezers because these units will then operate less efficiently and stored items may lose their quality and may also be difficult to locate.

ITEM PERISHABILITY

If all food products retained the same level of freshness, flavor, and quality while in storage, you would have little difficulty in maintaining proper product inventory levels. The shelf life of food products, however, varies greatly.

Figure 4.4 lists the difference in shelf life of some common foodservice items when properly stored in a dry storeroom or a refrigerator. Figure 4.5 lists the typical shelf life of some common foodservice items when properly stored in a refrigerator or freezer.

FIGURE 4.4 Shelf Life of Selected Products

Item	Storage Area	Shelf Life
Canned vegetables	Dry storeroom	12 months
Flour	Dry storeroom	3 months
Potatoes	Dry storeroom	14–21 days
Sugar	Dry storeroom	3 months
Bacon	Refrigerator	30 days
Butter	Refrigerator	14 days
Ground beef	Refrigerator	2–3 days
Lettuce	Refrigerator	3–5 days
Milk	Refrigerator	5–7 days
Steaks (fresh)	Refrigerator	14 days
Tomatoes	Refrigerator	5–7 days

FIGURE 4.5 Recommended Refrigeration and Freezer Storage Period Maximums

Cold Storage Chart

These short, but safe, time limits will help keep potentially hazardous foods from spoiling or becoming dangerous to eat. Because proper freezing keeps potentially hazardous foods safe indefinitely, recommended storage times are for quality only.

Product	Refrigerator: 41°F (5°C) or less	Freezer 0°F: (–18°C) or less
Eggs		
Fresh, in shell	3 to 5 weeks	Do not freeze
Raw yolks & whites	2 to 4 days	1 year
Hard cooked	1 week	Does not freeze well
Liquid pasteurized eggs, egg substitutes		
Opened	3 days	Does not freeze well
Unopened	10 days	1 year
Mayonnaise		
Commercial, refrigerate after opening	2 months	Do not freeze
Frozen dinners & entrées		
Keep frozen until ready to heat	—	3 to 4 months
Deli & vacuum-packed products		
Store-prepared (or homemade) egg, chicken, ham, tuna, & macaroni salads	3 to 5 days	Does not freeze well
Hot dogs & luncheon meats		
Hot dogs		
Opened package	1 week	1 to 2 months
Unopened package	2 weeks	1 to 2 months
Luncheon meat		
Opened package	3 to 5 days	1 to 2 months
Unopened package	2 weeks	1 to 2 months
Bacon & Sausage		
Bacon	7 days	1 month
Sausage, raw—from chicken, turkey, pork, beef	1 to 2 days	1 to 2 months
Smoked breakfast links, patties	7 days	1 to 2 months

Product	Refrigerator: 41°F (5°C) or less	Freezer 0°F: (−18°C) or less
Hard sausage—pepperoni, jerky sticks	2 to 3 weeks	1 to 2 months
Summer sausage labeled "Keep Refrigerated"		
Opened	3 weeks	1 to 2 months
Unopened	3 months	1 to 2 months
Ham, corned beef		
Corned beef, in pouch with pickling juices	5 to 7 days	Drained, 1 month
Ham, canned labeled "Keep Refrigerated"		
Opened	3 to 5 days	1 to 2 months
Unopened	6 to 9 months	Do not freeze
Ham, fully cooked		
vacuum sealed at plant, undated, unopened	2 weeks	1 to 2 months
Ham, fully cooked vacuum sealed at plant, dated, unopened	"Use-by" date on package	1 to 2 months
Ham, fully cooked		
Whole	7 days	1 to 2 months
Half	3 to 5 days	1 to 2 months
Slices	3 to 4 days	1 to 2 months
Hamburger, ground, & stew meat		
Hamburger & stew meat	1 to 2 days	3 to 4 months
Ground turkey, veal, pork, lamb, & mixtures of them	1 to 2 days	3 to 4 months
Fresh beef, veal, lamb, pork		
Steaks	3 to 5 days	6 to 12 months
Chops	3 to 5 days	4 to 6 months
Roasts	3 to 5 days	4 to 12 months
Variety meats—tongue, liver, heart, kidneys, chitterlings	1 to 2 days	3 to 4 months
Prestuffed, uncooked pork chops, lamb chops, or chicken breasts stuffed with dressing	1 day	Does not freeze well
Soups & stews		
Vegetable or meat added	3 to 4 days	2 to 3 months
Cooked meat leftovers		
Cooked meat & meat casseroles	3 to 4 days	2 to 3 months
Gravy & meat broth	1 to 2 days	2 to 3 months
Fresh poultry		
Chicken or turkey, whole	1 to 2 days	1 year
Chicken or turkey, pieces	1 to 2 days	9 months
Giblets	1 to 2 days	3 to 4 months
Cooked poultry leftovers		
Fried chicken	3 to 4 days	4 months
Cooked poultry casseroles	3 to 4 days	4 to 6 months
Pieces, plain	3 to 4 days	4 months
Pieces covered with broth, gravy	1 to 2 days	6 months
Chicken nuggets, patties	1 to 2 days	1 to 3 months
Pizza, cooked	3 to 4 days	1 to 2 months
Stuffing, cooked	3 to 4 days	1 month

Because food items have varying shelf lives, you must balance the need for a particular product with the optimal shelf life of that product. Serving items that are "too old" is a sure way to produce guest complaints. In fact, one of the quickest ways to determine the overall effectiveness of a foodservice manager is to *walk the boxes*. This means to take a tour of a facility's storage areas. If many products, particularly in the refrigerated areas, are moldy, soft, overripe, or rotten, it is a good indication of a foodservice operation that does not have an understanding of proper inventory levels based on the shelf lives of the items kept in inventory. It is also a sign that menu item sales forecasting methods (see Chapter 3) are either not in place or are not working well.

VENDOR DELIVERY SCHEDULE

It is the fortunate foodservice operator who lives in a large city with many vendors, some of whom may offer the same services and all of whom would like to have the operator's business. In many cases, however, you will not have the luxury of daily delivery. Your operation may be too small to warrant such frequent stops by a vendor, or your operation may be in such a remote location that daily delivery is not possible. Consider, for a moment, the difficulty you would face if you were the manager of a foodservice operation located on an offshore oil rig operating in the Gulf of Mexico. Clearly, in a case like that, a vendor willing to provide daily doughnut delivery is going to be hard to find! In all cases, it is important to remember that the cost to the vendor for frequent deliveries will be reflected in the prices the vendor charges to you.

POTENTIAL SAVINGS FROM INCREASED PURCHASE SIZE

Sometimes you will find that you can realize substantial savings by purchasing needed items in large quantities. This certainly makes sense if the total savings actually outweigh the added costs of receiving and storing the larger quantity. Remember, however, that there are costs associated with extraordinarily large purchases. These might include storage costs, spoilage, deterioration, insect or rodent infestation, or theft.

As a general rule, you should determine your ideal product inventory levels and then maintain your stock within those ranges. Only when the advantages of placing an extraordinarily large order are very clear should such a purchase be undertaken.

OPERATING CALENDAR

When an operation is involved in serving meals seven days a week to a relatively stable number of guests, the operating calendar makes little difference to inventory-level decision making. If, however, the operation opens on Monday and closes on Friday for two days, as is the case in many school foodservice accounts, the operating calendar plays a large part in determining desired inventory levels. In general, it can be said that an operator who is closing down, either for a weekend or for a season (as in the operation of a summer camp or seasonal hotel), should attempt to greatly reduce overall perishable inventory levels as the closing period approaches.

RELATIVE IMPORTANCE OF STOCK OUTAGES

In many foodservice operations, not having enough of a single food ingredient or menu item is simply not that important. In other operations, the shortage of even one menu item might spell disaster. For example, it might be all right for the local French restaurant to run out of one of the specials on Saturday night, but it is not difficult to imagine the problem of the McDonald's restaurant manager who runs out of French fries on that same Saturday night!

For the small operator, a mistake in the inventory level of a minor ingredient that results in an outage can often be corrected by a quick run to the grocery store. For the larger facility, such an outage may well represent a substantial loss of sales or guest goodwill. In the restaurant industry, when an item is no longer available on the menu, you "86" the item, a reference to restaurant slang originating in the early 1920s (86 rhymed with *nix*, a Cockney term meaning "to eliminate"). If you, as a manager, "86" too many items on any given night, the reputation of your restaurant is likely to suffer.

A strong awareness and knowledge of how critical outage factors are will help you determine appropriate product inventory levels. A final word of caution is, however, necessary. The foodservice operator who is determined never to run out of anything must be careful not to set inventory levels so high as to actually end up costing the operation more than if more realistic levels were maintained.

VALUE OF INVENTORY DOLLARS

In some cases, operators elect to remove dollars from their bank accounts and convert them to product inventory. When this is done, the operator is making the decision to value product more than dollars. If the dollars used to purchase inventory must be borrowed from the bank, rather than being available from operating revenue, a greater cost to hold the inventory is incurred because interest must be paid on the borrowed funds. In addition, a foodservice company of many units that invests too much of its money in inventory may find that funds for acquisition, renovation, or marketing the company are reduced. In contrast, a state institution that is given its entire annual budget at the start of its **fiscal year** (a year that is 12 months long but does not necessarily begin on January 1) may find it advantageous to use its purchasing power to acquire large amounts of inventory at the beginning of the year and at very low prices.

DETERMINING AMOUNTS IN FOOD INVENTORY

It is important for you to continually monitor the amount of products you have in inventory. Inventory levels may be determined by counting the item, as in the case of cans, or by weighing items, as in the case of meats. Volume (e.g., gallons, quarts, and the like) is another method of establishing product amounts. If an item is purchased by the pound, it is generally weighed to determine the amount on hand. If it is purchased by the piece or case, the appropriate unit to determine the item amount may be either pieces or cases. If, for example, canned pears are purchased by the case, with six cans per case, management might decide to count the items in terms of either cases or cans. That is, three cases of the canned pears might be considered as three items (when counted by the case) or as 18 items (when counted by the can). Properly used, either method will correctly establish the amount of product you have on hand and is acceptable.

FUN ON THE WEB!

Counting food and beverage inventories has historically been a very time-consuming task. However, advances in inventory-counting systems are occurring regularly. To see examples of various products designed to help restaurant managers control their inventory costs and speed up their inventory taking, enter "restaurant inventory management systems" in your favorite search engine and review the results.

DETERMINING AMOUNTS IN BEVERAGE INVENTORY

Determining amounts in inventory for liquor products is most often more difficult than determining these same levels for food. Food items, as well as beers and wines, can most often be counted for inventory purposes. Opened containers of spirits, however, must be valued also. It is the process of determining the amounts of product in these opened liquor containers that will present a challenge to you. Two inventory methods are commonly used to accomplish this goal:

1. Weight
2. Visual estimate

LIQUOR INVENTORY BY WEIGHT

The weight method of determining spirits inventories uses a scale or smart-device photograph of a liquor bottle's contents to "weigh" open bottles and determine their remaining contents. The product weight, in ounces, is then multiplied by the product cost per ounce to arrive at the value of the opened container's contents. This system is effective only if you remember to subtract the weight of the empty bottle itself from the total product's weight or if that feature is built into the smart-device app being used.

VISUAL ESTIMATE

Counting full bottles of spirits by sight is easy, but determining the quantities and values of partial bottles visually is more difficult. You can do it rather quickly and fairly accurately, however, if you estimate the amount remaining in open bottles by using the **tenths system.** This system requires that the inventory taker assign a value of 10/10 to a full bottle, 5/10 to a half bottle, and so on. Then, when inventory is taken, the partial bottle is visually examined and the appropriate "tenth" is assigned, based on the amount left in the bottles. Some operators use rulers to assist in this effort, since bottle shapes and sizes vary.

Although this system results only in an approximation of the actual amount in a bottle, many managers feel the tenths system is accurate enough for their purposes. It does have the advantage of being a rather quick method of determining inventory levels of open bottles.

In general, it is important to take liquor inventories at a time when the operation is closed so that product quantities on hand do not change when the inventory is being taken. It is also important that product contained in the lines of mechanical drink-dispensing systems be counted if the quantity of product in these lines is deemed to be significant.

FUN ON THE WEB!

Today's beverage managers benefit from the development of advanced technology systems that assist them in determining their liquor inventory levels. "Partender" is one good example of a company that uses Apple iOS (for iPhone, iPod Touch, and iPad) and Android apps to help managers use smart devices to quickly and accurately determine liquor inventory levels and values. Go to the company website to learn more about the ways advanced technology such as Partender's is being utilized to assist managers in completing their liquor and other product inventory tasks.

DETERMINING INVENTORY VALUES

Proper inventory control requires that you monitor both the amount and value of items in your inventory. Valuing, or establishing a dollar value for an inventory item, is performed using the following item inventory value formula:

Item amount × Item value = Item inventory value

An item's actual value can often be more complicated to determine than its amount. This is because the price you pay for an item may vary slightly each time you buy it. For example, assume that you bought curly endive for $2.20 per pound on Monday, but the same item cost you $2.50 per pound on Wednesday. On Friday, you see that you have one pound of the curly endive in your refrigerated walk-in. Is the value of the item $2.20 or $2.50?

Item value must be determined by using either the LIFO or the FIFO method. When the LIFO method is in use, the item's value is said to be the price paid for the least recent (oldest) addition to item amount. If the FIFO method is in use, the item value is said to be the price paid for the most recent (newest) product on hand. In the hospitality industry, most operators value inventory at its most recently known value; thus, FIFO is the more commonly used inventory valuation method.

Inventory value is determined using a form similar to the **inventory valuation sheet** shown in Figure 4.6. This inventory valuation sheet has a place for all inventory items, the quantity on hand, and the unit value of each item. There is also a place for the date the inventory was taken, a spot for the name of the person who counted the product, and another space for the person who extends (calculates) the monetary value of the inventory. It is recommended that these two be different individuals to reduce the risk of inventory valuation fraud.

FIGURE 4.6 Inventory Valuation Sheet

Unit Name: _____			Inventory Date: _____	
Counted By: _____			Extended By: _____	

Item	Unit	Item Amount	Item Value	Inventory Value
			Page Total	

Page _____ Of _____

The inventory valuation sheet should be completed each time the inventory is counted. It can be manually prepared or produced as part of an inventory evaluation software program. Regardless of the form used, the item's inventory value is determined using the inventory value formula. Thus, if we have five cases of fresh beets in our inventory and each case has a value of $20.00, the inventory value of our beets is:

> Item amount × Item value = Item inventory value
>
> or
>
> 5 cases × $20.00 per case = $100.00

The process of determining inventory value requires that you or a member of your staff count all food products on hand and multiply the value of the item by the number of units on hand. The process becomes more difficult when one realizes that the average foodservice operation has hundreds of items in inventory. Thus, "taking the inventory" can be a very time-consuming task. A **physical inventory**, one in which the food and beverage products are actually counted, must, however, be taken to determine your actual product usage. Some operators take this inventory monthly, others weekly or even daily to determine their inventory amounts on hand and as an aid to calculating their actual food and beverage usage and their product cost percentages (see Chapter 5).

HERE'S HOW IT'S DONE *4.1*

Determining the total value of your inventory items is an easy process. It simply requires that you multiply the number of units you have in inventory times the value of each unit. Then you sum each of the individual product values. In the foodservice industry, there are a variety of different units you will buy. Some examples include gallons, cases, pounds, bags, bottles (abbreviated btl.), boxes, and crates. Regardless of the unit in which an item is purchased, however, managers always use the same formula to establish the individual item's inventory value:

> Item amount × Item value = Item inventory value

When using this formula, the item amount is equal to the amount held in inventory. The item value is equal to the item's unit cost. Thus, the amount in inventory multiplied by the item's unit cost equals its inventory value. To illustrate, assume an inventory item is purchased in gallons. If 1.5 gallons are currently in inventory and if each gallon cost your operation $18.00, the calculation is:

> 1.5 gallon in inventory × $18.00 cost per gallon =
> $27.00 inventory value

As you can see from the following chart, regardless of the unit size used to count the amount in inventory, the process used to calculate item values is exactly the same.

After the value of each individual inventory item is calculated, it is easy to use addition to determine the value of your operation's total inventory.

As you will learn in Chapter 5, knowing the value of your inventory at the beginning and at the end of an accounting period is essential when you want to accurately calculate your operation's overall food cost for that accounting period.

Now, you know just how to do it!

Inventory Item	Amount on Hand	Item Value	Total Item Value
2-oz. coffee packets	1.5 cases	$18.00/case	$ 27.00
Pure maple syrup	1.5 gal.	$18.00/gal.	$ 27.00
Roquefort cheese	1.5 lb.	$18.00/lb.	$ 27.00
Sugar packets	1.5 boxes	$18.00/box	$ 27.00
Balsamic vinegar	1.5 bottles	$18.00/bottle	$ 27.00
Baking powder	1.5 cans	$18.00/can	$ 27.00
Asparagus (fresh)	1.5 crates	$18.00/crate	$ 27.00
		Total Inventory Value	**$189.00**

PRODUCT ISSUING AND RESTOCKING •————

Issuing is the formal process of removing needed beverage, food, and supply products from inventory. In smaller properties issuing may be as simple as entering the locked storeroom, selecting the product, and locking the door behind you. In a more complex operation, especially one that serves alcoholic beverages, this method is inadequate to achieve appropriate control.

The issuing of products should occur only after the product has been requisitioned. A **requisition** is a formal request to have products issued from storage. The act of requisitioning products from the storage area need not be unduly complex. Sometimes foodservice managers create difficulties for their workers by developing a requisition system that is far too time-consuming and complicated. The difficulty in such an approach usually arises because management hopes to equate products issued with products sold without taking a physical inventory. In reality, this process is difficult, if not impossible, to carry out.

Consider, for example, that you manage the bar area of Scotto's Supper Club. Scotto's is a high-volume steakhouse with an upscale clientele. If, on a given night, you attempt to match liquor issued to liquor sold, you would need to assume that all liquor issued on a given day is sold on the same day and that no liquor issued on a prior day was sold on the given day. This will, generally, not be the case. In the kitchen, some items issued today, for example ice cream, may be sold over several days; thus, in the same way as for liquor, food products issued will not relate exactly to products sold. It is simply good management to view an issuing system as one of providing basic product security and to view a total inventory control/cost system as a separate entity entirely. Given that approach, let us examine how an issuing system can be designed to help protect the security of food and beverage products.

Employees should always requisition food and beverage items based on management-approved estimates of future sales and product production schedules. Although special care must be taken to ensure that employees use the products for their intended purpose, maintaining product security can be achieved with relative ease if a few principles are observed:

1. Food, beverages, and supplies should be requisitioned only as needed based on approved production schedules.
2. Needed items should be issued only with management approval.
3. If a written record of issues is to be kept, each person removing food, beverages, or supplies from the storage area must sign, acknowledging receipt of the products.
4. Products that do not ultimately get used should be returned to the storage area, and their return should be recorded.

Some larger foodservice operators employ a full-time storeroom person to operate their requisition program. This process can sometimes be helpful because requisition schedules for tomorrow's food, for instance, can be submitted today, thus allowing storeroom personnel the time to gather the items from inventory prior to delivering them to the kitchen. Occasionally, products are even weighed and measured for kitchen personnel, according to the standardized recipes to be prepared. When this system is in place, the storeroom is often called an **ingredient room.**

Figure 4.7 illustrates the kind of food and supplies requisition form you might use at Scotto's Supper Club.

Note that the requested amounts and issued amounts may vary somewhat. In the case of rice, it is relatively easy to issue exactly the amount requisitioned because the rice can be weighed. In the cases of broccoli and rib roast, however, the nature of the product itself may make it impossible to exactly match the amount issued with the amount requisitioned. In other cases, the storeroom may be out of a requested item completely.

Note also that the total cost of issues is arrived at by computing the value of the issued amount, not the requisitioned amount. This is so because it is the value

FIGURE 4.7 Storeroom Requisition

	Storage Unit	Requested Amount	Issued Amount	Unit Cost	Total Cost
Item					
Rice	1 lb.	5 lb.	5.0 lb.	$0.25/lb.	$ 1.25
Broccoli	1 lb.	30 lb.	28.5 lb.	$0.90/lb.	$ 25.65
Rib roast	1 lb.	100 lb.	103.5 lb.	$8.40/lb.	$869.40
Total					$896.30

Unit Name: **Scotto's Supper Club** Requisition #: **0221** Date: **1/15**

To: Kitchen **X**   Requisition Approved By: **S.A.R.**
Bar _____   Requisition Filled By: **T.A.P.**

of the issued amount that has actually been removed from inventory and, thus, will ultimately be considered when determining amounts to purchase in the future and the cost of the products you sold.

It is important that a copy of the storeroom requisition form be sent to the person responsible for purchasing after it has been prepared so that this individual will know about the movement of products in and out of the storage areas and thus the amount of product that remains in inventory.

SPECIAL CONCERNS FOR ISSUING BEVERAGES

The basic principles of product issuing that apply to food and supplies also apply to beverages. There are, however, special concerns that must be addressed when issuing beverage products from liquor storerooms and wine cellars:

1. Liquor storeroom issues
2. Wine cellar issues

LIQUOR STOREROOM ISSUES

Although various systems could be used for issuing liquor, many managers favor the **empty for full system** of liquor replacement. In this system, each bartender is required to hold empty liquor bottles in the bar or a closely adjacent area. At the conclusion of the shift, or at the start of the next shift, each empty liquor bottle is replaced with a full one. The empty bottles are then either broken or disposed of, as local beverage law requires.

It is important to note that all liquor bottles issued from the liquor storage area should be visibly marked in a manner that is not easily duplicated. This allows management to ensure, at a glance, that all liquor to be sold is the property of the foodservice operation, and not that of a bartender who has produced his or her own bottle for the purpose of going into an illicit partnership with the operation. In a "partnership" of this type, the operation supplies the guest while the bartender provides the liquor and then pockets the product sales and profit! Although bottle marking will not completely

FIGURE 4.8 Wine Cellar Issues

Product	Vintage	Number of Bottles	Check #	Removed By
1. Bolla Soave	2004	2	60485 L	T.A.
2. Glen Ellen Cabernet Sauvignon	2003	1	60486 L	S.J.
3. Barton & Guestier Medoc	1999	1	Manager "comp"	S.A.R.
4. Copperridge Cabernet	Current stock	1	Kitchen	S.A.R.
5. Bolla Soave	2006	1	60500 M	S.J.
6. Copperridge Cabernet	Current stock	1	Bar stock	S.A.R.
7.				
8.				
9.				
10.				
11.				
12.				

Remarks: #4 Requested by Chef 1/15

#6 House Wine Sent to Bar Area 1/15

prevent dishonest bartenders from bringing in their own liquor, it will force them to pour their product into the operation's marked bottles and to dispose of their own empties, which makes revenue-related theft of this type quite difficult.

WINE CELLAR ISSUES

The issuing of wine from a wine cellar is a special case of product issuing because these sales cannot be predicted as accurately as sales of other alcoholic beverage products. That is, you may know that a given percentage of your guests are likely to select wine, but you are not likely to know the specific wines they will select. This is especially true in an operation where a large number of wines are contained on a wine list. If the wine storage area contains products valuable enough to remain locked, it is reasonable to assume that each bottled wine issued should be noted. You can use a form such as the one shown in Figure 4.8 to record your operation's wine-issuing activity.

A form of this type may be used to identify wine sold to guests, wine transferred to a bar area to fill guests' wine-by-the-glass orders, or for use in the kitchen. If the wine is to be sent to a guest as *complimentary,* or **comp,** that can be noted as well, along with the initials of the management personnel authorizing the comp. In the case of the wine cellar issue, the form itself should remain in the wine cellar for use by the wine-purchasing agent, and a copy should, on a daily basis, be sent to management for review.

RESTOCKING INVENTORY

Regardless of the methods used by employees to requisition food and beverage products or the systems management uses to issue these products, inventory levels in an operation will be reduced as sales are made. It will be your responsibility to monitor reductions in product inventories and purchase additional products as needed. Restocking your inventory is critical if product shortages are to be avoided and if products needed for menu item preparation are to be available.

Nothing is quite as traumatic for the foodservice manager as being in the middle of a busy meal period and finding that the operation is out of a necessary ingredient or frequently requested menu item. For most managers, however, it would be very time-consuming to monitor the amount of each ingredient, food product, and all supplies in inventory on a daily basis. The average foodservice operation stocks hundreds of ingredients and items, each of which may or may not be used every day. The task could be overwhelming.

Imagine, for example, the difficulty associated with monitoring, on a daily basis, the use of each sugar packet in a high-volume restaurant. Taking a daily inventory of the use of such a product would be akin to spending $10 to watch a penny! The effective foodservice manager knows that proper control involves spending time and effort where it is most needed and can do the most good. It is for this reason that many operators practice the ABC method of inventory control. To understand the principles utilized by the ABC inventory control system, however, you first must first fully understand the concepts of physical inventory and perpetual inventory.

PHYSICAL AND PERPETUAL INVENTORIES

A physical inventory system is one in which an actual physical count and valuation of all inventory on hand is taken at the close of an accounting period. A **perpetual inventory** system is one in which the entire inventory is counted and recorded, and then additions to and deletions from total inventory are recorded as they occur.

Both physical and perpetual inventories have advantages and disadvantages for the foodservice operator. The physical inventory, properly taken, is the most accurate of all because each item is actually counted and then valued. It is the physical inventory, taken at the end of the accounting period (the ending inventory), that is used in conjunction with the beginning inventory (the ending inventory value from the prior accounting period) to compute an operation's cost of food or beverages sold (see Chapter 5).

Despite its accuracy, however, the physical inventory suffers from a significant disadvantage: It is extremely time-consuming. Even with the use of software programs that can extend inventory (multiply number of units on hand by each unit's value) or handheld bar code scanners that assist in the process, counting each food and beverage item in storage can be a cumbersome and time-consuming task. This is so even for the well-trained individuals who will carefully count and weigh the inventoried items.

Perpetual inventory seeks to eliminate the need for frequent counting by adding to the inventory when appropriate (via receiving slips) and subtracting from inventory when appropriate (via requisitions or issues). Perpetual inventory is especially popular in monitoring liquor and wine inventories, where each product may have its own inventory sheet or, in some cases, a bin card.

A **bin card** is simply an index card (or line on a spreadsheet) that details additions to and deletions from a given product's inventory level. When using hard copy or electronic bin cards to monitor inventory levels managers need only review the cards, rather than take a physical inventory, to determine how much product is on hand at any point in time. Figure 4.9 illustrates the use of such a card. The accurate use of a bin card, or any other perpetual inventory system, requires that every addition to, and subtraction from, the products in inventory be carefully recorded.

As bar-code-reading hardware and software programs become more popular, additions and deletions to and from inventory are increasingly recorded electronically. In the ideal situation, perpetual inventory systems, regardless of

FIGURE 4.9 Bin Card

Product Name: Canadian Club			Bottle Size: 750 ml
Balance Brought Forward: 24			Date: 1/31
Date	In	Out	Total on Hand
2/1	4		28
2/2		6	22
2/3		5	17
2/4	12		29

the form they take, must be verified, on a regular basis, by an actual physical inventory.

Some managers prefer to use the same form for recording both the quantity and the price of an inventory item. This can be done by using a perpetual inventory card. **Perpetual inventory cards** are simply bin cards, similar to the one in Figure 4.9, that also includes the product's price. A new perpetual inventory card or spreadsheet line is created each time the product's purchase price changes, with the quantity of product on hand entered on the new card. This system allows for continual tracking of quantity of items on hand, as well as their prices.

Today, managers increasingly use computer spreadsheets and specialized inventory software to maintain perpetual inventories. In addition, some POS systems include inventory management components.

The accurate use of a perpetual inventory system requires that each change in product quantity be noted. However, employees, when in a hurry, may simply forget to update the perpetual system as they add or remove inventory items. Mistakes such as these will reduce the accuracy of the perpetual inventory. For this reason, it is not wise to depend solely on a perpetual inventory system for accurate cost calculations. There are, however, several advantages to the perpetual inventory system, among them the ability of the purchasing agent to quickly note quantity of product on hand without resorting to a daily physical inventory count.

The question of which of the two systems is best arises when making the decision about whether to use a physical or perpetual inventory system. Experienced managers know that neither is best, so they use the best of both systems.

ABC INVENTORY CONTROL

Utilizing the best features of physical and perpetual inventory systems is exactly what the ABC inventory system was designed to do. It separates inventory items into three main categories:

> **Category A** items are those that require tight control and the most accurate record keeping. These are typically high-value items, and though few in number, they can make up 70 to 80 percent of the total inventory value.
>
> **Category B** items are those that make up 10 to 15 percent of the inventory value and require only routine control and record keeping.
>
> **Category C** items make up only 5 to 10 percent of the inventory value. These items require only the simplest of inventory control systems.

Returning to the hypothetical example of Scotto's Supper Club, assume that the following 10 items are routinely held in your inventory:

1. Precut New York strip steak
2. Prepared horseradish
3. Eight-ounce chicken breasts (fresh)

4. Garlic salt

5. Onion rings

6. Crushed red pepper

7. Dried parsley

8. Lime juice

9. Fresh tomatoes

10. Rosemary sprigs

As can be seen, even with this short list, you have a variety of items in inventory. Some of these items, like the New York strip steak itself, are very valuable, highly perishable, and critical for the execution of your menu. Others, like the crushed red pepper, are much less costly, not highly perishable, and may less dramatically affect the operation if you ran out between deliveries. Clearly, these two items should not be treated the same for inventory purposes. The simple fact is that they are not equally critical to the operation's success. The ABC system helps you distinguish between those items that deserve special, perhaps daily, attention, and those items that you can safely spend less time managing.

To develop the A, B, and C categories, follow these steps:

1. Calculate monthly usage in units (e.g., pounds, gallons, cases, and the like) for each inventory item.

2. Multiply total item usage times its purchase price (unit value) to arrive at the total monthly amount of product usage.

3. Rank items from highest dollar usage to lowest.

In a typical ABC analysis, approximately 20 percent of the items held in inventory will account for about 70 to 80 percent of the total monthly product cost. These represent the A product category. It is not necessary that the line separating A, B, and C products be drawn the same for every operation. Many operators use the following guide, but it can be adapted as you see fit:

Category A—Top 20% of items
Category B—Next 30% of items
Category C—Next 50% of items

It is important to note that, although the percentage of items in category A is small, the percentage of total monthly product cost these items represent is large. Alternatively, the number of items in category C is large, but the total dollar value of product cost these items account for is rather small. It is important to note that the ABC inventory system is concerned with the monetary value of products, not the number of items. Returning to the Scotto's example may help make this distinction of the ABC system clear. One item on your menu is New York Strip Steak with Onion Ring. The preparation of this item is simple. Your cook sprinkles the steak with seasoning salt and cooks it to the guest's specification. The steak is then garnished with one large, deep-fried onion ring (which you buy frozen). In this example, these inventory items would likely be grouped as follows:

Scotto's Strip Steak	
Ingredient	**Inventory Category**
New York strip steak	A
Onion ring	B
Garlic salt	C

Figure 4.10 shows the complete result of performing an ABC analysis on the 10 ingredients items listed previously and then ranking those items in terms of their inventory value.

FIGURE 4.10 ABC Inventory Analysis on Selected Inventory Items

Item	Monthly Usage	Purchase Price	Monthly Usage $	Category
Precut New York strip steak	300 lb.	$ 7.50/lb.	$2,250.00	A
8-oz chicken breasts (fresh)	450 lb.	$ 2.10/lb.	$ 945.00	A
Fresh tomatoes	115 lb.	$ 0.95/lb.	$ 109.25	B
Onion rings	30 lb.	$ 2.20/lb.	$ 66.00	B
Rosemary sprigs	10 lb.	$ 4.50/lb.	$ 45.00	B
Prepared horseradish	4 lb.	$ 2.85/lb.	$ 11.40	C
Lime juice	2 qt.	$ 4.10/qt.	$ 8.20	C
Garlic salt	2 lb.	$ 2.95/lb.	$ 5.90	C
Crushed red pepper	1 oz.	$16.00/lb.	$ 1.00	C
Dried parsley	4 oz.	$ 4.00/lb.	$ 1.00	C

FIGURE 4.11 Guide to Managing ABC Inventory Items

Category	Inventory Management Techniques
A	1. Order only on an as-needed basis. 2. Conduct perpetual inventory on a daily or, at least, weekly basis. 3. Have clear idea of purchase point and estimated delivery time. 4. Conduct monthly physical inventory.
B	1. Maintain normal control systems; order predetermined inventory (par) levels. 2. Monitor more closely if sale of this item is tied to sale of an item in category A. 3. Review status quarterly for movement to category A or C. 4. Conduct monthly physical inventory.
C	1. Order in large quantity to take advantage of discounts if item is not perishable. 2. Stock constant levels of product. 3. Conduct monthly physical inventory.

The ABC inventory system specifically directs your attention to the areas where it is most needed. Controlling product costs, especially for category A items, is extremely important. Figure 4.11 details the differences in how you would manage items in the A, B, and C inventory categories.

The ABC system focuses management's attention on the essential few items in inventory, while focusing less attention on the many low-cost, slower-moving items. Again, it is important to note that management's time is best spent on the items of most importance. In the case of inventory management, these are the category A and, to a lesser degree, category B items.

The ABC system can also be used to arrange storerooms or to determine which items should be stored in the most secure areas. Regardless of the inventory management system used, however, whether it is the physical, perpetual, or ABC inventory, management must be strict in monitoring both withdrawals from inventory and the process by which inventory is restocked.

PURCHASE POINTS

When your inventories are properly controlled and issues from inventories are carefully recorded, you will be in an excellent position to determine when your inventories should be restocked. You can do so by creating a purchase point for each item you hold in inventory. A **purchase point** is the point at which an item should be reordered and its inventory level replenished. An item's purchase point can be identified by one of two methods:

1. As needed (just-in-time)
2. Par level

AS NEEDED

When you elect to use the **as-needed,** or **just-in-time,** method of determining an item's purchase point, you are basically purchasing food based on your prediction of unit sales and the sum of the ingredients (from standardized recipes) necessary to produce those sales. Then, no more than the absolute minimum of needed inventory level is purchased from your vendors. When this system is used, a buyer compiles a list of needed ingredients and submits it to management for approval to purchase. For example, in a hotel foodservice operation, the demand for 500 servings of a raspberries and cream torte dessert, to be served to a group in the hotel next week, would cause the responsible person to check the standardized recipe for this item (see Chapter 3) and determine the amount of raspberries and other key ingredients that should be ordered. Then that amount, and no more, would be ordered from the appropriate vendors.

PAR LEVEL

Foodservice operators may set predetermined purchase points, called **par levels,** for some inventory items. The par level is the amount of an item that should be held in inventory at all times. In the case of the raspberries and cream torte dessert referred to previously, it is likely that making the torte will require a few tablespoons of vanilla extract. It does not make sense, however, to order vanilla extract by the needed tablespoon. In fact, you are likely to find that you are restricted in the quantity of it you can buy due to the vendor's delivery minimum—namely, one bottle or one case. In instances such as this, or when demand for a product is relatively constant, you may decide that the use of an as-needed ordering system will not work as well as will identifying par levels for some items you sell.

When determining par levels, you actually establish both minimum and maximum amounts to be held in inventory. Many foodservice managers establish a minimum par level by computing working stock and then adding 25 to 50 percent more for safety stock. Then, an appropriate purchase point, or point at which additional stock is purchased, is determined. If, for example, you have decided that the inventory level for coffee should be based on a par system, the decision may be made that the minimum amount (based on your coffee usage) of coffee that should be on hand at all times is four cases. This would be the minimum par level. To ensure you never ran out of coffee, however, assume that you set the maximum par level of 10 cases. Although the inventory level in this situation would vary from a low of 4 cases to a high of 10 cases, you would be assured that you would never have too little or too much of this particular menu item.

When cases of coffee were to be ordered under this system, you would always attempt to keep the number of cases on hand between the minimum par level (4 cases) and the maximum par level (10 cases). The purchase point in this example might be 6 cases; that is, when your operation had 6 cases of coffee on hand, an order would be placed with the coffee vendor. The intention would be to get the total stock of coffee up to 10 cases before your supply got below 4 cases. Delivery might take one or two days, so 6 cases might be an appropriate purchase point.

Whether you use an as-needed system, a par-level system, or, as in the case of many operators, a combination of both systems, each ingredient or menu item should have a preset and management-designated inventory level or amount. As a rule, highly perishable items should be ordered on an as-needed basis, whereas items with a longer shelf life can often have their inventory levels set using a par-level system. The answer to the question, "How much of each ingredient should I have on hand at any point in time?" must come from you and from your estimate of future sales.

Restocking inventory requires the use of the purchase order (PO) described in Chapter 3. Before you can place an order, however, you will need to find out what you need! The process is much like going through your own home and making a shopping list before you go to the grocery store. Some managers say that they intuitively "know" what they need without looking at their storage areas, inventory valuation sheets, or records of requisitions and issues. If you have ever gone grocery shopping without a list, however, you know that you can easily miss a few items. For that reason, making a detailed assessment of your current inventory prior to placing orders is always a good idea.

A good way to make sure that you have checked all your in-storage items is to use a **daily inventory sheet** (Figure 4.12). A daily inventory sheet will have the items listed in your storage areas, their unit of purchase, and their par values preprinted on the sheet. In addition, the form will have the following columns: On Hand, Special Order, and Order Amount.

Having a preprinted list of all your items in storage and units of purchase is important so that you will not have to write down the items every time you take the inventory. The list should be arranged in the same order that you store the items so that you can quickly and easily locate your products. The par value should be listed so that you know how much inventory you should have in storage at any given time.

To use the daily inventory sheet, you would physically walk through your storage areas to determine which items (and amounts) you should order. Under the On Hand column, you would list how many of each item you have on hand—that is, sitting on the shelf. You also need to list any "special order" amounts needed above the par level. An example of this would be extra cases of perishables, such as strawberries, ordered for a banquet. Then, you must calculate the order amount as follows:

Par value − On hand + Special order = Order amount

In Figure 4.12, the order amount for hot wings would be calculated as follows:

Order Amount for Hot Wings

6 cases par value − 2 cases on hand + 3 cases special order = 7 cases to be ordered

FIGURE 4.12 Daily Inventory Sheet

Item	Description	Unit	Par Value	On Hand	Special Order	Order Amount
Hot wings	15 lb. IQF	case	6	2	3	7
Baby-back ribs	2–2 ½ lb.	case	3	1.5	1	3
Sausage links	96, 1 oz.	case	5			
Drummies	2–5 lb.	case	4			
Bologna	10 lb. avg.	each	3			
Beef pastrami	10 lb. avg.	each	4			
Slice pepperoni	10 lb. avg.	each	6			
All-beef franks	8/1, 10 lb.	case	7			

For example, if you have less than a whole purchase unit on hand, such as ½ case of baby-back ribs as in Figure 4.12, then you may need to round the order amount up to a full case as follows:

Order Amount for Baby-back Ribs
3 cases par value − 1.5 cases on hand + 1 case special order = 2.5 cases to be ordered : (rounded up to 3 cases)

Although the form in Figure 4.12 is called the daily inventory sheet, this does not mean that you have to check your inventory or prepare purchase orders on a daily basis. Rather, you should always make your "grocery lists" on, or as close as reasonably possible to, your normal ordering days.

MANAGING FOOD PRODUCTION ●————————————————

When you have ordered and received the food and beverage products you forecast will be purchased by your guests, your concern turns toward the most important function of all, controlling the food and beverage production process. If any single activity stands at the heart of foodservice management and cost control, this is it. To study this process, assume again that you are the manager of Scotto's Supper Club. As you prepare for another week of business, you review your sales history, sales forecasts, purchase orders, and menu specials. You do these things to begin taking the first step in controlling your food production costs.

CONTROLLING FOOD PRODUCTION COSTS

Often, those individuals who manage restaurants do so because they relish managing the **back of the house,** or kitchen production area, of their food facilities. Managing food production to produce tasty, attractive, nutritious, and cost-effective menu items is one of the most challenging and enjoyable aspects of foodservice management. Managing the food production process means controlling five key areas:

1. Waste
2. Overcooking
3. Overportioning
4. Improper carryover utilization
5. Inappropriate make-or-buy decisions

WASTE

Food losses through simple product waste will cause excessive food costs. This waste may be easy to observe, such as when an employee does not use a rubber spatula to get all of the salad dressing out of a 1-gallon jar, or as difficult to detect as the shoddy work of the salad preparation person who trims the lettuce just a bit more than management would prefer, resulting in a reduced amount of usable lettuce available to make salads and in higher salad costs.

Management must demonstrate its concern for the value of products on a daily basis. Each employee should be made to realize that wasting food directly affects the profitability of the operation and, thus, his or her own economic well-being. In general, food waste is most often the result of poor training or management's inattentiveness to detail. Unfortunately, some managers and employees feel that small amounts of food waste are unimportant. Your primary goal in reducing waste in the food production area should be to maximize product utilization and minimize the dangerous "it's only a few pennies' worth so it doesn't matter" syndrome.

OVERCOOKING

Cooking is simply the process of exposing food to heat. Excessive cooking, however, most often results in reduced product volume, whether the item cooked is roast beef or vegetable soup. This is so because many foods have high moisture contents and heating usually results in moisture loss. To minimize this loss, cooking times and methods listed on standardized recipes must be carefully calculated and meticulously followed.

It is important to recognize that, in many ways, excess heat is the enemy of both well-prepared foods and a manager's cost control efforts. Too much time on the steam table line or in the holding oven extracts moisture from products, reduces product quality, and results in fewer portions that are available for sale and service. The result is increased food cost. To illustrate, note that Figure 4.13 details the change in **portion cost,** which is the cost of producing one serving of a menu item, when the ending weight of a roast prime rib of beef is reduced due to overcooking.

If we assume that a properly cooked pan of roast prime rib of beef yields 50 servable pounds at a cost of $8.00 per pound, the total product cost would equal $400.00 (50 lb. × $8/lb. = $400).

When properly cooked, the roast beef would yield 100 eight-ounce portions, for a cost of $4.00 per portion. As you can see in Figure 4.13, however, increased cooking time or an excessive final product temperature will result in moisture loss, cause product shrinkage, and increase the item's portion cost.

Although the difference between a portion cost of $4.00 and $4.71 might seem small, it is the small numbers that can really add up and increase costs. Thus, it is the control of this type of production issue that separates the good foodservice manager from the outstanding one.

To control product loss due to overcooking, you must strictly enforce standardized recipe cooking times. This is especially true for items with high moisture content, such as meats, soups, stews, and baked goods. Moreover, extended cooking times can result in total product loss if properly prepared items are placed in an oven, fryer, steam equipment, or broiler and then forgotten until it is too late! It is, therefore, advisable to supply kitchen production personnel with small, easily cleanable timers and thermometers for which they are responsible. These can help substantially in reducing product losses due to overcooking.

FIGURE 4.13 Effect of Overcooking on Portion Cost

Portion Cost of 50 Pounds (800 Ounces) of Roast Prime Rib of Beef			
			50 lb. cost = $400
Preparation State	Ending Weight (oz.)	Number of 8-Ounce Portions	Portion Cost
Properly prepared	800	100	$4.00
Overcooked 15 min.	775	97	$4.12
Overcooked 30 min.	750	94	$4.26
Overcooked 45 min.	735	92	$4.35
Overcooked 60 min.	720	90	$4.44
Overcooked 75 min.	700	88	$4.55
Overcooked 90 min.	680	85	$4.71

HERE'S HOW IT'S DONE *4.2*

Portion cost is the amount it costs an operation to produce one serving of a menu item. Portion cost is one important factor in establishing the selling prices of menu items. For that reason and for many others, the ability to calculate a portion cost correctly is an important management skill.

In some cases, the calculation of the portion cost is very easy. For example, assume a manager sells fresh apples. The manager buys apples in 10-pound bags that contain 30 apples. Each bag costs $8.40. The manager would use division to calculate the portion cost for one apple:

$$\frac{\$8.40 \text{ cost per bag}}{30 \text{ apple portions per bag}} = \$0.24 \text{ portion cost}$$

In other situations, managers utilize the cost required to produce a standardized recipe when they calculate their portion costs. For example, assume a manager sells custard pie. The manager's standardized recipe for custard pie produces seven pies. Each pie will be cut into eight pieces. In this case, multiplication is required to determine how many portions the recipe will produce: 7 pies × 8 slices per pie = 56 slices, or pie portions.

If the cost of producing the standardized recipe, including the pastry for the crust, eggs, sugar, salt, vanilla, milk, and nutmeg, is $25.20, the manager would again use division and the same portion cost formula to calculate the cost of producing one slice of custard pie:

$$\frac{\$25.20 \text{ recipe cost}}{56 \text{ pie portions}} = \$0.45 \text{ portion cost}$$

Because the vast majority of items served by restaurateurs should always be produced from standardized recipes (see Chapter 3), it is easy to see why adherence to proper recipe production and proper portioning is so critical to accurately calculating and controlling an operation's portion costs.

OVERPORTIONING

No other area of food and beverage cost control has been analyzed and described as fully through articles, speeches, and even books as the control of portion size. There are two reasons for this. First, overportioning on the part of service personnel has the effect of increasing operational costs and may cause the operation to mismatch its production schedule with anticipated demand. For example, assume that 100 guests are expected and 100 products to be served to them are produced, yet overportioning causes you to be out of the product after only 80 guests have been served. The remaining 20 guests will be left clamoring for "their" portions, which, of course, no longer exist because, due to overportioning; these portions have already been served to other guests.

Also, overportioning must be avoided because guests always want to feel that they have received fair value for their money. If portions are large one day and small the next, guests may feel that they have been cheated on the second day. Consistency is a key to operational success in foodservice. Guests want to know exactly what they will get for their money.

It is not possible to state what a portion size should be because it is not advantageous to establish the same standard portion sizes for all foodservice operations. For example, the proper portion size of an entrée in a college residence hall feeding only male athletes should clearly be different from that of an extended-care facility whose typical resident might be over 75 years old. It is important for you to consider your clientele, ambiance, pricing structure, and desired quality standards prior to establishing appropriate portion sizes for your own operation. Once portion size for an item has been established, however, it is up to you to strictly enforce it.

Often, employees resist management's efforts to control portion size. When this is the case, it is a clear indication that management has failed in its mission to provide employees with a basic understanding that underlines the foodservice industry. Employees must be made to see that strict adherence to predetermined portion size is a benefit both to the guest and to the operation. Management must be sensitive, also, to the fact that it is the server who often must deal with the guest who complains about the inadequacy of portion size. Therefore, servers must be made to feel comfortable about predetermined portion sizes so that management, along with the employees, will want to maintain them.

FIGURE 4.14 Portion Cost Chart for Frozen Corn

Corn Portion Cost @ $2.80 per 3-lb. Box		
Number of Portions per 3-lb. Box	Portion Size (oz.)	Portion Cost (cents)
16	3.0	17.5
15	3.2	18.7
14	3.4	20.0
13	3.7	21.5

In many cases, tools are available that will help employees serve the proper portion size. Whether these tools consist of scales, scoops, ladles, dishes, or spoons, employees must have an adequate number of easily accessible portion-control devices if they are to use them. One commonly used tool that assists in portion control is the food scoop. **Food scoops** are sized based on the number of servings per quart of product served. Thus, a #12 scoop will yield 12 servings per quart. A #20 scoop will yield 20 servings per quart, and so on.

It is important to understand that many portion sizes are directly tied to the purchasing function. To serve a ¼-pound hot dog, for instance, one must purchase ¼-pound hot dogs. In a similar vein, if one full banana is sliced for addition to breakfast cereals, the purchasing agent must have been diligent in ordering and accepting only the banana size for which management has developed a specification.

Constant checking portion size served is an essential task of management. When incorrect portion sizes are noticed, they must be promptly corrected. If not, considerable cost increases can be incurred. Returning again to our example of Scotto's Supper Club, consider that you purchase, on occasion, and in accordance with your menu plan, 3-pound boxes of frozen yellow corn to be served as your vegetable of the day. Each box costs $2.80. With a total of 48 ounces (3 pounds × 16 ounces per pound = 48 ounces) and an established portion size of 3 ounces, you know that you should average 48 ounces/3 ounces per serving = 16 servings per box of corn. Figure 4.14 demonstrates the effect on total portion cost if one, two, or three servings are lost due to overportioning.

As Figure 4.14 shows, a small amount of overportioning on an item as inexpensive as corn costs the operation only a few cents per serving. Those few cents per serving, however, multiplied time after time, can mean the difference between a profitable operation and one that is only marginally successful. If your portion cost for corn should have been 17.5 cents ($2.80/16 portions = 17.5 cents per portion), but, due to overportioning, it rises to 21.5 cents ($2.80/13 portions = 21.5 cents per portion), then your food costs are 4.0 cents higher than they should be on this item. If Scotto's is open seven days a week and serves an average of 200 portions of corn per day, your total loss to overportioning for a year would be 365 days × 200 portions served per day × 0.04 loss per portion = $2,920 total loss, an amount that would be more than enough to buy your staff proper portioning tools. It is also an amount worthy of your attention and correction.

IMPROPER CARRYOVER UTILIZATION

As discussed earlier in this text, predicting guest counts is often an inexact process. Because this is true, and because most foodservice operators want to offer the same broad menu to the evening's last diner as was offered to its first, it is inevitable that some prepared food will remain unsold at the end of the operational day. These items are called **carryovers**, or in some operations, leftovers.

In some segments of the hospitality industry, carryovers are a potential problem area; in others, it is less of a concern. Consider, for example, the operation of a gelato shop. At the end of the day, any unsold gelato is simply held in the freezer until the next day with no measurable loss of either product quantity or quality. Contrast that situation, however, with a full-service cafeteria. If closing time is

8:00 P.M., management wishes to have a full product line, or at least some of each menu item, available to the guest who walks in the door at 7:55 P.M. Obviously, in five more minutes a large number of items will become carryovers. This cannot be avoided. A manager's ability to effectively integrate carryover items on subsequent days can make the difference between profits and losses in some operations.

You have learned that in almost every case, food products are at their peak of quality when they are delivered to your restaurant. From then on, storage, preparation, and holding activities often diminish product quality. These forces are especially at work in the area of carryovers. It is for this reason that production schedules must note carryover items on a daily basis. If this is not done, these items tend to get stored and then may get "lost" in walk-in refrigerators or freezers.

You should have a clear use in mind for each menu item that may have to be carried over. For example, broiled or sautéed fish may be used to prepare seafood chowder or bisque. Today's prime rib roast may be the key ingredient in tomorrow's beef stroganoff, and so on. Menu specials, substitutions, and employee meals can be sources of utilization for products like these. This utilization process can be creative and, if you involve your staff, quite effective.

It is important to understand that carryover foods seldom can be sold for their original value. Today's beef stew made from yesterday's prime rib will not likely be sold at prime rib prices. Carryovers generally mean reduced income relative to product value, and less profits; thus, it is critical that you strive to minimize carryovers.

Carryover items that are created should be properly labeled, wrapped, and rotated so that items can be found and reused easily, resulting in both greater employee efficiency in locating carryover items and reduced energy costs because refrigerator doors will be opened for shorter periods of time. Managers will find that requiring foods to be properly labeled and stored in clear plastic containers helps greatly in this regard.

INAPPROPRIATE MAKE OR BUY DECISIONS

Many foodservice operators choose to buy some food products that are pre-prepared in some fashion. These items, called **convenience foods,** or **ready foods,** can be of great value to your operation. Often, they can save dollars spent on labor, equipment, and hard-to-secure food products. They can also add menu variety beyond the skill level of the average kitchen crew. A disadvantage, however, is that these items tend to cost more on a per-portion basis. This is to be expected because these items most often must include a charge for the labor needed to make the item, enhanced packaging and, of course, the food item itself.

Convenience items are not, of course, an all-or-nothing operational decision. Nearly all foodservice operations today use canned products, sliced bread, precut produce, and the like—items that would have been considered convenience items years ago. Therefore, the question is not whether to use convenience items but, rather, it is which *convenience* items are best to use.

In general, the following guidelines are of value when determining whether to adopt the use of a convenience product:

1. Is the quality acceptable? This question must be answered from the point of view of the guest, not management alone.

2. Will the product save labor? Identifiable labor savings must be discovered if management is to agree that the convenience item will reduce overall costs.

3. Would it matter if the guest knew? If an operation has built its image on made-on-premise items, guests might react negatively if they know that an item has actually been prepared from a "boil in a bag" package or heated in a microwave oven.

4. Does the product come in an acceptable package size? If convenience items are not sold in a size that complements the operation, excessive waste can result.

5. Is the appropriate storage space available? Many convenience items must be stored in a refrigerated or frozen form. Your facility must have the needed storage capacity for these items.

Green and Growing!

A foodservice operation's cost of food is affected by a variety of factors. One such factor relates to the source reduction decisions made by the operation's suppliers. Where recycling occurs within the foodservice operation to reuse materials, source reduction is utilized by suppliers to minimize the amount of resources initially required to package, store, and ship the items they sell. The result of effective source reduction is a lessened impact on the environment and lower product costs.

Consider, for example, the difference in the producer's cost between packaging, storing, and shipping frozen orange juice concentrate (which foodservice operators will reconstitute on-site) and "ready-to-serve" juice. Not only will packaging costs be higher in the second case (because of the greater product volume), but the item's greater weight will also mean higher transportation costs. Storage costs, too, will be greater with the ready-to-serve item, as will the cost of disposing of used product containers.

Packaging and energy costs add up, and these costs will inevitably be passed on from the manufacturer to the foodservice operation. The result is higher food costs and potentially lowered profits. Creative source reduction efforts, however, can result in fewer wasted natural resources and lower food costs. Foodservice operators should encourage these efforts by purchasing quality products from those suppliers who take their source reduction responsibilities seriously and act on them.

FOOD PRODUCTION SCHEDULES

Foodservice managers are in charge of kitchen production. How much of each item to prepare each day may be a joint decision between you and your chef or kitchen production manager, but it is you who must ultimately take the responsibility for proper production decisions. A complete food production schedule process will require you to do the following:

- Maintain sales histories.
- Forecast future sales levels.
- Purchase and store needed food and beverage supplies.
- Plan daily production schedules.
- Issue needed products to production areas.
- Manage the food and beverage production process.

Planning daily production schedules is important because you will want to have both the products and the staff needed to properly service your guests. If, for example, you forecast that 50 chocolate cakes will be needed on a given day for the college residence hall you manage, then you must have both the products and the staff necessary to produce that number of cakes. In a similar manner, if you know that 500 pounds of ground beef patties must be cooked for your burger restaurant, then the ground beef and the staff to cook it must be available.

Ideally, the process of determining how much of each menu item to prepare on a given day is based on your sales forecast and would look as follows:

Prior-day carryover + Today's production = Today's sales forecast ± Margin of error

The margin of error amount should be small; however, projecting sales and guest counts is an imprecise science at best, so most foodservice managers will find that they should produce a small amount more than they anticipate selling each day. This minimizes the chances of running out of an important menu item. Of course, with some menu items, preparation does not begin until the sale is made. For example, in most cases, a New York strip steak will not actually be cooked until the guest orders it. An order for coconut cream pie, however, cannot be filled in the same manner because the pies must be made ahead. It is because of items like coconut cream pie that production sheets are necessary. Figure 4.15 demonstrates the production sheet in use at Scotto's.

FIGURE 4.15 Production Schedule Sheet

Unit Name: <u>Scotto's Supper Club</u>   Date: <u>1/15</u>

Menu Item	Sales Forecast	Planned Overage	Prior-Day Carryover	New Production	Total Available	Number Sold	Carryover
1. Prime Rib	85	5	15	75	90		
2. Broccoli	160	10	0	170	170		
3. Coconut Cream Pie	41	0	70	0	70		
4.							
5.							
6.							
7.							
8.							
9.							
10.							
11.							
12.							
13.							
14.							
15.							
16.							
17.							
18.							

Special Instructions: <u>Thaw turkeys for Sunday preparation</u>

Production Manager: <u>S. Anthony</u>

From Figure 4.15, you can see that you had 15 servings of prime rib left over from the prior day's operation. You would know that by looking at the carryover column of the *prior* day's production sheet or by taking a physical inventory. You anticipate sales of 85 servings of prime rib, and so it might seem that only 70 servings should be prepared (70 new servings plus 15 carryovers from the prior day equals 85). In fact, you would most likely prepare a number of new servings that is slightly higher than anticipated demand. The reason is simple: If you have more guests come in than anticipated or if more of the guests than you forecast actually select prime rib, you do not want to run out of the item. There is no industry-wide standard percentage that should be overproduced for a given item. The amount you plan to make will depend on a variety of factors, including your own knowledge of your guests and the importance of running out of a given item. Common overages tend to be 5 to 10 percent above normal sales forecasts. For purposes of this example, assume that five extra servings of prime rib is the amount of overproduction you feel is appropriate for this item. With estimated sales of 85 servings, you actually want to have 90 servings available.

In the case of broccoli, you make the decision not to carry over any broccoli that was not sold on the prior day. If any such product exists, it could be used to make soup or, if there is no appropriate use for it, discarded because the quality of previously cooked broccoli is not likely to be at the same high level as that of freshly cooked broccoli. Regardless of the type of operation you manage, you will likely find that some of your menu items simply do not retain their quality well enough to be are carried over for sale in their original form. These items must be discarded or utilized as an ingredient in a different dish. Again, in the case of broccoli, proposed production exceeds anticipated demand by a small margin (10 servings). In the case of the coconut cream pie, you make the decision to produce none on this particular day. This is because this item is made in large quantities, but not each day. With 70 servings available and an anticipated demand of 41, you have more than enough to sustain your operation through this day and, perhaps, the next as well, if the quality of the carried-over pies remains high.

At the end of the evening service period, you would enter the number sold in the appropriate column and make a determination on how much, if any, of each product you will carry over to the next day. Some foodservice managers preprint their production sheets listing all menu items and, thus, ensure that production levels for each major menu item are assessed on a daily basis. Others prefer to use the production sheet on an as-needed basis. When this is the case, it is used daily but only for the items to be prepared that day. Either method is acceptable, but production schedules are always critical to operational efficiency.

Consider the Cost

"How many dozen should I put in the proofer?" asked Elizabeth, the new baker at the Sands Cafeteria.

Rami El-Hussieny was the day shift operations manager and, unfortunately, he did not know how to answer Elizabeth's question. What she wanted to know was simple enough: How many dozen rolls should be placed in the proofer in anticipation of the night's dinner business?

The problem was that the frozen dinner roll dough used at the Sands Cafeteria needed to proof for at least two hours prior to being baked for 15 minutes. If too many rolls were proofed, they would never be needed, but they would still have to be baked and made into bread dressing or even tossed out. If too few dozen were proofed and the night was busier than anticipated, they would run out of "Fresh Baked Rolls" (one of the restaurant's signature items), and Rami knew that the night manager would be really upset. It was a daily guess, and sometimes Rami missed the guess!

He wondered if a prebaked roll with a shelf life of three or four days would, despite not having been baked on site, be the best solution to this problem.

1. What do you think is the main cause of Rami's difficulty?
2. Most foodservice managers would agree that fresh baked goods are very high quality and greatly enjoyed by their guests, yet many of these bake few, if any, products on-site. What are two specific reasons why higher-quality, made-on-site items are often not produced?
3. What is the relationship between product quality and product availability in this case study? Which product characteristic do you think is more important from the guest's point of view?

MANAGING BEVERAGE PRODUCTION

In its simplest, but also its least desired form, beverage production can consist simply of a bartender **free-pouring**, which is making a drink by pouring liquor from a bottle, but without carefully measuring the poured amount. In a situation such as this, it is very difficult to control product costs. At the other end of the control spectrum are automated beverage-dispensing systems that are extremely sophisticated control devices. The following are alternative beverage production control systems that you can use, based on the amount of control you feel is appropriate for your operation.

FREE-POUR

The lack of control resulting from free-pouring alcohol is significant. It should never be allowed in the preparation of the majority of drinks your bartenders will serve. It is appropriate in some settings, however, for example, in wine-by-the-glass sales. In this situation, the wine glass itself serves as a type of product control device. Large operations, however, may even elect to utilize an automated dispensing system for their wines by the glass. Also, it is most often necessary for a bartender to free-pour when he or she must add extremely small amounts of a product as a single ingredient in a multi-ingredient drink recipe. An example would be a bartender who must add a very small amount of dry vermouth when making a martini.

FUN ON THE WEB!

Bartenders faced with a guest order for a drink with which they are unfamiliar can quickly refer to the drink's recipe by using one of the many popular applications found on "smart" electronic devices which can access a virtually unlimited number of drink recipes. John Wiley & Sons offers the very popular *Mr. Boston* bartending guides in hard copy and in e-book formats. To learn more, go to: www.wiley.com. When you arrive, type "Mr. Boston" in the search bar.

JIGGER POUR

A **jigger** is a device (like a small cup) used to measure alcoholic beverages, typically in ounces and fraction of ounce quantities. Because jiggers are inexpensive, this control approach is also inexpensive. It is also quite portable. It is a good system to use in remote serving locations, such as a pool area, beach, guest suite, or banquet room. The disadvantage, of course, is that there is still room for employee overpouring error as well as the potential for bartender fraud (see Chapter 5).

METERED POUR SPOUT

In some situations, you may determine that a pour spout, designed to dispense a predetermined amount of liquor each time the bottle is inverted, makes good sense. Pour spouts are inserted into bottles and are available to dispense a variety of different quantities. When using a metered pour spout, the predetermined portion of product is dispensed whenever the bartender is called upon to serve that product.

FUN ON THE WEB!

Many managers find that metered pour spouts are very effective cost control tools. Metered spouts that dispense a predetermined amount of liquor ranging from ⅞ ounce to 1½ ounce are commonly available. In electronically monitored systems, every liquor shot served is pre-portioned and then recorded. At the end of each shift, managers can produce a pouring report that indicates how much money bartenders should have entered into the POS system or cash register based on the amount of liquor served. To review such systems, enter "alcoholic beverage control systems" in your favorite search engine, then review the results to see how electronically based metered systems can help managers control their liquor costs.

BEVERAGE GUN

In some large operations, beverage guns are connected directly to liquor bottles of various sizes. The gun may be activated by pushing a mechanical or electronic button built into the gun or the POS. In either case, the bartender may find, for example, that pushing a gin and tonic button on a gun device will result in the dispensing of a predetermined amount of both gin and tonic. Although the control features built into gun systems are many, their cost, lack of portability, and possible negative guest reaction can be limiting factors in their selection.

TOTAL BAR SYSTEM

The most expensive, but also the most complete, beverage production control solution is a **total bar system.** This system combines sales information with automated product dispensing information to create a complete revenue and production management system. Depending on the level of sophistication and cost, the total bar system can perform one or all of the following tasks:

1. Record beverage sale by brand.
2. Record who made the sale.
3. Record sales dollars and/or post the sale to a guest room folio (bill) in a hotel.
4. Measure and dispense liquor for drinks.
5. Add predetermined mixes to drink.
6. Reduce liquor values from beverage inventory value totals as drink sales are made.
7. Prepare liquor requisitions.
8. Compute liquor cost by brand sold.
9. Calculate gratuity on checks.
10. Identify payment method (e.g., cash, check, credit or debit card).
11. Record guest sales by table or check number.
12. Record date and time of sales.

RESPONSIBLE ALCOHOLIC BEVERAGE SERVICE

Alcohol sales are important in many foodservice operations. People have long been fond of alcoholic beverages regardless of where they are consumed, because they add greatly to the enjoyment of food and friends. In moderate doses, **ethyl alcohol,** the type of alcohol found in beverage products, acts as a mild tranquilizer. In excessive doses, however, it can become toxic, causing impaired judgment and, in some cases, even death. Clearly, a foodservice manager whose establishment serves alcoholic beverages must take great care in the serving of alcohols beverages and the monitoring of guests' alcohol intake.

As well, most states have now enacted third-party liability legislation, which, under certain conditions, holds your business and, in some cases, you, personally responsible for the actions of your guests who consume excessive amounts of alcoholic beverages in your operation. These legislative acts are commonly called **dram shop laws.** *Dram shop* is derived from the word *dram,* which refers to a small drink, and shop where such a drink was sold. Dram shop laws shift some of the liability for acts committed by an individual under the influence of alcohol from that individual to the server or operation that supplied the intoxicating beverage.

The responsible service of alcohol requires careful control of the amount of alcohol served to each guest. The proper management of a beverage operation requires strict adherence to control procedures for several reasons:

1. Beverage operations are subject to tax audits to verify sales revenue. In some states, these audits are unannounced.

2. Beverage operations can, in some cases, be closed down on the spot for the violation of a liquor law.

3. Employees in a bar may deceptively seek to become operational "partners" by bringing in their own beverage products to sell and then keeping sales revenue.

4. Detecting the disappearance of small amounts of beverage products is extremely difficult, as, for example, the loss of 8 ounces of beer from a multigallon keg.

Cost Control Around the World

The responsible service and consumption of alcohol is of concern to hospitality managers worldwide. As result, it is an important issue to members of hospitality associations worldwide. HOTREC is the umbrella group for trade associations representing hotels, restaurants, cafés, and similar establishments in Europe. HOTREC consists of 43 national trade associations representing the hospitality sector in 26 countries, from Portugal to Estonia and from Ireland to Cyprus.

HOTREC's principal purpose is to monitor and analyze developments in the European Union (EU) that have a direct impact on the hospitality industry. One important initiative HOTREC actively supports is the *Wine in Moderation Programme*.

The Wine in Moderation Programme is a pan-European initiative designed to promote responsibility and moderation in wine consumption. It seeks to educate the public about the social and health risks of excessive alcohol consumption and misuse. HOTREC members recognize that education is a powerful tool that can be used in efforts to encourage responsible alcohol service and consumption. You can learn more about the Wine in Moderation Programme and how managers working in every country can support its principles and its educational efforts to promote responsible drinking by entering "Wine in Moderation Programme" into your favorite search engine and then reviewing the information on the program's website.

Technology Tools

In this chapter, you learned about cost control concepts related to product storage, inventory management, issuing, and production. There are a variety of programs that assist managers in these areas. The programs available include those that:

1. Maintain product inventory values by food category (i.e., produce, meat, dairy, etc.).

2. Create "shopping lists" through production of daily inventory and comparison with production schedules.

3. Report par stock levels, daily storeroom issues, and daily product usage.

4. Maintain perpetual inventory.

5. Compute LIFO or FIFO inventory values.

6. Maintain inventory products database by vendor, storeroom location, product type, alpha order, etc.

7. Report below-par inventory levels.

8. Report daily cost of goods issued or sold.

9. Interface with handheld bar code readers for accurate inventory count and price extension.

10. Compute inventory loss rates.

11. Develop production schedules based on weekly, daily, or monthly sales forecasts.

12. Create product requisition (issues) lists based on forecasted sales.

In some cases, these software programs are designed to be self-standing. In other cases, the programs are designed to operate in conjunction with many of the advanced POS systems currently on the market.

For these reasons and others, serving standard sized drink portions is an absolute must for the beverage operation. Although direct reference by a bartender to a standardized recipe may be necessary for only a few types of drinks, standardized recipes that detail the quantity of beverage product management has predetermined as appropriate must be strictly adhered to. That is, if management has determined that bourbon and water should be a 1-ounce portion of bourbon and a 2-ounce portion of water, then both items should be measured by a jigger or another measuring device used to dispense these predetermined amounts.

Each drink sold in a bar must have a standardized recipe or, if the preparation of the alcoholic beverage is simple, such as a glass of wine or draft beer, a standardized portion size. These standards directly affect responsible guest service, guest satisfaction, and the ultimate profitability of the operation.

Apply What You Have Learned

Assume that you are the manager of a restaurant (serving casual Italian food) that is part of a national chain. Beverage sales account for 35 percent of your total sales, with one-half of those sales coming from diners and one-half from guests drinking in the bar area.

An e-mail message from your supervisor arrives, asking your opinion about the company converting from the manual bartending system currently in use to one that is fully automated. The system essentially controls and accounts for the quantity of alcohol poured when making drinks or serving beer or wine. Your written response to the following questions is requested.

1. How would such a system likely affect the control procedures in place at your restaurant?

2. How would guests sitting in the dining room likely perceive the system?

3. How would guests sitting at the bar likely perceive the system?

4. How would the system likely be perceived by your bartenders?

Key Terms and Concepts

The following are terms and concepts discussed in the chapter that are important for you as a manager. To help you review, please define the terms below.

inventory	tenths system	par level
LIFO (last in, first out)	inventory valuation sheet	daily inventory sheet
FIFO (first in, first out)	physical inventory	back of the house
potentially hazardous foods	issuing	portion cost
freezer burn	requisition	food scoop
two-key system	ingredient room	carryover
recodable electronic locks	empty for full system	convenience foods (ready foods)
cellar temperature	comp	free-pouring
oxidation	perpetual inventory	jigger
working stock	bin card	total bar system
safety stock	perpetual inventory card	ethyl alcohol
fiscal year	purchase point	dram shop laws
	as needed (just-in-time)	

Test Your Skills

You may download the Excel spreadsheets for the Test Your Skills exercises from the student companion website at www.wiley.com/college/dopson. Complete the exercises by placing your answers in the shaded boxes and answering the questions as indicated.

1. Olan Haynes is responsible for managing the inventory at the Dobie Road Retirement Center. Olan purchases a variety of items by the case, but he prefers to inventory all of these items in other ways.

   For example, he purchases beets by the case. Each case of beets contains 6 cans. But Olan wants to calculate his inventory value based on the number of cans of beets he has in inventory, not the number of cases. Use the following chart to calculate the preferred inventory unit value (e.g., dollars per can, jar, or bottle) that Olan should use for each item listed, based on the purchase unit cost of each item Olan holds in his inventory.

Inventory Item	Purchase Unit	Purchase Unit Cost	Preferred Inventory Unit	Inventory Units per Case	Preferred Inventory Unit Value $
Beets	1 case	$18.00	can	6	
Chicken base	1 case	$96.12	jar	12	
Catsup	1 case	$19.44	bottle	24	
Soy sauce	1 case	$22.80	gallon	4	
Cocoa mix	1 case	$21.50	bag	10	

2. Jack Stills operates the Spartan Restaurant. He is taking the end-of-month inventory in the restaurant's bar. When calculating the value of his spirits, he uses the "tenths" method of estimating product value. He has accounted for all of the spirits product held in his liquor storage area and is now calculating the value of his "behind the bar" inventory. He has completed this process for all of the products he serves except gin. Help him arrive at the ending inventory value for gin by completing the following portion of his Spirits inventory value sheet.

Product	Cost Per 750 ml Bottle	Amount on Hand (750 ml)	Product Value
Seagram's	$11.50	2.3	
Well Gin	7.50	4.6	
Bombay	17.50	2.2	
Bombay Sapphire	19.50	2.9	
Tanqueray	16.50	1.0	
Tanqueray Ten	19.00	1.7	
Tanqueray Rangpur	19.00	2.3	
Gordon's	10.75	1.5	
White Satin	22.50	0.8	
Total Value			

3. Kyle Minoge manages the four-person ingredient room staff at the 800-bed Parkview Hospital. One tool Kyle has developed to help monitor his inventory levels on a daily basis is a requisitions and issues record that records daily all of the inventory items requested by the kitchen's production staff and issued by Kyle's storeroom staff. The record Kyle maintains also indicates the monetary value of the issues made. Help Kyle complete part of yesterday's requisitions and issues record below.

Parkview Hospital Requisitions and Issues Record						
Item	Inventory Unit	Unit Cost	Requested Amount	Issued Amount	Issued Unit	Total Cost
Flour	25-lb. bag	$25.00	25 lb.	1	bags	
Beef base	1-lb. jar	$ 7.15	3 lb.	3	jars	
Roast beef (top round)	lb.	$ 6.24	50 lb.	54	pounds	
Potatoes (redskin)	40-lb. box	$15.00	78 lb.	2	boxes	
Broccoli (frozen)	3-lb. box	$ 2.55	61 lb.	21	boxes	

Why do you think the amount of roast beef, potatoes, and broccoli requested by the kitchen staff yesterday was different than the amount issued by Kyle's ingredient room staff?

4. Robin Christopher uses bin cards to manage the wine inventory at the Michelin-starred Riverside Restaurant. Each of the wines held in inventory has its own bin card. The bin card for Hundred Acre Cabernet, listed on the menu for $450 per bottle, is presented below, along with its purchase and sales activity for the month of October.

Make the appropriate entries on the card for the month of October to determine how much of this wine Robin should have in inventory on each of the days listed including the end of the month.

Bin Number: 237 Hundred Acre Cabernet,		Bottle Size: 750 ml	
Date	In	Out	Amount on Hand
Oct. 1			23
Oct. 3		2	
Oct. 8		1	
Oct. 10		5	
Oct. 12	12		
Oct. 14		2	
Oct. 15		2	
Oct. 17		4	
Oct. 19		5	
Oct. 21	12		
Oct. 23		2	
Oct. 25		3	
Oct. 30		3	
Oct. 31		1	

What would it mean if Robin took a physical inventory at the end of October and there was actually one bottle less in inventory than indicated on the wine's bin card? What would it mean if there was actually one bottle more than indicated on the wine's bin card?

5. Kesha Avril operates Rio Bravo. Rio Bravo is a small, fast-casual Mexican-style restaurant. Keisha would like to set up an ABC inventory system for monitoring some of her inventoried products. Keisha has listed below last month's usage for 20 key items she holds in inventory.

   a. Calculate Monthly Usage $, then see (b) and (c) below.

Item	Monthly Usage	Purchase Unit	Purchase Price per Unit	Monthly Usage $
Chicken breast	1,023	pound	$ 0.99	
Avocado	85	case	$19.50	
Corn tortillas	230	pound	$ 0.38	
Skirt steak	527	pound	$ 4.15	
Green peppers	7	case	$28.50	
Onions	2	bag	$44.00	
Parsley	4	crate	$18.00	
Tortilla chips	265	pound	$ 0.88	
Chili powder	12	pound	$ 4.60	
White cheddar cheese	28	pound	$ 3.50	
Sofrito	42	jar	$ 2.10	
Rice	6	bag	$45.00	
Cumin	10	pound	$ 6.38	
Iceberg lettuce	5	case	$18.50	
Cilantro	6	crate	$14.10	
Fresh tomatoes	16	lug	$11.50	
Sour cream	21	5-lb. carton	$ 4.25	
Pork butt	483	pound	$ 2.78	
Flour tortillas	200	pound	$ 0.88	
Tilapia fillets	61	pound	$ 2.95	

   b. After calculating Monthly Usage $, copy the table and paste below. After pasting, sort the table by Monthly Usage $, from largest to smallest.

   c. Assign each inventory item to an A, B, or C inventory category where the top 20 percent of the items (75 percent of the cost) are assigned to category A, the next 30 percent of the items (15 percent of the cost) are assigned to category B, and the remaining 50 percent of the items (10 percent of the cost) are assigned to category C.

Item	Monthly Usage	Purchase Unit	Purchase Price per Unit	Monthly Usage $	Inventory Category (ABC)
Don't forget to calculate the total after you sort ⟶ Total					

6. Lesley is the purchasing manager for an organic food restaurant with a banquet room. She needs to create the food purchase orders for tomorrow. Her par-value, on-hand, and special-order requirements are as follows. Help Lesley determine the amount of each item she needs to order. (*Spreadsheet hint*: Use the ROUNDUP function with zero decimals in the Order Amount column.)

Daily Inventory Sheet						
Item	Description	Unit	Par Value	On Hand	Special Order	Order Amount
Avocados	48 ct.	case	6	2	3	
Cauliflower	12 ct.	case	5	1		
Cucumbers	Medium	case	3	0		
Grapes	Red seedless	lug	4	1		
Lettuce	Green leaf, 24 ct.	case	5	2	4	
Lettuce	Romaine, 24 ct.	case	3	0.5		
Pears	D'Anjou	case	3	1		
Peppers	Green bell, med.	case	7	2	5	
Pineapples	7 ct.	case	4	0		
Potatoes	B reds	50-lb. bag	3	0.5		
Potatoes	Peeled, large	25-lb. bag	4	1	4	
Squash	Yellow #2	30-lb. case	5	2	2	
Strawberries	Driscoll	flat	3	1.5		

7. Maxine Wilson is the executive chef at the Plainview Air Force Base. Fajita Spiced Whitefish is one of Maxine's most popular items. Using the standardized recipe information below calculate the total recipe cost and the per portion cost for Maxine's Fajita Spiced Whitefish.

Fajita Spiced Whitefish
Yield in portions: 50   Portion size: 6 oz.

Ingredient	Amount	Recipe Cost	Procedure
Boneless whitefish fillet: 6 oz.	50 fillets	$103.20	Pat whitefish fillets dry.
Potato flakes; dry	1 lb. 8 oz.	$ 1.58	Mix potato flakes, cornstarch, flour, and seasoning to make a breading. Coat each fillet with the breading mixture.
Cornstarch	10 oz.	$ 0.96	
Flour, all-purpose	4 oz.	$ 0.25	
Fajita seasoning	10 oz.	$ 4.18	
Salt	4 oz.	$ 0.10	
Vegetable oil	4 cups	$ 2.73	Heat oil in fry pan. Place breaded fillet into hot oil, presentation side down. Cook until browned, then turn to brown other side. Remove from fry pan and drain.
	Total Recipe Cost		Portion Cost

8. Helen Lang is the manager at the Prime Rib House restaurant. Her best-selling menu item is the 10-ounce regular cut prime rib. Helen pays $8.97 a pound for the standing rib roasts she uses. When properly trimmed, cooked, and sliced, each 22-pound rib roast she buys will produce 25 regular cut slices weighing 10 ounces each. Tonight, Helen's production forecast calls for the cooking of two rib roasts. Calculate the portion cost of this item that Helen's operation would achieve if the following number of 10-ounce portions are actually served from the two cooked roasts.

Number of roasts	
Rib roast weight in lb.	
Total number of lb.	
Cost per lb.	
Total cost of ribs	

Rib Portions Served	Portion Cost
50	
48	
46	
44	
42	
40	

What two key areas of controlling production costs would Helen want to monitor to ensure that the two rib roasts cooked and served by her production staff have the lowest portion cost?

9. Mario Armando Perez is the kitchen manager at the Asahi Sushi House. Mario's restaurant offers five popular types of sushi roll. Mario keeps careful records of the number of each roll type sold, from which he computes each item's popularity index. For March 1, Mario estimates 150 guests will be served.

   Based on his experience, and to ensure he does not run out of any item, Mario would like to have extra servings (planned overage) of selected menu items available for sale. Using planned overage, the popularity index of his menu items, and his prior day's carryover information, help Mario determine the amount of new production needed and the total available for the day.

   At the end of the day, Mario also records his actual number sold in order to calculate his carryover amount for the next day. Using all of the information given, help Mario complete his kitchen production schedule for March 1.

Mario's Kitchen Production Schedule: March 1								
Menu Item	Popularity Index	Sales Forecast	Planned Overage	Prior Day Carryover	New Production	Total Available	Number Sold	Carryover
Spicy Tuna Roll	34%		5	6			52	
Salmon Special Roll	10%		5	2			12	
Spicy Shrimp Roll	30%		5	5			50	
California Roll	20%		5	2			30	
BBQ Eel Roll	6%		0	0			5	
Total to Serve	100%	150	20					

10. Overportioning alcoholic beverages most often causes a significant increase in beverage portion costs, and it will make it more difficult to ensure that an operation is practicing responsible alcoholic beverage service. As a result, overportioning when preparing and serving alcoholic beverages must be avoided.

    The underportioning of liquor caused by a bartender's failure to follow a drink's standardized recipe can also be a problem for an operation. What would be the likely result for an operation that consistently underportions the amount of liquor used in the drinks that it serves?

CHAPTER 5

Monitoring Food and Beverage Product Costs

OVERVIEW

This chapter teaches you how to calculate the product-related costs of making the menu items you sell. In addition, you will learn how to compare the product cost results you actually achieve to those you planned to achieve. The chapter concludes by identifying steps you can take to help ensure you meet your operation's profit goals by monitoring your product costs and then reducing those costs if they are too high.

Chapter Outline

- Cost of Sales
- Computing Cost of Food Sold
- Computing Cost of Beverage Sold
- Computing Costs with Transfers
- Utilizing the Cost of Sales Formula
- Reducing the Cost of Sales Percentage
- Technology Tools
- Apply What You Have Learned
- Key Terms and Concepts
- Test Your Skills

LEARNING OUTCOMES

At the conclusion of this chapter, you will be able to:
- Accurately calculate food and beverage costs and their cost percentages.
- Compare product costs achieved in an operation against the product costs the operation planned to achieve.
- Apply strategies designed to reduce an operation's cost of sales and its cost of sales percentage.

COST OF SALES

In Chapters 3 and 4, you learned how to properly purchase, receive, inventory and issue food and beverage products. You also learned in Chapter 1 that, when it follows the *Uniform System of Accounts for Restaurants*, an operation's food and beverage costs are reported two ways: (1) as a total dollar amount and (2) as a percentage of the operation's total sales.

The *USAR* recommends reporting food cost separately from beverage cost. When the amounts of an operation's individual food and beverage costs are combined, they are referred to as the operation's total **cost of sales.**

The ability to accurately calculate and report an operation's cost of sales is an important management skill. In nearly all foodservice operations, a manager's ability to control cost of sales will be used as a primary measure of that manager's competence and his or her abilities.

All restaurant managers must be able to calculate their actual food costs. In those operations that sell alcoholic beverages, the manager must also know how to calculate the operation's actual beverage costs. As well, managers should know how to estimate, or forecast, their future product costs. When they can do that accurately, they are able to compare the cost of sales their operations' actually achieve to the operations' cost of sales forecasts. If significant differences exist, they can take the steps needed to improve their operations product usage and, as a result, help to meet their profit goals.

COMPUTING COST OF FOOD SOLD

It is important to recognize that the cost of sales incurred by an operation in an accounting period is most often *not* equal to the amount of food purchases in that same accounting period. Because that is true, managers must use a very specific process to accurately calculate their cost of sales and cost of sales percentages. The cost of food sold formula they use to do so is shown in Figure 5.1.

It is important to recognize that an operation's cost of food sold is actually the dollar amount of all food sold *plus* the costs of any food which was thrown away, spoiled, wasted, or stolen. To best use the cost of food sold formula properly, managers must fully understand each of its individual parts.

BEGINNING INVENTORY

When calculating cost of food sold, **beginning inventory** is the dollar value of all food on hand at the beginning of an accounting period. It is determined by completing

FIGURE 5.1 Formula for Cost of Food Sold

> **Beginning Inventory**
>
> **PLUS**
>
> **Purchases = Food available for sale**
>
> **LESS**
>
> **Ending Inventory = Cost of food consumed**
>
> **LESS**
>
> **Employee Meals = Cost of food sold**

a physical inventory, which is an actual count and valuation of all foods in storage and/or in production areas (see Chapter 4).

If, when taking a physical inventory, products are undercounted, your food costs will ultimately appear higher than they actually are. If, on the other hand, you erroneously overstate the value of products in inventory, a process called **padding inventory,** your costs will appear artificially low.

It is important that managers take accurate physical inventories and, for the purpose of calculating food or beverage costs, to recognize that the beginning inventory for an accounting period is always the ending inventory amount from the prior accounting period. Thus, for example, an operation's ending inventory for January 31st will become the operation's beginning inventory for February 1st.

PURCHASES

Purchases are the sum cost of all food bought during the accounting period. The purchases amount is determined by properly summing the value of all delivery invoices and other bills for products purchased in the accounting period.

FOOD AVAILABLE FOR SALE

Food available for sale is the sum of the beginning inventory and purchases made during a specific accounting period. Some managers refer to food available for sale as **goods available for sale** because this term was commonly used prior to the publication of the most recent edition of the *USAR*. Regardless of the term used, each represents the value of all food that was available for sale during that accounting period.

ENDING INVENTORY

Ending inventory refers to the dollar value of all food on hand at the end of the accounting period. It also must be determined by completing an accurate physical inventory.

COST OF FOOD CONSUMED

The **cost of food consumed** is the actual dollar value of all food used, or consumed, by the operation. Again, it is important to note that this is not merely the value of all food sold but, rather, the value of all food no longer in the establishment due to sale, spoilage, waste, or theft. Cost of food consumed also includes the cost of any complementary meals served to guests as well as the value of any food (meals) eaten by employees.

EMPLOYEE MEALS

Employee meal cost is actually a labor-related, not food-related, cost (see Chapter 7). Free or reduced-cost employee meals are a benefit much in the same manner as medical insurance or paid vacation. Therefore, the value of this benefit, if provided, should not be recorded as a cost of food but, rather, as a cost of labor. The dollar value of food eaten by employees is *subtracted* from the cost of food consumed and *added* to the cost of labor to more accurately reflect an operation's true cost of food sold. Food products do not have to be consumed as a full meal in order to be valued as a labor cost. Soft drinks, snacks, and other food items consumed by employees are all considered employee meals for the purpose of computing cost of food sold. If records are kept on the number of employees consuming food each day, monthly employee meal costs are easily determined.

Some operators prefer to assign a fixed dollar value to each employee meal served in an accounting period rather than record the amount of food eaten by each employee. Thus, for example, if an operator assigns a value of $3.00 to each employee meal served and 1,000 meals are served in a month, the value of employee meals for that month would be $3,000 ($3.00 per meal × 1,000 meals served = $3,000).

COST OF FOOD SOLD

Cost of food sold, or cost of goods sold, is the actual amount of all food expenses incurred by the operation *minus* the cost of employee meals. It is not possible to accurately determine this number unless a beginning physical inventory has been taken at the start of the accounting period, followed by another physical inventory taken at the end of the accounting period.

Calculating actual cost of food sold on a regular basis is important because it is not possible to improve your food cost control efforts unless you first know what your food costs actually are. In nearly all operations, cost of food sold is calculated on at least a monthly basis because it is reported on the operation's income statement (P&L). In many operations, these same costs are calculated on a weekly or even on a daily basis!

FOOD COST PERCENTAGE

To properly analyze an operation's cost of sales for a specific accounting period, managers must first determine the amount of food used in that period and the amount of sales achieved in the same period. When they have done so, they can calculate their **food cost percentage**.

HERE'S HOW IT'S DONE 5.1

Managers calculate their food cost percentages by first accurately determining their cost of food sold and then dividing by their food sales:

$$\frac{\text{Cost of food sold}}{\text{Food sales}} = \text{Food cost \%}$$

Some foodservice managers, however, are more interested in how much it costs to serve each of their guests rather than their operations' food cost percentages. Operations in which this average cost of meals served value is important include military bases, hospitals, senior living facilities, school and college foodservice operations, and business organizations that provide free meals to their workers.

Whether the guests served are soldiers, patients, residents, students, or workers, calculating an operation's cost per meal is easy because it uses a variation of the basic food cost percentage formula. The formula

used to calculate the average cost of meals served in an operation is:

$$\frac{\text{Cost of food sold}}{\text{Total meals served}} = \text{Cost per meal}$$

For example, assume a manager's operation incurred $25,000 in cost of food sold during an accounting period. In that same accounting period, the manager served 10,000 meals. To calculate this operation's cost per meal, the manager applies the cost per meal formula. In this example:

$$\frac{\$25,000}{10,000 \text{ meals}} = \$2.50 \text{ per meal}$$

Whether managers are most interested in their cost of food percentage or in their cost per meal served, it is essential that they first calculate accurately the amount of their cost of food sold.

The formula used to compute an operation's food cost percentage is:

$$\frac{\text{Cost of food sold}}{\text{Food sales}} = \text{Food cost \%}$$

An operation's food cost percentage represents that portion of food sales that was spent on all food expenses. To illustrate, assume you managed an operation that achieved $50,000 in food sales in the current accounting period. In the period you spent $15,000 for food. Your food cost percentage for the period would be calculated as:

$$\frac{\$15,000}{\$50,000} = 30\%$$

COMPUTING COST OF BEVERAGE SOLD

The proper computation of a beverage cost percentage is identical to that of a food cost percentage, with one important difference. Typically, there is no equivalent for employee meals because the consumption of alcoholic beverage products by employees who are working should be strictly prohibited. Thus, "employee drinks" would never be considered as a reduction from overall beverage cost. However, it is important to recognize that an operation's **cost of beverage sold** is actually the dollar amount of all beverage products sold as well as the costs of all beverages that were given away, wasted, or stolen. The cost of beverage sold formula is shown in Figure 5.2.

BEVERAGE COST PERCENTAGE

To properly analyze an operation's **beverage cost percentage**, managers must first determine the amount of beverages used in that period and the amount of beverage sales achieved in the same period.

The formula used to compute an operation's beverage cost percentage is:

$$\frac{\text{Cost of beverage sold}}{\text{Beverage sales}} = \text{Beverage cost \%}$$

To illustrate, assume you managed an operation that achieved $100,000 in beverage sales in the current accounting period. In the period, you spent $18,000 for beverages. Your beverage cost percentage for the period would be calculated as:

$$\frac{\$18,000}{\$100,000} = 18\%$$

FIGURE 5.2 Formula for Cost of Beverage Sold

Beginning Inventory

PLUS

Purchases = **Beverages available for sale**

LESS

Ending Inventory = **Cost of beverage sold**

COMPUTING COSTS WITH TRANSFERS •⎯⎯⎯⎯

In some operations other reductions from, and additions to, food and beverage expenses must be considered when accurately calculating the operation's cost of goods sold. To illustrate, consider the situation you would face as a manager of Rio Lobo's, a popular Tex-Mex style restaurant that has a high volume of alcoholic beverage sales. To prepare your drinks, your bartenders use a large quantity of limes, lemons, and fruit juices issued from the kitchen. You would, of course, like your beverage cost percentage to reflect all of the costs associated with buying and using the beverages as well as the food ingredients needed in drink preparation. As a result, you must transfer the cost of any food ingredients used in drink production away from your cost of food sold and add them to your costs of beverage sold.

Assume further that, in this operation, your kitchen produces several standardized recipes that require the use of wines that are taken from your wine inventory as needed and beers that are issued from the bar. As a result you must transfer the cost of these wines and beers away from your cost of beverage sold and add them to your cost of food sold.

FIGURE 5.3 Rio Lobo Weekly Transfer Record

Location: Rio Lobo					Month/Date: 1/15–1/21	
Product Value						
Date	**Item**	**Quality**	**To Bar**	**From Bar**	**Issued By**	**Received By**
1/15	Lemons	6	$ 0.72		T. S.	B. H.
	Limes	2 (large)	1.28		T. S.	B. H.
	Cream	2 qt.	4.62		T. S.	B. H.
1/16	Chablis	1 gal.		$11.10	B. H.	T. S.
1/17	Coffee	2 lb.	10.70		T. S.	B. H.
1/18	Cherries	½ gal.	12.94		T. S.	B. H.
1/18	Lemons	4	0.48		T. S.	B. H.
	Limes (small)	12	2.24		T. S.	B. H.
	Ice cream (vanilla)	1 gal.	13.32		T. S.	B. H.
1/19	Pineapple juice	½ gal.	3.00		T. S.	B. H.
1/20	Tomato juice	1 case	20.00		T. S.	B. H.
1/20	Sherry	750 ml		6.70	B. H.	T. S.
1/21	Celery	1 bunch	0.54		T. S.	B. H.
Total Product Value			**$69.84**	**$17.80**		

The value of transfers to and from one operating unit to another should be recorded on a product transfer form. The form includes a space for the amount of product transferred, the product's value, and the individuals authorizing the transfers. Figure 5.3 shows the way in which a product transfer form would be used at Rio Lobo's for the *first week* of the month of January.

After all appropriate transfers have been made, accurate cost of beverage sold and cost of food sold calculations can be made.

Figure 5.4 illustrates the formulas you would use to calculate Cost of Food Sold and Cost of Beverage Sold at Rio Lobo's including transfers for the *entire month* of January.

FIGURE 5.4 Cost of Food Sold and Cost of Beverage Sold with Transfers

Accounting Period: 1/15–2/15

Unit Name: Rio Lobo's

Cost of Food Sold	
Beginning inventory	$25,000
PLUS	
Purchases	40,000
= Food available for sale	$65,000
LESS	
Ending inventory	$27,000
= Cost of food consumed	$38,000
LESS	
Food transfers from kitchen	5,000
PLUS	
Beverage transfers to kitchen	3,000
LESS	
Employee meals	1,000
= Cost of food sold	$35,000

Cost of Beverage Sold	
Beginning beverage inventory	$12,000
PLUS	
Purchases	18,000
= Beverages available for sale	$30,000
LESS	
Ending inventory	14,000
= Cost of beverage consumed	$16,000
PLUS	
Food transfers from kitchen	5,000
LESS	
Beverage transfers to kitchen	3,000
= Cost of beverage sold	$18,000

UTILIZING THE COST OF SALES FORMULA

When managers truly understand the cost of sales formulas for food and beverages, they are in a good position to perform three additional tasks that can improve the management of their operations:

1. Calculating cost of sales for individual product categories
2. Estimating daily cost of sales
3. Comparing actual costs to attainable costs

CALCULATING COST OF SALES FOR INDIVIDUAL PRODUCT CATEGORIES

In some cases, managers are interested in knowing the cost of sales for their individual inventory items or groups of items in addition to their overall cost of sales. To illustrate, consider the manager of Benjamin's steakhouse. In the month of January, Benjamin's achieved $190,000 in food sales. Figure 5.5 details Benjamin's food usage in five major inventory categories for the month.

In this case, the manager has decided to analyze her product usage in terms of five categories of food items. This is because, although she is interested in her overall food cost and food cost percentage, she is also interested in her meat cost percentage, as well as her product usage in other specific areas.

Calculating individual costs for her various product categories simply requires that she identify the desired product subcategories. She would then take beginning and ending inventories for each product category and then apply the cost of sales formula to determine the cost of the goods (products) sold in each category.

Because this manager understands the cost of sales formula, she can calculate food cost percentages by product category as well as calculate each category's proportion of her total cost, as shown in Figure 5.6.

Figure 5.6 shows that Benjamin's food cost percentage for January was 34.2 percent ($65,000 ÷ $190,000 = 34.2%). To calculate the food cost percentages in each category, the manager at Benjamin's uses $190,000 as the denominator in her food cost percentage calculations and the total amount of the cost of food sold in each product category as the numerator.

In some cases, managers want to know the proportion of total food cost accounted for by each product category. To calculate the proportion of total product cost percentage, the manager at Benjamin's would use the following formula:

$$\frac{\text{Cost in product category}}{\text{Total cost in all categories}} = \text{Proportion of total product cost}$$

FIGURE 5.5 Inventory by Product Category

Unit Name: Benjamin's						Date: January 31
	Meat	Seafood	Dairy	Produce	Other	Total
Beginning inventory	$26,500	$ 4,600	$ 7,300	$ 2,250	$23,000	$ 63,650
Purchases	33,800	17,700	4,400	15,550	1,800	73,250
Goods available	60,300	22,300	11,700	17,800	24,800	136,900
Ending inventory	28,000	10,900	6,000	4,500	21,000	70,400
Cost of food consumed	32,300	11,400	5,700	13,300	3,800	66,500
Employee meals	900	200	100	250	50	1,500
Cost of Food Sold	$31,400	$11,200	$ 5,600	$13,050	$ 3,750	$ 65,000

FIGURE 5.6 Food Cost Category % Percentage and Proportion of Total

Benjamin's Sales: $190,000			
Category	Cost of Food Sold	Food Cost %	Proportion of Total Product Cost (%)
Meat	$31,400	16.5%	48.3%
Seafood	11,200	5.9%	17.2%
Dairy	5,600	2.9%	8.6%
Produce	13,050	6.9%	20.1%
Other	3,750	2.0%	5.8%
Total	$65,000	34.2%	100.0%

Thus:

$$\frac{\text{Cost in meat category}}{\text{Total cost in all categories}} = \text{Proportion of total product cost}$$

In this example, that would be:

$$\frac{\$31,400}{\$65,000} = 48.3\%$$

By using the categories listed in Figure 5.6, this manager might be better able to determine when her costs are above those she would expect. Using the category food cost proportion approach, she would know, for example, that meats accounted for 48.3 percent of her total food usage in the month of January. She could compare this figure to the meat expense of prior months to determine whether her meat cost proportion is rising, declining, or staying constant. If her category cost or her overall percentages are higher than she anticipated, she must find out why and then take corrective action as necessary.

HERE'S HOW IT'S DONE 5.2

All managers should be interested in their overall product costs and cost percentages, but sometimes managers are also interested in their cost of goods sold percentages for individual food or beverage product categories. To see why, consider a manager who calculated her beverage cost percentage for last month and found it to be 22 percent. Utilizing a minor variation of the beverage cost percentage formula, the manager can calculate individual beverage cost percentages for beer, wine, and spirits sales as shown below.

Product	Sales	Cost of Beverage Sold	Beverage Cost (%)
Beer	$ 8,000	$1,600	20%
Wine	12,000	3,600	30%
Spirits	10,000	1,400	14%
Total	$30,000	$6,600	22%

Using beer as an example, the formula the manager would use to calculate her beverage cost percentage for "beer" is:

$$\frac{\text{Cost of beverage sold for beer}}{\text{Beer sales}} = \text{Beverage cost \% for beer}$$

In many cases, restaurant managers calculate separate cost of sales percentages or proportions only for certain items such as meats and seafoods. Similarly, beverage managers often calculate separate cost of sales percentages for their beer, wine, and liquor sales.

In this illustration, the manager may well gain more critical information about her operation by knowing the beverage cost percentages of her individual beverage categories than she would by knowing only her overall beverage cost percentage.

Today's modern POS systems routinely report an operation's product sales by category. Because that is so, managers utilizing the same product categories when taking their beginning and ending inventories can calculate individual product category cost percentages as well as the overall cost percentages achieved in their operations.

ESTIMATING DAILY COST OF SALES

The best managers want to know their cost of sales on a daily or weekly basis, rather than merely on a monthly basis. When they do, they can better address cost of sales-related problems as they occur. But you know that the accurate calculation of an operation's actual cost of sales requires its managers to conduct a physical inventory.

You could, of course, take a physical inventory every day. If you did, you could compute your operation's daily cost of sales. But taking an accurate physical inventory in most operations is a very time-consuming task. It would be convenient if you could have a close estimate of your food usage on a daily or weekly basis without the extra effort of a daily inventory count. Fortunately, such an approximation method exists. Figure 5.7 illustrates a six-column form, which you can use for a variety of purposes. One of them is to estimate food cost percentages on a daily or weekly basis.

To illustrate how the form is used, assume that you own an Italian restaurant that serves no liquor and caters to a family-oriented clientele. You would like to

FIGURE 5.7 Six-Column Form

Date: _____

_____   _____   _____

Weekday	Today	To Date	Today	To Date	Today	To Date

monitor your food cost percentage on a more regular basis than once per month, which is your regular accounting and inventory period. You have decided to use a six-column form to estimate your food cost percentage. Since you keep track of both daily sales and daily purchases, you can easily do so. In the space above the first two columns, you put the word "Sales." Above the middle two columns, you write "Purchases," and above the last two columns, you enter "Cost %."

You then proceed each day to enter your daily sales revenue in the column labeled Sales Today. Your invoices for food deliveries are totaled daily and entered in the column titled Purchases Today. Dividing the Purchases Today column by the Sales Today column yields the figure that is placed in the Cost % Today column.

Purchases to Date (the cumulative purchases amount) is divided by Sales to Date (the cumulative sales amount) to yield the Cost % to Date figure. A quick summary of the form is as follows:

Six-Column Food Cost % Estimate

1. $\dfrac{\text{Purchases today}}{\text{Sales today}} = \text{Cost \% today}$

2. $\dfrac{\text{Purchases to date}}{\text{Sales to date}} = \text{Cost \% to date}$

Figure 5.8 shows this information for your operation for the time period January 15 (Monday) to January 21 (Sunday).

As you can see, you buy most of your food at the beginning of the week, but sales are highest in the later part of the week. This is a common occurrence at many foodservice establishments. As can also be seen, your daily cost percentage ranges

FIGURE 5.8 Six-Column Food Cost Estimate

Date: 1/15–1/21

Weekday	Sales		Purchases		Cost %	
	Today	To Date	Today	To Date	Today	To Date
Monday	$ 850.40	$ 850.40	$1,106.20	$1,106.20	130.0%	130.0%
Tuesday	920.63	1,771.03	841.40	1,947.60	91.4%	110.0%
Wednesday	1,185.00	2,956.03	519.60	2,467.20	43.8%	83.5%
Thursday	971.20	3,927.23	488.50	2,955.70	50.3%	75.3%
Friday	1,947.58	5,874.81	792.31	3,748.01	40.7%	63.8%
Saturday	2,006.41	7,881.22	286.20	4,034.21	14.3%	51.2%
Sunday	2,404.20	10,285.42	0	4,034.21	0%	39.2%
Total	$10,285.42		$4,034.21		39.2%	

from a high of 130 percent (Monday) to a low of 0 percent (Sunday), when no deliveries are made. In the Cost % to Date column, however, the range is only from a high of 130 percent (Monday) to a low of 39.20 percent (Sunday).

In order for the six-column food cost to be an accurate estimate, you must make one important assumption: *For any time period you are evaluating, the beginning inventory and ending inventory amounts are the same.* In other words, over any given time period, you will have approximately the same amount of food on hand at all times. If this assumption is correct, the six-column food cost estimate is, in fact, a good indicator of your food usage.

If you assume that your inventory is constant (e.g., that beginning inventory equals ending inventory), the cost of sales formula indicates that your cost of food sold for the one-week period in this example would be a little less than $4,034.21, (39.20 percent of sales). Why a little less? Because the cost of food formula indicates that we must still subtract the value of employee meals, if any are provided, because they are an employee benefit and not a food expense.

How accurate is the six-column form for estimating product usage? For most operators, it is quite accurate and has the following advantages:

1. It is very simple to compute, requiring 10 minutes or less of data entry per day for most operations (the cells in a six-column Excel spreadsheet can be formulated to do the math for you).
2. It records both sales history and purchasing patterns.
3. It identifies problems before the end of the monthly accounting period.
4. By the ninth or tenth day, the degree of accuracy in the To Date column is very high.
5. It is a daily reminder to both management and employees that there is a very definite relationship between sales and expenses.

Those managers whose operations use an issuing system (see Chapter 4), rather than daily purchases, for recording their daily food usage can simply substitute "Issues" for "Purchases" in the six-column form and achieved the same cost of sales estimate results.

The use of a six-column food cost estimator is highly recommended for the operator who elects to conduct a physical inventory less often than every two weeks. Because it keeps costs uppermost in the minds of managers and employees alike, it is recommended that this cost estimate be posted where all employees can see it. It communicates daily to employees both sales and the costs required to generate those sales. It also provides a visual reminder of the importance of controlling product usage.

COMPARING ACTUAL COSTS TO ATTAINABLE COSTS

When managers can calculate their overall cost of sales amounts and percentages, and can even estimate these costs on a daily or weekly basis, they are in a good position to answer three important operational questions:

1. What are our actual product costs?
2. What should be our attainable product costs?
3. How close are we to our cost goals?

DETERMINING ACTUAL PRODUCT COST

In Chapter 3, you learned that every menu item sold in a restaurant should be produced from a standardized recipe to ensure product quality and consistency and to aid in product purchasing.

In addition to having a standardized recipe for each item, managers should have a standardized recipe cost sheet for each item. The **standardized recipe cost sheet** is simply a record of the ingredient costs required to produce a standardized recipe. Managers use standardized recipe cost sheets to calculate their total recipe costs and their individual portion costs.

A standardized cost sheet can be created using any basic spreadsheet software. The spreadsheet (or a manager using a manual calculator) simply multiplies the cost of each ingredient times the amount of the ingredient used. For example, if the cost of an ingredient in a recipe is $2.00 per cup and the standardized recipe calls for 3 cups, then the cost for this recipe ingredient is calculated as follows:

$2.00 cost per cup × 3 cups required = $6.00 ingredient cost

Standard spreadsheet programs are an excellent means of creating these records, doing the mathematical calculations and keeping the recipe costs current. Properly maintained, recipe cost sheets provide you with up-to-date information that can help with pricing decisions in addition to comparing your actual food and beverage costs with those you should incur.

Figure 5.9 shows the format you might use for a standardized recipe cost sheet if you operate Steamer's, a small soup and sandwich carryout kiosk. The recipe in this example is for beef stew, and it yields a total recipe cost of $43.46 and a cost

FIGURE 5.9 Standardized Recipe Cost Sheet

Unit Name: **Steamer's**	
Menu Item: **Beef Stew**	Recipe Number: **146**
Special Notes:	Recipe Yield: **40**
All ingredients weighed as edible	Portion Size: **8 oz.**
Portion (EP)	Portion Cost: **$1.09**

Ingredients		Ingredient Cost	
Item	**Amount**	**Unit Cost**	**Total Cost**
Corn, frozen	3 lb.	.60 lb.	$ 1.80
Tomatoes	3 lb.	1.40 lb.	4.20
Potatoes	5 lb.	0.40 lb.	2.00
Beef cubes	5 lb.	5.76 lb.	28.80
Carrots	2 lb.	.36 lb.	.72
Water	2 gal.	N/A	—
Salt	2 T	.30 lb.	.02
Pepper	2 t	12.00 lb.	.12
Garlic	1 clove	.80/clove	.80
Tomato juice	1 qt.	4.00 gal.	1.00
Onions	4 lb.	1.00 lb.	4.00
Total Cost			$43.46

Total Recipe Cost: $43.46   Recipe Type: Soups/Stews

Portion Cost: $1.09   Date Costed: 4/15

Previous Portion Cost: $1.01   Previous Dated Costed: 1/15 per serving (portion cost) of $1.09. Note that all ingredients are listed in their edible portion (EP) forms, a concept addressed in detail later in this chapter.

A standardized recipe cost sheet can be produced in seconds today using a personal computer. This formerly tedious task has become so simplified there is just no reason for management not to have accurate, up-to-date costing sheets for all its recipes. As a result, it easy for managers to know the precise portion costs that should be attainable when standardized recipes are followed carefully.

FUN ON THE WEB!

A number of companies offer recipe-costing programs for sale. These programs assist managers with portion cost calculation and much more.

To review programs of this type, enter "recipe costing software" in your favorite search engine. Pay special attention to those programs that interface (connect electronically) with an operation's POS and inventory management systems. One especially popular product offering of this type is "Food Trak," developed and marketed by Systems Concept Inc. Systems Concept Inc. is a Microsoft Gold Certified Partner, the highest level of partnership available through Microsoft. Watch for it in your search results.

Accurately calculating portion costs based on standardized recipe cost is important. However, some managers have difficulty computing total recipe costs because recipes often contain ingredient amounts that are used in a different quantity than they are purchased. For example, you may purchase soy sauce by the gallon, but your recipes may call for it to be added by the cup or tablespoon. In other cases, ingredients may be purchased in pounds or gallons but added to recipes in grams and liters. When situations such as this arise, an ingredient conversion table or chart similar to the one presented in Figure 5.10 must be used. This is so because recipe ingredient weights, measures, and sizes must be precisely computed if your recipe costs are to be accurate.

FUN ON THE WEB!

The USDA offers managers free recipe conversion information that can really speed up the recipe conversion process. To review this valuable resource and download a copy, go to: http://teamnutrition.usda.gov/Resources/rec_adjust.pdf.

Calculating recipe costs and portion costs accurately is important. For you to correctly calculate recipe costs, however, you must understand the concept of product yield and how it affects costs.

PRODUCT YIELD

Most foodservice products are delivered in the **as purchased (AP)** state. This refers to the weight or count of a product as it is delivered to the foodservice operator. For example, if a case of lettuce containing 24 heads is delivered to an operation, the lettuce will be delivered in its AP state.

Edible portion (EP) refers to the weight of a product after it has been cleaned, trimmed, cooked, and portioned. For example, after the 24 heads of lettuce delivered in AP state have been trimmed, washed and chopped, or otherwise prepared, the heads will be in the EP state.

AP refers to food products as the operator receives them, and EP refers to food products as the guest receives them. Foodservice buyers purchase ingredients at AP costs, but these items are served in their EP state. To determine actual recipe costs, it is often necessary to conduct a yield test to determine an ingredient's EP, rather than AP, costs.

FIGURE 5.10 Ingredient Conversion Table

Weight and Measure Equivalents	
Item	**Equivalent**
60 drops	1 teaspoon
3 teaspoons	1 tablespoon
2 tablespoons	1 liquid ounce
4 tablespoons	¼ cup
16 tablespoons	1 cup
2 cups	1 pint
2 pints	1 quart
4 quarts	1 gallon
4 pecks	1 bushel
16 ounces	1 pound
Select Spices*	
Pepper: 4.20 tablespoons	1 ounce
Salt: 1.55 tablespoons	1 ounce
Common Can Sizes	
Can Size	**Quantity**
No. 303	1¼ cups
No. 2	2½ cups
No. 2½	3½ cups
No. 5	7⅓ cups
No. 10	13 cups
Conversion Formulas		
To Convert	**Multiply**	**By**
Ounces to grams	Ounces	28.35
Grams to ounces	Grams	0.035
Liters to quarts	Liters	0.950
Quarts to liters	Quarts	1.057
Pounds to kilos	Pounds	0.45
Kilos to pounds	Kilos	2.20
Inches to centimeters	Inches	2.54
Centimeters to inches	Centimeters	0.39

*Spices have different conversions based on their individual weights.

A **yield test** is a procedure used for computing your actual EP costs on an AP product that will experience weight or volume loss during preparation.

To illustrate how a yield test results in the determination of actual product cost, assume you purchased 10 pounds of fresh carrots (AP) to be used for stew. You know that you will have product losses due to the peeling and trimming of the carrots. As a result, the original 10 pounds of fresh carrots for your stew will yield less than 10 pounds when the carrots are peeled and sliced into their EP state.

The formula used to calculate product yields is:

Product as purchased (AP) − Losses due to preparation = Product edible portion (EP)

Returning to the example of 10 pounds of fresh carrots, if one half pound of carrots is lost in their preparation, the product's EP yield would be calculated as:

10 lb. AP − 0.5 pounds loss due to preparation = 9.5 lb. EP

Many fresh produce items, as well as many meat and seafood items purchased in their AP state, will yield significantly reduced amounts when converted to their EP states. For meats and seafood, managers conduct a **butcher's yield test** that considers loss due to trimming inedible fat and bones, as well as losses due to cooking or slicing when they calculate their EP costs. A sample butcher's yield test showing the EP yield for the beef chuck used in the beef stew recipe previously presented is shown in Figure 5.11.

When performing yield tests managers are interested in a product's waste percentage and yield percentage. **Waste percentage** is the percentage of product lost due to cooking, trimming, portioning, or cleaning. For example, the yield test shown in Figure 5.11 indicates that that 8 pounds, or 128 ounces (8 lb. × 16 oz. = 128 oz.), of beef chuck will lose 3 pounds, or 48 ounces (3 lb. × 16 oz. = 48 oz.), during the preparation process. You can compute this item's waste percentage using the following formula:

$$\frac{\text{Product loss}}{\text{AP weight}} = \text{Waste \%}$$

In this example:

$$\text{Waste \%} = \frac{48 \text{ oz.}}{128 \text{ oz.}} = 0.375, \text{ or } 37.5\%$$

Once waste percentage has been determined, it is possible to compute an ingredient's yield percentage. **Yield percentage** is the percentage of product you will have remaining after cooking, trimming, portioning, or cleaning.

FIGURE 5.11 Butcher's Yield Test Results

Unit Name: <u>Steamer's</u>	Item: <u>Beef Cubes</u>	Date Tested: <u>1/1</u>
Specification: <u># 842</u>		Item Description: <u>Beef Chuck</u>
AP Amount Tested: <u>8 lb.</u>		
Price per Pound AP: <u>$3.60</u>		

Loss Detail	Weight	Use % of Original
AP	8 lb. 0 oz.	100.0%
Fat loss	1 lb. 2 oz.	14.1%
Bone loss	1 lb. 14 oz.	23.4%
Cooking loss	0	0%
Carving loss	0	0%
Total product loss (waste)	3 lb. 0 oz.	37.5%

Product yield: <u>62.5%</u>   **EP cost per pound: <u>$5.76</u>**

Yield test performed by: <u>L. D.</u>

Waste % + Yield % = 100%, so yield percentage can be calculated as shown in the following formula:

$$\text{Yield } \% = 1.00 - \text{Waste } \%$$

In the beef cubes example, the yield percentage is computed as:

$$\text{Yield } \% = 1.00 - 0.375 = 0.625, \text{ or } 62.5\%$$

Yield percentage is important because, if you know a product's yield percentage, you can compute the AP weight you must buy to yield the appropriate EP weight amount needed in your recipes. You can determine the amount of an AP ingredient you must have on hand by using the following formula:

$$\frac{\text{EP required}}{\text{Product yield } \%} = \text{AP required}$$

In the example recipe shown in Figure 5.9, with an EP required of 5 pounds of beef cubes, or 80 ounces (5 lb. × 16 oz. = 80 oz.), and a product yield percentage of 62.5 percent, or 0.625, the computation to determine the appropriate AP amount of beef chuck to buy to produce the beef stew recipe is:

$$\frac{80 \text{ oz.}}{0.625} = 128 \text{ oz.}$$

This can be converted to pounds:

$$\frac{128 \text{ oz.}}{16 \text{ oz.} / \text{lb.}} = 8 \text{ lb. AP required}$$

To check the preceding figures to verify that you should use a yield percentage of 0.625 when purchasing this item, you can proceed as follows:

$$\text{EP required} = \text{AP required} \times \text{Yield } \%$$

In this example,

$$\text{EP required} = 8 \text{ lb.} \times 0.625 = 5 \text{ lb.}$$

Another way to determine product yield percentage is to compute it directly using the following formula:

$$\frac{\text{EP weight}}{\text{AP weight}} = \text{Product yield } \%$$

In the beef cubes example, the EP weight needed in the recipe is equal to the product's AP weight of 8 pounds less the product's preparation loss of 3 pounds.

Thus, EP weight equals 5 pounds, and product yield percentage is computed as follows:

$$\frac{5 \text{ lb.}}{8 \text{ lb.}} = 62.5\%$$

Managers can only calculate recipe costs accurately if they know their edible portion costs. **Edible portion cost (EP cost)** is the portion cost of the item after cooking, trimming, portioning, or cleaning. The EP cost is useful to know because it represents the true cost of an ingredient or menu item based on its product yield.

It is important to note that in some cases, the same product may have different yields when purchased from different suppliers. As a result, managers should always use EP cost rather than AP prices to compare product prices offered from various suppliers. In general, you want to choose the supplier that offers the lowest EP cost for the same product, assuming the same specification or quality is being purchased.

To compute a product's actual EP cost, you simply divide the AP price per pound or unit by the product's yield percentage.

In our example, with an AP price per pound for beef chuck of $3.60 and a product yield of 0.625, the EP cost would be $5.76. This EP cost is computed using the EP cost formula:

$$\frac{\text{AP price / lb.}}{\text{Product yield \%}} = \text{EP cost / lb.}$$

In this example:

$$\frac{\$3.60 \text{ AP cost / lb.}}{0.625 \text{ product yield}} = \$5.76 \text{ EP cost / lb.}$$

You know now that your actual EP cost per pound when buying beef chuck with this particular specification, and from this supplier, is $5.76. You should conduct additional butcher yield tests if you are considering changing suppliers, modifying your beef chuck purchase specifications, or varying the quality level of the beef used in your recipe. In addition, it is usually a good idea to conduct yield tests on all of your meat and seafood items at least twice per year.

HERE'S HOW IT'S DONE 5.3

The formula managers use to calculate a product yield percentage is:

$$\frac{\text{EP weight}}{\text{AP weight}} = \text{Product yield \%}$$

Managers must understand the concept of a product yield percentage and how this percentage is calculated because it helps them answer two very important questions:

1. How much of a product should I buy?
2. What will the product cost?

How Much to Buy

To calculate how much of a product to buy, managers simply divide the EP amount that is needed in a recipe by the product's yield percentage. For example, if 15 pounds of a product is needed in its recipe-ready EP state and the product's yield is 75 percent, the manager must buy:

$$\frac{15 \text{ lb. EP needed}}{0.75 \text{ yield}} = 20 \text{ lb.}$$

When the manager buys 20 pounds of the product and achieves a 75 percent yield, 15 pounds of product in its EP state will be available.

What Will It Cost?

To find their true costs, managers must always price the ingredients used in their recipes in each ingredient's EP state, even when the product is purchased in an AP state. To calculate what a product will actually cost, managers divide the product's AP price by the product's yield percentage. For example, if a product is purchased by the pound in its AP state, the ingredient costs $6.00 per pound, and the product's yield is 75 percent, then the product's actual recipe-ready EP cost per pound will be:

$$\frac{\$6.00 \text{ / lb. AP}}{0.75 \text{ yield}} = \$8.00 \text{ / lb. EP}$$

When managers know how to calculate product yield percentages, they are better prepared to do a good job purchasing and accurately calculating the true portion costs of their standardized recipes.

Waste percentage and yield percentage can be known if records are kept on meat cookery, the cleaning and processing of vegetables and fruits, and the unavoidable losses that can occur in some products during portioning. Most recipes assume consistency in these areas, and good foodservice managers take the losses into account when making purchasing decisions. For example, in the beef stew recipe example, knowing that you will experience a yield percentage of 0.625 will help you determine exactly the right amount of meat to purchase. Good vendors are an excellent source for providing information related to trim and loss rates for standard products they sell. With this information, some operators even go so far as to add a minimum or required yield percentage as a part their product specifications.

DETERMINING OPERATIONAL EFFICIENCY

It is good for managers to be able to calculate their actual product cost. To manage your operation exceptionally well, however, you must be able to compare how well you are doing with how well you *should* be doing. This process of assessing how well you are doing begins with determining your attainable product cost.

Attainable product cost is defined as the cost of goods sold figure that should be achievable in your operation if avoidable losses were completely eliminated. Some managers refer to attainable product cost as standard cost, because these would be the costs they achieved if all of their units' operational standards were met.

When you compare attainable product cost to your actual product cost, you get a measure of your operation's efficiency. The formula for this **operational efficiency ratio** is:

$$\frac{\text{Actual product cost}}{\text{Attainable product cost}} = \text{Operational efficiency ratio}$$

To illustrate, assume again that you own Steamer's, the small soup and sandwich carryout kiosk referred to in the previous example. By calculating your recipe and portion costs, you determine your attainable product cost for a week to be $850. That is, if your operation is very efficient in its food usage, your cost of sales for the week should be $850. Assume further that you actually achieve a product cost of $850 for that week. Applying the operational efficiency ratio, your results would be:

$$\frac{\$850 \text{ actual product cost}}{\$850 \text{ attainable product cost}} = 100\%$$

These results represent perfection in the relationship between your attainable and actual operational results. In this example, your operation incurred no avoidable product loss.

Assume, however, that actual product costs were higher than attainable product cost; for example, $900. In that case, the operational efficiency ratio formula would be computed as:

$$\frac{\$900 \text{ actual product cost}}{\$850 \text{ attainable product cost}} = 105.9\%$$

In this scenario, you would know that your actual product usage, and thus your cost, was 5.9 percent higher than your attainable product cost goal.

A 100 percent operational efficiency ratio is rarely achieved, for a number of reasons. One key reason is that some product loss in a foodservice operation is virtually unavoidable. Consider, for example, the cost of a product such as fresh brewed coffee. Although you may be able to compute the portion cost of producing an 8-ounce cup of coffee, it is much more difficult to estimate the amount of product that must be discarded on a regular basis to ensure that guests are getting only freshly brewed coffee. Further, at the end of the day, it is likely that some brewed coffee will be discarded.

An additional reason why 100 percent operational efficiency ratios are rarely achieved is that every foodservice operation employs people, and people make errors at work. Despite these challenges, however, managers should strive to ensure their actual product costs are as close as possible to their attainable product costs.

In general, operational efficiency ratings in the range of 100 to 110 percent are attainable. Variance beyond that, however, can indicate serious product control problems. Ratios that are too high—that is, ratios above 110 percent—could be an indication of excessive waste, ingredient theft, spoilage, overportioning, or inaccurate recipe cost sheet computation.

Operating efficiency ratings that are too low, that is, ratings in the 80 to 90 percent range must also be avoided. Efficiency ratios such as these could be the result of miscalculation of the number of items sold, inaccurate ingredient costing, under portioning, incorrect standardized cost sheets, or errors in valuing inventory.

Many managers find that it is helpful to share operational efficiency ratio results with employees because an operation's staff should also be very interested in the answer to the fundamental question of: "How well are we doing?"

ACCEPTABLE AND UNACCEPTABLE VARIANCE

In Chapter 2, you learned how managers calculate their sales variance and their sales variance percentages. Using a similar approach, managers can calculate their product cost variances and product cost variance percentages. When comparing their actual product costs with their attainable product costs they use the following formula:

$$\frac{\text{Actual product cost} - \text{Attainable product cost}}{\text{Attainable product cost}} = \text{Cost percentage variance}$$

For example, assume a manager calculated her attainable product cost to be $8000 for a week. The manager's actual product cost was $8,500 for the week, resulting in a variance of $500 ($8,500 actual product cost − $8,000 attainable product cost = $500).

In this example, the manager's cost percentage variance would be calculated as:

$$\frac{\$8,500 - \$8,000}{\$8,000} = 6.25\%$$

Managers calculate and analyze their cost percentage variances because they realize they should not treat all variances from expected results in the same way. For example, a variance of one or two dollars from an expected result of several thousand dollars is small enough that it likely constitutes a very acceptable level of variation. A variance of one or two dollars from an expected result of nine dollars, however, might well be cause for concern and, thus, is likely unacceptable.

Figure 5.12 displays the operational efficiency ratios, dollar variances, and percentage variances that might result if you were to compute individual efficiency ratios on a variety of individual products in a steakhouse. The important concept here is a simple one: As a manager, your attention should be directed toward those areas where the need is greatest. In most cases, this means addressing large dollar variances and/or large percentage variances from your expected results.

FIGURE 5.12 Acceptable and Unacceptable Variance

Item	Actual Cost	Attainable Cost	Efficiency Ratio	Dollar Variance	Percentage Variance
Steaks	$1,010	$1,000	1.01	$10.00	1%
Coffee	$ 20	$ 10	2.00	$10.00	100%
Bolla Soave	$ 550	$ 500	1.10	$50.00	10%
Horseradish	$ 22	$ 20	1.10	$ 2.00	10%
Parsley	$ 45	$ 50	0.90	–$ 5.00	–10%

Results such as those shown in Figure 5.12 call upon you to make decisions about the acceptability of the variances you may encounter. Efficiency ratios in this example range from 0.90 to 2.00.

The $10.00 variance in actual steak cost is likely within an acceptable range because the expected cost was $1,000 and the efficiency ratio was 1.01. The $10.00 variance in coffee costs, however, is likely unacceptable because it represents actual costs that were twice as high as the expected coffee costs and that efficiency ratio is 2.00.

In a similar manner, the 10 percent variance in the cost of Bolla Soave wine represents $50 and thus may well be worth investigating, whereas the 10 percent parsley cost variation of $5.00 may be too small to merit your immediate attention.

Although it is not possible to determine one range of variance acceptability that is appropriate for all food facilities, it is important for you to establish variances from attainable costs that are acceptable for your own operation. When you do so, you will be able to easily identify those variations that must be investigated and corrected.

HERE'S HOW IT'S DONE *5.4*

In most cases, when managers calculate a cost percentage variance, they will generate a positive number. That is true because, in many cases, an operation's actual product costs will exceed its attainable or ideal product costs. In some cases, however, the cost variance percentage will be negative.

For example, assume a manager estimated he would incur $500 in salad dressing cost after serving 1,000 salads. After serving 1,000 salads, the manager's actual salad dressing cost was $450. To calculate the cost percentage variance, the manager applies the cost percentage variance formula:

$$\frac{\text{Actual product cost} - \text{Attainable product cost}}{\text{Attainable product cost}} = \text{Cost percentage variance}$$

In this example, the manager's cost percentage variance for salad dressing is:

$$\frac{\$440 - \$500}{\$500} = -12.0\%$$

In this example, the manager's salad dressing costs were 12 percent less than he had anticipated. There can be several reasons why an operation could achieve a negative cost percentage variance. One reason could be that the price paid for salad dressing by the operation was less than originally estimated. In that case, a negative cost percentage variance actually indicates good news for the operation.

It could be instead, however, that the operations' wait staff was serving less than the standardized amount of dressing on each guest's salad. Although this would cause a short-term decrease in the operation's per-salad dressing costs, the practice is also likely to cause a long-term decrease in guest satisfaction. For this reason, managers must investigate negative cost percentage variances indicating reduced costs just as thoroughly as they examine those positive cost percentage variances that indicate excessive costs.

Green and Growing!

Increasingly, foodservice operators recognize that most human activity, including their own businesses, leaves a "carbon footprint" on the planet. A carbon footprint is a measure of the impact human activities have on the environment in terms of the amount of greenhouse gases (carbon dioxide) produced. The term is useful for individuals and organizations to conceptualize their personal (or organizational) impact in contributing to global warming.

Examples of activities in which foodservice operations engage to help reduce their carbon footprint include the following:

- Buy food products locally.
- Monitor efficient energy usage regularly.

- Avoid the sale of bottled waters where the packaging and shipping of these items result in the unnecessary production of carbon dioxide.
- Use cold water for washing and cleaning when practical and sanitary.
- Reduce, reuse, and recycle!

Reduction of a business's carbon footprint is good for the environment and for business. Keep watching the hospitality trade press for an ever-increasing number of new strategies you can consider for reducing your own operation's carbon footprint!

REDUCING THE COST OF SALES PERCENTAGE

In some cases, managers who evaluate their product usage will find that their operations are extremely effective at utilizing their food and beverage products. In other cases, managers may find that their product-related costs are just too high to allow them to meet their profit goals. When that occurs, corrective action must be taken. To illustrate, assume a manager has a food cost percentage goal, or target, of 35 percent. In a specific accounting period, however, the manager's operation actually achieved a 38 percent food cost. In this example, the manager must take steps to reduce the excessive cost of sales percentage. Recall, however, that sales to customers mean costs are incurred. Increased sales mean increased costs. Therefore, despite missing his or her target, this manager's goal would not simply be to reduce overall product cost. Rather, the goal would be to maintain current (and increasing!) sales levels while achieving product costs that are at their proper proportion of sales. To do just that, restaurant managers must perform three important tasks:

1. Minimizing product loss in the kitchen
2. Minimizing product loss in the bar
3. Optimizing overall cost of sales percentage

MINIMIZING PRODUCT LOSS IN THE KITCHEN

Loss of food products can happen when control systems do not prevent losses incurred while products are in storage, losses due to overcooking or overportioning, and loses due to employee theft. It's especially important to have programs in place that will minimize the chances of product theft by employees. Although all kitchens can expect to experience small amounts of employee-related product loss, such as an employee eating an apple in secret, or nibbling a carrot where the supervisor cannot see it, extensive loss of product must be prevented.

Most kitchen-related theft deals with the removal of food products, rather than money, from the premises. This is because, unlike bartenders, few kitchen production workers also handle cash. Kitchen workers can, however, work with service personnel to defraud the operation (see Chapter 11). In addition, many kitchen workers will have direct have access to valuable food and beverage products. The following product security tips are helpful when designing control systems to ensure the safety and security of food (and beverage) products:

Product Security Tips

1. Keep all storage areas locked and secure.

2. Issue food only with proper authorization and management approval.

3. Monitor the use of all carryovers.

4. Do not allow food to be prepared unless a guest check or other written request precedes the preparation.

5. Maintain an active inventory management system.

6. Ensure that all food received is signed for by the appropriate receiving clerk.

7. Do not pay suppliers for food products without an appropriate and signed invoice.

8. Do not use "petty cash" to pay for food items unless a receipt and the product can be produced.

9. Conduct systematic physical inventories of all level A, B, and C products.

10. Do not allow employees to remove food from the premises without management's specific approval.

MINIMIZING PRODUCT LOSS IN THE BAR

Employee product theft can occur in either the bar or the kitchen production areas, but it is often more prevalent in the bar areas. Experienced food and beverage managers seem to have an endless supply of stories related to theft in bar operations. Indeed, bar theft is one of the most frequent types of thefts in the foodservice industry. Although it may well be impossible to halt all kinds of bar theft, the following are activities you should watch for to help ensure the opportunities for product theft in a bar are minimized.

ORDER FILLED BUT NOT RUNG UP

In the "order filled but not rung up" case, the bartender delivers the drink as requested by the guest or server, but the drink sale is never recorded in the POS system, and the bartender simply pockets the amount of the sale. As a result, the sales as recorded in the POS will be equal to the amount of money in the cash drawer. All drinks should be recorded by the POS system to prevent this type of theft. Management's vigilance is critical to ensure that no drink is prepared until after the order is properly recorded (entered in the POS or rung up on the cash register).

OVER- AND UNDERPOURING

When bartenders overpour, they are stealing from the operation. When they underpour, they are shortchanging the guest. Remember that your bartenders will pour the appropriate amount if you always insist that they do so. When bartenders underpour, they may be making up for drinks they have given away or sold but have not rung up. When they overpour, they may be doing so for their friends or for the extra tips this activity may yield. In either case, management must prevent such behavior.

Proper portion size in the spirits area is ensured through the enforced use of jiggers, metered devices, or other mechanical or electronic equipment. In the case of draft beer, **head size**—that is, the amount of foam on top of the glass—directly affects portion size and portion cost, and, thus, it too must be controlled.

FUN ON THE WEB!

Product loss related to draft beer can be due to either employee theft or to improper dispensing issues (e.g., wrong service temperature, too much carbonation, improperly cleaned beer lines). As a result, draft beer dispensing systems and their maintenance is a critical area of concern for bar managers. A variety of quality dispensing systems are on the market. To review them, enter "draft beer product control" in your favorite search engine, then carefully review the results.

DILUTION OF PRODUCT

Often called *watering down* the drinks, this method of bar or storeroom theft involves adding water to the product to make up for spirits that have either been stolen or given away. It is especially easy to water down products such as gin, vodka, rum, or tequila because these clear spirits will not change color with the addition of water. Detection of this type of theft is often difficult. Periodic sampling of a known-proof alcohol against bar stock by a knowledgeable food and beverage director is one of the defenses against such bartender fraud. Since each alcohol product has a particular specific gravity or weight associated with it, you may also check for product dilution through the use of a **hydrometer**, which identifies specific gravity. If water has been added to the bottle of liquor, the specific gravity will change from the value originally associated with that liquor.

PRODUCT SUBSTITUTION

When a specific call brand liquor has been ordered and paid for by a guest, it should, of course, be served to that guest. If, however, a bartender substitutes a less expensive well liquor for the call brand, while charging the guest for the higher priced call liquor, the bartender may intend to keep the difference in the prices paid for the two items. This has the effect of shortchanging guests, who paid higher prices for premium liquor drinks they did not receive. Conversely, if guests have ordered well drinks, but the bartender makes their drinks from premium or super premium call liquors, guests have received more value than they will pay for and the operation is shortchanged.

Although it is impossible to list all types of product-related bar thefts, it is important to note that they can and do occur. Conscientious managers should hire honest bartenders, train them well, and demand that they follow all house policies. Perhaps the best advice of all is simply to be vigilant. Watch the bar area carefully, or enlist the aid of a **spotter**, a professional who, for a fee, will observe the bar operation. Commonly known as **mystery shoppers**, spotters pose as anonymous customers but, during their unannounced visits, they observe workers carefully and later report to management any unusual or inappropriate behavior by bartenders or service staff.

Although alcoholic beverage theft most often occurs during the normal operation of the bar, in some operations it may also occur in other areas. Consider, for example, a couple who wish to serve champagne to their guests at their upcoming wedding reception. The reception will be held in a local hotel. It is estimated that 10 cases of champagne will be required to serve all the guests. The hotel's food and beverage director orders 12 cases of champagne because it would not be appropriate to run out during the reception. The newlyweds will pay for each bottle used. Potential difficulties could arise in two ways.

In the first, more champagne is used than should have been used because the bartenders serve guests in larger than normal glasses or they pour larger than normal portions. Because portion sizes are not controlled, the safe service of alcohol during the reception could be questionable. As well, the bride and groom will be charged for the extra product consumed. This will raise their bill for the reception needlessly and will likely decrease their satisfaction with the event.

In the second scenario, 12 cases are ordered and 10 cases of champagne are used, as planned, but the hotel's bartending staff also steals 1 case. The result is that only 1 case is available to be returned to inventory. The bartenders maintain that all 11 cases were served. Management, trusting the integrity of the bartenders, would likely call on the guests to pay for 1 extra case of product. Imagine, however, the embarrassment if the bride and groom demand that management produce the empty bottles from 11 cases! As these two scenarios illustrate, management must be vigilant to ensure that alcoholic beverage products are never stolen from the operation or from its guests.

To control drink production, it is also important to designate portion size and glassware to be used. This helps ensure that the portion size of the drink is appropriate and consistent with the guest's visual perception of a full glass. The ice to be used in drinks is also important for controlling drink production.

What does ice have to do with standardized beverage production? A lot! Large ice cubes will leave space between them when scooped into a glass. This will permit a larger amount of mixers to be added, which may dilute the drink more than intended. By contrast, smaller cubes or (especially) shaved ice will pack a glass and permit less of the mixer to be added. This may, in turn, give the impression of a stronger drink. A second difference created by ice size is that large cubes have less exposed surface area and will melt (and dilute the drink) at a slower pace than smaller cubes. As a result, in the bar area, you should select an ice machine that makes ice in a form that you feel best fits your view of proper spacing in the glass and that possesses the most desirable melting characteristics.

FUN ON THE WEB!

Several companies sell advanced automatic beverage-dispensing systems. One of the best known is Berg. To see its products, enter "Berg Liquor Controls" in your favorite search engine. Go to Berg's site and then click "Why Liquor Control."

Some companies sell high-quality commercial ice machines. Scotsman is one of those. To learn more about machines that produce ice cubes, nuggets and flakes, enter "Scotsman ice machines" in your favorite search engine, locate its site, and then click: "Products" to review the ice production options available to foodservice managers.

DIRECT THEFT

Alcohol is a highly desirable product for many employees; therefore, its direct theft is always a possibility. This is especially true in a beverage service area that is secluded or in which bartenders have direct access to product inventory and ease of exit. Proper controls as well as strict rules limiting the access of employees to beer, wine, and liquor storage areas should help deter and detect this sort of theft.

It is also important to remember that not all alcohol sales take place in a traditional, designated bar area. Because of this, additional problem areas related to beverage product control include:

1. In-room minibars
2. Bottle sales
3. Open bars
4. Banquet operations

IN-ROOM MINIBARS

Minibars, typically containing bottled and canned beer, 100-ml wine bottles, and 50-ml liquor bottles, are popular in hotels that cater to upscale travelers. The control issue here is one of matching requests by the hotel's housekeeping department for bottle replacement with actual guest usage. Some large hotels deal with this issue by having a single individual or even a department charged with the responsibility of refilling the minibars. Many modern minibars record liquor sales electronically as products are removed by guests but such records still must be carefully monitored to ensure that items issued from storage are indeed used to restock the minibars and are not lost to employee theft.

BOTTLE SALES

When liquor sales are made by the bottle, either through room service in a hotel, or at a reception area, the control issue is one of verifying bottle count. The guest and the operation must both be treated fairly in such a transaction. In the case of full-bottle sales to a guest room, the guest should be required to sign a receipt confirming acceptance of the product. This is the only way to avoid potential mis-understandings about cost.

In the case of receptions or banquets, guests should be charged only for empty bottles, or, in the case of a purchase of a specified number of bottles, should be shown both full and empty bottles equal to the number used and charged for the event. In an effort to protect both the establishment and the guest from employee theft, the thoughtful beverage manager will mark the bottles for receptions or banquets in a way that is not easily duplicated. Marking bottles helps prevent employees from bringing in their own empty bottles and then removing full ones at the event host's expense.

OPEN BARS

Open bars (hosted bars) are those in which no charge is made to guests for the individual drinks they consume but, when the bar is closed, one total amount is charged to the host or sponsor of the open bar. Open bars are common, especially at events such as weddings, special-occasion parties, and cocktail receptions. Unfor-tunately, because the individual drinker is not paying for each drink, the open-bar situation can sometimes create an "all you can drink" mindset among guests and bartenders. Because that can be the case, consumption by individual drinkers at open bars must be carefully monitored.

The production control issues associated with open bars fall into one of two main categories: namely, portion size and accountability. At open bars guests can sometimes cajole bartenders into serving drinks with larger than normal amounts of alcohol. This must, of course, be prevented. Bartenders, as well as guests, must understand that, although it may be an open bar, someone will be paying the bill at the end of the event. The hosts of the open bar have the right to expect reasonable portion control if they are paying on a per-drink or per-bottle-used basis. If the foodservice operation has established a per-person charge for the open bar, overpor-tioning costs will have to be absorbed by the operation. This means strict control of portion size and total liquor consumption per guest must be carefully monitored.

As great an issue as overportioning is, accountability looms larger and larger on the horizon as an area of legitimate cost control concern for the effective beverage manager. Recall from Chapter 4 that dram shop legislation increasingly holds liquor sellers responsible for the actions of those they serve. As a result, bartenders who work open bars should be specially trained to spot signs of guest intoxication. As difficult as it may sometimes be, guests should be made aware that it is illegal, in all states, to serve an intoxicated guest. To do so puts the entire food and beverage operation at risk.

Some managers have virtually eliminated the open-bar concept, preferring to go to a coupon system where each coupon issued is good for one drink, and the number of coupons issued, rather than the number of drinks served, can be controlled. Although the possibility exists that coupons can be shared and, thus, given to an intoxicated guest, the coupon system does demonstrate an attempt by management to exercise reasonable care, an effort that may prove vital in their defense in the event of dram shop–related litigation.

BANQUET OPERATIONS

The sale of alcoholic beverages during a seated banquet usually takes the form of bottled-wine sales. Guests may be provided with a set number of bottles on the table, to be shared by those seated at the table. Alternatively, as they consume their wine, they can be served by the banquet wait staff. It is the latter method that presents the greatest product control problems because the host of the event will be charged by either the number of bottles served or the number of guests served. If the payment is based on the number of bottles served, the bottles should be marked and the empties made available for inspection by either the guest or the banquet captain. If the sale is based on the number of glasses poured, then both the host of the event and the beverage operation must be in agreement as to the desired portion size and the total number of portions allowed to be served to each guest, table, or to the entire group.

OPTIMIZING OVERALL COST OF SALES PERCENTAGE

After management has determined what an operation's costs actually are, and has compared them to what the operation's costs should be, it may often be found that Walt Kelly's Pogo comic character was correct when he said, "*We have met the enemy, and he is us!*"

Foodservice managers (and their bosses) often seem to be on a never-ending quest to reduce food and beverage production costs. Although you must remember to guard against inappropriate cost cutting efforts, you may, in some cases, find yourself managing an operation where food and beverage production costs, when expressed as a percentage of sales, are simply too high and must be reduced. As you design strategies to reduce your product costs, it is helpful to review potential solutions based on the cost of sales equation.

You have learned that the product cost percentage equation is deceptively easy to state. In its simplest form, it can be represented as:

$$\frac{A}{B} = C$$

where:

A = Cost of products sold

B = Sales

C = Cost percentage

This formula can, however, become extremely complex. Its analysis occupies many a food organization staff meeting and can give the foodservice operator many sleepless nights! Essentially, six basic cost reduction strategies are available to influence this rather simple formula. A quick algebra lesson, however, prior to our discussion of these six approaches may be useful.

In general, the rules of algebra reveal the following things about any $A/B = C$ formula:

- If A is unchanged and B increases, C decreases.
- If A is unchanged and B decreases, C increases.
- If A increases at the same proportional rate B increases, C remains unchanged.
- If A decreases and B is unchanged, C decreases.
- If A increases and B is unchanged, C increases.

Put into foodservice management terms, these same algebraic statements can be translated as follows:

- If product costs can be kept constant while sales increase, the product cost percentage goes down.
- If product costs remain constant but sales decline, the cost percentage increases.
- If product costs go up at the same rate sales go up, the cost percentage will remain unchanged.
- If product costs can be reduced while sales remain constant, the cost percentage goes down.
- If product costs increase with no increase in sales, the cost percentage will go up.

In general, foodservice managers work to control the variables that impact product cost percentage and seek to reduce the overall value of C in the cost percentage equation. The six cost reduction approaches used to optimize overall product cost percentage, along with a summary of each approach, are presented here to help you devise your own cost reduction strategies:

How to Reduce Overall Product Cost Percentage
1. Ensure that all products purchased are sold.
2. Decrease portion size relative to price.
3. Vary recipe composition.
4. Alter product quality.
5. Achieve a more favorable sales mix.
6. Increase price relative to portion size.

To reduce your product costs, you will ultimately select an appropriate strategy from this relatively small number of alternatives. These strategies can be applied to excessive food costs or to excessive beverage costs. It is the careful selection and mixing of these approaches to cost control that differentiate the successful operator from the unsuccessful one.

To illustrate, assume that you own and operate a family style restaurant. You compute your actual food cost percentage for last month and have determined that it was 4 percentage points higher than you had planned. If you have approximately six cost-reducing options available to you, by the mathematics law of permutations, this means you have ($6 \times 5 \times 4 \times 3 \times 2$), or 720 possible combinations of these six differing cost reduction methods. No wonder, then, there is so much information written about reducing product costs!

It is not the authors' contention that all product cost reduction methods are exhausted by these six approaches, but rather the approaches are presented here as a means of systematically analyzing the various cost percentage reduction alternatives that are available to most managers.

ENSURE THAT ALL PRODUCT PURCHASED IS SOLD

These seven words have tremendous implications. They include all phases of professional purchasing, receiving, storage, inventory, issuing, production, service, and cash control. Perhaps the hospitality industry's greatest challenge in the area of cost control is ensuring that all products, once purchased, do indeed generate cash sales that are ultimately deposited into the operation's bank account!

DECREASE PORTION SIZE RELATIVE TO PRICE

Product cost percentages are directly affected by portion size. Too often, foodservice managers and bar operators assume that their standard portion sizes must conform to some unwritten rule of uniformity. This is simply not the case. Most guests would prefer a smaller portion size of higher quality ingredients than the reverse. In fact, one problem some restaurants have is that their portion sizes are simply too large. The result is excessive food loss because uneaten products must be thrown away. It is important to remember that portion sizes are determined by the foodservice manager and, as a result, they are variable.

To see the impact of portion size on product cost percentage review the data in Figure 5.13. This figure presents the significant effect on liquor cost percentage of varying the standard drink size served in an operation using $16.00 per liter as the standard cost of liquor and assuming 0.8-ounce evaporation per 33.8-ounce (1-liter, or 1,000-ml) bottle, and a standard $7.00 selling price per drink.

Note that, in this example, the manager's product cost percentage ranges from 6.93 percent when a 1-ounce portion is served, to a 13.85 percent product cost when a 2-ounce portion is served.

Portion size directly affects product cost percentage and guest perceptions of value delivered. As a result, when establishing your portion sizes, you should take all of the variables affecting your operation into account. These may include your location, pricing structure, competition, and the clientele you are seeking to attract.

VARY RECIPE COMPOSITION

Experienced managers know that even the simplest standardized recipes can often be varied somewhat. For example, what is the proper amount of beef and the proper amount of carrots to use when making 100 servings of high-quality beef stew? Because the cost of beef exceeds the cost of carrots, 100 servings of beef stew made with increased amounts of beef will cost more than 100 servings made with increased amount carrots. The question of what constitutes an ideal recipe composition must be answered by management. The answer to that question, for each standardized recipe utilize in an operation, will directly affect the operations' overall food cost percentage.

Similarly, the proportion of alcohol to mixer has a profound effect on beverage cost percentages. In some cases, the amount of alcohol used in drinks can be reduced,

FIGURE 5.13 Impact of Drink Size on Liquor Cost Percentage at Constant Selling Price of $7.00 per Drink

Drink Size	Drinks per Liter	Cost Per Liter	Cost Per Drink (cents)	Sales Per Liter	Liquor Cost % Per Liter
2 oz.	16.5	$16.00	97.0	$115.50	13.85%
1¾ oz.	18.9	$16.00	84.7	$132.30	12.09%
1½ oz.	22.0	$16.00	72.7	$154.00	10.39%
1¼ oz.	26.4	$16.00	60.6	$184.80	8.66%
1 oz.	33.0	$16.00	48.5	$231.00	6.93%

yet overall drink sizes can actually be increased. This can be done, for example, by increasing the proportion of lower-cost standardized drink recipe ingredients such as milk, juices, and soda and reducing the proportion of higher-costs spirit products. Utilization of the strategy often contributes to a feeling of satisfaction by the guest, while allowing the operator to reduce beverage costs and increase profitability.

ALTER PRODUCT QUALITY

In nearly all cases, higher-quality products cost an operator more than lower-quality products. That is certainly true for managers purchasing food and beverages. As a result, one way to achieve cost savings is to reduce product quality. This area must be approached with great caution, however, because you do not want to offer inferior quality. Rather, you should always strive to purchase the quality of product appropriate for its intended use.

For example, managers may find that less expensive canned asparagus can be excellent when used in a baked casserole dish, but the same canned product is likely an unacceptable substitution for the freshly cooked asparagus accompanying a $45.00 rib-eye steak.

Similarly, a specific coffee liqueur such as Kahlua, when called for by a guest, must, of course, be used to prepare that guest's drink. It may be quite acceptable, however, to use a non-brand name and lower-cost coffee liqueur for the many specialty drinks (e.g. Black Russian, Brave Bull, Black Magic, or Sombrero) that include coffee liqueur as an ingredient. In this example, a lower-cost generic-type coffee liqueur might be used for these specific drinks with totally satisfactory results. With appropriate experience and care, you can determine the quality of ingredients that best serve your operation and your guests and then purchase only that specific quality.

When managers find that an appropriate ingredient, rather than the highest-cost ingredient, provides good quality and good value to guests, they might be able to reduce product costs by using product substitution. But recall that managers must be very careful in this area. Lower-quality products may cost an operator less, but customers may also perceive that menu items made from these lower-quality ingredients provide reduced levels of value to them, and that reaction by guests must always be avoided.

Consider the Cost

"You're our food guru. They are offering the same size pizza as we do, but for $2.00 less. How can they do that?" asked Kevin Gustafson to Sara Leiboda. Sara was the director of operations for the seven-unit Brooklyn Pizza House restaurants. Kevin was the company president. The Brooklyn Pizza House was known for its mid-priced, high-quality, deep dish–style pizza.

Located near the main campus at State University, the company's target market is students who attend the school. The advertising programs in use by the company are clever and effective. Business and profits are good. But now Kevin and Sara were discussing the new $9.99 pizza promotion that had just been announced by their major competitor.

"They changed their cheese topping formulation Kevin," replied Sara. "They increased their use of pizza cheese by another 25 percent. One of my friends works in their central production kitchen. That's where they process and prepackage the pizza ingredients for delivery to their stores. My friend says they changed their 75/25 mozzarella/pizza cheese ratio to a 50/50 ratio. As you know, we only use 100 percent mozzarella cheese on all of our pizzas.

"Why would they do that?" asked Kevin.

"Well," replied Sara, "it's simple. Pizza cheese is a processed cheese product that costs quite a bit less than high-quality mozzarella. Pizza cheese can actually contain as little as 51 percent real cheese and still be sold as pizza cheese. It melts O.K., but it can't compare to real mozzarella in taste. By using it, they can reduce their per-pizza costs and, because their costs are lower, they can even reduce their selling prices. That's what they did. I guess they think it will increase their sales, reduce their food cost percentage, and ultimately increase their profits.

1. Why do you think this competitor decided to reduce the quality of cheese used in its pizzas?

2. Do you think students at the university will notice the change? Would you advise Kevin and Sara to make the same change to their pizza formulation? Why or why not?

ACHIEVE A MORE FAVORABLE SALES MIX

Experienced managers know that their customers' item selection decisions will have a direct and significant impact on the product cost percentages that will be achieved in these managers' operations. This is so because an operation's product cost percentages are determined in large part by the operation's sales mix.

Sales mix is defined as the series of guest purchasing decisions that result in a specific food or beverage cost percentage. Sales mix affects overall product cost percentage anytime guests have a choice among several menu selections, each selection having its own unique product cost percentage.

To see a simple example of how sales mix can directly affect an operation's product costs, assume a quick service restaurant offered only three menu items for sale. In this restaurant, the manager also offers a special "value meal" that includes one of each item, as shown in Figure 5.14.

From the data in Figure 5.14, it is easy to see that if, on a specific day, 100 percent of the restaurant's customers bought a hamburger and nothing else, the operation's product cost for that day would be 37.6 percent.

If, on another day, 100 percent of the restaurant's customers bought a soft drink and nothing else, the product cost percentage for that day would be 15.2 percent. Similarly, if every customer purchased only the "value meal" on a specific day, the operation would achieve a 33.1 percent product cost on that day. In this example, it is easy to see that the operation's actual product cost will be largely determined by the mix of the individual product costs resulting from the menu item choices made by the operation's customers.

To show a more realistic example of the effect of sales mix on product costs, assume that you are the food and beverage director at the Raider Resort, a 400-room beachfront hotel property on the Gulf Coast of Texas. In addition to your regular restaurant, you monitor your beverage sales in three serving areas:

1. *Banquets:* The beverages served in receptions prior to meal events. These sales are made in your grand ballroom, foyer, or outdoors. Banquet beverages are also served during banquet meal functions.

2. *The Starlight Bar:* An upscale bar with soft piano music that typically appeals to hotel guests who are 55 years and older.

3. *Harry O's:* A bar with indoor and poolside seating. Contemporary top-40 music played in the evenings draws a younger crowd interested in mingling and dancing.

You compute a separate beverage cost percentage for each of these beverage outlets. Figure 5.15 details the separate operating results recently achieved in each location. It also shows the overall (combined) beverage cost percentage achieved in all three units when calculated using the beverage cost percentage formula introduced earlier in this chapter.

In this example, assume that you know each beverage location uses the same portion size for all standard drinks. Well and call liquors, as well as wine-by-the-glass brands, are the same in all three locations. In this resort setting, you dislike

FIGURE 5.14 Four-item menu

Menu Item	Product Cost	Selling Price	Product Cost %
Hamburger	$1.50	$3.99	37.6%
French Fries	$0.50	$1.99	25.1%
Soft Drink	$0.15	$0.99	15.2%
Value Meal	$2.15	$6.49	33.1%

FIGURE 5.15 Raider Resort

Monthly Beverage Percentage Report			
Location	Cost of Beverages	Beverage Sales	Beverage Cost %
Banquets	$20,500	$ 80,000	25.6%
Starlight Bar	10,350	45,500	22.7%
Harry O's	16,350	67,000	24.4%
Total	$47,200	$192,500	24.5%

the difficulty associated with serving draft beer; thus, beer is sold in cans or bottles only. All three bars offer the same beer choices.

In addition, bartenders are typically rotated on a regular basis through every serving location. Given all that, should you be concerned that your beverage cost percentage varies so greatly by service location? The answer, in this case, is that you most likely have no cause for concern. In this situation, it is clear that your sales mix, and not poor control systems, have primarily determined your beverage cost percentage in each individual location.

A closer examination of the three outlets, as shown in Figure 5.16, reveals how this can happen.

Although product cost percentages are the same in each location for the individual beverage categories, the overall beverage cost percentages in the three units

FIGURE 5.16 Raider Beverage Outlets

Monthly Beverage Percentage Recap			
#1 Outlet Name: Banquets			Month: January
Product	Cost of Beverages	Beverage Sales	Beverage Cost %
Beer	$ 2,500	$10,000	25.0%
Wine	12,000	40,000	30.0%
Spirits	6,000	30,000	20.0%
Total	$20,500	$80,000	25.6%
#2 Outlet Name: Starlight Bar			
Product	Cost of Beverages	Beverage Sales	Beverage Cost %
Beer	$ 3,750	$15,000	25.0%
Wine	1,500	5,000	30.0%
Spirits	5,100	25,500	20.0%
Total	$10,350	$45,500	22.7%
#3 Outlet Name: Harry O's			
Product	Cost of Beverages	Beverage Sales	Beverage Cost %
Beer	$11,250	$45,000	25.0%
Wine	2,100	7,000	30.0%
Spirits	3,000	15,000	20.0%
Total	$16,350	$67,000	24.4%

FIGURE 5.17 Raider Resort

Beverage Sales Percentage Recap				
Unit	Beer	Wine	Spirits	Total Sales
Banquets	12.5%	50.0%	37.5%	100%
Starlight Bar	33.0%	11.0%	56.0%	100%
Harry O's	67.0%	10.5%	22.5%	100%

is not the same. The reason that each unit varies in total beverage cost percentage is due to sales mix, the guests' overall preference for the specific product choices offered for sale. In other words, guests, and not management alone, have helped to determine the final beverage cost percentages in each of the units.

Managers can directly help to influence guest selection and sales mix by such techniques as strategic pricing, effective menu design, and creative marketing, but to some degree it will always be the guest who will determine an operation's overall cost percentage. This is so because it is customers and their choices that determine an operations' sales mix.

In the example of the Raider Resort, it is easy to analyze the sales mix by examining Figure 5.17, a detailing of the beverage products selected by guests in each beverage outlet.

Each sales percent in Figure 5.17 was computed using this formula:

$$\frac{\text{Item dollar sales}}{\text{Total beverage sales}} = \text{Item \% of total beverage sales}$$

Therefore, in the case of beer sales in the banquets area, and using the data from Figure 5.16:

$$\frac{\text{Banquet beer sales}}{\text{Total banquet beverage sales}} = \text{\% banquet beer sales}$$

or

$$\frac{\$10,000}{\$80,000} = 12.5\%$$

As indicated, each beverage outlet operates with a unique sales mix. Figure 5.17 shows that in the banquet area the sales mix is heavy in wines and spirits, the choice of many guests when they are at a reception or dining out.

The Starlight Bar clientele is older, and their preferred drink tends to be spirits. Harry O's, on the other hand, caters to a younger crowd that, in this example, prefers beer. It is important to remember that, despite controls that are in place, costs that are in line, and effective management policies, variations in product cost percentages can still occur due to sales mix, rather than other factors. Experienced managers recognize this fact, and as a result, they monitor sales mix carefully to determine its impact on the overall product cost percentages of both food and beverages.

Because you now understand sales mix, you can recognize that the effective marketing and promotion of good (lower product cost) items can help you reduce your product cost percentage and increase your profitability, while allowing the portion size, recipe composition, and product quality of your menu items to remain constant.

Cost Control Around the World

It is easy to see that sales mix has a significant impact on an operation's product cost percentages. This is true with food, and it is especially true in the area of alcoholic beverages because the drinking preferences of local customers vary greatly across the globe.

You can readily see this by reviewing the alcoholic beverage consumption patterns of countries that consume the most beer, wine, and spirits per capita. This brief table indicates the countries where per capita consumption of beer, wine, and spirits vary.

It is easy to see that a multinational restaurant offering its guests beer, wine, and spirits choices could experience very different sales results in the countries shown in the table based solely on the preferences of the country's alcoholic beverage drinkers. Thus, a manager of a steakhouse in Berlin, Germany, will very likely experience a different beverage sales mix than will a manager operating the same steakhouse in Florence, Italy, or in Moscow, Russia. Foodservice managers working internationally must monitor and carefully review the impact local dining and drinking preferences will have on their sales mix and, as a result, on their product cost percentages.

Consumption Rank	Beer	Wine	Spirits
1	Czech Republic	Luxembourg	Russia
2	Ireland	France	Thailand
3	Germany	Italy	Bahamas

Source: LiveScience Staff, "Global Alcohol Consumption: Top 20 Booze-Drinking Countries," *LiveScience* (Feb. 15, 2012).

INCREASE PRICE RELATIVE TO PORTION SIZE

In many cases, managers facing rising product cost percentages feel they simply must increase their selling prices. Although increasing prices is often relatively easy to do, this area must be approached with the greatest caution of all. There is no bigger temptation in foodservice than to raise prices in an effort to counteract management's ineffectiveness at controlling product costs. This temptation must be resisted.

There are times, of course, when selling prices on selected menu items must be increased. This is especially true in inflationary times or in terms of unique product shortages. Price increases should be considered, however, only when all other alternatives and needed steps to control costs have been considered and effectively implemented. Any price increases passed on to guests should reflect only increases in your costs, not your inefficiency.

While in most cases, it is important to keep menu prices low, some operators may be afraid to charge 25 or 50 cents more for similar menu items than their competition. In some instances, keeping prices in line with competitors' prices is a good strategy. More frequently, however, decor, quality of product, and service may allow you to charge higher prices than your competitors. Experienced managers know that, given the proper facility ambiance, most guests will not react negatively to small variances in prices because it is perceived value, not price alone, which drives a guest's purchase decision.

You have learned that managing the food and beverage production process is a complex task and that it must be accomplished with the utmost skill. In fact, the goal of all your purchasing and production systems should be to deliver to guests only high-quality products sold at a fair price. It is important that your food and beverage products are prepared correctly and at an appropriate cost to you, but it is just as important to ensure that these products are sold to guests at prices that help ensure your operation's profitability. For that reason, the important task of properly pricing your menu items will be the topic of the next chapter.

Technology Tools

In the past, restaurants were slow to install technological tools in kitchen areas where production staff could easily use them. Increasingly, however, these installations are being made. In a professional kitchen, cost control efforts are often shared between management and the production staff. Advanced technology programs available for kitchen production use include those that can help both you and your production staff members:

1. Perform nutrition-related analysis of menu items, including:
   a. Recipe nutrient analysis
   b. Diet analysis
   c. FDA (Food and Drug Administration) food labels
   d. Diabetic exchange
   e. Weight management components
2. Calculate total recipe costs and per portion costs.
3. Compute product yield and product waste percentages.
4. Compute actual versus ideal costs based on product issues.
5. Estimate and compute daily food cost.
6. Maintain product usage records by:
   a. Vendor
   b. Product
   c. Food category
   d. Individual menu item
   e. Ingredient
7. Compare portions served to portions produced to monitor overportioning and waste.
8. Report food and beverage product usage variances based on actual sales.
9. Suggest usage for carryover products.
10. Conduct "make versus buy" calculations on convenience items to optimize employee productivity and minimize costs.

FUN ON THE WEB!

Many of the software programs available for assisting in foodservice operations are geared toward commercial restaurants. Some of the very best programs, however, have been developed for the institutional foodservice market.

To view the product features offered by two of these companies, search the Internet to locate the website of Computrition, a company that was originally formed to assist health care facility foodservice operators. Next, locate the home page of the Cbord Group, a company that was formed to assist foodservice managers operating campus dining facilities.

Apply What You Have Learned

Jennifer Tye is the manager of a fine dining restaurant chain that serves its guests a variety of traditional Southern dishes prepared with the very finest of ingredients. It is most famous for its upscale version of Chicken Fried Steak.

At Jennifer's restaurant, this dish (beef steak, seasoned, breaded, and then pan fried) is prepared using USDA Prime rib-eye steak. As the price of rib-eye has increased, Jennifer's food cost percentage on this item has risen dramatically.

Currently, Jennifer is considering whether the selling price of this dish should be increased significantly or if she should take other steps to help reduce her overall product cost percentage.

1. What issues should Jennifer consider prior to making this decision?

2. What alternatives to raising prices do you think are available to Jennifer?

3. What would you advise Jennifer to do?

Key Terms and Concepts

*T*he following are terms and concepts discussed in the chapter that are important for you as a manager. To help you review, please define the terms below.

cost of sales	beverage cost percentage	operational efficiency
beginning inventory	standardized recipe cost	ratio
padding inventory	sheet	head size
purchases	as purchased (AP)	hydrometer
food available for sale	edible portion (EP)	spotter
goods available for sale	yield test	mystery shopper
ending inventory	butcher's yield test	open bar
cost of food consumed	waste percentage	hosted bar
employee meal cost	yield percentage	sales mix
cost of food sold	edible portion cost	
food cost percentage	(EP cost)	
cost of beverage sold	attainable product cost	

Test Your Skills

You may download the Excel spreadsheets for the Test Your Skills exercises from the student companion website at **www.wiley.com/college/dopson**. Complete the exercises by placing your answers in the shaded boxes and answering the questions as indicated.

1. Belinda Gates is the manager at the Roasted Pepper restaurant. Belinda records her monthly food and beverage sales separately. She also follows the *USAR* recommendation and thus separately calculates her product costs for food, beverages, and her overall cost of sales. Help Belinda complete this portion of her monthly operating records by calculating her total cost of sales and all of her cost of sales percentages for the month.

Roasted Pepper: Sales and Cost of Sales		
	This Month	**Percent**
SALES		
Food	$ 90,000	75%
Beverages	30,000	25%
Total Sales	$120,000	100%
COST OF SALES		
Food	$ 25,200	
Beverages	6,600	
Total Cost of Sales		

2. Saint John's Hospital foodservice director, Herman Zindu, has a problem. He has the following information about his operation for the month of April, but has forgotten how to compute cost of food sold for the month. Use Herman's figures to compute actual cost of food sold for his operation.

   Could Herman have computed this figure if he had not taken a physical inventory on April 30? Why or why not?

Inventory March 31			$22,184.50
April Purchases:			
Meats		$11,501.00	
Dairy		6,300.00	
Fruits and vegetables		9,641.00	
All others foods		32,384.00	
Total Purchases			
Number of employees eating monthly	2,550		
Cost per employee meal	$ 1.25		
Inventory on April 30			$23,942.06

Beginning inventory	
Purchases	
Goods available for sale	
Ending inventory	
Cost of food consumed	
Employee meals (30 days)	
Cost of food sold	

3. Spike Dykes operates the student foodservice in a dormitory at Clairmont College. Spike is interested in calculating his "Food Cost per Student Meal Served." Data about his costs and meals served for the spring semester can be found in the following table. Help Spike complete the table.

In which months did Spike achieve his lowest and highest cost per meal? Spike wants his average cost per meal for the semester to be below $3.00. Did he achieve this goal?

	Jan	Feb	March	April	May	Total
Beginning inventory	$22,500	$21,750	$26,500	$25,500	$16,000	
Purchases	$65,000	$64,750	$63,000	$64,500	$64,300	
Goods available for sale						
Ending inventory	$21,750	$26,500	$25,500	$16,000	$12,000	
Cost of food consumed						
Employee meals	$ 5,750	$ 5,500	$ 5,250	$ 5,000	$ 4,850	
Cost of food sold						
Meals served	20,750	20,100	21,500	21,250	19,000	
Cost per meal						

4. Jana Foster is the general manager for a new restaurant in the Champos Restaurants chain. This new facility is located in a beachfront resort town, and sales there are excellent. The problem, according to Jana's regional manager, is that the new operation is consistently operating at a beverage cost percentage higher than the company average. Jana's regional manager has flown to Jana's town to see why her beverage cost percentage is too high. The prices set by the company for all restaurants are $3.00 for beer, $3.50 for wine, $5.00 for spirits (nonfrozen specialty drinks), and $7.00 for frozen specialty drinks.

Help Jana compare her beverage cost percentages with the following company averages.

Company Averages				
Product	Product Mix	Cost of Beverages	Beverage Sales	Beverage Cost %
Beer	30%	$24,336	$121,680	
Wine	20%	20,280	81,120	
Spirits (nonfrozen specialty drinks)	30%	30,420	121,680	
Spirits (frozen specialty drinks)	20%	24,336	81,120	
Total				

Jana's Beachfront Restaurant				
Product	Product Mix	Cost of Beverages	Beverage Sales	Beverage Cost %
Beer	15%	$14,700	$ 73,500	
Wine	5%	6,125	24,500	
Spirits (nonfrozen specialty drinks)	15%	18,375	73,500	
Spirits (frozen specialty drinks)	65%	95,550	318,500	
Total				

Look at the sales mix and the beverage cost percentages of both the company and the beachfront restaurant. Explain why Jana's total beverage cost percentages are consistently higher than the company averages. What would you advise Jana to tell her regional manager?

5. "Fast Eddie" Green operates a restaurant in the casino town of Taloona. He is checking over the work of his assistant manager, who has been newly hired. One of the jobs of the assistant manager is to complete daily the six-column food cost estimate. "Fast Eddie" finds that, although the purchase and sales data are there for the first 10 days of the accounting period, the form has not been completed. Complete the form for "Fast Eddie" so that he can go home.

| Weekday | PURCHASES | | SALES | | COST % | |
	Today	To Date	Today	To Date	Today	To Date
1/11	$ 1,645.80		$ 3,842.50			
1/12	2,006.40		2,970.05			
1/13	1,107.20		2,855.20			
1/14	986.24		3,001.45			
1/15	1,245.60		3,645.20			
1/16	2,006.40		4,850.22			
1/17	0.00		6,701.55			
1/18	1,799.90		3,609.20			
1/19	851.95		2,966.60			
1/20	924.50		3,105.25			
Total						

6. Elaine is the director of foodservice at a large retirement center, and she has asked Gerry, one of her managers, to investigate the costs involved in adding a carving station to the regular Sunday brunch menu. Gerry is trying to decide which carved meats could be served. He must first determine the EP costs and yields of the various kinds of meats. Help him calculate the EP cost and yield of an inside round of beef.

Butcher's Yield Test Results

Unit Name: Elaine's   Date Tested: May 20

Item: Inside Round

Specification: # 138

AP Amount Tested: 20 lb.

Price per Pound AP: $6.00

Loss Detail	Pounds	Ounces	Total Ounces	% of Original
AP weight	20 lb.	0 oz.		
Fat loss	3 lb.	6 oz.		
Bone loss	2 lb.	4 oz.		
Cooking loss	1 lb.	12 oz.		
Carving Loss	0	8 oz.		
Total Production Loss				
EP Weight				

Net product yield %:

Yield test performed by: GW

EP cost per pound:

7. Lebron operates "Ham from Heaven," a sandwich shop specializing in slow roasted spicy ham sandwiches. Currently, Lebron buys bone-in hams and roasts them in-house. These hams cost $2.99 per pound and produce a 58 percent usable yield. Semi-boneless hams of the same quality cost $3.99 per pound, with a 78 percent yield. Boneless hams of the same quality would cost $6.99 per pound and produce a 96 percent yield. Calculate the EP cost per pound of each alternative.

   Choose the alternative you would recommend to Lebron and explain your reason for choosing it. Specifically, what factors would influence your decision?

Ham from Heaven			
	AP Price per Pound	Yield	EP Cost per Pound
Bone-in ham			
Semi-boneless ham			
Boneless ham			

8. Maxine Wilson is the director of dietary services at State College. Each semester, Maxine carefully monitors the average cost of serving her students dinner in the residence halls. Maxine's attainable costs and actual food costs for the most recently completed semester are shown below. Calculate the efficiency ratio, dollar variance, and percentage variance in each of Maxine's product categories and her total dinner cost per student below.

   What was the overall percentage variance for Maxine's dinner cost per student? Is this cause for concern?

   Which product category showed the highest percentage variance? What do you think may have caused this variance?

Product Category	Actual Cost	Attainable Cost	Efficiency Ratio	Dollar Variance	Percentage Variance
Meat	$1.09	$1.06			
Seafood	$0.55	$0.41			
Fruits	$0.48	$0.51			
Vegetables	$0.46	$0.45			
Dairy products	$0.29	$0.28			
Desserts	$0.25	$0.30			
Cost Per student (dinner)	$3.12	$3.01			

9. Nancy operates a takeout cookie store in the mall. Business is good, and guests seem to enjoy the products. Her employees, mostly young teens, are a problem because they seem to like the products also. Nancy takes a physical inventory on a weekly basis. This week, her total cost of goods sold figure was $725.58. Nancy has determined that this week she will also compute her attainable food cost and her operational efficiency ratio. Help Nancy by completing the following information using the attainable food cost form.

After completing the form, give Nancy five suggestions to keep her employees from eating all of her profits.

Attainable Food Cost

Unit Name: <u>Nancy's</u>

Date Prepared: <u>1/22</u>   Time Period: <u>1/15 to 1/21</u>

Prepared By: <u>S.L.</u>

Item	Number Sold in Dozens	Cost per Dozen	Total Cost	Menu Price per Dozen	Total Sales
Chocolate chip	85	$1.32		$3.40	
Macadamia	60	$1.61		$4.10	
Coconut chip	70	$0.83		$2.95	
Fudge	141	$1.42		$3.80	
M & M	68	$1.39		$3.40	
Soft drinks	295	$0.16		$0.85	
Coffee	160	$0.09		$0.75	
Attainable product cost					

Actual product cost: _____

Attainable product cost: _____

Operational efficiency ratio: _____

Attainable food cost %: _____

---

10. This chapter introduced six different action steps managers could take to reduce their cost of food and cost of food percentages when they encounter rising costs. In some foodservice settings, such as schools, colleges, and correctional and health care facilities, however, managers are allotted a fixed amount of money to spend per meal served and this amount may only be adjusted on an annual basis. Thus, managers of these facility types cannot readily increase their prices in the face of rising costs. Review the six alternative cost reduction strategies presented in the chapter and identify three specific actions you would recommend noncommercial foodservice managers could take to stay within their budgets during times of rapidly rising product costs.

CHAPTER 6

Managing Food and Beverage Pricing

OVERVIEW

This chapter begins by teaching you about the different kinds of menus you will encounter as a hospitality manager. The types of menus offered directly affect the prices managers can charge for their menu items. Knowledge of various menu formats can also help you reduce costs through effective utilization of your food and beverage products as well as better utilization of your staff. This chapter examines and analyzes, in detail, the factors that influence the prices you will charge for the menu items you will sell.

Finally, the chapter explains the procedures used to assign individual menu item prices based on cost and collected sales data. By understanding the pricing process you can help ensure that your menu items will generate the sales revenue you need to meet your profit goals.

Chapter Outline

- Menu Formats
- Menu Specials
- Factors Affecting Menu Pricing
- Assigning Menu Prices
- Special Pricing Situations
- Technology Tools
- Apply What You Have Learned
- Key Terms and Concepts
- Test Your Skills

LEARNING OUTCOMES

At the conclusion of this chapter, you will be able to:
- Choose the best menu format for a specific foodservice operation.
- Identify the variables to be considered when establishing menu prices.
- Assign menu prices to menu items based on the items' costs, popularity, and profitability.

181

MENU FORMATS •————————————————————

If you have determined that your purchasing, receiving, storing, issuing, and production controls are well in line, you have an excellent chance of reaching your profit goals. It is possible to find, however, that even when these areas are well managed, food and beverage costs are still too high to achieve your profit targets. When this is the case, the problem may well lie in the fundamental areas of menu format, product pricing, or both.

Menus are one of the most effective ways managers can communicate with their guests. In a foodservice operation, the term "menu" actually means two things. First, the "menu" refers to the items available for sale to guests. Secondly, the term "menu" refers to the specific way items available for sale are presented or communicated to guests. Alternatives for menu presentation include websites, printed paper menus, on-premise menu display boards or blackboards, and even oral recitation by servers.

Some facilities create separate menus for their food and alcoholic beverage products. Other operators find it more appropriate to have menus that combine both their food and beverage offerings. Regardless of the choice the business makes, the menu provides an excellent opportunity to build impulse sales or to communicate the special products and services a facility has to offer.

With the advent of computers and inexpensive on-premise color printing capabilities, many operators find that they can create their own menus for a very low cost. As a result, they can change their menus more frequently than they would have been able to in the past. In addition, they can create menu **tip-ons,** which are smaller menu segments clipped to more permanent menus. Tip-ons can prove very effective in influencing your customers' impulse buying.

Menus and their design can vary greatly so it makes good sense to examine menu formats before addressing the topic of how to price menu items. Menu formats in foodservice establishments generally fall into one of the following three major categories:

1. Standard menu
2. Daily menu
3. Cycle menu

Each of these formats can help your efforts to control food costs if they are used in the proper setting.

STANDARD MENU

The **standard menu** is the same every day. It can be printed and handed to guests, displayed in the operation, or recited by service staff. It is the menu format most common in commercial restaurants. Examples of commercial restaurants that utilize the standard menu include Cracker Barrel, Red Lobster, Applebee's, and Outback Steakhouses. You may periodically add or delete a menu item, but the standard menu generally remains unchanged on a day-to-day basis. There are many operational advantages to such a menu format. First, the standard menu simplifies your ordering process. The menu remains constant each day, so it is easy to know which products must be purchased to produce the menu items offered for sale.

Second, guests tend to have a good number of choices when selecting from a standard menu. This is true because virtually every item that can be produced by the kitchen is available for selection by each guest entering the operation.

A third advantage of the standard menu is that guest preference data are easily obtained because the total number of menu items that will be served stays constant and, thus, is generally smaller than in some alternative menu formats. As you learned in Chapter 3, menu item sales histories can be used to accurately compute menu item popularity and that makes it easier to create production schedules and buy needed ingredients. In addition, standard menus often become marketing tools for your operation because guests soon become familiar with and return for their favorite menu items.

The standard menu tends to be most popular in those segments of the food service business where the guest selects the location of the dining experience, as contrasted with situations where a guest's choice is restricted. Examples of restricted-choice situations include cafeterias in college residence halls where students are required to dine in on-campus, a hospital where patients during their stay must choose their menu selections from that hospital only, and an elementary school's cafeteria.

Despite its many advantages, the standard menu does have drawbacks from a cost control standpoint. First, standard menus often do not allow for easy utilization of carryovers. In fact, in many cases, items that are produced for a standard menu and remain unsold must be discarded because the next day their quality will not be acceptable to guests. An example is a quick-service restaurant that produces too many hamburgers for a busy dinner period and does not sell all of them. Indeed, for some quick-service restaurants, a burger that is made but not sold within five minutes (or less) is discarded. Contrast that cost control strategy with one that says that cooked burgers not sold within five minutes will be chopped and added to the house specialty chili, and it is easy to see how menu design and the specific items placed on the menu can directly affect food costs and food cost control.

A second disadvantage of the standard menu is its lack of ability to respond quickly to market changes and product cost changes. For example, a restaurant that does not list green beans on the menu cannot take advantage of the seasonal harvest of green beans, a time when they are at their peak in freshness and can be purchased at a very low price. Conversely, if management has decided that its two house vegetables will be broccoli and corn, even considerable price increases in these two items will have to be absorbed by the operation because these two menu items are listed on the permanent (standard) menu. This can cause serious problems if the ingredients needed to produce listed menus item increase significantly in price. An extreme example of this kind of problem was found in a quick-service seafood restaurant chain that found it was paying almost three times what it had the previous year for a seafood item that constituted approximately 80 percent of its menu sales. A foreign government had restricted fishing for this product off its shores, and the price the operation paid for the fish it offered on its menu skyrocketed. This chain was nearly devastated by this turn of events. Needless to say, management quickly moved to add chicken, lower-cost seafood products, and even seafood pastas to the menu to counter the effect of this very large price increase.

Whenever possible, you should monitor food prices with an eye to making seasonal adjustments that emphasize foods when their costs are low and deemphasizes those foods when their costs are high. The standard menu, however, makes this quite difficult. Some restaurant groups respond to this problem by changing their standard menu on a planned schedule. They develop a standard menu for the summer, for example, and another for the winter. In this way, they can take advantage of seasonal cost savings and add some variety to their menus (by introducing new items and removing less popular ones), but still maintain the core menu items for which they are known. By doing so, they continue to enjoy the cost-related benefits of offering a standard menu while minimizing the disadvantages of using such a menu format.

DAILY MENU

In some restaurants, you might elect to operate without a standard menu and, instead, implement a **daily menu,** that is, a menu that changes every day. This format is especially popular in some upscale restaurants where the chef's daily creations are viewed with great anticipation, and even some awe, by eager guests. The daily menu offers some advantages over the standard menu. For example, management can respond very quickly to changes in ingredient or item prices. In fact, that is one of the daily menu's great advantages. In addition, carryovers are less of a problem because any product unsold from the previous day has at least the potential of being incorporated, often as a new dish, into the next day's menu.

Every silver lining has its cloud, however. For all its flexibility, the daily menu is recommended only for very special situations due to the tremendous control drawbacks associated with its implementation. First, item popularity data are difficult to obtain because the items on any given day may never have been served in that particular combination. Thus, the preparation of specific items in certain quantities can be pure guesswork, and this is most often an inefficient way of determining production schedules.

Second, it may be difficult to plan to have the necessary ingredients on hand to prepare the daily menu if the menu is not known well ahead of time. How does one decide on Monday whether one should order tuna steaks or sirloin steaks for the menu on Thursday? Obviously, this situation requires that even the daily menu be planned far enough in advance to allow an operation's purchasing agent to select and order the items necessary to produce the daily menu.

Third, the daily menu may sometimes serve as a marketing tool, but it can just as often serve as a disappointment to guests who had a wonderful menu item the last time they dined at a particular establishment and have now returned only to find that their favorite item is not being served. On a positive note, it is very unlikely that any guest will get bored with a routine at a daily menu restaurant because the routine is, in fact, no routine at all.

Both the standard menu and the daily menu have control advantages and disadvantages. A third menu format, the cycle menu, is an effort by management to enjoy the best aspects of both of these approaches and to minimize their respective disadvantages.

CYCLE MENU

A **cycle menu** is a menu that is in effect for a specific time period. The length of the cycle refers to the length of time the menu is in effect. Thus, we refer to a 7-day cycle menu, a 21-day cycle menu, a 30-day cycle menu, or one of any other length of time.

Cycle menus are utilized most often by institutions such as colleges and universities, hospitals, assisted living facilities, correctional facilities, and other settings where the same guest, or the same type of guest, is served every day.

Typically, a cycle menu is repeated on a regular basis. For example, a particular cycle menu could consist of four 7-day periods. If each of the four periods were labeled as A, B, C, and D, the cycle periods could rotate as illustrated in Figure 6.1.

Cost Control Around the World

In the United States, the daily à la carte menu is by far the style that is most commonly used by restaurants. When managers use an à la carte menu, guests select individual menu items and each menu item is priced separately. As a result, for example, guests ordering from an à la carte menu might or might not choose an appetizer to begin their meal. Similarly, guests might or might not choose a dessert to complete their meals. In all cases, with the à la carte menu, guests choose what they want and are charged only for the items they select.

In many other parts of the world, including most of Europe, the **prix fixe** (pronounced "prefix") **menu** is the more common style. When an operation offers a prix fixe menu, guests choose from a predetermined list of items presented as a multicourse meal. The items included in the meal are then sold at one set price. Thus, for example, a guest selecting roast chicken for an entrée might also receive crab bisque as an appetizer, crème brûlée as a dessert, and a choice of coffee or tea as a beverage. In this example, the guest would pay one set (fixed) price for all of the items included in their prix fixe menu selection.

Each menu style has its advantages and disadvantages, and each is popular in different parts of the world. But managers must be very aware of the differences between these two menu styles because the differences directly affect the way managers using each format make appropriate pricing decisions for their operations.

FIGURE 6.1 Sample Cycle Menu Rotation

Days	Cycle
1–7	A
8–14	B
15–21	C
22–28	D
29–35	A
36–42	B
43–49	C
50–56	D
57–63	A

Within each cycle, the individual menu items offered to guests will vary on a daily basis. For example, cycle menu A might consist of the following seven dinner items:

Day 1	Monday	Cheese Enchiladas
Day 2	Tuesday	Turkey and Bread Dressing
Day 3	Wednesday	Corned Beef and Cabbage
Day 4	Thursday	Fried Chicken Strips
Day 5	Friday	Stir Fried Lobster
Day 6	Saturday	Lasagna
Day 7	Sunday	Beef Pot Roast

These same menu items will be served again when cycle menu A repeats itself on days 29 through 35.

Day 29	Monday	Cheese Enchiladas
Day 30	Tuesday	Turkey and Bread Dressing
Day 31	Wednesday	Corned Beef and Cabbage
Day 32	Thursday	Fried Chicken Strips
Day 33	Friday	Stir-Fried Lobster
Day 34	Saturday	Lasagna
Day 35	Sunday	Beef Pot Roast

In the typical case, cycle menus B, C, and D would consist of many (or all) different menu items. In this manner, no menu item will be repeated more frequently than desired by management.

Cycle menus make the most sense when guests dine with you on a very regular basis, either through the choice of the individual, such as a college student or summer camper eating in a dining hall, or through the choice of an institution, such as a hospital or correctional facility. In cases like this, menu variety is very important. The cycle menu provides a systematic method for incorporating that variety into the menu. At a glance, the foodservice manager can determine how often, for example, fried chicken strips will be served per week, month, or year, and how frequently bread dressing rather than saffron rice is served with baked chicken. In this respect, the cycle menu can offer more choice to the guest than will the standard menu. With cycle menus, production personnel can be trained to produce a wider variety of foods than with the standard menu, thus expanding their skills, but requiring fewer skills than might be needed with a daily menu concept.

Cycle menus also have the advantage of being able to systematically incorporate today's carryovers (see Chapter 4) into tomorrow's finished product. This is an extremely important cost-related advantage. Also, because of its cyclical nature, management should have a good idea of guest preferences and, thus, be able to schedule and plan production to a greater degree than with the daily menu.

Purchasing, too, is simplified because the menu is known ahead of time, and menu ingredients that will appear on all the different cycles can be ordered with ample lead time. Inventory levels are easier to maintain as well because, as is the case with the standard menu, product usage is well known. Even price reductions in item costs (e.g., incorporating the use of lower cost and locally grown produce during peak harvest periods) can be incorporated into cycle menu planning, thus lowering costs and maximizing product quality.

To illustrate the differences and the impact of operating under the three different menu systems, consider the case of Larry, Moe, and Curly Jo, three foodservice operators who wish to serve roast turkey and dressing for their dinner entrée on a Saturday night in April. Larry operates a restaurant with a standard menu. If he is to print a standard menu that allows him to serve turkey in April, and does not do a menu reprint, he will be required to offer the same item in January and June. If he is to utilize any carryover parts of the turkey, he must offer a second turkey item on his menu, which also must be made available every day. Larry is not sure all the trouble and cost is worth it!

In addition, consider the expense involved in a national chain restaurant with thousands of outlets. If this turkey dinner menu item needed to be changed in any way, reprints of menus reflecting the change would likely be very costly. If Larry is the **CEO (chief executive officer)**, the highest ranking member of a national or international foodservice organization, any decision he makes to change the standard menu to incorporate new items would indeed be a major undertaking.

Moe operates a restaurant with a daily menu. For him, serving roast turkey and dressing on a Saturday in April is quite easy. His problem, however, is that he has no idea how much to produce because he has never before served this item at this time of the year and on this specific evening in his restaurant. Also, few of the guests he has served in the past year are likely to know in advance about his decision to serve the menu item. What if no one orders it?

Curly Jo operates on a cycle menu. She can indeed put roast turkey and dressing on the cycle. If it sells well, she will keep it on the cycle menu. If it does not, it will be removed from the next cycle. Curly Jo makes a note to herself that she should record how well it sells and leave a space in the cycle for the utilization of any carryover product that might exist within the next few days. The advantages of the cycle menu, in this specific situation, are quite apparent.

MENU SPECIALS

Regardless of the menu format used, you can generally incorporate relatively minor menu changes on a regular basis. This can be accomplished through the offering of daily or weekly **menu specials**—that is, menu items that will appear on the menu as you desire and then are removed when the items are sold or it is discontinued. These daily or weekly specials are most often an effort on the part of management to provide menu variety, take advantage of low-cost raw ingredients, utilize carryover products, or test-market the potential of new menu items.

The menu special is a powerful cost control tool. Properly utilized, it helps shape the future menu by testing guest acceptance of new menu items while providing opportunities for you to respond to the challenges of using carryovers or other food and beverage products you have in inventory.

FACTORS AFFECTING MENU PRICING •────────

Regardless of the menu format utilized, managers must carefully determine their menu items' selling prices. A great deal of important information has been written in the area of menu pricing and menu pricing strategy. A great deal of nonsense has also been written. For the serious foodservice operator, menu pricing is a topic that deserves its own significant consideration and study. Menu pricing is directly related to cost control by virtue of the basic profit formula presented in Chapter 1:

Revenue − Expenses = Profit

FUN ON THE WEB!

Revenue management is the term hospitality professionals use to describe the process of monitoring and determining selling prices. Revenue management is an important process in hotels and restaurants. Effective revenue management requires an understanding of consumer buying behavior, product costs, and customer-centric revenue optimization. John Wiley publishes a popular book specifically on this topic. To review the book go to the Amazon website.

When you arrive, enter "Revenue Management for the Hospitality Industry; Hayes and Miller" in the search bar.

When foodservice operators find that profits are too low, they frequently question whether their prices (and thus their revenues) are too low. It is important to remember, however, that revenue and price are not synonymous terms.

Revenue means the amount spent by all guests. It is the amount of money an operation takes in. **Selling price** (price) refers to the amount charged to one guest for his or her purchase. Thus, total revenue is generated by the following formula:

Price × Number sold = Total revenue

From this formula, it can be seen that there are actually two components of total revenue. Price is one component, and the other is the number of items sold. It is most often true that as selling price increases the number of items sold will decrease. For this reason, price increases must be evaluated based on their impact on total revenue and not on price alone.

To illustrate how price and number sold affect total revenue, assume that you own a quick-service restaurant (QSR) chain. You are considering raising the price of small drinks from $1.00 to $1.25. Figure 6.2 illustrates the possible effects of this price increase on total revenue in a single one of your units. Note especially that, in at least one alternative result, increasing your selling price will actually have the effect of *reducing* your total revenue.

Experienced foodservice managers know that increasing prices without giving added value to guests can result in higher prices but, frequently, lower revenue because of a reduction in the number of guest purchases. This is true because guests demand a good **price/value relationship** when making a purchase. The price/value relationship simply reflects guests' view of how much value they are receiving for the prices they are paying.

Perhaps no area of hospitality management is less understood than the area of pricing. This is not surprising when you consider the many factors that play a part in the pricing decision. For some foodservice operators, inefficiency in cost control

FIGURE 6.2 Alternative Results of Selling Price Increases

Old Price	New Price	Number Served	Total Revenue	Revenue Result
$1.00		200	$200.00	
	$1.25	250	$312.50	Increase
	$1.25	200	$250.00	Increase
	$1.25	160	$200.00	No change
	$1.25	150	$187.50	Decrease

is passed on to guests in the form of higher prices. In fact, sound pricing decisions should always be based on establishing a positive price/value relationship in the mind of the guest.

Is important to recognize that most foodservice operators face fairly similar product costs when they purchase the ingredients needed to produce the items they sell. Whether the product on the menu is pancakes or Prime Rib, wholesale prices for needed raw ingredients may vary only slightly from one supplier to the next. In some cases, this variation is due to volume buying, whereas in others, it is the result of the relationship established with the vendor. Regardless of the source, the fact remains that variations in prices that operators pay for ingredients are often small relative to potential variations in menu prices. This becomes easier to understand when you realize that a menu item's selling price is most often a function of much more than its product cost. In fact, menu prices are significantly affected by all of the following factors:

Factors Influencing Menu Price

1. Economic conditions
2. Local competition
3. Service levels
4. Guest type
5. Product quality
6. Portion size
7. Ambience
8. Meal period
9. Location
10. Sales mix

ECONOMIC CONDITIONS

The economic conditions that exist in a local area or even in an entire country can have a significant impact on the prices that restaurant managers can charge for their menu items. When an economy is robust and growing, managers generally have a greater ability to charge higher prices for the items they sell. When a local economy is in a recession or is weakened by other events, a manager's ability to raise or even maintain prices in response to rising costs may be more limited. In most cases, managers will not have the ability to directly influence the strength of their local economy. It is the manager's job, however, to monitor local economic conditions and to carefully consider these conditions when establishing menu prices.

LOCAL COMPETITION

While the prices charged by competitors may be important, this factor is often too closely monitored by the typical foodservice operator. It may seem to some managers that the average guest is vitally concerned with low price and nothing more. In reality, small variations in price generally make little difference to the buying behavior of the average guest.

If a group of young professionals goes out for pizza and beer after work, the major determinant will not likely be whether the selling price for the beer is $4.00 in one establishment or $4.25 in another. This small variation in price is simply not likely to be the major factor in determining which operation the group of young professionals will choose to visit. Other factors will be more important.

Your competition's selling price is somewhat important when establishing price, but it is a well-known fact in foodservice that someone can always sell a lesser-quality product for a lesser price. The price competitors charge for their products can be useful information in helping you arrive at your own selling price. It should not, however, be the only determining factor in your pricing decisions.

Successful foodservice operators spend their time focusing on building guest value in their own operation and not in attempting to mimic the efforts of the competition. Despite the fact that many managers feel customers only want low prices, it is important to remember that, in the consumer's mind, higher prices are most often associated with higher-quality products and, thus, with a better price/value relationship.

SERVICE LEVELS

The service levels that an operation provides its guests directly affect the prices the operation can charge. Most guests expect to pay more for the same product when service levels are higher. Thus, for example, the can of soda sold from a vending machine is generally less expensive than a similar-sized soda served by a human being. In a like manner, many pizza chains charge a lower price, for example, for a large pizza that is picked up by the guest than for that same pizza when it is delivered to the guest's door. This is as it should be. The hospitality industry is, in fact, a service industry, and the cost of delivering a pizza is greater than the cost incurred when a guest picks the pizza up.

Because service levels impact pricing directly, as the personal level of service increases in an operation, selling prices may also be increased. This personal service may range from the delivery of products as in the delivered pizza example, to a manager's decision to improve customer service by increasing the number of servers in a busy dining room and, thus, improving service quality by reducing the number of guests each worker must serve.

These examples should not imply that extra income from increased menu prices must go only to pay for extra labor required to increase service levels. Guests are willing to pay more for increased service levels, but this higher price should cover extra labor cost and provide for extra profit as well. In the hospitality industry, those companies that have been able to survive and thrive over the years have done so because of their uncompromising commitment to high levels of guest service, and they charge menu prices that reflect those service levels.

GUEST TYPE

All guests want good value for their money. But some guest types are simply less price sensitive than others. The question of what represents good value varies by the type of clientele. An example of this can clearly be seen in the pricing decisions of convenience stores across the United States. In these facilities, food products such as premade sandwiches, fruit, drinks, cookies, and the like are sold at relatively high prices. The guests these stores cater to, however, value speed and convenience above all else. For this speed and convenience, the customers are willing to pay a premium price.

In a like manner, guests at an expensive steakhouse restaurant are less likely to respond negatively to small variations in drink prices than are guests at a corner neighborhood tavern. A thorough understanding of who their guests are and what these guests value most is critical to the ongoing success of foodservice managers as they established their operations' menu prices.

PRODUCT QUALITY

In nearly every instance, a guest's quality perception of any specific menu item offered for sale in the foodservice business can range from very low to very high. These perceptions are the direct result of how the guest views a restaurant's menu offerings. These perceptions are directly affected by food quality; but they should never be shaped by the guest view of a menu item's wholesomeness or safety. All foods must be wholesome and safe to eat. In most cases, guests' perceptions of quality will be based on a variety of factors, only one of which is product quality. Visual product quality and grade of ingredients, as well as portion size and service level, are additional factors that impact a guest's view of overall product quality.

To illustrate, consider that, when most foodservice guests think of a "hamburger" they actually think, not of one product, but of a range of products. A hamburger, in these guests' minds, may include a rather small burger patty on a regular bun, wrapped in paper and served in a sack. If so, expectations will be that its price will be low.

If, however, the guests' thoughts turn to an 8-ounce gourmet "Kobe steakburger" presented with avocado slices and alfalfa sprouts on a fresh-baked, toasted, whole-grain bun and served for lunch in a white-tablecloth restaurant, the purchase price expectations of the guests will be much higher and so will their expectations of service levels provided.

As an effective foodservice manager, you will often choose from a variety of quality levels and delivery methods when developing product specifications and, consequently, planning your menus and establishing your prices. To illustrate, if you select the market's cheapest bourbon as your well brand, you will likely be able to charge less for drinks made from it than your competitor who selects a better brand. Your guests' perceptions of your drink quality levels, however, may also be perceived to be lower than your competitors. To be successful, managers should select the product quality levels that best represent their target markets' anticipated desires as well as their operations' own pricing and profit goals.

PORTION SIZE

Portion size plays a large role in determining menu pricing. Portion size is an often-misunderstood concept, yet it is probably the second most significant factor (next to sales mix) in overall pricing. The great chefs know that people "eat with their eyes first!" This relates to presenting food that is visually appealing. It also impacts size and pricing. A burger and fries that fill an 8-inch plate may well be lost on an 11-inch plate. On the 8-inch plate, guests may perceive high levels of value. On the 11-inch plate, guest perceptions of value delivered for price paid may be significantly reduced.

Portion size, then, is a function of both product quantity and presentation. It is no secret why successful cafeteria chains use smaller-than-average dishes to plate their food. For their guests, the image of price to value when dishes appear full comes across loud and clear.

In some dining situations, particularly in an "all you care to eat" operation, the previously mentioned principle again holds true. The proper dish size is just as critical as the proper size scoop or ladle when serving the food. Of course, in a traditional table service operation, management must control portion size because the larger the portion size, the higher the product costs. One very good way to determine whether portion sizes are too large is simply to watch the dishwashing area and see what comes back from the dining room as uneaten. In this regard, the dishroom operator becomes an important player in the cost control team.

Many of today's health-conscious consumers prefer lighter food with more choices in fruits and vegetables. The portion sizes of these items can often be boosted at a fairly low increase in cost. At the same time, average beverage sizes are increasing, as are the size of many side items such as French fries. Again, some of these tend to be lower-cost items. This can be good news for the foodservice operator if prices can be increased to adequately cover the costs of providing the larger portion sizes.

Every menu item should be analyzed with an eye toward determining if the quantity (portion size) being served is the "optimum" quantity. You would like to serve this amount, of course, but no more. The effect of portion size on menu price is significant, and it will be your job to establish and maintain control over your desired portion sizes.

AMBIENCE

If people ate only because they were hungry, few restaurants would be open today. People eat out for a variety of reasons, some of which have little to do with the food itself. Fun, companionship, time limitations, adventure, and variety are just a few reasons diners cite for eating out rather than eating at home. For the foodservice operator who provides an attractive ambience, menu prices can reflect this. **Ambience** is the feeling or overall mood created in an operation. Ambience is affected by an operation's decor, staff uniforms, music, and other factors that directly affect its atmosphere.

When ambience is a major customer draw, managers find they are selling much more than food and, thus, may justly charge higher menu prices. In most cases, however, foodservice operations that count too heavily on ambience alone to carry their business generally start out well but are not ultimately successful. Excellent product quality with outstanding service goes much further over the long run than do clever restaurant designs. Ambience may, however, draw guests to a service location for the first time. When this is true, prices may be somewhat higher if the quality of products provided to guests also supports the higher price structure.

MEAL PERIOD

In some cases, diners expect to pay more for an item served in the evening than for that same item served at a lunch period. Sometimes this is the result of a smaller "luncheon" portion size, but in other cases the portion size, as well as service levels, may be the same in the evening as earlier in the day. This is true, for example, in buffet restaurants that charge a different price for lunch than they charge for dinner, perhaps expecting that guests on their lunch break will spend less time in the restaurant and thus eat less. You must exercise caution in this area however. Guests should clearly understand why a menu item's price changes with the time of day. If this cannot be answered to the guest's satisfaction, it may not be wise to implement a time-sensitive pricing structure.

LOCATION

Location can be a major factor in determining price. One needs look no further than America's many themed amusement parks, movie theaters, or sports arenas to see evidence of this. Foodservice operators in these locations are able to charge premium prices because they have, in effect, a monopoly on food sold to the visitors. The only all-night diner on the interstate highway exit is in much the same situation. Contrast that with an operator who is just one of several seafood restaurants on a restaurant row in a seaside resort town. In this case, it is unlikely that an operation will be able to charge prices significantly higher than its competitors.

It used to be said of restaurants that success was due to three things: location, location, and location! This may have been true before so many foodservice operations opened in the United States. There is, of course, no discounting the value of an excellent restaurant location, and location alone can indeed influence price in some cases. Location does not, however, guarantee long-term success. Location can be an asset or a liability. If it is an asset, menu prices may reflect that fact. If location is indeed a liability, menu prices may actually need to be lower to attract a sufficient clientele to ensure the operation achieves its total revenue and profit goals.

SALES MIX

Of all the pricing-related factors addressed thus far, sales mix most heavily influences the menu pricing decision; just as guest purchase decisions will influence total product costs (see Chapter 5). Recall that sales mix refers to the specific menu items selected by guests. Managers can respond to this situation by employing a concept called price blending. **Price blending** refers to the process of pricing products with different individual cost percentages in a way that achieves a favorable overall product cost percentage.

The ability to blend prices is a useful skill and one that is well worth mastering. To illustrate, assume that you are the operations vice president for a chain of upscale hamburger restaurants known as Texas Red's. Assume also that you hope to achieve an overall food cost of 40 percent in your units. For purposes of simplicity, assume that Figure 6.3 illustrates the three products you sell and their corresponding selling price if each is priced to achieve a 40 percent food cost.

In Chapter 5, you learned that the formula for computing food cost percentage is:

$$\frac{\text{Cost of food sold}}{\text{Food sales}} = \text{Food cost \%}$$

FIGURE 6.3 Unblended Price Structure

Texas Red's Burgers			
Menu Item	Item Cost	Desired Food Cost	Proposed Selling Price
Hamburger	$1.50	40%	$3.75
French Fries	0.32	40%	0.80
Soft Drinks (12 oz.)	0.18	40%	0.45
Total	$2.00	40%	$5.00

This formula can be worded somewhat differently for a single menu item without changing its accuracy:

$$\frac{\text{Cost of specific food item sold}}{\text{Food sales of that item}} = \text{Food cost \% of that item}$$

It is important to understand that when a single menu item is sold, the food sales of that item equal its selling price. The principles of algebra allow you to rearrange the formula as follows:

$$\frac{\text{Cost of specific food item sold}}{\text{Food cost \% of that item}} = \text{Food sales (selling price) of that item}$$

Thus, in Figure 6.3, the hamburger's selling price is

$$\frac{\$1.50}{0.40} = \$3.75$$

Note that, in Figure 6.3 all products are priced to sell at a price that yield a 40 percent food cost. As a result, sales mix—that is, the individual menu selections of guests—would not affect this operation's overall food cost percentage. The sales mix resulting from this pricing strategy could, however, have very damaging results on your profitability. The reason is very simple. If you use the price structure indicated, your drink prices are too low. Most guests expect to pay far in excess of 45 cents for a soft drink at a quick-service restaurant. You run the risk, in this example, of attracting many guests who are interested in buying only soft drinks at your restaurants. Your burger by itself, however, may be priced too high relative to your competitors. However, if you use the price-blending concept, and if you assume that each guest coming into your restaurants will buy a burger, French fries, and a soft drink, you can create a different menu price structure and still achieve your overall cost objective, as seen in Figure 6.4.

Note that, in this example, you actually achieve a total food cost slightly lower than 40 percent. Your hamburger price is now less than $2.50 and more likely in line with your local competitors. Note also, however, that you have assumed each guest coming to Texas Red's will buy one of each item. In reality, of course, not all guests will select one of each item.

Some guests will not elect fries, whereas others may stop in only for a soft drink. It is for this reason that popularity indexes discussed in Chapter 3 and sales mix records addressed in Chapter 5 are so critical. These sales-related histories let you know exactly what your guests are buying when they visit your operation. With this information, you can better develop your pricing strategy. To illustrate how this works, assume that you monitored a sample of 100 guests who came into one of your Texas Reds units and found the results presented in Figure 6.5.

FIGURE 6.4 Blended Price Structure

Texas Red's Burgers			
Menu Item	Item Cost	Proposed Food Cost %	Proposed Selling Price
Hamburger	$1.50	60.2%	$2.49
French Fries	0.32	21.5%	1.49
Soft Drinks (12 oz.)	0.18	16.5%	1.09
Total	$2.00	39.4%	$5.07

FIGURE 6.5 Sample Sales Mix Data

Texas Red's Burgers						
Total Sales: $449.25				Guests Served: 100		
Total Food Cost: $180.20				Food Cost %: 40.1%		

Menu Item	Number Sold	Item Cost	Total Food Cost	Selling Price	Total Sales	Food Cost %
Hamburger	92	$1.50	$138.00	$2.49	$229.08	60.2%
French Fries	79	0.32	25.28	1.49	117.71	21.5%
Soft Drink (12 oz.)	94	0.18	16.92	1.09	102.46	16.5%
Total			$180.20		$449.25	40.1%

As you can see from Figure 6.5, you can use the price-blending concept to achieve your overall cost objectives if you have a good understanding of how many people buy each menu item. In this example, you have achieved the 40 percent food cost you sought. It matters little if the burger has a 60.2 percent food cost if the burger is sold in conjunction with the appropriate number of soft drinks and fries. Obviously, there may be a cost-related danger if your guests begin to order nothing but hamburgers when they come to your establishment. That, however, is unlikely. Again, careful monitoring of guest preferences will allow you to make price adjustments, as needed, to keep your overall costs and prices in line.

A word of caution regarding the manipulation of sales mix and price blending is in order. Because price itself is one of the factors that impact item popularity, a change in menu price may cause a change in customer buying habits. If, in an effort to reduce overall product cost percentage, you were to increase the selling price of soft drinks at Texas Red's, for example, you might find that a higher percentage of guests would elect *not* to purchase a soft drink. This could have the effect

Green and Growing!

You have now been introduced to at least 10 factors that may influence the prices you charge for the items you sell. In the future, Leadership in Energy and Environmental Design (LEED) certification achieved by your operation may well constitute another such factor. The LEED rating system developed by the US Green Building Council (USGBC) evaluates facilities on a variety of standards. The rating system considers sustainability, water use efficiency, energy usage, air quality, construction and materials, and innovation. Currently, the maximum LEED score that can be achieved is 69 points, and operations scoring 26 or more points earn one of the following ratings:

Certified: 26–32 points

Silver: 33–38 points

Gold: 39–51 points

Platinum: 52–69 points

In many cases, when LEED certification is pursued, the initial construction cost of a building will be higher than the current industry standard. However, these costs are recovered by the savings incurred over time due to the lower-than-industry-standard operational costs that are typical of a LEED-certified building. In the foodservice business, these initial costs may also be mitigated by the fact that, increasingly, consumers are willing to pay more to dine in LEED-certified operations. In addition, LEED-certified buildings are healthier for workers and for diners. The LEED certification creates benefits for building owners, employees, and guests. Look for a continuing increase in its importance to your guests.

of actually increasing your overall product cost percentage because fewer guests would choose to buy the one item you sell that has an extremely low food cost percentage. Experienced managers know that understanding sales mix as well as the concept of price blending will have a major impact on their overall menu pricing philosophies and strategies.

FUN ON THE WEB!

To evaluate restaurants' pricing strategies based on reviewers' perceptions of these operations service levels, guest type, product quality, ambience, location, and much more, you can go to the website operated by Zagat.

First, use your favorite search engine to locate and go to the Zagat home page. When you arrive, choose a city. Then click on your specific restaurant criteria or just click on "Most Popular." Click any restaurant for a review that includes a features list, reviewers' ratings, prices, and much more. Look at several restaurant reviews. Pay special attention to reviewer comments that are directly related to pricing.

ASSIGNING MENU PRICES

The methods used to assign menu prices in food service operations are often as varied as the managers who utilize the methods. In general, however, menu prices in food and beverage operations have historically been determined on the basis of one of the following two concepts:

1. Product cost percentage
2. Product contribution margin

PRODUCT COST PERCENTAGE

This method of pricing is based on the idea that the cost of producing an item should be a predetermined percentage of the item's selling price. As was illustrated earlier in this chapter, if you have a menu item that costs $1.50 to produce, and your desired cost percentage equals 40 percent, the following formula can be used to determine what the item's menu price should be:

$$\frac{\text{Cost of specific food item sold}}{\text{Food cost \% of that item}} = \text{Food sales (selling price) of that item}$$

or

$$\frac{\$1.50}{0.40} = \$3.75$$

Thus, given a $1.50 food cost, the recommended selling price of this item would be $3.75. If that item is sold for $3.75, then a 40 percent food cost should be achieved for that item. A check of this work can also be done using the food cost percentage formula:

$$\frac{\$1.50}{\$3.75} = 0.40, \text{ or } 40\%$$

FIGURE 6.6 Pricing-Factor Table

Desired Product Cost %	Pricing Factor
20	5.000
23	4.348
25	4.000
28	3.571
30	3.333
33⅓	3.000
35	2.857
38	2.632
40	2.500
43	2.326
45	2.222

When management uses a predetermined or target food or beverage cost percentage to price menu items, it is stating its belief that product cost in relationship to selling price is of most importance.

Experienced foodservice managers know that a second method of calculating selling prices based on predetermined cost percentage goals can be used. This method uses a pricing factor or multiplier that can be assigned to each desired food or beverage cost percentage. This factor, when multiplied by an item's portion cost, will result in a selling price that yields the desired product cost percentage. Figure 6.6 details such a pricing factor table.

In each case, the factor is calculated by the following formula:

$$\frac{1.00}{\text{Desired product cost \%}} = \text{Pricing factor}$$

Thus, if a manager was attempting to calculate the pricing factor needed to price menu items while achieving a product cost of 40 percent, the manager's computation would be

$$\frac{1.00}{0.40} = 2.50$$

To return to our example, if you want to achieve a 40 percent food cost and if your item costs $1.50 to produce, then the computation is:

$$\text{Pricing factor} \times \text{Food cost} = \text{Menu price}$$

or

$$2.5 \times \$1.50 = \$3.75$$

As can be seen, these two methods of arriving at the proposed selling price yield identical results. One mathematical formula simply relies on division, whereas the other relies on multiplication. The decision about which formula to use is completely up to you. With either approach, the selling price will be determined with a goal of achieving a specified food or beverage cost percentage for each item sold.

HERE'S HOW IT'S DONE *6.1*

To calculate the selling price of a menu item when applying the food cost percentage method you must know two things:

1. The cost of the menu item
2. The food cost percentage you wish to achieve

When you know those two things, you can choose to calculate selling prices using either division or multiplication. You will always get the same answer. To illustrate, assume you know that an entrée costs $4.50 to make. You wish to achieve a 25 percent food cost on the menu item.

Division

To determine the proper selling price using division, you simply divide the cost of the menu item by the food cost percentage you wish to achieve. In this example:

$$\frac{\$4.50 \text{ Menu item cost}}{25\% \text{ Desired food cost}} = \$18.00 \text{ Selling price}$$

Multiplication

To determine the proper selling price using multiplication, you must first know the pricing factor that is associated with your desired food cost. In this example, the desired food cost is 25 percent, so the pricing factor to use (from Figure 6.6) is 4.

$$\$4.50 \text{ Menu item cost} \times 4 \text{ Pricing factor} = \$18.00 \text{ selling price}$$

If you don't have a pricing factor table readily available to you, you can easily calculate the pricing factor you should use simply by dividing your desired food cost percentage into 100. In this example:

$$100 \div 25\% \text{ Desired food cost} = 4 \text{ Pricing factor}$$

In many settings, such as "all-you-can-eat" buffets and banquet-style meals, foodservice managers cannot determine a single portion cost, but rather, must calculate their selling prices based on their **plate costs**. A plate cost is simply the sum of all product costs included in a single meal (or *plate*) served to a guest for one fixed price. In such settings, prices are determined in exactly the same manner as they are for an individual menu item. To illustrate, assume you manage the foodservice operation at an exclusive Country Club. The club specializes in wedding receptions. Assume, further, that a bride and groom holding their reception at your facility have selected a meal from your banquet menu that resulted in your operation incurring the following plate costs:

Pre-meal reception	$ 4.50
Dinner	11.00
Dessert	2.00
Beverages (nonalcoholic)	3.00
Total plate cost	$20.50

Assume also that you sought to achieve a 40 percent product cost on each of your banquet meals. Utilizing the pricing factor method, the computation is:

$$2.5 \text{ pricing factor} \times \$20.50 \text{ plate cost} = \$51.25$$

In this example, with a total plate cost of $20.50 and a desired food cost of 40 percent, the selling price of your banquet meal would be $51.25.

PRODUCT CONTRIBUTION MARGIN

Some foodservice managers prefer an approach to menu pricing that focuses on each of their menu item's contribution margin rather than their product cost percentages. **Contribution margin** is defined as the amount that remains after the product cost of the menu item is subtracted from the item's selling price. Contribution margin, then, is the amount that a menu item "contributes" to pay for labor and all other expenses and provide for a profit. Thus, if an item sells for $3.75 and the product cost for this item is $1.50, the contribution margin is computed as:

$$\text{Selling price} - \text{Product cost} = \text{Contribution margin}$$

$$\text{or}$$

$$\$3.75 - \$1.50 = \$2.25$$

When this approach is used, the formula for determining selling price is:

Product cost + Contribution margin desired = Selling price

Establishing menu price using this philosophy is a matter of combining product cost with a predetermined contribution margin. Management's role here is to determine the desired contribution margin for each menu item. When using this approach, you are likely to establish different contribution margins for various menu items or groups of items. For example, in a restaurant where items are priced separately, entrées might be priced with a contribution margin of $2.50 each, desserts with a contribution margin of $1.25, and drinks, perhaps, with a contribution margin of $0.75. Those managers who rely on the contribution margin approach to pricing do so in the belief that the average contribution margin per item is a more important consideration in pricing decisions than is the product cost percentage.

PRODUCT COST PERCENTAGE OR PRODUCT CONTRIBUTION MARGIN

Although the debate over the "best" pricing method for food and beverage products is likely to continue for some time, you should remember to view pricing as an important process that has as its end goal the establishment of a desirable price/value relationship in the mind of your guests.

Regardless of whether the pricing method used is based on product cost percentage, contribution margin, or even a completely different approach, the selling price selected must provide for a predetermined operational profit. For this reason, it is important that the menu not be priced so low that no profit is possible nor so high that you will not be able to sell a sufficient number of items to make a profit. In the final analysis, it is the customer who will eventually determine what your sales will be on any given item. Being sensitive to required profit as well as to your guests' needs, wants, and desires is critical to an effective pricing strategy.

Consider the Cost

"We have to lower our price or we'll just get killed," said Hoyt Jones, director of operations for the seven-unit Binky's Sub shops. Binky's was known for its modestly priced, but very high-quality, sandwiches and soups. Business and profits were good, but now Hoyt and Rachel, who served as Binky's director of marketing, were discussing the new $4.99 "*Foot-Long Deal*" sandwich promotion that had just been rolled out by their major competitor, an extremely large chain of sub shops that operated over 5,000 units nationally and internationally.

"They just decided to lower their prices to appeal to value-conscious customers," said Hoyt.

"But how can they do that and still make money?" asked Rachel.

"There's always a less expensive variety of ham and cheese on the market," replied Hoyt. "They use lower-quality ingredients than we do. We charge $6.99 for our foot-long sub. That wasn't bad when they sold theirs at $5.99. Our customers know we are worth the extra dollar. Now that they are at $4.99 . . . I don't know, but I think they are going to kill us in the market. We need to do something—fast."

1. How large a role do you believe "cost" likely played into the decision of this competitor to reduce its sandwich prices? Explain your answer.

2. Do you think the typical foodservice customer will consistently pay a higher price for better-quality food and beverage products? Give a specific example to support your answer.

3. Assume you were the president of Binky's Subs. What steps would you instruct Hoyt and Rachel to take to address this specific pricing challenge?

SPECIAL PRICING SITUATIONS

Some pricing decisions faced by foodservice managers call for a unique approach. In many cases, pricing is used as a way to influence guests' purchasing decisions or to respond to particularly complex situations. The following are examples of these special pricing situations:

1. Coupons
2. Value pricing
3. Bundling
4. Salad bars and buffets
5. Bottled wine
6. Beverages at receptions and parties

COUPONS

Coupons are a popular way to vary menu price. Essentially, there are two types of coupons in use in the hospitality industry. The first type generally allows guests to get a free item when they buy an additional item. This **buy one, get one (BOGO)** approach has the effect of reducing by 50 percent the selling price of the couponed item.

With the second type of coupon generally utilized, some form of restriction is placed on the coupon's use. For example, the coupon might only be accepted at a certain time of day, or a reduction in price granted by the coupon's use might be available only if the guest purchases a specific designated menu item, such as a coupon for $3 off a lunch entrée or $4 off a dinner entrée.

Whichever coupon type is offered, coupons have the effect of reducing sales revenue from individual guests in the hope that the total number of guests will increase to the point that total sales revenue will increase.

VALUE PRICING

Value pricing refers to the practice of reducing prices on selected menu items in the belief that, as in couponing, the total number of guests served will increase to the point that total sales revenue also increases. A potential danger with value pricing is that if guest counts do not increase significantly, total sales revenue may, in fact, decline rather than increase.[1]

Many credit the Wendy's chain with first establishing value pricing, but currently its use is widespread, as is evident by the large number of 99-cent and $1.00 "value priced" menu items for sale in the major quick-service restaurant (QSR) segment chains.

BUNDLING

Bundling refers to the practice of selecting specific menu items and pricing them as a group so that the single menu price of the group is lower than if the items in the group were purchased individually. The most common example is the combination meals offered by many quick-service restaurants. In many cases, these bundled

---

[1]See D. K. Hayes and V. L. Huffman, "Value Pricing: How Low Can You Go?" *The Cornell Quarterly* (February, 1995), pp. 51–56.

meals consist of a sandwich, French fries, and a drink. These bundled meals, often promoted as "value meals" or "combo meals," encourage guests to buy one of each menu item rather than only one or two of them.

The bundled meal is generally priced so competitively that a strong value perception is established in the guest's mind.

SALAD BARS AND BUFFETS

The difficulty in establishing one set price for either a salad bar or a buffet is that the amount eaten and, thus, the total serving costs incurred by an operation will vary from one guest to the next. For example, a person weighing 100 pounds will, most likely, consume fewer products from a buffet than will a 300-pound person. The general industry practice, however, is that each of these two guests would pay the same price to go through the salad bar or buffet line.

Short of charging guests for the amount they actually consume (a product-weighing approach that has been tried by some commercial operators but with only limited success); when offering an all-you-care-to-eat salad bar or a buffet, a single selling price must be established. This price must be based on a known "average" plate cost for the diner who is given the all-you-can-eat option. This can be accomplished rather easily if product usage record keeping is accurate and timely.

Regardless of the buffet items to be sold, their usage must be accurately recorded. Consider the situation of Mei, the manager of Lotus Gardens, a Chinese restaurant where patrons pay one price but may return as often as they like to a buffet line. Mei finds that a form like the one presented in Figure 6.7 is helpful in recording both product usage and guests served. Note that Mei uses the ABC method to determine her menu items. She does so because total food costs on a buffet line or salad bar are a function of two things:

- How much is eaten
- What is eaten

FIGURE 6.7 Salad Bar or Buffet Product Usage

Unit Name: <u>Lotus Gardens</u>							Date: <u>1/15 (Dinner)</u>
Menu Item	Category	Beginning Amount	Additions	Ending Amount	Total Usage	Unit Cost	Total Cost
Sweet and Sour Pork	A	6 lb.	44 lb.	13 lb.	37 lb.	$4.40/lb.	$162.80
Bean Sprouts	B	3 lb.	17 lb.	2 lb.	18 lb.	$1.60/lb.	$ 28.80
Egg Rolls	B	40 each	85 each	17 each	108 each	$0.56 each	$ 60.48
Fried Rice	C	10 lb.	21.5 lb.	8.5 lb.	23 lb.	$0.60/lb.	$ 13.80
Steamed Rice	C	10 lb.	30 lb.	6.5 lb.	33.5 lb.	$0.40/lb.	$ 13.40
Wonton Soup	C	2 gal.	6 gal.	1.5 gal.	6.5 gal.	$4.00/gal.	$ 26.00
Total Product Cost							$305.28

Total Product Cost: <u>$305.28</u>

Guests Served: <u>125</u>

Cost per Guest: <u>$2.44</u>

To establish her prices, Mei notes the amount of product she puts on the buffet to begin the dinner meal period (Beginning Amount), adds any additional amounts placed on the buffet during the meal period (Additions), and calculates the amount of usable product left at the end of the meal period (Ending Amount). From this information, Mei can compute her total product usage and her total product cost per guest.

Based on the data in Figure 6.7, Mei knows that her total product cost for dinner on January 1 was $305.28. She can then use the following formula to determine her buffet product cost per guest:

$$\frac{\text{Total buffet product cost}}{\text{Guests served}} = \text{Buffet product cost per guest}$$

or

$$\frac{\$305.28}{125} = \$2.44$$

On this day, Mei had a per-guest portion cost (plate cost) of $2.44. She can use this information to establish a menu price that she feels is appropriate for helping her reach her profit goals. To illustrate, assume that Mei uses the product cost percentage approach to establishing menu price. She determines that a 25 percent food cost is her goal. Using the pricing factor table in Figure 6.6, Mei would use the following formula to establish her per-person buffet price:

$$4.0 \text{ pricing factor} \times \$2.44 \text{ per-person cost} = \$9.76 \text{ selling price}$$

For marketing purposes, and to ensure her desired food cost percentage, Mei may well round her buffet selling price up to, say, $9.99 per person. The significant point to remember here is that the amount consumed by any individual guest is less important than the average amount consumed by each guest. That is so because it is the consumption of the average, or typical, guest that is used to establish the menu price.

It is important to recognize that Mei's buffet cost per guest will likely vary somewhat each day. This is not a cause for great concern. Minor variations in product cost per guest should be covered adequately if the selling price is properly established. By monitoring buffet costs on a regular basis, Mei can be assured that she has control over the costs per guest and an appropriate selling price.

Mei knows that the secret to keeping selling prices low in a salad bar or buffet situation is to apply a variation of the ABC inventory approach (see Chapter 4). That is, A items, which are expensive, should be no more than approximately 20 percent of the total product available. The B items, which are moderate in price, should be about 30 percent of the item offerings, and C items, which are inexpensive, should be 50 percent of the offerings. Using this approach, a menu listing of items can be prepared to ensure that only items that stay within these predetermined ranges are offered to guests.

BOTTLED WINE

Few areas of restaurant industry pricing create more controversy than that of pricing wines by the bottle. The reason for this may be the incredible variance in cost among different **vintages,** or years of wine production, as well as the quality of alternative wine offerings. If your foodservice operation will sell wine by the bottle, it is likely that you will have some wine products that appeal to value-oriented guests and other, higher priced wines that are preferred by guests seeking these superior wines.

An additional element that affects wine pricing is the fact that many wines that are sold by the bottle in restaurants are also sold in retail grocery or liquor stores.

Thus, guests may have a very good idea of what a similar bottle of wine would cost them if it were purchased in either of these locations. How you decide to price the bottled-wine offerings on your own menu will definitely affect your guest's perception of the price/value relationship offered by your operation.

Properly pricing wine by the bottle calls for skill and insight. Consider the case of Claudia, who owns and manages a casual-dining Armenian restaurant. Using the product cost percentage method of pricing, Claudia attempts to achieve an overall wine product cost in her restaurant of 25 percent. Thus, when pricing her wines and using the pricing factor table in Figure 6.6, Claudia multiplies the cost of each bottled wine she sells by four to arrive at her desired selling price. Following are the four wines she wants to sell and the costs and selling prices associated with each type:

Wine	Product Cost	Selling Price	Product Cost %
1	$ 4.00	$16.00	25%
2	$ 6.00	$24.00	25%
3	$15.00	$60.00	25%
4	$20.00	$80.00	25%

After reviewing the selling prices established using a product cost percentage approach, Claudia decides that she would like to explore the contribution margin approach to wine pricing. She therefore computes the contribution margin (Selling price – Product cost = Contribution margin) for each wine she sells and finds the following results:

Wine	Selling Price	Product Cost	Contribution Margin
1	$16.00	$ 4.00	$12.00
2	$24.00	$ 6.00	$18.00
3	$60.00	$15.00	$45.00
4	$80.00	$20.00	$60.00

Her conclusion, after evaluating the contribution margin approach to pricing and what she believes to be her customers' perception of the price/value relationship she offers, is that she may be hurting sales of wines 3 and 4 by pricing these products too high, even though they are currently priced to achieve the same 25 percent product cost as wines 1 and 2. She also determines that the selling price of Wine 1 may actually be too low because it yields only a $12.00 contribution margin.

In the case of bottled wine, the contribution margin approach to price can often be used to your advantage. Guests are often quite price conscious when it comes to bottled wine. When operators seek to achieve profits guests feel are inappropriate, bottled-wine sales may decline. After reviewing all of her price-related information, Claudia develops her own bottled wine pricing strategy, as shown:

Wine	Product Cost	Selling Price	Contribution Margin	Product Cost %
1	$ 4.00	$19.00	$15.00	21.1%
2	$ 6.00	$22.00	$16.00	27.3%
3	$15.00	$33.00	$18.00	45.5%
4	$20.00	$39.00	$19.00	51.3%

Note that, although selling price has been increased in the case of wine 1, it has been reduced for wines 2, 3, and 4. Contribution margin is still higher for wine 4 than for wine 1. The difference, however, is not as dramatic as before. Product cost percentages have, of course, been altered due to the price changes Claudia is proposing. Note, also, that the **price spread,** defined as the range between the lowest and the highest priced menu item, has been drastically reduced. Whereas the price spread was previously $16.00 to $80.00, it is now $19.00 to $39.00. This reduction in price spread may assist Claudia in selling more of the higher-priced wine because her guests may be more comfortable with the price/value relationship perceived under this new pricing approach. It is important to remember, however, that Claudia must monitor sales and determine if her new strategy is successful.

In general, it may be stated that pricing bottled wine only by the product percentage method is a strategy that may result in overall decreased bottled-wine sales. In this specific pricing situation, the best approach to establishing selling price calls after evaluating both your product cost percentage and your contribution margin.

BEVERAGES AT RECEPTIONS AND PARTIES

Pricing beverages for open-bar receptions and similar special events can be challenging and the reason for this is very simple. Each consumer group can be expected to behave somewhat differently when attending an open-bar or hosted-bar function. Clearly, we would not expect the guests at a formal political fund-raising cocktail reception to consume as many drinks during a one-hour reception as a group of fun-loving individuals celebrating a favorite team's victory in a championship football game.

Establishing a price per person in these two situations may well result in quite different numbers. One way to solve this problem is to charge each of the guests for what they actually consume. In reality, however, many party hosts want their guests to consume beverage products without having them pay for each drink. When this is the case, you could elect to charge the host on a per-drink-consumed basis, or charge the host on a per-person (served), per-hour basis. When charging on a per-person, per-hour basis, you must have a good idea of how much the average attendee will consume during the length of the party or reception so that an appropriate price can be established.

To illustrate beverage pricing in a hosted bar situation assume that you are the food and beverage director at the Carlton, a luxury hotel. Ms. Swan, a potential food and beverage guest, approaches you with the idea of providing a one-hour champagne reception for 100 guests prior to an important dinner that she is considering booking at your facility. This guest would like all of the attendees to drink as much champagne during the reception as they care to.

Ms. Swan's specific question is: "How much will I be charged for the reception if 100 guests attend?" Clearly, an answer of "I don't know," or, "It depends on how much they drink," is inappropriate. It is, of course, your business to know the answer to such questions, and you can know. If you are aware, from past events and records you have kept, what the average consumption for a group of this type has been previously, you can establish an appropriate price. To do so, records for this purpose must be maintained. Figure 6.8 is an example of one such management tool that can be used to provide the information you will need.

Note that average consumption of any beverage product type can be recorded. In this example, assume that you had recently recorded the data from the Gulley wedding, an event very similar to the one requested by Ms. Swan. In this case, a wedding reception, which also requested champagne, was held for 97 guests. The product cost per guest for that event, based on your records in Figure 6.8, equaled $3.37.

FIGURE 6.8 Beverage Consumption Report

Event: Gulley Wedding				Date: 1/15		
Unit Name: The Carlton Hotel						
Beverage Type	**Beginning Amount**	**Additions**	**Ending Amount**	**Total Usage**	**Unit Cost**	**Total Cost**
Liquor A						
B						
C						
D						
E						
F						
G						
Beer A						
B						
C						
D						
E						
Wine A						
B						
C						
D						
Other: Champagne:						
A. Sparkling	8 bottles	24	9	23	$6.00/btl.	$138.00
B. Sparkling Pink	8 bottles	24	11	21	$9.00/btl.	$189.00
Total Product Cost						$327.00

Total Product Cost: $327.00

Guests Served: 97   Cost per Guest: $3.37

Based on what you know about the drinking pattern of similar groups, you could now use either the product cost percentage method or the contribution margin pricing method to establish your per-person reception price.

For purpose of illustration, assume that you used the product contribution margin approach to pricing alcoholic beverage receptions. Further assume that the contribution margin you desire per person served is $15.00. The established selling price using the contribution margin formula would be:

Product cost + Desired contribution margin = Selling price

In this example:

$ 3.37	(Per-person product cost)
+ $15.00	(Desired contribution margin)
= $18.37	Selling price per person

Armed with this historical information, as well as that from as many other similar events you have served in the past, you are better prepared to answer Ms. Swan's question: "How much will I be charged for my reception if 100 guests attend?"

Monitoring your product costs and then assigning reasonable menu prices based on these costs is a major part of your job as a foodservice manager. You must be able to perform this task well. Increasingly, however, the cost of labor, as well as the cost of food and beverage products, has occupied a significant portion of the typical foodservice manager's cost control efforts. In fact, in some foodservice facilities, the costs of labor and employee benefits provided exceed that of the food and beverage products sold. Because labor cost control is so important, in the next chapter we will turn our attention to the unique set of skills and knowledge you must acquire to adequately manage and control your operation's labor costs.

Technology Tools

In this chapter you learned about the menu formats you most often encounter as a hospitality manager, as well as the factors affecting menu prices and the procedures used to assign individual menu item prices based on cost and sales data. The mathematical computations required to evaluate the effectiveness of individual menu items and to establish their prices can be complex, but there are a wide range of software products available that can help you to do the following:

1. Develop menus and cost recipes.
2. Design and print menu "specials" for meal periods or happy hours.
3. Compute and analyze menu item and overall food cost percentage.
4. Compute and analyze menu item and overall contribution margin.
5. Price banquet menus and bars based on known product costs.
6. Evaluate the profitability of individual menu items.
7. Estimate future item demand based on past guest purchase patterns.
8. Assign individual menu item prices based on management-supplied parameters.

Menu analysis and pricing software is often packaged as part of a larger software program. Its importance, however, is great. It is an area that will continue to see rapid development in the future as software makers seek additional ways to improve their menu pricing-related products.

FUN ON THE WEB!

Advances in menu management software continue to occur rapidly. Increasingly, restaurateurs are looking for programs that will give them many options to choose from when designing their own sales tracking (and pricing) processes. The point of success (POS) company is one such maker of advanced software programs designed specifically for restaurants and bars. You can visit their website where you will be able to compare the features of their "standard" and "premium" POS software programs. Which would you choose?

Apply What You Have Learned

Dominic Carbonne owns Hungry Henry's pizza, a four-unit chain of take-out pizza shops in a city of 60,000 people (with an additional 25,000 college students attending the local state university). Recently, a new chain of pizza restaurants has opened in town. The products sold by this new chain have lesser quality and use lesser quantity of ingredients (cheese, meat, fruit, and vegetable toppings) and are also priced 25 percent less than Hungry Henry's equivalent size pizza.

Dominic has seen his business decline somewhat since the new chain opened. This is especially true with the college students:

1. How would you evaluate the new competitor's pricing strategy?

2. What steps would you advise Dominic to take to counter this competitor?

3. Describe three specific strategies restaurants can use to communicate "quality, rather than low price," to his potential customers.

Key Terms and Concepts

The following are terms and concepts discussed in the chapter that are important for you as a manager. To help you review, please define the terms below.

tip-on (menu)	menu specials	value pricing
standard menu	selling price	bundling
daily menu	price/value relationship	vintage
cycle menu	ambience	price spread
à la carte (menu)	price blending	
prix fixe (menu)	plate cost	
CEO (chief executive officer)	contribution margin	
	buy one, get one (BOGO)	

Test Your Skills

You may download the Excel spreadsheets for the Test Your Skills exercises from the student companion website at www.wiley.com/college/dopson. Complete the exercises by placing your answers in the shaded boxes and answering the questions as indicated.

1. Carlita operates a take-out only pizza parlor that specializes in four-cheese pizzas. Carlita offers four different pizza sizes and she knows what it costs to make each size. Help her calculate her food cost percentage and contribution margin for each size pizza.

Pizza Size	Product Cost	Selling Price	Food Cost %	Contribution Margin
Small	$3.10	$ 9.99		
Medium	$4.10	$11.99		
Large	$5.10	$13.99		
Extra Large	$6.10	$15.99		

Which pizza size do you think is Carlita's most profitable? Why?

2. Bill owns Bill's Burger Barn, and he is dissatisfied with his consistently high food cost percentage. In an effort to drop his food cost percentage below 35 percent, he has decided to incorporate price blending into his pricing strategy. He has developed three combo items, and he wants to find out if his food cost percentage has been lowered after the first week of sales. Help Bill calculate the food cost percentage for his combo items.

Bill's Burger Barn Combo						
Number Item	Number Sold	Product Cost	Total Cost	Selling Price	Total Sales	Food Cost %
Hamburger	200	$1.50		$3.49		
French Fries (large)	185	$0.40		$1.60		
Soft Drink (16 oz.)	190	$0.20		$1.35		
Total						

Bill's Bacon Cheeseburger Combo						
Number Item	Number Sold	Product Cost	Total Cost	Selling Price	Total Sales	Food Cost %
Bacon Cheeseburger	160	$1.65		$4.29		
Onion Rings	135	$0.30		$1.40		
Soft Drink (16 oz.)	155	$0.20		$1.35		
Total						

Bill's Chicken Sandwich Combo						
Number Item	Number Sold	Product Cost	Total Cost	Selling Price	Total Sales	Food Cost %
Chicken Sandwich	75	$1.10		$3.15		
French Fries (large)	75	$0.40		$1.60		
Soft Drink (16 oz.)	75	$0.20		$1.35		
Total						

Should Bill continue with this pricing strategy?

3. Tonekwa has priced her menu items using the product cost percentage method in the past. She has asked her evening shift manager to price new menu items, and she believes that he will feel more comfortable using the factor method to price the new items. Help Tonekwa convert her desired product cost percentages to factors. (*Spreadsheet hint:* Use the ROUND function for the "Factor" column to three decimal places.)

Pricing Factor Table	
Desired Product Cost %	**Pricing Factor**
18%	
21%	
22%	
24%	
26%	
31%	
32%	
36%	
37%	
41%	
42%	
44%	
46%	

4. Bess and David own two small diners in a midsize city in Oklahoma. Bess has primary responsibility for the diner in the suburbs, and David has primary responsibility for the diner in the inner city. The menu items and product costs are the same in both diners, but the market in the inner city demands lower menu prices than that in the suburbs. So Bess has set her desired product cost percentage at 40 percent, and David's desired product cost percentage is 42 percent because he can't charge as much as Bess. Bess likes to use the product cost percentage method to price menu items and David likes to use the factor method. Help both of them determine their selling prices. (*Spreadsheet hint:* Use the ROUND function for "Pricing Factor" column to three decimal places.)

Bess and David's Diner–Suburbs (Bess)

Desired Product Cost Percentage: 40%

Product Cost Percentage Method

Menu Item	Product Cost	Desired Product Cost Percentage	Selling Price
Chicken Breast Dinner	$2.25		
Seafood Platter	$3.45		
Steak Dinner	$4.99		
Turkey Sandwich	$1.25		
Pork Chop	$2.45		
Hamburger	$1.50		
Cheeseburger	$1.75		
French Fries	$0.45		
Meat Loaf	$1.25		
Small Drink	$0.35		

Bess and David's Diner–Inner City (David)

Desired Product Cost Percentage: 42%

Factor Method

Menu Item	Product Cost	Pricing Factor	Selling Price
Chicken Breast Dinner	$2.25		
Seafood Platter	$3.45		
Steak Dinner	$4.99		
Turkey Sandwich	$1.25		
Pork Chop	$2.45		
Hamburger	$1.50		
Cheeseburger	$1.75		
French Fries	$0.45		
Meat Loaf	$1.25		
Small Drink	$0.35		

5. Frankie Marie owns Frankie's Cafeteria in a small southern town. She has decided to price her menu items using the contribution margin method. She has determined the following contribution margins for her food categories:

Contribution Margins:

Salad: $1.20
Entrées: $4.25
Desserts: $1.50
Drinks: $1.10

Help her price her menu items.

Contribution Margin Approach			
Menu Item	Product Cost	Desired Contribution Margin	Selling Price
Salads			
Dinner Salad	$0.30		
Macaroni Salad	$0.55		
Potato Salad	$0.65		
Carrot and Raisin Salad	$0.40		
Bavarian Salad	$0.60		
Entrées			
Liver and Onions	$2.50		
Steak Patty	$2.75		
Meatloaf	$2.85		
Chicken Fried Steak	$2.10		
Fried Catfish	$2.35		
Chicken Casserole	$2.25		
Turkey and Dressing	$2.55		
Desserts			
Chocolate Cream Pie	$0.75		
Coconut Cream Pie	$0.75		
Pecan Pie	$1.25		
Chocolate Cake	$0.60		
Pudding	$0.20		
Jell-O	$0.20		
Carrot Cake	$0.70		
Drinks			
Coffee	$0.15		
Tea	$0.15		
Soft Drink	$0.15		

6. Gabriel Hinojosa owns Gabriel's Tex-Mex Restaurant, an extremely popular, 250-seat establishment in a large California city. Gabriel has decided to offer a four-hour Sunday brunch buffet for his guests because he thinks he can achieve a guest count of 625 (2½ turns). Last Sunday, June 1, he offered the buffet for the first time, and he charged $12.00 per guest. However, he only served 400 people. He believes he could attract more guests if he offered the buffet at a lower price. He collected information on last Sunday's buffet product usage, and he used the ABC method to put his menu items into categories. His desired food cost percentage is 40 percent. Help him complete the buffet product usage report. (*Spreadsheet hint:* Use the ROUND function for "Cost per Guest" and "Desired Selling Price Based on Cost" to two decimal places.)

   After completing this analysis, what should be Gabriel's selling price? If he uses this new selling price and he serves 625 guests next Sunday, June 8, will his total revenue increase? If so, by how much?

Buffet Product Usage (Sunday, June 1): Gabriel's Tex-Mex Restaurant

Menu Item	Category	Unit	Beginning Amount	Additions	Ending Amount	Total Usage	Unit Cost	Total Cost
Steak Fajitas	A	lb.	20	60	6		$4.50	
Chicken Fajitas	A	lb.	15	70	10		$4.00	
Carne Asada	A	lb.	10	50	4		$4.25	
Cheese Enchiladas	B	lb.	2	80	15		$2.00	
Beef Enchiladas	B	lb.	3	60	10		$2.50	
Enchiladas Verde	B	lb.	1	70	8		$2.00	
Chili Rellenos	B	lb.	10	45	5		$2.75	
Tacos	C	each	0	150	20		$0.30	
Bean Chalupas	C	each	0	175	5		$0.25	
Tortilla Soup	C	gal.	2	10	4		$0.30	
Spanish Rice	C	lb.	5	70	12		$0.20	
Refried Beans	C	lb.	15	75	6		$0.20	
Sopapillas	C	each	25	200	30		$0.15	
Total Product Cost								

Guests Served: 400

Total Product Cost:

Cost per Guest:

Desired Food Cost %: 40%

Desired Selling Price Based on Cost:

Revenues, June 1:

Projected Revenues, June 8:

Difference:

7. JoAnna is the foodservice director at Reading Hospital. She has just started a new menu program to offer guests visiting hospitalized patients "guest trays" so the patients and their guests can eat together. She has been offering her guest-tray program for one month, and it has been popular. She would like to know her average selling price per guest (check average) to see if she needs to change the price of her menu items. She would like to keep her average selling price above $11.50. Given the following information, and the fact that JoAnna priced each menu item with an $8.00 per guest tray contribution margin, calculate her average selling price for the month.

Menu Item	Number Sold	Product Cost	Contribution Margin	Selling Price	Total Sales
Hunter's Chicken	2,560	$3.50			
Jambalaya	750			$11.75	
Grilled Salmon	1,200	$4.50			
Beef Tenderloin	500			$16.50	
Vegetarian Cheese Bake	1,210	$2.75			
Total					

Average Selling Price

Did JoAnna achieve her desired average selling price per guest? Does she need to change her prices?

8. Ming has recently inherited the Quick Wok restaurant started by her parents. It is located in a busy strip shopping area surrounded by many office complexes, but it is also near many quick-service restaurants. The Quick Wok has been successful because of the quality of its food, but Ming feels that it could do even better at lunchtime if she could create a value meal option to appeal to the price-conscious consumer. Because both a McDonald's and a Wendy's are within a quarter-mile of her store, she has determined that her own value meal menu item needs to be priced at $1.00. She creates a stir-fry dish that, when served with white rice, has a portion cost of 65 cents. Her beverages have a cost of 20 cents. The beverages already sell for $1.00 each, and she does not want to raise this price.

She believes she could sell 75 of the new value meals per day if she offers the stir-fry dish at $1.00. As well, she seeks an overall product cost percentage of 35 percent. From historical data, she knows that 80 percent of her customers purchase a drink with their meals.

Based on the information given, calculate the overall product cost percentage of the value meals and beverages. Would you advise Ming to "go for it"? Why or why not?

Value Meal and Beverage						
Menu Item	Number Sold	Item Cost	Total Cost	Selling Price	Total Sales	Food Cost %
Stir Fry Dish	75					
Beverage						
Total						

How many beverages must be sold in addition to the value meals if Ming is to achieve her target food cost percentage goal? Is this number feasible? *Spreadsheet hint:* You will have to arrive at the number sold of beverages by trial and error. Specifically, start with 60 and increase or decrease the number until you reach a total food cost percentage of 35 percent. This Test Your Skills problem is designed to show you how changes in the number of items (beverages) sold affect total food cost percentage.

Number of Beverages to Achieve Target Overall Food Cost Percentage						
Menu Item	Number Sold	Item Cost	Total Cost	Selling Price	Total Sales	Food Cost %
Stir Fry Dish	75					
Beverage						
Total						

9. Jackson Daniels is the director of food and beverage at the Foxfire Country Club. In June, Jackson's club hosted three weddings. Each wedding featured a four-hour hosted bar paid for by the bride and groom. The consumption data from each event is listed below. Complete the missing data in the report, and then help Jackson answer the questions that follow:

	Number of Guests Served	Beer Cost	Wine Cost	Spirit Cost	Total Cost	Cost per Guest
June 07	250	$500	$ 400	$600		
June 14		$650	$1,225		$2,875	$5.75
June 21	400	$525	$1,000	$675		
Total						

a. What do you think should be Jackson's "best estimate" of the cost to the Club of providing a four-hour hosted bar at weddings?

b. If Jackson seeks to ensure a 20 percent beverage cost, what should be his selling price, per guest, for a four-hour hosted bar?

c. Would you recommend Jackson charge half of the amount in the answer in part b for a two-hour hosted bar? Explain your answer.

10. One criticism of both the product cost percentage and contribution margin methods used for determining menu prices is that both are based primarily on the cost of food (or beverages) and ignore the cost of labor. In many foodservice operations, however, the cost of labor equals or even exceeds the cost of food and beverages. Do you foresee the cost of labor playing an increasing role in the calculation of menu prices? Explain your answer.

CHAPTER 7

Managing the Cost of Labor

OVERVIEW

This chapter explains the techniques that managers use to control labor costs by establishing and monitoring labor cost standards. Factors that affect labor productivity as well as methods for improving labor productivity are presented. This chapter teaches you how to schedule employees based on established labor productivity standards, as well as how to compute a labor cost percentage and other measures of labor productivity used in the foodservice industry.

Chapter Outline

- Labor Expense in the Hospitality Industry
- Evaluating Labor Productivity
- Maintaining a Productive Workforce
- Measuring Current Labor Productivity
- Managing Payroll Costs
- Reducing Labor-Related Costs
- Technology Tools
- Apply What You Have Learned
- Key Terms and Concepts
- Test Your Skills

LEARNING OUTCOMES

At the conclusion of this chapter, you will be able to:
- Identify the factors that affect employee productivity.
- Develop labor standards and employee schedules used in a foodservice operation.
- Analyze and evaluate actual labor utilization.

LABOR EXPENSE IN THE HOSPITALITY INDUSTRY •——

You have learned that having the correct amount of food and beverage products available to serve your guests is important. Knowing how those products should be prepared and served is also vital. To see why, consider the case of Pauline. She manages the open-to-the-public cafeteria located in a large urban hospital. Both hospital staff and patients' visitors, who constitute the majority of her cafeteria guests, have good things to say about the quality of her food. They complain often, however, about the slowness of her cafeteria line, the soiled tables during the busy lunch hour, and the frequent running out of items at the salad bars. Pauline often feels that she needs more employees. She knows, however, that her current staff is actually larger than it was a few years ago. She also knows that she now serves more guests each day than she has in the past. Her question is, "Do I have the right number of employees scheduled to work, and at the right times, for the number of guests I am serving today?" Unfortunately for her, Pauline is so busy "helping" her employees get through the meal periods that there seems to be little time for thinking about and planning the strategies and techniques she needs to apply if she is to solve her labor-related customer service problems.

In years past, when labor was relatively inexpensive, Pauline might have responded to her need for more workers by simply hiring more employees. Today's foodservice manager, however, does not have that luxury. In today's increasingly costly labor market, you must learn the supervisory skills needed to maximize the effectiveness of your staff and the cost control skills required to evaluate their efforts. That is because labor is a significant foodservice operating cost. In fact, in some foodservice establishments, the cost of labor actually exceeds the cost of food and beverage products.

Today's competitive labor market indicates that, in the future, foodservice managers will likely find it even more difficult to recruit, train, and retain an effective team of employees. Therefore, the control of labor expenses takes on a greater level of importance than ever before. In some sectors of the foodservice industry, a reputation for long hours, poor pay, and undesirable working conditions has caused some high-quality employees to look elsewhere for more satisfactory jobs or careers. It does not have to be that way, and it is up to you to help ensure that in your organization it is not.

When labor costs are adequately controlled, management has the funds necessary to create desirable working conditions and pay a wage that will attract the very best employees. In every service industry, better employees mean better guest service and, ultimately, better business profits.

LABOR EXPENSE DEFINED

Payroll is the term generally used to refer to the salaries and wages you will pay your employees. **Labor expense** includes salaries and wages, but it also includes other labor-related costs. These include:

1. FICA (Social Security) taxes, including taxes due on employees' tip income
2. FUTA (Federal unemployment taxes) state unemployment taxes
3. Workers' compensation
4. Group life insurance
5. Health insurance, including:

   Medical

   Dental

   Vision

   Disability

6. Pension/retirement plan payments

7. Employee meals

8. Employee training expenses

9. Employee transportation costs

10. Employee uniforms, housing, and other benefits

11. Vacation/sick leave/personal days

12. Tuition reimbursement programs

13. Employee incentives and bonuses

Not every operation will incur all of the costs listed. But some operations will have all of these and more. You can be sure, however, that regardless of the facility you manage, you will incur some labor-related expenses in addition to wages and salaries. The critical question you must answer is, "How much should I spend on payroll and other labor expenses to deliver the quality of products and service that I feel is appropriate?" Before you can hope to answer that question, it is important that you understand well the individual components that make up payroll and labor expense.

FUN ON THE WEB!

In the United States, the Patient Protection and Affordable Care Act (ACA) was signed into law in 2010. This health insurance-related law directly affects the benefit costs incurred by many food service organizations. To learn more about the ACA, and its requirements go to: http://www.healthcare.gov/law/index.html.

PAYROLL

Payroll refers to the gross pay received by an employee in exchange for his or her work. That is, if an employee earns $10.00 per hour and works 40 hours for his or her employer, the gross paycheck (the employee's paycheck before any mandatory or voluntary deductions) would be $400 ($10.00 per hour × 40 hours = $400). This gross amount is considered a payroll expense.

If the employee earns a salary, that salary amount is also a payroll expense. A **salaried employee** generally receives the same income per week or month regardless of the number of hours worked. Thus, if a salaried employee is paid $700 per week when he or she works a complete week, that $700 is included in payroll expense. Salaried employees are actually more accurately described as **exempt employees** because their duties, responsibilities, and level of decisions make them "exempt" from the overtime provisions of the federal government's Fair Labor Standards Act (FLSA). Exempt employees do not receive overtime for hours worked in excess of 40 per week and are expected by most organizations to work the number of hours needed to do their jobs.

FUN ON THE WEB!

The designation of which workers can (and cannot) be considered exempt employees is governed by the US Department of Labor and the Fair Labor Standards Act (FLSA).

Minimum allowable salary levels are also determined by the Wage and Hour Division (WHD) of this department. To learn more about wages that must be paid to exempt and to nonexempt employees, go to: www.dol.gov/whd/.

FIXED PAYROLL VERSUS VARIABLE PAYROLL

When you manage a foodservice facility, you must make choices regarding the number and type of employee you will hire to help you serve your guests. Some employees are needed simply to open the doors for the minimally anticipated business. **Minimum staff** is the term used to describe the least number of employees, and the least number of payroll dollars, needed to operate a business. For example, in a small operation, this may include only one manager, one server, and one cook. The cost of providing payroll to these three individuals would be its minimum staff payroll.

Suppose, however, that the operation anticipated much greater volume on a given day. The increased number of guests expected means that the operation may need more cooks and more servers, as well as cashiers, dishroom personnel, and, perhaps, more supervisors to handle the additional workload. Clearly, these additional staff positions create a work group that is far larger than the minimum staff, but it is needed to adequately service the anticipated number of guests.

Payroll costs may be fixed or variable. **Fixed payroll** refers to the amount an operation pays in salaries. This amount, in most cases, is fixed because it remains unchanged from one pay period to the next unless the individual receiving the pay separates employment from the organization or is given a raise.

Variable payroll consists primarily of those dollars paid to hourly employees. Thus, variable payroll is the amount that should "vary" with changes in sales volume. Generally, as you anticipate increased volume levels in your facility, you may need to add additional hourly and, sometimes, additional salaried employees. The distinction between fixed and variable labor is an important one. As a manager, you may have little direct control over your fixed labor expense, whereas you will have nearly 100 percent control over variable labor expenses that are above your minimum staff levels.

LABOR EXPENSE

Unlike payroll expense, labor expense refers to the total of all costs associated with maintaining your workforce. Labor expense includes employee taxes and benefits costs and is always larger than payroll expense.

The actual amount of taxes and employee benefits paid for by a specific operation can vary greatly. Some expenses, such as payroll taxes and contributions to workers' unemployment and workers' compensation programs, are mandatory for all employers. Other benefit payments, such as those made for employee insurance and retirement programs, are voluntary and vary based on the benefits a business chooses to offer its employees. As employment taxes and benefit costs increase an operation's labor expense will increase even if payroll expense remains constant.

Most foodservice operators have total control over their payroll expense. It is, therefore, often referred to as a *controllable* labor expense. Other labor expenses, such as taxes and some benefits, over which an operator has little or no control, are commonly called *noncontrollable* labor expenses. In reality, however, you can exert some control over these noncontrollable labor expenses, such as a foodservice manager who works very hard to ensure a well-trained workforce in a safe environment and thereby achieves a lower rate on workers' compensation, accident, and health insurance for his or her employees.

In this chapter, we deal primarily with payroll-related expenses. This is in keeping with the concept that these are the most controllable of labor-related expenses. To determine how much payroll is needed to operate your business, you must be able to determine how much work must be done and how much work each employee can perform. If too few employees are scheduled to work, poor service and reduced sales can result, because guests may choose to go elsewhere in search of superior food and service levels. If too many employees are scheduled, payroll and other labor-related expenses will be too high, resulting in reduced profits. The best solution to this challenge is to know how many employees are needed given the estimated number of guests you will serve. To determine this number of employees, you must have a clear idea of the **productivity** of each of your employees. Productivity is the amount of work performed by an employee in a fixed period of time.

EVALUATING LABOR PRODUCTIVITY

There are many ways to assess labor productivity. In general, productivity is measured by the **productivity ratio** as follows:

$$\frac{\text{Output}}{\text{Input}} = \text{Productivity ratio}$$

To illustrate this formula, assume a restaurant employs 4 servers and it serves 60 guests. Using the productivity ratio formula, the output is guests served; the input is servers employed, as follows:

$$\frac{60 \text{ guests}}{4 \text{ servers}} = 15 \text{ guests per server}$$

This formula demonstrates that, for each server employed, 15 guests can be served. The productivity ratio is 15 guests to 1 server (15 to 1) or, stated another way, 1 server per 15 guests (1/15).

There are several ways of defining foodservice output and input; thus, there are several types of productivity ratios. Some of these are presented later in this chapter.

All of these productivity ratios can be helpful in determining the answer to the key question, "How much should I spend on labor?" The answer, however, is even more complicated than it might seem at first. In the preceding example, you know that, on average, 1 of your servers can serve 15 guests. But how many guests will a slow server serve? How about your best server? How much do you pay the most productive server? Your least productive? Are you better off scheduling your best server if you anticipate 20 guests, or should you schedule two of your slower servers? How can you help the slower server become an average or above-average server? At what cost? These are the types of questions that must be answered daily if you are to effectively manage your total payroll costs.

Foodservice operators must develop their own methods for managing payroll because every foodservice unit is different. Consider the differences between managing payroll costs at a small, quick-service food kiosk in a shopping mall and a large banquet kitchen in a 1,000-room convention hotel. Although the methods used to manage payroll costs may vary somewhat, it is always true that payroll costs can and should be managed.

MAINTAINING A PRODUCTIVE WORKFORCE

Before we address how managers calculate and utilize productivity ratios, it is important to understand the factors that make employees more productive because these factors directly affect employee productivity.

The following are 10 key employee-related factors that directly affect levels of employee productivity:

Ten Key Factors Affecting Employee Productivity

1. Employee selection
2. Training

3. Supervision
4. Scheduling
5. Breaks
6. Morale
7. Menu
8. Convenience food use versus scratch preparation
9. Equipment/tools
10. Service level desired

EMPLOYEE SELECTION

Choosing the right employee from the beginning is vitally important in developing a highly productive workforce. Good foodservice managers know that proper selection procedures go a long way toward establishing the kind of workforce that can be both efficient and effective. This involves matching the right employee with the right job. The process begins with the development of the job description.

JOB DESCRIPTION

A **job description** is a listing of the tasks that must be accomplished by the employee hired to fill a particular position. For example, in the case of a room service delivery person in a large hotel, the tasks might be listed as indicated on the job description shown in Figure 7.1.

A job description should be maintained for every position in every foodservice operation. From the job description, a job specification can be prepared.

FIGURE 7.1 Job Description

Job Description	
Unit Name: <u>Thunder Lodge Resort</u>	Position Title: <u>Room Service Delivery Person</u>
PRIME TASKS:	
1. Answer telephone to receive guest orders	7. Balance room service cash drawer
2. Set up room service trays in steward area	8. Clean room service setup area at conclusion of shift
3. Deliver trays to room, as requested	9. Other duties, as assigned by supervisor
4. Remove tray covers upon delivery	10.
5. Remove soiled trays from floors	11.
6. Maintain guest check control	12.
Special Comments: Hourly rate excludes tips. Uniform allowance is $45.00 per week	
Salary Range: <u>$10.00–$12.25/hour</u>	Signature: <u>Matt V.</u>

FIGURE 7.2 Job Specification

Job Specification

Unit Name: <u>Thunder Lodge Resort</u>   Position Title: <u>Room Service Delivery Person</u>

Personal Characteristics Required:

1. Good telephone skills; speaks clearly, speaks easily understood English

2. Ability to operate point of sale (POS) systems

3. Detail oriented

4. Pleasant personality

5. Discreet

Special Comments: <u>Good grooming habits are especially important in this position, as</u>

<u>employee will be a primary guest contact person.</u>

Job Specification Prepared By: <u>Matt V.</u>

JOB SPECIFICATION

A **job specification** is a listing of the personal characteristics needed to perform the tasks contained in a job description. Figure 7.2 shows the job specification that would match the job description shown in Figure 7.1.

As can be seen, this position requires a specific set of personal characteristics and skills. When a room service delivery person is hired, the job specification requirements (specs) must be foremost in management's mind. If the job specs do not exist or are not followed, it is likely that employees may be hired who are simply not able to be highly productive. Each employee hired must be able to do, or be trained to do, the tasks indicated in the employee's job description.

It will be your role to develop and maintain both job descriptions and job specifications so that employees know what their jobs are and so that you know the characteristics your employees must have, or be trained in, to do their jobs well. Managers selecting new employees have several important tools available to them. These include:

1. Applications
2. Interviews
3. Preemployment testing
4. Background/reference checks

APPLICATIONS

The **employment application** is a document completed by the candidate for employment. It will generally list the name, address, work experience, and related information of the candidate. It is important that each employment candidate for each position be required to fill out in person, or online, an identical application, and that his or her application be kept on file for each candidate who is ultimately selected for a position.

INTERVIEWS

From the employment applications submitted, you will select some candidates for the personal interview process. It is important to realize that the types of questions that can be asked in the interview process are highly regulated. As a result, job interviews, if improperly performed, can subject an employer to significant legal liability. For example, if a candidate is not hired based on his or her answer to—or refusal to answer—an inappropriate question, that candidate may have the right to file a lawsuit.

What questions can and cannot be asked of potential employees? The Equal Employment Opportunity Commission suggests that all employers consider the following three issues when deciding whether to include a particular question on an employment application or in a job interview:

1. Does this question tend to screen out minorities or females?
2. Is the answer needed to judge this individual's competence for performance of the job?
3. Are there alternative, nondiscriminatory ways to judge the person's qualifications?

In all cases, questions asked both on the application and in the interview should focus on the applicant's ability to do a job, and nothing else.

PREEMPLOYMENT TESTING

Preemployment testing is a common way to help improve employee productivity. In the hospitality industry, preemployment testing will generally fall into one of the following categories:

1. Skills tests
2. Psychological tests
3. Drug screening tests

Skills tests allow an applicant to show that he or she can complete a task. Example activities could include drink production for bartenders, computer application tests for those involved in using word processing or spreadsheet tools, or food production tasks for cooks and chefs.

Psychological testing can include personality tests, tests designed to predict mental performance, or tests of mental ability.

Preemployment drug testing is used by some organizations to determine if an applicant uses illegal drugs. Such testing is allowable in most states, and it can be a very effective tool for reducing insurance rates and potential employee liability issues.

BACKGROUND/REFERENCE CHECKS

Increasingly, hospitality employers are utilizing background checks prior to hiring employees in selected positions. Common verification points include the following:

- Name
- Social Security number
- Address history
- Dates of past employment and duties performed
- Education/training
- Criminal background
- Credit history

Background checks, like preemployment testing, can leave an employer subject to litigation if the information secured during a check is false or is used in a way that violates federal or state employment laws. In addition, if the information is improperly disclosed to third parties, it could violate the employee's right to privacy. Not conducting background checks on some positions can, however, subject the employer to potential litigation under the doctrine of **negligent hiring**, that is, a failure on the part of an employer to exercise reasonable care in the selection of employees. When background checks are performed, a candidate for employment should be asked to sign a consent form authorizing you to conduct the background check.

FUN ON THE WEB!

For government information regarding labor issues and laws in the United States, explore the US Department of Labor website at **www.dol.gov.** Click on "Site Map" then review the "Find It by Topic" list. You will find important information on hiring, minimum wage and overtime pay, family and medical leave, employment discrimination, and much more.

Green and Growing!

Consumers are increasingly aware that when they support businesses committed to sustainability, their dollars make an impact socially and environmentally. As a result, influential and leading-edge thinkers concerned about society and the environment seek out companies that share their health, social, and environmental interests and priorities. So committed are they that they are, on average, willing to spend 20 percent more than the typical guest for products that conform to their values and lifestyle.

In a similar manner, environmentally conscious workers are increasingly aware that a company's care for the environment most often is also reflected in its care for its employees. As a result, companies espousing genuine commitment to the environment attract a more committed and, as a result, higher-quality staff. These workers tend to value health, the environment, social justice, personal development, and sustainable living. They want to contribute their efforts to companies that share those values, and their numbers are growing.

Do you have to be "certified" as green to attract these environmentally conscious employees? That is, do you have to be a "perfect" green facility? No. But you cannot just pretend that you are, either. Workers easily see beyond false claims of care, in part because they share information so freely and easily via Web pages, Twitter "tweets," blogs, and chat rooms. The more environmentally friendly, socially responsible, and healthy you are known to truly be, the easier it will be for prospective employees who share these goals to find you—because they *are* looking.

TRAINING

Perhaps no area under your control holds greater promise for increased employee productivity than effective training. In too many cases, however, training in the hospitality industry is poor or almost nonexistent. Highly productive employees are usually well-trained employees, and, frequently, employees with low productivity have been poorly trained. Every position in a foodservice operation should have a specific, well-developed, and ongoing training program.

Effective training will improve job satisfaction and instill in employees a sense of well-being and accomplishment. It will also reduce confusion, product waste, and loss of guests. In addition, supervisors find that a well-trained workforce is easier to manage than one in which employees are poorly trained. An additional advantage of a well-trained workforce is that management will be more effective because of reduced stress, in terms of both work completion and interpersonal relationships.

Effective training begins with a good **orientation program**. An orientation program prepares a new worker for success on his or her job. The following list includes some of the concerns that most employees have when they start a new job. You should identify which items are relevant to your new employees and take care to provide them information in each area, in either written or verbal form.

Potential Orientation Program Information

1. Payday
2. Annual performance review
3. Probationary period

4. Dress code
5. Telephone call, cell phone use policy
6. Smoking policy
7. Uniform allowance
8. Disciplinary system
9. Educational assistance
10. Work schedule
11. Mandatory meetings
12. Tip policy
13. Transfers
14. Employee meal policy
15. Sexual harassment policy
16. Lockers/security
17. Jury duty
18. Leave of absence
19. Maternity leave
20. Alcohol/drug policy
21. Employee assistance programs
22. Tardy policy
23. Sick leave policy
24. Vacation policy
25. Holidays and holiday pay
26. Overtime pay
27. Insurance
28. Retirement programs
29. Safety/emergency procedures
30. Grievance procedures

Orientation and training programs need not be elaborate. They must, however, be consistent and continual. Hospitality companies can train in many different areas. Some training seeks to influence attitudes and actions, for example, when training to prevent work-related harassment is presented. In other cases, training may be undertaken to assist employees with stress or other psychologically related job aspects.

In most cases, the training you will be responsible for as a unit manager is **task training**—the training undertaken to ensure an employee has the skills to meet productivity goals. The development of a training program for any task requires managers to:

1. Determine how the task is to be done.
2. Plan the training session.
3. Present the training session.
4. Evaluate the session's effectiveness.
5. Retrain at the proper interval.

DETERMINE HOW THE TASK IS TO BE DONE

Often, jobs can be done in more than one way. When management has determined how a task should be completed, however, that method should be made part of the training program and should be strictly maintained unless a better method can be demonstrated and successfully implemented. If this is not done, employees will find that "anything goes," and product consistency, along with service levels, will vary tremendously.

PLAN THE TRAINING SESSION

Properly planning for a training session involves answering key questions:

1. Who should be trained?
2. Who should do the training?
3. Where should the training occur?
4. When should the session occur?
5. What tools, materials, or supplies are needed to conduct the session?
6. What should the length of the session be?
7. How frequently should the sessions occur?
8. How and where will the attendance and completion records regarding each training session offered be kept?

Good training sessions are the result of a need felt by management to train personnel matched with a management philosophy that training is important. Taking time to effectively plan training sessions is a good way for you to let employees know that you take the training process seriously.

Whether the training session is self-paced, an interactive program delivered via the Internet, a DVD, a hands-on demonstration, a group discussion, or a lecture-style presentation, time spent planning your training sessions is time well spent.

PRESENT THE TRAINING SESSION

Many managers feel that they have no time for training. But good management is about teaching, encouraging, and coaching others. As a result, you must find the time to train. Managers interested in the long-term success of their operations and employees will often set aside time each week to conduct training. Some managers maintain that all of the training in their unit must be **OJT** (on-the-job training). They feel that structured training either takes too long or is inappropriate. In nearly all cases, this is not correct and is a major cause of the rather low rate of productivity so prevalent in some parts of the hospitality industry.

The best training sessions are presented with enthusiasm and an attitude of encouragement. Make sure that training is presented not because employees "don't know" but because management wants them to "know more." Involve employees in the presentation of training exercises. Seek their input in the sessions. Ask questions that encourage discussion, and always conclude the sessions on a positive note.

A brief, but effective, plan for each session could be to:

1. Tell the employees what you hope to teach them, and why.
2. Present the session.
3. Reemphasize the main points and discuss why they are important.
4. Ask for questions to ensure understanding.

EVALUATE THE SESSION'S EFFECTIVENESS

There is a saying in education, "If the student hasn't learned, then the teacher hasn't taught." This concept, when applied to hospitality training, implies that simply presenting a training session is not enough. Training should result in change. Either employees improve and gain new skills, knowledge, or information, or they have not learned. If you know this to be the case, you must evaluate the training session. This process can be as simple as observing an employee's behavior (to test skill acquisition), or as detailed as preparing written questions for employees to answer (to test knowledge application and retention).

Post-training evaluation should also be directed at how the sessions were conducted. Were they too long? Were they planned well? The evaluation of training is as important as its delivery. Both the content of the session and the delivery itself should be evaluated because employees who are well trained are more productive, are more highly motivated, and provide better service to guests.

RETRAIN AT THE PROPER INTERVAL

Humans learn, unlearn, and relearn on a regular basis. The telephone number you might have known so well 10 years ago might now be gone from your memory. Similarly, the friend or teacher's name you knew well at one time and felt you would never forget may be forgotten. In the same way, employees who are well trained in an operation's policies and procedures need to be constantly reminded and updated if their skill and knowledge levels are to remain high.

Performance levels can decline because of a change in the operational systems you have in place or changes in equipment used. When this is true, you must retrain your employees. Training a workforce is one, if not the best, method of improving employee productivity. Effective training costs a small amount of time in the short run, but pays off extremely well in dollars in the long run. Managers who have risen to the top in the hospitality industry have some specific characteristics and traits. Chief among these is their desire to teach and encourage their employees and, thus, get the best results from each and every one of them.

SUPERVISION

All employees require proper supervision. This is not to say that all employees want to be told what to do. Proper supervision means assisting employees in improving productivity. In this sense, the supervisor is a helper and facilitator who provides employee assistance. Supervising should be a matter of assisting employees to do their best, not just identifying their shortcomings. It is said that employees think one of two things when they see their boss approaching:

1. Here comes help!

or

2. Here comes trouble!

For those supervisors whose employees feel that the boss is an asset to their daily routine, productivity gains are remarkable. Supervisors who see their position as one of power, or who see themselves as taskmasters, can only rarely maintain the quality workforce necessary to compete in today's competitive market.

It is important to remember that it is the employee, not management, who services the guest. When supervision is geared toward helping employees an operation's guests benefit, and, as a result, the operation benefits. This is why, in most foodservice operations, it is so important for managers to be **on-the-floor**, in other words, in the dining or service area, during meal periods. Greeting guests, solving bottleneck problems, maintaining food quality, and ensuring excellent service are all tasks of the foodservice manager during the service period. When employees see that management is committed to providing high-quality customer service, and is there to assist employees in delivering that level of service, worker productivity will improve.

SCHEDULING

Even with highly productive employees, poor employee scheduling by management can result in low productivity ratios. Consider the example in Figure 7.3, where management has determined a schedule for pot washers in a unit that is open for three meals per day.

FIGURE 7.3 Two Alternative Schedules

Schedule A

	7:30 to 8:30	8:30 to 9:30	9:30 to 10:30	10:30 to 11:30	11:30 to 12:30	12:30 to 1:30	1:30 to 2:30	2:30 to 3:30	3:30 to 4:30	4:30 to 5:30	5:30 to 6:30	6:30 to 7:30	7:30 to 8:30	8:30 to 9:30	9:30 to 10:30	10:30 to 11:30
Employee 1	■	■	■	■	■	■	■	■								
Employee 2	■	■	■	■	■	■	■	■								
Employee 3									■	■	■	■	■	■		■
Employee 4									■	■	■	■	■	■	■	■

Total Hours = 32

Schedule B

	7:30 to 8:30	8:30 to 9:30	9:30 to 10:30	10:30 to 11:30	11:30 to 12:30	12:30 to 1:30	1:30 to 2:30	2:30 to 3:30	3:30 to 4:30	4:30 to 5:30	5:30 to 6:30	6:30 to 7:30	7:30 to 8:30	8:30 to 9:30	9:30 to 10:30	10:30 to 11:30
Employee 1	■	■	■	■	■	■	■	■								
Employee 2					■	■	■	■	■	■	■	■				
Employee 3									■	■	■	■	■	■	■	■

Total Hours = 24

In Schedule A, four employees are scheduled for 32 hours at a rate of $9.00 per hour. Pot washer payroll, in this case, is $288 per day (32 hours/day × $9.00/ hour = $288 per day). Each shift, breakfast, lunch, and dinner, has two employees scheduled.

In Schedule B, three employees are scheduled for 24 hours. At the same rate of $9.00 per hour, payroll is $216 per day (24 hours/day × $9.00/hour = $216 per day). Wages, in this case, are reduced by $72 ($288 − $216 = $72), and further savings will be realized due to reduced employment taxes, benefits, employee meal costs, and other labor-related expenses. Schedule A assumes that the amount of work to be done is identical at all times of the day. Schedule B covers both the lunch and the dinner shifts with two employees but assumes that one pot washer is sufficient in the early-morning period as well as very late in the day.

When scheduling is done to meet projected demand, productivity ratios will increase. If production standards are to be established and monitored, management must do its job in ensuring that employees are scheduled only when needed to meet the sales or volume anticipated. Returning to our formula for computing the productivity ratio, Figure 7.4 assumes that 600 pots are to be washed, and as a result, shows the effect on the productivity ratio of different scheduling decisions.

Proper scheduling ensures that the correct number of employees is available to do the necessary amount of work. If too many employees are scheduled, productivity ratios will decline. If too few employees are scheduled, customer service levels may suffer or necessary tasks may not be completed on time or as well as they should be.

Work in a foodservice operation tends to occur in peaks and valleys, and the foodservice manager is often faced with uneven demands regarding the number of employees needed. Different days of the week may also require different levels of staffing. In a restaurant located in a hotel that caters to business travelers, for example, the slow period might be a weekend when most business travelers are at home rather than staying in the hotel.

In an upscale restaurant, on the other hand, the slow period may be during the week, with volume picking up on the weekends. For the weekend increase in business, the manager might hire part-time employees to handle the higher volume. To further complicate matters, some operations are faced with seasonal variations. In a college dining facility, the summers may be slow, or the operation may even be closed, whereas a beach resort may be extremely busy during that same time period.

Demand can also vary from hour to hour because people in the United States tend to eat in three major time periods. In restaurants doing strong lunch business, 5 cooks and 15 servers may be necessary. At 3:00 in the afternoon at the same restaurant, one cook and one server may find themselves with few guests to serve.

Scheduling efficiency during the day can often be improved through the use of the **split-shift**, a technique used to match individual employee work shifts with peaks and valleys of customer demand. In using a split-shift, the manager would, for example, require an employee to work a busy lunch period, be off in the afternoon, and then return to work for the busy dinner period.

Employee scheduling in the hospitality industry can be challenging. It is important, however, that it be done well. Productivity standards help the foodservice operator match workload to the number of needed employees.

FIGURE 7.4 Effect of Scheduling on Productivity Ratios

Number of Pots to Be Washed	Number of Pot Washers Scheduled	Productivity Ratio
600	4	150 pots/washer
600	3	200 pots/washer

BREAKS

Most employees simply cannot work at top speed for eight hours straight. They have both a physical and mental need for breaks from their work. These breaks give them a chance to pause, collect their thoughts, converse with their fellow employees, and, in general, prepare for the next work session. Employees who are given frequent, short breaks will outproduce those who are not given any breaks. It simply makes no sense, then, for management to behave as if they begrudge their staff the breaks that are so beneficial to the organization, as well as to the employee.

Federal law does not mandate that all employees be given breaks but some states do. As a result, foodservice supervisors often must determine both the best frequency and the best length of designated breaks. In some cases, however, and especially regarding the employment of students and minors, both federal and state law may mandate special workplace requirements for employees. As a professional manager, you will need to be familiar with these laws if they apply to your operation.

FUN ON THE WEB!

Visit the website of the department or agency responsible for enforcing youth employment laws in your state. To do so, enter "child labor laws" and the name of your state in your favorite search engine, then view the results to learn about any special laws or regulations that apply to minors working in that state.

MORALE

Employee morale is not often mentioned in discussions about controlling food-service labor costs. Yet, as experienced managers will attest, it is impossible to overestimate the financial value of a highly motivated employee or crew. Although it is a truism that employees motivate themselves, it is also true that effective managers can create an environment that makes it easy for employees to want to be motivated.

History is filled with examples of teams and groups who have achieved goals that seemed impossible, but were accomplished because they were highly motivated. Serving people should be fun. It should be exciting. If this sense of fun and excitement can be instilled in foodservice employees their work also becomes fun and exciting.

Work groups with high morale share common traits. In general, these groups work in an environment where:

1. A vision has been created.
2. The vision is constantly communicated to employees.
3. The vision is shared and embraced by both management and employees.

Creating a vision is nothing more than finding a "purpose" for the workforce. Any manager who communicates that the purpose for a pot washer is simply to clean pots cannot expect to have a fired-up, turned-on employee. Yet, pot washers can have high morale. They can be a critical part of management's overall purpose for the work crew. Consider, for purposes of illustration, some of the following techniques you could use to communicate a customer service vision to your pot washers, a group of workers not normally viewed as one having direct customer contact:

1. If your unit has been, as it should be, free from cases of foodborne illness, part of the credit goes to your pot-washing staff. Recognize them for this achievement on a quarterly basis.

2. Conduct regular "pot-washing station inspections." Score the area for cleanliness on a scale of 1 to 100. Present each pot washer with a certificate when the area score exceeds 90. If it does not exceed 90, increase training until it does!

3. Recognize your "best" pot washer(s) at an annual employee recognition luncheon or dinner for:

    a. Best attendance

    b. Best productivity

    c. Cleanest work area

    d. Most improved

    e. Most thorough

    f. Most often in proper uniform

    g. Safest worker

4. Include a pot washer on your safety committee. Publicly recognize all safety committee members on a regular basis.

5. Make it a point to go to the pot-washing area on a daily basis to thank those employees for a job well done. Emphasize the importance of their efforts.

6. Encourage food production employees (your pot washers' internal customers) to take the time to thank the pot washers for their hard work and valuable contributions to the food production process.

If the purpose or vision that management proposes is only a financial profit for the organization or its owners, employees will rarely share the vision, even if it is strongly communicated. If management's vision, however, includes the vital importance of each employee's efforts, then each employee can share that vision. A shared purpose between management and employee is important for the development and maintenance of high morale. It is just not enough for management to feel that employees should be "glad to have a job." This type of attitude by management results in high employee turnover and lost productivity.

Employee turnover can be high in some sections of the hospitality industry. By some estimates, it exceeds 200 percent per year. You can measure turnover in your own operation by using the following formula:

$$\frac{\text{Number of employees separated}}{\text{Number of employees in workforce}} = \text{Employee turnover rate}$$

For example, assume that you have a total of 50 employees in your foodservice operation. In the past year, you replaced 35 employees. Your turnover rate is computed as follows:

$$\frac{35 \text{ employees separated}}{50 \text{ employees in workforce}} = 70\% \text{ turnover rate}$$

Employee separation is the term used to describe employees who have either quit, been terminated, or in some other manner have "separated" themselves from the operation. The number of employees in the workforce refers to the average number of people employed by the operation during a given time period. It is computed by adding the number of employees at the beginning of the time period being evaluated to the number of employees at the end of the same period and dividing the sum by two.

Some foodservice operators prefer to distinguish between voluntary separation and involuntary separation. A **voluntary separation** is one in which the employee

HERE'S HOW IT'S DONE *7.1*

The formula used to calculate employee turnover rate is a simple one:

$$\frac{\text{Number of employees separated}}{\text{Number of employees in workforce}} = \text{Employee turnover rate}$$

Number of employees separated is the numerator in the formula. It simply refers to the number of employees that have left the organization during a defined accounting period; such as a month or a year.

Number of employees in workforce is the denominator in the formula. It represents the *average* number of workers employed in an organization. For that reason, managers calculating their employee turnover rates must identify the number of employees on staff at the beginning of the accounting period and the number on staff at the end of the accounting period. They then divide by two (2) to get the average number of employees on staff.

For example, in an organization that employed 40 people at the beginning of the year but, due to increase sales, employed 50 people at the end of the year, the calculation for the number of employees in the workforce calculation would be:

$$\frac{40\,(\text{beginning of the period employees}) + 50\,(\text{end of the period employees})}{2} = 45 \text{ number of employees in workforce}$$

If 18 employees were replaced during the year, the employee turnover rate for this operation would be:

$$\frac{18}{45} = 40\% \text{ turnover}$$

Using the *average* number of employees in the workforce when calculating an operation's turnover rate makes the turnover rate formula more accurate because it accounts for increases or decreases in the total number of staff members employed in the operation during the time period for which the employee turnover rate is being calculated.

made the decision to leave the organization. This may be due, for example, to retirement, a better opportunity in another organization, or relocation to another town. An **involuntary separation** is one in which management has caused the employee to separate from the organization. This may have been, for example, terminating the employee because of poor attendance or violation of procedures or policy or as a result of a reduction in the workforce.

Some managers want to know the amount of turnover that is voluntary compared to that which was involuntary. For example, excessively high voluntary turnover rates may be a signal that wages and salaries are too low to keep your best employees. High involuntary turnover rates might mean that employee screening and selection techniques need to be reviewed and improved. If it is your preference, you can modify the turnover formula to create these two ratios:

$$\frac{\text{Number of employees involuntarily separated}}{\text{Number of employees in workforce}} = \text{Involuntary employee turnover rate}$$

$$\frac{\text{Number of employees voluntarily separated}}{\text{Number of employees in workforce}} = \text{Voluntary employee turnover rate}$$

Whether separation is involuntary or voluntary, turnover is expensive. In both cases, an operation will incur employee turnover costs that are both actual and hidden. Actual costs, such as those involved in advertising the position vacancy, interviewing and new employee training time required are easy to determine. The hidden costs are harder to quantify but can cost dearly in an operation with a high turnover rate. Increased china and glassware breakage may result as a new dishwasher learns the job. A new server may provide slower customer service, or a new cook may cause an increase in waste or improperly prepared food.

Good foodservice managers regularly calculate and closely monitor their turnover rates. High turnover rates can mean trouble. Low turnover rates most often means that employee morale is high and workers feel good about the operations that employ them.

MENU

A major factor in employee productivity is the foodservice operation's actual menu. The items that you elect to serve on your menu will have a profound effect on your employees' ability to produce the items quickly and efficiently.

In general, the more variety of menu items a kitchen is asked to produce, the less efficient that kitchen will be. Of course, if management does not provide the guest with enough choices, loss of sales may result. Clearly, neither too many nor too few menu choices should be offered. The question for management is, "How many are too many?" The answer depends on the operation, the skill level of employees, and the level of menu item variety management feels is necessary to properly service its guests.

Menus that continuously expand are costly, in many ways. The quick-service unit that elects to specialize in hamburgers can prepare them quickly and efficiently. If the same restaurant decides to add pizza, tacos, salads, tofu wraps, and fried chicken strips, its management may find that not only are employees less productive but also guests are confused as to what the operation really is. Again, the dilemma management faces is to serve the widest variety of menu items possible but not so many as to reduce employee productivity.

Although the number of menu items produced is important, so is the type of item. Obviously, a small diner with one deep-fat fryer will have production problems if the day's specials are fried fish, fried chicken, and a breaded fried vegetable platter! Menu items must be selected to complement the skill level of the employees and the equipment available to produce the menu items. Most foodservice operations change their menu fairly infrequently. Print and signage costs are often high, and restaurateurs are most often reluctant to radically change their product offerings. Thus, it is extremely important that the initial menu items selected by management are items that can be prepared efficiently and serviced well. If this is done, productivity rates will be high, and so will guest satisfaction.

CONVENIENCE FOOD USE VERSUS SCRATCH PREPARATION

Few, if any, foodservice operators today make all of their menu items from scratch. Indeed, there is no real agreement among operators as to what *scratch cooking* or *on-site cooking* truly is. Canned fruits, frozen seafood, and ready-to-bake pastries are examples of foods that would not be available to many guests if it were not for the fact that they were processed to some degree before they were delivered to the foodservice operator's door. At one time, presliced white bread was even considered by some in foodservice as a convenience food. Today, of course, this is considered a staple.

Some foods, such as canned cheese sauce, can be modified by an operator to produce a unique item. This can be done by the addition of special ingredients according to the standardized recipe, with the intent of creating a product served only by that foodservice operation.

The decision of whether to "make" or "buy" a specific menu item involves two major factors. The first is, of course, product quality. In general, if an operation can make a product that is superior to the one it can buy from a supplier, it should produce that item. The second factor, product cost, is also a major issue. It is possible that management determines that a given menu item can be made in-house and that it is a superior product. The cost of preparing that product, however, may be so great that it is simply not cost effective to do so. Fortunately, convenience products are becoming more quality driven and less expensive due to advances in technology and increased competition among the major food suppliers.

To illustrate the impact on labor costs of the make versus buy decision, consider the situation that would arise if you managed a quick-service Mexican restaurant. One of the items that you use is frijoles; cooked and seasoned pinto beans, which are mashed prior to serving.

Assume that you use 50 edible portion (EP) pounds of these beans per day. You can buy the seasoned beans in cans for 80 cents per pound. Your EP cost per pound with the canned product includes only the cost of the beans. In addition, you would incur the labor cost required to open the cans and heat the beans, as well as the cost of cooking fuel.

If you were to make the frijoles from scratch, assume your food cost would go down to 36 cents per pound; the price you would pay for dried pinto beans and needed seasonings. This represents a savings in food cost of over 50 percent. In this example, it appears that making this menu item from scratch would save your operation money. The complete story, however, can only be viewed when you also consider the labor cost required to produce the frijoles.

Figure 7.5 details the hypothetical costs involved in the decision that you must make, assuming a usage of 50 pounds of product per day and a labor cost of $11.00 per hour to both cook the beans and clean up the production process.

As you can see in this example, you would experience a reduction in your cost of food if you made the frijoles from scratch but an *increase* from $11.00 to $44.00 in the cost of labor because your own employees must now complete the cooking process. In the case of frijoles, your decision might well be to purchase the convenience item, if it is of acceptable quality, rather than make it from scratch because the *overall* food and labor cost would be less.

Management, often in consultation with kitchen production staff, must address a large number of make-or-buy decisions. It is important to note, however, that these decisions affect both food *and* labor costs. One cannot generally achieve significant food cost savings items without expending additional labor dollars. Conversely, when a manager elects to buy a convenience item, rather than make the item from scratch, food costs tend to rise, but labor costs most often would decline. In general, labor productivity in your operation will rise when you elect to buy, rather than make from scratch, any item that you cannot produce efficiently. This may be due to specialized skills required, as is the case with some purchased gourmet bakery items, or it could simply be a case of your supplier having the tools and equipment necessary to do a time-consuming task at a great savings to you, such as the case of buying a prechopped, frozen onion. It is important, however, that you do not fall into the trap of electing to buy more convenience-type items without reducing your labor expenditures. When that happens, you lose in terms of both higher food costs and higher-than-required labor costs.

FIGURE 7.5 Frijoles: 50 Pounds

Component	Cost of Convenience Product	Cost of Scratch Product
Beans	$40.00 ($0.80/lb.)	$18.00 ($0.36/lb.)
Seasoning	0	2.00
Labor	11.00 (1 hour)	44.00 (4 hours)
Fuel	1.40	4.40
Total Cost	$52.40	$68.40

EQUIPMENT/TOOLS

In most cases, foodservice productivity ratios have not increased as much in recent years as have those of other businesses. Much of this is due to the fact that we are a labor-intensive, not machine-intensive, industry. In some cases, equipment improvements have made kitchen work easier. Slicers, choppers, and mixers have replaced human labor with mechanical labor. However, robotics and automation are not yet a part of our industry in any major way. Nonetheless, it is critical for you to understand the importance of a properly equipped workplace and how that improves productivity. This can be as simple as understanding that a sharp knife cuts more quickly and better than a dull one or as complex as deciding which wireless system will be used to provide data and communication links to the 1,000 stores in a quick-service restaurant chain. In either case, management must ask itself a fundamental question: "Am I providing my employees with the tools necessary to do their job effectively?" The key word in that question is *effectively*. If the proper tools are provided but they are mounted at the wrong height, placed in the wrong location, or unavailable at the right time, the tools will not be used effectively. Similarly, if the proper tools are provided but employees are not adequately trained in their use, productivity gains will not occur. In all cases, it is part of your job to provide your employees with the tools they need to do their jobs quickly and effectively.

SERVICE LEVEL DESIRED

It is simply a fact that the average quick-service employee can serve more guests in an hour than the best server at an exclusive fine dining restaurant. The reason for this is quite obvious. In the quick-service operation speed, not total level of service rendered, is of the utmost importance. In the fine dining restaurant, service is to be more elegant and the personal service delivered is of a much higher level. Thus, when you vary service levels, you also vary employee productivity ratios.

In the past, foodservice managers focused very heavily on speed of service. Although that is still important today, many operators are finding that guests expect and demand higher levels of service than ever before. If this trend continues, one could expect that foodservice productivity levels will tend to go down. To prevent this from happening, foodservice operators will need to become very creative in finding ways to improve employee productivity in other areas (for example, through training and improved morale) so that these "savings" can be used to provide the higher level of customer service demanded by today's sophisticated foodservice consumer.

Now that we have closely examined factors that directly impact employee productivity and know what management can do to affect them, we return to the original question, "How many employees are needed?" The key to knowing how many are needed to effectively operate a foodservice unit lies in developing and applying productivity standards.

There are several measures of employee productivity used in the foodservice industry. You will learn about the most popular of these and examine their weaknesses and strengths. In the final analysis, the best productivity measure for any unit you manage is the one that makes the most sense for your unique operation.

MEASURING CURRENT LABOR PRODUCTIVITY •——

There is a variety of ways managers measure productivity in the hospitality industry. We will examine six of them:

1. Labor cost percentage
2. Sales per labor hour

3. Labor dollars per guest served

4. Guests served per labor dollar

5. Guests served per labor hour

6. Revenue per available seat hour (RevPASH)

LABOR COST PERCENTAGE

Perhaps the most commonly used measure of employee productivity in the food-service industry is the **labor cost percentage.** It is computed as:

$$\frac{\text{Cost of labor}}{\text{Total sales}} = \text{Labor cost \%}$$

A labor cost percentage allows an operation's managers to measure the cost of labor used to generate a known quantity of sales. It is important to realize, however, that there are actually several ways managers could define cost of labor. You should select the one that makes the most sense for your own operation. Cost of labor, as previously mentioned, includes both payroll and total labor costs, including benefits. To measure productivity, you may elect, for example, to include only hourly staff wages or staff wages and salary costs, but not total labor costs. This approach makes sense if, for example, in your operation you have the ability to control only your payroll costs and not your total labor costs. Remember, however, that when comparing your labor cost percentage with those of other foodservice units, it is important that you make sure both your unit and the one you are comparing use the same formula for your computations. If you do not, your comparisons will not accurately reflect true differences between the units.

Controlling the labor cost percentage is extremely important in the foodservice industry because it is often used to assess the effectiveness of a manager. If labor cost percentage increases beyond what is expected, management will be held accountable.

Labor cost percentage is a popular measure of productivity, in part, because it is so easy to compute and analyze. Consider the case of Roderick, a foodservice manager in charge of a table service restaurant in a year-round theme park. The unit is popular and has a $20 per guest check average. Roderick uses only payroll (staff wages and management salaries) when determining his overall labor cost percentage because he does not have easy access to the actual cost of taxes and benefits provided to his employees. These labor-related expenses are considered by Roderick's supervisor to be noncontrollable and beyond Roderick's immediate influence.

Roderick has computed his labor cost percentage for each of the last four weeks using the labor cost percentage formula. His supervisor has given Roderick a goal of 35 percent for the four-week period. Roderick feels that he has done well in meeting that goal. Figure 7.6 shows Roderick's four-week performance.

FIGURE 7.6 Roderick's 4-Week Labor Cost % Report

Week	Cost of Labor	Total Sales	Labor Cost %
1	$ 7,100	$18,400	38.6%
2	8,050	21,500	37.4%
3	7,258	19,100	38.0%
4	6,922	24,800	27.9%
Total	$29,330	$83,800	35.0%

Using the labor cost percentage formula and the data in Figure 7.6, Roderick's labor cost percentage is calculated as:

$$\frac{\text{Cost of labor}}{\text{Total sales}} = \text{Labor cost \%}$$

That is,

$$\frac{\$29,330}{\$83,800} = 35\%$$

While Roderick did achieve a 35 percent labor cost for the four-week period, Madeline, his supervisor, is concerned because she received many negative comments in week 4 regarding poor service levels in Roderick's unit. Some of these were even posted online, and Madeline is concerned about the postings' potential impact on future visitors to the park's foodservice operations. When she carefully analyzes the numbers in Figure 7.6 she sees that Roderick far exceeded his goal of a 35 percent labor cost in weeks 1 through 3 and then reduced his labor cost to 27.9 percent in week 4.

Although the monthly overall average of 35 percent is within budget, she knows all is not well in this unit. Roderick elected to reduce his payroll in week 4, and yet it is clear from the negative guest comments that, at a 27.9 percent labor cost, service to his guests suffered. That is, too few employees were on staff to provide the necessary guest attention. As you can see, one disadvantage of using an overall labor cost percentage is that it can hide daily or weekly highs and lows.

In Roderick's operation, labor costs were too high the first three weeks and too low in the last week, but he still achieved his overall target of 35 percent. Recall from the discussion about percentages in Chapter 1 that the total labor cost of 35 percent indicates that, for each dollar of sales generated, 35 cents was paid to the employees who assisted in generating those sales. In many cases, a targeted labor cost percentage is viewed as a measure of employee productivity and, to some degree, management's skill in controlling labor costs.

In addition to its tendency to mask productivity highs and lows, labor cost percentage has some additional limitations as a measure of productivity. Notice, for example, what happens to this measure of productivity if all of Roderick's employees are given a 5 percent raise in pay. If this were the case, Roderick's labor cost percentages for last month would be calculated as shown in Figure 7.7.

Note that labor now accounts for 36.8 percent of each dollar sales value. It is important to realize that Roderick's workforce did not become less productive simply because they got a 5 percent increase in pay.

Labor cost percentage varies with changes in the price paid for labor. When the price paid for labor increases, labor cost percentage increases. When the price paid for labor decreases, labor cost percentage decreases. Because of this, using labor cost percentage alone to evaluate workforce productivity can sometimes be misleading.

FIGURE 7.7 Roderick's 4-Week Revised Labor Cost % Report (Includes 5% pay increase)

Week	Original Cost of Labor	5% Pay Increase	Cost of Labor (with 5% Pay Increase)	Total Sales	Labor Cost %
1	$ 7,100	$ 355.00	$ 7,455.00	$18,400	40.5%
2	8,050	402.50	8,452.50	21,500	39.3%
3	7,258	362.90	7,620.90	19,100	39.9%
4	6,922	346.10	7,268.10	24,800	29.3%
Total	$29,330	$1,466.50	$30,796.50	$83,800	36.8%

FIGURE 7.8 Roderick's 4-Week Revised Labor Cost % Report: (Includes 5% Increase in Selling Price)

Week	Cost of Labor	Original Sales	5% Selling Price Increase	Sales (with 5% Selling Price Increase)	Labor Cost %
1	$ 7,100	$18,400	$ 920	$19,320	36.7%
2	8,050	21,500	1,075	22,575	35.7%
3	7,258	19,100	955	20,055	36.2%
4	6,922	24,800	1,240	26,040	26.6%
Total	$29,330	$83,800	$4,190	$87,990	33.3%

To see another example of the limitations of labor cost percentage as a measure of labor productivity, consider the effect on labor cost percentage of increasing selling prices. Return to the data in Figure 7.6 and assume that Roderick's unit raised all menu prices by 5 percent prior to the beginning of the month. Figure 7.8 shows how an increase of this size in his selling prices would affect his labor cost percentage.

Note that increases in selling prices (assuming no decline in guest count or changes in buying behavior) will result in decreases in the labor cost percentage. Alternatively, lowering selling prices without increasing total revenue will result in increased labor cost percentage.

Although labor cost percentage is easy to compute and widely used, it is difficult to use as a measure of productivity over time because it depends on labor dollars spent and sales dollars received for its computation. Even in relatively noninflationary times, wages do increase and menu prices are adjusted. Both activities affect labor cost percentage but not worker productivity. In addition, institutional foodservice settings, which often have no dollar sales figures to report, can find that it is not easily possible to measure labor productivity using labor cost percentage because they generally calculate and report guest counts or number of meals served rather than sales dollars earned.

SALES PER LABOR HOUR

It has been said that the most perishable commodity any foodservice operator buys is the labor hour. When labor is not productively used, it disappears forever. It cannot be "carried over" to the next day, like an unsold head of lettuce or a slice of turkey breast. It is for this reason that some foodservice operators prefer to measure labor productivity in terms of the amount of sales generated for each labor hour used. This productivity measure is called **sales per labor hour**. The formula for computing this measure of labor productivity is:

$$\frac{\text{Total sales}}{\text{Labor hours used}} = \text{Sales per labor hour}$$

In this formula, labor hours used is simply the sum of all labor hours paid for by the operation in a specific sales period. Consider Roderick's labor usage and the resulting sales per labor hour information presented in Figure 7.9.

In this example, sales per labor hour ranged from a low of $19.50 in week 1 to a high of $28.66 in week 4. Operators who compute sales per labor hour do so because they feel it is a better measure of labor productivity than the labor cost percentage.

Sales per labor hour will vary with changes in selling prices (as does the labor cost percentage), but it will not vary based on changes in the price paid for

FIGURE 7.9 Roderick's 4-Week Sales per Labor Hour

Week	Total Sales	Labor Hours Used	Sales per Labor Hour
1	$18,400	943.5	$19.50
2	21,500	1,006.3	$21.37
3	19,100	907.3	$21.05
4	24,800	865.3	$28.66
Total	$83,800	3,722.4	$22.51

labor. In other words, increases and decreases in the price paid per hour of labor will not affect this productivity measure. On the negative side, however, sales per labor hour neglects to consider the hourly amount paid to employees per hour to generate the sales. As a result, a foodservice unit paying its employees an average of $10.00 per hour could, using this type of measure for labor productivity, have the same sales per labor hour as a similar unit paying $12.00 for each hour of labor used. Obviously, the manager paying $10.00 per hour has paid less for an equally productive workforce if the sales per labor hour used are the same in the two units.

Many managers, particularly those managing commercial foodservice operations, like utilizing the sales per labor hour productivity measure because records on both the numerator (total sales) and the denominator (labor hours used) are readily available. However, depending on the record-keeping system employed, it might be more difficult to determine total labor hours used than total labor dollars spent. This is especially true when large numbers of employees are paid by salary rather than those paid by the hour. The efforts of both salaried managers and hourly paid staff should be considered when computing a facility's overall sales per labor hour used.

LABOR DOLLARS PER GUEST SERVED

Had Roderick preferred, he might have measured his labor productivity in terms of the labor dollars spent per guest served his operation. This productivity measure is called **labor dollars per guest served**. The formula for this measure is:

$$\frac{\text{Cost of labor}}{\text{Guests served}} = \text{Labor dollars per guest served}$$

Using Roderick's data, the labor dollars per guest served computation would be as shown in Figure 7.10.

FIGURE 7.10 Roderick's 4-Week Labor Dollars per Guest Served

Week	Cost of Labor	Guests Served	Labor Dollars per Guest Served
1	$ 7,100	920	$7.72
2	8,050	1,075	$7.49
3	7,258	955	$7.60
4	6,922	1,240	$5.58
Total	$29,330	4,190	$7.00

In this example, the labor dollars expended per guest served for the four-week period would be computed as follows:

$$\frac{\$29,330}{4,190} = \$7.00$$

Using this measure of productivity, it is fairly easy to see why Roderick experienced guest complaints during the fourth week of operation. Note that in the first three weeks, he "supplied" his guests with more than $7.00 of guest-related labor costs per guest served, but in the fourth week that amount fell to less than $6.00 per guest.

As is the case with labor cost percentage, labor dollars per guest served is limited in that it will vary based on the price paid for labor. It is not, however, affected by changes in menu prices.

GUESTS SERVED PER LABOR DOLLAR

A variation on the formula of labor dollars per guest served is to reverse the numerator and denominator to create a new productivity measure, which is **guests served per labor dollar**. The formula for this measure of labor productivity is:

$$\frac{\text{Guests served}}{\text{Cost of labor}} = \text{Guests served per labor dollar}$$

Had Roderick wanted to use the guests served per labor dollar, his labor productivity data could have been calculated as is presented in Figure 7.11.

In this situation, Roderick served, for the four-week average, a total of 0.143 guests for each labor dollar expended. As a measure of labor productivity, guests served per labor dollar spent has several advantages. First, it can be used by food-service units, such as institutions, that do not routinely record dollar sales figures. Also, this measure is relatively easy to compute because you are very likely to keep records of the total number of guests you serve on a daily basis.

GUESTS SERVED PER LABOR HOUR

Guests served per labor hour is another powerful and popular measure of labor productivity:

$$\frac{\text{Guests served}}{\text{Labor hours used}} = \text{Guests served per labor hour}$$

The *guests served per labor hour* productivity measure is especially powerful because it includes neither dollar sales figures nor labor dollar expense in its computation. That means it is free from variations due to changes in menu selling prices and changes in the price paid for labor.

FIGURE 7.11 Roderick's 4-Week Guests Served per Labor Dollar

Week	Guests Served	Cost of Labor	Guests Served per Labor Dollar
1	920	$ 7,100	0.130
2	1,075	8,050	0.134
3	955	7,258	0.132
4	1,240	6,922	0.179
Total	4,190	$29,330	0.143

FIGURE 7.12 Roderick's 4-Week Guests Served per Labor Hour

Week	Guests Served	Labor Hours Used	Guests Served per Labor Hour
1	920	943.5	0.975
2	1,075	1,006.3	1.068
3	955	907.3	1.053
4	1,240	865.3	1.433
Total	4,190	3,722.4	1.126

Guests served per labor hour is strong in its ability to measure productivity gains across time due to changes that are unrelated to selling prices or wages paid. It is also extremely useful in comparing similar operating units in areas with widely differing wage rates or selling prices. Thus, it is popular with multiunit corporations comparing operational units in diverse geographic regions. It is also useful in comparing dissimilar facilities with similar wages and selling prices because it can help identify areas of weakness in management scheduling, employee productivity, facility layout and design, or other factors that can affect labor productivity.

Had Roderick elected to evaluate his workforce productivity through the use of the guests served per labor hour formula, his data would look like that shown in Figure 7.12.

As the data show, Roderick's guests served per labor hour ranges from a low of 0.975 guests per hour (week 1) to a high of 1.433 guests per hour (week 4). The average for the four-week period is 1.126 guests served per labor hour (4,190 guests served ÷ 3,722.4 hours used = 1.126 guests per labor hour). Note that, in week four, the number of guests served per worker hour used was higher than in previous weeks, the result of which was poor guest service and the source of Roderick's increased customer complaints.

Managers who use guests served per labor hour as a measure of productivity generally do so because they like its focus on service levels and not merely costs. However, it may be more difficult and time consuming to compute this measure of productivity

Consider the Cost

"You wanted to see me, sir?" said Francis to the clearly agitated guest seated at the six-top table in the corner of Chez Lapin, the upscale French Bistro-style restaurant that Francis managed.

"I've been waiting 10 minutes for my waiter to bring us our check. And as slow as he's been, it will probably take another 10 minutes to process my credit card. I just want to pay and leave. The food was fine, but this service is ridiculous!"

"I'm really sorry, sir. I'll find your server," replied Francis, as he glanced around the dining room. As he did, he noticed several unbussed tables that were littered with dirty dishes, as well as the hostess stand where the line of guests waiting to be seated hadn't gotten any smaller in nearly an hour.

When Francis entered the kitchen looking for the disgruntled guest's server, he was surprised to see several of the line cooks relaxing on the production line.

"How's it going back here tonight?" asked Francis, as he glanced around the kitchen.

"No problems. Just waiting for the orders to come in boss," replied Sasha, the sous chef in charge of the production line. "We're keeping up easily."

Assume that all of the workers at Chez Lapin are well trained and highly motivated:

1. Do you think the servers are likely doing their best to provide good service to the restaurant's guests? If you believe so, then why was the guest in this scenario unhappy?

2. What do you think is the cause of a consistently long line of waiting diners when there are numerous vacant, but unbussed, tables in the dining room?

3. The sous chef in this case said, "We're keeping up easily." Do you think that means they are being very efficient and, thus, very productive? Explain your answer.

because you must compute the number of labor hours used as well as make decisions on how to define a guest. For example, in an outdoor café, a guest who orders a cup of coffee is indeed a guest, but he or she requires much less service than one who consumes a full meal. Unless you decide differently, however, the guests served per labor hour productivity measure would treat these two guests in the same manner.

REVENUE PER AVAILABLE SEAT HOUR (RevPASH)

The final assessment of productivity that you should know about is also the newest. Dr. Sheryl E. Kimes has developed and advocates the use of **revenue per available seat hour (RevPASH)** as a way to measure the efficiency with which commercial restaurants manage their operations. RevPASH helps managers evaluate both how much guests purchase and how quickly they are served. It does so primarily by assessing average sales per guest (check average) you learned about in Chapter 2 and the average duration of guests' dining experiences. Duration is simply the length of time customers occupy a seat or table.

Although you will not generally have the ability to directly control the menu items your guests will purchase, the time it takes them to eat, or how long they linger after eating, RevPASH can give you a good idea of the speed at which your kitchen produces your menu items and the time it takes your service personnel deliver them.

To calculate RevPASH, you must be able to identify the number of diners you serve each hour, as well as the amount these guests spend (revenue). Typically, this information is easily retrieved from your operation's point of sale (POS) system. In addition, you must know the number of dining room seats available to your guests as well as the number of hours those seats were available. The formula for this measure of productivity is:

$$\frac{\text{Revenue}}{\text{Available seat hours}} = \text{Revenue per available seat hour (RevPASH)}$$

To illustrate, assume that Roderick's operation had 100 seats and that it was open for dinner from 5:00 to 10:00 P.M. Figure 7.13 shows the revenue his operation generated during each of the hours he was open last Friday.

Roderick calculates the total available seat hours in his operation simply by taking the number of seats available for guests and multiplying that number by the number of hours those seats are available: (Available seats × Hours of operation = Available seat hours). Note that, on average, Roderick fills 80 percent of his seats at a RevPASH of $40.70.

FIGURE 7.13 Revenue per Available Seat Hour (RevPASH)

				For: Last Friday Night
Hour	Available Seats	Guests Served	Revenue	RevPASH
4–5 P.M.	0	0	$ 0.00	$ 0.00
5–6 P.M.	100	25	1,500.00	15.00
6–7 P.M.	100	75	3,700.00	37.00
7–8 P.M.	100	100	5,200.00	52.00
8–9 P.M.	100	100	5,150.00	51.50
9–10 P.M.	100	100	4,800.00	48.00
10–11 P.M.	0	0	0.00	0.00
Total	500	400	$20,350.00	$40.70

% Seats Sold = 400/500 = 80%

His operation is most efficient from 7:00 to 10:00 P.M., as can be determined by a higher than average ($40.70) RevPASH for each of these hours. If Roderick could add incentives to attract or move diners to earlier times (5:00 to 6:00 P.M.), or perhaps stay open later (10:00 to 11:00 P.M.), an increase in his RevPASH and his potential profit could be considerable.

Also, note that if Roderick could increase his seat turnover (i.e., if in one hour he served 120 guests in 100 seats), his operation's RevPASH could also increase significantly. It is important to realize that RevPASH does not directly utilize the price paid for labor in its evaluation of operational efficiency. Managers using this measure, however, gain valuable information about when their operations' labor needs are the greatest. They can then use that information to efficiently schedule workers for each hour the operation is serving guests.

It is widely believed that work really does magically expand to meet (and often exceed!) the number of people available to do the job, and so measures of productivity must be available to guide management in making labor productivity assessments. Figure 7.14 summarizes the six productivity measures addressed in this chapter and lists some advantages and disadvantages associated with each. You may

FIGURE 7.14 Productivity Measures Summary

Measurement	Advantages	Disadvantages
Labor cost % = Cost of labor / Total sales	1. Easy to compute 2. Most widely used	1. Hides highs and lows 2. Varies with changes in price of labor 3. Varies with changes in menu selling price
Sales per labor hour = Total sales / Labor hours used	1. Fairly easy to compute 2. Does not vary with changes in the price of labor	1. Ignores price per hour paid for labor 2. Varies with changes in menu selling price
Labor dollars per guest served = Cost of labor / Guests served	1. Fairly easy to compute 2. Does not vary with changes in menu selling price 3. Can be used by non–revenue-generating units	1. Ignores average sales per guest and, thus, total sales 2. Varies with changes in the price of labor
Guests served per labor dollar = Guests served / Cost of labor	1. Fairly easy to compute 2. Does not vary with changes in menu selling price 3. Can be used by non–revenue-generating units	1. Ignores average sales per guest and, thus, total sales 2. Varies with changes in the price of labor
Guests served per labor hour = Guests served / Labor hours used	1. Can be used by non–revenue-generating units 2. Does not change due to changes in price of labor or menu selling price 3. Emphasizes serving guests rather than reducing costs	1. Time consuming to produce 2. Ignores price paid for labor 3. Ignores average sales per guest and, thus, total sales
RevPASH = Revenue / Available seat hours	1. Measures overall efficiency in seating and selling products to guests 2. Identifies most and least efficient serving periods 3. Assesses how much guests buy and how long it takes to serve them their selections	1. Most suitable for commercial operations 2. Varies with changes in menu selling price 3. Does not utilize the price paid for labor in its calculation 4. Requires a detailed data collection/reporting system

select one or more of the measures described previously or create your own measure. In most cases, it is recommended that you monitor your labor cost percentage (the easiest measure to compute) and at least one other measure of productivity if you are truly serious about controlling labor-related expenses.

SIX-COLUMN DAILY PRODUCTIVITY REPORT

Many operators, upon selecting a labor productivity measure, prefer to compute that measure on a daily, rather than on a weekly or monthly, basis. This can be done by using a six-column form similar to the one introduced in Chapter 5.

A six-column form for Roderick's restaurant sales and labor cost in week 1 is presented in Figure 7.15.

To estimate daily labor cost percentage (Cost of labor/Total sales = Labor cost %), the amounts in the Today columns are divided to create the Labor Cost % Today column, just as the amounts in the To Date columns are divided to create the Labor Cost % to Date column.

Roderick's daily labor cost percentage during Week 1 ranged from a low of 31.2 percent (day 7) to a high of 47.8 percent (day 2). The labor cost percentage for the week was 38.6 percent. Again, you can see the effect of averaging highs and lows when using measures of labor productivity.

Any of the six productivity-related measures can be calculated on a daily basis using a modification of the six-column form. Figure 7.16 details the method to be used to establish six-column forms for each of the six productivity measures presented in this chapter. When using the six-column report, it is important to remember that the To Date column value, on any given day, is always the sum of the values of all the preceding Today columns, including the current day.

FIGURE 7.15 Six-Column Labor Cost %

Unit Name: **Roderick's**   Date: 1/15–1/21

Weekday	Cost of Labor		Sales		Labor Cost %	
	Today	To Date	Today	To Date	Today	To Date
1	$ 800	$ 800	$ 2,000	$2,000	40.0%	40.0%
2	880	1,680	1,840	3,840	47.8%	43.8%
3	920	2,600	2,150	5,990	42.8%	43.4%
4	980	3,580	2,300	8,290	42.6%	43.2%
5	1,000	4,580	2,100	10,390	47.6%	44.1%
6	1,300	5,880	4,100	14,490	31.7%	40.6%
7	1,220	7,100	3,910	18,400	31.2%	38.6%
Total	$7,100		$18,400		38.6%	

FIGURE 7.16 Six-Column Labor Productivity Form

Measure of Productivity	Columns 1 & 2	Columns 3 & 4	Columns 5 & 6
Labor cost % = $\frac{\text{Cost of labor}}{\text{Total sales}}$	Cost of Labor Today Cost of Labor to Date	Sales Today Sales to Date	Labor Cost % Today Labor Cost % to Date
Sales per labor hour = $\frac{\text{Total sales}}{\text{Labor hours used}}$	Sales Today Sales to Date	Labor Hours Used Today Labor Hours Used to Date	Sales per Labor Hour Today Sales per Labor Hour to Date
Labor dollars per guest served = $\frac{\text{Cost of labor}}{\text{Guests served}}$	Cost of Labor Today Cost of Labor to Date	Guests Served Today Guests Served to Date	Labor Dollars per Guest Served Today Labor Dollars per Guest Served to Date
Guests served per labor dollar = $\frac{\text{Guests served}}{\text{Cost of labor}}$	Guests Served Today Guests Served to Date	Cost of Labor Today Cost of Labor to Date	Guests Served per Labor Dollar Today Guests Served per Labor Dollar to Date
Guests served per labor hour = $\frac{\text{Guests served}}{\text{Labor hours used}}$	Guests Served Today Guests Served to Date	Labor Hours Used Today Labor Hours Used to Date	Guests Served per Labor Hour Today Guests Served per Labor Hour to Date
Revenue per available seat hour = $\frac{\text{Revenue}}{\text{Available seat hours}}$	Revenue (Sales) Today Revenue (Sales) to Date	Available Seat Hours Today Available Seat Hours to Date	RevPASH Today RevPASH to Date

DETERMINING COSTS BY LABOR CATEGORY

Because of the various approaches used to measure effectiveness, it is not surprising that many operators find a single measure of their labor productivity is insufficient for their needs. Consider the case of Otis, the owner and operator of a restaurant called the Squirrel Flats Diner, which services both backpacking tourists and loggers taking a break from work at a nearby logging camp. Otis's sales last month were $100,000. His labor costs were $30,000. Thus, his labor cost percentage was 30 percent ($30,000 ÷ $100,000 = 0.30). Otis, however, knows more about his labor cost percentage than this overall number alone tells him. Figure 7.17 shows the method Otis uses to compute his overall labor cost percentage.

FIGURE 7.17 Labor Cost % for Squirrel Flats Diner

Time Period: 1/1–1/31		Sales: $100,000
Labor Category	**Cost of Labor**	**Labor Cost %**
Production	$12,000	12%
Service	9,000	9%
Sanitation	3,000	3%
Management	6,000	6%
Total	$30,000	30%

Note that Otis divides his labor expense into four distinct labor subcategories. Production includes all those individuals who are involved with preparing the food Otis sells. Service includes all the servers and cashiers involved in delivering the food to guests and receiving guest payments. Sanitation consists of the individuals responsible for ware washing and after-hour cleanup of the establishment. Management includes the salaries of Otis's two supervisors.

By establishing four labor categories, Otis has a better idea of where his labor dollars are spent than if only one overall figure had been used. Just as it is often helpful to compute food cost percentages by category (see Chapter 5), it is often helpful to calculate more than one labor cost percentage or other measure of labor productivity.

Notice in Figure 7.17 that the sum of Otis's four labor cost percentage subcategories equals the amount of his total labor cost percentage:

$$12\% + 9\% + 3\% + 6\% = 30\%$$

You may establish any number of labor subcategories that makes sense for your own unique operation. Of course, you can apply any measure of labor productivity to these labor subcategories. There are three important points to remember when determining labor productivity measures by subcategory:

1. Be sure to include all the relevant data, whether it is amount spent, hours used, sales generated, or guests served.
2. Use the same method to identify the numerator and denominator for each category.
3. Compute an overall total to ensure that the sum of the categories is consistent with the overall total.

Keep these points in mind as you examine Figure 7.18, which details Otis's second measure of labor productivity. He has selected guests served per labor dollar as a supplement to his computation of labor cost percentage. Otis feels that this second measure helps him determine his effectiveness with guests without losing sight of the total number of dollars he spends on payroll expense. The formula he uses for this computation is:

$$\frac{\text{Guests served}}{\text{Cost of labor}} = \text{Guests served per labor dollar}$$

Note that each labor category in Figure 7.18 yields a different *guests served per labor dollar* figure. As could be expected, when labor dollars in a category are low, guests served per labor dollar in that category is relatively high. This is

FIGURE 7.18 Guests Served per Labor Dollar for Squirrel Flats Diner

Guests Served: 25,000		Time Period: 1/1–1/31
Labor Category	Cost of Labor	Guests Served per Labor Dollar
Production	$12,000	2.083
Service	9,000	2.778
Sanitation	3,000	8.333
Management	6,000	4.167
Total	$30,000	0.833

clearly demonstrated in the Sanitation category of Figure 7.18. When labor dollars expended are high, as in the Total category, guests served per labor dollar is lower.

With the exception of RevPASH, each of the measures of labor productivity presented in this chapter can be subcategorized in any logical manner that is of value to management. The purpose of computing numbers such as these is, of course, that they are valuable in developing staff schedules and estimating future payroll costs. For example, assume that in one month Otis finds his labor cost percentage has exceeded his goal of 30 percent. By computing his guests served per labor dollar subcategory values, Otis can quickly see exactly where he has exceeded his goal and, thus, where he needs to make adjustments. In addition, if Otis knows that next month he is projecting 30,000 guests, he can estimate his labor costs for each subcategory. For example, by following the rules of algebra and adding the word "estimated," the guests served per labor dollar formula can be restated as follows:

$$\frac{\text{Number of estimated guests served}}{\text{Guests served per labor dollar}} = \text{Estimated cost of labor}$$

From the data in Figure 7.18 and using the Production subcategory as an example, Otis estimates his production labor costs in a month where 30,000 guests are anticipated as follows:

$$\frac{30,000 \text{ guests served}}{2.083 \text{ guests per dollar}} = \$14,402.30$$

Using this estimation method, Otis knows his production-related costs for the month should be approximately \$14,402. Using the same estimated cost of labor formula, Otis can project and budget different labor costs for each of his subcategories, as well as his overall labor cost total. Using this information, Otis can prepare an employee schedule that uses the planned for amount of payroll cost and no more.

MANAGING PAYROLL COSTS

Professional foodservice operators always manage their payroll costs. Essentially, the management of payroll costs is a four-step process:

Step 1. Determine productivity standards.
Step 2. Forecast sales volume.
Step 3. Schedule employees using productivity standards and forecasted sales volume.
Step 4. Analyze results.

STEP 1. DETERMINE PRODUCTIVITY STANDARDS

The first step in controlling payroll costs is to determine productivity standards for your operation. A **productivity standard** is defined as a guideline that constitutes an appropriate productivity ratio in your foodservice operation. Thus, a productivity standard might be a particular labor cost percentage, or a specific number of guests served per labor dollar expended, or any other predetermined productivity ratio

FIGURE 7.19 Labor Cost % Summary

Unit Description	Labor Cost %
Unit 1	34.1%
Unit 2	35.5%
Unit 3	34.3%
Unit 4	35.2%
District Average	34.8%
Company Average	34.0%
Industry Average	35.5%

you want to utilize. In other words, you must find the answers to the questions of how long it should take an employee to do a job and how many employees it takes to do the complete job.

A productivity standard, then, is simply management's expectation of the productivity ratio of each employee. Establishing productivity standards for every employee is an essential management task and the first step in controlling payroll costs.

Thus far, we have discussed some methods of measuring current productivity ratios based on historical sales and expense data. This tells you where you are in relation to productivity, but it does not say where you should be. To illustrate this concept, assume that you have decided to buy and operate a franchise unit within a themed steakhouse chain. Currently, four units of the same chain exist in your immediate geographic area, which has been designated a district by the **franchisor**, the entity responsible for selling and maintaining control over the franchise brand's name.

The area franchisor representative who monitors labor productivity by using labor cost percentage has shared the following data with you, as shown in Figure 7.19.

The figures for units one to four represent labor cost percentages in those franchise steakhouse units in your district. The district average is the unweighted mean of those four units. Company average refers to the overall labor cost percentage in of the units franchised by the steakhouse chain you are joining. Industry average refers to the average labor cost percentage reported by theme-style steakhouses of the type similar to the one you will own and operate.

Using the data presented in Figure 7.19, you could begin to establish your own desired productivity measures and goals. Your restaurant is not yet open, so you face the problem of not having historical data from your own unit to help you. Of course, this is always the case when opening new restaurants, but it is also true when significantly changing the theme, decor, or menu of an existing restaurant.

Using your own judgment and the information you do have available, you could choose as your labor cost goal the lowest labor cost percentage (unit one); the highest (unit two); the district, company, or industry average; or even some other number not included in this listing. Any of these numbers could become your target, or ideal, labor cost percentage. In the final analysis, you must use whatever data you have available, as well as your own insight, to establish an appropriate productivity standard for your operation. Productivity standards are typically based on the following types of information:

1. Unit history

2. Company average

3. Industry average
4. Management experience
5. A combination of two or more of the above

In this case, you might choose to begin with a 35 percent labor cost as one of your productivity standards. This figure is close to the district average (34.8%) and is likely an aggressive, but realistic, goal for your first year. As mentioned previously, you would likely want to choose at least one more measure of productivity to help you monitor your labor efficiency. In the years to come, you would want to effectively manage the factors that affect productivity, carefully monitor your actual productivity using the productivity measures you select and then establish a productivity goal that is both realistic and attainable.

STEP 2. FORECAST SALES VOLUME

Sales volume forecasting (see Chapter 2), when combined with established labor productivity standards, allows you to determine the number of employees that should be needed to effectively service your guests. All foodservice units must forecast sales volume if they are to supply an adequate number of employees to service that volume. This forecasting may be done in terms of either sales dollars or number of guests to be served.

An important, but frequently misunderstood, distinction must be made between forecasting sales volume and forecasting the number of employees needed to service that volume. The distinction is simply that, as a manager, you will view guests coming to your operation in "block" fashion, that is, in groups at a time. Employees, on the other hand, are added to your schedule one individual at a time and, thus, will significantly affect productivity measures. A brief example will make this clear. Ted owns a small shop that sells only specialty coffees. His service staff productivity standard is one server for each 30 guests. Thus, he schedules his employees as shown in Figure 7.20.

When 30 or fewer guests are expected, Ted needs only one server on duty. In effect, each time a block of 30 guests is added, Ted must add another server. Thus, if Ted anticipates 20 guests one day and 30 the next, no change in staff is necessary. That is, an addition of 10 extra guests does not dictate the addition of another server. On the other hand, if Ted anticipates 30 guests one day and 40 the next, an additional staff person is required because Ted has introduced a new block of guests.

It does not matter how much of the new block actually arrives; Ted has staffed for all of it. He hopes, of course, that all or nearly the entire block of guests will arrive because this will keep his cost per guest served lower. If only a small portion of the block comes, Ted's cost per guest served will rise unless he takes some action to reduce his labor-related expense.

FIGURE 7.20 Ted's Coffee Shop Staffing Guide

Number of Guests Anticipated	Number of Servers Needed
1–30	1
31–60	2
61–90	3
91–120	4

STEP 3. SCHEDULE EMPLOYEES USING PRODUCTIVITY STANDARDS AND FORECASTED SALES VOLUME

Forecasting sales volume is important to labor cost control because it begins to take managers out of the past and present and allows them to project into the future and significantly influence what will likely happen then.

To illustrate how established productivity standards (Step 1) are combined with sales forecasts (Step 2) to develop employee schedules (Step 3), consider Darla, the foodservice director at Langtree, a private college enrolling a high percentage of female students. Darla is responsible for operating both a residence hall feeding situation (Geier Hall) and an open snack bar/cafeteria (Lillie's Cafeteria and Snack Bar).

Geier Hall houses 1,000 young women. Lillie's Cafeteria and Snack Bar is open to all students, staff, and faculty of the school. Darla is committed to controlling all of her labor-related expense. As such, she has carefully monitored her past labor productivity ratios, those of other similar schools, and national averages. In addition, she has considered the facilities she operates, the skill level and morale of her workforce, and the impact of her aggressive training program on her employees' future productivity.

Because Lillie's generates a daily sales figure, Darla has determined that productivity in this operation should be measured using a labor cost percentage and that it should be able to operate at a labor cost of 30 percent.

In the residence hall, where dollar sales figures are replaced with daily guest counts, she has decided that her labor productivity measure should be guests served per labor hour. Her goal is a ratio of 30 to 1—that is, 30 guests served per labor hour expended. Darla may now develop her labor cost expense budget in terms of both dollars (Lillie's) and labor hours used (Geier Hall).

Figure 7.21 shows how Darla would establish her labor budget for Lillie's using her productivity standards, her sales forecast, and the labor cost percentage formula. Recall that the labor cost percentage formula is calculated as:

$$\frac{\text{Cost of labor}}{\text{Total sales}} = \text{Labor cost \%}$$

If you include the words *forecasted, standard,* and *budget* and then apply the rules of algebra, the labor cost percentage formula can be restated as follows:

$$\text{Forecasted total sales} \times \text{Labor cost \% standard} = \text{Cost of labor budget}$$

Thus, the cost of labor budget amount in the preceding formula becomes Darla's forecasted, or targeted, labor expense. To determine, for example, her targeted labor expense budget for Lillie's in week 1, and assuming her sales forecast for Lillie's for the period was $6,550, Darla would compute her labor budget as:

$$\$6,550 \times 30\% = \$1,965$$

Figure 7.22 illustrates how Darla would establish a budget for total number of labor hours to be used to service Geier Hall residents. Recall that, in this food facility, sales refers to the number of guests served rather than dollars, and this is reflected in Darla's sales forecast. Also, remember that the guests served per labor hour formula is defined as follows:

$$\frac{\text{Guests served}}{\text{Labor hours used}} = \text{Guests served per labor hour}$$

FIGURE 7.21 Labor Budget for Lillie's Cafeteria and Snack Bar Using Labor Cost %

Time Period	Forecasted Total Sales	Labor Cost % Standard	Cost of Labor Budget
Week 1	$ 6,550	30%	$1,965
Week 2	6,850	30%	2,055
Week 3	6,000	30%	1,800
Week 4	8,100	30%	2,430
Total	$27,500	30%	$8,250

If you include the words *forecasted, standard,* and *budget* and follow the rules of algebra, the guests served per labor hour formula can be restated as follows:

$$\frac{\text{Forecasted number of guests served}}{\text{Guests served per labor hour standard}} = \text{Labor hour budget}$$

Using week one in Figure 7.22 as an example, and assuming 20,000 meals would be served, the computation would be:

$$\frac{20,000 \text{ forecasted guests}}{30 \text{ guests served per labor hour standard}} = 666.7 \text{ labor hours}$$

Note that in Figures 7.21 and 7.22, Darla could have varied her weekly productivity standard and still have produced a four-week budget. In other words, on weeks when volume was high, she could have elected to reduce her desired labor cost percentage or increase the guests served per labor hour standard. This can be a logical course of action if the operator feels that increased volume can have the effect of reducing the cost percentage of fixed labor or can increase the number of guests served per labor hour by staff persons in specific positions, such as cashiers and managers. Experience tells Darla, however, that, in her case, a standard labor productivity ratio that remains unchanged across the four weeks is her best option.

From the labor hour budgets she developed, Darla can now schedule her production staff in terms of dollars to be spent for labor (Lillie's) and labor hours to be used (Geier Hall). She must be careful to schedule employees only when they are needed. To do this, she must forecast her volume in time blocks smaller than one-day segments. Perhaps, in her case, volume should be predicted in three periods (breakfast, lunch, and dinner) in the residence hall, and in one- or two-hour blocks in her snack bar/cafeteria

To see how Darla might schedule her residence hall staff during week 1 of her four-week projection, assume that Darla's weekly projection of sales volume for Geier Hall is as presented in Figure 7.23.

FIGURE 7.22 Labor Budget for Geier Hall Using Guests Served per Labor Hour

Time Period	Forecasted Number of Guests Served	Guests Served per Labor Hour Standard	Labor Hour Budget
Week 1	20,000	30 guests/hour	666.7
Week 2	18,600	30 guests/hour	620.0
Week 3	18,100	30 guests/hour	603.3
Week 4	17,800	30 guests/hour	593.3
Total	74,500	30 guests/hour	2,483.3

FIGURE 7.23 Weekly Labor Hour Budget for Geier Hall

Day	Forecasted Number of Guests Served	Guests Served per Labor Hour Standard	Labor Hour Budget
1	3,000	30 guests/hour	100.0
2	2,900	30 guests/hour	96.7
3	2,900	30 guests/hour	96.7
4	2,850	30 guests/hour	95.0
5	3,000	30 guests/hour	100.0
6	2,700	30 guests/hour	90.0
7	2,650	30 guests/hour	88.3
Total	20,000	30 guests/hour	666.7

On any given day, Darla can match her volume projections with budgeted labor hours or dollars. To see exactly how she would use this information to determine her employees' schedules, let us examine day 1 in Figure 7.23, a day when Darla projects 3,000 guests (meals) served and 100 labor hours needed. She knows that she should "spend" no more than 100 total hours for labor on that day. She also knows, from recording her productivity ratio in the past (Figure 7.24), where she has spent her labor hours in prior time periods. Thus, Darla should invest approximately 60 hours (100 hours available × 0.60 average usage) for production employees, 30 hours for service employees, and 10 hours of management time for Monday if she is to stay within her labor budget while providing an adequate number of workers in each of the three categories of labor she monitors regularly.

Presented in a different way, Darla knows that, to stay within her labor goals, each labor category will have its own unique guests served per labor hour ratio, as noted in Figure 7.25. It is important to note that, although guests served per labor hour varies by labor category, the overall total yields 30 guests per labor hour used, which is Darla's productivity standard. Darla's employee schedule for the production area on Monday might look as shown in Figure 7.26.

FIGURE 7.24 Recap of Past Percentage of Total Usage by Category

Geier Hall	
Labor Category	% of Total
Production	60%
Service	30%
Management	10%
Total	100%

FIGURE 7.25 Recap of Guests Served per Labor Hour

Geier Hall			
Labor Category	Forecasted Number of Guests Served	Labor Hour Standard	Budgeted Guests Served per Labor Hour
Production	3,000	60	50
Service	3,000	30	100
Management	3,000	10	300
Total	3,000	100	30

FIGURE 7.26 Employee Schedule

Unit Name: <u>Geier Hall</u>				Date: Monday 1/1
Labor Category: <u>Production</u>		Shift: <u>A.M. and P.M.</u>		Labor Budget: <u>60 hours</u>

Employee Name	Schedule	Hours Scheduled	Rate	Total Cost
Sally S.*	6:00 A.M.–2:30 P.M.	8	N/A	N/A
Tom T.*	6:30 A.M.–3:00 P.M.	8		
Steve J.*	8:00 A.M.–4:30 P.M.	8		
Lucy S.*	10:00 A.M.–6:30 P.M.	8		
Janice J.	7:00 A.M.–11:00 A.M.	4		
Susie T.	6:30 A.M.–10:30 A.M.	4		
Peggy H.	10:30 A.M.–1:30 P.M.	3		
Marian D.	2:00 P.M.–5:00 P.M.	3		
Larry M.*	11:00 A.M.–7:30 P.M.	8		
Jill D.*	1:00 P.M.–7:30 P.M.	6		
Total		60	N/A	N/A

*Includes 30-minute meal break.

Because employee schedules are based on the number of hours to be worked or dollars to be spent, an employee schedule form similar to the one in Figure 7.26 can be an effective tool in a daily analysis of labor productivity. Because labor is purchased on a daily basis it should be monitored on a daily basis. The labor schedule should even be adjusted as needed during the day. This constant adjustment is a key to the quick-service industry's profitability because schedule modifications by good managers in this segment of the industry are implemented hourly, not daily! In other words, if customer demand is lower than expected, employees can be released from the schedule to reduce labor costs. If volume is higher than expected, additional employees should be available on an "as needed" basis.

Some foodservice managers practice an **on-call** system in which employees who are off duty are assigned to on-call status. This means that these employees can be contacted by management on short notice to fill in for other employees who are absent. On-call employees may also be called in to work if customer demand suddenly increases. State laws vary regarding the compensation that must be paid to these on-call employees; thus, managers who use this method should know about existing state laws and their own company policies regarding the practice before it is implemented.

Other managers practice a **call-in** system, in which employees who are off-duty are required to check in with management on a daily basis to see if the predicted sales volume is such that they may be needed. This is a particularly good way to make rapid changes in staffing because of unforeseen increases in projected sales volume while minimizing the payment of overtime wages. **Overtime wages,** are those that must be paid at a higher than normal rate. Overtime wages should generally be held to a minimum and should require documented management approval before they are authorized.

In the case of Geier Hall, the Rate and Total Cost columns in Figure 7.26 are not computed because, in this unit, they are not part of the productivity measure (recall that guests served per labor hour relies on neither cost of labor nor sales revenue for its computation). They would, of course, be filled out when determining the cost of the schedule for Lillie's snack bar because, in that unit, it is labor dollars, not hours used, that is used to calculate the productivity standard. In all cases, an employee schedule, reviewed on a daily basis, should be established for each operating unit, labor category, and individual worker if managers are to match labor usage with projected volume.

Cost Control Around the World

Employee scheduling is directly affected by the laws, union contracts, and even the customs of the country in which a business operates. For example, Figure 7.27 details the amount of paid vacation earned by employees (who have worked at least one year) in several different countries in which US foodservice companies typically do business.

Additional regulations that can directly affect management's scheduling of employees include local child labor laws, overtime wage payment requirements, and union contract terms. The best managers ensure that their employee schedules always comply with the laws and requirements in place in those countries in which their operations are located.

FIGURE 7.27 Annual Earned Vacation Time

Country	Vacation Time Earned
Australia	No law, but 4 weeks is standard
France	5 weeks
Germany	4 weeks
Hong Kong	7 days
Mexico	6 days
Poland	18 days
Puerto Rico	15 days
South Africa	21 consecutive days
Spain	30 days
Sweden	5 weeks
Turkey	12 days
United Kingdom	EC directive (4 weeks annual leave)
Ukraine	24 calendar days
United States	*No national requirement. Two weeks is common but not mandatory.*

STEP 4. ANALYZE RESULTS

Darla has done a good job of using established labor standards and volume projections in building her employee schedule. To complete the job of managing labor-related expense, she should analyze her results.

Figure 7.28 details Lillie's actual and budgeted operating result for the first four weeks of the year.

To determine the percentage of budget, the following formula, introduced in Chapter 1, is used:

Actual amount ÷ Budgeted amount = % of budget

Note that total sales were somewhat less than budgeted (98%), whereas total labor cost dollars were somewhat higher than budgeted (102%). Consequently, labor cost percentage was somewhat higher than anticipated—in other words, a 31 percent actual result compared to a 30 percent budget percentage. Notice also that, when sales are projected perfectly (week 3) but labor dollars are overspent,

FIGURE 7.28 Labor Recap for Lillie's Actual versus Budgeted Labor Cost

Week	Sales			Labor Cost			Labor Cost %	
	Budgeted	Actual	% of Budget	Budgeted	Actual	% of Budget	Budgeted	Actual
1	$ 6,550	$ 6,400	98%	$1,965	$1,867	95%	30%	29%
2	6,850	7,000	102%	2,055	2,158	105%	30%	31%
3	6,000	6,000	100%	1,800	1,980	110%	30%	33%
4	8,100	7,600	94%	2,430	2,430	100%	30%	32%
Total	$27,500	$27,000	98%	$8,250	$8,435	102%	30%	31%

the resulting labor cost percentage will be too high (33%). Conversely, when labor costs are exactly as budgeted (week 4) but sales volume does not reach its estimate, labor cost percent will similarly be too high (32%).

It may seem that a 1 percent variation in overall labor cost percentage is insignificant. In fact, in this case it represents $185 ($8,435 actual cost − $8,250 budgeted cost = $185). However, if a foodservice company achieved sales of $30,000,000 per year, exceeding planned labor cost by 1 percent would represent a $300,000 ($30,000,000 × 0.01 = $300,000) per year cost overrun! Small percentages can add up. Only management can determine what constitutes a significant labor cost variation. Darla may well want to review standard scheduling techniques with her supervisors because she exceeded her budgeted labor cost in two of the four weeks shown. In Darla's case, $185 may well be a significant budget variation.

When referring to labor costs, some foodservice operators use the term **standard labor cost**—that is, the labor cost needed to meet established productivity standards—rather than budgeted cost. If productivity standards are used to establish budgeted labor costs, then the two terms are synonymous. It is important to recognize that actual labor costs will often vary somewhat from standard labor costs unless guest counts and/or revenues can be predicted perfectly (which, of course, is rarely the case). We can, however, compare budgeted labor expense with actual results to determine if the reasons for the variation from budget are valid and acceptable to management. The complete process for establishing the labor schedule is summarized in the checklist contained in Figure 7.29.

FIGURE 7.29 Ten-Point Labor Schedule Checklist

☐ 1. Monitor historical operational data (or alternative data if historical data are not available).

☐ 2. Identify productivity standards.

☐ 3. Forecast sales volume.

☐ 4. Determine budgeted labor dollars or hours.

☐ 5. Divide monthly budget into weekly budgets.

☐ 6. Divide weekly budget into daily budgets.

☐ 7. Segment daily budget into meal period budgets.

☐ 8. Build schedule based on the budget.

☐ 9. Analyze service levels during schedule period.

☐ 10. Review and adjust productivity standards as needed.

REDUCING LABOR-RELATED COSTS

If through your analysis you find that your labor costs are too high, problem areas must be identified and corrective action must be taken. If the overall productivity of your work group cannot be improved, other action must be taken. The approaches that managers take to reduce labor-related costs are different for fixed payroll costs than for variable payroll costs. Figure 7.30 indicates strategies managers can use to reduce labor-related expense in each of these two categories. Notice that you can only decrease variable payroll expense by increasing productivity, improving the scheduling process, eliminating employees, or reducing wages paid. Fixed payroll expense can be reduced (as a percentage of revenue) by increasing sales volume.

One too-often-ignored way of increasing employee productivity, and thus reducing labor-related expense, is through employee empowerment. Employee empowerment results from a decision by management to fully involve employees in the decision-making process as far as guests and the employees themselves are concerned. **Empowerment** refers simply to the fact that, whereas it was once customary for management to make all decisions regarding every facet of the operational aspects of its organization and present them to its employees as inescapable facts to be accomplished, employees can be given the power to get involved.

Employees can be empowered to make critical decisions concerning themselves and, most importantly, those concerning guests. Many foodservice employees work closely with guests. Many guest-related problems in the hospitality industry can be easily solved when employees are given the power to make it "right" for the guest. Management has found in many cases that, through a well-planned and consistently delivered training program, and by empowering their employees, they are nurturing a loyal and committed workforce that is more productive, is supportive of management, and is willing to go the extra mile for guests. Doing so builds repeat sales and profits.

FUN ON THE WEB!

Monthly journals and daily Web briefings are important sources of management information related to managing employees. The Society for Human Resource Management (SHRM) is a great source of human resource management–related information. Visit its website. While you are there, browse "Publications." Also consider a daily reading of the "HR News" column.

FIGURE 7.30 Reducing Labor-Related Expense Percentage

Labor Category	Actions
Fixed	1. Improve productivity.
	2. Increase sales volume.
	3. Combine jobs to eliminate fixed positions.
	4. Reduce wages paid to fixed-payroll employees.
Variable	1. Improve productivity.
	2. Schedule appropriately to adjust to changes in sales volume.
	3. Combine jobs to eliminate variable positions.
	4. Reduce wages paid to variable employees.

Technology Tools

As labor costs continue to increase, and as labor cost management becomes increasingly important to the profitability of restaurateurs, the tools available to manage these costs have significantly improved and increased as well.

Current software programs enable you to manage and control labor costs by helping you perform the following tasks:

1. Maintain employment records, such as:
   a. Required employment documents (e.g., applications, I-9s, W-2s)
   b. Tax data
   c. Pay rates
   d. Earned vacation or other leave time
   e. Subcategories of labor data
   f. Benefits eligibility
   g. Training records
2. Conduct and record the results of online or computer-based training programs.
3. Compute voluntary and involuntary employee turnover rates by department.
4. Track employee days lost due to injury or accident.
5. Maintain employee availability records (requested days off, vacation, or mandated leave).
6. Develop employee schedules and interface employee schedules with time-clock systems.
7. Monitor overtime wages costs.
8. Maintain job descriptions and job specifications.
9. Develop and maintain daily, weekly, and monthly productivity reports, including:
   a. Labor cost percentage
   b. Sales per labor hour
   c. Labor dollars per guest served
   d. Guests served per labor dollar
   e. Guests served per labor hour
   f. Optimal labor costs based on actual sales achieved
10. Interface employee scheduling software with forecasted sales volume software in the POS system.

FUN ON THE WEB!

Innovation in management tools that aid in managing payroll costs is not always aimed toward larger companies. Intuit is a company that produces a popular payroll program for smaller operators as well as the widely used Quick Books accounting program. To review the payroll program, go to the Intuit website. When you arrive, select "Intuit online payroll."

Apply What You Have Learned

*T*eddy Fields is the kitchen manager at the Tanron Corporation International Headquarters. The facility he helps manage serves 3,000 employees per day. Teddy very much needs an additional dishwasher. He is now interviewing Wayne, who is an excellent candidate with five years of experience and who is now washing dishes at the nearby Roadway restaurant.

Teddy normally starts his new dishwashers at $10.00 per hour. Wayne states that he currently makes $11.25 per hour, a rate that is higher than all but one of Teddy's current dishwashers. Wayne states that he simply will not leave his current job to take a pay cut.

1. Should Teddy offer to hire Wayne at a rate higher than most of his current employees? Why or why not?

2. Assume you answered no to question one above, what would you say to Wayne?

3. Assume you answered yes to question 1 above; what would you say to your current dishwashing employees if in the future Wayne shared his pay information with them?

Key Terms and Concepts

The following are terms and concepts discussed in the chapter that are important for you as a manager. To help you review, please define the terms below.

payroll	preemployment drug testing	guests served per labor dollar
labor expense	negligent hiring	guests served per labor hour
salaried employee	orientation program	revenue per available seat hour (RevPASH)
exempt employee	task training	productivity standard
minimum staff	OJT	franchisor
fixed payroll	on-the-floor	on-call
variable payroll	split-shift	call-in
productivity	employee separation	overtime wages
productivity ratio	voluntary separation	standard labor cost
job description	involuntary separation	empowerment
job specification	labor cost percentage	
employment application	sales per labor hour	
skills test	labor dollars per guest served	
psychological testing		

Test Your Skills

You may download the Excel spreadsheets for the Test Your Skills exercises from the student companion website at www.wiley.com/college/dopson. Complete the exercises by placing your answers in the shaded boxes and answering the questions as indicated.

1. Serrena owns a gourmet coffee shop. In Serrena's operation, payroll costs for hourly employees and salaried employees are calculated separately. Serrena recorded the revenue her operation generated last month as well as the amount she spent for hourly staff and for salaried managers. Calculate Serrena's last month labor cost percentages for her hourly staff and for her salaried employees as well as her total payroll cost and total payroll cost percentage.

	Payroll Last Month	Payroll Percent
Revenue	$135,000	
Cost of Hourly Staff	29,500	
Cost of Salaried Managers	6,500	
Total Payroll		

2. Rosa is the manager of a fine-dining Italian restaurant in a large Midwest city. She has experienced high turnover with her hourly employees over the past several months because they say that she isn't paying competitive wages. More employees have threatened to leave if she doesn't give them a raise. She has determined that she can compete with local restaurants if she raises the hourly wage from $8.00 per hour to $8.50, a 6.25 percent increase. Rosa is concerned about what this will do to her labor cost percentage. Her current labor cost is 35 percent, and she feels that 38 percent is the highest labor cost ratio she can maintain and still make a profit. Using last month's data, help Rosa calculate the effect of a 6.25 percent increase in wages. Can she give the employees what they want and still make a profit?

Week	Original Cost of Labor	Raise in Dollars	Total Cost of Labor	Sales	Labor Cost %
1	$10,650			$27,600	
2	12,075			32,250	
3	10,887			28,650	
4	10,383			37,200	
Total					

3. Jennifer operates Joe Bob's Bar-B-Q Restaurant. She specializes in beef brisket and blackberry cobbler. Her operation is very popular. The following data is taken from her last month's operation. She would like to establish labor standards for the entire year based on last month's figures because she believes that a month represents a good level of both customer service and profitability for her operation. Jennifer has an average guest check of $12 and an overall average payroll cost of $8 per hour.

   a. Use Jennifer's last month's operating results to calculate the following productivity standards: labor cost percentage, sales per labor hour, labor dollars per guest served, guests served per labor dollar, and guests served per labor hour. (*Spreadsheet hint:* Use the ROUND function to two decimal places for "Guests Served per Labor Hour" because you will use it in part c.)

Operating Results for Joe Bob's		
Week	Number of Guests Served	Labor Hours Used
1	7,000	4,000
2	7,800	4,120
3	7,500	4,110
4	8,000	4,450
Total	30,300	16,680

Calculate:

Average guest check	$12
Average wage per hour	$ 8
Total sales	
Total labor cost	

Productivity Measurement	Productivity Standard
Labor cost percentage	
Sales per labor hour	
Labor dollars per guest served	
Guests served per labor dollar	
Guests served per labor hour	

b. Jennifer has subdivided her employees into the following categories: meat production, bakery production, salad production, service, sanitation, and management. She wants to develop a sales per labor hour standard for each of her labor categories. She believes this will help her develop future labor budgets based on forecasted sales. Help Jennifer calculate this standard based on her current usage of labor hours.

Labor Category	% of Labor Hours Used	Labor Hours	Sales per Labor Hour
Meat production	25%		
Bakery production	15%		
Salad production	10%		
Service	20%		
Sanitation	20%		
Management	10%		
Total	100%		

c. Now that Jennifer has calculated her productivity standards, she would like to use them to develop a labor hours budget for each day next week. She has forecasted 8,000 guests, and she wants to use the guests served per labor hour standard that was calculated in part a. Use this information to develop a labor hours budget for Jennifer.

Day	Forecasted Number of Guests Served	Guests Served per Labor Hour Standard	Labor Hours Budget
1	900		
2	925		
3	975		
4	1,200		
5	1,400		
6	1,600		
7	1,000		
Total	8,000		

4. Mikel owns Mikel's Steak House, a popular dining establishment just outside of town on a busy state highway. Mikel uses labor cost percentage as his productivity measure, but he has been calculating it only once per month. Since his monthly costs have been higher than he expected, Mikel has decided that he needs a daily measure of his labor cost percentage to better control his costs.

   a. Calculate Mikel's daily labor cost percentage using the six-column daily productivity report, which follows.

Six-Column Labor Cost Percentage						
Unit Name: Mikel's Steak House				Date: 3/1–3/7		
	Cost of Labor		Sales		Labor Cost %	
Weekday	Today	To Date	Today	To Date	Today	To Date
1	$ 950		$ 2,520			
2	1,120		2,610			
3	1,040		2,720			
4	1,100		2,780			
5	1,600		3,530			
6	1,700		4,100			
7	1,300		3,910			
Total						

   b. Mikel wants to keep his labor cost percentage at 37 percent. Given the results of his six-column daily productivity report for the first week of March, will he be able to achieve his labor cost percentage standard if he continues in the same manner for the remainder of the month? If not, what actions can he take to reduce both his fixed and his variable labor-related expenses?

5. Jeffrey operates a high-volume, fine-dining restaurant called the Baroness. His labor productivity ratio of choice is guests served per labor hour. His standards for both servers and bus persons are as follows:

   Servers = 10 guests per labor hour

   Bus persons = 25 guests per labor hour

   On a busy day, Jeffrey projects the following volume in terms of anticipated guests. His projections are made in one-hour blocks. Determine the number of labor hours Jeffrey should schedule for each job classification for each time period.

   How often in the night should Jeffrey check his volume forecast to ensure that he achieves his labor productivity standards and, thus, is within budget at the end of the evening? (*Spreadsheet hint:* Format "Server Hours Needed" and "Bus person Hours Needed" to one decimal place.)

Volume/Staff Forecasting for Saturday: The Baroness			
Time	Forecasted Number of Guests Served	Server Hours Needed	Busperson Hours Needed
11:00–12:00	85		
12:00–1:00	175		
1:00–2:00	95		
2:00–3:00	30		
3:00–4:00	25		
4:00–5:00	45		
5:00–6:00	90		
6:00–7:00	125		
7:00–8:00	185		
8:00–9:00	150		
9:00–10:00	90		
10:00–11:00	45		
Total	1,140		

6. Steve is in trouble. He has never been a particularly strong labor cost control person. He likes to think of himself more as a "people person." His boss, however, believes that Steve must get more serious about controlling labor costs or he will make Steve an unemployed people person! Steve estimates his weekly sales and then submits that figure to his boss, who then assigns Steve a labor budget for the week. Steve's operating results and budget figures for last month are presented below.

   a. Compute Steve's % of Budget figures for both sales and labor cost. Also, fill in the columns for Budget and Labor Cost % per week for the five-week accounting period.

Operating Results: Steve's Airport Deli								
	Sales			Labor Cost			Labor Cost %	
Week	Budget	Actual	% of Budget	Budget	Actual	% of Budget	Budget	Actual
1	$2,500	$2,250		$ 875	$ 900			
2	1,700	1,610		595	630			
3	4,080	3,650		1,224	1,300			
4	3,100	2,800		1,085	1,100			
5	2,600	2,400		910	980			
Total								

   b. Do you feel that Steve has significant variations from budget? Why do you think Steve's boss assigned Steve a lower labor cost percentage goal during week 3? How do you feel about Steve's overall performance? What would you do if you were Steve's boss? If you were Steve?

7. Jordan is the new western regional manager for the Lotus House, an Asian buffet restaurant chain. Her territory consists of 12 stores in four states. Last week, she received the following data from her stores. Compute Jordan's labor cost by store, by state, and for her region.

	Sales	Cost of Labor	Labor Cost%
California			
Store 1	$ 91,000.00	$34,500.00	
Store 2	106,500.00	38,750.00	
Store 3	83,500.00	31,500.00	
Total			
Oregon			
Store 1	$ 36,800.00	$12,250.00	
Store 2	61,000.00	18,750.00	
Store 3	52,000.00	17,500.00	
Total			
Washington			
Store 1	$ 47,500.00	$14,750.00	
Store 2	46,500.00	15,000.00	
Store 3	45,500.00	15,000.00	
Total			
Nevada			
Store 1	$ 53,000.00	$17,250.00	
Store 2	56,000.00	18,500.00	
Store 3	55,100.00	17,250.00	
Total			
Region			

Can Jordan compute the average labor cost percentage for her region by summing the labor cost percentages of the four states and dividing by four? Why or why not? How is the overall labor cost percentage for her region computed?

8. Ravi Shah is the food and beverage director at the St. Andrews Golf Course and Conference Center. The facility is a popular place for weddings, and Ravi finds that on many Friday and Saturday nights, the banquet space at St. Andrews is completely booked. That is good news, but Ravi also finds that Allisha, the one full-time (paid $20.00 per hour) employee he has utilized as a supervisor for the banquet area, is averaging 15 hours overtime per week.

Ravi is considering three alternative courses of action:

1. Maintain the status quo and pay Allisha for 55 hours per week.

2. Create a salaried position, schedule the employee who holds the position 55 hours per week, and pay that individual $50,000 per year.

3. Split the job into two part-time positions of 30 and 25 hours per week and pay these employees $22.50 per hour.

Assume the following:

- Overtime is paid at 1.5 times the normally paid rate.
- The operation's benefit package for part-time employees is 20 percent of the wages paid to them.
- The operation's benefit package for full-time employees is 35 percent of the wages paid to them.
- All full-time employees receive two weeks paid vacation per year.

Which of these three courses of action will cost the facility the most money? The least? If you were Ravi, which of these alternatives would you implement? Why?

	Hours Worked	Pay per Hour	Pay per Week	Weeks in a Year	Pay before Benefits	Benefits	Annual Pay with Benefits
Alternative 1							
Total							
Alternative 2							
Alternative 3							
Total							

9. Luis manages Havana, a 150-seat full-service restaurant featuring Cuban and other Caribbean-style menu items. His restaurant is open for dinner from 5:00 to 11:00 P.M. Luis was excited to read, in one of the industry publications to which he subscribes, an article explaining RevPASH. In the past, Luis used labor cost percentage to create his allowable labor cost budget. Luis now wants to calculate RevPASH, as well as continue to use labor cost percentage, to establish his *hourly* allowable labor cost budget. He has created a form (below) to calculate each of these measures.

Luis is a good manager. When his dining room is slower, he encourages his servers to aggressively sell appetizers and desserts to increase his check average. When the restaurant is very busy, he encourages his servers to stress the quick turn of tables to minimize guest wait times and maximize the number of guests that can be served. As a result, and based on his historical records, when he serves 100 or fewer guests per hour, the restaurant achieves a $20.00 per guest check average. When 101–150 guests are served per hour, the check average drops to $18.00 per guest. When over 150 guests are served per hour, Havana achieves a $16.00 per guest check average.

Consider Luis's forecast, shown in the following, of the number of guests he will serve this coming Friday night, and then calculate his forecasted RevPASH for each hour he will be open. Next, help him find out how much he can spend for labor for each hour he will be open. Assume Luis's target is a 30 percent labor cost at all times. (*Spreadsheet hint:* Calculate Total Check Average *after* Total Revenue and Total Guests Served have been calculated.)

Havana Forecast for: __This FRIDAY Night__						
Hour	Available Seats	Guests Served	Check Average	Revenue	RevPASH	Allowable Cost Based on 30% Labor Cost
5–6 P.M.		50				
6–7 P.M.		100				
7–8 P.M.		150				
8–9 P.M.		175				
9–10 P.M.		125				
10–11 P.M.		75				
Total						
% Seats Sold =						

a. What percentage of his total seats available does Luis believe he will fill on Friday night? What overall check average does he estimate he will achieve?

b. What would be Luis's forecast for his hourly and overall RevPASH on this day?

c. What would be Luis's labor budget for each hour his restaurant will be open, as well as the total amount that could be spent for labor that night?

d. What are some specific steps Luis might take to improve his RevPASH on Fridays from 5 to 6 P.M.? From 8 to 9 P.M.?

10. In this chapter, you learned about the importance of employee training when seeking to improve worker productivity. The old foodservice adage that "Training doesn't cost—it pays!" is true. With creative thinking, even the cost of acquiring quality-training materials can be made very reasonable.

Assume you were the director of foodservices for a school district that included 20 elementary, middle, and high schools. You seek to provide training to the 100 foodservice employees working in your district. Name five specific steps you could take to identify and secure low-cost training materials that could be utilized at a minimum "cost-per-employee" to be trained.

CHAPTER 8

Controlling Other Expenses

OVERVIEW

This chapter explains the management of foodservice costs that are neither food, beverage, nor labor. These costs can represent 15 percent, or even more, of an operation's sales revenue and must be controlled well if your financial goals are to be achieved in the operations you manage.

The chapter teaches how to identify the other expense costs you can directly control, as well as those considered to be non-controllable expenses. In addition, it details how to express other expenses in terms of both other expenses per guest served and other expenses as a percentage of sales revenue.

Chapter Outline

- Other Expenses
- Controllable and Non-controllable Other Expenses
- Fixed, Variable, and Mixed Other Expenses
- Monitoring Other Expenses
- Managing Other Expenses
- Technology Tools
- Apply What You Have Learned
- Key Terms and Concepts
- Test Your Skills

LEARNING OUTCOMES

At the conclusion of this chapter, you will be able to:

- Classify other expenses as being either controllable or non-controllable.
- Categorize other expenses in terms of being fixed, variable, or mixed.
- Compute other expense costs in terms of cost per guest and as a percentage of sales.

OTHER EXPENSES

In nearly all cases, food, beverage, and labor expenses represent the largest cost areas you will encounter as a foodservice manager. In addition to food, beverage, and labor expense, there "other" operating expenses you must pay. These other expenses can account for a significant amount of the total cost of operating your foodservice unit. They include a variety of items. Examples include advertising, utility bills, the repair and maintenance of equipment, insurance, property taxes and mortgage payments (if a building is owned by the operation), or rent/lease payments (if the building is owned by others).

Some of these other expenses are directly under the control of management. When following the USAR, these types of expense are reported on an operation's income statement as **other controllable expenses**. Some other expenses, however, are not directly controllable by management and, as a result, these are reported on the income statement as **non-controllable expenses**.

Managing your other expenses will be just as important to your success as controlling food, beverage, and payroll expenses. Remember that the profit margins in many restaurants can be small, so the control of all costs is critically important. Even in those situations that are traditionally considered nonprofit, such as hospitals, nursing homes, and educational institutions, all costs must be controlled because dollars that are wasted in the foodservice area will not be available for use in other important areas of the institution.

You must look for ways to control all of your expenses, but sometimes the environment in which you operate will influence some of your operating costs in positive or in negative ways. An excellent example of this is in the area of energy conservation and waste recycling. Energy costs are one of the other expenses examined in this chapter. In the past, serving water to each guest upon arrival in a restaurant was simply **standard operating procedure (SOP)** for many operations. But the rising cost of energy and increased awareness of the effect on the environment of wasted resources caused many foodservice operations to implement a policy of serving water only on request rather than with each order, or of selling bottled water instead of serving "free" tap water.

Guests have found these changes quite acceptable, and the savings in the expenses related to glass washing, equipment usage, energy, and cleaning supplies, as well as labor, are significant. In a similar manner, many operators today are finding that recycling fats and oils, cans, jars, and paper products can be good not only for the environment but also for their bottom line. Recycling these items reduces your cost of routine trash disposal, and, in some communities, the recycled materials themselves have a cash value.

FUN ON THE WEB!

Use Less Stuff is an organization that seeks to help conserve natural resources and reduce waste. Its website is a great place to learn about source reduction, packaging, and waste reduction. Look at this site for ideas on how to cut other operating expenses through energy conservation, source reduction, and recycling. Especially note the Use Less Stuff (ULS) report. Also browse through the site for additional and valuable reports, articles, and links to other interesting green-oriented sites.

CONTROLLABLE AND NON-CONTROLLABLE OTHER EXPENSES

It is helpful for managers to consider other expenses in their operations in terms of the expenses being either controllable or non-controllable. To see why, consider the case of Steve, the owner of a neighborhood tavern/sandwich shop. Most of Steve's sales revenue comes from the sale of beer, sandwiches, and his special pizza. Steve is free to decide on the monthly amount he will spend on advertising. Advertising expense, then, is under Steve's direct control and is considered to be a controllable other expense.

Some of his other expenses, however, are not under his control. For example, the licenses needed to sell products are a familiar form of a non-controllable expense. The state in which Steve operates charges a liquor license fee to all those operations that serve alcoholic beverages. If his state increases the liquor license fee, Steve is required to pay the additional fee. In this situation, the alcoholic beverage license fee would be considered a non-controllable expense, that is, an expense that is outside of Steve's immediate control.

As an additional example, assume that you own a franchised quick-service unit that sells takeout chicken. Your store is part of a nationwide chain of such stores. Each month, your store is assessed a $500 advertising and promotion fee by the chain's regional headquarters. The $500 is used to purchase television advertising time for the chain. This $500 charge is a non-controllable operating expense because it is set by the franchisor and it must be paid each month.

A controllable expense is one in which decisions made by the foodservice manager can have the effect of either increasing or reducing the expense. A non-controllable expense is one that the foodservice manager can neither increase nor decrease. Management has some control over controllable expenses but usually has little or no control over non-controllable expenses. Because this is true, managers should focus their attention primarily on controllable, rather than non-controllable, expenses. In all likelihood, it is your ability to manage your controllable other expenses that will most influence how your cost control abilities are evaluated.

It is important to recognize that the items categorized as other expenses can constitute almost anything in the foodservice business. If your restaurant is a floating ship, periodically scraping the barnacles off the boat is categorized as an other expense. If an operator is serving food to oil field workers in Alaska, heating fuel for the dining rooms and kitchen is an other expense, and probably a very large one! If a company has been selected to serve food at the Olympics in a foreign country, airfares for its employees might be a significant other expense.

Each foodservice operation will have a unique list of required other expenses. It is not possible, therefore, to list all imaginable expenses that could be incurred by every foodservice operator. The expenses that are incurred, however, should be recorded and reported in a meaningful way. For example, some restaurants will incur napkin, straw, paper cup, and plastic lid costs. All of these costs could be conveniently reported under a general grouping, or cost category such as "Paper Supplies and Packaging."

Similarly, nearly all bars will incur expense for items such as stir sticks, paper coasters, tiny plastic swords, and small paper umbrellas. These costs might be combined and reported in a cost category such as "Bar utensils and supplies."

When cost groupings are used, they should make sense to the operator and should be specific enough to let the operator know exactly what is in the category. Although some operators prefer to make up their own other expense cost categories, the cost categories suggested in this text are recommended in the *Uniform System of Accounts for Restaurants, USAR*. The individual other expense cost categories generally recommended by the *USAR* are divided into two primary groups:

1. Other Controllable Expenses
2. Non-controllable Expenses

Within each of these two major other expenses groups, recommended groupings for individual cost categories are:

1. Other Controllable Expenses
   - Direct Operating Expenses
   - Music and Entertainment
   - Marketing
   - Utilities
   - General and Administrative Expenses
   - Repairs and Maintenance

2. Non-controllable Expenses
- Occupancy Costs
- Equipment Rental
- Depreciation and Amortization
- Corporate Overhead (multiunit restaurants)
- Management Fees
- Interest Expense

Within each of the two primary other expense cost subcategories, an operation's individual other expenses can be even further detailed to aid managers in their reporting and decision-making. For example, the *USAR* suggests the following individual costs be reported under the "Other Controllable Expenses" subcategory of "Utilities."

Utilities

- Electricity
- Gas
- Heating Oil and Other Fuel
- Recycling Credits
- Trash Removal
- Water and Sewage

Similarly, those expenses that are non-controllable may be detailed within their individual cost categories. For example, the *USAR* suggests the following individual costs be reported under the "Non-controllable Expenses" subcategory of "Occupancy Costs."

- Rent—Minimum or Fixed Amount
- Rent—Percentage Rent Amount
- Rent—Parking Spaces
- Ground Rent
- Common Area Maintenance
- Insurance on Building and Contents
- Other Municipal Taxes
- Personal Property Taxes
- Real Estate Taxes

FUN ON THE WEB!

If your restaurant plays background music, hosts live bands or karaoke nights, or contracts with DJs to play recorded music, your facility will be required to pay artists royalties for the music your guests will hear (or sing!). The following groups represent those artists and companies who produce music. Go to their websites to see how and why you will interact with them.

The American Society of Composers, Authors and Publishers (ASCAP). ASCAP is a membership association of over 450,000 US composers, songwriters, lyricists, and music publishers of every kind of music. Through agreements with affiliated international societies, ASCAP also represents hundreds of thousands of music creators worldwide.

BMI. BMI is an American performing rights organization that represents more than 550,000 songwriters, composers, and music publishers in all genres of music. The non–profit-making company collects license fees on behalf of the American and international artists that it represents.

SESAC. SESAC was founded in 1930, making it the second-oldest performing rights organization in the United States. SESAC's repertory, once limited to European and gospel music, has diversified to include today's most popular music, including R&B/hip-hop, dance, rock classics, country, Latina, contemporary Christian, jazz, and the television and film music of Hollywood.

One major purpose of the *USAR* is to give managers and owners guidance on how to best report the individual other expenses their businesses incur. The reasons why this is important will become very clear in Chapter 9 (Analyzing Results Using the Income Statement) of this text.

While all other expenses incurred by a foodservice operation will affect the amount of profit it produces, in most cases, managers are best served by devoting their attention to controllable, rather than to non-controllable, other expenses.

FIXED, VARIABLE, AND MIXED OTHER EXPENSES

Although it is important to recognize all costs as either controllable or non-controllable, it is also important to understand that, as a foodservice manager, some of the costs you will incur will stay the same each month, whereas others will vary. For example, if you elect to lease a building to house a restaurant and cocktail lounge you operate, your lease payment will likely require you to pay the same amount each month for the lease.

In some other instances, the amount you pay for an expense will vary based on the success of your business. Because each guest served will receive at least one napkin, the expenses a manager would incur for paper cocktail napkins used in a cocktail lounge will increase as the number of guests served increases and will decrease as the number of guests served decreases. As an effective cost control manager, it is important to recognize the difference between expenses that are fixed and those expenses that vary as your revenue varies.

A **fixed expense** is one that remains constant despite increases or decreases in sales volume. A **variable expense** is one that generally increases as sales volume increases and decreases as sales volume decreases. A **mixed expense** is one that has properties of both a fixed and a variable expense. To illustrate all three of these expense types, consider Jo Ann's Hot Dogs, a midsize, freestanding restaurant located near a shopping mall, where Jo Ann sells upscale Chicago-style hot dogs.

Assume that Jo Ann's average sales volume is $136,000 per month. Assume also that rent for her building and parking area is fixed at $8,000 per month. Each month, Jo Ann computes her rent as a percentage of total sales, using the following other expenses cost percentage formula:

$$\frac{\text{Other expenses}}{\text{Total sales}} = \text{Other expenses cost \%}$$

In this case, the Other Expenses category she is interested in looking at is rent; therefore, the formula becomes:

$$\frac{\text{Rent expense}}{\text{Total sales}} = \text{Rent expense cost \%}$$

Jo Ann has computed her rent expense percentage for the last six months. The results are shown in Figure 8.1.

Note that Jo Ann's rent expense percentage ranges from a high of 6.67 percent (February) to a low of 4.88 percent (May), yet it is very clear that rent itself was a constant, or fixed, amount of $8,000 per month. Thus, rent, in this lease arrangement, is considered to be a fixed expense.

It is important to note that, although the dollar amount of her rent expense is fixed, her rent expense percentage declines as her volume increases. Thus, the rent payment as a percentage of sales or cost per item sold is not fixed. This is true because as sales volume increases, the number of guests contributing to rent expense also increases; thus, it takes a smaller percentage amount of each guest's sales revenue to generate the $8,000 Jo Ann needs to pay her rent.

FIGURE 8.1 Jo Ann's Fixed Rent

			For Period: 1/1–6/30
Month	**Rent Expense**	**Sales**	**Rent %**
January	$8,000	$121,000	6.61%
February	$8,000	$120,000	6.67%
March	$8,000	$125,000	6.40%
April	$8,000	$130,000	6.15%
May	$8,000	$164,000	4.88%
June	$8,000	$156,000	5.13%
6-Month Average	$8,000	$136,000	5.88%

It makes little sense for Jo Ann to be concerned about the fact that her rent expense percentage varies monthly. If Jo Ann is comfortable with the six-month average rent percentage (5.88%), she is in control of and managing her other expense "rent" category. If, however, Jo Ann feels that her rent expense percentage is too high, she has only two options. She must increase sales, and thereby reduce her rent expense percentage, or she must negotiate a lower monthly rental with her landlord.

When rent, or any type of other cost, is fixed, the expense as expressed by the percentage of sales will vary with sales volume. The total amount of the expense, however, does not change in response to changes in sales volume.

Some restaurant lease payment arrangements are not fixed, but, rather, are based on the sales revenue an operator achieves in the leased facility. To illustrate, assume that Jo Ann has a lease arrangement of this type, requiring her to pay 5 percent of her monthly sales revenue as rent. If that were the case, Jo Ann's monthly lease payments would be completely variable, as shown in Figure 8.2.

Note that the dollar amount of Jo Ann's rent under this arrangement ranges from a low of $6,000 (February) to a high of $8,200 (May). The percentage of her sales revenue that is devoted to rent, however, remains fixed at 5 percent.

A third type of lease that is common in the hospitality industry illustrates the fact that some other expenses are mixed, that is, there is both a fixed and a variable component to this type of expense. Figure 8.3 demonstrates such a lease arrangement. In it, Jo Ann pays a flat rent amount of $5,000 per month plus 1 percent of total sales revenue.

Under this arrangement, a major portion ($5,000) of Jo Ann's lease is fixed, whereas a smaller amount (1% of revenue) is variable because the amount Jo Ann

FIGURE 8.2 Jo Ann's Variable Rent

			For Period: 1/1–6/30
Month	**Sales**	**Rent %**	**Rent Expense**
January	$121,000	5.00%	$6,050
February	$120,000	5.00%	$6,000
March	$125,000	5.00%	$6,250
April	$130,000	5.00%	$6,500
May	$164,000	5.00%	$8,200
June	$156,000	5.00%	$7,800
6-Month Average	$136,000	5.00%	$6,800

FIGURE 8.3 Jo Ann's Mixed Rent

For Period: 1/1–6/30

Month	Sales	Fixed Rent Expense	1% Variable Rent Expense	Total Rent Expense
January	$121,000	$5,000	$1,210	$6,210
February	$120,000	$5,000	$1,200	$6,200
March	$125,000	$5,000	$1,250	$6,250
April	$130,000	$5,000	$1,300	$6,300
May	$164,000	$5,000	$1,640	$6,640
June	$156,000	$5,000	$1,560	$6,560
6-Month Average	$136,000	$5,000	$1,360	$6,360

must pay each month varies based on her sales revenue. Mixed expenses of this type are common and often include items such as some energy costs, garbage pickup, cell phone use, some franchise fees, and other expenses where the operator must pay a base amount and then additional amounts are paid as usage or sales volume increases.

In summary, the total dollar amount of fixed expenses does not vary with sales volume, whereas the total dollar amount of variable expenses changes as volume changes. As a percentage of total sales, however, a fixed expense percentage decreases as sales increase, and a variable-expense percentage will not change with changes in sales.

A mixed expense has both fixed and variable components; therefore, as sales increase, the mixed-expense percentage decreases while the total dollar amount of the mixed expense increases. Figure 8.4 shows how fixed, variable, and mixed expenses are affected by increases in an operation's sales volume.

A convenient way to remember the differences between fixed, variable, and mixed expenses is to consider a paper napkin holder and napkins on a cafeteria line. The napkin holder is a fixed expense. One holder is sufficient, whether you serve 10 guests at lunch or 100 guests. The napkins themselves, however, are a variable expense. As you serve more guests (assuming each guest takes one napkin), you will incur a greater paper napkin expense. The cost of the napkin holder and napkins, if considered together, would be a mixed expense.

For some very large restaurant chains, it makes sense to separate some mixed expenses into their fixed and variable components, whereas smaller operations may elect, as in the case of the napkin holder and napkins, to combine these expenses. The company you work for may make the choice of how to account for other expenses, or you may be free to record other expense costs in a manner you feel is best for your own operation.

Effective managers know they should not categorize controllable, non-controllable, fixed, variable, or mixed costs in terms of being either "good" or "bad." Some expenses are, by their very nature, related to sales volume. Others are not. It is important to

FIGURE 8.4 Fixed, Variable, and Mixed Expense Behaviors as Sales Volume Increases

Expense	As a Percentage of Sales	Total Dollars
Fixed Expense	Decreases	Remains the same
Variable Expense	Remains the same	Increases
Mixed Expense	Decreases	Increases

remember that, in most cases, the goal of management is not to reduce, but rather to increase variable expenses in direct relation to increases in sales volume.

Expenses are required if you are to service your guests. In the example of the paper napkins, it is clear that management would prefer to use 100 paper napkins at lunch rather than 10. As long as the total cost of servicing guests is less than the amount charged to guests, increasing the number of guests served will increase variable other expenses, but it will increase profits as well.

Normal variations in expense percentages that relate only to whether an expense is fixed, variable, or mixed should not be of undue concern to management. It is only when a fixed expense is too high or a variable expense is out of control that management should act. This is called the concept of **management by exception.** That is, if the expense is within an acceptable variation range, there is no need for management to intervene. You must take corrective action only when operational results are outside the range of acceptability. This approach keeps you from over-reacting to minor variations in expense, but allows you to monitor all-important expense-related activities.

MONITORING OTHER EXPENSES

When managing other expenses, two control and monitoring calculations can be helpful to you:

1. Other expense cost percentage
2. Other expense cost per guest

Each alternative can be used effectively in specific management situations; thus, it is important for you to understand both.

As you learned earlier in this chapter, the other expenses cost percentage is computed as follows:

$$\frac{\text{Other expenses}}{\text{Total sales}} = \text{Other expenses cost \%}$$

Thus, for example, in a situation where a restaurant you operate incurs an advertising expense of \$5,000 in a month, serves 10,000 guests, and achieves sales of \$78,000 for that same month, you would compute your advertising expense percentage for that month as follows:

$$\frac{\$5,000}{\$78,000} = 6.4\%$$

The other expense cost per guest is computed as follows:

$$\frac{\text{Other expense}}{\text{Number of guests served}} = \text{Other expense costs per guest}$$

Using the preceding formula, you would compute your advertising expense cost per guest as follows:

$$\frac{\$5,000}{10,000 \text{ guests}} = \$0.50 \text{ per guest}$$

The computation required to calculate an other expense percentage requires that the other expense cost category be divided by total sales. In many cases,

HERE'S HOW IT'S DONE *8.1*

The best managers know how to calculate their other expense costs as a percentage of sales as well as on a "per guest" basis. To do both, three pieces of information must be known:

1. Total sales
2. Amount of other expense
3. Number of guests served

To calculate other expenses as a percent of sales, use this formula:

$$\frac{\text{Other expenses}}{\text{Total sales}} = \text{Other expenses cost \%}$$

To calculate other expenses on a per guest basis, use this formula:

$$\frac{\text{Other expense}}{\text{Number of guests served}} = \text{Other expense costs per guest}$$

To practice applying these two formulas, assume a restaurant achieved the following operating results:

1. Total sales = $250,000
2. Amount of other expense = $3,750
3. Number of guests served = 50,000

In this example, the operation's other expense percentage is:

$$\frac{\$3,750 \text{ other expense}}{\$250,000 \text{ total sales}} = 1.5\% \text{ other expense cost}$$

In this example, the operation's other expenses when calculated on a per-guest basis is:

$$\frac{\$3,750 \text{ other expense}}{50,000 \text{ guests served}}$$
$$= \$0.075 \text{ per guest (or 7.5 cents per guest)}$$

this approach yields useful management information. In some cases, however, this computation alone may not provide adequate information; therefore, using the concept of other expense cost per guest can be very useful.

To illustrate, consider the following example: Scott operates Chez Scot, an exclusive, fine-dining establishment in a suburban area of a major city. One of Scott's major other expenses is linen. He uses both linen tablecloths and napkins. Scott's partner, Joshua, believes that linen costs are a variable operating expense and should be monitored through the use of a linen cost percentage figure. In fact, says Scott's partner, records indicate that the linen cost percentage has been declining over the past five months; therefore, current control systems must be working. As is evident in Figure 8.5, the linen cost percentage has indeed been declining over the past five months.

Scott, however, is convinced that there are linen control problems. He has monitored linen costs on a cost per guest basis. His information is presented in Figure 8.6, and it validates Scott's concern. There is indeed a control problem in the linen area.

Figures 8.5 and 8.6 both show that a linen control problem does exist; yet Figure 8.6 shows it most clearly because it is plain that linen cost per guest has risen from $1.06 in January to its May high of $1.22.

FIGURE 8.5 Chez Scot Linen Cost Percentage

Month	Total Sales	Linen Cost	Cost %
January	$ 68,000	$ 2,720	4.00%
February	70,000	2,758	3.94%
March	72,000	2,772	3.85%
April	71,500	2,753	3.85%
May	74,000	2,812	3.80%
Total	$355,500	$13,815	3.89%

FIGURE 8.6 Chez Scot Linen Cost per Guest

Month	Linen Cost	Number of Guests Served	Cost per Guest
January	$ 2,720	2,566	$1.06
February	2,758	2,508	$1.10
March	2,772	2,410	$1.15
April	2,753	2,333	$1.18
May	2,812	2,305	$1.22
Total	$13,815	12,122	$1.14

Chez Scot is enjoying increased sales ($68,000 in January vs. $74,000 in May), but its guest count is declining (2,566 in January vs. 2,305 in May). The average sale per guest (check average) has obviously increased. This is a good sign because it indicates that each guest is spending more. The fact that fewer guests are being served per month should, however, result in a *decrease* in demand for linen and, thus, a decline in total linen cost. In fact, on a per-person basis, linen costs are up. Scott is correct to be concerned about possible problems in the area of linen control.

Calculating other expense cost per guest may also be useful in a situation where the foodservice manager normally receives no daily payments and thus has no daily dollar sales figures. Consider, for example, a college residence hall dining situation where paper products such as cups, napkins, straws, and lids are placed on the serving line to be used by the students while eating their meals. Students utilizing this dining hall pay a per-semester dining fee rather than pay for each meal eaten.

In this situation, Juanita, the cafeteria manager, wonders whether students are taking more of these items than is normal. The problem is, of course, that she is not exactly sure what "normal" usage is when it comes to supplying paper products to her students. Juanita belongs to an industry trade association that asks its members to supply annual cost figures to a central location where the costs are tabulated and reported back to the membership. Figure 8.7 shows the tabulations for last year from five different colleges in addition to those of Juanita's school.

Juanita has computed her paper products cost per student for the year and has found it to be higher than at P. University and the University of T., but lower than O. University, C. State University, and A. State University. Juanita's costs appear to be in line in the paper goods area. If, however, Juanita hopes to reduce paper products cost per student even further, she could, perhaps, call or arrange a visit to either P. University or the University of T. to observe their operations and/or purchasing techniques.

The other expense cost per guest formula is of value any time management believes it can be helpful or when lack of a sales figure makes the computation of other expense cost percentage impossible. While other expenses are often reported monthly, they may also be monitored on a more frequent basis. Figure 8.8 presents a

FIGURE 8.7 Average Paper Product Cost

Institution	Cost of Paper Products	Number of Students	Paper Product Cost per Student
O. University	$140,592	8,080	$17.40
C. State University	$109,200	6,500	$16.80
P. University	$122,276	7,940	$15.40
University of T.	$184,755	11,300	$16.35
A. State University	$ 61,560	3,600	$17.10
5-University Average	$123,676.60	7,484	$16.53
Juanita's Institution	$ 77,220	4,680	$16.50

FIGURE 8.8 Six-Column Cost of Paper Products

	Other Expense Cost		Number of Guests Served		Cost per Guest	
Juanita's Institution					Date: 4/1–4/8	
Weekday	Today	To Date	Today	To Date	Today	To Date
Monday	$ 145.50	$ 145.50	823	823	$0.18	$0.18
Tuesday	200.10	345.60	751	1,574	0.27	$0.22
Wednesday	417.08	762.68	902	2,476	0.46	$0.31
Thursday	0	762.68	489	2,965	0	$0.26
Friday	237.51	1,000.19	499	3,464	0.48	$0.29
Saturday	105.99	1,106.18	375	3,839	0.28	$0.29
Sunday	0	1,106.18	250	4,089	0	$0.27
Monday	157.10	1,263.28	841	4,930	0.19	$0.26
Total	$1,263.28		4,930		$0.26	

six-column form that can be used to track both daily and monthly cumulative cost per guest figures for paper products. It is maintained by inserting Other Expense Cost and Number of Guests Served in the first two sets of columns. The third set of columns, Cost per Guest, is obtained by applying the other expense cost per guest formula.

Green and Growing!

Increasingly, foodservice managers are finding that creative "green" initiatives benefit their operations in many ways, including those that reduce other expenses. "Trayless dining" is just such an example. College foodservice operators find that when serving trays are removed from cafeteria lines, diners take less food (because they only want to carry what they know they will eat). In typical cases, trayless operations experience a 30–50 percent reduction in food and beverage waste (and in the long run, a likely reduction in the "waist" lines of students!).

Without trays to wash, water consumption is also decreased. In fact, one large foodservice operator reports that trayless dining saves about 200 gallons of water for every 1,000 meals served by reducing the number of trays and dishes that must be washed. The result is a decrease in other expenses, such as water, utilities, and cleaning products as well as reduced labor costs. Of course, the removal of trays doesn't just eliminate waste and save money. It also fits into popular campus themes of green living and sustainability, making trayless dining an excellent example of a win-win-win situation for operators, those they serve, and the environment.

MANAGING OTHER EXPENSES

Managers are responsible for reducing and controlling their operation's other expenses. It is important to remember that each foodservice manager will face his or her own unique set of other expenses. A restaurant on a beach in southern Florida may well undertake the expense of purchasing hurricane insurance, while a similar restaurant in Colorado would not. Each foodservice operation is unique.

Effective operators are those who are constantly on the lookout for ways to reduce unnecessary additions to any of their other expense categories. For most managers, however, the effective control of other expenses must include special attention to three key cost areas:

- Food and beverage operations
- Equipment maintenance and repair
- Occupancy costs

MANAGING OTHER EXPENSES RELATED TO FOOD AND BEVERAGE OPERATIONS

In many respects, the other expenses related to food and beverage operations should be treated just like food and beverage expenses. For instance, in the case of cleaning supplies, linens, uniforms, and the like, products should be ordered, inventoried, and issued in the same manner used for food and beverage products.

Recall that, in most cases, reducing the total dollar amount of variable cost expenses is generally not desirable because, in fact, each additional sale will bring additional variable expense. In this case, although total variable expenses may increase, the positive impact of the additional sales on fixed costs will serve to reduce an operation's overall other expense percentage. It is also true that an operation's fixed costs can only be reduced when they are measured as a percentage of total sales. This is done, of course, by increasing an operation's total sales.

To see how this occurs, let's examine a shaved-ice kiosk called Igloo's located in the middle of a small mall parking lot. Figure 8.9 demonstrates the impact of volume increases on both total other expense and other expense cost percentage. In this example, some of the other expenses related to food and beverage operations are fixed and others are variable. The variable portion of other expense, in this example, equals 10 percent of gross sales. Fixed expenses equal $150.

FUN ON THE WEB!

Rising utility costs are a food production expense that should be of concern to everyone who manages a food-service operation. Energy conservation is not only good for your country; it's also good for your operation's bottom line. Energy Star is a government program designed to encourage efficient energy use. For information related to reducing energy costs, visit: **www.energystar.gov.** When you arrive, click on "Guidelines for Energy Management."

Note that the variable expense shown in Figure 8.9 increases from $100 to $1,500 as sales increase from $1,000 to $15,000. But, when that occurs, total other expense percentage drops from 25 percent of sales to 11 percent of sales. Thus, for managers seeking to reduce their percentage of other expense costs directly related to food and beverage operations, increases in sales are quite helpful!

FIGURE 8.9 Igloo's Fixed and Variable Other Expenses

Sales	Fixed Expense	Variable Expense (10%)	Total Other Expense	Other Expense Cost %
$ 1,000	$150	$ 100	$ 250	25.00%
$ 3,000	$150	$ 300	$ 450	15.00%
$ 9,000	$150	$ 900	$1,050	11.67%
$10,000	$150	$1,000	$1,150	11.50%
$15,000	$150	$1,500	$1,650	11.00%

Consider the Cost

"The piece looks great, but tell me about the prices one more time," said Nigel, the manager of the Old Dublin Pub. Nigel was talking to Alice Petoskey, the sales representative for Image Custom Printing.

Nigel had asked Alice for a quote on producing a flyer that would advertise the pub's St. Patrick's Day festivities to be held in just one month. Nigel planned to offer special menu items on that day, as well as discounted prices on the Irish-made beers he offered on tap. He had also arranged to hire a band to play traditional Irish music. He was now considering how best to advertise the event and all of the special activities he had planned at the pub on that day.

He and Alice were discussing prices for printing the beautiful flyer Alice's company had designed for him.

"Okay," replied Alice, "There is a one-time design and setup fee of $300.00, no matter how many pieces we print. After that fee, the flyers are $0.50 per copy if you buy less than 1,000 copies, $0.40 per copy if you buy between 1,000 and 10,000 copies, and, like I was telling you, the best deal for you is if you buy more than 10,000 copies. Then the price per copy goes down to only $0.25!"

1. What would Nigel's total payment to Alice's company be if he purchases 500 flyers? 6,000 flyers? 11,000 flyers? Use the following table to help you with your answer.

Number of Copies	Cost per Copy	Setup Fee	Total Cost

2. What additional flyer-related costs will Nigel incur if he decides to purchase the advertising flyers from Alice?

3. Assume you are Nigel. What additional and potentially lower-cost advertising alternatives would you want to consider prior to agreeing to buy the flyers from Alice's company?

Utility services costs are an extremely important category of other expenses related to food and beverage operations. To produce their menu items, serve, and clean up, restaurants typically use thousands of gallons of water, consume significant amounts of natural gas (generally used for cooking and water heating), and utilize a large number of **kilowatt-hours (kWh)**—the measure of electrical usage—each month.

Like food and labor costs, energy usage costs can be controlled. This process starts by understanding just where your restaurant uses its energy. Although the heating and cooling costs incurred by a restaurant in Alaska will be different from those of a restaurant in Arizona, the usage pattern shown in Figure 8.10 is a typical one. Your utility costs can (and should) be controlled, and learning and teaching your staff about the information in Figure 8.11 is a good way to start the process.

FIGURE 8.10 Typical Restaurant's Energy Consumption Pattern

Activity	Energy Use %
Cooking	32%
Heating (building)	19%
Cooling (building)	18%
Heating (water)	13%
Refrigeration	11%
Lighting	6%
Administrative	1%
Total	100%

FIGURE 8.11 Ten Commonsense Energy Tips for Restaurateurs

1. Turn It Off
   - Turn off lights, cooking equipment, and exhaust fans when they are not being used.
   - Activate the standby mode for office equipment, in-house computers, and printers to effectively put these pieces of equipment "to sleep" when not in use.

2. Keep It Closed
   - Keep refrigerator doors closed.
   - Keep outside doors, if any, to the kitchen closed to minimize heating and cooling loss.

3. Turn It Down
   - Set air-conditioning units at 76°F (24.5°C) for cooling.
   - Set heating systems at 68°F (20°C) for heating.
   - Reduce the temperature of your hot water heater (where appropriate).
   - Adjust heating/cooling temperature settings when you close your operation for the night.

4. Vent It
   - Use ceiling fans to help recirculate dining room air.
   - Retrofit exhaust hoods with both low- and high-speed fans in dish room, food preparation, and cooking areas.

5. Change the Bulbs
   - Replace incandescent bulbs with fluorescent. They use 75 percent less electricity and last 10 times as long.
   - Install photocell light sensors (motion detectors) where appropriate (storage areas and the like) to activate lighting only when needed.

6. Watch the Water
   - Run dishwashers only when they are full.
   - Replace/repair leaking faucets immediately.
   - Insulate all hot water pipes.
   - Install "water-saver" spray nozzles in dish areas.

7. Cook Right
   - Stagger preheat times for equipment to minimize surcharges for high-energy use.
   - Bake during off-peak periods.
   - Idle cooking equipment (between meal periods) at reduced temperatures where appropriate.

8. Seal It
   - Caulk and weather-strip cracks and openings around doors, windows, vents, and utility outlets.
   - Check freezer, refrigerator, and walk-in seals and gaskets for cracks or warping. Replace as needed.

9. Maintain It
   - Change air filters on a regular basis (monthly during peak heating and cooling seasons).
   - Clean grease traps on ventilation equipment.
   - Clean air conditioner and refrigeration condenser/evaporator coils at least every three months.
   - Oil, lube, clean, and repair equipment as needed to maximize operating efficiency.

10. Get Help
   - Take advantage of any advisory services offered by your local utility company and governmental agencies.
   - Talk to your **heating, ventilation, and air-conditioning (HVAC)** repair person for tips on minimizing energy and maintenance costs with your particular HVAC system. It's like getting a free energy management consultant!

MANAGING OTHER EXPENSES RELATED TO EQUIPMENT MAINTENANCE AND REPAIR

Any skilled craftsman knows that keeping his or her tools clean and in good working order will make them last longer and perform better. The same is true for tools and equipment in foodservice facilities. A properly designed and implemented preventive maintenance program can go a long way toward reducing equipment failure and, thus, decreasing equipment and facility-related costs. Proper care of mechanical equipment not only prolongs its life but also reduces operational costs. As prices for water, gas, and other energy sources needed to operate facilities continue to rise, you must implement a facility repair and maintenance program that seeks to discover and treat minor equipment and facility problems before they become major problems.

One way to help ensure that costs are as low as possible is to use a competitive-bid process before awarding contracts for services you require. For example, if you hire a carpet cleaning company to clean your dining room carpets monthly, it is a good idea to annually seek competitive bids from new carpet cleaners. This can help to reduce your costs by ensuring that the carpet cleaner you select has given you a price that is competitive with other service providers in the area. For general maintenance contracts in such areas such as the kitchen or for mechanical equipment, elevators, or grounds, it is recommended that these contracts be put out for bid at least once per year. This is especially true if the dollar value of the contract is large.

To help control equipment maintenance and repair costs, air-conditioning, plumbing, heating, and refrigerated units should be inspected at least yearly, and kitchen equipment, such as dishwashers, slicers, and mixers, should be inspected at least monthly for preventive maintenance purposes. A form similar to the one shown in Figure 8.12 is useful in this process.

FIGURE 8.12 Equipment Inspection Report

Unit Name: <u>Your Restaurant</u>   Time Period: <u>1/1–1/31</u>

Item Inspected	Inspection Date	Inspected By	Action Recommended
A. Refrigerator #6	1/1	D.H.	Replace gasket
B. Fryer	1/7	D.H.	Inspected, no maintenance needed
C. Ice Machine	1/9	D.H.	Drain, de-lime
D.			
E.			

Some foodservice managers operate facilities that are large enough to employ their own full-time maintenance staff. If this is the case, make sure these employees have copies of the operating and maintenance manuals of all equipment. These documents can prove invaluable in the reduction of equipment and facility-related operating and repair costs.

FUN ON THE WEB!

Record keeping is one of the most important aspects of a preventive maintenance program. To see examples of software programs developed to help you record and plan preventive maintenance activities for your equipment, enter "restaurant equipment maintenance software" into your favorite search engine and review the results.

Cost Control Around the World

In a large number of cases, those who operate American chain restaurants outside the United States will experience equipment repair and replacement costs that are higher than their US-based counterparts. That's because, in many cases, a franchised restaurant's popularity is tied closely to the type of equipment or facility it requires for the production of its most popular menu items. When these key facility-related pieces of equipment are missing because repair service or spare parts are not readily available in foreign countries, the results can be disastrous.

For example, imagine a McDonald's with a US-built fryer that needs a replacement part, a Dairy Queen with a malfunctioning "Blizzard" machine, or a Rainforest Cafe with a defective sound system. You can easily see how the character (and popularity) of those restaurants would be significantly and negatively altered if one or more of these critical pieces of equipment were unavailable for a significant amount of time.

In many cases, foodservice operators will find it more difficult to build, service, and maintain their physical facilities in foreign countries. This is especially true if the company has not identified a dependable, cost-effective, and local service representative for the building they occupy or the major equipment they utilize.

FUN ON THE WEB!

Finding reliable service and repair for foodservice equipment is always an issue for managers. This is especially the case for those operators whose restaurants are located in less-populated areas of the world or in areas where service on popular equipment is hard to obtain. Fortunately, some quality companies do offer virtually "worldwide" sales and service. To view one such company, go to the "Hobart" company's website.

When you arrive at the site, click "Locate Hobart in Your Region" to view a list of the international sales and service centers maintained by this high-quality foodservice equipment and consulting company.

MANAGING OCCUPANCY COSTS

Occupancy costs refer to those expenses incurred by a foodservice unit that are related to occupying and paying for its physical facility (building). For the foodservice manager who is not the owner, the majority of occupancy costs will be non-controllable. Rent, mortgages, taxes, and interest on debt are real costs but are most often beyond the immediate control of the unit manager. However, if you own the facility you manage, occupancy costs are a primary determinant of both profit on your sales and return on dollars invested in your operation.

If your occupancy costs are too high because of unfavorable rent or lease arrangements or due to excessive debts and required loan repayments, you may face extreme difficulty in generating profits. Food, beverage, labor, and other controllable operating expenses can only be managed to a point—beyond that, efforts to reduce costs excessively can result in decreased product quality, reduced guest service levels and lower guest satisfaction. If occupancy costs are unrealistically high, no amount of effective cost control can help "save" the operation's profitability.

Total controllable and non-controllable other expenses in an operation can range from 5 to 15 percent or even more of the unit's total sales. Experienced managers know that, although other expenses are sometimes considered to be minor expenses, they are extremely important to overall operational profitability. This is especially true in a situation where the number of guests you serve is fixed, or nearly so, and the prices you are allowed to charge for your products is fixed as well. In a case such as this, your ability to control your operation's other expenses will be vital to your success.

In this and the previous chapters of this text, you have learned a great deal about the ways managers control their food, labor, and other expense costs. In the next chapter, you will learn how foodservice managers report and then analyze their actual operating results.

Technology Tools

Those expenses that are related to neither food nor labor were introduced in this chapter. Depending on the specific foodservice operation, these costs can represent a significant portion of the operation's total expense requirements. As a result, controlling these costs is just as important as controlling food- and labor-related costs. Software and hardware that can be purchased to assist in this area include applications that relate to:

1. Assessing and monitoring utilities cost
2. Minimizing energy costs via the use of motion-activated sensors
3. Managing equipment maintenance records
4. Tracking marketing costs/benefits
5. Menu and promotional materials printing hardware and software
6. Analysis of communications costs (telephone tolls, websites, and social media)
7. Analysis of all other expense costs on a "cost per guest" basis
8. Analysis of all other expense costs on a "cost per dollar sale" basis
9. Comparing building/contents insurance costs across alternative insurance providers
10. Software programs designed to assist in the preparation of the income statement, balance sheet, and the statement of cash flows
11. Income tax management
12. Income tax filing

The unique needs of an individual restaurant will heavily influence which other expense software programs and applications would be helpful. At a minimum, most independent operators should computerize their records related to taxes at all levels to ensure accuracy, safekeeping, and timeliness of required filings.

Apply What You Have Learned

Hyewon Kim owns her own catering business. She continually monitors her other expense costs, including the cost of liability insurance for drivers of her catering vans. This year, Hyewon's auto insurer advises her that insurance rates for her coverage will increase by 15 percent next year. The insurance company also states that if Hyewon will institute a preemployment drug-testing program for those employees who will drive her vans, there will be no insurance rate increase.

Hyewon does not currently require potential employees to agree to be drug-tested prior to becoming employed in her business, but it is legal to do so in her state.

1. If you were Hyewon, would you implement the drug-testing program? Why or why not?

2. What additional costs will Hyewon incur if such a program were implemented?

3. What should Hyewon tell potential employees about her reason for implementing a preemployment drug-testing program? What should she do if a potential employee refuses to agree to the test?

Key Terms and Concepts

The following are terms and concepts discussed in the chapter that are important for you as a manager. To help you review, please define the terms below.

other controllable
  expenses
non-controllable
  expenses
standard operating
  procedure (SOP)

fixed expense
variable expense
mixed expense
management by
  exception
kilowatt-hour (kWh)

heating, ventilation,
  and air-conditioning
  (HVAC)
occupancy costs

Test Your Skills

You may download the Excel spreadsheets for the Test Your Skills exercises from the student companion website at www.wiley.com/college/dopson. Complete the exercises by placing your answers in the shaded boxes and answering the questions as indicated.

1. Sophia owns and operates a restaurant featuring Lobster Rolls and Fried Cod Sandwiches. She is evaluating her revenue and expenses for last month. Help Sophia assess her operation's profit and other expense performance by completing the following revenue and expense worksheet.

Sophia's Restaurant	Amount	Percentage
Sales	$75,000	100%
Total Cost of Food	25,000	33.3%
Total Cost of Labor	20,000	26.7%
Other Controllable Expenses	10,000	
Non-controllable Expenses	5,000	
Profit		

2. Susie operates a restaurant in the ski resort town of Asvail. She has decided to group her Other Expenses categories in terms of either fixed expenses or variable expenses. Place an X in the Variable Expense column for those expenses that vary with sales volume. For expenses that do not vary with sales, place an X in the Fixed Expense column.

Other Expenses	Variable Expense	Fixed Expense
Linen rental		
Piano rental		
Ice		
Insurance		
Pension plan payments		
Snow shoveling fees (parking lot)		
Paper products		
Kitchen equipment lease (mixer)		
Long-term debt payment		
Real estate tax		

3. Tutti owns a fine-dining restaurant in a suburb of a major coastal city. Last year, her sales were not as high as she would have liked. To help increase her sales volume, Tutti decided to hire a sales consultant, Tina Boniner, to help bring in more customers.

Tutti hired Tina on a trial basis for the first six months of the year. Tina was paid a fixed fee of $1,000 per month and a commission of 1 percent of all sales. At the end of June, Tutti wants to evaluate whether she should hire Tina for the next six months. Calculate Tutti's sales consultant cost percentage.

Mixed Expense—Sales Consultant					For Period: 1/1–6/30
Month	Sales	Fixed Fee	1% Variable Expense	Total Expense	Cost %
January	$81,000				
February	80,000				
March	88,000				
April	92,000				
May	110,000				
June	108,000				
6-Month Total/Average					

a. Tutti has decided that she cannot spend more than 2.2 percent of total sales for Tina's services. Based on the six-month average cost percentage, can Tutti afford to hire Tina for another six months?

b. Last year's average monthly sales for the first six months was $80,000. Based on this year's sales data, has Tina done a good job at increasing sales? Should she be hired again?

4. John owns and operates the End Zone Steakhouse. He would like to turn the operation over to his son Zeke, a graduate of Spartacus High School. Zeke, however, has no foodservice background. Zeke would like to prove that he can effectively operate the restaurant and that he would be good at controlling costs. Operating cost categories for the restaurant, in terms of other expenses, are as follows. Place an X in the Controllable column for those operating expenses that Zeke could control. If he could not control the cost, place an X in the Non-controllable column.

Other Expenses	Controllable	Non-controllable
Real estate tax		
Menu printing		
Professional musicians		
Interest on long-term debt		
Charitable donations		
Cleaning supplies		
Flowers and decorations		
Licenses and permits		

5. Shanna operates a lounge in an extremely popular downtown convention hotel. The hotel regularly operates around the 80 percent occupancy mark, and its lounge, Luigi's, is very often filled to capacity. On weeks when business at the hotel is slower, Shanna attempts to build local sales by scheduling a variety of popular bands to play on the stage. She must select one band to play on Saturday night, six weeks from now, when the hotel is not busy. She has kept records of the costs and sales volume of the last four bands she has booked.

a. Compute both band expense percentage and cost per guest served. Based on the cost percentage of the bands, which one should Shanna select for booking?

Expense percentage and Cost per Guest Served—Bands						
Unit Name: Luigi's Lounge						
Date	Band	Band Expense	Lounge Sales	Cost %	Number of Guests Served	Cost per Guest Served
1/15	Tiny and the Boys	$1,400	$11,400		1,425	
2/15	Shakin' Bill and the Billfolds	$1,900	$12,250		1,980	
3/15	La Noise	$2,000	$12,000		2,005	
4/15	The Hoppers	$2,000	$10,250		2,100	

b. Would your answer change if you knew Shanna charged a $5.00 cover charge to enter the lounge on the nights she has a band, and that the cover charge is reported separately from the lounge sales? If so, which band would you choose?

Date	Band	Number of Guests Served	Cover Charge per Guest	Total Cover Charges	Lounge Sales	Total Sales
1/15	Tiny and the Boys	1,425			$11,400	
2/15	Shakin' Bill and the Billfolds	1,980			$12,250	
3/15	La Noise	2,005			$12,000	
4/15	The Hoppers	2,100			$10,250	

6. Marjorie manages a 200-seat, white-tablecloth restaurant in an upscale neighborhood. Since her guests expect her tablecloths and napkins to be really white, she sends her linens to a local laundry service daily. The laundry service charges her by the piece. She wants to keep track of her laundry cost per guest to see if she can use the information to control her laundry costs better. Help her complete her six-column cost per guest report. She has budgeted $0.60 per guest on average. How is she doing at controlling her laundry costs?

Six-Column Cost per Guest—Laundry Service						
Unit Name: Marjorie's					Date: 5/1–5/7	
	Laundry Service Cost		Number of Guests Served		Cost Per Guest	
Weekday	Today	To Date	Today	To Date	Today	To Date
1	$225		400			
2	204		375			
3	200		350			
4	240		425			
5	275		450			
6	300		500			
7	230		420			
Total						

7. Josiam operates the foodservice at Springdale Valley school system. He has just been informed by City Power, the electrical company in his area, that the rate per kilowatt-hour (kWh) for the school system's kitchens will be rising from $0.085 per kWh to $0.092 per kWh beginning next academic year (September). Based on last year's bill, what was each kitchen's electricity usage?

Assuming no operating changes, how much more will be spent next year? Who are some of Josiam's best resources for discovering ways to limit electricity usage in the kitchens?

School	Electricity Cost Last Year	Number of kWh Used Last Year	Cost per kWh Estimate Next Year	Estimated Electricity Cost for Next Year
Springdale Elementary	$ 6,800.00		0.092	
Jefferson Elementary	7,650.00		0.092	
Clinton Middle School	10,200.00		0.092	
Tri-Valley High School	12,750.00		0.092	
Total	$37,400.00		0.092	

8. Enrique has located the perfect spot for his restaurant. It is 3,000 square feet in the local mall, and the mall managers have given him the following monthly lease options:

Option 1: Pay a flat fee of $2.00 per square foot per month.

Option 2: Pay a flat fee of $3,000 per month plus 5 percent of food sales.

Enrique estimates that his sales for the coming year will be as shown below. Calculate the monthly lease amount for both options.

Which lease option should Enrique choose? Why?

Month	Sales Forecast	Option 1			Option 2		
		No. of Square Feet	Flat Fee per Square Foot	Monthly Lease $	Flat Fee per Month	Five % of Sales	Monthly Lease $
Jan	$ 65,000						
Feb	55,000						
Mar	65,000						
April	70,000						
May	80,000						
June	70,000						
July	70,000						
Aug	85,000						
Sept	90,000						
Oct	95,000						
Nov	110,000						
Dec	135,000						
Total							

9. Libbey Hocking is the owner of the Hummingbird, an all-organic restaurant featuring fresh salads and a variety of vegetarian entrée dishes. As part of a dining room redesign, she is replacing all of the glassware in her 100-seat restaurant. Libbey would like to purchase 40 dozen glasses. Her glassware vendor has offered her similarly styled glassware at three different quality levels. The highest-quality glassware would cost Libbey $50.00 per dozen. The average life expectancy of these glasses is 1,000 uses before they either break or chip. A lower-priced, mid-quality glass sells for $35.00 per dozen and has an expected life of 750 uses. The least-expensive glasses sell for $26.00 per dozen and have an expected life of 500 uses. Help Libbey get more information to assess her best purchase choice by completing the following product cost comparison worksheet. (*Spreadsheet hint:* Format the "Per Use Cost" column to five decimal places.)

Hummingbird's Glassware Purchase Worksheet

Product Durability	Price per Dozen	Number of Dozens	Total Cost	Total Number of Glasses	Per Glass Cost	Estimated Uses Per Glass	Per Use Cost
Highest							
Middle							
Lowest							

a. Based on cost per use only, which quality glass should Libbey purchase?

b. What non–purchase price factors might influence Libbey's choice of glassware?

c. If you were Libbey, which product alternative would you select? Explain your answer.

10. The cost of maintaining an effective website as well as its social media presence is an increasingly important marketing cost for every foodservice operation. Name some specific "Other Expense" costs that you feel could be reduced through the effective use of an operation's website and social media presence.

CHAPTER 9

Analyzing Results Using the Income Statement

OVERVIEW

This chapter explains what you will do to analyze the cost effectiveness of your operation. It teaches you how to read and use the income statement, the financial document that is also known as the profit and loss (P&L) statement. It explains techniques used to analyze your sales volume as well as your food, beverage, labor, and other expenses. Finally, the chapter shows you how to review the income (P&L) statement to analyze your operation's profitability.

Chapter Outline

- Introduction to Financial Analysis
- Uniform System of Accounts
- Income Statement (*USAR* Format)
- Analysis of Sales/Volume
- Analysis of Food Expense
- Analysis of Beverage Expense
- Analysis of Labor Expense
- Analysis of Other Expenses
- Analysis of Profits
- Technology Tools
- Apply What You Have Learned
- Key Terms and Concepts
- Test Your Skills

LEARNING OUTCOMES

At the conclusion of this chapter, you will be able to:
- Prepare an income (P&L) statement.
- Analyze sales and expenses using the income statement.
- Evaluate a facility's profitability using the income statement.

INTRODUCTION TO FINANCIAL ANALYSIS •————————

Far too many foodservice managers find that they collect information, fill out forms, and enter and receive numbers from their point-of-sale (POS) system, calculators, or computers with little regard for what they should do with all of the data they have collected.

Some have said that managers often make poor decisions because they lack information, but when it comes to the financial analysis of a hospitality operation, the opposite is usually true. Foodservice managers, more often than not, find themselves awash in numbers! It is an important part of your job to sift through this information and select for analysis those numbers that can shed light on exactly what is happening in your operation. Among other things, you will want to know:

How much money did we take in?

How much money did we spend?

How much profit did we make?

This information is necessary to effectively operate your business. It also may be required by groups that are directly or indirectly involved with the financial operation of your facility. For example, local, state, and federal financial records relating to taxes and employee wages must submitted to the appropriate governmental authorities on a regular basis. In addition, records showing the financial health of an operation may need to be submitted to new suppliers to establish an operation's credit worthiness.

If a foodservice operation has both operating partners and investors, those partners and investors will certainly require accurate and timely updates that focus on the financial health of the business. Owners, stockholders, and investment bankers may all have an interest in the day-to-day effectiveness of an operation's management. For each of these groups, and of course, for the foodservice organization's own managers, a systematic and accurate examination of operational efficiency on a regular basis is critical.

As a professional foodservice manager, you will be very interested in examining your operation's cost of doing business. Documenting and analyzing sales, expenses, and profits is sometimes called **cost accounting**, but a more appropriate term for the process is **managerial accounting**, a term that reflects the importance managers place on this process. In this text, we use the term *managerial accounting* when referring to documenting, analyzing, and managing information related to an operation's sales, expenses, and profits.

It is important for you to be aware of the difference between **bookkeeping**, the process of simply recording and summarizing financial data, and managerial accounting, the actual analysis of that data. As an example, a POS system can be programmed to provide data about food and beverage sales per server. Management can, if it wishes, track by shift, the relative sales effort of each service employee. If this is done with the goal of examining the data to increase training needed by less productive servers or to reward the most productive ones, the POS system has, in fact, added information that is valuable and has assisted in the unit's operation.

If, on the other hand, information describing server effectiveness is dutifully recorded on a daily basis, filed away or sent to a regional office, and is then left to collect dust, the POS system has actually harmed the operation by taking management's time away from the more important task of running the business. It has converted the manager's role from that of skilled cost analyst to one of a bookkeeper (record keeper) only. This type of situation must be avoided at all times because you need to maximize your effectiveness by being in the production area or dining room during high-service periods rather than in the office catching up on your paperwork.

Bookkeeping is essentially the summarizing and recording of data. Managerial accounting involves the summarizing, recording, and, most important, analysis and use of that data. As a professional foodservice manager, you are also a managerial accountant!

You do not have to be a **certified management accountant (CMA)** or a **certified public accountant (CPA)** to analyze data related to foodservice revenue and expense. This is not meant to discount the value of an accounting professional that can assist a manager. It is important to establish, however, that it is the professional foodservice manager, not an outside expert, who is most qualified to assess the effectiveness of the foodservice team in controlling costs while providing the service levels desired by management. The analysis of operating data, a traditional role of the accountant, must also be part of your role as a manager. The process is not complex and, in fact, is one of the most fun and creative aspects of a foodservice manager's job.

It is important to recognize that a good foodservice manager is, in fact, a manager first and not an accountant. It is also important, however, for you to be able to read and understand financial information and be able to speak intelligently and confidently with the many parties outside your operation who will read and use the information produced by accountants. This information will be crucial to your operation's overall health and success. It can also provide data that will assist you in improving the quality of your management decisions.

It is also important to know that, by federal law, it is an operation's management (not its accountants) that is called on to verify the accuracy of the financial data it reports. In the past, some managers in some industries have fraudulently reported their financial information. As a direct result, the United States Congress, in 2002, passed the **Sarbanes–Oxley Act (SOX)**. Technically known as the Public Company Accounting Reform and Investor Protection Act, the law provides criminal penalties for those found to have committed accounting fraud. Sarbanes–Oxley (SOX) covers a whole range of corporate governance issues, including the regulation of those who are assigned the task of verifying a company's financial health. Ultimately, Congress determined that a company's implementation of proper financial reporting techniques is not merely good business, it is the law, and violators are subject to fines or even prison terms!

FUN ON THE WEB!

The 2002 Sarbanes–Oxley Act became law to help rebuild public confidence in the way corporate America governs its business activities. The Act has far-reaching implications for the tourism, hospitality, and leisure industry. To examine an overview of its provisions, go to http://www.sec.gov/about/laws.shtml.

When you arrive at the site, select "Sarbanes-Oxley Act of 2002."

UNIFORM SYSTEM OF ACCOUNTS

Financial reports related to the operation of a foodservice facility are of interest to management, stockholders, owners, creditors, governmental agencies, and, often, the general public. To ensure that this financial information is presented in a way that is both useful and consistent, a **uniform system of accounts** has been established for many areas of the hospitality industry. In Chapter 1 you learned that the National Restaurant Association, for example, has developed the *Uniform System of Accounts for Restaurants (USAR)*.

Uniform systems of accounts also exist for hotels, clubs, nursing homes, schools, and hospitals. Each system seeks to provide a consistent and clear manner in which managers working in those areas can record sales, expenses, and the overall financial condition of their specific organizations. Sales categories, expense classifications, and methods of computing relevant ratios are included in the uniform systems of accounts. These uniform systems are often made available by the national trade or professional associations involved with each hospitality segment.

It is important to note that the uniform systems of accounts are guidelines, not a mandated methodology. Small foodservice operations, for example, may use the

USAR in a slightly different way than will large operations. In all cases, however, operators who use the uniform system of accounts "speak the same language," and it is truly useful that they do so. If operators prepared financial records in any manner they wished, it is unlikely that the many external audiences who must use them could properly interpret the reports. As a result, it is important that managers secure a copy of the applicable uniform system of accounts for their operations and then become familiar with its basic formats and reporting principles.

FUN ON THE WEB!

Look at the following site to review *The Uniform System of Accounts for the Lodging Industry*. Go to the Educational Institute of the American Hotel and Lodging Association website. When you arrive search for "Uniform System of Accounts for the Lodging Industry 10th Revised Edition" to see a synopsis of the book and, if you wish, to place an order.

FUN ON THE WEB!

Hospitality managers can learn what they need to know about reporting and analyzing their financial results in books devoted specifically to that subject. One of the very best books available is *Managerial Accounting for the Hospitality Industry*.

You can review the latest edition of the book at www.wiley.com. Enter the title in the search bar to explore the book's table of contents and, if you wish, to place an order.

INCOME STATEMENT (*USAR* FORMAT) •————————

The income statement is a summary report that describes the sales achieved, the money spent on expenses, and the resulting profit generated by a business in a specific time period. Despite its formal title as the "statement of income and expense," it is popularly referred to as the income statement, the profit and loss statement, or the P&L, the shortened title introduced in Chapter 1.

The P&L is a manager's most important tool for cost control. Properly designed P&Ls show the revenue and expenses of a business at a level of detail deemed best by the owners of the business and that conforms to the appropriate uniform system of accounts (e.g., for restaurants, hotels, clubs, or other industry segment).

P&Ls show the operating profits of a business. But the word profit can mean different things to different managers; therefore, the P&L statement can be somewhat confusing if you are not familiar with it. To see why, assume that someone asked you how much money you "made" on your last job. You could answer by telling the amount of gross earnings you achieved (your pay before taxes), or you could just as accurately answer by telling your net earnings (after-tax earnings) or your *take-home* pay. In either case, you would be accurately communicating the amount that you "earned," but the two answers you would provide would be very different. In a similar manner, some business operators consider profit to be what they earn before they pay income taxes, whereas others reserve the term *profit* for their after-income tax earnings.

A precise definition of exactly what is meant by the term *profit* must be established for each P&L statement if it is to be helpful and communicate information accurately. In all cases, however, one purpose of the P&L statement is to identify **net income**, which is the profit generated after all expenses of the business have been paid.

Figure 9.1 details two years of P&L statements presented in a *USAR*-recommended format for Joshua's Inc., a foodservice complex that includes a cocktail lounge, two

FIGURE 9.1 Joshua's Income Statement (P&L)[1]

	Last Year	%	This Year	%
Joshua's Inc. Last Year versus This Year				
SALES				
Food	$ 1,891,011	82.0%	$ 2,058,376	81.0%
Beverage	415,099	18.0%	482,830	19.0%
Total Sales	$2,306,110	100.0%	$2,541,206	100.0%
COST OF SALES				
Food	$ 712,587	37.7%	$ 767,443	37.3%
Beverages	94,550	22.8%	96,566	20.0%
Total Cost of Sales[2]	$ 807,137	35.0%	$ 864,009	34.0%
LABOR				
Management	$128,219	5.6%	$ 142,814	5.6%
Staff	512,880	22.2%	571,265	22.5%
Employee Benefits	99,163	4.3%	111,813	4.4%
Total Labor	$ 740,262	32.1%	$ 825,892	32.5%
PRIME COST	$1,547,399	67.1%	$1,689,901	66.5%
OTHER CONTROLLABLE EXPENSES				
Direct Operating Expenses	$ 122,224	5.3%	$132,143	5.2%
Music & Entertainment	2,306	0.1%	7,624	0.3%
Marketing	43,816	1.9%	63,530	2.5%
Utilities	73,796	3.2%	88,942	3.5%
General & Administrative Expenses	66,877	2.9%	71,154	2.8%
Repairs & Maintenance	34,592	1.5%	35,577	1.4%
Total Other Controllable Expenses	$ 343,611	14.9%	$ 398,970	15.7%
CONTROLLABLE INCOME	$ 415,100	18.0%	$ 452,335	17.8%
NON-CONTROLLABLE EXPENSES				
Occupancy Costs	$ 120,000	5.2%	$ 120,000	4.7%
Equipment Leases	–	0.0%	–	0.0%
Depreciation & Amortization	41,510	1.8%	55,907	2.2%
Total Non-controllable Expenses	161,510	7.0%	175,907	6.9%
RESTAURANT OPERATING INCOME	$ 253,590	11.0%	$ 276,428	10.9%
Interest Expense	86,750	3.8%	84,889	3.3%
INCOME BEFORE INCOME TAXES	$ 166,840	7.2%	$ 191,539	7.5%
Income Taxes	65,068	2.8%	76,616	3.0%
NET INCOME	$ 101,772	4.4%	$ 114,923	4.5%

[1] Income Statement format is based on the *USAR*, 8th ed., with the inclusion of income taxes and net income.
[2] All percentages are computed as a percentage of Total Sales except Cost of Sales line items, which are based on their respective category sales.

dining areas, and banquet space. Joshua prepares his P&L statement for the calendar year period of January 1 through December 31.

In some operations, a fiscal year that differs from a calendar year (see Chapter 4) is used to prepare P&Ls. Fiscal year reporting may be used in seasonal resorts, noncommercial facilities such as schools and colleges, and any other situation in which it makes good sense for the operation to do so.

P&Ls should be prepared for any accounting period that is helpful to management. As a result, managers may prepare annual, quarterly, monthly, or even weekly P&Ls.

As can be seen in Figure 9.1, last year Joshua's operation generated $2,306,110 in total sales and achieved a net income of $101,772. This year, when the corporation generated total sales revenue of $2,541,206, Joshua achieved a net income of $114,923. The question Joshua must ask himself, of course, is, "How good is this performance?"

It is important to note that each food service operation's P&L statement could be formatted slightly differently than the P&L shown in Figure 9.1 even when it follows the *USAR*. All income statements, however, typically will take a very similar, rather than identical, approach to reporting revenue and expense.

Note that, although the detail is much greater, the layout of Joshua's P&L is similar in structure to the abbreviated P&L presented in Chapter 1 as Figure 1.3. Both statements list revenue first, then expenses, and finally, the difference between the revenue and expense figures. If this number is positive, it represents a profit. If expenses exceed revenue, a loss, represented by a negative number or a number in brackets, is shown. Operating at a loss is often referred to as operating "in the red," based on an old practice of using red ink to write down debts or losses. Regardless of the color of the ink, operating at a loss can cause an operator to shed a few tears!

To help ensure that your operation does not produce a loss, you need to know some important components of the *USAR* income statement format. The *USAR* can best be understood by dividing it into four major sections: (1) sales, (2) prime cost, (3) other controllable expenses, and (4) non-controllable expenses.

Referring to Figure 9.1, the Sales category includes the revenue generated by all of the food and beverage purchases made by Joshua's guests. The Prime Cost section of Joshua's P&L details the amount that was spent for food and beverages as well as the total amount spent for labor. **Prime cost** is defined as an operation's total cost of sales added to its total labor cost. Prime cost is clearly listed on the P&L because it is an excellent indicator of management's ability to control cost of sales and labor; the two largest expenses in most food service operations.

The prime cost concept is important because when prime costs are excessively high it makes it very difficult to generate a sufficient amount of profit in a food service operation. This can be so even when controllable and non-controllable other expenses are kept well in line. While each restaurant operation is different, prime costs in the range of 60 to 70 percent are common for full-service operations, while prime costs below 60 percent are most common in limited or quick service operations.

The Other Controllable Expenses categories for Joshua's include entries for:

Direct operating expenses

Music & entertainment

Marketing

Utilities

General & administrative expenses

Repairs & maintenance

The Non-controllable Expenses categories listed on Joshua's P&L include:

Occupancy costs

Equipment leases

Depreciation and amortization

Although interest expense and income taxes are not included in the non-controllable expenses section of the *USAR*-format P&L, they are commonly regarded as nonoperating, and non-controllable expenses. Therefore, these costs can be assessed within the fourth section of the income statement.

Note that, when following the *USAR,* the foodservice manager arranges the four main sections of a P&L in order from most controllable to least controllable. Knowing what the four main sections of the income statement contain allows you to focus on those things over which you have the most control as a foodservice manager. When you focus on these controllable areas, you can better manage your time and make the most out of your efforts to control costs.

Managers most often choose **restaurant operating income** (the operating income subtotal before interest expense is subtracted) or **income before income taxes** (the operating income after interest expense is subtracted, but before income taxes are subtracted) as the most relevant indicators of management performance. This is because most managers do not have interest expenses or taxes in their direct span of control. As you know, the government controls taxes; to paraphrase Benjamin Franklin, the only sure things in life are death and taxes. So, the foodservice manager has little control over the amount of money "Uncle Sam" gets every year. Regardless of the specific income subtotal assessed, in all cases managers must be clear about how it will reflect on their ability to manage the operation based on their control (or lack of control) of the costs represented by the subtotal.

Note, also, that each revenue and expense category in Figure 9.1 is expressed both in terms of its whole dollar amount and its percentage of total sales. All ratios are calculated as a percentage of total sales except the following:

- Food costs are divided by food sales.
- Beverage costs are divided by beverage sales.

When calculating food and beverage cost percentages, the food and beverage expenses are the numerator while their respective food and beverage sales are the denominator. Food costs and beverage costs are among the most controllable items on the income statement; thus it helps Joshua to separate these sales and costs out of the aggregate and evaluate these individual expense areas more carefully. Notice, also, that Joshua's accountant presents this year's P&L statement along with last year's P&L statement in a side-by-side comparison because this can help Joshua assess changes in costs and analyze trends in his business.

Another facet of the uniform system of accounts that you should know about is the supporting schedule. The income statement as shown in Figure 9.1 is an **aggregate statement.** This means that all details associated with the sales, costs, and profits of the foodservice establishment are summarized on the P&L statement. Although this summary gives the manager an overall look at the performance of the operation, detailed expenses within each cost category are not included directly on the statement. These details can be found in **supporting schedules.** Each line item on the income statement should be accompanied by a supporting schedule that outlines all of the information that the manager needs to know about that category to operate the business successfully.

For example, in Figure 9.1, Direct Operating Expenses could have an accompanying supporting schedule that details costs incurred for uniforms, laundry and linen, china and glassware, silverware, and the like. These expenses can also be broken down by percentage of total direct operating expenses. In addition, the supporting schedule should have a column in which notes can be made about the costs it includes.

Figure 9.2 is an example of a supporting schedule that would accompany Joshua's Income Statement (Figure 9.1). Note that the Total Direct Operating Expenses, $132,143 in the Direct Operating Expense Schedule, matches exactly with this year's Direct Operating Expenses as listed on the income statement.

The type of information and the level of detail that are included on supporting schedules are left up to the manager, based on what is appropriate for the manager's

FIGURE 9.2 Direct Operating Expenses Schedule

Type of Expense	Expense	% of Direct Operating Expenses	Notes
Uniforms	$ 13,408	10.15%	
Laundry and Linen	40,964	31.00%	
China and Glassware	22,475	17.01%	Expense is higher than budgeted because china shelf collapsed on March 22.
Silverware	3,854	2.92%	
Kitchen Utensils	9,150	6.92%	
Linen	2,542	1.92%	
Cleaning Supplies	10,571	8.00%	
Paper Supplies	2,675	2.02%	
Bar Uniforms	5,413	4.10%	
Menus and Wine Lists	6,670	5.05%	Expense is lower than budgeted because the new wine supplier agreed to print the wine lists free of charge.
Exterminating	1,803	1.36%	
Flowers and Decorations	9,014	6.82%	
Licenses	3,604	2.73%	
Total Direct Operating Expenses	$132,143	100.00%	

operation. The schedules are used to collect the information needed to give additional detail about sales or costs and to determine problem areas and potential opportunities for improving each item on the income statement.

The P&L statement is only one of several documents owners use to help evaluate the success of a business. The P&L statement alone, however, yields important information that is critical to the development of future management plans and budgets.

The analysis of P&L statements is a fun and very creative process if basic procedures are well understood. In general, managers who seek to discover all that their P&L will tell them undertake the following areas of analysis:

1. Sales/volume
2. Food expense
3. Beverage expense
4. Labor expense
5. Other controllable and non-controllable expense
6. Profits

Using the data from Figure 9.1, each of these areas will be reviewed in order.

ANALYSIS OF SALES/VOLUME

As discussed earlier in this text, foodservice operators can measure sales in terms of either dollars generated or number of guests served. In both cases, an increase in sales volume is usually to be desired. A sales increase or decrease must, however, be analyzed carefully if you are to truly understand the revenue direction of your business.

STEPS IN COMPUTING SALES MEASURES

Consider the sales portion of Joshua's P&L statement, as detailed in Figure 9.3. Based on the data from Figure 9.3, Joshua can compute his overall sales increase or decrease using the following steps:

Step 1. Determine sales for this accounting period.

Step 2. Calculate the following: this period's sales minus last period's sales.

Step 3. Divide the difference in Step 2 by last period's sales to determine the sales percentage variance (increase or decrease).

For Joshua, the sales percentage variance is as indicated in Figure 9.4. To illustrate the steps outlined for calculating sales variance using Total Sales as an example, we find:

Step 1. $2,541,206

Step 2. $2,541,206 − $2,306,110 = $235,096

Step 3. $235,096 ÷ $2,306,110 = 10.2%

The P&L statement shows Joshua has achieved an overall increase in total sales of 10.2 percent. There are several ways total sales could have increased in the current year:

1. The same number of guests was served, but at a higher check average.
2. More guests were served at the same check average.
3. More guests were served at a higher check average.
4. Fewer guests were served, but at a higher check average.

FIGURE 9.3 Joshua's P&L Sales Comparison

Sales	Last Year	% of Sales	This Year	% of Sales
Food Sales	$1,891,011	82.0%	$2,058,376	81.0%
Beverage Sales	415,099	18.0%	482,830	19.0%
Total Sales	$2,306,110	100.0%	$2,541,206	100.0%

FIGURE 9.4 Joshua's P&L Sales Variance

Sales	Last Year	This Year	Variance	Variance %
Food Sales	$1,891,011	$2,058,376	$167,365	+ 8.9%
Beverage Sales	415,099	482,830	67,731	+16.3%
Total Sales	$2,306,110	$2,541,206	$235,096	+10.2%

FIGURE 9.5 Joshua's P&L Sales Comparison with 5% Menu Price Increase

Sales	Last Year	Adjusted Sales (Last Year × 1.05)	This Year	Variance	Variance %
Food Sales	$1,891,011	$1,985,561.55	$2,058,376	$ 72,814.45	+ 3.67%
Beverage Sales	415,099	435,853.95	482,830	46,976.05	+10.78%
Total Sales	$2,306,110	$2,421,415.50	$2,541,206	$119,790.50	+ 4.95%

To examine which of these possibilities was responsible for the total sales increase, Joshua may need to apply a sales adjustment technique. To see why, assume that Joshua raised his prices for food and beverage by 5 percent at the beginning of the year. If this was the case, and he wishes to determine his actual sales increase, he must first consider the impact of that 5 percent menu price increase. The procedure he would use to adjust his sales variance to include the menu price increases is as follows:

Step 1. Increase the prior-period (last year) sales by the amount of the price increase.

Step 2. Subtract the result in Step 1 from this period's sales.

Step 3. Divide the difference in Step 2 by the value of Step 1.

Thus, in our example, Joshua would follow these steps to determine his real (after selling price adjustments) sales increase.

In the case of total sales, the procedure would be as follows:

Step 1. $2,306,110 × 1.05 = $2,421,415.50

Step 2. $2,541,206 − $2,421,415.50 = $119,790.50

Step 3. $119,790.50 ÷ $2,421,415.50 = 4.95%

Figure 9.5 details the results that are achieved if this 5 percent adjustment process is completed for all sales areas. Joshua's total sales figure would be up this year by 4.95 percent if he adjusted it for a 5 percent menu price increase. Thus, although Joshua's overall sales did increase significantly this year, approximately half of the increase was due to increased menu prices rather than to additional guest purchases.

There is still more, however, that the P&L can tell Joshua about his sales. If he has kept accurate guest count records, he can compute his sales per guest (check average) amount. With this information, he can determine whether his sales are up because he is serving more guests or because he is serving the same number of guests but each one is spending more per visit or because some of both has occurred.

In fact, if each guest is spending quite a bit more per visit, Joshua may even have experienced a *decrease* in total guest count yet still achieved an increase in total sales. If this were the case, he would want to know about it because it may be quite unrealistic to assume that revenue will continue to increase over the long run if the number of guests visiting the establishment is declining.

OTHER FACTORS INFLUENCING SALES ANALYSIS

In some foodservice operations special factors must be taken into consideration before sales revenue can be accurately analyzed. To illustrate, consider the situation you would face if you owned a restaurant across the street from a professional basketball arena. If you were to prepare a P&L that compared sales from this May to sales generated last May, the number of home basketball games in May for this professional team in each of the two periods (which could vary) would have to be determined before you could make valid conclusions about guest count increases or decreases because the number of home games would directly affect your sales levels.

FIGURE 9.6 Hot Dog! Sales Data

	Last Year	This Year	Variance	Variance %
Total Sales (October)	$17,710.00	$17,506.00	−$ 204	−1.2%
Number of Operating Days	22 days	21 days	1 day	
Average Daily Sales	$ 805.00	$ 833.62	$28.62	+3.6%

Similarly, if a foodservice facility is open only Monday through Friday, the number of operating days contained in two given accounting periods may be different for the facility. When this is the case, percentage increases or decreases in sales volume must be based on average daily sales, rather than the total sales figure.

To illustrate this, consider Hot Dog!, a hot dog stand that operates in the city center of a large metropolitan area only on Monday through Friday. In October of this year, the stand was open for 21 operating days. Last year, however, because of the number of weekdays and weekend days in October, the stand operated for 22 days. Figure 9.6 details the comparison of sales for the stand, assuming no increase in menu selling prices this year when compared with last year's selling prices.

At first glance, it would appear that October sales this year are 1.2 percent lower than last year, but in reality, average daily sales are up 3.6 percent! Are sales for October up or down? Clearly, the answer must be qualified in terms of monthly or daily sales. For this reason, effective foodservice managers must be careful to consider all of the relevant facts before making determinations about an operation's overall sales direction.

Every critical factor must be considered when evaluating sales revenue, including the number of operating meal periods or days; changes in menu prices, guest counts, and check averages; and holidays and special events. Only after carefully reviewing all details of this type can you truly assess whether an operation's sales are increasing or decreasing.

ANALYSIS OF FOOD EXPENSE

In addition to sales analysis, the P&L statement, whether created weekly, monthly, quarterly, or annually, provides information about other areas of operational interest. For the effective foodservice manager, the analysis of food expense is a matter of major concern.

Figure 9.7 details the food expense portion of Joshua's P&L as detailed in the Cost of Sales: Food Expense Schedule.

FIGURE 9.7 Joshua's P&L Cost of Sales: Food Expense Schedule

	Last Year	% of Food Sales	This Year	% of Food Sales
Food Sales	$1,891,011	100.0%	$2,058,376	100.0%
Cost of Sales: Food				
Meats and Seafood	297,488	15.7%	$ 343,063	16.7%
Fruits and Vegetables	94,550	5.0%	127,060	6.2%
Dairy	55,347	2.9%	40,660	2.0%
Baked Goods	16,142	0.9%	22,870	1.1%
Other	249,060	13.2%	233,790	11.4%
Total Cost of Food Sales	$ 712,587	37.7%	$ 767,443	37.3%

FIGURE 9.8 Joshua's P&L Variation in Food Expense by Category

Category	Last Year %	This Year %	Variance %
Meats and Seafood	15.7	16.7	+1.0
Fruits and Vegetables	5.0	6.2	+1.2
Dairy	2.9	2.0	−0.9
Baked Goods	0.9	1.1	+0.2
Other	13.2	11.4	−1.8
Total Cost of Food Sold %	37.7	37.4	−0.4

It is important to remember that the numerator of the food cost percentage equation is cost of food sold, whereas the denominator is total food sales, rather than total food and beverage sales.

With total cost of food sold this year of $767,443, and total food sales of $2,058,376, the total food cost percentage is 37.3 percent ($767,443 ÷ $2,058,376 = 37.3%). A food cost percentage can be computed in a similar manner for each subcategory of food. For instance, the food cost percentage for the category Meats and Seafood for this year would be computed as follows:

$$\frac{\text{Meats and seafood costs}}{\text{Total food sales}} = \text{Meats and seafood cost \%}$$

or

$$\frac{\$343,063}{\$2,058,376} = 16.7\%$$

At first glance, it appears that Joshua has done well for the year and that his total cost of goods sold expense has declined 0.4 percent, from 37.7 percent overall last year to 37.3 percent this year. This is true. Closer inspection of Figure 9.7, however, indicates that, although the categories Dairy and Other showed declines, Meats and Seafood, Fruits and Vegetables, and Baked Goods showed increases.

Figure 9.8 shows the actual differences in food cost percentage for each of Joshua's food categories. Although it is true that Joshua's overall food cost percentage is down

Cost Control Around the World

You have learned that the *USAR* contains suggestions for preparing income statements primarily for businesses operated in the United States. However, income statements prepared in other countries can vary in format from the income statements prepared according to *USAR* recommendations. One good example of this relates to the concept of profits. In the United Kingdom, for example, income statements are routinely prepared in a way that clearly indicates an operation's **gross profit**. Gross profit is calculated as:

Total sales − Total cost of sales = Gross profit

Many operators feel gross profit is a key number because it assesses food and beverage sales and those food and beverage-related costs that can and should be directly controlled by the manager on a daily basis. Earlier editions of the USAR actually included gross profit calculations, but the most recent edition does not. In many other countries, however, gross profit remains a key entry on the income statement.

The proper preparation of income statements and understanding the concept of gross profit are both good examples of the expanded knowledge many food service managers must have when they are responsible for businesses operating in countries that establish their own preferred systems for reporting a food service unit's operating results.

by 0.4 percent, the variation among categories is quite significant. It is clearly to his benefit to subcategorize food products so that he can watch for fluctuations within and among groups rather than merely monitor his increase or decrease in overall food costs. Without such a breakdown of categories, he will not know exactly where to look if food costs get too high.

Sometimes food costs rise because the purchase prices of needed ingredients rise. In other cases, food costs rise because too much food is held in inventory, resulting in excessive product loss or theft. It would be helpful for Joshua to determine how appropriate the inventory levels are for each of his product subgroups so that he can adjust the inventory sizes if needed. To do this, Joshua must be able to compute his food inventory turnover.

FOOD INVENTORY TURNOVER

Inventory turnover refers to the number of times the total value of an operation's inventory has been purchased and replaced in an accounting period. Each time the cycle is completed once, we are said to have "turned" the inventory. For example, if you normally keep $100 worth of oranges on hand at any given time and last month's usage of oranges was $500, you would have replaced your orange inventory five times that month. The formula used to compute a food inventory turnover is:

$$\frac{\text{Cost of food consumed}}{\text{Average inventory value}} = \text{Food inventory turnover}$$

Note that it is cost of food consumed (see Chapter 5), rather than cost of food sold, that is used as the numerator in this ratio. This is because all food usage should be tracked so that you can better determine what is sold, wasted, spoiled, pilfered, and provided to employees as employee meals.

Inventory turnover is a measure of how many times an operation's inventory value is purchased and sold to guests. In the foodservice industry, we are, of course, interested in high inventory turnover as it relates to increased sales. If a 5 percent profit is made on the sale of an inventory item, we would like to sell (turn) that item as many times per year as possible. If, in this example, the item were sold from inventory only once per year, one 5 percent profit would result. If the item turned 10 times, however, a 5 percent profit on each of the 10 sales would result. But managers must ensure that a high inventory turnover is caused by increased sales and not by increased food waste, food spoilage, or employee theft.

Joshua can compute an overall food inventory turnover or he can compute inventory turnovers for each of his food categories. To compute his inventory turnover for each food category Joshua must first establish his average inventory value for each food category. The average inventory value is computed by adding the beginning inventory value for a food category for this period to the ending inventory value of the food category for this period and then dividing by two, using the following formula:

$$\frac{\text{Beginning inventory value} + \text{Ending inventory value}}{2} = \text{Average inventory value}$$

From his inventory records, Joshua creates the data recorded in Figure 9.9.

To illustrate the computation of average inventory value, note that Joshua's Meats and Seafood beginning inventory for this year was $16,520, whereas his ending inventory for that category was $14,574. His average inventory value for

FIGURE 9.9 Joshua's P&L Average Inventory Values

Inventory Category	This Year Beginning Inventory	This Year Ending Inventory	Average Inventory Value
Meats and Seafood	$16,520	$14,574	$15,547
Fruits and Vegetables	1,314	846	1,080
Dairy	594	310	452
Baked Goods	123	109	116
Other	8,106	9,196	8,651
Total	$26,657	$25,035	$25,846

that category is $15,547 [($16,520 + $14,574) ÷ 2 = $15,547]. All other categories and the total average inventory value are computed in the same manner.

Now that Joshua has determined the average inventory values for his food categories, he can compute the inventory turnovers for each of these. As you recall from Chapter 5, Cost of Food Consumed is identical to Cost of Food Sold when no reduction is made in cost as a result of employee meals. That is the case at Joshua's facility because he charges employees full price for menu items that he sells to them as employee meals. Therefore, employee meals are included in regular food cost because a normal food sales price is charged for these meals. Figure 9.10 shows the result of his computations using the food inventory turnover formula for this year.

To illustrate, Joshua's Meats and Seafood inventory turnover is 22.1 ($343,063 ÷ $15,547 = 22.1). That is, Joshua purchased, sold, and replaced his meat and seafood inventory, on average, 22 times this year. Note that all other food categories and the total inventory turnover are computed in the same manner. Note also that in categories such as fruits and vegetables, dairy, and baked goods, the turnovers are very high, reflecting the perishability of these items. Joshua's overall inventory turnover is 29.7.

If Joshua's *target* inventory turnover for the year was 26 times (every two weeks), then he should investigate why his actual inventory turnover is higher. It could be because of his increase in sales, which is a good sign of his restaurant's performance. Or it could be due to excessive waste, pilferage, or spoilage.

Alternatively, if his inventory turnover was less than 26 times per year, and his target was 26 times, the difference could be due to lower sales or overstocking of his inventory. Joshua could be buying excess inventory at a bulk discount (which is an intentional management decision to save money), or he might be purchasing too much due to poor inventory management. He should use inventory turnover analysis to help him determine how he can most effectively control his product costs in the future.

FIGURE 9.10 Joshua's P&L Food Inventory Turnover

Inventory Category	Cost of Food Consumed	Average Inventory	Inventory Turnover
Meats and Seafood	$343,063	$15,547	22.1
Fruits and Vegetables	127,060	1,080	117.6
Dairy	40,660	452	90.0
Baked Goods	22,870	116	197.2
Other	233,790	8,651	27.0
Total/ Average	$767,443	$25,846	29.7

ANALYSIS OF BEVERAGE EXPENSE •——————————

Joshua's P&L (Figure 9.1) shows beverage sales for this year of $482,830. With total sales of $2,541,206, beverages represent 19 percent of Joshua's total sales ($482,830 ÷ $2,541,206 = 19%). Also from Figure 9.1, beverage costs for this year are shown as $96,566; thus, Joshua's beverage cost percentage, which is computed as cost of beverages divided by beverage sales, is 20 percent ($96,566 ÷ $482,830 = 20%).

To completely analyze the beverage expense category, Joshua would compute his beverage cost percentage, compare that to his planned or targeted beverage expense, and compute a beverage inventory turnover rate using the same inventory turnover formula he utilized for his food products.

If an operation carries a large number of rare and expensive wines, its overall beverage inventory turnover rate will be relatively low. Conversely, those beverage operations that sell their products such as beer and spirits primarily by the glass are likely to experience inventory turnover rates that are quite high. The important concept here is to compute the turnover rates at least once per year (or more often if needed) to gauge whether inventory sizes should be increased or decreased.

High beverage inventory turnovers accompanied by frequent product outages may indicate inventory levels that are too low, whereas low inventory turnover rates and many slow-moving inventory items may indicate the need to reduce beverage inventory levels.

Figure 9.1 shows that last year's beverage cost percentage was 22.8 percent ($94,550 ÷ $415,099 = 22.8%). This, at first glance, would indicate that beverage costs have been reduced, not in total dollars spent, because sales were higher this year than last year, but in percentage terms. In other words, a beverage cost percentage of 22.8 percent last year versus 20 percent this year indicates a 2.8 percent overall reduction.

Assume, for a moment, however, that Joshua raised drink prices by 10 percent this year over last year. Assume also that Joshua pays, on average, 5 percent more for beverages this year compared with last year. After making those assumptions, is his beverage operation more efficient this year than last year, less efficient, or the same? To determine the answer to this important question in the beverage or any other expense category, Joshua must make adjustments to both his sales and his cost figures. Similar to the method for adjusting sales, the method for adjusting expense categories for known cost increases is as follows:

Step 1. Increase the prior-period expense by the amount of the cost increase.

Step 2. Determine appropriate sales data, remembering to adjust prior-period sales, if applicable.

Step 3. Divide costs determined in Step 1 by sales determined in Step 2.

Thus, in our example, Joshua's beverage expense last year, adjusted for this year's costs, would be $94,550 × 1.05 = $99,277.50.

His beverage sales from last year, adjusted for this year's menu prices, would be $415,099 × 1.10 = $456,608.90.

His last year's beverage cost percentage, adjusted for increases in this year's costs and selling prices, would be computed as follows:

$$\frac{\$99,277.50}{\$456,608.90} = 21.7\%$$

In this case, Joshua's real cost of beverage sold has, in fact, declined this year, although not by as much as he had originally thought. That is, a 21.7 percent adjusted cost for last year versus a 20 percent cost for this year equals a reduction of 1.7 percent, not 2.8 percent as originally determined.

In nearly all cases, food and beverage expense categories must be adjusted in terms of both their costs and menu selling prices if truly accurate comparisons are to be made over longer periods of time. For example, when older foodservice managers remember back to the time when they purchased hamburger for $0.59 per pound, it is important to recall that the quarter-pound hamburger they made from it may have sold for $0.59 also! The 25 percent resulting product cost percentage is no different from today's operator paying $3.00 a pound for ground beef and selling the resulting quarter-pound burger for $3.00.

It is not possible to compare efficiency in food and beverage usage from one time period to the next unless you are making that comparison in equal terms. As product costs increase or decrease and as menu prices change, they may affect changes in food and beverage expense percentages. As an effective manager, you must determine if variations in product usage and cost percentages are caused by real changes in your operation or simply by differences in the price you pay for your products or by changes in your selling (menu) prices.

ANALYSIS OF LABOR EXPENSE

From Figure 9.1, it is interesting to note that, although the total dollars Joshua spent on labor increased greatly from last year to this year, his labor cost percentage increased only slightly. This was true in the Management and Staff categories, as well as the Employee Benefits category. Recall that whenever your labor costs are not 100 percent variable, increasing sales volume will help you decrease your labor cost percentage, while the total dollars you spend on labor will increase. The reason for this is simple. When total dollar sales volume increases, fixed labor cost percentages will decline. In other words, the dollars paid for fixed labor will consume a smaller percentage of your total revenue. Thus, as long as any portion of total labor cost is fixed (management's salaries, for example), increasing volume will have the effect of reducing an operation's labor cost percentage.

Variable labor costs increase with sales volume increases, but the percentage of revenue they consume should stay relatively constant. When you combine a declining percentage (fixed labor cost) with a constant percentage (variable labor cost), you should achieve a reduced overall percentage, although your total labor dollars expended will increase as sales increase.

Is important to note that serving additional guests will most often cost an operation additional labor dollars. That, in itself, is not a bad thing. In most foodservice situations, you want to serve more guests. If labor expenses are controlled properly you will find that an increase in the number of guests served, and the sales generated by these additional guests, will still result in increased labor costs required to service those guests. You must be careful, however, to always ensure that increased labor costs are at the appropriate level for increases achieved in sales volume.

Remember, too, that declining costs of labor are not always a sign that all is well in a foodservice unit. Declining costs of labor may be the result of significant reductions in the number of guests served. If, for example, a foodservice facility produces poor-quality products and provides poor service, guest counts can be expected to decline, as would the cost of labor required to service those guests who do remain. Labor dollars expended by management would decline, but it would be an indication of improper, rather than effective, management.

An effective foodservice manager seeks to achieve reductions in operational expense because of improved operational efficiencies, not because of reduced sales.

Figure 9.11 details the labor cost portion of Joshua's P&L. Note that all the labor-related percentages he computes are based on his total sales, that is, the combination of his food and beverage sales. This is different from computing expense percentages for food and beverages because food cost percentage is determined using food sales as the denominator and beverage cost percentage computations

FIGURE 9.11 Joshua's P&L Labor Cost

Labor Cost	Last Year	% of Total Sales	This Year	% of Total Sales
Management	$128,219	5.6%	$142,814	5.6%
Staff	512,880	22.2%	571,265	22.5%
Employee Benefits	99,163	4.3%	111,813	4.4%
Total Labor Cost	$740,262	32.1%	$825,892	32.5%

use beverage sales as a denominator. Thus, Joshua's total management, staff and employee benefits expense percentage for this year is computed as:

$$\frac{\text{Total labor cost}}{\text{Total sales}} = \text{Labor cost \%}$$

or

$$\frac{\$825,892}{\$2,541,206} = 32.5\%$$

A brief examination of the labor portion of Joshua's P&L would indicate an increase in both dollars spent for labor and labor cost percentage. Just as adjustments must be made for changes in sales and food and beverage expenses before valid expense comparisons can be made, so too must adjustments be made for changes, if any, in the price an operator pays for labor.

In Joshua's case, assume that all employees were given a **cost of living adjustment (COLA)**, or pay raise, of 5 percent at the beginning of this year. Recall from Chapter 7 that this, coupled with an assumed 10 percent menu price increase, would indeed have the effect of changing the operation's overall labor cost percentage, even if its labor productivity did not change.

From Figure 9.11, Joshua can see that his actual labor cost percentage increased from 32.1 percent last year to 32.5 percent this year, an increase of 0.4 percent. To adjust for the changes in the cost of labor and his selling prices, if these indeed occurred, Joshua uses assessment techniques similar to those previously detailed in this chapter. Thus, based on the assumption of a 5 percent increase in the cost of labor and a 10 percent increase in the average menu selling price, he adjusts both sales and cost of labor, using the same steps as those employed for adjusting food or beverage cost percentage, and computes a new labor cost for last year as follows:

Step 1. Determine sales adjustment: $2,306,110 × 1.10 = $2,536,721

Step 2. Determine total labor cost adjustment: $740,262 × 1.05 = $777,275.10

Step 3. Compute adjusted labor cost percentage: $777,275.10 ÷ $2,536,721 = 30.6%

As can be seen, last year Joshua's P&L would have indicated a 30.6 percent labor cost percentage *if* he had operated under this year's increased labor costs and this year's selling prices. This is certainly an area that Joshua would want to investigate. The reason is simple. If he were exactly as efficient this year as he was last year, and if he assumed a 10 percent menu price increase and a 5 percent labor cost increase, Joshua's cost of labor for this year should have been computed as follows:

This year's sales × Last year's adjusted labor cost % = This year's projected labor cost

or

$2,541,206 × 0.306 = $777,609.04

Put in another way, if Joshua were just as efficient with his labor this year as he was last year, he would have expected to spend 30.6 percent of sales for labor this year, given his 5 percent payroll increase and 10 percent menu price increase. In actuality, Joshua's labor cost was $48,282.96 higher ($825,892 actual labor cost this year − $777,609.04 projected labor cost this year = $48,282.96). A variation in labor cost this large should obviously be of concern to Joshua, and he should examine it closely.

Increases in payroll taxes, benefit programs, and employee turnover can all affect labor cost percentage. Although, for our example, we assumed that employee benefits (including payroll taxes, insurance, etc.) increased at the same 5 percent rate as did salaries and wages, these are, of course, different expenses and may increase at rates higher or lower than salary and wage payments to employees. Indeed, one of the fastest-increasing labor-related costs for foodservice managers today is the cost of health insurance benefit programs. This is especially the case with the recent passage of the Patient Protection and Affordable Care Act (**Affordable Care Act**), the federal law mandating, in some situations, that foodservice employers provide health care insurance for their employees.

Controlling and evaluating total labor cost is an important part of your job as a hospitality manager. In fact, many managers feel it is more important to control labor costs than product costs because, for many of them, labor and labor-related benefit costs comprise a larger portion of their operating budgets than do food and beverage product costs.

ANALYSIS OF OTHER EXPENSES

An analysis of other expenses should be performed each time the P&L is produced. Figure 9.12 details the other expenses listed on Joshua's P&L statement.

Joshua's other expenses consist of both other controllable expenses and non-controllable expenses, and he must review these carefully.

FIGURE 9.12 Joshua's P&L Other Expenses

	Last Year	% of Total Sales	This Year	% of Total Sales
Other Controllable Expenses				
Direct Operating Expenses	$122,224	5.3%	$132,143	5.2%
Music & Entertainment	2,306	0.1%	7,624	0.3%
Marketing	43,816	1.9%	63,530	2.5%
Utilities	73,796	3.2%	88,942	3.5%
General & Administrative Expenses	66,877	2.9%	71,154	2.8%
Repairs & Maintenance	34,592	1.5%	35,577	1.4%
Total Other Controllable Expenses	$343,611	14.9%	$398,970	15.7%
Non-controllable Expenses				
Occupancy Costs	$120,000	5.2%	$120,000	4.7%
Equipment Leases	0	0%	0	0%
Depreciation & Amortization	41,510	1.8%	55,907	2.2%
Total Non-controllable Expenses	$161,510	7.0%	$175,907	6.9%

In Joshua's operation, other expenses have increased from last year's levels. To see why, each individual expense category must be reviewed. Note that his Repairs and Maintenance expense category is higher this year than it was last year. This is one area in which he both expects and approves a cost increase. It is logical to assume that kitchen repairs will increase as a kitchen ages. In that sense, a kitchen is much like a car. Even with a good preventative maintenance program, Joshua does not expect an annual decline in kitchen repair expense. In fact, he would be somewhat surprised and concerned should this category be smaller this year than in the previous year because his sales were higher and likely caused more wear and tear on his one year older kitchen equipment.

In the same way, his contributions to his state and national association political action funds, charged to General and Administrative expenses, could be up significantly. This could be acceptable due to Joshua's belief that he, as part of the hospitality industry, needs to make his voice heard to his local and national political leaders. Because of that, membership in state and national trade associations simply make good sense and their costs are justified.

A complete analysis of other expenses could prove difficult for Joshua if he is not sure how he compares with others in his area or with operations of a similar nature. For comparison purposes he is able to use industry trade publications to get national averages on other expense categories. One helpful source Joshua can use is an annual publication, *The Restaurant Industry Operations Report*, published by the National Restaurant Association and prepared by Deloitte & Touche (it can be ordered through the National Restaurant Association's website).

For operations that are a part of a corporate chain, unit managers can most often receive comparison data from district and regional managers, who can supply performance information from similar units operating in the city, region, state, and nation.

Consider the Cost

"Wow!" I can't believe the size of the electricity bill this month," said Wendy. She was talking to Matt, the assistant manager of the Aussie Steakhouse in Phoenix, Arizona, where Wendy served as general manager.

"Is it higher than last month?" asked Matt.

"It's a lot higher," replied Wendy. "I thought it would be a little higher because it was really hot last month."

"So our usage was up?" asked Matt.

"Yes," said Wendy, "and the rate per kilowatt-hour we pay is up from last year, too. It seems like that rate goes up a little more every year."

"Is the bill so high it will affect our monthly bonus?" asked Matt. "I hope not," he continued, "because we had a great month last month, and I was really counting on the extra money in my next check."

"I don't know," said Wendy. "Let me get the calculator and we'll see."

1. What would be the likely effect on both the dollar amount and the cost of utilities as a percent of sales reported on the monthly P&L of the Aussie Steakhouse if there were:

   a. An increase in the amount of electricity used in the restaurant?

   b. An increase in the cost per unit (kilowatt-hour) of the electricity consumed?

   c. An increase in the number of guests served by the restaurant?

2. In this scenario it appears that if the cost of other expenses in this restaurant is too high, its managers might not achieve their monthly bonus. Do you believe the cost of electricity is a controllable or non-controllable operating expense?

3. Regardless of your answer to the previous question, what are at least three specific actions Wendy and Matt could take to address their rising electricity costs?

ANALYSIS OF PROFITS

As can be seen in Figure 9.1, profit for Joshua's, Inc. is represented by the "net income" figure located at the bottom of the income statement. In fact, because of its location on the income statement, some managers even refer to this number as *the bottom line*.

In addition to being evaluated on the basis of their ability to generate profit dollars, foodservice managers are often evaluated on their ability to achieve targeted profit margins. A **profit margin** represents the amount of profit generated on each dollar of sales. Profit margin represents that portion of a dollar's sale that is returned to the operation in the form of profits. For that reason, profit margin is also referred to as **return on sales, or ROS**. This year, Joshua's profit margin is 4.5 percent. For each dollar of sales generated at Joshua's, 4.5 cents profit was made. Joshua calculates his profit margin using the following formula:

$$\frac{\text{Net income}}{\text{Total sales}} = \text{Profit margin}$$

or

$$\frac{\$114,923}{2,541,206} = 4.5\%$$

For the foodservice manager, perhaps no number is more important than profit margin (ROS). This percentage is often considered to be the most telling indicator of a manager's overall effectiveness at generating revenues and controlling costs in line with forecasted results.

Although it is not possible to state what a "good" ROS figure should be for all restaurants, industry averages, depending on the specific restaurant segment, can range from 1 percent to over 20 percent.

Some operators prefer to use Restaurant Operating Income (see Figure 9.1) as the numerator for their profit margin (ROS) calculations instead of Net Income. This is because, in most cases, an operation's interest expense is a cost established by the operation's owners, not its managers. As a result, amounts paid for interest are not truly reflective of a manager's ability to generate a profit.

Regardless of the manner in which profits are viewed, and profit margins are calculated, it is most important to recognize that food service operators ultimately bank "dollars" and not "percentages." Clearly, a manager whose operation achieves a 15 percent ROS on revenues of $2,000,000 is going to generate more profits than a manager who achieves a 20 percent ROS on revenues of $500,000. Because that is true, effective managers are concerned about both the dollar amount of profit they generate and their ROS percentage.

Joshua's ROS results of this year ($114,923 or 4.5% of sales) represent an improvement over last year's figure of $101,772, or 4.4 percent of total sales. Thus, he has shown improvement both in the dollar size of his net income and in the size of net income as related to total sales. In Chapter 2, you learned how to calculate a sales variance and a sales variance percentage. The variance amount and percentage variance between last year's net income and this year's net income can be calculated using similar formulas.

Joshua can compute the variance in his net income by subtracting net income last year from net income this year as follows:

$$\text{Net income this year} - \text{Net income last year} = \text{Net income variance}$$

or

$$\$114,923 - \$101,772 = \$13,151$$

Joshua can then compute his net income variance percentage as follows:

$$\frac{\text{Net income this year} - \text{Net income last year}}{\text{Net income last year}} = \text{Percentage variance}$$

or

$$\frac{\$114,923 - \$101,772}{\$101,772} = 12.9\%$$

An alternative, and shorter, formula for computing the percentage variance is as follows:

$$\frac{\text{Variance}}{\text{Net income last year}} = \text{Percentage variance}$$

or

$$\frac{\$13,151}{\$101,772} = 12.9\%$$

Yet another way to compute the percentage variance is to use a math shortcut, as follows:

$$\frac{\text{Net income this year}}{\text{Net income last year}} - 1 = \text{Percentage variance}$$

or

$$\frac{\$114,923}{\$101,772} - 1 = 12.9\%$$

or

$$1.129 - 1 = 12.9\%$$

How much of this improvement is due to improved operational methods versus increased sales will depend, of course, on how much Joshua actually did increase his sales relative to increases in his costs. Monitoring selling price, guest count, sales per guest, operating days, special events, and actual operating costs is necessary for accurate profit comparisons. Without knowledge of each of these areas, the effective analysis of profits becomes a risky proposition.

HERE'S HOW IT'S DONE 9.1

Sometimes managers simply want to know the difference between two numbers. For example, they may want to know the difference between the amount of money spent this year for food compared to the amount of money spent for food last year, or the amount of profit earned this year compared to the amount of profit earned last year. Calculating the difference, or variance, between any two numbers simply requires the use of subtraction.

Sometimes, however, managers know they will gain more information when they calculate the percentage variance between two numbers. Calculating a percentage variance is a two-step process that is easy to do once you learn how.

To illustrate, assume you wish to calculate the percentage variance between last year's profits and this year's profits. Last year's profit was $300,000. This year's profit is $310,500. The two-step process for calculating variance percentage in this example is:

Step 1. Subtract last year's number from this year's number. In this example, that would be:

$$\$310,500 - \$300,000 = \$10,500$$

Step 2. Divide the difference calculated in Step 1 by last year's number. In this example, that would be:

$$\$10,500 \div \$300,000 = .035, \text{ or } 3.5\%$$

That tells the manager that this year's profit is 3.5 percent *higher* than last year's profit.

Or, you can use a shortcut by dividing this year's number by last year's number and subtracting 1. In this example, that would be:

$$(\$310,500 \div \$300,000) - 1 = 3.5\%$$

The identical two-step process works when a number from this year is *smaller* than a number from last year. To illustrate, assume last year's profit was $312,000 and

profit this year is $297,600. The two-step process for calculating variance percentage in this case is:

Step 1. Subtract last year's number from this year's number. In this example, that would be:

$$\$297,600 - \$312,000 = -\$14,400 \text{ (Note that this is a negative number!)}$$

Step 2. Divide the difference calculated in Step 1 by last year's number. In this example, that would be:

$$-\$14,400 \div \$312,000 = -.046, \text{ or } -4.6\%$$

That tells the manager that this year's profit was 4.6 percent *lower* than last year's profit.

Using the short cut again, you can divide this year's number by last year's number and subtract 1. In this example, that would be:

$$(\$297,600 \div \$312,000) - 1 = -4.6\%$$

With a little practice, you will be able to calculate and assess the percentage difference between any two numbers with ease!

Green and Growing!

Some foodservice operators think that adopting a sustainable, or "green," operations viewpoint inevitably means putting planet before profit. They would argue that businesses can survive only if they put profits first, so that is where their focus should be. In the long run, of course, an organization's purpose must include a focus on both profit and planet. It is true that an unprofitable business will not stay in business long. It is also true that "planet-friendly" management yields many positive financial outcomes for businesses, as well as for the health of the local communities these businesses count on to support them.

For example, the simple act of buying local (to minimize transportation costs and environmental impact) produces an additional reward: community connection. Buying local creates relationships with those who produce food and keeps money flowing through a local economy, resulting in a healthier community.

There are additional positive outcomes from the local food movement. For example, as more hospitality businesses use local, seasonal, sustainably raised food, more fresh fruits and vegetables may be consumed, resulting in positive nutrition and health impacts within the community. The long-term result may be a reduction in health-care costs. Perceptive foodservice operators now clearly recognize that profits, planet, and people all benefit from an operation's green commitment.

Technology Tools

This chapter introduced the concept of management analysis as it relates to sales, expenses, and profits. In this area, software is quite advanced, and there are many tools available to assist you. The best of these will help you:

1. Analyze operating trends (sales and costs) over management-established time periods.
2. Analyze food and beverage costs.
3. Analyze labor costs.
4. Analyze other expenses.
5. Analyze profits.
6. Compare operating results of multiple profit centers within one location or across several locations.
7. Interface with an operation's point-of-sale (POS) system or even incorporate it completely.
8. "Red flag" areas of potential management concern.
9. Evaluate the financial productivity of individual servers, day parts, or other specific time periods established by management.
10. Compare actual to budgeted results and compute variance percentages as well as suggest revisions to future budget periods based on current operating results.

Apply What You Have Learned

Terri Settles is a registered dietitian (RD). She supervises five hospitals for Maramark Dining Services, the management company the hospitals have selected to operate their foodservice operations. Her company produces a monthly and annual income statement for each hospital.

1. Discuss five ways in which income statements can help Terri do her job better.
2. What would a hospital do with "profits" or surpluses made in the food-service area?
3. What effect will "profit" or "loss" have on the ability of Terri's company to continue to manage the foodservice operations for these hospitals?

Key Terms and Concepts

The following are terms and concepts discussed in the chapter that are important for you as a manager. To help you review, please define the terms below.

cost accounting
managerial accounting
bookkeeping
certified management
   accountant (CMA)
certified public
   accountant (CPA)
Sarbanes-Oxley
   Act (SOX)

uniform system of
   accounts
net income
prime cost
restaurant operating
   income
income before income
   taxes
aggregate statement

supporting schedules
gross profit
inventory turnover
cost of living adjustment
   (COLA)
Affordable Care Act
profit margin
return on sales (ROS)

Test Your Skills

You may download the Excel spreadsheets for the Test Your Skills exercises from the student companion website at www.wiley.com/college/dopson. Complete the exercises by placing your answers in the shaded boxes and answering the questions as indicated.

1. Jacob operates a Sicilian-themed restaurant that does a significant amount of carryout pizza business. Jacob's P&L has been designed to indicate the sales levels achieved in his dining room, carryout business, and bar. The revenue Jacob achieved this month and last month is indicated on the partial P&L shown below. Calculate Jacob's total sales for this month and last month as well as the variances and percentage variances in each of his revenue categories then answer the questions that follow.

Jacob's Restaurant				
	Last Month	This Month	Variance	Variance %
Sales				
Dining Room	$84,500	$86,250		
Carry-out	15,000	15,500		
Bar	13,500	12,750		
Total Sales				

   a. Did Jacob's total sales this month increase or decrease when compared to last month's sales?

   b. In what revenue-producing area(s) did Jacob's sales increase?

   c. In which sales area did Jacob experience the greatest dollar increase?

   d. In which sales area did Jacob experience the greatest percentage increase?

   e. In which sales area did Jacob's sales not improve?

2. Roscco Burnett is the manager of a New York–style delicatessen. Roscco's boss has established performance targets that determine the amount of bonus Roscco will receive each month. Roscco's performance is evaluated in five separate categories. Roscco receives a 2 percent bonus for each of the five targets he achieves. He earns a 2 percent bonus when:

   a. His food cost is 30 percent or less.

   b. His total cost of sales is 31 percent or less.

   c. His labor cost is 22 percent or less for the "Staff" category.

   d. His total labor cost is 35 percent or less.

   e. His prime costs are less than 63 percent.

If he achieves all five of his targets, the maximum bonus Roscco can achieve is 10 percent of his monthly salary. Review the targets established for Roscco's performance, complete Roscco's P&L Sales and Prime Cost sections, and then answer the question that follows.

Roscco's P&L Sales and Prime Cost		
	This Month	**%**
SALES		
Food	$71,500	
Beverage	9,250	
Total Sales		
COST OF SALES		
Food	$22,250	
Beverage	2,200	
Total Cost of Sales		
LABOR		
Management	$ 4,750	
Staff	16,252	
Employee Benefits	6,225	
Total Labor Cost		
PRIME COST		

What percent of his monthly salary will Roscco receive as a bonus this month?

3. Aafreen is the owner of a restaurant that features Pakistani and American cuisine. She operates on a calendar year and prepares a monthly P&L as well as a year-to-date (YTD) P&L. Aafreen is preparing her P&L for June. She has entered the amounts and calculated her percentages for the month. She has also entered her YTD revenue and expense amounts. Help Aafreen complete her P&L by calculating her missing YTD percentages.

Income Statement, June 201X				
	June	%	YTD	%
SALES				
Food	$55,200	82.5%	$331,200	
Liquor	4,450	6.7%	27,500	
Beer	3,550	5.3%	20,500	
Wine	3,700	5.5%	23,250	
Total Sales	$66,900	100.0%	$402,450	
COST OF SALES				
Food	$17,150	31.1%	$101,750	
Liquor	1,140	25.6%	6,400	
Beer	875	24.6%	4,850	
Wine	1,150	31.1%	8,750	
Total Cost of Sales	$20,315	30.4%	$121,750	
LABOR				
Management	$ 4,750	7.1%	$ 28,500	
Staff	13,525	20.2%	79,500	
Employee Benefits	4,225	6.3%	23,750	
Total Labor	22,500	33.6%	131,750	
PRIME COST	$42,815	64.0%	$253,500	
OTHER CONTROLLABLE EXPENSES				
Direct Operating Expenses	$ 3,450	5.2%	$ 22,450	
Music & Entertainment	275	0.4%	1,850	
Marketing	1,150	1.7%	7,250	
Utilities	1,850	2.8%	12,450	
General & Administrative Expenses	2,950	4.4%	18,150	
Repairs & Maintenance	950	1.4%	3,850	
Total Other Controllable Expenses	10,625	15.9%	66,000	
CONTROLLABLE INCOME	$13,460	20.1%	$ 82,950	
NON-CONTROLLABLE EXPENSES				
Occupancy Costs	$ 5,900	8.8%	$ 35,400	
Equipment Leases	1,150	1.7%	6,900	
Depreciation & Amortization	1,350	2.0%	8,500	
Total Non-controllable Expenses	$ 8,400	12.6%	$ 50,800	
RESTAURANT OPERATING INCOME	$ 5,060	7.6%	$ 32,150	
Interest Expense	725	1.1%	4,350	
INCOME BEFORE INCOME TAXES	$ 4,335	6.5%	$ 27,800	
Income Taxes	1,735	2.6%	11,120	
NET INCOME	$ 2,600	3.9%	$ 16,680	

4. Faye manages Faye's Tea Room in a small suburban town. She sells gourmet food and a variety of teas. This year, Faye increased her selling prices by 5 percent, and she increased her wages by 10 percent. Faye's condensed P&L follows. Help her calculate her variance and variance percentage from last year to this year. Use her adjusted sales and labor cost to provide a more accurate picture of her performance this year.

Increase in Selling Prices					
Increase in Wages					
Faye's Condensed P&L					
	Last Year	Adjusted Sales and Labor (for Last Year)	This Year	Variance	Variance %
Sales	$1,865,000		$2,315,000		
Cost of Food	615,450		717,650		
Cost of Labor	540,850		671,350		
Other Expenses	428,950		486,150		
Total Expenses					
Profit					

5. a. Rudolfo owns Rudolfo's Italian Restaurante in the Little Italy section of New York City. He wants to compare last year's costs to this year's costs on his food expense schedule to see how he performed in each food category. Help Rudolfo complete his schedule.

Rudolfo's Food Expense Schedule				
	Last Year	% of Food Sales	This Year	% of Food Sales
Food Sales	$2,836,517		$3,087,564	
Cost of Food Sold				
Meats and Seafood	$ 386,734		$ 445,982	
Fruits and Vegetables	122,915		165,178	
Dairy	71,951		52,858	
Baked Goods	20,985		29,731	
Other	323,778		303,927	
Total Cost of Food Sold				

b. In addition to calculating the food cost percentage for each of his food categories, Rudolfo wishes to calculate his inventory turnover for the year. Help Rudolfo complete his inventory turnover table below. Assume that cost of food sold, part a., and cost of food consumed, part b., are the same for Rudolfo's.

Rudolfo's inventory turnover target for this year was 32 times. Did he meet his target? If not, what may have caused this?

Rudolfo's Food Inventory Turnover					
Inventory Category	This Year's Beginning Inventory	This Year's Ending Inventory	Average Inventory Value	Cost of Food Consumed	Inventory Turnover
Meats and Seafood	$21,476	$17,489		$445,982	
Fruits and Vegetables	$ 1,708	$ 1,015		$165,178	
Dairy	$772	$372		$ 52,858	
Baked Goods	$160	$131		$ 29,731	
Other	$10,538	$11,035		$303,927	
Total					

6. Jaymal is director of club operations for five military bases in Florida. He has just received year-end income statements for each base. Information from the revenue and labor portion of those statements is shown below. Jaymal wants to use the current year's data to create next year's budget. Assume that Jaymal is happy with his labor productivity in each unit and that both wages and revenue in each will increase 2 percent next year. Calculate how much Jaymal should budget for revenue and labor in each unit. Also, calculate what Jaymal's labor cost percentage will be for each unit if he meets his budget. (*Spreadsheet hint*: Use the ROUND function to one decimal place for Projected Labor Cost %.)

Projected increase in wages		
Projected increase in revenues		

	This Year's Results		Next Year's Budget		
Location	This Year's Labor Cost	This Year's Revenue	Projected Labor Cost	Projected Revenue	Projected Labor Cost %
Pensacola	$ 285,000	$ 980,500			
Daytona	$ 197,250	$ 720,000			
Fort Myers	$ 235,500	$ 850,250			
Tampa	$ 279,750	$ 921,750			
Miami	$1,190,250	$3,720,000			

7. Ron MacGruder is senior vice president of acquisitions for Yummy Foods. Yummy is a large multinational food service company. It owns over 2,000 restaurants. Among its famous brands are a chain of pizza parlors, a Mexican carryout group, a chain of fried chicken stores, and a large group of fried fish stores. Ron is constantly on the lookout for growing food service concepts that could be purchased at a fair price and added to the Yummy group. One such concept that is currently available for sale is a small but expanding group of upscale Thai restaurants called Bow Thais. The current owners wish to sell the 17-unit chain and retire to Florida. They proudly point to the fact that both their sales and profits have increased in each of the last three years. Revenue has more than doubled this year compared to two years ago. Profits have risen from just $600,000 two years ago to over $1,000,000 this year. In addition, the Bow Thais chain consisted of 6 units two years ago, 12 units last year, and 17 units this year.

Develop a summary P&L for each of Bow Thais' last three years showing revenue, expenses, and profit. Next compute a "per unit" revenue, expense, profit, and profit margin level for each of the three years for which you have data.

Would you advise Ron to buy the company? Why or why not?

	Revenue	Expenses	Profit	No. of Units	Revenue per Unit	Expenses per Unit	Profit per Unit	Profit Margin %
2 Years Ago	$ 6,500,000		$ 600,000					
Last Year	$ 9,900,000		$ 800,000					
This Year	$13,500,000		$1,010,000					

8. Basil Bakal is the newly appointed food and beverage director at Telco Industries. Telco creates and markets software apps developed for use with iPods. The company has 500 employees and operates its own cafeteria and executive dining room, where it daily offers free lunches to all employees.

Basil's employee cafeteria serves between 375 and 425 lunches per day. Approximately 50 more meals per day are served in the executive dining room. Basil has created his own modified version of a P&L for use in his operation. Calculate the percentages of meals served in the employee cafeteria and executive dining room and the costs per meal served, and then answer the questions that follow.

a. How much more did it cost (cost of sales per meal) Basil to serve a meal in the executive dining room than it did in the employee cafeteria? Why do you think that would be so?

b. Basil's modified P&L combines all labor costs when calculating cost per meal served. Why do you think he elected not to allocate labor costs between the two serving areas? How could he do so?

c. Assume you were on the board of directors of Telco. How would you decide how much more money you should allocate to Basil's area next year to account for rising food prices? Who would you expect to provide you with the information you need to make an informed decision about the appropriate size of this increase?

Telco Industries Food Services Department		
	Meals Served Last Year	% of Total Meals Served
NUMBER OF MEALS SERVED		
Cafeteria	104,250	
Executive Dining Room	12,150	
Total Served		
	Total Cost $	Per Meal Cost $
COST OF SALES		
Cafeteria	$248,750	
Executive Dining Room	48,450	
Total Cost of Sales		
LABOR		
Management	73,332	
Staff	171,108	
Employee Benefits	61,110	
401(k) Match	25,350	
Total Labor		
PRIME COST		
OTHER CONTROLLABLE EXPENSES		
Direct Operating Expenses	113,515	
Utilities	96,000	
General & Administrative Expenses	46,669	
Repairs & Maintenance	21,510	
Total Other Controllable Expenses		

9. Lucir manages a German restaurant in a large western city. The restaurant's owner wants to know how well Lucir did this year at generating sales, controlling costs, and providing a profit. The owner promised Lucir that he would give her a raise if she increased return on sales (profit margin) by at least 1 percent. Complete Lucir's P&L.

   Should Lucir receive a raise?

Lucir's P&L				
	Last Year	%	This Year	%
SALES				
Food	$2,647,415		$2,675,889	
Beverage	498,119		965,660	
Total Sales				
COST OF SALES				
Food	$ 855,104		$1,074,420	
Beverages	104,005		115,879	
Total Cost of Sales				
LABOR				
Management	$ 192,330		$ 204,227	
Staff	576,989		581,260	
Employee Benefits	118,996		122,994	
Total Labor				
PRIME COST				
OTHER CONTROLLABLE EXPENSES				
Direct Operating Expenses	$ 146,669		$ 145,357	
Music & Entertainment	2,767		8,386	
Marketing	52,579		69,883	
Utilities	88,555		97,836	
Administrative & General Expenses	80,252		78,269	
Repairs & Maintenance	41,510		39,135	
Total Other Controllable Expenses				
CONTROLLABLE INCOME				
NON-CONTROLLABLE EXPENSES				
Occupancy Costs	$ 144,000		$ 132,000	
Equipment Leases	0		0	
Depreciation & Amortization	49,812		61,498	
Total Non-controllable Expenses				
RESTAURANT OPERATING INCOME				
Interest Expense	104,100		93,378	
INCOME BEFORE INCOME TAXES				
Income Taxes	235,146		343,150	
NET INCOME				

10. In this chapter you learned that a P&L statement is used to report revenue, expense, and profit. In many cases, noncommercial foodservice operators, such as those responsible for schools, colleges and universities, and health-care facilities, including retirement complexes, nursing homes, and hospitals, are severely restricted in their ability to increase their revenues. This is because the operating budgets of such facilities are fixed annually based on the number of meals estimated to be served. Also, such facilities do not seek to earn a "profit" in the traditional sense of the word. In these non-commercial operations, however, the preparation and thoughtful analysis of monthly P&L statements is still considered essential. Why do you believe this is so?

CHAPTER 10

Planning for Profit

OVERVIEW

This chapter shows you how to analyze your menu so you can identify which menu items contribute the most to your profits. In addition, it teaches you how to determine the sales dollars and guest volume levels you must achieve to break even and to generate a profit in your operation. Finally, the chapter shows you how to establish an operating budget and presents techniques you can use to monitor your effectiveness in staying within your budget.

Chapter Outline

- Financial Analysis and Profit Planning
- Menu Analysis
- Cost/Volume/Profit Analysis
- The Budget
- Developing the Budget
- Monitoring the Budget
- Technology Tools
- Apply What You Have Learned
- Key Terms and Concepts
- Test Your Skills

LEARNING OUTCOMES

At the conclusion of this chapter, you will be able to:
- Analyze a menu for profitability.
- Prepare a cost/volume/profit (break-even) analysis.
- Establish a budget and monitor performance to the budget.

FINANCIAL ANALYSIS AND PROFIT PLANNING •———

In addition to analyzing the profit and loss (P&L) statement (see Chapter 9), you should also undertake a thorough study of three additional areas of analysis that will assist you in planning for profit:

1. Menu analysis
2. Cost/volume/profit (CVP) analysis
3. Budgeting

Menu analysis concerns itself with the profitability of the individual menu items you sell. CVP analysis deals with the sales dollars and volume required by your foodservice unit to avoid an operating loss and to make a profit. The process of budgeting allows you to plan your next year's operating results by projecting your sales, expenses, and profits and then developing a budgeted P&L statement.

Some foodservice operators "hope for profit" instead of "planning for profit." Although hoping is an admirable pursuit when playing the lottery, it does little good when managing a foodservice operation. Smart managers know that preplanning is the key to achieving the cost and profit goals that will keep them in business.

MENU ANALYSIS •———

Effective managers want to know the answer to a basic operational question: "How does the sale of a particular menu item contribute to the overall success of my operation?" The answer to such a question can sometimes be provided by applying mathematics, but numbers are only one component of menu analysis. There are others to consider.

Consider the case of Danny, who operates a successful family restaurant, called The Mark Twain, in rural Tennessee. The restaurant has been in his family for three generations. One item on the menu is mustard greens with scrambled eggs. It does not sell often, but both mustard greens and eggs are ingredients in other, more popular items. Why does Danny keep the item in a prominent spot on the menu? The answer is simple and has little to do with finance. The menu item was Danny's grandfather's favorite. As a thank-you to his grandfather, who started the business and inspired Danny to become service and guest oriented, the menu item survives every menu reprint.

Menu analysis is about more than just analyzing numbers. It involves marketing, sociology, psychology, and a good deal of emotion. Remember that guests respond best not to weighty financial analyses, but rather to menu item descriptions, placement on the physical menu, price, and current popularity. Although the financial analysis of a menu is indeed done "by the numbers," you must realize that while those numbers are an important part, they are merely one part, of the complete menu analysis process.

For the serious foodservice manager, the analysis of a menu deserves special study. Many components of the menu, such as item pricing, layout, design, and copy, all play an important role in the overall success of a foodservice operation. If you investigate the menu analysis methods that have been widely used by professional food service managers in recent times, you will find that each method seeks to perform a menu analysis using one or more of the following operational variables with which you are familiar:

• Food cost percentage
• Item popularity
• Contribution margin
• Selling price
• Variable expenses
• Fixed expenses

FIGURE 10.1 Three Methods of Menu Analysis

Method	Variables Considered	Analysis Method	Goal
1. Food cost %	a. Food cost % b. Popularity	Matrix	Minimize overall food cost %
2. Contribution margin	a. Contribution margin b. Popularity	Matrix	Maximize contribution margin
3. Goal value	a. Contribution margin % b. Popularity c. Selling price d. Variable cost % e. Food cost %	Algebraic equation	Achieve predetermined profit % goals

Although there are many variations, three of the most popular systems of menu analysis are shown in Figure 10.1. They represent the three major philosophical approaches to menu analysis. The **matrix analysis** referenced in Figure 10.1 provides a method for comparisons between menu items. A matrix allows menu items to be placed into categories based on whether they are above or below overall menu item averages for factors such as food cost percentage, popularity, and contribution margin.

Each approach to menu analysis has its proponents and detractors, but an understanding of each will help you as you attempt to develop your own philosophy of menu analysis.

FOOD COST PERCENTAGE

Menu analysis that focuses on food cost percentage is the oldest and most traditional method used. When analyzing a menu using the food cost percentage method, you are seeking menu items that have the effect of minimizing your overall food cost percentage. The rationale for this is that a lowered food cost percentage leaves more of the sales dollar to be spent for other operational expenses.

A criticism of the food cost percentage approach is that, when it is used, items that have a higher food cost percentage may be removed from the menu in favor of items that have a lower food cost percentage, but when purchased by guests, these lower food cost percentage items may also contribute fewer dollars to overall profit.

To illustrate the use of the food cost percentage menu analysis method, consider the case of Maureen, who operates a steak and seafood restaurant near the beach in a busy resort town. Maureen sells seven items in the entrée section of her menu. The items and information related to their popularity, selling price, portion cost, and contribution margin (see Chapter 6) for a one-week period in January are presented in Figure 10.2.

The numbers in the rows of Figure 10.2 are calculated as follows:

Individual Menu Item Rows:

> Number Sold and Selling Price can be obtained from the POS system.
>
> Total Sales = Number Sold × Selling Price
>
> Item Cost (food only) can be obtained from a standardized recipe cost sheet.
>
> Total Cost = Number Sold × Item Cost
>
> Item Contribution Margin = Selling Price − Item Cost
>
> Total Contribution Margin = Number Sold × Item Contribution Margin
>
> Food Cost % = Total Cost/Total Sales *or* Item Cost/Selling Price

FIGURE 10.2 Maureen's Menu Analysis Worksheet

Date: 1/15–1/21

Menu Item	Number Sold	Selling Price	Total Sales	Item Cost	Total Cost	Item Contribution Margin	Total Contribution Margin	Food Cost %
Strip Steak	73	$17.95	$ 1,310.35	$ 8.08	$ 589.84	$ 9.87	$ 720.51	45%
Coconut Shrimp	121	16.95	2,050.95	5.09	615.89	11.86	1,435.06	30%
Grilled Tuna	105	17.95	1,884.75	7.18	753.90	10.77	1,130.85	40%
Chicken Breast	140	13.95	1,953.00	3.07	429.80	10.88	1,523.20	22%
Lobster Stir-Fry	51	21.95	1,119.45	11.19	570.69	10.76	548.76	51%
Scallops/Pasta	85	14.95	1,270.75	3.59	305.15	11.36	965.60	24%
Beef Medallions	125	15.95	1,993.75	5.90	737.50	10.05	1,256.25	37%
Total	700		$11,583.00		$4,002.77		$7,580.23	
Weighted Average	100	$16.55	$ 1,654.71	$ 5.72	$ 571.82	$10.83	$1,082.89	35%

Total Row:
The totals in the Number Sold, Total Sales, Total Cost, and Total Contribution Margin columns are calculated by simply adding the numbers in those columns.

Average/Weighted Average Row:
To calculate the values in the Weighted Average row do the weighted average calculations in the following order:

AVERAGE/WEIGHTED AVERAGE	CALCULATION
Average number sold	700 Total number sold/7 menu items = 100
Average total sales	$11,583.00 Total sales/7 menu items = $1,654.71
Weighted average selling price	$1,654.71 Average total sales/100 Average number sold = $16.55
Average total cost	$4,002.77 Total cost/7 menu items = $571.82
Weighted average item cost	$571.82 Average total cost/100 Average number sold = $5.72
Average total contribution margin (CM)	$7,580.23 Total CM/7 menu items = $1,082.89
Weighted average item contribution margin (CM)	$1,082.89 Average total CM/100 Average number sold = $10.83
Weighted average food cost %	$571.82 Average total food cost/$1,654.71 Average total sales = 35%

To analyze her menu using the food cost percentage method, Maureen separates her items based on two variables:

1. Food cost percentage
2. Popularity (number sold)

Maureen's overall food cost is 35 percent (rounded), so she considers any individual menu item with a food cost percentage above 35 percent to be high in food cost percentage, whereas any menu item with a food cost below 35 percent will be considered low.

In a similar way, with a total of 700 entrées served in this accounting period and seven possible menu choices, each menu item would sell 700/7, or 100 times, if all were equally popular. Given that fact, Maureen determines that any item that sold more than 100 times during this week's accounting period will be considered high (above average) in popularity, whereas any item selling less than 100 times will be considered low (below average) in popularity. Having made these determinations, Maureen produces a matrix labeled as follows:

		Popularity	
		Low	**High**
High		1 High food cost % Low popularity	2 High food cost % High popularity
Food Cost %			
Low		3 Low food cost % Low popularity	4 Low food cost % High popularity

Based on the number sold and food cost percentage data in Figure 10.2, Maureen can classify her menu items in the following manner:

Square	Characteristics	Menu Item
1	High food cost % Low popularity	Strip Steak, Lobster Stir-Fry
2	High food cost % High popularity	Grilled Tuna, Beef Medallions
3	Low food cost % Low popularity	Scallops/Pasta
4	Low food cost % High popularity	Coconut Shrimp, Chicken Breast

Note that each menu item can be placed in one, and only one, of the four squares. Using the food cost percentage method of menu analysis, Maureen would like as many menu items as possible to fall within square 4. These items have the characteristics of being low in food cost percentage but high in popularity, or guest acceptance. Thus, both coconut shrimp and chicken breast have below-average food cost percentages and above-average popularity.

When developing a menu that seeks to minimize food cost percentage, items in the fourth square are highly desirable because the low food cost percentage of the individual items helps keep the operation's overall food cost percentage low and the items sell very well. These items are, of course, kept on the menu. They should be well promoted and have high menu visibility. Promote them to your best guests and take care not to develop and attempt to sell a menu item with a higher food cost percentage that is similar enough in nature that it could detract from the sales of these lower-cost items.

The characteristics of the menu items that fall into each of the four matrix squares are unique and, thus, should be managed differently. Because of this, items that fall into each individual square require a special marketing strategy, depending on their matrix location. These strategies can be summarized as shown in Figure 10.3.

FIGURE 10.3 Analysis of Food Cost Matrix Results

Square	Characteristics	Problem	Marketing Strategy
1	High food cost % Low popularity	Marginal due to both high product cost and lack of sales	a. Remove from the menu. b. Consider current food high product cost trends to determine if the item itself is unpopular or if its method of preparation is. c. Survey guests to determine current wants regarding this item. d. If this is a high-contribution-margin item, consider reducing price and/or portion size.
2	High food cost % High popularity	Marginal due to high product cost menu	a. Increase price. b. Reduce prominence on the menu. c. Reduce portion size. d. "Bundle" the sale of this item with one that has a lower cost and, thus, provides better overall food cost %.
3	Low food cost % Low popularity	Marginal due to lack of sales	a. Relocate on the menu for greater visibility. b. Take off the regular menu and run as specials. c. Reduce menu price. d. Eliminate other unpopular menu items in order to increase demand for this one.
4	Low food cost % High popularity	None	a. Promote well. b. Increase visibility on the menu.

It can be quite effective to use the food cost percentage method of menu evaluation. It is fast, easy to calculate, and time-tested. Remember that if you achieve too high a food cost percentage, you run the risk that not enough percentage points will remain to generate a profit on your sales.

In spite of its popularity, however, the food cost percentage menu analysis method has limitations. For example, most foodservice operators would say it is better to achieve a 20 percent food cost on a menu item than a 40 percent food cost. Consider, however, a chicken dish that sells for $5.00 and costs you just $1.00 to make. This item yields a 20 percent food cost ($1.00 food cost ÷ $5.00 selling price = 20% food cost), and there are $4.00 ($5.00 − $1.00 = $4.00) remaining to pay for the labor and other expenses of serving this guest.

Compare that sale to a sale made to the same guest buying a steak for $10.00 that costs you $4.00 to make. Your food cost percentage would be 40 percent ($4.00 food cost ÷ $10.00 selling price = 40% food cost). In this case, however, there would be $6.00 ($10.00 − $4.00 = $6.00) remaining to pay for the labor and other expenses of serving this guest. Clearly, in this example it would be better to sell more steak than chicken, despite the steak's higher food cost percentage. In this example, steak has a larger contribution margin than chicken. For this reason, many operators prefer to analyze their menus using a contribution margin matrix.

CONTRIBUTION MARGIN

When analyzing a menu using the contribution margin approach, the operator seeks to produce a menu that maximizes the menu's overall contribution margin. Recall from Chapter 6 that contribution margin is defined as the amount that remains after the product (food or beverage) cost of a menu item is subtracted from that item's selling price.

HERE'S HOW IT'S DONE *10.1*

Recall that contribution margin for an individual menu item is the amount of money remaining from the item's selling price after the product cost of making the item has been subtracted. The formula for calculating a contribution margin for a menu item is:

Item selling price − Item product cost = Item contribution margin

To illustrate, if a menu item sells for $10 and it cost $2.00 to make it, the item's contribution margin is $8.00. In this example, the menu item's contribution margin is calculated as:

$10.00 Selling price − $2.00 Product cost = $8.00 Contribution margin

Remember, also, that when calculating the contribution margin of a menu item, it is important to include the cost of the item as well all of that item's accompaniments such as bread, salads, side dishes, and garnishes that are also presented to the guest when the menu item is ordered.

The cost of these accompaniments can be significant and must be included in the calculation of the item's contribution margin. For example, if the item that sells for $10.00 and costs $2.00 to make is served with a side vegetable that cost $0.50, the true contribution margin of the item would be calculated as:

$10.00 Selling price − $2.00 Product cost − $0.50 Side vegetable cost = $7.50 Contribution margin

Contribution margin is the amount that you will have available to pay for your labor, your controllable and non-controllable other expenses, and to keep for your profit. Thus, from Figure 10.2, if an item on Maureen's menu, such as strip steak, sells for $17.95 and the product cost for the item is $8.08, the contribution margin per menu item would be computed as follows:

Selling price − Item cost = Contribution margin per menu item
or
$17.95 − $8.08 = $9.87

When contribution margin is the driving factor in analyzing a menu, the two variables used for the analysis are contribution margin and item popularity.

To illustrate the use of the contribution margin approach to menu analysis, the data in Figure 10.2 are again used. In this case, Maureen must again separate her items based on high or low popularity. Doing so gives the same results as those obtained when using the food cost percentage method; thus, any item that sells 700/7, or 100 times, or more is considered to be a high-popularity item, whereas any menu choice selling less than 100 times would be considered low in popularity.

Some menu analysis experts maintain that any menu item that achieves at least 70 percent of the average number sold be considered a high-popularity menu item, whereas those that sell below 70 percent of the average should be considered low-popularity. However, to illustrate the procedure, we will be using the average number of items sold (in this case, 100 items sold) for our calculations.

When computing average contribution margin for the entire menu, Maureen must follow two steps. First, to determine the total contribution margin for the menu, the following formula is used:

Total sales − Total item (product) costs = Total contribution margin
or
$11,583.00 − $4,002.77 = $7,580.23

Because 700 total menu items were sold, you can determine the average contribution margin per item using the following formula:

$$\frac{\text{Total item contribution margin}}{\text{Number of items sold}} = \text{Average contribution margin per item}$$

or

$$\frac{\$7,580.23}{700} = \$10.83$$

To develop the contribution margin matrix, you proceed along much the same lines as with the food cost percentage matrix. In this case, average item popularity is 100 and average item contribution margin is $10.83. The matrix is developed as follows:

Popularity

Contribution Margin		Low	High
	High	1 High contribution margin Low popularity	2 High contribution margin High popularity
	Low	3 Low contribution margin Low popularity	4 Low contribution margin High popularity

Maureen now classifies her menu items according to the contribution margin matrix in the following manner:

Square	Characteristics	Menu Item
1	High contribution margin Low popularity	Scallops/Pasta
2	High contribution margin High popularity	Coconut Shrimp, Chicken Breast
3	Low contribution margin Low popularity	Strip Steak, Lobster Stir-Fry
4	Low contribution margin High popularity	Grilled Tuna, Beef Medallions

Again, when completing this analysis, each menu item can be placed in one, and only one, matrix square. Using the contribution margin method of menu analysis, Maureen would like as many of her menu items as possible to fall within square 2—that is, high contribution margin and high popularity.

From her analysis, Maureen knows that both coconut shrimp and chicken breast yield a higher than average contribution margin. In addition, these items sell very well. Just as Maureen seeks to give high menu visibility to items with low food cost percentage and high popularity when using the food cost percentage method of menu analysis, she seeks to give that same visibility to items with high contribution margins and high popularity when using the contribution margin approach.

Each of the menu items that fall in the other squares requires a special marketing strategy, depending on its square location. These strategies are summarized as shown in Figure 10.4.

A frequent, and legitimate, criticism of the contribution margin approach to menu analysis is that it tends to favor high-priced menu items over low-priced

FIGURE 10.4 Analysis of Contribution Margin Matrix Results

Square	Characteristics	Problem	Marketing Strategy
1	High contribution margin Low popularity	Marginal due to lack of sales	a. Relocate on menu for greater visibility. b. Consider reducing selling price.
2	High contribution margin High popularity	None	a. Promote well. b. Increase prominence on the menu.
3	Low contribution margin Low popularity	Marginal due to both low contribution margin and lack of sales	a. Remove from menu. b. Consider offering as a special occasionally, but at a higher menu price.
4	Low contribution margin High popularity	Marginal due to low contribution margin	a. Increase price. b. Reduce prominence on the menu. c. Consider reducing portion size.

ones because higher-priced menu items, in general, tend to have the highest contribution margins. Over the long term, this can result in sales techniques and menu placement decisions that tend to put in the guest's mind a higher check average than the operation may warrant or desire. This may not be desirable at all. Alternatively, the successful menu strategy related to the many **quick-service restaurants (QSRs)** that offer $0.99, $1.00, or $1.99 value menu items is certainly not one of maximizing contribution margin, but rather is one of seeking to increase total revenue.

Some users of the contribution margin method of menu analysis refer to it as **menu engineering** and classify the squares used in the analysis with colorful names. The most common of these are "plow horses" (square 1) because these items have high contribution margins but are less popular, "stars" (square 2), because these items are popular and also have high contribution margins, "dogs" (square 3) because these have low contribution margins and are not popular, and "puzzles" or sometimes "challenges" (square 4) because these menu items are highly popular but return lower than average contribution margins to the operator.

The selection of either food cost percentage or contribution margin as a menu analysis technique is really an attempt by the foodservice operator to answer the following questions:

- Are my menu items priced correctly?
- Are the individual menu items selling well enough to warrant keeping them on the menu?
- Is the overall profit margin on my menu items satisfactory?

The use of either the matrix-based food cost or contribution margin menu analysis system to answer these questions is, the authors believe, overly simplistic for use in today's increasingly sophisticated foodservice operations.

Because of the limitations of matrix analysis, neither the matrix food cost nor the matrix contribution margin approach is truly effective in analyzing menus. This is the case because, mathematically, the axes on the matrix are determined by the mean (average) of food cost percentage, contribution margin or sales level (popularity). When this is done, some items will always fall into the less desirable categories. This is so because, in matrix analysis, high food cost percentage, for instance, really means food cost percentage above that operation's average, or arithmetic mean. Obviously, then, some items must always fall above and below the average regardless of their contribution to operational profitability. Eliminating the poorest items only shifts other items into undesirable categories.

To illustrate this significant drawback to matrix analysis, consider the following example. Assume that Homer, one of Maureen's competitors, sells only four items, as follows:

Homer's No. 1 Menu	
Item	Number Sold
Beef	70
Chicken	60
Pork	15
Seafood	55
Total	200
Average sold	50 (200/4)

After conducting a matrix analysis, Homer may elect to remove the pork item because its sales level is below the average of 50 items sold. If Homer adds turkey to the menu and removes the pork, he could get the following results:

Homer's No. 2 Menu	
Item	Number Sold
Beef	65
Chicken	55
Turkey	50
Seafood	30
Total	200
Average sold	50 (200/4)

As can be seen, the turkey item drew sales away from the beef, chicken, and seafood dishes and did not increase the total number of menu items sold. In this case, it is now the seafood item that falls below the menu average. Should that item be removed because its sales are now below average? Clearly, this might not be wise. Removing the seafood item might serve only to draw sales from the remaining items to the seafood's replacement item. The same type of result can occur when you use a matrix to analyze food cost percentage or contribution margin. As someone once stated, half of us are below average in everything. Thus, the matrix approach, because of its average-based format, inherently forces some items to be below average.

An additional and increasingly relevant criticism of both the food cost percentage and contribution margin analysis methods relates to the fact that the results of both are determined by the price operators pay for food or beverage products. As increasing numbers of operators find they pay more for labor to produce their menu items than for the ingredients to make them, some managers question any menu analysis system that ignores labor and other important costs.

How, then, can an operator answer important questions related to menu price, sales volume, and overall profit margin? One answer is to avoid the overly simplistic and ineffective matrix analysis and employ all, or even part, of a more powerful and effective method of menu analysis called goal value analysis.

FUN ON THE WEB!

Some companies have developed menu engineering software designed to help managers analyze their menus. To view the menu analysis offerings of current software producers, enter "menu engineering software" in your favorite search engine and review the results.

GOAL VALUE ANALYSIS

Goal value analysis was introduced by Dr. David Hayes and Dr. Lynn Huffman in a 1985 article titled "Menu Analysis: A Better Way," published by the respected and refereed hospitality journal *The Cornell Quarterly*.

Ten years later, at the height of what was known as the *value pricing* debate (i.e., extremely low pricing strategies used to drive significant increases in guest counts) the effectiveness of goal value analysis was again proved in a second article, "Value Pricing: How Low Can You Go?" which was also published in *The Cornell Quarterly* in 1995. Ultimately, the system was reviewed and its usefulness expanded by Dr. Lea Dopson of the University of North Texas.

Goal value analysis uses the power of an algebraic formula to replace less sophisticated menu averaging techniques. Before the widespread introduction of computerized spreadsheet programs, some managers found the computations required to use goal value analysis challenging. Today, however, such computations are easily made using standard spreadsheet programs such as Microsoft's Excel.

The advantages of goal value analysis are many, including ease of use, accuracy, and the ability to simultaneously consider more variables than is possible with two-dimensional matrix analysis. Mastering the power of goal value analysis can truly help you design menus that are effective, popular, and, most important, profitable.

Goal value analysis is used to evaluate each menu item's food cost percentage, contribution margin, and popularity. Unlike the two previous matrix-based analysis methods introduced, however, it also includes the analysis of the menu item's nonfood variable costs as well as its selling price. Returning to the data in Figure 10.2, we see that Maureen has an overall food cost percentage of 35 percent. In addition, she served an average of 100 guests per menu item at an entrée check average of $16.55. If we knew about Maureen's overall fixed and variable expenses (see Chapter 8) we would know a great deal more about the profitability of each of Maureen's menu items. Goal value analysis evaluates that profitability information.

One difficulty encountered when seeking to evaluate a menu item's profitability is that the assignment of nonfood variable costs to individual menu items can be a challenge. The issue is complex. It is very likely true, for example, that different items on Maureen's menu require differing amounts of labor to prepare. For instance, the strip steak on her menu is purchased precut and vacuum-sealed. Its preparation simply requires opening the steak package, seasoning the steak, and placing it on a broiler. The lobster stir-fry, on the other hand, is a complex dish that requires cooking and shelling the lobster, cleaning and trimming the vegetables, then preparing the item when ordered by quickly cooking the lobster, vegetables, and a sauce in a wok. Thus, the variable labor cost of preparing the two dishes is very different.

It is assumed that Maureen responds to these differing costs by charging more for a more labor-intensive dish and less for one that is less labor intensive. Other dishes require essentially the same amount of labor to prepare; thus, their variable labor costs have less impact on individual menu item's selling prices. Because that is true, for analysis purposes, most operators find it convenient to assign variable costs to individual menu items based on their *average* labor and other variable costs. For example, if labor and other variable costs are 30 percent of total sales, all menu items may be assigned that same variable cost percentage of their selling price.

For the purpose of her goal value analysis, Maureen determines her total variable costs. These are all the costs that vary with her sales volume, excluding the cost of the food itself. She computes those variable costs from her P&L statement (see Chapter 9) and finds that they account for 30 percent of her total sales. Using this information, Maureen assigns a variable cost of 30 percent of selling price to each menu item.

Having compiled the information in Figure 10.2, Maureen can use the algebraic goal value formula to create a specific target, or goal value, for her entire menu, and then use the same formula to compute the goal value of each individual menu item. Menu items that achieve goal values higher than that of the menu's overall goal value will contribute greater than average profit percentages. As the goal value for an item increases, so too does its profitability percentage. Assuming that Maureen's average food cost percentage, average number of items sold per menu item, average selling price (check average), and average variable cost percentage all meet the overall profitability goals of her restaurant, each individual menu item's goal value can be analyzed to assess that item's contribution to profits. The goal value formula is:

$$A \times B \times C \times D = \text{Goal value}$$

where

$A = 1.00 - \text{Food cost \%}$
$B = \text{Item popularity}$
$C = \text{Selling price}$
$D = 1.00 - (\text{Variable cost \%} + \text{Food cost \%})$

Note that A in the preceding formula is really the contribution margin *percentage* of a menu item. D is the *percentage* amount available to fund fixed costs and provide for a profit after all variable costs (including food) are accounted for.

Maureen uses this formula to compute the goal value of her overall menu and finds that:

$$A \qquad \times B \quad \times C \quad \times D \qquad\qquad = \text{Goal value}$$
$$(1.00 - 0.35) \times 100 \times \$16.55 \times [1.00 - (0.30 + 0.35)] = \text{Goal value}$$

or

$$0.65 \qquad \times 100 \times \$16.55 \times 0.35 \qquad\qquad = 376.5$$

According to this formula, any menu item whose goal value equals or exceeds 376.5 will achieve profitability that equals or exceeds that of Maureen's overall menu. The computed goal value carries no unit designation; that is, it is neither a percentage nor a dollar figure because it is really a numerical target or score.

Figure 10.5 details the goal value data Maureen needs to complete a goal value analysis on each of her seven individual menu items. Figure 10.6 details the results of Maureen's goal value analysis. Note that she has calculated the goal values of her menu items and listed them in order of highest to lowest goal value. She has also inserted her overall menu goal value in the appropriate rank order.

Note that the grilled tuna falls slightly below the profitability of the entire menu, whereas the strip steak and lobster stir-fry fall substantially below the overall goal value score. Should the strip steak and lobster stir-fry be replaced? The answer, most likely, is no if Maureen is satisfied with her current target food cost percentage, profit margin, check average, and guest count.

FIGURE 10.5 Maureen's Goal Value Analysis Data

Item	Food Cost % (in decimal form)	Number Sold	Selling Price	Variable Cost % (in decimal form)
Strip Steak	0.45	73	$17.95	0.30
Coconut Shrimp	0.30	121	$16.95	0.30
Grilled Tuna	0.40	105	$17.95	0.30
Chicken Breast	0.22	140	$13.95	0.30
Lobster Stir-Fry	0.51	51	$21.95	0.30
Scallops/Pasta	0.24	85	$14.95	0.30
Beef Medallions	0.37	125	$15.95	0.30

FIGURE 10.6 Goal Value Analysis Results

Rank	Menu Item	A	B	C	D	Goal Value
1	Chicken Breast	(1 − 0.22)	140	$13.95	[1 − (0.30 + 0.22)]	731.2
2	Coconut Shrimp	(1 − 0.30)	121	16.95	[1 − (0.30 + 0.30)]	574.3
3	Scallops/Pasta	(1 − 0.24)	85	14.95	[1 − (0.30 + 0.24)]	444.3
4	Beef Medallions	(1 − 0.37)	125	15.95	[1 − (0.30 + 0.37)]	414.5
	Overall Menu Goal Value	*(1 − 0.35)*	*100*	*$16.55*	*[1 − (0.30 + 0.35)]*	*376.5*
5	Grilled Tuna	(1 − 0.40)	105	17.95	[1 − (0.30 + 0.40)]	339.3
6	Strip Steak	(1 − 0.45)	73	17.95	[1 − (0.30 + 0.45)]	180.2
7	Lobster Stir-Fry	(1 − 0.51)	51	21.95	[1 − (0.30 + 0.51)]	104.2

Every menu will have items that are more or less profitable than others. In fact, some operators develop items called **loss leaders**. A loss leader is a menu item that is priced very low, sometimes even below its total cost, for the purpose of drawing large numbers of guests to the operation and thus increasing total revenue. If, for example, Maureen has the only operation in town that serves outstanding lobster stir-fry, that item may, in fact, contribute to the overall success of the operation by drawing people who will buy it, whereas others dining with them may order menu items that are more profitable.

The accuracy and value of goal value analysis is well documented. Used properly, it is a convenient way for management to evaluate the profitability, sales volume, and pricing characteristics of menu items. Because all of the values needed for the goal value formula are readily available, management need not concern itself with puzzling through endless decisions about item replacement.

Items that do not achieve the targeted goal value tend to be deficient in one or more of the key areas of food cost percentage, popularity, selling price, or variable cost percentage. In theory, all menu items have the potential of reaching the goal value. Management may, however, determine that some menu items can best serve the operation as loss leaders, an approach illustrated by the continued use of "value" menu items by leading chains in the QSR segment.

To better understand goal value analysis, consider the formula results for Maureen's strip steak:

Strip Steak

$$
\begin{aligned}
A \quad &\times B \times C \quad \times D &= \text{Goal value} \\
(1.00 - 0.45) \quad &\times 73 \times \$17.95 \times [1 - (0.30 + 0.45)] &= \text{Goal value} \\
0.55 \quad &\times 73 \times \$17.95 \times 0.25 &= 180.2
\end{aligned}
$$

This item did not meet the goal value target. Why? There can be several answers. One is that the item's 45 percent food cost is too high. This can be addressed by reducing portion size or changing the item's recipe or garnish; these actions could have the effect of reducing the item's portion cost and, thus, its food cost percentage, which has the effect of increasing the A value.

A second approach to improving the goal value score of the strip steak is to work on improving the B value, that is, the number of times the item is sold. This may be done through improved placement on the menu, increased merchandising, or, because it is one of the more expensive items on the menu, incentives to wait staff for selling this item.

Menu price (variable C) is in line with the rest of the menu but could be adjusted upward. Of course, any upward price adjustments in C may well result in declines in the number of items sold (*B* value)! Increases in the menu price will also have the effect of decreasing the food cost percentage and the variable cost percentage of the menu item (and increasing the contribution margin). This is because selling price (sales) is the denominator of the food cost percentage and variable cost percentage equations.

Obviously, the changes you undertake as a result of any menu analysis are varied and can be complex. As you gain experience in knowing the tastes and behavior of your guests, however, your skill in menu-related decision making will quickly improve.

Sophisticated users of the goal value analysis system can, as suggested by Lendal Kotschevar, in *Management by Menu* 4th ed. (www.wiley.com), modify the goal value formula to increase its accuracy and usefulness even more. In the area of variable costs, a menu item might be assigned a low, medium, or high variable cost. If overall variable costs equal 30 percent, for example, management may choose to assign a variable cost of 25 percent to those items with very low labor costs attached to them, 30 percent to others with average labor costs, and 35 percent or more to others with even higher costs. This adjustment affects only the *D* variable of the goal value formula and can be made quite easily.

Goal value analysis will also allow you to make better decisions more quickly. This is especially true if you know a bit of algebra and realize that anytime you determine a desired overall goal value and know any three of the four variables contained in the formula, you can solve for the fourth unknown variable by using goal value as the numerator and placing the known variables in the denominator.

Figure 10.7 shows you how to solve for each unknown variable in the goal value formula.

To illustrate how the information in Figure 10.7 can be used, let's return to the information in Figure 10.6 and assume that, after Maureen talks with many of her customers and, based on their comments, she feels the 12-ounce strip steak she is offering is too large for many of her guests and that is why its popularity (*B* value) is low. Thus, Maureen elects to take three actions:

1. She reduces the portion size of the item from 12 ounces to 9 ounces, resulting in a reduction in her food cost from $8.08 to $6.10.

2. Because she knows her guests will likely be hesitant to pay the same price for a smaller steak, she also reduces the selling price of this item by $1.00 to $16.95. She feels that this will keep the strip steak from losing any popularity resulting from the reduction in portion size. Her new food cost percentage for this item is 36 percent ($6.10 ÷ $16.95 = 36%).

3. Since the labor required to prepare this menu item is so low, she assigns a below-average 25 percent variable cost to its *D* value.

Maureen now knows three of the goal value variables for this item and can solve for the fourth. Maureen knows her *A* value (1.00 − 0.36), her *C* value ($16.95), and her *D* value [1.00 − (0.25 + 0.36)]. The question she would ask is this: "Given this

FIGURE 10.7 Solving for Goal Value Unknowns

Known Variables	Unknown Variables	Method to Find Unknown
A, B, C, D	Goal value (GV)	$A \times B \times C \times D$
B, C, D, GV	A	$\dfrac{GV}{B \times C \times D}$
A, C, D, GV	B	$\dfrac{GV}{A \times C \times D}$
A, B, D, GV	C	$\dfrac{GV}{A \times B \times D}$
A, B, C, GV	D	$\dfrac{GV}{A \times B \times C}$

newly structured menu item, how many must be sold to make the item achieve the targeted goal value and thus contribute to profits?" The answer requires solving the goal value equation for B, the number sold.

From Figure 10.7, recall that, if B is the unknown variable, it can be computed by using the following formula:

$$\frac{\text{Goal value}}{A \times C \times D} = B$$

In this case:

$$\frac{376.5}{(1.00 - 0.36) \times \$16.95 \times [1.00 - (0.25 + 0.36)]} = B$$

Thus:

$$89 = B$$

According to the formula, 89 servings of strip steak would have to be sold to achieve Maureen's target goal value. An easy, alternative way to determine the effects of changes made to menu items is to use an Excel spreadsheet. Once you put the formulas in a spreadsheet, it is then easy to see how changes made to food costs, number of items, selling prices, and variable costs affect item goal values.

Goal value analysis is also powerful because it is not, as is matrix analysis, dependent on past performance to establish profitability but can be used by management to establish future menu targets. You can use it to establish a desired food cost percentage, target popularity figure, selling price, or variable cost percentage.

To illustrate, assume that Maureen wishes to achieve a greater profit margin and a $17.00 entrée average selling price for next year. She plans to achieve this through a reduction in her overall food cost to 33 percent and her other variable costs to 29 percent. Her overall menu goal value formula for next year, assuming no reduction or increase in guest count, would be as follows:

A	$\times B$	$\times C$	$\times D$	= Goal value
$(1.00 - 0.33)$	$\times 100$	$\times \$17.00$	$\times [1.00 - (0.29 + 0.33)]$	= Goal value
		or		
0.67	$\times 100$	$\times \$17.00$	$\times 0.38$	$= 432.8$

Thus, each item on next year's menu should be evaluated with the new goal value in mind. It is important to remember, however, that Maureen's actual profitability will be heavily influenced by sales mix (see Chapter 5). Thus, all pricing, portion size, and menu placement decisions become critical. Note that Maureen can examine each of her menu items and determine whether she wishes to change any of the items' individual characteristics to meet her goals. It is at this point that she must remember that she is a foodservice operator and not merely an accountant. A purely quantitative approach to menu analysis is neither practical nor desirable. Menu analysis and pricing decisions are always a matter of experience, skill, insight, and educated predicting because it is difficult to know in advance how changing the characteristics of any one menu item may affect the sales mix of the remaining items.

COST/VOLUME/PROFIT ANALYSIS

Many foodservice operators find that some accounting periods are more profitable than others. Often, this is because sales volume is higher or costs are lower during certain periods. The ski resort that experiences tremendous sales during the ski season but has a greatly reduced volume or may even close during the summer season is a good example. Profitability, then, can be viewed as existing on a graph similar to Figure 10.8.

FIGURE 10.8 Cost/Volume/Profit Graph

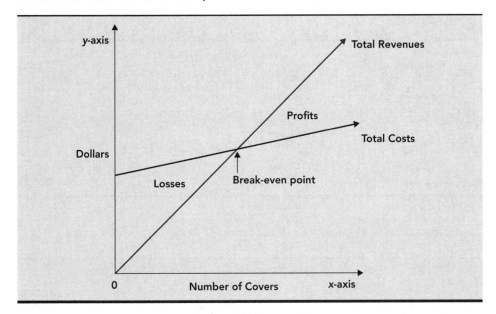

The *x*-axis in Figure 10.8 represents the number of covers sold in a foodservice operation. The *y*-axis represents the costs/revenues in dollars. The Total Revenues line starts at zero because if no covers are sold, no dollars are generated. The Total Costs line starts farther up the *y* axis because fixed costs are incurred even if no covers are sold. The point at which the two lines cross (intersect) is called the **break-even point**.

At the break-even point, operational expenses are exactly equal to sales revenue. Stated in another way, when sales volume in your operation equals the sum of your total variable and fixed costs, your break-even point has been reached. Below the break-even point, costs are higher than revenues, so losses occur. Above the break-even point, revenues exceed costs, so profits are made.

Most operators would like to know their break-even point on a daily, weekly, or monthly basis. In effect, by determining the break-even point, the operator is answering the question: "How much sales volume must I generate before I begin to make a profit?"

Beyond the break-even point, you will want to answer another question: "How much sales dollars and volume must I generate to make my desired profit level?" To answer this question, you must conduct a **cost/volume/profit (CVP) analysis**. A CVP analysis helps predict the sales dollars and volume required to achieve desired profit (or break-even) based on your known costs. You can perform a CVP analysis either by constructing a CVP graph or by arithmetical calculation. Although there are advantages to both methods, the arithmetical calculation is typically the most accurate. You can make CVP calculations to determine the dollar sales volume required to break even and/or achieve a desired profit, or to determine the number of guests (covers) that must be served to break even.

To see how a CVP analysis is conducted, consider the case of Jennifer, who operates an Asian restaurant. Based on her income statement and sales records from last month, Jennifer has converted her P&L statement to a **contribution margin income statement**, as shown in Figure 10.9. A contribution margin income statement simply shows P&L items in the categories of total sales, variable costs, contribution margin, fixed costs, before-tax profit, taxes, and after-tax profit.

As you have learned, foodservice expenses can generally be classified as either fixed or variable. Of course, some expenses have both a fixed and a variable component and, thus, in reality, are mixed costs (see Chapter 8). For the purpose of engaging in a CVP analysis, however, it is necessary for the operator to assign costs to either a fixed or a variable category, as Jennifer has done. In addition, her **contribution margin for overall operation** is defined as the dollar amount that contributes to paying an operation's fixed costs and providing for a profit.

FIGURE 10.9 Contribution Margin Income Statement

Jennifer's			
Total sales	$125,000	Sales per guest	$12.50
Variable costs	50,000	Guests served	10,000
Contribution margin	75,000		
Fixed costs	60,000		
Before-tax profit	15,000		
Taxes (40%)	6,000		
After-tax profit	$ 9,000		

Contribution margin for overall operation at Jennifer's is calculated as:

Total sales − Variable costs = Contribution margin for overall operation

or

$125,000 − $50,000 = $75,000

Jennifer can also view her contribution margin income statement in terms of per-unit (guest) and percentage sales, variable costs, and contribution margin, as shown in Figure 10.10.

Notice the box in Figure 10.10 that includes per unit (guest) and percentage calculations for sales per guest (selling price, (SP)), variable costs (VC), and contribution margin (CM). Note also that fixed costs are not calculated as per unit or as a percentage of sales. This is because fixed costs do not vary with sales volume increases or decreases.

To calculate these numbers, the following steps are taken:

Step 1. Divide total sales, variable costs, and contribution margin by the number of guests served (units) to get per-guest (per-unit) values:

$$\frac{SP}{Unit} = \frac{\$125,000}{10,000 \text{ units}} = \$12.50$$

$$\frac{VC}{Unit} = \frac{\$50,000}{10,000 \text{ units}} = \$5.00$$

$$\frac{CM}{Unit} = \frac{\$75,000}{10,000 \text{ units}} = \$7.50$$

$$\frac{SP}{Unit} - \frac{VC}{Unit} = \frac{CM}{Unit}$$

$$\$12.50 - \$5.00 = \$7.50$$

FIGURE 10.10 Contribution Margin Income Statement with per-Unit and Percentage Calculations

Jennifer's			
Total sales	$125,000		
Variable costs	50,000	**Per Unit (Guest)**	**Percentage**
Contribution margin	75,000	SP $12.50	100%
Fixed costs	60,000	VC 5.00	40%
Before-tax profit	15,000	CM $ 7.50	60%
Taxes (40%)	6,000	Guests served = 10,000	
After-tax profit	$ 9,000		

Step 2. Divide VC/Unit by SP/Unit, and CM/Unit by SP/Unit to get percentage values:

$$SP\% = 100\%$$

$$VC\% = \frac{\$5.00}{\$12.50} = 40\%$$

$$CM\% = \frac{\$7.50}{\$12.50} = 60\%$$

$$SP\% - VC\% = CM\%$$

$$100\% - 40\% = 60\%$$

After Jennifer's P&L statement has been converted to a contribution margin income statement and per-unit values and percentages have been calculated, she can determine her operational break-even point and the sales required to achieve her desired profit. She wants to do this based both on dollar sales and on the number of units (guests) required to be served.

To determine the dollar sales required to break even, Jennifer uses the following formula:

$$\frac{\text{Fixed costs}}{\text{Contribution margin }\%} = \text{Break-even point in sales}$$

or

$$\frac{\$60,000}{0.60} = \$100,000$$

Thus, Jennifer must generate $100,000 in sales per month before she begins to make a profit. At a sales volume of less than $100,000, she is operating at a loss. In terms of the number of guests that must be served to break even, Jennifer uses the following formula:

$$\frac{\text{Fixed costs}}{\text{Contribution margin per unit (per guest)}} = \text{Break-even point in guests served}$$

or

$$\frac{\$60,000}{\$7.50 \text{ per guest}} = 8,000 \text{ guests (units/covers)}$$

Now assume that Jennifer has decided that next month she will plan for $12,000 in after-tax profits. To determine sales dollars and needed guests (covers) to achieve her after-tax profit goal, Jennifer uses the following formula:

$$\frac{\text{Fixed costs} + \text{Before-tax profit}}{\text{Contribution margin }\%} = \text{Sales dollars to achieve desired after-tax profit}$$

Jennifer knows that her after-tax-profit goal is $12,000, but the preceding formula calls for before-tax profit. To convert her after-tax profit to before-tax profit, Jennifer must compute the following:

$$\frac{\text{After-tax profit}}{1 - \text{Tax rate}} = \text{Before-tax profit}$$

or

$$\frac{\$12,000}{1 - 0.40} = \$20,000$$

Now that Jennifer knows her before-tax profit goal of $20,000, she can calculate the sales dollars needed to achieve her targeted after-tax profit as follows:

$$\frac{\text{Fixed costs} + \text{Before-tax profit}}{\text{Contribution margin \%}} = \text{Sales dollars to achieve desired after-tax profit}$$

or

$$\frac{\$60,000 + \$20,000}{0.60} = \$133,333.33$$

Thus, Jennifer must generate $133,333.33 in sales to achieve her desired after-tax profit of $12,000. In terms of calculating the number of guests that must be served to make her desired profit, Jennifer uses the following formula:

$$\frac{\text{Fixed costs} + \text{Before-tax profit}}{\text{Contribution margin per unit (guest)}} = \text{Guests to be served to achieve desired after-tax profit}$$

or

$$\frac{\$60,000 + \$20,000}{\$7.50 \text{ per guest}} = 10,666.67 \text{ guests (covers)}$$

Round up from 10,667.67 to 10,667. You *must always* round the number of guests *up* because (1) a guest (person) does not exist as a fraction, and (2) it is better to slightly overstate the number of guests to achieve break-even or desired profits than to understate the number and risk a loss or reduce profit. It is better to be safe than sorry!

Also note that once you round the number of guests up to 10,667, you should adjust the total sales dollars to reflect this. Thus, $10,667 \times \$12.50 = \$133,337.50$ sales to achieve the desired after-tax profit is more accurate than $133,333.33, which you calculated using CM percentage. The variation in these two sales dollar levels is due to rounding. This difference is minimal and might not even warrant adjustment unless an exact sales dollar amount is required based on number of guests.

When calculating sales and covers needed to achieve break-even and determine desired after-tax profits, you can easily apply the proper formula if you remember that:

1. Contribution margin percentage is used to calculate sales dollars.
2. Contribution margin per unit is used to calculate sales volume in units (guests or covers).

Once you fully understand the CVP analysis concept, you can predict any sales level for break-even or after-tax profits based on your selling price, fixed costs, variable costs, and contribution margin. You can also make changes in your selling prices and costs to improve your ability to break even and achieve your desired profit levels. This is where menu pricing and cost control concepts covered in this book come into play. As you make changes in your control areas, you will be able to manage your operation efficiently so that losses can be prevented and planned profits can be achieved.

LINKING COST/VOLUME/PROFIT ANALYSIS WITH GOAL VALUE ANALYSIS

Cost/volume/profit analysis is used to establish targets for the entire operation, whereas goal value analysis evaluates individual menu items against those operational targets. Goal value analysis is based on an operation's goals related to food cost, other variable costs, selling price, and number of covers. If, for example, the CVP analysis suggests that covers needed to generate desired profits will not likely be achieved, costs should be evaluated.

If food and labor costs are reduced to generate a more reasonable sales figure in CVP analysis by increasing contribution margin, then those changes affect the desired food and variable costs in goal value analysis. In addition, desired selling price (check average) and number of covers in goal value analysis should be set based on results from CVP analysis.

The direct relationship between goal value analysis and CVP was first presented by Dr. Lea Dopson, "Linking Cost-Volume-Profit Analysis with Goal Value Analysis in the Curriculum Using Spreadsheet Applications," *The Journal of Hospitality Financial Management* 12 (1) (2004), 77–80.

These two forms of analysis are strategically linked, as follows:

Cost/Volume/Profit Analysis	Goal Value Analysis
Food cost % from contribution margin income statement	Food cost % goal
Guests served to achieve desired after-tax profit	Total average number of covers per menu item goal
Selling price	Selling price goal
Labor and other variable cost % from contribution margin income statement	Variable cost % goal

To illustrate the linkage between goal value analysis and CVP analysis consider Priscilla's Mexican Restaurant. It operates in a major metropolitan area in north Texas. Priscilla, the restaurant's owner, conducted a CVP analysis and goal value analysis for the month of June (30 days).

Figure 10.11 shows how her CVP analysis links with her goal value analysis. The following table shows the specific links between Priscilla's two analyses (see also italicized numbers in Figure 10.11).

Cost/Volume/Profit Analysis	Priscilla's CVP	Goal Value Analysis	Priscilla's GV
Food cost % from contribution margin income statement	32%	Food cost % goal	32%
Guests served to achieve desired after-tax profit	18,334/30 days = 611	Total average number of covers per menu item goal	611/7 menu items = 87
Selling price	$15.00	Selling price goal	$15.00
Labor and other variable cost % from contribution margin income statement	28%	Variable cost % goal	28%

By looking at these two analyses, you can learn how the overall goals of the operation affect menu item profitability. Conversely, you can see how changes you make to menu items affect the overall profitability of the operation.

FIGURE 10.11 Linking Cost/Volume/Profit with Goal Value Analysis

Priscilla's Mexican Restaurant: June

	Per Unit (Guest)	Percentage
SP	$15.00	100%
VC	$ 9.00	60%
CM	$ 6.00	40%

CVP Analysis

Fixed costs	$ 90,000.00	
Desired after-tax profit	$ 12,000.00	
Tax rate	40%	
Before-tax profit	$ 20,000.00	
Break-even point in guests served	15,000	Rounded up = 15,000
Break-even point in sales dollars	$225,000.00	
Guests served to achieve desired after-tax profit	18,333.3	Rounded up = 18,334
Sales dollars to achieve desired after-tax profit	$275,010.00	

Contribution Margin Income Statement for June

Units sold		18,334	
Revenues		$275,010.00	100.00%
Food cost		88,003.20	32.00%
Labor & other variable costs		77,002.80	28.00%
Total variable costs		165,006.00	60.00%
Contribution margin		110,004.00	40.00%
Fixed costs		90,000.00	
Before-tax profit		20,004.00	7.27%
Taxes		8,001.60	
After-tax profit		$ 12,002.40	4.36%
Total average number of covers/night	611	Average number of covers/items sold	87

Goal Value Analysis Data

Item	Food Cost %	Number Sold	Selling Price	Variable Cost %
Fajita Plate	38%	86	$18.13	28%
Grande Dinner	35%	116	$17.41	28%
Menudo	25%	48	$12.16	28%
Mexican Salad	24%	75	$13.91	28%
Burrito Dinner	28%	73	$15.66	28%
Chimichanga Dinner	33%	97	$17.41	28%
Enchilada Dinner	26%	131	$10.41	28%
Overall Menu (Goal Value)	32%	87	$15.00	28%

Goal Value Analysis Results

Item	Food Cost %	Number Sold	Selling Price	Variable Cost %	Goal Value
Grande Dinner	35%	116	$17.41	28%	485.7
Enchilada Dinner	26%	131	$10.41	28%	464.2
Chimichanga Dinner	33%	97	$17.41	28%	441.3
Mexican Salad	24%	75	$13.91	28%	380.6
Burrito Dinner	28%	73	$15.66	28%	362.2
Overall Menu (Goal Value)	*32%*	*87*	*$15.00*	*28%*	*355.0*
Fajita Plate	38%	86	$18.13	28%	328.7
Menudo	25%	48	$12.16	28%	205.7

MINIMUM SALES POINT

Every foodservice operator should know his or her break-even point. The concept of minimum sales point is related to the break-even concept. **Minimum sales point (MSP)** is the sales volume required to justify keeping an operation open during a given period of time. At sales levels below the MSP, the operation is not profitable. At sales levels above the MSP, enough revenue is being taken in to make a contribution to profits. The information needed to calculate the MSP is:

1. Food cost percentage
2. Minimum payroll cost needed for the time period
3. Variable cost percentage

Fixed costs are eliminated from the calculation because, even if the volume of sales in an extended opening period equals zero, fixed costs still exist and must be paid. To illustrate, consider the situation of Richard, who is trying to determine whether he should close his steakhouse at 10:00 P.M. or 11:00 P.M.

Richard wishes to compute the sales volume necessary to justify staying open the additional hour. He can make this calculation because he knows that his food cost equals 40 percent, his minimum labor cost to stay open for the extra hour equals $150, and his variable costs (taken from his P&L statement) equal 30 percent. In calculating MSP, Food cost % + Variable cost % is the **minimum operating cost**. Richard applies the MSP formula as follows:

$$\frac{\text{Minimum labor cost}}{1 - \text{Minimum operating cost}} = \text{MSP}$$

or

$$\frac{\text{Minimum labor cost}}{1 - (\text{Food cost \%} + \text{Variable cost \%})} = \text{MSP}$$

In this case, the computation would be as follows:

$$\frac{\$150}{1 - (0.40 + 0.30)} = \text{MSP}$$

or

$$\frac{\$150}{1 - (0.70)} = \text{MSP}$$

or

$$\frac{\$150}{0.30} = \$500 \text{ MSP}$$

If Richard can achieve a sales volume of $500 in the 10:00 to 11:00 P.M. time period, he should stay open. If this level of sales is not possible, he should close the operation at 10:00 P.M. Richard can also use MSP to determine the hours his operation are most profitable. Of course, some managers may not have the authority to close their operations, even when remaining open is not very profitable. Corporate policy, contractual hours, promotion of a new unit, competition, and other factors must all be taken into account before the decision should be made to modify operational hours.

THE BUDGET

In most managerial settings, you will be responsible for preparing and maintaining a budget (see Chapter 1) for your foodservice operation. This budget, or financial plan, will detail the operational direction of your unit and your expected financial results. The techniques used in managerial accounting will show you how close your actual performance conformed to your budget, and will provide you with the information you need to make any needed changes to your operational procedures or budget process. This will help ensure that your operation achieves the goals of your financial plan.

It is important to note that the budget should not be a static (unchanging) document. Rather, it should be modified and fine-tuned as managerial accounting presents data about sales and costs that affect the direction of the overall operation. For example, if you own a dance club featuring Latin music, and you find that a major competitor in your city has closed its doors, you may quite logically determine that you want to increase your estimate of the number of guests who will come to your club. This would, of course, affect your projected sales revenue, your costs, and, in most cases, your profitability. Not to do so might allow you to meet and even exceed your original sales and profit goals but would ignore a significant event that very likely will affect your financial plan for the club.

In a similar manner, if you are the manager of a New York–style delicatessen specializing in salads, sliced meats, and related items, and you find through your purchase orders that the price you pay per pound for the high-quality beef briskets used to make your corned beef has doubled since last month, you must adjust your budget or you will find that you have no chance of staying within your food cost guidelines. Again, the point is that budgets should be closely monitored through the use of managerial accounting, which includes the thoughtful analysis of operating data.

Just as the P&L tells you about your past performance, the budget is developed to help you predict and achieve your future goals. In effect, the budget tells you what must be done if predetermined cost and profit objectives are to be met. In this respect, you are attempting to modify the profit formula, as presented in Chapter 1. With a well-thought-out and attainable budget, your profit formula would change from:

Revenue − Expenses = Profit

to

Budgeted revenue − Budgeted expenses = Budgeted profit

FIGURE 10.12 Advantages of Budgeting

1. It is the best means of analyzing alternative courses of action and allows management to examine alternatives prior to adopting a particular one.
2. It forces management to examine the facts regarding what must be done to achieve desired profit levels.
3. It provides a standard for comparison, which is essential for good controls.
4. It allows management to anticipate and prepare for future business conditions.
5. It helps management to periodically carry out a self-evaluation of the organization and its progress toward its financial objectives.
6. It provides a communication channel whereby the organization's objectives are passed along to its various departments.
7. It encourages department managers who have participated in the preparation of the budget to establish their own operating objectives and evaluation techniques and tools.
8. It provides management with reasonable estimates of future expense levels and serves as an instrument for setting proper menu prices.
9. It identifies time periods in which operational cash flows may need to be supplemented from other sources.
10. It communicates realistic financial performance to owners, investors, and the operation's managers.

To prepare a budget and stay within it helps ensure attainable results. Without such a plan, you must guess how much to spend and how much sales you should anticipate. The effective foodservice operator builds his or her budget, monitors it closely, modifies it when necessary, and achieves desired results. Yet, many operators do not develop a budget. Some say that the process is too time consuming. Others feel that a budget, especially one shared with the entire organization, is too revealing. Budgeting can also cause conflicts. This is true, for example, when dollars budgeted for new equipment must be used for either a new kitchen stove or a new beer-tapping system. Obviously, in this example, the kitchen manager and the beverage manager may hold different points of view on where these funds would best be spent!

Despite the fact that some operators avoid budgets, they are extremely important. The advantages for having and using a budget are summarized in Figure 10.12.

Budgeting is best done by the entire management team, for it is only through participation in the process that the whole organization will feel compelled to support the budget.

Foodservice budgets can be considered as one of three main types:

1. Long-range budget
2. Annual budget
3. Achievement budget

LONG-RANGE BUDGET

The **long-range budget** is typically prepared for a period of three to five years into the future. Although it is not highly detailed it does provide a long-term view about where the operation should be going. It is particularly useful in those cases where additional operational units may increase sales volume and accompanying expense.

To illustrate, assume that you are preparing a budget for a corporation you own. Your corporation has entered into an agreement with an international franchise company to open 45 sub shops in malls across the United States and Canada. You will open a new store approximately every month for the next four years. To properly plan for your revenue and expense in the coming four-year period, a long-range budget for your company will be necessary.

ANNUAL BUDGET

The annual, or yearly, budget is the type most operators think of when the term *budget* is used. As it states, the **annual budget** is for a one-year period or, in some cases, one season. This would be true, for example, in the case of a children's summer camp that is open and serving meals only while school is out of session and campers are attending; or in the case of a ski resort that opens in late fall/early winter but closes in the spring when the snow melts.

It is important to remember that an annual budget need not follow a calendar year. In fact, the best time period for an annual budget is the one that makes sense for the operation. A college foodservice director in the United States, for example, would want a budget that covers the time period of a school year, that is, from the fall of one year through the spring of the next. For a restaurant whose owners have a fiscal year that is different from a calendar year, the annual budget may coincide with either the fiscal year or the calendar, as the owners prefer.

It is also important to remember that an annual budget need not consist of 12 one-month periods. Although many operators prefer one-month budgets, some prefer budgets consisting of 13 separate 28-day periods. Other mangers may prefer to use quarterly (three-month) or even weekly budgets to plan for revenues and costs throughout the budget year.

ACHIEVEMENT BUDGET

The **achievement budget** is always of a shorter range, perhaps a month or a week. It provides current operating information and, thus, assists in making current operational decisions. A weekly achievement budget might, for example, be used to predict the number of gallons of milk needed for this time period or the number of servers to be scheduled on Tuesday night.

DEVELOPING THE BUDGET

Some managers think it is very difficult to establish a budget, and so they simply do not do it. Creating a budget is not that complex. You can learn to do it and do it well. To establish any type of budget, you need to have the following information:

1. Prior-period operating results (if available)
2. Assumptions of next-period operations
3. Goals
4. Monitoring policies

To examine how prior-period operating results, assumptions of next-period operations, and goals drive the budgeting process, we will consider the case of Levi, who is preparing the annual foodservice budget for his 100-bed health-care facility. This section addresses prior-period operating results, assumptions, and goals, and the final section looks more closely at monitoring the budget.

PRIOR-PERIOD OPERATING RESULTS

Levi's facility serves patient meals to an average of 80 patients per day and he serves approximately 300 additional meals per day to staff and visitors. His department is allotted a fixed dollar amount by the facility's administration for each meal he serves.

His operating results for last year are detailed in Figure 10.13. Patient and additional meals served were determined by actual count. Revenue and expense

FIGURE 10.13 Levi's Last-Year Operating Results

Patient Meals Served: 29,200   Revenue per Meal: $3.46

Additional Meals Served: 109,528

Total Meals Served: 138,728

	Amount	Percentage
Total Department Revenue	$480,000	100%
Cost of Food	192,000	40%
Cost of Labor	153,600	32%
Other Expenses	86,400	18%
Total Expense	$432,000	90%
Profit	$ 48,000	10%

figures were taken from Levi's income (P&L) statements at the year's end. It is important to note that Levi must have this information if he is to do any meaningful profit planning. Foodservice unit managers who do not have access to their past operating results are at a tremendous managerial disadvantage. Levi has his operational summaries and the data that produced them. Because he knows how he has operated in the past, he is now ready to proceed to the assumptions section of the planning process.

ASSUMPTIONS OF NEXT-PERIOD OPERATIONS

If Levi is to prepare a budget with enough value to serve as a useful guide and enough flexibility to adapt to a changing environment, he must factor in the assumptions he and others feel will affect his operation in the coming year.

Although each management team will arrive at its own conclusions given the circumstances of its own operation, in this example, Levi makes the following assumptions regarding next year:

1. Food costs will increase by 3 percent.
2. Labor costs will increase by 5 percent.
3. Other expenses will rise by 10 percent due to a significant increase in utility costs.
4. Revenue received for all meals served will be increased by no more than 1 percent.
5. Resident occupancy averaging 80 percent of his facility's capacity will remain unchanged.

Levi makes these assumptions after discussions with his facility administrators, suppliers and labor union leaders, after review of his own records, and, most importantly, by his knowledge of the operation itself.

In the commercial sector, when arriving at realistic future performance assumptions, operators must also consider new or reduced levels of competition, changes in traffic patterns, variations in product costs, and national food trends. At the highest level of foodservice management, assumptions regarding the acquisition of new units or the introduction of new products directly affect the budgeting process.

As an operator, Levi predicts items 1, 2, and 3 by himself, whereas his own supervisor has given him input about items 4 and 5. Given these assumptions, Levi can establish realistic operating goals for next year.

Green and Growing!

Budgeting for utility costs is one of a foodservice operator's biggest challenges. This is due to both the instability of energy prices and the impact of the weather on usage. Both of these factors should lead cost-conscious and planet-conscious managers to consider all possible strategies for reducing energy usage. For many operators, these strategies should include:

1. Investigating the installation of smart lighting systems that automatically turn off lights when storage areas are vacant.

2. Replacing all incandescent lighting with an appropriate type of electric discharge lamp (such as fluorescent, mercury vapor, metal halide, or sodium) wherever possible.

3. Using dual-flush, low-flow, or waterless toilets to reduce water waste.

4. Installing low-flow faucet aerators on all sinks to cut water usage by as much as 40%—from a standard 4 gallons per minute to a cost-saving 2.5 gallons a minute.

5. Implementing an effective preventive maintenance program for all cooking equipment, including frequent and accurate temperature recalibrations.

6. Reducing waste disposal costs by implementing effective source reduction plans as well as pre- and post-production recycling efforts.

The benefits to implementing strategies such the preceding are twofold. They will improve an operation's bottom line and reduce its carbon footprint. Those results are good news for a business's P&L, and they directly benefit the business's current, as well as its future, customers.

ESTABLISHING OPERATING GOALS

Given the assumptions he has made, Levi considers his operating goals for the coming year. He will develop these goals (targets) for each of the following areas:

1. Meals served
2. Revenue
3. Food costs
4. Labor costs
5. Other expenses
6. Profit

MEALS SERVED

Given the assumption of no increase in patient occupancy, and in light of his results from last year, Levi budgets to prepare and serve 29,200 patient meals (80 meals per day × 365 days = 29,200 meals). He feels, however, that he can increase his visitor and staff meals somewhat by being more customer-service driven and by offering a wider selection of lower calorie and lighter items on the facility's cycle menu. He decides, therefore, to raise his goal for additional meals from the 109,528 served last year to 115,000 for the coming year. Thus, his budgeted total meals to be served will equal 144,200 meals (29,200 patient meals + 115,000 visitor and staff meals = 144,200 total meals).

REVENUE

Levi knows that his total revenue is to increase by only 1 percent. His revenue per meal will thus be $3.46 × 1.01 = $3.49. With 144,200 meals estimated to be served, Levi will receive $503,258 (144,200 × $3.49 = $503,258) if he meets his meals-served budget.

HERE'S HOW IT'S DONE *10.2*

When preparing budget forecasts, a manager often must project either an increase or a decrease in a known sales or expense amount. For example, assume a manager spent $80,000 for utilities last year. The manager is preparing next year's budget and believes that next year utility costs will *increase* by 5 percent. This manager can forecast next year's utility cost in two different ways that will yield the same result.

The first way requires the manager to multiply last year's utility costs times the 5 percent projected increase and then *add* the resulting number to last year's utility costs. It is a two-step process:

Step 1: Calculate the amount of the projected increase:

$$\$80,000 \times .05 = \$4,000$$

Step 2: Add the amount of the projected increase to last year's cost to arrive at next year's estimated cost:

$$\$80,000 + \$4,000 = \$84,000$$

The second way to arrive at the same number is faster because it requires only one step. That is so because the manager in this example is actually projecting next year's utility cost to be 105 percent (100% + 5% = 105%) of this year's cost. When using this approach the one-step calculation is:

Step 1:

$$\$80,000 \times 1.05 = \$84,000$$

What if the manager assumes an amount of sales or expense will decrease? When projecting a sales or expense *decrease*, the same math principles apply. To illustrate, assume the manager will implement cost savings approaches projected to *reduce* total utility costs by 5 percent. Using the two-step approach, the calculation is:

Step 1: Calculate the amount of projected decrease:

$$\$80,000 \times .05 = \$4,000$$

Step 2: Subtract the amount of the projected decrease from last year's cost to arrive at next year's estimated cost:

$$\$80,000 - \$4,000 = \$76,000$$

The faster way to arrive at the same projected decreased amount requires only one step. That is possible because the manager is actually projecting next year's utility cost to be 95 percent of this year's cost (100% − 5% = 95%).

1. When using this approach, the one-step calculation is:

Step 1:

$$\$80,000 \times .95 = \$76,000$$

Both the two steps and the one step approach yield the same answer.

Choose the method you like best!

FOOD COSTS

Levi is planning to serve more meals, so naturally he expects to spend more on food. In addition, he assumes that this food will cost, on average, 3 percent more than it did last year. To determine a food budget, Levi computes the estimated food cost for 144,200 meals as follows:

1. Last year's food cost per meal = Last year's cost of food/Total meals served = $192,000/138,728 = $1.38 per meal

2. Last year's food cost per meal + 3% Estimated increase in food cost = $1.38 × 1.03 = $1.42 per meal

3. $1.42 × 144,200 Meals to be served this year = $204,764 estimated cost of food this year

LABOR COSTS

Levi is planning to serve more meals, so he also expects to spend more on the labor needed to prepare and serve the extra meals. In addition, he assumes that this labor will cost, overall, 5% more than last year. To determine a labor budget, Levi computes the estimated labor cost for 144,200 meals to be served as follows:

1. Last year's labor cost per meal = Last year's cost of labor/Total meals served = $153,600/138,728 = $1.11 per meal
2. Last year's labor cost per meal + 5% Estimated increase in labor cost = $1.11 × 1.05 = $1.17 per meal
3. $1.17 × 144,200 Meals to be served this year = $168,714 Estimated cost of labor this year

OTHER EXPENSES

Levi assumes a 10 percent increase in other expenses, and, thus, they are budgeted as last year's amount plus an increase of 10 percent. Thus, $86,400 × 1.10 = $95,040.

Based on his assumptions about next year, Figure 10.14 details Levi's budget summary for next year.

Cost Control Around the World

To illustrate one of the many ways in which the global economy affects financial reporting in the foodservice industry, consider the challenges and opportunities facing Inez Magana. Inez is the Southern Region Director of Operations for El Pollo Salsa, a restaurant chain with units in the United States, Caribbean, Mexico, Brazil, and other South American countries. She oversees 150 company-owned stores. One of Inez's most important tasks is to accurately prepare income and expense forecasts and annual budgets for her restaurants.

It is a fundamental principle of accounting that the financial performance of a business should be reported in an identifiable **monetary unit**. A monetary unit is simply defined as a specific and recognized currency denomination. Typically, financial statements are prepared in the currency of the country in which the business is based. Thus, in Inez's case, the US dollar is the monetary unit used for preparing many, but not all, of her financial forecasts.

At first, it might appear easy to ensure that financial summaries are prepared in the currency denomination used by the company whose records are being reported. But, in reality, fulfilling the monetary unit reporting principle can be quite complex. Consider that Inez operates restaurants internationally and her restaurants' sales and expenses are reported as follows:

- Sales and expense in her American restaurants are reported in US dollars.
- Sales and expense in her Mexican restaurants are reported in Mexican pesos.
- Sales and expense in her Brazilian restaurants are reported in Brazilian reals.
- Sales and expense in her Dominican Republic restaurants are reported in Dominican Republic pesos.
- Sales and expense in her Bolivian restaurants are reported in Bolivian bolivianos.
- Sales and expense in her Aruban restaurants are reported in Aruban florins.

The ability to move easily back and forth among international currencies when reporting financial results for restaurants operating in various countries is just one of the many skills international managers must master to do their jobs well.

FUN ON THE WEB!

Managers who must prepare budgets using monetary units other than US dollars can take advantage of many free-to-use currency calculators. These calculators allow managers to enter amounts in any international currency and have those amounts automatically converted to their US dollar equivalent. Alternatively, they can use the calculators to enter a US dollar amount and have that amount converted to a chosen international currency.

To review one or more of these helpful tools, enter "Currency converter" in your favorite search engine, then choose a site offering a free converter and try it yourself!

FIGURE 10.14 Levi's Budget for Next Year

Patient Meals Budgeted: 29,200   Budgeted Revenue per Meal: $3.49

Visitor and Staff Meals Budgeted: 115,000

Total Meals Budgeted: 144,200

	Amount	Percentage
Total Budgeted Revenue	$503,258	100.0%
Budgeted Expenses		
Cost of Food	$204,764	40.7%
Cost of Labor	168,714	33.5%
Other Expenses	95,040	18.9%
Total Expense	$468,518	$93.1%
Profit	$ 34,740	6.9%

PROFIT

Note that the increased costs Levi will be forced to bear, when coupled with his minimal revenue increase, will cause his profit to fall from $48,000 for last year to a projected $34,740 for the coming year. If this is not acceptable, Levi must either increase his revenue beyond his original assumption or look to his operation for ways to reduce costs.

Levi has now developed concrete guidelines for his operation. Since his supervisor approves his budget as submitted, Levi is now ready to implement and then monitor his new budget.

MONITORING THE BUDGET

An operational plan has little value if management does not use it. In general, the budget should be regularly monitored and analyzed in each of the following three areas:

1. Revenue
2. Expenses
3. Profit

REVENUE ANALYSIS

If revenue falls below projected levels, the impact on profits can be substantial. Simply put, if revenues fall far short of projections, it may be difficult or even impossible for you to meet your profit goals. If revenue consistently exceeds your projections, the overall budget must be modified or the expenses required to produce the increased sales will soon exceed the originally predicted amounts. Effective managers compare their actual revenue to budgeted revenue on a regular basis.

Increases in operational revenue should result in proportional total dollar increases in variable expense budgets. Fixed expenses, because they do not vary with volume, need not be adjusted for increases (or decreases) in revenue. For those foodservice operations with more than one meal period, monitoring budgeted sales volume may mean monitoring each meal period.

Consider the case of Rosa, the night (P.M.) manager of a college cafeteria. She feels that she is busier than ever, but her boss, Lois, maintains that there can be no increase in Rosa's labor budget because the overall cafeteria sales volume is exactly in line with budgeted projections.

FIGURE 10.15 College Cafeteria Annual Revenue Budget Summary

			Time Period: <u>First 6 Months</u>
Meal Period	**Annual Budget**	**Actual To Date**	**% of Budget**
A.M.	$480,500	$166,698	35%
P.M.	350,250	248,677	71%
Total	$830,750	$415,375	50%

Figure 10.15 shows the complete story of the sales volume generation at the college cafeteria after the first six months of their fiscal year. Note that the year is half (50 percent) completed at the time of this analysis.

Based on the sales volume she generates, Rosa should indeed have an increase in her labor budget for the P.M. meal period. The amount of business she is generating in the evenings is substantially higher than budgeted. Note that she is halfway through her budget year, but has already generated 71 percent of the annual revenue forecasted by the budget. This, however, does not mean that the labor budget for the entire cafeteria should be increased. In fact, the labor budget for the A.M. shift should likely be reduced because those dollars would be better used for labor needed to serve meals in the evening meal period.

Some foodservice operators relate revenue to the number of seats they have available in their operation. As a result, they sometimes budget based on **sales per seat**, the total revenue generated by a facility divided by the number of available seats in the dining area(s). The size of a foodservice facility affects both total investment and operating costs, therefore this can be a useful number. The formula for the computation of sales per seat is:

$$\frac{\text{Total sales}}{\text{Available seats}} = \text{Sales per seat}$$

To illustrate this, assume that, if Rosa's cafeteria has 120 seats, her P.M. sales per seat thus far this year would be as follows:

$$\frac{\$248,677}{120} = \$2,072.31$$

The A.M. sales per seat, given the same number of seats, would be computed as follows:

$$\frac{\$166,698}{120} = \$1,389.15$$

As you can see, Rosa's sales per seat at night are much higher than that of her A.M. counterpart. Of course, part of that may be due to the fact that evening menu items in the cafeteria may sell for more, on average, than do breakfast and lunch items.

Some commercial foodservice operators relate revenue to the number of square feet their operations occupy. These operators budget revenues based on a **sales per square foot** basis. This is a very common approach in shopping centers and malls where occupation costs are determined in large degree by the number of square feet a foodservice operation leases from the space's owner.

The computation of sales per square foot is quite similar to that used in Rosa's sales per seat calculation. The formula for sales per square foot is:

$$\frac{\text{Total sales}}{\text{Total square footage}} = \text{Sales per square foot}$$

Regardless of how it is measured, when sales volume is lower than originally projected, management must seek ways to increase revenue or to reduce costs. As stated earlier, one of management's main tasks is to generate guests, whereas the staff's main task is to service these guests to the best of their ability.

There are a variety of marketing methods used for increasing sales volume, including increased advertising, price discounting, the use of coupons, and the offering of specials. For the serious foodservice manager, a thorough study of the modern techniques of foodservice marketing is mandatory if you are to be ready to meet all the challenges you will face.

EXPENSE ANALYSIS

Effective foodservice managers are careful to monitor operational expense because costs that are too high or too low may be cause for concern. Just as it is not possible to estimate future sales volume perfectly, it is also not possible to estimate future expense perfectly because, as you have learned, some expenses will vary as sales volume increases or decreases.

To know that an operation spent $800 for fruits and vegetables in a given week becomes meaningful only if we know what the sales volume for that week was. Similarly, knowing that $500 was spent for labor during a given lunch period can be analyzed only in terms of the amount of sales achieved in that same period.

To help them make expense assessments quickly, some operators elect to utilize the **yardstick method** of calculating expense standards so determinations can be made as to whether variations in expenses are due to changes in sales volume or other reasons, such as waste or theft.

To illustrate the yardstick method, consider the case of Marion, who operates a college cafeteria during nine months of the year in a small southeastern city. Marion has developed both revenue and expense budgets. His problem, however, is that variations in revenue cause variations in expense. This is true in terms of food products, labor, and other expenses. As a truly effective manager, he wishes to know whether changes in his actual expenses are due directly to these variations in revenues or are due to inefficiencies in his operation.

DEVELOPING YARDSTICK STANDARDS FOR FOOD COSTS

To begin his analysis, Marion establishes a purchase standard for food products using a seven-step model.

Step 1. Divide total inventory into management-designated subgroups (categories); for example, meats, produce, dairy, and groceries.

Step 2. Establish dollar value for subgroup purchases during the prior accounting period.

Step 3. Establish sales volume for the prior accounting period.

Step 4. Determine percentage of purchasing dollar spent for each food category.

Step 5. Determine percentage of revenue dollar spent for each food category.

Step 6. Develop weekly sales volume and associated expense projection. Compute percentage cost to sales for each food category and sales estimate.

Step 7. Compare weekly revenue and expense to projection. Take corrective action if necessary.

FIGURE 10.16 Marion's College Cafeteria Food Data

		Last School Year (9 Months)
Total Sales: $450,000		Average Sales per Month: $50,000
Purchases		
Meats	$ 66,600	
Fish/Poultry	36,500	
Produce	26,500	
Dairy	20,000	
Groceries	18,300	
Total	$167,900	

To develop his yardstick standards for food, Marion collects data from last year as shown in Figure 10.16.

Assuming that Marion has created a revenue estimate of $52,000 per month for this year and that he was satisfied with both last year's food cost percentage and profits, he can now follow the steps outlined previously to establish his yardstick standards for food. Marion estimates a weekly sales volume of $52,000/4, or $13,000, for this year.

Marion's Yardstick Standards for Food

Step 1. Meats
Fish/Poultry
Produce
Dairy
Groceries

Step 2.
Meats	$ 66,600
Fish/Poultry	36,500
Produce	26,500
Dairy	20,000
Groceries	18,300
Total	$167,900

Step 3. $450,000 total revenue in prior period (9 months)

Step 4.
Meats	$ 66,600 ÷ $167,900 =	39.7%
Fish/Poultry	$ 36,500 ÷ $167,900 =	21.7%
Produce	$ 26,500 ÷ $167,900 =	15.8%
Dairy	$ 20,000 ÷ $167,900 =	11.9%
Groceries	$ 18,300 ÷ $167,900 =	10.9%
Total	$167,900	100.0%

Step 5.
Meats	$ 66,600 ÷ $450,000 =	14.8%
Fish/Poultry	36,500 ÷ $450,000 =	8.1%
Produce	26,500 ÷ $450,000 =	5.9%
Dairy	20,000 ÷ $450,000 =	4.4%
Groceries	18,300 ÷ $450,000 =	4.1%
Total	$167,900	37.3%

Step 6.

Category	% Cost to Total Cost	% Cost to Total Sales	Weekly Sales Estimate				
			$11,000	$12,000	$13,000	$14,000	$15,000
Meat	39.7%	14.8%	$ 1,628	$ 1,776	$ 1,924	$ 2,072	$ 2,220
Fish/Poultry	21.7%	8.1%	891	972	1,053	1,134	1,215
Produce	15.8%	5.9%	649	708	767	826	885
Dairy	11.9%	4.4%	484	528	572	616	660
Groceries	10.9%	4.1%	451	492	533	574	615
Total	100.0%	37.3%	$ 4,103	$ 4,476	$ 4,849	$ 5,222	$ 5,595

Note that, to compute the data for Step 6, you must multiply % cost to total sales by the weekly sales estimate. For example, when using the sales estimate of $13,000 for a week, the meat budget would be computed as:

$$0.148 \times \$13,000 = \$1,924$$

Similarly, the cost estimate for fish/poultry would be computed as follows:

$$0.081 \times \$13,000 = \$1,053$$

Step 7. Analysis

Marion can now compare his budgeted expense with actual performance over several volume levels. In a week in which sales volume equals $14,000, for example, Marion expects that total meat used for that period, according to his yardstick measure, will equal approximately $2,072 ($14,000 × 14.8% = $2,072).

If his meat usage exceeds $2,072 for the period, he knows exactly where to direct his attention. Using the yardstick system, Marion can easily monitor any expense over any number of differing volume levels. The yardstick method of purchase estimation is especially helpful for those operations that experience great variation in sales volume. An operation that has a slow season and a busy season, for instance, may find that the use of this method is quite helpful in monitoring expenses.

DEVELOPING YARDSTICK STANDARDS FOR LABOR COSTS

Just as Marion used the yardstick method to estimate food expense at varying sales volume levels, he can also use it to estimate labor cost expenditures at those various levels. To develop a labor yardstick, he follows these steps:

Step 1. Divide total labor cost into management-designated subgroups—for example, servers, cooks, ware washers, and bartenders.

Step 2. Establish dollar value spent for each subgroup during the prior accounting period.

Step 3. Establish sales volume for the prior accounting period.

Step 4. Determine percentage of labor dollar spent for each subgroup.

Step 5. Determine percentage of revenue dollar spent for each labor category.

Step 6. Develop weekly sales volume and associated expense projection. Compute % cost to sales for each labor category and sales estimate.

Step 7. Compare weekly revenue and expense to projection. Correct if necessary.

Marion collected labor-related data from last year's reporting period as shown in Figure 10.17.

FIGURE 10.17 Marion's College Cafeteria Labor Data

		Last School Year (9 Months)
Total Sales: $450,000		Average Sales per Month: $50,000
Labor Costs		
Management	$ 40,000	
Food Production	65,000	
Service	12,000	
Sanitation	18,000	
Total	$135,000	

It is important to note that Marion can develop a labor yardstick based on various measures of labor productivity including guests served, labor hours worked, or, as is his preference here, labor cost percentage.

To develop the labor standard based on labor cost percentage, Marion follows the seven-step process outlined below.

Marion's Yardstick Standards for Labor

Step 1. Management
        Food Production
        Service
        Sanitation

Step 2. Management $ 40,000
        Food Production   65,000
        Service   12,000
        Sanitation   18,000
        Total $135,000

Step 3. $450,000 total revenue in prior period (9 months)

Step 4. Management $ 40,000 ÷ $135,000 =   29.6%
        Food Production   65,000 ÷ $135,000 =   48.2%
        Service   12,000 ÷ $135,000 =   8.9%
        Sanitation   18,000 ÷ $135,000 =   13.3%
        Total $135,000   100.0%

Step 5. Management $ 40,000 ÷ $450,000 =   8.9%
        Food Production   65,000 ÷ $450,000 =   14.4%
        Service   12,000 ÷ $450,000 =   2.7%
        Sanitation   18,000 ÷ $450,000 =   4.0%
        Total $135,000   30.0%

Step 6.

Category	% Cost to Total Cost	% Cost to Total Sales	Weekly Sales Estimate				
			$11,000	$12,000	$13,000	$14,000	$15,000
Management	29.6%	8.9%	$ 979	$ 1,068	$ 1,157	$ 1,246	$ 1,335
Food Production	48.2%	14.4%	1,584	1,728	1,872	2,016	2,160
Service	8.9%	2.7%	297	324	351	378	405
Sanitation	13.3%	4.0%	440	480	520	560	600
Total	100.0%	30.0%	$ 3,300	$ 3,600	$ 3,900	$ 4,200	$ 4,500

Note that, to compute the data for Step 6, Marion must multiply % cost to total sales by his weekly sales estimate. For example, using the sales estimate of $13,000, the management portion of the budget would be computed as follows:

$$\$13{,}000 \times 0.089 = \$1{,}157$$

The food production cost expense estimate, based on the same weekly sales, would be computed as:

$$\$13{,}000 \times 0.144 = \$1{,}872$$

Step 7.   Analysis

It is now easy for Marion to identify exactly where his labor variations, if any, are to be found.

The yardstick method may, of course, be used for any operational expense, be it food, labor, or one of the many other expenses you will incur. Today, the use of spreadsheet formulas allows those operators who are skilled at using them to easily calculate their estimated expenses at any level of actual revenue. In all cases, however, you must monitor your actual expenditures as they relate to budgeted expenditures, while keeping changes in sales volume in mind.

Consider the Cost

Sophia Lancaster is the registered dietitian (RD) responsible for all dietary services at Parker Meridian Memorial Hospital. Her operation consists of two departments. The first, and largest, is patient feeding. It consists of the tray line staff and the majority of her food production staff.

The second department is the public cafeteria, which includes special dining areas for hospital staff and a large dining area for visitors. Each year, she submits to her supervisor an annual labor expense budget broken down by month for each of her two departments.

On June 1, and after four months of consideration and planning, Sophia and her staff were excited to implement a new public cafeteria menu. The response from hospital visitors was excellent. The dining room staff reported that there were many positive comments about the foods selected for the new menu, and the production staff reported a 25 percent increase in the amount of food prepared for cafeteria service. Sophia had only budgeted for a 5 percent sales increase because of the new menu, so she was very happy.

On July 7, when Sophia's assistant, Jason, brought her the financial reports for the month of June, he was concerned. "I think we are in big trouble, Boss," he said. "We spent a lot more on cafeteria labor last month than we budgeted!"

1. What do you think is the cause of Sophia's labor budget overage in the cafeteria?

2. Do you think that going "over" budget in this situation is a good thing or a bad thing? Why?

3. If you were Sophia, would you reexamine your cafeteria labor budget for future operating periods? Why or why not?

PROFIT ANALYSIS

As business conditions change, changes in the budget are to be expected. This is because budgets are based on a specific set of assumptions and if these assumptions change, so too will the budgets. Assume, for example, that you budgeted $1,000 in January for snow removal from the parking lot attached to the restaurant you own in New York state. If unusually severe weather causes you to spend $2,000 for snow removal in January instead, the assumption (normal levels of snowfall) was incorrect and the budget will be incorrect as well.

Ultimately, budgeted profit levels must be realized if an operation is to provide adequate returns for owner and investor risk. Consider the case of James, the operator of a foodservice establishment with excellent sales but below-budgeted profits.

James budgeted a 5 percent profit on $2,000,000 of sales; and thus, $100,000 profit ($2,000,000 sales × 0.05 profit = $100,000) was planned.

At year's end, however, James achieved $2,000,000 in sales but only $50,000 profit; or 2.5 percent of sales ($50,000 ÷ $2,000,000 = 2.5%). If the operation's owners feel that $50,000 is an adequate return for their risk, James's professional services may be retained. If they do not, he could lose his job, even though the operation is profitable.

Remember that your goal is not merely to generate a profit, but rather, to generate budgeted profit. In most cases, you will be rewarded only when you meet this goal because a primary purpose of management is to generate the profits needed to continue the business. Budgeting for these profits is a fundamental step in the process.

Analyzing the success of achieving budget forecasts is of tremendous managerial concern. If profit goals are to be met, safeguarding incoming money, the operational revenue you generate, is very critical. It is to that task that we turn our attention in the next chapter, because the proper collection of money and accounting for guest payment of services is one of the final steps in a successful food and beverage cost control system.

Technology Tools

This chapter introduced the concepts of conducting individual menu item analysis and identifying a break-even point for your operation. When this break-even point is known, an effective operational budget can be produced. The chapter concluded with a discussion of the importance of developing and monitoring a budget. Although menu analysis software is often packaged as part of a larger program and is somewhat limited, software designed for overall break-even analysis and budgeting is readily available. Software in this area is available to help you:

1. Evaluate item profitability based on:
   a. Food cost percentage
   b. Popularity
   c. Contribution margin
   d. Selling price
2. Conduct menu matrix analysis.
3. Perform break-even analysis.
4. Budget revenue and expense levels.
5. Budget profit levels.
6. Assemble and produce budgets based on days, weeks, months, years, or other identifiable accounting periods.
7. Conduct performance to budget analysis.
8. Maintain performance to budget histories.
9. Blend budgets from multiple profit centers (or multiple units).
10. Perform budgeted cash flow analysis.

For commercial operators, it is simply not wise to attempt to operate an effective foodservice unit without a properly priced menu and an accurate budget that reflects accurate sales and expense estimates.

Apply What You Have Learned

*A*nanda Fields is the CEO of a company that operates a very large number of quick-service restaurants. Recently, competitors have been increasing sales at their restaurants at a faster rate than Ananda's. Joseph Smiley, vice president of operations, is encouraging Ananda to introduce a new line of higher-priced, higher-quality, and higher-contribution-margin items to increase sales and improve profits.

Sonya Miller, her vice president for marketing, is recommending that Ananda introduce a "value" line of products that would be priced very low but that could also have the effect of significantly increasing traffic to the stores.

1. Do you think more customers would be attracted using Joseph's recommendation or Sonya's?

2. What factors would cause Ananda to choose one menu recommendation over the other?

3. What impact will Ananda's menu decision have on the image projected by her stores? What can she do to influence this image?

Key Terms and Concepts

The following are terms and concepts discussed in the chapter that are important for you as a manager. To help you review, please define the terms below.

matrix analysis
quick-service
   restaurant (QSR)
menu engineering
goal value
   analysis
loss leaders
break-even point

cost/volume/profit
   (CVP) analysis
contribution margin
   income statement
contribution margin for
   overall operation
minimum sales point
   (MSP)

minimum operating cost
long-range budget
annual budget
achievement budget
monetary unit
sales per seat
sales per square foot
yardstick method

Test Your Skills

You may download the Excel spreadsheets for the Test Your Skills exercises from the student companion website at www.wiley.com/college/dopson. Complete the exercises by placing your answers in the shaded boxes and answering the questions as indicated.

1. Boniso operates Boniso's Mexican Restaurant in an urban city in the South. He has worked hard at setting up cost control systems, and he is generally happy with his overall results. However, he is not sure if all of his menu items are providing profitability for his restaurant. He decides to use food cost matrix and contribution margin matrix analyses to study each of his menu items.

   a. Complete his menu analysis worksheet.

Menu Analysis Worksheet								
Menu Item	Number Sold	Selling Price	Total Sales	Item Cost	Total Cost	Item Contribution Margin	Total Contribution Margin	Food Cost %
Fajita Plate	147	$12.95		$4.92				
Enchilada Dinner	200	$ 9.95		$3.48				
Menudo	82	$ 6.95		$1.74				
Mexican Salad	117	$ 7.95		$2.39				
Chalupa Dinner	125	$ 8.95		$2.51				
Burrito Dinner	168	$ 9.95		$3.25				
Taco Dinner	225	$ 5.95		$1.55				
Total								
Weighted Average								

b. Using the results of Boniso's menu analysis worksheet (in part a), fill in the appropriate average food cost, popularity, and contribution margin in the blanks below. Then, place the menu items in the appropriate squares in the matrices.

Food Cost Matrix

High Food Cost % (Above _____ %)		
Low Food Cost % (Below _____ %)		
	Low Popularity (Below _____ sales)	High Popularity (Above _____ sales)

Contribution Margin Matrix

High Contribution Margin (Above $ _____)		
Low Contribution Margin (Below $ _____)		
	Low Popularity (Below _____ sales)	High Popularity (Above _____ sales)

2. Garikai is a manager at Boniso's Mexican Restaurant (from the previous question), and he believes that goal value analysis, rather than Boniso's matrix analysis, is a better way to study the profitability of his menu items.

a. Using the following goal value analysis data, help Garikai analyze the restaurant's menu items.

Goal Value Analysis Data				
Item	Food Cost % (in decimal form)	Number Sold	Selling Price	Variable Cost % (in decimal form)
Fajita Plate	0.38	147	$12.95	0.28
Enchilada Dinner	0.35	200	$ 9.95	0.28
Menudo	0.25	82	$ 6.95	0.28
Mexican Salad	0.30	117	$ 7.95	0.28
Chalupa Dinner	0.28	125	$ 8.95	0.28
Burrito Dinner	0.33	168	$ 9.95	0.28
Taco Dinner	0.26	225	$ 5.95	0.28
Overall Menu (Goal Value)	0.32	152	$ 8.95	0.28

After computing the following goal values, sort (in descending rank order) by goal value. Be sure to include the overall menu in the appropriate rank order. *Spreadsheet hint:* Calculate the goal values by placing the ENTIRE Goal Value formula for each item in the Goal Value column as follows: (1 − Food Cost %) × Item Popularity × Selling Price × (1 − (Variable Cost % + Food Cost %)). The table will not sort correctly if partial calculations for Goal Value exist in columns A, B, C, or D. For example, DO NOT calculate (1 − Food Cost %) in the A column or (1 − (Variable Cost % + Food Cost %)) in the D column.

Goal Value Analysis Results					
Item	"A" Food Cost % (in decimal form)	"B" Number Sold	"C" Selling Price	"D" Variable Cost % (in decimal form)	Goal Value

b. After analyzing his menu items, Garikai believes he can improve the chalupa dinner by lowering the selling price to $8.55. He believes that this lower price will increase number of chalupa dinners sold to 150. However, the change in price will increase both his food cost percentage and variable cost percentage to 29 percent for the chalupa dinner.

   If he makes these changes, will the chalupa dinner meet or exceed the overall menu goal value? Should Garikai make these changes?

Results of Changes Made to Chalupa Dinner					
Item	"A" Food Cost % (in decimal form)	"B" Number Sold	"C" Selling Price	"D" Variable Cost % (in decimal form)	Goal Value
Chalupa Dinner					

3. Eunice manages a Thai restaurant in a primarily Asian section of a major West Coast city. She is interested in determining dollar sales and number of guests needed to break even and to generate her desired profits. Her check average (selling price) is $16.00, her variable cost per unit (guest) is $5.60, and her fixed costs are $170,000.

   a. Complete the following grid, and determine her before-tax profit.

	Per Unit (Guest)	Percentage
SP		
VC		
CM		

Fixed costs	$170,000.00
Desired after-tax profit	$24,000.00
Tax rate	40%
Before-tax profit	

   b. Using the information from part a, calculate the following. (*Spreadsheet hint:* Use the ROUNDUP function for "Rounded up—Break-even point in guest served" and "Rounded up—Guests served to achieve desired after-tax profit.")

Break-even point in sales dollars		

Break-even point in guests served		Rounded up =	

Sales dollars to achieve desired after tax profit		

Guests served to achieve desired after tax profit		Rounded up =	

c. Based on her calculations, Eunice doesn't think that she can attract as many guests as she needs to achieve her desired after-tax profit. Therefore, she has decided to make some changes to improve her situation. Due to these changes, she has been able to reduce her selling price by $1.00, decrease her variable cost percentage by 5%, and lower her fixed costs by $5,000. After these changes, what are Eunice's sales dollars and guests served to achieve her after-tax profit? Complete the following grid and calculations. (*Spreadsheet hint:* Use the ROUNDUP function for "Rounded up—Guests served to achieve desired after-tax profit.")

	Per Unit (Guest)	Percentage
SP		
VC		
CM		

Fixed Costs	

Sales dollars to achieve desired after tax profit	

Guests served to achieve desired after tax profit		Rounded up =	

4. Sinqobile runs a restaurant in an East Coast city that specializes in African-American cuisine. She has compiled her sales and cost data from last year, and she wants to develop a budget for this year. She has projected the following increases for this year:

Projected Increases

Meals served	3%
Selling price per meal	2%
Cost of food	5%
Cost of labor	10%
Other expenses	2%

Using this information, help Sinqobile complete her budget.

	Last Year	Budget
Meals served	122,000	
Selling price per meal	$12.50	

Last year's food cost per meal:

Last year's food cost per meal + Estimated increase:

Estimated cost of food this year:

Last year's labor cost per meal:

Last year's labor cost per meal + Estimated increase:

Estimated cost of labor this year:

	Last Year $	Last Year %	Budget $	Budget %
Revenue	$1,525,000.00			
Cost of food	$ 610,000.00			
Cost of labor	488,000.00			
Other expenses	245,760.00			
Total expenses	$1,343,760.00			
Profit	$ 181,240.00			

The owner of the restaurant has requested that Sinqobile make at least a 10 percent profit for this year. Based on her budget figures, is she likely to meet this goal? If not, what can she do to achieve a 10 percent profit?

5. Sitabiso manages an executive dining room in an office building of a major food manufacturing company. Her sales, on average, run between $17,000 and $21,000 per week. She has decided to use yardstick standards for labor to predict labor costs for varying sales levels. With these data, she can determine if variations in her expenses are due to changes in sales volume or other reasons such as waste or theft. She has compiled information from last year to help her predict her weekly labor costs. Using this information, help Sitabiso complete her yardstick standards for labor. (*Spreadsheet hint:* Use the ROUND function for "% Cost to Total Sales" column. Also, round to 3 decimal places, e.g., 0.123 or 12.3%.)

Yardstick Standards for Labor			
Total Sales:	$900,000	Average Sales per Month: $75,000	
Labor Costs:			
Management	$ 84,000		
Food Production	143,000		
Service	27,600		
Sanitation	34,200		
Total	$288,800		

Category	% Cost to Total Cost	% Cost to Total Sales	Weekly Sales Estimate				
			$17,000	$18,000	$19,000	$20,000	$21,000
Management							
Food production							
Service							
Sanitation							
Total							

6. Toni Lamazza is developing next year's foodservice budget for the Springdale school system, consisting of 17 different schools in a two-county area. Toni knows the revenue she will get from the school board, but is not sure how much the board will give her to pay for anticipated increases in employee benefits. Complete the chart below to help Toni determine the amount employee benefits can increase and still allow her to show a budget surplus.

   At what level of employee benefit cost increase will Toni have a "break-even" budget? How much would her surplus/deficit be if benefits increase by 20 percent?

	Current Budget	Budget with Employee Benefits Increases			
		5% Increase	10% Increase	15% Increase	20% Increase
Revenue	$ 7,000,000	$7,000,000	$7,000,000	$7,000,000	$7,000,000
Cost of Food	$ 2,095,000	$2,095,000	$2,095,000	$2,095,000	$2,095,000
Cost of Payroll	$ 3,700,000	$3,700,000	$3,700,000	$3,700,000	$3,700,000
Cost of Employee Benefits	$ 700,000				
Other Expenses	$ 400,000	$ 400,000	$ 400,000	$ 400,000	$ 400,000
Total Costs	$6,895,000				
Budget Surplus/ Deficit	$ 105,000				

7. J. D. McAllister is really happy. He has just succeeded in securing a $2,000,000 bank loan with a variable percentage interest rate to build his dream restaurant. J. D.'s loan is for 25 years, and it carries an interest rate that is set at 7 percent for the first year (this year). Thus, his first year's monthly interest payments will be $14,136. An experienced restaurateur, J. D. has prepared the following annual budget for this year.

Annual Budget for This Year	
Total Sales	$2,046,000.00
Variable Costs	
Food	429,660.00
Beverage	257,796.00
Labor	572,880.00
Other Variable Costs	171,864.00
Total Variable Costs	$1,432,200.00
Fixed Costs (excluding loan repayment)	$ 239,568.00
Loan Repayment (7% interest)	169,632.00
Total Fixed Costs	$ 409,200.00
Before Tax Profit	$ 204,600.00
Taxes (40%)	81,840.00
After Tax Profit	$ 122,760.00

J. D.'s interest rate will likely vary over the life of the loan because it is tied to the prime interest rate established by the Federal Reserve Board (part of the federal government). Assume the Fed increases interest rates next year by 0.5 percent, and thus J. D.'s interest rate moves to 7.5 percent. As a result, his new monthly loan repayment will be $14,780.

Also assume that his total variable cost percentage and fixed costs (excluding the increased loan repayment) will be the same next year, and his check average (selling price) will be $20 per cover. With the higher mortgage payment, what sales dollars and number of guests served will J. D. need to achieve next year to maintain the same number of after-tax profit dollars as he budgeted for this year?

	Per Unit (Guest)	Percentage
SP		
VC		
CM		

Fixed costs (excluding loan repayment)

Loan repayment (7.5% interest)

Total fixed costs

Desired after-tax profit

Tax rate

Before-tax profit

Sales dollars to achieve desired after-tax profit

Guests served to achieve desired after-tax profit

8. V. K. Sing is the manager of the Knight Kap restaurant. V. K. is preparing his budget for next year and would like to estimate his beverage revenue and expense. V. K. kept careful sales and cost records from last year, and these are listed below.

	Guests Served	Selling Price	Beverage Cost
Beer	3,500	$ 8.50	$1.70
Wine	4,800	$16.00	$4.80
Spirits	2,500	$12.00	$1.80

V. K. has made the following assumptions about next year:

- The cost he will pay for alcoholic beverages will increase by 2 percent in all of the beverage categories.
- V. K. will increase the selling price of all alcoholic beverages by 5 percent.
- The number of guests served will increase by 2 percent for beer, 2 percent for wine, and 3 percent for spirits.

To help V. K. prepare next year's beverage revenue and expense budget, calculate the following for each of his three beverage types:

1. Forecasted total beverage revenue
2. Forecasted total beverage cost
3. Forecasted beverage cost percentage

Projected Changes (Percentage Increases or Decreases)			
	Guests Served	Selling Price	Beverage Cost
Beer			
Wine			
Spirits			

Forecasted Beverage Revenue and Expense Forecast: Knight Kap						
	Guests Served	Selling Price	Beverage Cost	Total Beverage Revenue	Total Beverage Cost	Beverage Cost %
Beer						
Wine						
Spirits						
Total						

9. The Wheatfield Valley golf course has been owned by the Miley family for two generations. Currently, it is managed by Cyrus Miley, a graduate of State University, where he majored in hospitality management. Last year was a good one for the golf course. Now Cyrus is preparing next year's operating budget. He has gathered a great deal of information to help him prepare the best budget possible. After carefully analyzing that information, Cyrus predicts that next year the course will experience:

- A 5 percent increase in food sales
- A 3 percent increase in beverage sales
- No change in food or beverage product cost percentage
- Salaries and wages (management and staff) that will increase 4.5 percent
- Employee benefits that will increase 10 percent
- An increase of 2.5 percent in each Other Expense category
- No change in Occupancy Costs and Depreciation & Amortization
- Interest payments of $1,000 per month
- Tax payments that are estimated to be 25 percent of income before income taxes

Calculate this year's operating percentages for the food and beverage department on the budget worksheet provided, and then using his assumptions about next year, create Cyrus's new operating budget in dollars and percentages.

The Wheatfield Valley Golf Course
F&B Department
Budget Worksheet for Next Year

	This Year Actual $	%	Next Year Budget $	%
SALES				
Food	$173,250.00			
Beverage	56,750.00			
Total Sales				
COST OF SALES				
Food	$ 58,250.00			
Beverages	9,375.00			
Total Cost of Sales				
LABOR				
Management	$ 9,000.00			
Staff	27,250.00			
Employee Benefits	6,200.00			
Total Labor				
PRIME COST				
OTHER CONTROLLABLE EXPENSES				
Direct Operating Expenses	$ 13,200.00			
Utilities	5,975.00			
General & Administrative Expenses	6,375.00			
Repairs & Maintenance	1,750.00			
Total Other Controllable Expenses				
CONTROLLABLE INCOME				
NON-CONTROLLABLE EXPENSES				
Occupancy Costs	$ 15,000.00			
Equipment Leases	0.00			
Depreciation & Amortization	4,200.00			
Total Non-controllable Expenses				
RESTAURANT OPERATING INCOME				
Interest Expense	$ 12,000.00			
INCOME BEFORE INCOME TAXES				
Income Taxes	$ 15,356.25			
NET INCOME				

10. Menu analysis is typically associated with commercial foodservice operators who charge individual selling prices for their menu items. In many cases, however, noncommercial (nonprofit) foodservice operators receive a fixed amount of money per guest served regardless of the menu items selected by the guest. Those managers in charge of foodservice in a college residence hall's cafeteria, a senior living facility, and a military base are just three of many such examples.

Despite the differences in how they charge for the items they serve, however, managers in both commercial and noncommercial operations are concerned about guest acceptance of the menu items they offer. What are some specific ways formal menu analysis (e.g., goal value analysis) can help noncommercial managers address this important issue?

CHAPTER 11

Maintaining and Improving the Revenue Control System

OVERVIEW

This chapter will teach you the principles of revenue control, which includes protecting your sales revenue from external and internal threats of theft. This chapter will also teach you how to establish an effective revenue security system, which is a series of checks and balances that will help you protect your revenue from the time it is collected from your guests to the time it is deposited in your bank and properly spent.

Chapter Outline

- Revenue Security
- External Threats to Revenue Security
- Internal Threats to Revenue Security
- Developing the Revenue Security System
- The Complete Revenue Security System
- Technology Tools
- Apply What You Have Learned
- Key Terms and Concepts
- Test Your Skills

LEARNING OUTCOMES

At the conclusion of this chapter, you will be able to:
- Identify internal and external threats to revenue.
- Create effective countermeasures to combat internal and external theft.
- Establish and monitor a complete and effective revenue security system.

REVENUE SECURITY

In Chapter 1, you learned that Revenue − Expenses = Profit. A close examination of that formula has led some foodservice operators to state that 50 percent of their time should be focused on managing revenue and 50 percent on managing expenses. This is actually quite reasonable because all of the cost control systems you can develop will be of little use if you are unable to collect the revenue generated by your restaurant, deposit that revenue into your bank account, and spend it only on legitimate expenses.

Errors in revenue collection or security can be the result of simple employee mistakes or, in some cases, outright theft by either guests or employees. An important part of your job is to devise revenue security systems that protect your operation's income, whether you receive it in the form of cash, checks, credit or debit card receipts, coupons, meal cards, or any other method of guest payment.

In its simplest form, revenue control and security is a matter of matching products sold with money received. Thus, an effective revenue security system ensures that the following five formulas reflect what really happens in your foodservice operation:

1. Documented product requests = Product issues
2. Product issues (by the kitchen or bar) = Guest charges
3. Total charges = Sales receipts
4. Sales receipts = Sales (bank) deposits
5. Sales deposits = Funds available to pay legitimate expenses (called accounts payable)

The potential for guest or employee theft or fraud exists in all of the preceding areas, so it is important for you to remain alert to irregularities that can help you know if either is taking place.

To illustrate problems that could occur, assume that you own a chain of 10 coffee/dessert shops. You call your units The Pie Parlor. You sell freshly baked gourmet pies of many varieties, all for the same price of $2 per slice or $15 for a whole pie. A whole pie consists of eight slices. In addition, you sell coffee for $2 per cup. Assume that Figure 11.1 details your sales record on a Monday for

FIGURE 11.1 Sales Record

Unit Name: The Pie Parlor #6			Date: 1/15
Item	Number Sold	Selling Price	Total Sales
Apple Pie			
Slices	60	$ 2.00	$ 120.00
Whole	11	15.00	165.00
Pumpkin Pie			
Slices	40	2.00	80.00
Whole	14	15.00	210.00
Cherry Pie			
Slices	75	2.00	150.00
Whole	5	15.00	75.00
Peach Pie			
Slices	25	2.00	50.00
Whole	10	15.00	150.00
Coffee	200	2.00	400.00
Total			$1,400.00

unit 6, which is one of your 10 stores. If you have in place a good system of controlling your revenue, you should have total receipts (revenue) of $1,400 for January 15 at this unit. If, in fact, at the conclusion of the day you have only $1,300 in actual revenue, a security problem exists, not perhaps in the control of products but rather in the control of receipts. If you were short $100 in revenue per day for each of your 10 units, and you were open 360 days per year, your revenue loss for the year would be a staggering $360,000 ($100 short × 10 units × 360 days = $360,000)!

There are several reasons why you might have a revenue shortage. An examination of the potential problems you might be facing will be helpful as we proceed to examine revenue security systems designed to address these issues. Revenue security problems can exist in either of the following areas:

1. External threats to revenue security
2. Internal threats to revenue security

EXTERNAL THREATS TO REVENUE SECURITY

Both guests and employees can be threats to revenue. As a result, your facility could have lost sales revenue because of guests defrauding your foodservice operators. This activity can take a variety of forms, and a very common one is for a guest to **walk, or skip, the bill** or guest check. Guests are said to have walked, or skipped, a guest check when they consume products but then leave the foodservice operation without paying their bills. This type of theft is not generally present in, for example, a quick-service restaurant (QSR) where payment is collected before, or at the same time, the food is given to the guest.

In cases where a guest is in a busy dining room, however, it is quite possible for one or more members of a dining party to slip outside while the server is busy with other guests. In any case, the loss of revenue to your business can be substantial if you do not take the necessary steps to reduce this type of theft. The fact is, in a busy restaurant it can sometimes be relatively easy for a guest or an entire party to leave without settling their bill unless everyone on your staff is extremely vigilant. To help reduce this type of guest theft, implement the steps in Figure 11.2.

It is, of course, also possible that a guest simply forgets to settle his or her bill and leaves the establishment without paying. However, if many of your guests walked their bills on your day of $1,400 sales in our Pie Parlor example, you would, of course, find that the products had indeed been consumed, but the money in your cash drawer would not equal the sales value of the pie and coffee products issued by the kitchen to your waitstaff, who then served the products to your guests.

In addition to skipping a bill, another form of external theft you must be aware of is that used by the quick-change artist. A **quick-change artist** is a guest who, having practiced the routine many times, attempts to confuse a cashier. In his or her confusion, the cashier gives the guest too much change. For example, a guest who should have received $5 in change may use a confusing routine to secure $15. To prevent this from happening, you must train your cashiers well and instruct them to notify management immediately if there is any suspicion of attempted fraud to your operation through quick-change routines by a guest.

Another form of external theft that you must guard against is that of a guest using counterfeit money. **Counterfeit money** is an imitation of currency intended to be passed off fraudulently as real money. Counterfeit money used by guests will not be honored as legal currency by banks. Therefore, counterfeit money deposited by a restaurant manager will result in the ultimate loss of revenues if the perpetrator is not caught. You will have an exercise in the Test Your Skills section of this chapter that will help you learn how to identify counterfeit money.

FIGURE 11.2 Steps to Reduce Guest Walks, or Skips

1. If the custom of your restaurant is that guests order and consume their food prior to your receiving payment, instruct servers to present the bill for the food promptly when the guests have finished.
2. If your facility has a cashier in a central location in the dining area, have that cashier available and visible at all times.
3. If your facility operates in such a manner that each server collects for his or her own guest's charges, instruct the servers to return to the table promptly after presenting the guest's bill to secure a form of payment.
4. Train employees to be observant of exit doors near restrooms or other areas of the facility that may provide an unscrupulous guest the opportunity to exit the dining area without being easily seen.
5. If an employee sees a guest leave without paying the bill, management should be notified immediately.
6. Upon approaching a guest who has left without paying the bill, the manager should ask if the guest has inadvertently "forgotten" to pay. In most cases, the guest will then pay the bill.
7. Should a guest still refuse to pay or flee the scene, the manager should note the following on an incident report:
   a. Number of guests involved
   b. Amount of the bill
   c. Physical description of the guest(s)
   d. Vehicle description if the guests flee in a car, as well as the license plate number if possible
   e. Time and date of the incident
   f. Name of the server(s) who actually served the guest
8. If the guest is successful in fleeing the scene, the police should be notified. In no case should your staff members or managers be instructed to attempt to physically detain the guest. The liability that could be involved should an employee be hurt in such an attempt is far greater than the value of a skipped food and beverage bill.

USE OF CARDS AS BILL PAYMENT

In our advanced technology society, fewer and fewer consumers carry large amounts of cash, and many facilities are reluctant to accept personal checks. Thus, most foodservice operations (including QSRs), now accept a variety of "plastic" forms of bill payment. Since the 1960s, credit cards and travel and entertainment (T&E) cards have been the most common form of plastic guest payment at most restaurants. Today, guests increasingly pay their bills with debit cards.

Also known as "bank" cards, **credit cards** are simply a system by which banks loan money to consumers as the consumer makes purchases. The loans typically carry interest. Merchants such as restaurants and hotels accepting the cards for payment are charged a fee (by the banks) for the right to allow their customers to pay by credit card. Examples of credit cards are Visa and MasterCard.

Travel and entertainment (T&E) cards are a payment system by which the card issuer collects full payment from the card users on a monthly basis. These card companies do not typically assess their users interest charges. Rather, they rely on larger fees collected from the merchants who accept the cards to make their profits. Examples of T&E cards are American Express (Amex) and Diners Club. In some cases, the fees charged by T&E card issuers are so high some restaurateurs do not accept them.

Debit cards are now an extremely popular form of guest payment. In this system, the funds needed to cover the user's purchase are automatically transferred from the card user's bank account to the entity issuing the debit card. As with bank cards and T&E cards, merchants accepting debit cards are assessed a fee for the right to do so.

If restaurant managers are to ensure that they collect all of the money they are due from payment card companies, they must effectively manage the **interface** (electronic connection) between the various payment card issuers and their restaurant. That interface is typically provided by the restaurant's **merchant service provider** (**MSP**). An MSP plays an important role as the restaurant's coordinator/manager of payment card acceptance and funds collection.

It is important to understand that payment card issuers as well as MSPs who are assisting restaurants do so for a price. The card issuer will charge the restaurant a fee and the MSP will charge a variety of fees, including setup fees, per transaction fees, programming fees, statement fees, and fees related to managing the card interface. These interface-related fees may include equipment purchase charges (or leases) and connectivity fees.

In most cases, restaurants have little option but to accept the most popular of payment cards. The MSP selected, however, will vary, and so will the amount of fees it charges. Overall, the MSP generally keeps 10 to 20 percent of all the payment card–related fees you will pay, and the card issuing company (Visa, MasterCard, and others) receives the balance. At the end of the month, you will get a statement displaying the total transactions and the various fees you paid (because the fees are withdrawn by the MSP before your revenue is deposited in your bank account). Thus, for example, an operation may receive a total of $97.50 from a transaction in which a guest originally paid her $100.00 guest check using a payment card.

It is important to remember that maintaining the quality of relationship between your MSP and the restaurant's revenue is just as important as maintaining adequate control over the cash your restaurant accepts. This is so because, in most cases, a restaurant accepting payment cards does not actually "receive" immediate cash from its card sales but, rather, it will be credited via **electronic funds transfer** (**EFT**) the money it is due after all fees have been paid. If a restaurant's POS/MSP interface is faulty or mismanaged, the result can be slow processing, increased errors, omissions, and even disappearing sales!

Unfortunately, the number of stolen and fraudulent payment cards in use today is very high. It is, therefore, important for the foodservice operator to check the validity of the payment card before accepting it for payment. The federal government has passed a law prohibiting the fraudulent use of credit cards. Individuals who fraudulently use credit cards in interstate commerce to obtain goods or services of $1,000 or more in any given year could be subject to fines of up to $10,000 and prison terms of up to 10 years; yet payment card fraud continues.

In addition, issues of identity theft of customers are possible. The chance for a foodservice employee to defraud the customer through **credit card skimming** is always a concern. Skimming is the theft of credit card information used in an otherwise legitimate transaction. It is typically done by a dishonest employee, such as a server or bartender, who has easy access to a guest's payment card information. In the most common case, the employee secretly records the guest's name, credit card number and the three- or four-digit security code number found on the back of the card. This information can be written down by the employee, or photographed/ scanned on various mobile devices. The information is later used to make unauthorized purchases on that guest's payment card. One way to limit this activity is to provide handheld credit card scanners at the actual point of sale so that customers never lose sight of their cards.

Fortunately, payment card security has come a long way since the early introduction of these cards. Today, payment cards are issued with three-dimensional designs, magnetic strips, encoded numbers, cardholder photos, and other features that reduce the chance of guest fraud as well as theft of the card user's personal information by unscrupulous employees. In addition, today's electronic payment card verification (interface) systems, including Apple Pay and others like it, are fast, accurate, and designed to reduce the chances of income loss by your business.

To ensure that you can collect your money from the MSP that administers your account, your staff will be required to follow the specific procedures of the various

FIGURE 11.3 Credit and Debit Card Verification

1. Confirm that the name on the card is the same as that of the individual presenting the card for payment. Drivers' licenses or other acceptable forms of identification can be used.
2. Examine the card for any obvious signs of alteration.
3. Confirm that the card is indeed valid, that is, that the card has not expired or is not yet in effect.
4. Compare the signature on the back of the card with the one produced by the guest paying with the card.
5. The employee processing the charge should initial the credit card receipt.
6. Credit card charges that have not yet been processed should be kept in a secure place to limit the possibility that they could be stolen.
7. Do not issue cash in exchange for credit card charges.
8. Do not write in tip amounts for the guest. Only the guest should supply these, unless the "tip" is, in truth, a mandatory service charge and that fact has been communicated in advance to the guest.
9. Tally credit card charges on a daily basis, making sure to check that the above procedures have been followed. If they have not, corrective action should immediately be taken to ensure compliance.
10. Ensure that only managers approve all cardholder challenges or requests for charge card payment reversals occurring after a guest's card has been charged.

payment card companies. If you agree to accept credit, T&E, and/or debit cards for payment, you should become very familiar with the procedures required by each card issuer and follow them carefully. To enhance your chances of collecting your money from these companies and to reduce the risk of fraudulent card use, insist that your staff follow the steps in Figure 11.3.

FUN ON THE WEB!

Each card issuer has developed specific procedures that merchants must follow if they are to accept the card for payment. To review the procedures of some of the major issuers of payment cards, go to one or more of the card issuers' websites. Enter the following in your favorite browser:

VISA (for Visa cards)

MASTERCARD (for Master Cards)

DISCOVERNETWORK (for Discover cards)

AMERICANEXPRESS (for American Express cards)

When you arrive at the sites, enter the word "Merchants" in the site's search bar.

INTERNAL THREATS TO REVENUE SECURITY

Most foodservice employees are honest, but some are not. In addition to protecting your revenue from unscrupulous guests, you must protect it from those few employees who may attempt to steal the revenue your facility has earned from sales. Cash is the most readily usable asset in a foodservice operation, and it is a major target for dishonest employees. In general, theft from service personnel is usually not a matter of removing large sums of cash at one time, because this is too easy for management to detect. Rather, service personnel may use a variety of techniques to cheat an operation of a small amount at a time.

One of the most common server theft techniques involves the omission of recording the guest's order. In this situation, the server does not record the sale in the operation's POS, but charges the guest and pockets the revenue from the sale. To reduce this possibility, all sales must be recorded in the POS system or on a guest check if management is to develop a system that matches products sold to revenue received. A **guest check** is simply a written record of what the guest purchased and how much the guest was charged for the item(s). The use of paper or electronic guest checks is standard in the industry today because guest checks also serve as the way employees take guest orders and communicate the orders to those employees responsible for filling them. A rule when using guest checks is that no food or beverage should be issued to a server unless the server first records the sale on a guest check.

Modern point-of-sale (POS) systems assign unique numbers to each guest check they create. This POS feature eliminates duplicate guest check fraud and is one of the main reasons even the smallest of foodservice operations should utilize an electronic POS system. Complete revenue control is a matter of developing the checks and balances necessary to ensure that the value of products sold and the amount of revenue received equal each other.

Another method of service personnel fraud is one in which the server gives the proper guest check to the guest, collects payment, and then destroys the guest check but keeps the money. In this case, you would find that the money you collected equaled the sum of the guest checks you have, but, of course, the actual amount of product you served would not be equal to that indicated on the guest checks. For this reason, POS systems operate on a precheck/postcheck system for guest checks.

In a **precheck/postcheck system**, the dining room server writes guest orders on a piece of paper for subsequent entry into a POS terminal called a **user workstation**. The terminal records the items ordered and then displays the order in the production area. In some systems, the order may even be printed in the production area. Increasingly, this method of entering guest orders can be accomplished in one step instead of two. Handheld and wireless at-the-table order entry devices now allow servers (and guests in some cases!) to enter precheck orders directly into an operation's POS system. This direct data entry system is fast, and it eliminates mistakes made when transferring handwritten guest orders to the POS system.

Regardless of how the prechecked guest check is created, kitchen and bar personnel are, in this system, prohibited from issuing any products to the server without a uniquely numbered, prechecked guest check. When the guest is ready to leave, the cashier retrieves the prechecked guest check and prepares a postcheck bill for the guest to pay. The postcheck total includes the charges for all of the prechecked items ordered by the guest plus any service charges and taxes due. The guest then pays the bill. In a precheck/postcheck system, products ordered by the guest, prechecked by the server, and issued by the kitchen or bar should match the items and money collected by the cashier.

There can be reasons why initial prechecked sales totals do not match the amount of money collected by the cashier. Many times, guests place orders and then change their minds, adding or subtracting from their original orders. In other cases, a guest might return an ordered item and, depending on the reason for the item's return, the guest might not be charged for it. For these types of reasons, the question of who can make deletions (voids, returns, reductions) to a prechecked guest check is a potential security concern to the restaurant manager and should be closely controlled.

Another method of employee theft involves failing to finalize a sale recorded on the precheck and pocketing the money. To prevent such theft, management must have systems in place to identify open checks during and after each server's work shift. **Open checks** are those that have been used to authorize product issues from the kitchen or bar but that have not been collected for (closed) and thus have not been added to the operation's sales total.

Unless all open checks are ultimately closed out and presented to guests for payment, the value of menu items issued will not equal the money collected for those items.

The totals of guest checks rung on the POS during a predetermined period are electronically tallied, so management can compare the sales recorded by the POS with the money actually contained in the cash drawer. For example, a cashier working a shift from 7:00 A.M. to 3:00 P.M. might have recorded $1,000 in sales (including taxes) during that time period. If that were in fact the case, and if no errors in handling change occurred, the cash drawer should contain the $1,000 in sales revenue (in addition to the amount that was in the drawer at the beginning of the shift).

If the drawer contains less than $1,000, it is said to be **short**; if it contains more than $1,000, it is said to be **over**. Cashiers rarely steal large sums directly from the cash drawer because such theft is easily detected, but management must make it a policy that any cash shortages or overages will be investigated. Some managers believe that only cash shortages, not overages, need to be monitored. This is not the case. Consistent cash shortages may be an indication of employee theft or carelessness and should, of course, be investigated. Cash overages, too, may be the result of sophisticated theft by the cashier. Essentially, a cashier who is defrauding an operation because he or she knows that management does not investigate overages may remove $18.00 from a cash drawer, but falsify (reduce) the operation's sales records by $20.00. The result is a $2.00 cash "overage"!

Even if you have controls that make internal theft difficult, the possibility of significant fraud still exists. Consequently, some companies protect themselves from employee dishonesty by bonding their employees. **Bonding** is simply a matter of management purchasing an insurance policy against the possibility that an employee(s) will steal.

Through the process of bonding an employer can be covered for the loss of money or other property sustained through dishonest acts of a "bonded" employee. Bonding can cover many types of acts including larceny, theft, embezzlement, forgery, misappropriation, or other fraudulent or dishonest acts committed by an employee, alone or in collusion with others. Essentially, a business can select from several bonding options. These are:

- Individual—covers one employee (e.g., a restaurant's bookkeeper)
- Position—covers all employees in a given position (e.g., all bartenders or all cashiers)
- Blanket—covers all employees

If an employee has been bonded and an operation can determine that he or she was indeed involved in the theft of a specific amount of money, the operation will be reimbursed for all or part of the loss by the bonding company. Although bonding will not completely eliminate theft, it is relatively inexpensive and well worth the cost to ensure that all employees who handle cash or other forms of operational revenue are bonded. Because the bonding company may require detailed background information on employees prior to agreeing to bond them, it is also an excellent preemployment check to verify an employee's track record in prior jobs.

The scenarios discussed in this chapter do not list all possible methods of revenue loss, but it should be clear that you must have a complete revenue security system if you are to ensure that all products sold generate sales revenue that finds its way into your bank account. It is important to remember that even good revenue control systems present the opportunity for theft if management is not vigilant or if two or more employees conspire to defraud the operation (**collusion**). Figures 11.4 and 11.5 outline common methods of theft and procedures managers can use to minimize theft by service employees.

FUN ON THE WEB!

The POS systems available to foodservice operators range from the very simple to the highly sophisticated. To see a few POS companies' range of products, enter "restaurant POS systems" in your favorite search engine and review the features of one or more of the POS systems they offer for sale.

FIGURE 11.4 Common Methods of Theft by Service Employees

- Omit recording the guest's order and keep the money.
- Use the same guest check more than once.
- Destroy the guest check or voids the sale but keep the money.
- Enter another server's password in the POS and keep the money.
- Fail to finalize sale and keep the money.
- Charge guests for items not purchased and then keep the overcharge.
- Change the totals on payment card charges after the guest has left.
- Enter additional payment card charges and pocket the cash difference.
- Incorrectly add legitimate charges to create a higher than appropriate total, with the intent of keeping the overcharge.
- Purposely shortchange guests when giving back change, with the intent of keeping the extra change.
- Charge higher than authorized prices for products or services, record the proper price, and then keep the overcharge.
- Add a coupon to the cash drawer and simultaneously remove sales revenue equal to the value of the coupon.
- Declare a check to be complimentary after the guest has paid the bill.
- Engage in collusion between two or more employees to defraud the operation.

Consider the Cost

"The beauty of our system," said Phil Larson, "is that you can monitor the actions of all your employees and all your managers."

Phil was talking to Gene Monteagudo, chief operating officer for Fazziano's Fast Italian Kitchens, a chain of 150 casual dining and carryout Italian food restaurants. Gene had called POS-Video Security, the company Phil represented, because, for the second time this year, one of Gene's regional managers had discovered a case of employee/manager collusion. Working together, the employee and manager stole revenue from their restaurant by manipulation of their unit's POS system.

"I'm pretty sure I see how your company's product would have detected our most recent theft problem, but go over it one more time," said Gene.

"Okay, Gene, I'd be glad to," said Phil. "Essentially, our new system goes beyond traditional surveillance methods by synchronizing the video with the data mined from your POS system to create detailed, customized video reports. Potentially fraudulent activity such as manager overrides, coupons or comps, or even a cash drawer being open for too long, is tracked and the corresponding video surveillance can be searched by transaction number. Data reports and streaming video, both real time and stored, can be accessed securely on a PC or handheld device via a Web browser."

"So, for example," replied Gene, "when a sales void occurs, your system identifies the portion of videotape that was recording at the time of the void and would then allow my regional managers to view just that portion of the video so they could see what was going on in the store at the precise time of that transaction."

"Exactly," said Phil.

1. What types of employee fraud do you think could be uncovered utilizing the technology offered by POS-Video Security's new product?

2. Do you think that the behavior of most dishonest cashiers and managers would be changed if they knew their actions were being video recorded?

3. What issues should Gene consider as he evaluates the potential benefits to be gained from the purchase of an advanced technology control system such as the one offered by Phil's company?

We now turn our attention to the development of an effective revenue control system. It may not be possible to prevent all types of theft, but a good revenue control system can help determine if, in fact, a theft has occurred and also help you establish procedures to prevent losses in your operation.

FIGURE 11.5 Procedures to Minimize Theft by Service Employees

- Require a written (or POS produced) guest check recording each sale.
- Assign unique numbers to each guest check created.
- Use a precheck/postcheck system.
- Do not allow employees to share POS passwords and require employees to change their passwords frequently.
- Close out open checks.
- Monitor overs/shorts.
- Perform voids by supervisor only.
- Deny cashiers access to unredeemed cash value coupons.
- Require special authorization from management to "comp" guest checks.
- Develop a system of checks and balances.
- Bond employees (acquire an insurance policy against employee theft).

DEVELOPING THE REVENUE SECURITY SYSTEM

An effective revenue security system will help you accomplish the following five important tasks:

1. Verification of product issues
2. Verification of guest charges
3. Verification of sales receipts
4. Verification of sales deposits
5. Verification of accounts payable

You must consider each of these five areas when developing your total revenue security system. In many cases, each foodservice operation you manage will have a different manner of both selling products and accounting for revenue. It is useful, however, to view the revenue control system for any unit in terms of these five key points and how they relate to each other.

In an ideal world, a product would be sold, its sale recorded, its selling price collected, the funds deposited in the foodservice operation's bank account, and the cost of providing the product paid for, all in a single step. Rapid advances in the area of computers, smart cards, and digital wallets are making this a near reality for more foodservice operators each day. The following example from the grocery industry helps illustrate just how this works.

A grocery store customer uses his or her bank-issued debit card when buying a frozen entrée dinner. The cashier, in this instance, uses a scanner to read the bar code printed on the frozen entrée dinner. The following actions then take place:

- The amount the shopper owes the store is recorded in the POS system and the sale itself is assigned a tracking number (verification of product issued/sold).
- The sale amount is displayed for the guest who is asked to confirm its correctness; if it is correct, the shopper pays and a receipt is printed for the shopper (verification of guest charge).
- The store POS system records the amount of the sale as well as the form of payment used by this shopper (verification of sales receipt).
- The shopper's debit card number is attached to this specific sales tracking number and a transfer of funds takes place from the shopper's account to that of the grocery store (verification of sales deposit).
- The funds on deposit in the grocery store's bank account are available to pay for the purchase of additional frozen entrée dinners (verification of accounts payable).

Of course, not all foodservice operations have the technological sophistication to duplicate exactly the system described in our grocery store example. Foodservice operators should, however, adapt the technology they currently have available to the development of good revenue control systems.

In all cases, the foodservice manager should have a thorough understanding of how the revenue security system works and, thus, what is required to maintain it. To illustrate the five-step process of revenue security, consider the situation of Faris, who operates a Lebanese restaurant in New York City.

Faris considers his restaurant to be a family-oriented establishment. It has a small cocktail area and 100 guest seats in the dining room. Total revenue at Faris's exceeds $1 million per year. When he started the restaurant, he did not give a tremendous amount of thought to the design of his revenue control system because he was in the restaurant at all times. Due to his success, however, he spends more and more of his time developing a second restaurant and, thus, needs both the security of an adequate revenue security system and the ability to review it quickly to evaluate the sales levels in his original store. Thus, Faris has begun to develop a revenue security system, concentrating on the following formula:

Product issues = Guest charges = Sales receipts = Sales deposits = Funds available for accounts payable

Faris knows that the first goal he must achieve is that of verifying his product issues.

STEP 1. VERIFICATION OF PRODUCT ISSUES

The key to verification of product issues in the revenue security system is to follow one basic rule: *No product shall be issued from the kitchen or bar unless a permanent record of the issue is made.*

In its simplest terms, this means that the kitchen should not fill any server request for food unless that request has been documented in this step of the control system. In some restaurants, the server request for food or beverages will take the form of a multicopy, written guest check, designed specifically for the purpose of revenue control. When this is the case, the top copy of this multicopy form would generally be sent to the kitchen or bar. The guest check, in this case, becomes the documented request for the food or beverage product. For those operations utilizing a POS system, the "guest check" consists of an electronic record of product issues. When this is the case, a guest's order information is viewed by the production staff on a computer terminal, or, in other cases, the POS system prints a hard copy of the order for use by the production staff. In this case, the software within the computer keeps the permanent record of the request. In every case, however, there should be a permanent documented order that authorizes the kitchen to prepare food or the bar to prepare a drink. In a quick-service restaurant also, no food should be given to the guest unless that sale has been recorded. If a foodservice operation elects to supply its employees with meals during work shifts, these meals, too, should be recorded in the system.

In the bar, this principle of verifying all product sales is even more important. Bartenders should be instructed never to issue a drink unless that drink has first been recorded in the POS system. This should be the procedure, even if the bartender is working alone.

This rule regarding product issuing is important for two reasons. In the first place, requiring a permanent documented order ensures that there is a record of each product sale. Second, this record of product sales can be used to verify both proper inventory usage and product sales totals. Faris enforces this basic rule by requiring that no menu item be served from his kitchen or the bar without the sale first being entered into his POS system.

If his verification of product sales system is working correctly, Faris will find that the following formula should hold true:

$$\text{Documented product requests} = \text{Product issues}$$

Experienced foodservice operators know that it is possible for employees to issue products *without* a document product request when:

1. Two or more employees work together to defraud the operation. Collusion of this type can be discovered when managers have a system in place to carefully count the number of items removed from inventory and then compare that number to the number of products that were actually issued.

2. A single employee (such as a bartender working alone) is responsible for both making and filling the product request. In this case also, managers will uncover this type of fraud when they carefully compare the number of items (or servings) removed from inventory with the number of recorded product issues.

STEP 2. VERIFICATION OF GUEST CHARGES

When the production staff is required to prepare and distribute products only in response to a properly documented request, it is critical that those documented

FIGURE 11.6 Sample Guest Check

			Faris's		Phone #: <u>123-4567</u>
Date	Table	Server	Guests	**Check Number** 123456	
Items Ordered					Price
Subtotal					
Tax					
Gratuity					
Total					

<u>Guest Receipt</u>					
Date	Table	Server	Guests	Check Number 123456	Total

requests result in charges to the guest. It makes little sense to enforce a verification of product issues step without also requiring the service staff to ensure that guest charges match these requests. This concept can be summarized as follows: *Product issues must equal guest charges.*

There are a variety of ways this can be achieved. If managers use manually generated guest checks as a primary control device, the managerial goal is to ensure that product issues equal guest check totals. If they do, all issued products will result in appropriate charges to the guest. Figure 11.6 is a sample of a guest check that could be in use at Faris's. Note that the check is numbered on both the top and the bottom, or guest receipt portion.

If guest checks are used as a control device, it is important to remember that the numbers on the checks are of no operational value if the checks are not tightly controlled. Each guest check must be accounted for, and employees must know that they will be held responsible for each check they are issued. This is because an unscrupulous employee could present a guest check for payment to a guest, then destroy the check and keep the money. For this reason, "lost" guest checks should always be accounted for. To keep track of the checks issued to service personnel, managers use a guest check control form. Figure 11.7 is an example of such a form that could be used at Faris's.

Note that this control form recognizes that some guest checks can be lost or damaged. When using the guest check system of verifying guest charges, you must be aware of these incidents when they occur and must investigate when it is determined that a check is missing. Each lost or destroyed check should be "approved" by management. That is, management should know why and how each missing check came to be missing!

FIGURE 11.7 Sample Guest Check Control Form

Faris's

Date: <u>1/15</u>   Shift: <u>Lunch</u>

Check Numbers Issued			Check Numbers Returned				
From	To	Issued To	From	To	Checks Used	Checks Accounted for	Number Missing
00001	00100	Beth	00055	00100	45	44	1
00101	00200	Sally	00130	00200	70	70	0
00201	00300	Gerry	00264	00300	36	36	0

Unaccounted Checks:

Check Number	Issued To	Explanation	Manager's Initials
00035	Beth	Torn by accident	D.K.H.

A POS system simplifies the task of guest check control by creating a unique transaction number (guest check) for each server request. That is, a documented request for products generates, within the POS system, a guest check that is matched to that request. Guest checks cannot be "lost" on purpose, because the POS keeps a record of each transaction, as well as attempts by employees to request a product, receive it from the kitchen or bar, and then *void* (subtract) the charge from the guest's bill. Guest check control is another significant advantage enjoyed by operators who utilize their POS systems properly.

When properly implemented, this second step of the revenue control system will result in the following formula:

Product issues = Guest charges

Faris has now implemented two key revenue control principles. The first one is that no product can be issued from the kitchen or bar unless the order is documented; the second one is that all guest charges must match product issues.

With these two systems in place, Faris can deal with many problems. If, for example, a guest has "walked" his or her check, the operation would have a duplicate record of the transaction. The POS would have recorded which products were sold to this guest, which server sold them, and perhaps additional information, such as the time of the sale, the number of guests in the party, and, of course, the sales value of the products.

The POS system Faris utilizes also ensures that service personnel do not attempt to write one item on the guest check but charge the guest a higher or lower price. This would be possible in a manual check system, and those operators who utilize such systems must perform a periodic audit of checks to help detect this type of fraud.

To complete this aspect of his control system, Faris implements a strict policy regarding the documentation of employee meals. This has the added advantage of giving him a monthly total of the value of employee meals. Recall that he needs this figure to accurately compute his cost of food consumed (see Chapter 5).

Faris is now ready for the next major component in a revenue security system, that is, the actual collection of guest payments; his operation's sales receipts.

STEP 3. VERIFICATION OF SALES RECEIPTS

Sales receipts, as defined in this step, refer to actual revenue received by the cashier or other designated personnel, in payment for products served. In Faris's case, this means all sales revenue from his restaurant and lounge. This essential principle can be summarized as follows: *Both the cashier and a member of management must verify sales receipts.*

Verifying sales receipts is more than a simple matter of counting cash at the end of a shift. In fact, cash handling, although it is an important part of the total sales receipt reconciliation, is only one part of the total sales receipt verification system. To illustrate this, consider Figure 11.8, the form Faris uses to verify his total sales receipts. The form indicates that both the cashier and a supervisor make the sales receipt verification. Although this will not prevent possible collusion by this pair, it is extremely important that sales receipt verification be a two-person process.

Faris wishes to ensure that the amount of cash and checks in his cash drawer, as well as his payment card charges, matches the dollar amount that he has charged his guests. If this is so, he has accounted for all of his sales receipts, given that he has controlled both product issues and guest charges. As you can see, the form presented in Figure 11.8 details both the guest charges recorded in the POS system and the money Faris has collected.

In most operations, individual guest charges are recorded only in the POS system. This is the case, for example, in a cafeteria or QSR, where food purchases

FIGURE 11.8 Sales Receipt Report

		Faris's
		Performed By:
Date: 1/15		Cashier: Tammi F.
Shift: Dinner		Supervisor: Faris L.

Revenue per Guest Check		
Guest check totals	$7,500.00	
Service charges	450.00	
Tax	618.00	
Total guest check revenue		$8,568.00

Receipts

Charge cards		
VISA	893.00	
MasterCard	495.00	
Discover	1,200.00	
American Express	975.00	
Total charge card receipts	$3,563.00	

Cash		
Twenties and larger	$4,840.00	
Tens	1,480.00	
Fives	240.00	
Ones	196.00	
Change	68.20	
Total cash	$6,824.20	
Less: Bank	$ 500.00	
Tip-outs	1,320.00	
Net cash receipts		$5,004.20
Net total receipts		$8,567.20
Variance check revenue to net receipts		$ (0.80)

are totaled and paid for at the same time. It is also true in any operation using a precheck/postcheck POS system. In such instances, the POS system provides an accurate total of guest and other charges. Receipts collected should equal these charges. In those operations still using a manual guest check system, the sum of the individual check totals (charges to guests) should equal the amount of revenue (sales receipts) collected.

If Faris's revenue security system is working properly, he knows that the following formula should be in effect:

Total charges = Sales receipts

Note that the function of Figure 11.8 is to require Faris's staff to reconcile total charges with actual revenue (sales receipts). Overages or shortages are entered and, if they exceed predetermined allowable limits, are investigated by management.

Service charges, the second entry on the form, are special charges assessed to guests. Faris assesses a service charge of 15 percent on all parties larger than eight persons. Hotel often assess a service charge on all food and beverages sold in their meeting spaces. Note that total charges consist of all sales, service charges, and taxes. This is the total amount of revenue the operation should have received on this date.

Sales receipts refer to all forms of revenue, such as cash, checks (if accepted), and payments made by credit or debit cards. In addition, note that Faris must subtract the value of his starting cash bank and any tip-outs, or gratuities, due to service personnel. These gratuities are typically added to payment card vouchers by the guest, but paid out to the service personnel by management either in cash or in their paychecks because such tip income is taxable to the server.

Note, also, that Figure 11.8 has a space to indicate cash overages and shortages (variance of total charges to net total receipts). Some foodservice operators allow no variance whatsoever. Others routinely ignore minor variances. It will be up to you, as the manager, to determine the level of variance you are comfortable with as far as this reconciliation is concerned.

STEP 4. VERIFICATION OF SALES DEPOSITS

It is strongly recommended that only management make the actual bank deposit of daily sales revenue. A cashier or other clerical assistant may complete the deposit slip, but management alone should bear the responsibility for monitoring the actual deposit of sales. This concept can be summarized as follows: *Management must personally verify all bank deposits.*

This involves the actual verification of the contents of the deposit and the process of matching bank deposits with actual sales. These two numbers obviously should match. That is, if you deposit Thursday's sales on Friday, the Friday deposit should match the sales amount of Thursday. If it does not, you have experienced some loss of revenue that has occurred after your cashier has reconciled sales receipts to guest charges. **Embezzlement** is the term used to describe employee theft where the embezzler takes company funds he or she was entrusted to keep and diverts them to personal use. Embezzlement is a crime that often goes undetected for long periods of time because many times the embezzler is a trusted employee. Falsification of, or destroying, bank deposits is a common method of embezzlement. To prevent this activity, you should take the following steps to protect your deposits:

1. Make bank deposits of cash and checks daily if possible.
2. Ensure that the person preparing the deposit is not the one making the deposit—unless you or the manager do both tasks. Also, ensure that the individual making the daily deposit is bonded.
3. Establish written policies for completing **bank reconciliations**, the regularly scheduled comparison of the business's deposit records with the bank's acceptance records. Payment card funds transfers to a business's bank account should be reconciled each time they occur. Increasingly, cash and payment card reconciliations can be accomplished on a daily basis via the use of online banking features.
4. Review and approve written bank statement reconciliations at least once each month.
5. Change combinations on safes periodically and share the combinations with the fewest employees possible.
6. Require that all cash-handling employees take regular and uninterrupted vacations on a regular basis so that another employee can assume and uncover any improper practices.
7. Employ an outside auditor to examine the accuracy of deposits on an annual basis.

If verification of sales deposits is done correctly and no embezzlement is occurring, the following formula should hold true:

Sales receipts = Sales deposits

STEP 5. VERIFICATION OF ACCOUNTS PAYABLE

Accounts payable, as defined in this step, refers to the legitimate amount owed to a vendor for the purchase of products or services. The basic principle to be followed when verifying accounts payable is: *The individual authorizing the purchase should verify the legitimacy of the vendor's invoice before it is paid.*

Vendor payments are an often-overlooked potential threat to the security of a restaurant's revenue. Of course, a restaurant should pay all of its valid expenses (invoices for payment). However, both external vendors and the restaurant's employees can attempt to defraud a foodservice operation through the manipulation of invoices.

For example, consider again the case of Faris. One day, he receives an invoice for fluorescent light bulbs. The invoice is for over $400, yet the invoice lists only two dozen bulbs as having been delivered. This is clearly a large overcharge. Faris is not familiar with this specific vendor, but the delivery slip included with the invoice was, in fact, signed (six weeks ago) by his receiving clerk. Quite likely, in this case, Faris and his operation are the victims of a bogus invoice scam by the vendor, and that scam threatens his facility's revenue.

Businesses, churches, and fraternal and charitable organizations are routinely targeted for invoice payment scams. The typical supplier scam involves goods or services that you would routinely order. These include items such as copier paper, toner and maintenance supplies, equipment maintenance contracts, or classified advertising. Dishonest suppliers can take advantage of weaknesses in an organization's purchasing procedures or of unsuspecting employees who may not be aware of their fraudulent practices. In addition, the supplies delivered by these bogus firms are most often highly overpriced and of poor quality.

In a revenue system that is working properly, the following formula should be in effect:

Sales deposits = Funds available for accounts payable

Funds available for accounts payable should, of course, only be used to pay legitimate expenses that result from a purchase that can be verified by authorized personnel within the hospitality operation.

SPECIAL REVENUE COLLECTION SITUATIONS

In some situations, guests are not billed immediately upon finishing their meal, beverages, or reception, but are **direct billed** for their charges. This is often the case in hotel food and beverage operations as well as those restaurants with banquet facilities. When this is the case, creditworthy guests are sent a bill for the value of the products they have consumed after their event is over. When this form of billing is employed, it is important that the invoice accurately reflects all guest charges. Consider, for example, the case of Faris, who agrees to provide a wedding banquet. The guest who arranged the event guarantees a count of 90 guests, but on the evening of the dinner, 100 guests actually attend. The guest should be billed for 100 if all were served, and payment by the guest should reflect that. In this manner, the principles of revenue control are still in place; that is, guest charges should equal revenue collected. Figure 11.9 is an example of a banquet event order/invoice (guest check) that Faris could use to bill customers.

Accounts receivable is the term used to refer to guest charges that have been billed to the guest but not yet collected. Too high an accounts receivable amount should be avoided because the foodservice operation has paid for the products consumed by the guest and the labor to serve the products but has not yet collected from the guests for these. In addition, collecting money after a guest has left your operation can be more difficult as time passes. For these reasons, you must be diligent in promptly collecting accounts receivable.

In addition to direct billing, other special revenue collection systems may be in place. For example, consider the drink ticket, or coupon, often sold or issued in hotel

FIGURE 11.9 Banquet Event Order/Invoice

Faris's	**Date 1/15**

Banquet Event Order/Invoice

Day of Event: _____ Date of Event: _____

Time of Event: _____ to _____ Time Ready By: _____

Type of Event: _____ Location: _____

Expected Count: _____ Guaranteed Count: _____ Final Count: _____

Organization Hosting Event: _____

Organization Contact Person: _____

Organization Address: _____

Organization Telephone: _____ Fax: _____ E-mail: _____

Price: _____ Tax: _____ Service Charge: _____ %

Deposit Amount: _____ Deposit Received: _____

Total Amount Due: _____ Payment Due Date: _____

Menu	Setup (Style of Room, A/V)
	Linen
Wines/Liquors	**Decor/Flowers**

Signature of Guest: _____ Date: _____

Signature of Manager: _____ Date: _____

reception areas for use at cocktail receptions. These coupons should be treated as if they were cash, for, in fact, they are its equivalent. Thus, those individuals who are selling the coupons should not be the same ones as those dispensing the beverages. In addition, the collected drink coupons should equal the number of drinks served. The recording form required to verify this will vary, based on each operation's drink price policy, but such a record should be developed and used.

Another special pricing situation is the reduced-price coupon. Coupons are popular in the hospitality industry and can take a variety of forms, such as 50 percent off a specific purchase, "buy-one-get-one-free" (BOGO) promotions, or a program whereby a guest who buys a predetermined number of items or meals gets the next one free. In all of these cases, the coupon should be treated as its cash equivalent because, from a revenue control perspective, these coupons are equivalent to cash.

THE COMPLETE REVENUE SECURITY SYSTEM

If he follows the steps outlined in the preceding pages, Faris will now have completed the development of his revenue security system. Its five key principles are:

1. No product shall be issued from the kitchen or bar unless a permanent record of the issue is made.

2. Product issues must equal guest charges.

3. Both the cashier and a member of management must verify sales receipts.

4. Management must personally verify all bank deposits.

5. Management or the individual authorizing the purchase should verify the legitimacy of the vendor's invoice before it is paid.

It is possible to develop and maintain a completely manual revenue control system. That is, each of the five major components of the revenue control system described in this chapter could be instituted without the aid of a computer or even a cash register. In today's world, however, such an approach is both wasteful of time and suspect in accuracy. The simple fact is that the amount of information you need to effectively operate your business grows constantly. Guest dining choices, vendor pricing, inventory levels, payroll statistics, and revenue control are simply a few of the issues involving the huge amount of data collection and manipulation your business demands.

Fortunately, inexpensive POS systems that can help you easily and quickly assemble the data you need to make good management decisions are readily available. It is dangerous, however, for a foodservice manager to expect that a POS system will "bring" control to an operation. That happens rarely! A POS system will, however, take good control systems that have been carefully designed by management and add to them in terms of speed, accuracy, or additional information.

If you hope to improve your revenue security or any other cost control system in the operation, your POS system will be of immense value. If, however, your operation has no controls and you are not committed to the control process, your POS will simply become a high-tech adding machine, used primarily to sum guest purchases and nothing more. Properly selected and utilized, however, POS systems play a crucial role in the implementation of a complete revenue security system.

Green and Growing!

In most foodservice operations, the use of sophisticated information technology (IT) systems continues to grow. Operators can purchase POS systems designed to gather and analyze more operational and customer-related data than ever before.

These same POS systems provide an excellent example of how companies seeking to reduce energy consumption and become more environmentally responsible can do so in every area of their operations. Considering the purchase of a "green" POS system means choosing energy-efficient systems designed for upgradability, expandability, and long life. By using energy-efficient POS equipment for longer periods of time, operating costs are reduced and landfill waste lessened. Green-oriented operators can also insist that POS system manufacturers do their part by utilizing sustainable shipment packaging materials. For example, by switching from Styrofoam packaging to recycled and reusable paper packaging, the average packaging footprint can be reduced by an estimated 50 percent.

Some recently introduced POS solutions consume less energy than a standard 100-watt light bulb! Efficiency advancements such as these help operators save money from high energy costs, while also helping to relieve the stress of excess energy consumption on the environment. When foodservice operators "grow green" by purchasing refurbished computer equipment for use in their cost and revenue control systems, they may be able to save even more money. Both of these approaches to POS system implementation (choosing new or refurbished equipment) allow operators to aggressively pursue their profit goals in an environmentally friendly fashion.

Technology Tools

In this chapter, the principles of revenue control were introduced. In years past, the manual counting of money and balancing of cashier drawers was time consuming and, in most cases, tedious. With the advent of credit and debit card sales, the process has become easier, but its importance has not diminished. Protecting sales revenue from external and internal threats of theft requires diligence and attention to detail. The POS software and specialized hardware now on the market that can help in this area includes those that:

1. Maintain daily cash balances from all sources, including those of multiunit and international operations.
2. Reconcile inventory reductions with product issues from kitchen.
3. Reconcile product issues from kitchen with guest check totals.
4. Reconcile guest check totals with revenue totals.
5. Create over and short computations by server, shift, and day.
6. Balance daily bank deposits with daily sales revenue and identify variances.
7. Maintain database of returned checks.
8. Maintain accounts receivable records.
9. Maintain accounts payable records.
10. Maintain records related to the sale and redemption of gift cards.
11. Interface back-office accounting systems with data compiled by the operation's POS system.
12. Interface budgeting software with revenue generation software.
13. Create income statements, statements of cash flows, and balance sheets.

It is important to note that interfacing (electronically connecting) the various software programs you select is very helpful. For example, a program that forecasts sales revenue and also supplies that data to the software program you are using to schedule labor hours needed will be more effective and helpful to you than one that does not directly connect to the scheduling feature. In a similar manner, a software program that compares sales recorded on the POS with daily bank deposits is preferable to one that does not connect these two independent but correlated functions.

Apply What You Have Learned

Donald Wright worked for 15 years as a snack bar cashier for the Sports Arena managed by Stanley Harper's company. Donald had twice won the company's "Employee of the Year" award, and Stanley considered Donald a valued and trusted employee who had, on many occasions, performed above and beyond the call of duty.

Stanley was surprised when newly installed video surveillance equipment confirmed that Donald, despite rules against it, had, on several occasions, given free food and beverages to friends who had visited the arena.

On the advice of the company's human resource representative, Stanley is documenting, in writing, his decision on handling the situation.

1. Assume you are Stanley, and draft a letter to Donald indicating the consequences of his actions.

2. Do you believe an employee caught defrauding his/her employer should ever be given a second chance? If so, under what circumstances?

3. What impact will Stanley's decision in this case have if, in the future, other employees are caught stealing?

Key Terms and Concepts

*T*he following are terms and concepts discussed in the chapter that are important for you as a manager. To help you review, please define the terms below.

walk/skip (the bill)
quick-change artist
counterfeit money
credit cards
travel and entertainment
  (T&E) cards
debit cards
interface
merchant service provider
  (MSP)

electronic funds transfer
  (EFT)
credit card skimming
guest check
precheck/postcheck
  system
user workstation
open check
short
over

bonding
collusion
embezzlement
bank reconciliation
accounts payable
direct billed
accounts receivable

Test Your Skills

You may download the Excel spreadsheets for the Test Your Skills exercises from the student companion website at www.wiley.com/college/dopson. Complete the exercises by placing your answers in the shaded boxes and answering the questions as indicated.

1. Trisha Sangus manages a large hotel. Recently, her hotel controller identified a problem in one of the hotel dining rooms. Essentially, Stevie, one of the evening cashiers, was voiding product sales after they had been rung up on the POS, and then removing an equal amount of money from the cash drawer so that the drawer balanced at the end of the shift. What procedures would you recommend to Trisha to prevent a further occurrence of this type of incident? Assume that a precheck/postcheck guest check system is in place.

2. Counterfeit money is a problem for all US businesses, including those in the hospitality industry. The US Department of Treasury has developed educational aids to assist managers who must train those who handle cash. To do so, they have compiled information that is critical in the detection of imitation currency and coins.

   Go to the US Secret Service website to learn about how to detect counterfeit money: **www.secretservice.gov.** Under "Investigations" click "Know Your Money," and then click "How to Detect Counterfeit Money" and "If You Suspect a Note Is Counterfeit" to learn more about this threat to revenue security. When you are done, prepare a training session appropriate for cashiers who may routinely be responsible for the detection of counterfeit money. Include a memo to your cashiers detailing what they should actually do if they suspect a bill is counterfeit.

3. Mary Margaret and Blue are the owners/operators of an extremely upscale bakery goods boutique, and they are interested in a complete asset control system that includes protection of both products and revenue. Identify two control devices/procedures that they could implement to help them control revenue security in the following areas, and explain your reason for choosing each.

   a. Product issues

   b. Guest charges

c. Sales receipts

d. Sales deposits

e. Accounts payable

4. Each of the following payment methods allows for potential employee and/or guest theft. Assume that Debbie operates a semiprivate country club where club members and the general public may purchase products in a variety of settings. Using Figures 11.4 and 11.5 and the section on direct billing as a guide, identify at least two potential methods of theft for each of the following, as well as a description of the specific procedures Debbie should implement to prevent such theft.

a. Guest pays cashier directly.

b. Guest pays server at the table.

c. Guest is direct billed.

Which system would you favor using?

5. Denise Cronin operates a quick-service sandwich restaurant in a busy section of a major downtown area. Last week, the POS system in Denise's operation reported the following guest charges, and Denise, upon verifying cash on hand at the end of each day, generated the following sales receipts. Determine Denise's daily and weekly overage and shortage amounts.

Does Denise have a cash control problem? How often in a day do you believe Denise should balance her sales receipts with her guest charges? Why?

Day	Sales Receipts	Guest Charges	Over/(Short)
Monday	$3,587.74	$3,585.28	
Tuesday	$3,682.22	$3,693.35	
Wednesday	$3,120.35	$3,110.54	
Thursday	$2,985.01	$3,006.27	
Friday	$4,978.80	$4,981.50	
Saturday	$6,587.03	$6,588.82	
Sunday	$1,733.57	$1,737.93	
Total			

6. Allison Holmes has just been promoted to the job of regional beverage manager at Appleboy's Restaurants. Her district includes six successful units. In one unit, Allison suspects that Ron, the restaurant manager, and Tony, the bar manager, have collaborated to defraud their restaurant by serving cash-paying guests at the bar, not ringing up the sales, and then splitting the revenue collected from those guests.

Since the unit's cash drawers are always in balance, no one has previously investigated the possibility of employee theft in this unit. What are some indications of such fraudulent activity that would lend support to Allison's suspicions? How would you suggest Allison find out if she is actually correct?

7. Kathy, the general manager, was shocked to discover that the thief in her successful seafood restaurant was Dan, her own dining room supervisor. Dan had used his detailed knowledge of weaknesses in the POS data monitoring system Kathy had designed to void legitimate sales after the fact and thus

defraud the restaurant out of an average of $800.00 in revenue per day, every day, for the past six months. When finally confronted, Dan confessed to the thefts, citing a gambling problem as the reason for his actions.

The information below details Kathy's reported revenue, food cost, labor cost, other costs, and profit for the past 180 days. Calculate the potential financial performance in dollars and percentages her restaurant would have achieved had it not been for Dan's actions. (*Spreadsheet hint*: Food Cost, Labor Cost, and Other Costs will be the same for Actual $ and Potential $.)

Kathy's Restaurant Performance				
Revenue Stolen				
	Actual %	Actual $	Potential $	Potential %
Revenue	100.0%	$1,566,000		
Food Cost	37.0%			
Labor Cost	29.0%			
Other Costs	26.5%			
Profit	7.5%			

a. How much profit in dollars did Kathy lose because of Dan's fraudulent activities (difference between potential and actual)?

b. How much profit percent did Kathy lose because of Dan's fraudulent activities (difference between potential and actual)?

c. List three things that Kathy could have done to minimize the potential for Dan's illegal activity.

8. Kim owns a small bar in a suburban town, and he caters to the "after five" business crowd. He has been experiencing his heaviest business on Wednesday, Thursday, and Friday evenings, so he has recently hired an extra bartender for those shifts. As part of his standard operating procedures, he requires all spills to be recorded on a spill report. His average drink price is $7.00, and his spillage has historically been running about 3 percent of sales.

The information below details Kim's Spillage Report for last week. Calculate the dollar and percentage spilled to see how well Kim's bartenders are doing as compared to the historical average of 3 percent. Does Kim have any controls problems? If so, what may be the contributing factors from a revenue security perspective, and how might he correct them?

Kim's Spillage Report					
Day	Sales Receipts	# Spilled	Average Drink Price	$ Spilled	% of Sales Spilled
Monday	$1,563.00	6	$7.00		
Tuesday	$1,647.00	8	$7.00		
Wednesday	$1,936.00	20	$7.00		
Thursday	$2,045.00	23	$7.00		
Friday	$2,251.00	25	$7.00		
Saturday	$1,574.00	7	$7.00		
Sunday	$1,412.00	5	$7.00		
Total					

9. Erica is the Special Events Coordinator of a large hotel, and she is reviewing her end of event reports after a wedding reception she has just managed. The bride and groom had planned on 300 guests, and they only wanted champagne and wine served. Based on an average of 3 drinks consumed per guest and an average of 5 drinks served per bottle, Erica had estimated the number of bottles she should serve for the reception. Below is the report that her banquet captain prepared on actual bottles used at the reception. The actual number of attendees at the reception was 250 guests.

   The information below shows beverage usage at the wedding reception. Calculate the difference in planned versus used beverages, and the difference, if any, in number of guests served versus estimated. Are there any unusual discrepancies based on the number of actual reception attendees (250 guests)? Should Erica be concerned about these numbers? If so, what might Erica do to investigate these concerns?

Beverage Usage Report

Beverage Selection	# of Guests Selecting	Average Drinks per Bottle	Estimated Bottles	Used Bottles	Difference in Bottles Used	Difference in # of Drinks Served	Average Drinks per Guest	Difference in # of Guests Served
Champagne	100	5		30			3	
Wine	200	5		48			3	
Total		5					3	

10. Sometimes it can be difficult to determine whether errors made in the payment of an operation's bills (when they are uncovered by an audit) represent intentional fraud or simply are mistakes resulting from an employee's poor training or lack of knowledge.

   Assume an audit uncovered duplicate invoice payments made to three different food vendors over a 90-day period. The payments were made to them by the individual in your operation who is responsible for accounts payable. What specific action would you take to determine whether the individual's mistakes were intentional or simply exposed weaknesses in your accounts payable system?

GLOSSARY

28-day period. Accounting method that divides a year into 13 equal periods of 28 days each.

À la carte (menu). A menu format in which guests select individual menu items and each menu item is priced separately.

Acceptance hours. The hours of the day in which an operation is willing to accept food and beverage deliveries.

Accounting period. A period of time—that is, hour, day, week, or month—in which an operator wishes to analyze revenue and expenses.

Accounts payable. The legitimate amount owed to a vendor for products or services rendered.

Accounts receivable. The term used to refer to guest charges that have been billed to the guest but not yet collected.

Achievement budget. A forecast or estimate of projected revenue, expense, and profit for a period of a month or a week. It provides current operating information and, thus, assists in making current operational decisions.

Affordable Care Act. Formally known as the Patient Protection and Affordable Care Act; the federal law designed to expand health-care coverage for US citizens.

Aggregate statement. Summary of all details associated with the sales, costs, and profits of a foodservice establishment.

Alcoholic beverages. Those products that are meant for consumption as a beverage and that contain a significant amount of ethyl alcohol. They are classified as beer, wine, or spirits.

Ambience. The feeling or overall mood created in an operation by its decor, staff uniforms, music and other factors that directly affect its atmosphere.

Annual budget. A forecast or estimate of projected revenue, expense, and profit for a period of one year.

AP. See *As purchased.*

As needed (Just-in-time). A system of determining the purchase point by using sales forecasts and standardized recipes to decide how much of an item to place in inventory.

As purchased (AP). This term refers to the weight or count of a product as delivered to the foodservice operator.

Attainable product cost. The cost of goods consumed figure that should be achievable given the product sales mix of a particular operation.

Auditors. Those individuals responsible for reviewing and evaluating proper operational procedures.

Average (mean). The value arrived at by adding the quantities in a series and dividing the sum of the quantities by the number of items in the series.

Average sales per guest (check average). The mean amount of money spent per customer during a given financial accounting period. Often referred to as check average.

Back of the house. The kitchen production area of a foodservice establishment.

Bank reconciliation. A comparison of a business's deposit and disbursements records with its bank's acceptance and disbursement records.

Beer. A fermented beverage made from grain and flavored with hops.

Beginning inventory. The dollar value of all products on hand at the beginning of the accounting period. This amount is determined by completing a physical inventory.

Beverage costs. The costs related to the sale of alcoholic beverages.

Beverage cost percentage. The ratio of an operation's beverage costs to its beverage sales. The formula used to calculate beverage cost percentage is: Cost of beverage sold ÷ Beverage sales = Beverage cost percentage.

Bid sheet. A form used to compare prices among many vendors in order to select the best prices.

Bin card. An index card with both additions to and deletions from inventory of a given product. To facilitate its use, the card is usually affixed to the shelf that holds the given item. Used in a perpetual inventory system.

Bonding. Purchasing an insurance policy to protect the operation in case of employee theft.

Bookkeeping. The process of recording and summarizing financial data.

Break-even point. The point at which operational expenses are exactly equal to sales revenue.

Budget/plan. A forecast or estimate of projected revenue, expense, and profit for a defined accounting period. Often referred to as plan.

Bundling. The practice of selecting specific menu items and pricing them as a group in such a manner that the single menu price of the group is lower than if the items in the group were purchased individually.

Business dining. Food is provided as a service to the company's employees either as a no-cost (to the employee) benefit or at a greatly reduced price.

Butcher's yield test. A procedure designed to identify losses due to the trimming of inedible fat and bones in meat as well as losses due to the meat's cooking or slicing.

Buy one, get one (BOGO). A marketing technique in which buyers who purchase a single item receive a second item of equal or lesser value for no additional charge.

Call-in. A system whereby employees who are off duty are required to check in with management on a daily basis to see if the volume is such that they may be needed.

Call liquors. Those spirits that are requested (called for) by a particular brand name.

Carryover. A menu item prepared for sale during a meal period but carried over for use in a different meal period.

Check average. See *Average sales per guest.*

Cellar temperature. The range of temperatures (approximately 50°F to 57°F (12°C to 14°C) highly recommended for the long term storage of many types of bottled wines.

CEO (chief executive officer). The highest-ranking leader/manager in an organization.

Certified management accountant (CMA). A professional designation and certification program designed for accounting and financial management professionals and administered by the Institute of Management Accountants, Inc.

Certified public accountant (CPA). A professional designation indicating the passing of a standardized examination (The Uniform Certified Public Accountant Examination) demonstrating the highest levels of competency in accounting.

Cherry picker. A customer who buys only those items from a supplier that are the lowest in price among the supplier's competition.

COLA. See *Cost of living adjustment.*

Collusion. Secret cooperation between two or more individuals that is intended to defraud an operation.

Comp. Short for the word *complimentary,* which refers to the practice of management giving a product to a guest without a charge. This can be done for a special customer or as a way of making amends for an operational error.

Contract price. A price mutually agreed on by supplier and operator. This price is the amount to be paid for a product or products over a prescribed period of time.

Contribution margin. The profit or margin that remains after product cost is subtracted from an item's selling price.

Contribution margin for overall operation. The dollar amount that contributes to covering fixed costs and providing for a profit.

Contribution margin income statement. A financial summary that shows P&L items in terms of sales, variable costs, contribution margin, fixed costs, and profit.

Cost. See *Expenses.*

Convenience foods (Ready foods). A menu item or ingredient that has been purchased pre-prepared to reduce on-site labor cost or to enhance product consistency.

Conversion factor (recipe). A mathematical formula that yields a number (factor) managers use to convert a recipe that produces a known yield to the same recipe producing a desired yield. The formula used to calculate a recipe conversion factor is: Yield desired ÷ Current yield = Conversion factor.

Cost accounting. See *Managerial accounting.*

Cost of beverage sold. The value of all beverage products sold as well as the costs of all beverages given away, wasted, or stolen in a defined accounting period.

Cost of food consumed. The actual dollar value of all food used, or consumed, by the operation.

Cost of food sold. The dollar amount of all food actually sold, thrown away, wasted, or stolen, plus or minus transfers from other units, minus employee meals.

Cost of living adjustment (COLA). A term used to describe a raise in employee pay.

Cost of sales. The combined value of the food and beverage costs used to produce a known quantity of revenue in a defined accounting period.

Cost/volume/profit (CVP) analysis. Method that helps predict the sales dollars and volume required to achieve desired profit (or break-even) based on known costs.

Count (product size). Term used to designate size. Size as established by number of items per pound or number of items per container.

Counterfeit money. An imitation of currency intended to be passed off fraudulently as real money.

Credit card skimming. The theft of credit card information used in an otherwise legitimate transaction.

Credit cards. Cards in a payment system by which banks loan money to consumers as the consumer makes purchases. The loans typically carry interest.

Credit memo. An addendum to the vendor's delivery slip (invoice) that reconciles differences between the delivery slip and the purchase order.

Cycle menu. A menu that is in effect for a predetermined length of time, such as 7 days or 14 days.

Daily inventory sheet. A form that lists the items in storage, the unit of purchase, and the par value. It also contains the following columns: on hand, special order, and order amount.

Daily menu. A menu that changes every day.

Debit cards. Cards in a payment system by which the funds needed to cover the user's purchase are automatically transferred from the user's bank account to the entity issuing the debit card.

Delivery invoice. A vendor's record of the amount due for items delivered to a customer.

Desired profit. The profit that an owner seeks to achieve on a predicted quantity of revenue.

Direct billed. Guests are not billed immediately upon consuming products and services, but are sent a bill for the value of the products and services after their visit or event is over.

Draft beer. The term used to identify beer products sold in a keg.

Dram shop laws. The term used to describe a series of legislative acts that, under certain conditions, hold businesses and, in some cases, individuals, personally responsible for the actions of guests who consume excessive amounts of alcoholic beverages. These "laws" shift the liability for acts committed by an individual under the influence of alcohol from that individual to the server or operation that supplied the intoxicating beverage.

Edible portion (EP). This term refers to the weight or count of a product after it has been trimmed, cooked, and portioned.

Electronic funds transfer (EFT). Provides for the electronic payment and collection of money and information; EFT is safe, secure, efficient, and less expensive than paper check payments and collections.

Embezzlement. The term used to describe theft of a type where the money, entrusted to the embezzler for business purposes, is diverted to the embezzler by his or her fraudulent action.

Employee meals cost. Free or reduced-cost meals that are employee benefits and are labor-related, not food-related, costs.

Employee separation. An event that describes employees who quit, are dismissed, or in some other manner have their employment with an operation terminated.

Employment application. A formal document, completed by a candidate for employment, which lists the name, address, work experience, and related information of the candidate.

Empowerment. Giving employees the power to make decisions.

Empty for full system. The bartender is required to retain empty liquor bottles, and then each empty liquor bottle is replaced with a full one at the beginning of the next shift. The empty bottles are then either broken or disposed of, as local beverage law requires.

Ending inventory. The dollar value of all products on hand at the end of the accounting period. This amount is determined by completing a physical inventory.

EP. See *Edible portion.*

Ethics. The choices of proper conduct made by an individual in his or her relationships with others.

Ethyl alcohol. The type of alcohol contained in intoxicating beverage products.

Exempt employees. Salaried employees whose duties, responsibilities, and level of decisions make them "exempt" from the overtime provisions of the US government's Fair Labor Standards Act (FLSA). Exempt employees are expected, by most organizations, to work whatever hours are necessary to accomplish the goals of the organization.

Expenses. The price paid to obtain the items required to operate the business. Often referred to as cost.

Extended price. The price per unit multiplied by the number of units. This refers to a total unit price on a delivery slip or invoice.

FIFO. See *First-in, first-out.*

First-in, first-out (FIFO). Term used to describe a method of storage in which the operator intends to sell his or her oldest product before selling the most recently delivered product.

Fiscal year. Start and stop dates for a 365-day accounting period. This period need not begin in January and end in December.

Fixed average. The average amount of sales or volume over a specific series or time period; for example, first month of the year or second week of the second month.

Fixed expense. An expense that remains constant despite increases or decreases in sales volume.

Fixed payroll. Those dollars spent on employees, such as managers, receiving clerks, and dietitians, whose presence is not generally directly dependent on the number of guests served.

Food available for sale. The sum value of the beginning inventory of food and all food purchases made by an operation during a defined accounting period.

Food cost percentage. The portion of food sales that was spent on food expenses.

Food costs. The dollar costs associated with actually producing the menu item(s) a guest selects.

Food scoop. A portion control device sized based on the number of servings per quart of product served. Thus, for example, a #12 scoop will yield 12 servings per quart.

Franchisor. The entity responsible for selling and maintaining control over the franchise name. (Alternative spelling: franchiser.)

Free-pouring. Pouring liquor from a bottle without measuring the poured amount.

Freezer burn. A form of deterioration in product quality resulting from poorly wrapped or excessively old items stored at freezing temperatures.

Goal value analysis. A menu pricing and analysis system that compares goals of the foodservice operation to performance of individual menu items.

Goods available for sale. The sum of the beginning inventory and purchases. It represents the value of all food that was available for sale during the accounting period.

Gross profit. Covers Sales through Total Gross Profit on the *Uniform System of Accounts for Restaurants* income statement. Consists of food and beverage sales and costs that can and should be controlled by the manager on a daily basis.

Guest check. A written record of what was purchased by the guest and how much the guest was charged for the item(s).

Guest count. The number of individuals served in a defined time period.

Guests served per labor dollar. A calculation used to measure worker productivity. The formula used to calculate guests served per labor dollar is: Guests served ÷ Cost of labor = Guests served per labor dollar.

Guests served per labor hour. A calculation used to measure worker productivity. The formula used to calculate guests served per labor hour is: Guests served ÷ Labor hours used = Guests served per labor hour.

Head size. The amount of space on the top of a glass of beer that is made up of foam. Thus, a glass of beer with one inch of foam on its top is said to have a one-inch head.

Heating, ventilation, and air-conditioning (HVAC). The mechanical system used to provide heating and cooling to buildings.

House wine. The term used to indicate the type of wine to be served in the event a specific brand-name product is not requested by the guest.

Hosted bar. An arrangement in which no charge is made to guests for the individual drinks they consume at an event but, when the bar is closed, one total amount is charged to the event's host or sponsor. Also referred to as an "open" bar.

Hydrometer. An instrument used to measure the specific gravity of a liquid.

Ideal expense. Management's view of the correct or appropriate amount of expense necessary to generate a given quantity of sales.

Income before income taxes. A term utilized in the *Uniform System of Accounts for Restaurants (USAR)* indicating an operation's remaining revenue after subtracting all of its operating expenses but before subtracting the amounts of any income taxes that are due.

Income. Net income. See *Profit.*

Income statement. See *Profit and loss statement (P&L).*

Ingredient room. A storeroom or section of a storeroom where ingredients are weighed and measured according to standardized recipes and then delivered to the appropriate kitchen production area.

Interface. Electronic connection for the purpose of sharing data.

Inventory. All of a foodservice operation's currently stored food and beverage products.

Inventory turnover. The number of times the total value of inventory has been purchased and replaced in an accounting period.

Inventory valuation sheet. A form that documents all inventory items, the quantity on hand, and the unit value of each item.

Involuntary separation. Management causes the employee to separate from the organization (fires the employee).

Issuing. The process of supplying food or beverage products from storage by management for use in an operation.

Jigger. A bar device used to measure predetermined quantities of alcoholic beverages. Jiggers usually are marked in ounces and portions of an ounce, for example, 1 ounce or 1½ ounces.

Job description. A listing of the tasks to be performed in a particular position.

Job specification. A listing of the personal skills and characteristics needed to perform those tasks pertaining to a particular job description.

Keg beer. See *Draft beer.*

Kilowatt-hours. The measure of electrical usage.

kWh. See *Kilowatt-hours.*

Labor costs. See *Labor expense.*

Labor cost percentage. A measure of employee productivity calculated as: Cost of labor ÷ Sales = Labor cost percentage.

Labor dollars per guest served. A calculation used to measure worker productivity. The formula used to calculate labor dollars per guest served is: Cost of labor ÷ Guests served = Labor dollars per guest served.

Labor expense. All expenses (costs), including payroll, required to maintain a workforce in a foodservice operation.

Last-in, first-out (LIFO). Term used to describe a method of storage in which the operator intends to sell his or her most recently delivered product before selling the older product.

LIFO. See *Last-in, first-out.*

Liquors. Fermented beverages that are distilled to increase their alcohol content. Also referred to as *spirits.*

Long-range budget. A forecast or estimate of projected revenue, expense, and profit for a period of three to five years.

Loss leader. A menu item that is priced very low for the purpose of drawing large numbers of customers to the operation.

Management by exception. If an expense is within an acceptable variation range, there is no need for management to intervene. Management takes corrective action only when operational results are outside the range of acceptability.

Managerial accounting. The process of documenting and analyzing sales, expenses, and profits. Sometimes referred to as cost accounting.

Matrix analysis. A method for comparisons between menu items. A matrix allows menu items to be placed into categories based on whether they are above or below overall menu item averages such as food cost percentage, popularity, and contribution margin.

Menu engineering. A popular name for one variation of the contribution margin method of menu analysis and that classifies menu items as stars, puzzles, plow horses, or dogs.

Menu specials. Menu items that will appear on the menu and be removed when they are either consumed or discontinued. These daily or weekly specials are an effort to provide variety, take advantage of low-cost raw ingredients, utilize carryover products, or test market potential of new menu items.

Merchant service provider (MSP). A merchant service provider is the restaurant's coordinator/manager of payment card acceptance and funds collection, and it provides the electronic connection between payment card issuers and their merchants.

Minimum operating cost. Food cost percentage plus variable cost percentage used in calculating minimum sales point.

Minimum sales point (MSP). The dollar sales volume required to justify staying open.

Minimum staff. The term used to designate the least number of employees, or payroll dollars, required to operate a facility or department within the facility.

Mixed drink. A drink made with one or more liquors (spirits) and other ingredients. Also referred to as a *cocktail.*

Mixed expense. An expense that has properties of both a fixed and a variable expense.

Monetary unit. A specific currency denomination, for example, US dollar, British pound, or Japanese yen.

MSP. See *Minimum sales point.*

Mystery shopper. An individual employed by management to pose as an anonymous customer who, during an unannounced visit, observes an operation and reports the observations back to management. Also referred to as a "Spotter."

Negligent hiring. Failure on the part of an employer to exercise reasonable care in the selection of employees.

Net income. The profit realized after all expenses and appropriate taxes for a business have been paid.

Non-controllable expense. An expense that the foodservice manager can neither increase nor decrease.

Occupancy costs. Expenses related to occupying and paying for the physical facility that houses the foodservice unit.

OJT. See *On-the-job training.*

On-call. A system whereby selected employees who are off duty can be contacted by management on short notice to cover for other employees who are absent or to come to work if customer demand suddenly increases.

On-the-floor. In the dining area.

On-the-job training (OJT). A method of training in which workers are training while they actually are performing their required tasks.

Open bar. A bar in which no charge for an individual drink is made to the customer, thus establishing an all-you-can-drink environment. Sometimes referred to as a hotel bar.

Open check. A guest check that has been used to authorize product issues from the kitchen or bar in an operation, but that has not been collected for (closed) and thus the amount of the open check has not been added to the operation's sales total.

Operational efficiency ratio. A calculation used to measure an operation's attainable product costs to its actual product cost. The formula used to calculate an operational efficiency ratio is: Actual product cost ÷ Attainable product cost = Operational efficiency ratio.

Orientation program. A program usually held during the first week of an employee's job that provides information about important items such as dress code, disciplinary system, tip policy, lockers/security, sick leave policy, and retirement programs.

Other controllable expenses. Non-food and beverage costs that can be directly influenced by management action. Examples include advertising expense, utility costs, and the costs of repair and maintenance of equipment.

Other expenses. The expenses of an operation that are neither food, beverage, nor labor.

Over. Term used when the total amount of money in a cash drawer is more than the total amount of money that should be there based on sales receipts.

Overtime wages. Employee wages that, by law or policy, must be paid at a higher than normal rate.

Oxidation. A process that occurs when oxygen comes in contact with bottled wine, resulting in a deterioration of the wine product.

P&L. See *Profit and loss statement.*

Padded inventory. The term used to describe the inappropriate activity of adding a value for nonexisting inventory items to the value of total inventory in an effort to understate actual costs.

Par level. A system of determining the purchase point by using management-established minimum and maximum allowable inventory levels for a given inventory item.

Payroll. Total wages and salaries paid by a foodservice operation to its employees.

Percent. The number "out of each hundred." Thus, 10 percent means 10 out of each 100. This is computed by dividing the part by the whole.

Percentage variance. The change in sales, expressed as a percentage, that results from comparing two operating periods.

Performance to budget. The percentage of the budget actually spent on expenses.

Perpetual inventory. An inventory control system in which additions to and deletions from total inventory are noted as they occur.

Perpetual inventory card. A bin card that includes the product's price at the top of the card, allowing for continual tracking of the quantity of an item on hand and its price.

Physical inventory. An inventory control system in which an actual or physical count and valuation of all inventory on hand is taken at the close of each accounting period.

Plan. See *Budget*.

Plate cost. The sum cost of all product costs included in a single meal (or "plate") served to a guest for one fixed price.

PO. See *Purchase order*.

Point-of-sale (POS) system. A system for controlling hospitality operations' cash and product usage by using a computer processor and, depending on the size of the operation, additional computer hardware, communication devices, and/or software.

Popularity index. The percentage of total guests choosing a given menu item from a list of menu alternatives.

Portion cost. The product cost required to produce one serving of a menu item.

POS. See *Point of sales*.

Potentially hazardous foods. Foods that must be carefully handled for time and temperature control to keep them safe to consume.

Precheck/postcheck system. The server records the order (prechecks) on a guest check when the order is given to him or her by the guest. The products ordered by the guest, prechecked by the server and issued by the kitchen or bar, should match the items and money collected by the cashier (postcheck).

Predicted number to be sold. A method of determining the number of a given menu item that is likely to be sold if the total number of customers to be served is known.

Preemployment drug testing. A preemployment test used to determine if an applicant uses drugs. It is allowable in most states and can be a very effective tool for reducing insurance rates and potential employee liability issues.

Premium liquors. Expensive call liquors.

Price blending. The process of assigning prices based on product groups for the purpose of achieving predetermined cost objectives.

Price comparison sheet. A listing of several vendors' bid prices on selected items that results in the selection of a vendor based on the best price.

Price spread. The difference in price on a menu between the lowest and highest priced item of a similar nature.

Price/value relationship. The guests' view of how much value they are receiving for the price they are paying.

Prime cost. An operation's total cost of sales added to its total labor cost.

Prix fixe (menu). A menu format in which guests select a preset group of menu items and then pay one set (fixed) price for all of the menu items included in the grouping.

Product mix. See *Sales mix*.

Product specification (spec). A detailed description of an ingredient or menu item. Also referred to as a spec.

Product yield. The amount of product remaining after cooking, trimming, portioning, or cleaning.

Productivity. The amount of work performed by a worker in a set amount of time.

Productivity ratio. This formula refers to the total unit output divided by the total unit input.

Productivity standard. Management's expectation of the productivity ratio of each employee. Also, management's view of what constitutes the appropriate productivity ratio in a given foodservice unit or units.

Profit. The dollars that remain after all expenses have been paid. Often referred to as net income.

Profit and loss statement (P&L). A detailed listing of revenue and expenses for a given accounting period. Also referred to as an income statement.

Profit margin. This formula refers to net income divided by total revenues. Also referred to as return on sales.

Psychological testing. Preemployment testing that can include personality tests, tests designed to predict performance, or tests of mental ability.

Pull date (beer). Expiration date on beverage products, usually beers, after which they should not be sold.

Purchase order (PO). A listing of products requested by the purchasing agent. The purchase order lists various product information, including quantity ordered and price quoted by the vendor.

Purchase point. The point in time when an item held in inventory reaches a level that indicates it should be reordered.

Purchases. The sum cost of all food purchased during the accounting period. Determined by adding all properly tabulated invoices for the accounting period.

Quick-service restaurant (QSR). A quick-service restaurant offers a limited menu and is designed for the convenience of customers who want their food fast.

Quick-change artist. A guest who, having practiced the routine many times, attempts to confuse the cashier so that the cashier, in his or her confusion, will give the guest too much change.

Recipe-ready. A recipe ingredient that is cleaned, trimmed, cooked, and generally completed, save for its addition to the recipe.

Recodable electronic locks. A locking system that allows management to issue multiple keys and to identify precisely the time an issued key was used to access the lock, as well as to whom that key was issued.

Refusal hours. Those hours of the day in which an operation refuses to accept food and beverage deliveries.

Reporting period. The process of reporting a time period for which records are being maintained. This may be of the same duration as an accounting period.

Requisition. When a food or beverage product is requested from storage by an employee for use in an operation.

Restaurant operating income. A term utilized in the *Uniform System of Accounts for Restaurants (USAR)* indicating an operation's remaining revenue after subtracting all operating expenses except costs those designated as corporate overhead, interest expense and other income (expense).

Return on sales (ROS). Often referred to as profit margin. This formula refers to net income divided by total revenues. The ROS can also be stated in whole dollar terms.

Revenue. The term used to indicate the dollars taken in by the business in a defined period of time. Often referred to as sales.

Revenue per available seat hour (RevPASH). The amount of hourly income generated by each available seat in a foodservice operation.

Rolling average. The average amount of sales or volume over a changing time period; for example, the last 10 days or the last three weeks.

ROS. See *Return on sales*.

Safety stock. These are additions to par stock, held as a hedge against the possibility of extra demand for a given product. This helps reduce the risk of being out of stock on a given item.

Salaried employee. An employee who receives the same income per week or month regardless of the number of hours worked.

Sales. See *Revenue*.

Salaried employee. An employee who receives the same income per week or month regardless of the number of hours worked.

Sales forecast/projected sales. A prediction of the number of guests to be served and the revenues they will generate in a defined, future time period.

Sales history. A record of sales achieved by an operator in a given sales outlet during a specifically identified time period.

Sales mix. The series of consumer-purchasing decisions that result in a specific food and beverage cost percentage. Sales mix affects overall product cost percentage any time menu items have varying food and beverage cost percentages.

Sales per labor hour. A calculation used to measure worker productivity. The formula used to calculate sales per labor hour is: Total sales ÷ Labor hours used = Sales per labor hour.

Sales per seat. The total revenue generated by a facility divided by the number of seats in the dining area.

Sales to date. The cumulative sales figures reported during a given financial accounting period.

Sales per square foot. A measure of an operation's revenue as it relates to the number of square feet the operation occupies. The formula used to calculate sales per square foot is: Total sales ÷ Total square footage = Sales per square foot.

Sales variance. An increase or decrease from previously experienced or predicted sales levels.

Sales volume. The number of units sold.

Sarbanes–Oxley Act (SOX). Technically known as the Public Company Accounting Reform and Investor Protection Act, the law provides criminal penalties for those found to have committed accounting fraud. The SOX covers a whole range of corporate governance issues, including the regulation of those who are assigned the task of verifying a company's financial health.

Scoop (food). See *food scoop*.

Selling price. The total amount paid by guests for the purchase of a singly priced item.

Shelf life. The period of time an ingredient or menu item maintains its freshness, flavor, and quality.

Short. Term used when the total amount of money in a cash drawer is less than the total amount of money that should be there based on sales receipts.

Shorting. When the vendor is unable to deliver the quantity of item ordered for the appointed delivery date.

Skills tests. Preemployment tests such as typing tests for office employees, computer application tests for those involved in using word processing or spreadsheet tools, or food production tasks, as in the case of chefs.

Skip. See *Walk*.

SOP. See *Standard operating procedure*.

Spec. See *Product specification*.

Spirits. Fermented beverages that are distilled to increase the alcohol content of the product.

Split shift. A scheduling technique used to match individual employee work shifts with the peaks and valleys of customer demand.

Spotter. An individual employed by management for the purpose of inconspicuously observing bartenders and waitstaff in order to detect any fraudulent or policy-violating behavior.

Standard labor cost. The labor cost needed to meet established productivity standards.

Standard menu. A printed and otherwise fixed menu that stays the same day after day.

Standard operating procedure (SOP). Term used for the way something is done in normal business operations.

Standardized recipe. The procedures to be used for consistently preparing and serving a given menu item.

Standardized recipe cost sheet. A record of the ingredient costs required to produce an item sold by a foodservice operation.

Statement of income and expense. The accounting tool used to report an operation's revenue, expenses, and profit for a defined time period. Also known as the income statement, the profit and loss statement, and the P&L.

Supporting schedules. List of all details associated with each line item on the income statement.

Sustainable development. A variety of Earth-friendly practices and policies designed to meet the needs of the present population without compromising the ability of future generations to meet their own needs.

Task training. The training undertaken to ensure an employee has the skills to meet productivity goals.

Tenths system. A liquor inventory valuation system that requires the inventory taker to assign a product value based on a visual inspection of a bottle's content. For example, a value of 10/10 is assigned for a full bottle, 5/10 is assigned to a half bottle, and so on.

Tip-on (menu). A small menu segment clipped to a larger and more permanent list of menu items.

Total bar system. An automated set of procedures that combine sales information with product dispensing information to create a complete beverage revenue and production control program.

Travel and entertainment (T&E) cards. Cards in a payment system by which the card issuer collects full payment from the card users on a monthly basis. These card companies do not typically assess their users' interest charges.

Two-key system. A system to control access to storage areas.

Uniform systems of accounts. A recommended and standardized (uniform) set of accounting procedures used for categorizing and reporting revenue and expense.

Uniform System of Accounts for Restaurants (USAR). The recommended and standardized (uniform) set of accounting procedures used for categorizing and reporting revenue and expense in the restaurant industry.

User workstation. A computer terminal used only to ring up food and beverage orders.

Value pricing. The practice of reducing all or most prices on the menu in the belief that total guest counts will increase to the point that total sales revenue also increases.

Variable expense. An expense that generally increases as sales volume increases and decreases as sales volume decreases.

Variable payroll. Those dollars expended on employees whose presence is directly dependent on the number of guests served. These employees include servers, bartenders, and dishwashers, for example. As the number of guests served increases, the number of these individuals required to do the job also increases. As the number of guests served decreases, variable payroll should decrease.

Vintage. The specific year(s) of production for a wine.

Vintner. Wine producer.

Voluntary separation. An employee makes the decision to leave the organization.

Walk/skip (the bill). A term used to describe a customer who has consumed a product, but leaves the foodservice operation without paying the bill. Also known as a skip.

Waste percentage. This formula is defined as product loss divided by AP weight and refers to product lost in the preparation process.

Weighted average. An average that combines data on the number of guests served and how much each has spent during a given financial accounting period.

Well liquors. Those spirits that are served by an operation when the customer does not specify a particular brand name.

Wine. A fermented beverage made from grapes, fruits, or berries.

Wine list. A menu of wine offerings.

Working stock. The quantity of goods from inventory reasonably expected to be used between deliveries.

Yardstick method. Method of calculating expense standards so determinations can be made as to whether variations in expenses are due to changes in sales volume or other reasons, such as waste or theft.

Yield percentage. This formula is defined as one minus waste percentage and refers to the amount of product available for use by the operator after all preparation-related losses have been taken into account.

Yield test. A procedure used to determine actual EP ingredient costs. It is used to help establish actual costs on a product that will experience weight or volume loss in preparation.

INDEX